Routledge Handbook of Contemporary Malaysia

The *Routledge Handbook of Contemporary Malaysia* offers a broad, analytical survey of Malaysia. It provides a comprehensive survey of significant topics in Malaysian politics, economy, and society today, focussing on issues, institutions, and trends. It is divided into four thematic sections, which are all introduced by the editor:

- Domestic politics
- Economics
- Social policy and social development
- International relations and security.

Now available in paperback, the volume brings together an international team of experts: an interdisciplinary mix of forty contributors from Malaysia and elsewhere, including many of the leading specialists on Malaysian affairs. The chapters included in the volume form an accessible and fascinating window onto contemporary Malaysia. They each introduce a different aspect of the Malaysian polity, economy, or society, offering both historical perspective and a current assessment or investigation. Designed for general readers and specialists alike, chapters may be read individually – each stands on its own – or conjointly.

Up-to-date, interdisciplinary, and academically rigorous, the *Handbook* will be of interest to students, academics, policymakers, and others in search of reliable information on Malaysian politics, economics, and society.

Meredith L. Weiss is Professor of Political Science at the University at Albany, State University of New York, USA. She is the author of *Student Activism in Malaysia: Crucible, Mirror, Sideshow* (2011) and *Protest and Possibilities: Civil Society and Coalitions for Political Change in Malaysia* (2006), and editor of several volumes, most recently *Political Participation in Asia: Defining and Deploying Political Space* (2018), with Eva Hansson.

Routledge Handbook of Contemporary Malaysia

Edited by Meredith L. Weiss

Routledge
Taylor & Francis Group
LONDON AND NEW YORK

First published in paperback 2018

First published 2015
by Routledge
2 Park Square, Milton Park, Abingdon, Oxon OX14 4RN

and by Routledge
711 Third Avenue, New York, NY 10017

Routledge is an imprint of the Taylor & Francis Group, an informa business

British Library Cataloguing-in-Publication Data
A catalogue record for this book is available from the British Library

Library of Congress Cataloging-in-Publication Data
Routledge handbook of contemporary Malaysia / [edited by] Meredith L. Weiss.
pages cm
Includes bibliographical references and index.
ISBN 978-0-415-81673-1 (hardback) – ISBN 978-1-315-75624-0 (ebook)
1. Malaysia–Politics and government. 2. Malaysia–Social conditions.
3. Malaysia–Economic conditions. I. Weiss, Meredith L. (Meredith Leigh),
1972- editor of compilation. II. Welsh, Bridget, 1967- Elections in Malaysia.
Contains (work):
DS597.2.R66 2015
959.506–dc23
2014011134

ISBN: 978-0-415-81673-1 (hbk)
ISBN: 978-1-138-31280-7 (pbk)
ISBN: 978-1-315-75624-0 (ebk)

Typeset in Bembo
by Taylor & Francis Books

Contents

Figures

Tables

Boxes

Contributors

Editorial Board

Editorial Assistant

Xiaoye She

Abdul Rahman Embong is Professor in Sociology of Development and Principal Fellow at the Institute of Malaysian & International Studies (IKMAS), Universiti Kebangsaan Malaysia. He was President of the Malaysian Social Science Association between 2000 and 2010, and is currently the Association's Advisor. He has written many books, including *State-led Modernization and the New Middle Class in Malaysia* (2002).

Afif Pasuni is Associate Research Fellow in the Malaysia Programme, S. Rajaratnam School of International Studies (RSIS), Singapore, and writes on Southeast Asian affairs, focusing mostly on Malaysian politics. He has contributed to journals, newspapers, and publications such as *Southeast Asian Affairs*, *Journal of Current Southeast Asian Affairs*, *East Asia Forum*, *The Nation*, *The Straits Times*, and *The Malaysian Insider*.

Athi S.M. is a Research Fellow at the Institute of the Malay World and Civilization (ATMA), Universiti Kebangsaan Malaysia. His research area is labour studies with particular interest in social and spatial mobility. He is a doctoral candidate at the University of Amsterdam, the Netherlands and currently in the final stage of his PhD thesis research.

William Case joined City University of Hong Kong as Director of the Southeast Asia Research Centre (SEARC) and Professor in the Department of Asian and International Studies. He has held teaching or visiting research positions at the University of Malaya in Kuala Lumpur, Malaysia, the National University of Malaysia, the University (Institute) MARA in Shah Alam, Malaysia, Chulalongkorn University in Bangkok, Thailand, the Centre for Strategic and International Studies (CSIS) in Jakarta, Indonesia, and the Yuchengko Centre at De La Salle University in Manila, the Philippines. He has published extensively on Southeast Asian politics and political economy in academic journals and media outlets.

Chee Heng Leng is Visiting Professor, Women's Development Research Centre (KANITA), Universiti Sains Malaysia. Her research interest is in the political economy of healthcare and migration studies. She co-edited *Health Care in Malaysia: Dynamics of Provision, Financing and Access* (jointly with Simon Barraclough, 2007).

James Chin is Professor of Political Science and Head of the School of Arts & Social Sciences, Monash University, Malaysia Campus. In addition to his academic work, he is a member of the Advisory Board, Centre for Public Policy Studies (CPPS) and Senior Fellow, Institute for Democracy and Economic Affairs (IDEAS). He was previously Senior Visiting Research Fellow, Institute of South East Asian Studies (ISEAS), Singapore.

Karminder Singh Dhillon, PhD (Boston) is currently heading the Centre for Expertise Development at the National Institute of Public Administration Malaysia. He has previously served at the Ministry of Defense, Institute of Diplomacy and Foreign Relations and the Prime Minister's Department. He is author of *Malaysian Foreign Policy in the Mahathir Era 1981–2003: The Dilemmas of Development* (2009).

Greg Felker is Associate Professor of Politics at Willamette University in Salem, Oregon, USA. He has also taught at the Hong Kong University of Science & Technology, the University of Maryland, College Park, USA, and Chulalongkorn University, Thailand. His research interests lie in the comparative and international political economy of Southeast Asia.

Goh Ban Lee is a Fellow in the Penang Institute and a columnist for *The Sun* newspaper in Malaysia, focusing on urban governance. He has a PhD from University of California, Los Angeles, USA. Among his publications are *Non-compliance – A Neglected Agenda in Urban Governance* (2002) and *Counselling Local Councils* (2007).

Alberto G. Gomes is Professor of Anthropology and Director of the Centre for Dialogue at La Trobe University, Australia. His books on the Orang Asli include *Malaysia and the 'Original People'* (with R. Dentan, K. Endicott, and B. Hooker, 1997), *Looking for Money* (2004), and *Modernity and Malaysia* (2007).

Anantha Raman Govindasamy is Senior Lecturer in Politics at Universiti Malaysia Sabah. He holds a PhD in Politics from Flinders University, Australia. His work focuses on politics, economics, and culture in Malaysia. His most recent publications include 'The Islamisation of Malaysia: Religious Nationalism in the Service of Ethnonationalism' (with Michael Barr, 2010) and 'Indian and Rural Displacement: Exclusion from Region Building in Malaysia' (2010).

Heng Pek Koon is Assistant Professor and ASEAN Studies Center Director at American University's School of International Service. She is also Contract Chair of the Maritime Southeast Asia Area Studies programme at the US State Department's Foreign Service Institute. Specialising in Malaysia's ethnic politics and regional integration, she earned her PhD from London University's School of Oriental and African Studies, UK.

Adnan A. Hezri is Director of Technology, Environment, and Sustainability (TiES) at the Institute of Strategic and International Studies (ISIS) Malaysia. Dr Hezri studies comparative public policy, specialising in natural resources policy and governance. His visiting appointments include Adjunct Fellow at the Fenner School of Environment and Society, the Australian National University and Associate Fellow of the Academy of Sciences Malaysia.

Amarjit Kaur is Emeritus Professor of Economic History at the University of New England, Australia. Her research interests include labor history, international labour migration, forced migration and the Indian Diaspora. Her recent publications include *Proletarian and Gendered Mass Migrations* (2013) (co-edited with Dirk Hoerder); *Wage Labour in Southeast Asia* (2004); and *Mobility, Labour Migration and Border Controls in Asia* (2006) (co-edited with Ian Metcalfe).

Kuik Cheng-Chwee is currently a postdoctoral fellow at the Princeton–Harvard China and the World Program. He is on leave from Universiti Kebangsaan Malaysia. He researches on China–Southeast Asia relations and weaker states' alignment behaviour. His publications include 'The Essence of Hedging: Malaysia and Singapore's Response to a Rising China' (2008) and 'China's Evolving Multilateralism in Asia' (2008).

Lai Yew Meng is Senior Lecturer in Politics and International Relations at Universiti Malaysia Sabah. His research interests include Malaysian politics, Japanese and Chinese foreign policy, and East Asian security. Lai is the co-editor of *Security Studies: A Reader* (with Christopher W. Hughes, 2011) and the author of *Nationalism and Power Politics in Japan's Relations with China: A Neoclassical Realist Interpretation* (2013).

Hwok-Aun Lee is Senior Lecturer in the Department of Development Studies, University of Malaya, Malaysia. He obtained a PhD in Economics from the University of Massachusetts, Amherst, USA, and has researched and published on affirmative action, inequality, labour, social policy, discrimination, and education.

Molly N.N. Lee is an education consultant from Malaysia. Her professional expertise is in higher education, teacher education, ICT in education, and education for sustainable development. Her recent academic publications include *Management of Research and Innovation in Malaysia and Globalizing Practices in Asian Universities* (2013).

Joseph Chinyong Liow is Associate Dean and Professor at the S. Rajaratnam School of International Studies, Nanyang Technological University, Singapore. He is the author of *Islam, Education, and Reform in Southern Thailand: Tradition and Transformation* (2009), *Piety and Politics: Islamism in Contemporary Malaysia* (2009), and *Dictionary of the Modern Politics of Southeast Asia*, 4th edn (2014), and editor of a four-volume series of essays on Islam, *Islam in Southeast Asia: Critical Concepts* (Routledge).

Carolin Liss is currently a Research Fellow at the Peace Research Institute, Frankfurt, Germany. She is the author of *Oceans of Crime: Maritime Piracy and Transnational Security in Southeast Asia and Bangladesh* (2011) and articles on piracy, terrorism, and the privatisation of maritime security in Asia and Africa.

John Liu is a human rights activist currently attached to the Bangkok-based Asian Forum for Human Rights and Development (FORUM-ASIA). He was previously coordinator of Suara Rakyat Malaysia (SUARAM). He has authored a number of publications, including several editions of SUARAM's annual human rights reports and FORUM-ASIA's *Internet and Social Media in Asia: Battleground for Freedom of Expression* (2012). Liu holds an MA in Development Studies from the London School of Economics, UK.

Francis Loh Kok Wah was, until 2012, Professor of Politics in Universiti Sains Malaysia, Penang, Malaysia. His latest books are *Old vs New Politics in Malaysia* (2009) and *Building Bridges, Crossing Boundaries* (editor, 2010). He sat on the SSRC Global Security Committee (2000–03) and has consulted for UNDP and the Forum of Federations. He is president of Aliran, a multiethnic NGO in Malaysia.

Carolina López C. is Senior Research Fellow at the University of Malaya, Malaysia. She runs the Centre for Dialogue & Transformation, where applied research is conducted concerning conflict transformation and psychosocial healing in post-conflict societies. Among her publications are *Teoría ideológica-estructural, a macro y micro nivel: Antología de escritos teóricos*, 'The Struggle for Wholeness: Addressing Individual and Collective Trauma in Violence-ridden Societies', and 'Ideological-Structural Analysis, Micro and Macro-theory of Intercivilizational Dialogue' (all 2004).

Norma Mansor is currently Professor in the Department of Administrative Studies and Politics and Director of the Social Security Research Centre, University of Malaya, Malaysia. She has written nearly 100 academic reports, articles, and chapters in books on topics including public policy, public administration, and governance. She serves as reviewer and editorial board member of several journals.

Ong Kian Ming was elected as the Member of Parliament for Serdang in May 2013 representing the Democratic Action Party (DAP). He holds a PhD in Political Science from Duke University, an MPhil from the University of Cambridge, and a BSc from the London School of Economics (LSE). He was formerly a political researcher and analyst as well as a management consultant.

Cecilia Ng is an independent researcher and women's rights advocate. She was previously with the Women's Development Research Centre (KANITA), Universiti Sains Malaysia and Universiti Putra Malaysia. She is active in women's groups in Malaysia and has been involved in research, training, and advocacy on gender issues since the early 1980s. Recently Cecilia was appointed as one of the Directors of the Penang Women's Development Corporation (PWDC), a state-run body established to promote gender equality and social justice.

Pang Khee Teik is a Malaysian arts consultant, activist, curator, photographer, and writer. He has an MA in Gender and Sexuality from Birkbeck, University of London, UK, under the Chevening Scholarship. He was formerly the director of The Annexe Gallery, editor of arts website Kakiseni.com, and co-founder of sexuality rights festival Seksualiti Merdeka.

Por Heong Hong, PhD candidate, School of Social Sciences, Universiti Sains Malaysia (USM), is also a research assistant for a project on medical tourism. She is currently writing up her thesis, *Nation and Bodies Reimagined: The Politics of Healthcare in Post-war Peninsular Malaysia, 1945–2012.* Her research interests include political economy and the cultural history of healthcare.

Arnold Puyok is Senior Lecturer in Politics and International Relations, Universiti Malaysia Sarawak. Dr Puyok's areas of expertise are ethnic politics, the politics of state and federal relations, electoral politics, and politics and society. His works on contemporary Malaysian politics, especially Sabah and Sarawak, have been published in *Asian Journal of Political Science*, *Journal of Contemporary Southeast Asia*, and *Kajian Malaysia*. He also regularly contributes to *The Malaysian Insider*, *Malaysiakini*, and *East Asia Forum*.

Raja Noriza Raja Ariffin received her Master of City and Regional Planning from the California State University, Fresno, USA and her Doctor of Philosophy from the Institute of Planning, University of Nottingham, UK. Her research interests are in the areas of urban governance, transportation, quality of life, and policy analysis. She is the Head of the Department of Administrative Studies and Politics, Faculty of Economics and Administration, University of Malaya, Malaysia.

Kathy Rowland has over eighteen years' experience in the arts, working as an advocate, producer, writer, and editor. In 2001, she co-founded the online arts magazine www.kakiseni.com, and was its Managing Editor until 2008. She edited and introduced *Huzir Sulaiman: Collected Plays 1998–2012* (2012) and *Krishen Jit: An Uncommon Position, Selected Writings* (2003). She is currently a Lecturer at the Faculty for Creative Industries at LASALLE College of the Arts Singapore.

Ruhanas Harun is Professor in the Department of Strategic Studies at the National Defence University of Malaysia (UPNM). Her research focuses on foreign policy and national security, both within the ASEAN region and between Southeast Asia and Europe. She holds an MA from the University of Paris – Sorbonne, France.

Shamsul A.B. is Distinguished Professor and Founding Director, Institute of Ethnic Studies, Universiti Kebangsaan Malaysia. An anthropologist by training, his academic interests cover the broader field of social science, with an empirical focus on Malaysia and the Malay-speaking world. Since 2007, he has edited the module for the compulsory 'Ethnic Relations Course' in which all new students in Malaysia's twenty public universities must enrol.

Xiaoye She is currently a PhD candidate in political science at University at Albany, State University of New York (SUNY), USA. She also holds an MA in Economics and a dual BA in Southeast Asian Studies and Economics. Her current research concentrates on comparative political economy and public policy, with a focus on issues of macroeconomic policy and structural reform, as well as urbanisation and social policy in developing and transitioning contexts.

tan beng hui works on issues around gender and sexuality in Malaysia. Her recent contributions include a study on the politicisation of ethnicity, religion, and sexuality, and a chapter on women and inclusive growth that appeared in the country's first National Human Development Report. She has also been actively engaged in the local women's movement for over two decades.

Jeff Tan is a political economist and Associate Professor at the Aga Khan University, Institute for the Study of Muslim Civilisations (AKU–ISMC) in London, UK. His research interests include privatisation (in particular infrastructure and water), entrepreneurship and industrialisation, and his publications on Malaysia have covered these areas.

Eric C. Thompson is Associate Professor of Sociology at the National University of Singapore. His research interests include transnational networking, urbanism, agrarian transitions, and ASEAN regionalism. His work has appeared in *American Ethnologist*, *Political Geography*, *Asian Studies Review*, *Contemporary Sociology*, and *Contemporary Southeast Asia* among others. He is author of *Unsettling Absences: Urbanism in Rural Malaysia* (2007) and co-editor of *Cleavage, Connection and Conflict in Rural, Urban, and Contemporary Asia* (with Tim Bunnell and D. Parthasarathy, 2012).

Helena Varkkey is Senior Lecturer at the Department of International and Strategic Studies, University of Malaya, Malaysia. She carries out research on the political economy of agribusiness in Southeast Asia, with a focus on transboundary pollution. She has recently published journal articles in *Asia Pacific Viewpoint* and *Environmental Hazards*.

Meredith L. Weiss is Associate Professor of Political Science at the University at Albany, State University of New York, USA. She is the author of *Student Activism in Malaysia: Crucible, Mirror, Sideshow* (2011) and *Protest and Possibilities: Civil Society and Coalitions for Political Change in Malaysia* (2006), as well as numerous journal articles and chapters, and editor of several volumes, most recently *Electoral Dynamics in Malaysia: Findings from the Grassroots* (2014).

Bridget Welsh is Associate Professor of Political Science at Singapore Management University. She received her doctorate from Columbia University, USA, language training at Cornell University (FALCON), USA, and bachelor's degree from Colgate University, USA. She has authored/edited multiple books and articles on Southeast Asian politics. Her latest book is entitled *Democracy Denied: The Malaysia GE13* (2014).

Yeoh Seng Guan is Senior Lecturer in the School of Arts and Social Sciences, Monash University, Malaysia. He is an urban anthropologist who works primarily on the interfaces between cities, religion, and civil society in Southeast Asia. He is editor of *The Other Kuala Lumpur: Living in the Shadows of a Globalising Southeast Asian City* (2014) and *Media, Culture and Society in Malaysia* (2010).

Glossary

ABIM	Angkatan Belia Islam Malaysia, Malaysian Muslim Youth Movement
AFC	Asian financial crisis (1997–98)
AKAR	Parti Angkatan Keadilan Rakyat
Ali-Baba	Subcontracting arrangements between Malays ('Ali') and Chinese ('Baba')
Allah	'God' in Arabic
AMCJA	All-Malaya Council of Joint Action
APEC	Asia-Pacific Economic Cooperation
ARF	ASEAN Regional Forum
ASEAN	Association of Southeast Asian Nations
ASG	Abu Sayyaf Group
Bahasa Indonesia	The language of Indonesia, which is very similar to Bahasa Malaysia
Bahasa Melayu/Malaysia	Malay/Malaysian language
Bangsa Malaysia	Malaysian race or Malaysian nation
BCIC	Bumiputera Commercial and Industrial Community
BERJAYA	Parti Bersatu Rakyat Jelata Sabah
BERSIH	Gabungan Pilihanraya Bersih dan Adil, Coalition for Clean and Fair Elections
BN	Barisan Nasional, National Front; Malaysia's ruling coalition
BNM	Bank Negara Malaysia, Malaysian National Bank
Bumiputera	Literally, 'princes of the soil'; Malays and indigenous people of Malaysia
CAHCP	Coalition Against Health Care Privatization
CAP	Consumers' Association of Penang
CEDAW	Convention on the Elimination of All Forms of Discrimination Against Women
CHC	Citizens' Healthcare Coalition
CIQ	Customs, Immigration and Quarantine
Consociationalism	A structure of government in vertically segmented (e.g. ethnically plural) states, in which leaders of each community share power
DAP	Democratic Action Party; part of Pakatan Rakyat
DEO	District education officer
DRG	Diagnostic-related group
EAEC	East Asian Economic Caucus

EAEG	East Asian Economic Grouping
EAS	East Asia Summit
EC	Election Commission
EEZ	Exclusive economic zones
EOI	Export-oriented industrialisation
EPF	Employees' Provident Fund
EPU	Economic Planning Unit
ETP	Economic Transformation Programme
FAMA	Federal Agriculture Marketing Authority
FDI	Foreign direct investment
FELDA	Federal Land Development Authority
FPMPAM	Federation of Private Medical Practitioners' Associations Malaysia
FTA	Free trade agreement
FTZ	Free trade zones
GAM	Gerakan Aceh Merdeka, Free Aceh Movement
GE	General election
Gerakan	Parti Gerakan Rakyat Malaysia, Malaysian People's Movement Party; part of the BN
GFC	Global financial crisis
GLC	Government-linked corporations
GMM	Global Movement of Moderates
GP	General practitioner
GST	Goods and services tax
Hari Raya Qurban	Also known as the Festival of Sacrifice, it is celebrated when pilgrims return home after performing the Hajj in Mecca. On this special occasion, a cow is slaughtered to commemorate Allah's forgiving Ibrahim (Abraham), freeing him from the promise to sacrifice his son Ismail, as had been commanded
HEI	Higher education institution
HICOM	Heavy Industries Corporation of Malaysia
HINDRAF	Hindu Rights Action Force
IC	Identity card
ICT	Information and communications technology
IDC	Immigration detention camps
ILO	International Labour Organization
IMB	International Maritime Bureau
IMF	International Monetary Fund
IMP	Independence of Malaya Party
ISA	Internal Security Act
ISI	Import-substitution industrialisation
Islam Hadhari (IH)	Civilizational Islam
ISMA	Ikatan Muslimin Malaysia, Malaysian Muslim Solidarity
JAIS	Jabatan Agama Islam Selangor, Selangor Islamic Religious Department
JAKOA	Jabatan Kemajuan Orang Asli, Department of Orang Asli Development
JHEOA	Jabatan Hal Ehwal Orang Asli, Department of Aboriginal Affairs; currently JAKOA

JI	Jemaah Islamiyah
Kampung	Village
KDM	Kadazandusun (or Kadazan Dusun) Murut
Kenduri	A festive meal prepared by Malays to celebrate special occasions
Keris	Malay ceremonial knife
Ketuanan Islam	Muslim supremacy
Ketuanan Melayu	Malay supremacy or Malay hegemony
KMM	Kumpulan Mujahidin Malaysia, Malaysia Mujahidin Movement
Konfrontasi	Indonesia's military campaign (1963–66) against the formation of the Federation of Malaysia from the union of peninsular Malaya, Singapore, Sabah, and Sarawak
LDP	Liberal Democratic Party; part of the BN
LP	Labour Party
MAF	Malaysian Armed Forces
MALSINDO	Trilateral agreement among Singapore, Malaysia and Indonesia to combat piracy in the Malacca Strait
MARA	Majlis Amanah Rakyat, Council of Trust for Indigenous People
MARDI	Malaysian Agricultural Research and Development Institute
Masuk Melayu	Literally 'to enter Malayness', this term is used to connote a person's conversion to Islam
MCA	Malaysian Chinese Association; part of the BN
MCCBCHST	Malaysian Consultative Council for Buddhism, Christianity, Hinduism, Sikhism and Taoism
MCP	Malayan Communist Party
MDP	Malaysian Democratic Party
Menteri besar	Chief minister of a Malaysian state
Merdeka	Independence
MGGI	Malaysian Gender Gap Index
MIC	Malaysian Indian Congress; part of the BN
MILF	Moro Islamic Liberation Front (Philippines)
MMA	Malaysian Medical Association
MMEA	Malaysian Maritime Enforcement Agency
MoE	Ministry of Education
MOF	Ministry of Finance/Treasury
MOH	Ministry of Health
MoHE	Ministry of Higher Education
MPOC	Malaysian Palm Oil Council
MRSM	Maktab Rendah Sains MARA (Majlis Amanah Rakyat, Council of Trust for the People), MARA junior science college
MTM	Monetary Transmission Mechanism
MUIS	Majlis Ugama Islam Sabah, Sabah Islamic Council
Murtad	Apostasy, committed when a Muslim chooses to leave the Islamic faith
MWFCD	Ministry of Women, Family and Community Development
NCP	National Cultural Policy
NEAC	National Economic Action Council
NEB	National Education Blueprint
NEM	New Economic Model

NEP	New Economic Policy
NFPE	Non-financial public enterprise
NHESP	National Higher Education Strategic Plan
NIC	Newly industrialised country
NUP	National Urbanisation Policy
OPP	Outline Perspective Plan
OPR	Overnight policy rate
Orang Asli	Indigenous people
OSA	Official Secrets Act
Pakatan	Pakatan Rakyat, People's Alliance
Parti Perikatan	Alliance Party, a coalition among UMNO, MCA and MIC; forerunner of the BN
PAS	Parti Islam SeMalaysia, Pan-Malaysian Islamic Party; part of Pakatan Rakyat
PASOK	Pertubuhan Kebangsaan Nanukragong Bersatu
PBB	Parti Persaka Bumiputera Bersatu; part of the BN
PBDS	Parti Bansa Dayak Sarawak
PBRS	Parti Bersatu Rakyat Sabah; part of the BN
PBS	Parti Bersatu Sabah, Sabah United Party; part of the BN
PCDOM	Primary Care Doctors of Malaysia
PDS	Parti Demokratik Sabah
Pekemas	Parti Keadilan Masyarakat Malaysia
PEMUDA	Pasukan Petugas Khas Pemudahcara Perniagaan, Special Task Force to Facilitate Business
Perkasa	Pertubuhan Pribumi Perkasa Malaysia, Malaysian Indigenous Empowerment Organisation
PERMAS	Persatuan Rakyat Malaysia Sarawak
Pernas	Perbadanan Nasional Berhad, Malaysia's 'Franchise Business Partner'
PETRONAS	Petroliam Nasional Berhad, National Petroleum Corporation
PKR	Parti Keadilan Rakyat, People's Justice Party; part of Pakatan Rakyat
PN	Parti Negara
PNB	Permodalan Nasional Berhad, National Equity Corporation
PPPA	Printing Presses and Publications Act
PR	Parti Rakyat; Pakatan Rakyat
PRS	Parti Rakyat Sarawak; part of the BN
PSD	Public Service Department
PUNB	Perbadanan Usahawan Nasional, National Entrepreneurial Corporation
PUTERA	Pusat Tenaga Rakyat
RCI	Royal Commission of Inquiry
RDI	Research, development and innovation
ReCAAP	Regional Cooperation Agreement on Combating Piracy and Armed Robbery against Ships in Asia
Reformasi	Political reform movement launched in 1998
RELA	Ikatan Relawan Rakyat Malaysia, Peoples' Voluntary Corps
RMN	Royal Malaysian Navy

ROS	Registrar of Societies
SAPP	Sabah Progressive Party
SCA	Sabah Chinese Association
SCCP	Sabah Chinese Consolidated Party
SED	State education department
SF	Socialist Front
SNAP	Sarawak National Party
SOE	State-owned enterprises
SPDP	Sarawak Progressive Democratic Party; part of the BN
SPM	Sijil Pelajaran Malaysia, Malaysian Certificate of Education
STPM	Sijil Tinggi Pelajaran Malaysia, Malaysian Higher Education Certificate
SUHAKAM	Human Rights Commission of Malaysia
SUPP	Sarawak United Peoples' Party; part of the BN
SWP	Sarawak Workers Party
TPP	Trans-Pacific Partnership
Ummah	Global community of Muslims
UMNO	United Malays National Organisation; lead party in the BN
UNDP	United Nations Development Programme
UNPKO	United Nations Peacekeeping Operations
UPKO	United Pasokmomogun Kadazandusun Murut Organisation; part of the BN
USNO	United Sabah National Organization
UUCA	Universities and University Colleges Act
VAT	Value-added tax
VAW	Violence against women
Vision 2020	Prime Minister Mahathir's plan for Malaysia to achieve fully developed status by the year 2020 (in Malay, *Wawasan 2020*)
WAO	Women's Aid Organisation
WCC	Women's Centre for Change
WHO	World Health Organization
Yang Di-Pertuan Agong	King, elected from among Malaysia's hereditary state-level sultans
ZOPFAN	Zone of Peace, Freedom and Neutrality

A brief introduction to Malaysia

Meredith L. Weiss

No country can be adequately captured in a single volume, however intellectually or physically weighty. A complete picture of all that comprises 'contemporary Malaysia' would hence clearly be beyond the possible scope of this volume. And yet, our aim is for more than a set of static descriptions or assessments. Instead, this volume presents a series of thoughtful, hopefully thought-provoking engagements with different dimensions of Malaysian politics, economics, and society. Each chapter can stand on its own; taken together, however, they offer an especially rich perspective on the extraordinary complexity of modern Malaysia. This brief introduction lays the ground for the more substantive chapters that follow, offering a sketch of key moments and attributes, then an overview of the volume as a whole.

Malaysia: a snapshot

Malaysia has never had the benefit or option of isolation. Located along key sea-lanes, at the tip of the Southeast Asian landmass, what is now Malaysia grew out of shifting suzerainty of wide-reaching empires, localised sultanates, and ideological flows. These tides left more than material artefacts. Two were most important: the entry and spread of Islam in the fourteenth and fifteenth centuries, then the arrival of the first Europeans shortly thereafter. Islam has remained. (See the chapter by Liow and Afif for the contemporary political implications of the faith's ever-greater entrenchment.) Europeans – first the Portuguese, next the Dutch, then, more extensively and intensively, the British – have since departed. But these paired influences arguably did more than any other exogenous or common internal factors to shape Malaysian culture, identity, institutions, and borders.

Malaysia today is a constitutional monarchy, with a federal, parliamentary framework. Most power, as well as most fiscal resources, is vested in the central government and bureaucracy, although Sabah and Sarawak reserve somewhat greater authority (and largesse to dispense) than their peninsular counterparts. (See the chapters on federalism by Francis Loh Kok Wah and on public administration by Norma Mansor and Raja Noriza Raja Ariffin for details.) Singapore was briefly part of the Federation of Malaysia upon its formation, but left after a mere two years, in 1965. Local elections have been suspended altogether in Malaysia since the mid-1960s, although Goh Ban Lee makes the case for their reinstatement in his chapter here.

An upwardly mobile, newly industrialised country, Malaysia aspires to attain fully developed status by the year 2020. Now, it is considered an upper-middle-income state, with a reasonably diversified, generally open, export-oriented economy, but also a significant state sector and role in development (see the chapter by Greg Felker for more on Malaysia's developmentalist framework). As the chapters by Hwok-Aun Lee, Helena Varkkey, Jeff Tan, and Xiaoye She in particular detail, politics and economics are closely intertwined in Malaysia. The multi-ethnic Barisan Nasional (BN, National Front) coalition, and especially its dominant partner, the United Malays National Organisation, use the rewards of economic development not only to enrich fortunate elites (see William Case's chapter for a discussion of this key stratum), but also to cultivate support – and make real progress along human development and economic indicators – among the public. It is in large part by way of such distributions that the BN (or its progenitor, the tripartite Alliance) has retained power at the federal level and in most states since independence.

That said, while Malaysia is classified as a competitive electoral authoritarian, or simply semi-democratic/semi-authoritarian state – multiparty, competitive elections are held regularly, as Bridget Welsh describes, but those elections fall short of free and fair, and civil liberties face significant curbs, as John Liu explains – its politics are far from static. A heated campaign and closely fought election that culminated in Malay–Chinese riots in May 1969 ushered in new controls on political discourse and mobilisation. Even so, the past two decades in particular have seen rising popular mobilisation, in forms ranging from artistic production (see the chapter by Kathy Rowland) to mass street protests (Anantha Raman Govindasamy details three exemplars of such mobilisation). The elections of 2008 and 2013 were especially noteworthy, not only for the loss of the BN's two-thirds majority in parliament (sufficient to pass constitutional amendments), but also for the apparent solidification of a two-coalition order, as Ong Kian Ming posits in his chapter. Nor are the roster of hardest-fought issues fully consistent. Some, like education (see the chapter by Molly N.N. Lee) and healthcare (Chee Heng Leng and Por Heong Hong) are perennial concerns; others, such as gender equality (tan beng hui and Cecilia Ng), sexuality rights (Pang Khee Teik), or environmental sustainability (Adnan A. Hezri), are newly or unevenly politicised.

As the chapter by Shamsul A.B. and Athi S.M. details, among the key legacies of British rule was an ethnically segmented (and accordingly catalogued) society, reflected in a carefully moulded economic order. The constructed categories of 'Malay', 'Chinese', and 'Indian' are omnipresent in Malaysian socio-political life, albeit with important permutations in the two offshore states of Sabah and Sarawak (see the chapters by James Chin and Arnold Puyok in particular). The category *bumiputera*, literally, 'sons of the soil', includes both the narrow Malay majority and Malaysia's relatively small percentage (higher in East Malaysia) of indigenous peoples. *Bumiputera* enjoy political, cultural, and economic privilege in Malaysia, as a result of both a constitutionally decreed special status and that position's operationalisation in far-reaching, deeply entrenched affirmative action policies. Economic inequality and policies generate perennial tensions, not least due to this structural preference, but questions of the extent to which the Malays' special position should translate into cultural, and specifically religious, sovereignty are today especially fraught, as the chapter by Carolina López C. in particular details. Meanwhile, the Malaysian social fabric is changing in fundamental ways, with increasingly prevalent migrant labour, both skilled and otherwise (see Amarjit Kaur's chapter), and rural–urban flows; on the impacts of the latter dynamic in rural and urban areas, see the chapters by Eric C. Thompson and Yeoh Seng Guan, respectively.

Domestic permutations and polity trajectories notwithstanding, Malaysia has remained throughout, too, a key player within the Association of Southeast Asian Nations (ASEAN) and a sometimes-fiery middle-power state on the global stage; in his chapter, Karminder Singh Dhillon lays out and evaluates Malaysia's array of foreign policy objectives. Aspiring to, and achieving, prominence among trading states, among Muslim-identified states in the Organisation of the Islamic Conference, and in security alliances alike (see the chapters by Lai Yew Meng and Carolin Liss), Malaysia claims more prominence than its small size might suggest. (The chapters by Heng Pek Koon, Kuik Cheng-Chwee, and Ruhanas Harun assess Malaysia's relations with the US, China, and Europe, respectively.) Yet even in this policy domain, changes in leadership, fluctuating priorities, and the inevitable buffeting of booms and crises make for a never-dull picture.

Overview of the volume

As noted above, this volume cannot hope to be fully comprehensive. Rather it aspires to be thorough and analytical – to lay out relevant facts and background on a wide range of issues and topics, then to make something of those details: to draw conclusions, to test theorised relationships among factors, to offer suggestions, to venture predictions. Moreover, while the volume is purposely biased toward present-day Malaysia, the chapters are sensitive to history and context, and some are more pointedly historical in their approach.

The chapters are divided among four sections: domestic politics, economics, social policy and social development, and international relations and security. In reality, these sections necessarily overlap – Islam, for instance, as not just a faith, but a social cleavage, an ideology and/or a strategic priority colours all four sections – but the contributions within each section are generally more directly complementary than those across sections. Each author had relatively free rein in deciding how to structure and orient his or her chapter. The authors come from a range of backgrounds – most, but not all, are academics; the majority, but not all, are Malaysians (locally based or expatriate); and they run the gamut of most presumed-relevant socio-political cleavages in Malaysia – so their perspectives are obviously multifarious. In short, our aim with this volume is to capture manifold perspectives on and paradoxes within Malaysia as a state and a nation, more to provoke further reflection and debate than with the pretence of offering pat answers.

Part I
Domestic politics

Overview

Meredith L. Weiss

As Malaysia achieved independence in 1957, deeply entrenched racial pillarisation and class stratification foretold a difficult political path ahead, despite a high degree of elite consensus. Indeed, Malaysia today is home to multiple visions and histories: as the chapters that follow detail, Malaysian politics is hardly monolithic. That variety comes through across states and regions within the country (e.g. the economic and cultural differences marking east and west coast, urban and rural areas, or peninsular and East Malaysia); across administrative levels, however much attention tends to focus on national, and secondarily, state-level, politics; and across subsets of voters, whether seen in terms of ethnicity, religion, gender, age, or socioeconomic class.

Bridget Welsh homes in on these distinctions in her chapter on elections in Malaysia. The lion's share of political discussion and research alike in Malaysia centre around elections, held and respected with near-unbroken regularity since independence, at both the federal and state levels. Yet however prolific studies of elections may be, they tend to hover at the elite level, on the one hand, and to characterise voters as though in homogenous (and especially ethnic) blocs, on the other. Recent studies have foregrounded other dimensions – from other social cleavages (religion, region, gender, etc., though notably, seldom class), to the role of state largesse and developmentalism, to the sway of media and messaging. Moreover, recent praxis in Malaysia has not only raised questions of electoral integrity, but suggested a turn toward increasing citizen engagement and empowerment. Even so, whether elections could usher in regime change remains uncertain.

In his chapter on political parties and coalitions, Ong Kian Ming engages with elections from a different angle. He notes that a combination of social structure as well as institutional legacies and advantages conspires to sustain the incumbent Barisan Nasional (National Front, BN) and stymie alternatives. That said, the rise and solidification recently of Pakatan Rakyat (People's Alliance) as a coherent, seemingly cohesive alternative signals a shift to a two-coalition order, rather than a single behemoth versus disparate small challengers. Indeed, Ong suggests that the effective number of parties/coalitions (the real number of players) is, and long has been, right about two, taking into account initiatives for opposition coordination since 1990. Regardless, while Sabah and Sarawak have likewise shifted toward a two-party system, with local parties having lost ground there, patterns and issues on the ground have long differed between the peninsula and East Malaysia.

Our focus next turns to the elites within those parties, whom William Case deems increasingly testy, riven by both inter- and intra-party rivalries. Prevailing conventional wisdom, he suggests, tends to assume greater stability and cohesiveness than is borne out in fact. Separating out issues of elite relations and relative statuses from questions of regime (in)stability, Case forces a reassessment of patronage flows, elite pacts, and (sometimes sordid, bare-knuckled) contests. The fight, he notes, is at least as fraught within the single dominant party, given the spoils and status at stake, as it is between that party and its partners or rivals. While like Ong, Case notes shifts in these parties over time, he finds that what has changed is less the fact of elite fractiousness than the axes on which squabbling elites align.

We turn next to perhaps the most fraught of these axes, at least on the mass level – religion – with Joseph Chinyong Liow and Afif Pasuni's chapter on political Islam and Arnold Puyok's, on Christians' political mobilisation. Liow and Afif note the entanglement of Islamism with ethnicity, on the one hand, and electoral pressures, on the other. While Islam has a long history of being central to Malay society, the parameters of Islamism in politics have shifted, as parties compete both within the Malay community and across ethnic lines; with the proliferation of Islamic civil society movements; with the rotation of key leaders as well as ideational currents; and with the ascendance of particular issues – for instance, recent tensions over questions of religious freedom. Arnold Puyok, meanwhile, notes the unduly little attention given to the role of the Christian Church and its leaders in Malaysian politics, despite their recent assertiveness. While that engagement has been driven in part by the rise of political Islam, coupled with apparent limitations on the space for and religious freedom of non-Muslims in the polity, Christian mobilisation – particularly in Sabah and Sarawak, given their larger proportion of Christians and different patterns of engagement – has its own distinctive issues and dynamics.

The next three chapters divide Malaysia by geographic and administrative level, rather than social cleavages per se. Francis Loh explores Malaysia's federal structure. The country's thirteen states have relatively little authority (although Sabah and Sarawak have greater, if diminishing, rights; see below), due to historical and institutional legacies, the lack of a clear demographic basis for state divisions, and political exigency. A combination of constitutional design and the evolution of political and economic processes over time has fostered a top-heavy institutional structure, now tested by the fact of opposition-led governments in a larger share of states since 2008 than previously. The federal government has taken steps, ranging from withholding resources to removing services from state control by way of privatisation, to prevent the transfer of financial resources or administrative authority to opposition-controlled states, but such tactics increasingly spark tensions even with BN-led states.

James Chin homes in on the most administratively distinctive states in that latter category, Sabah and Sarawak. He reminds us that these two states, while both firmly in the BN camp, differ not just from their peninsular counterparts, but from each other in important ways. The BN has essayed to solidify a similar sort of BN dominance in East Malaysia as on the peninsula, helped in that effort by (or in conjunction with) not just an increasing population share for Muslims over the past few decades, but also Muslim dominance in the state legislature and a 'Muslim-first' policy framework. Non-Muslim Bumiputera and Chinese have been politically marginalised, with little chance of change, particularly so long as the BN – now heavily reliant on East Malaysian support – remains in power at the federal level.

With Goh Ban Lee's chapter, we delve deeper among administrative strata, to the local government level. The balance of authority in Malaysia rests squarely with the federal government, not just vis-à-vis the states, but also local government. Particularly in the absence of long-since-abolished local elections, the role of local authorities has diminished and the lines between this level and those above have blurred. Distributional and other decisions are heavily tilted toward the federal government, even though it is state governments that create local authorities and appoint office-holders, and that otherwise retain significant authority over the local level. Moreover, problems of poor documentation, the opacity of procedures, and lack of both compliance with and enforcement of regulations has resulted in a lack of local government accountability and effectiveness.

Norma Mansor and Raja Noriza Raja Ariffin share some of these critiques, but take a broader view of Malaysia's public administration. They chart the stages of development of the public administration, from a hierarchical and stripped-down model under British rule, to an expanded and more hands-on developmental apparatus, to embrace of a neoliberal new public management framework, to more recent reforms. They note improvements to regulations and processes related to doing business, the greater inclusion of public input in policy-making, and continuing efforts to overhaul outdated or no longer adequate or germane institutions and processes, in light of changing priorities and economic conditions.

Finally, Anantha Raman Govindasamy homes in on a very different sort of politics: the recent efflorescence of hands-on, large-scale, extra-electoral citizens' protests. He offers the Coalition for Clean and Fair Elections (BERSIH), Hindu Rights Action Force (HINDRAF), and Pertubuhan Pribumi Perkasa Malaysia (Perkasa, Malaysian Indigenous Empowerment Organisation) as examples of an increasingly active, politically engaged civil society. While in the electoral realm, as Welsh details, ethnicity is still highly salient (especially in the cases of HINDRAF and Perkasa), Bersih in particular underscores the possibility also for multiracial initiatives. This spate of mobilisation, he suggests, is tied to electoral developments, including the relative decline of the BN and rise of Pakatan, but also is both the outgrowth and cause of citizens' apparent increasing influence on government decision-making.

1

Elections in Malaysia

Voting behaviour and electoral integrity

Bridget Welsh

Of all the countries in Southeast Asia, Malaysia's elections have arguably received the most academic attention. Since the country received its independence in 1957, there have been thirteen general elections, regularly held within five-year intervals with the exception of the eighteen-month emergency period after the May 1969 racial riots. As elections have become highly institutionalised, the study of Malaysian elections has been a flourishing research area, dominating the discussion of politics. Despite the broadening of civil society and political contestation outside of the campaign periods, elections serve as defining points in the country's political history, be it the recent May 2013 and March 2008 polls or the pivotal historic 1955 and 1969 contests. By way of an example, less than a year after the 2013 polls, no fewer than three journal special issues, three books and multiple articles have been devoted to understanding the electoral process and outcome (Case 2013; Chin 2013a; Kee 2013; Khoo 2013; Ufen 2013; Weiss 2013; Welsh 2013, 2014).

This chapter looks at research on contemporary elections in Malaysia. The chapter is necessarily selective in its approach and coverage. The purpose is to draw together central themes and evaluate how elections are being understood, rather than to provide a comprehensive review. Attention centres on two important themes: voting behaviour and electoral integrity. This attention to political behaviour and the rules and norms governing polls reflects two comparatively recent threads in the studies of Malaysian elections. The focus is on national-level general elections (GEs).[1]

The richness of recent studies lends considerable optimism regarding our understanding of elections in Malaysia. Our knowledge of Malaysians as voters has expanded, with increasing attention to different political identities and social cleavages. We also find that public attention to electoral reform has fostered in-depth research on how Malaysia administers elections and the impact of these administrative rules and procedures. As elections have become more competitive in the last decade, more attention is also centring on how elections may allow changes in leaders and policies. In short, we appreciate the multiple roles that citizens, campaigns, rules and institutions play in shaping electoral outcomes. Nevertheless, as will be developed below, considerable questions remain unanswered, not least of which is whether elections in Malaysia will offer its citizens the opportunity for regime change.

From elites to citizens: frameworks of voters and voting

With high turnouts, averaging over 70 percent since independence, it is fitting to begin with how voters have been studied. In two of the most comprehensive early studies on Malaysian elections, Ratnam and Milne (1967) and Vasil (1972) provide a detailed overview of the participants, parties and performance during the 1964 and 1969 GEs, respectively. These works set the standard for research on elections in their scope and richness and began a pattern that has occurred regularly in Malaysian scholarship – a focus on reporting on the election itself. The thrust of these initial works was on the winners and losers, allowing for resilience in these studies over time. One of the defining features of these early studies, however, was the largely missing Malaysian voter. The attention to the election primarily highlighted the elites participating in the process as candidates and their campaigns. Voters were largely missing ingredients in the initial analytical works, as an elite focus on interpreting elections emerged.

While a preoccupation with elites would persist in election studies – as it does in other analyses of politics in Malaysia – an appreciation of ordinary citizens would evolve gradually. Voters began to be framed as groups, primarily as ethnic communities. The dominance of ethnicity in Malaysian politics is a persistent feature in the analysis of voting behaviour, with the framing of ethnicity initially derived from the race-linked Malay–Chinese–Indian–Other (MCIO) conceptualisation that parallels the ethnic composition and identity of the leading peninsular-based political parties.[2] In 1957, the dominant party, the United Malays National Organisation (UMNO), forged a coalition with the Malaysian Chinese Association (MCA) and Malaysian Indian Congress (MIC), forming what was known as the Alliance. After 1969, the Alliance was expanded to include more political parties, particularly those in the two states of Sabah and Sarawak in East Malaysia, and renamed the National Front or Barisan Nasional (BN). While nominally more multi-ethnic, the main opposition parties historically in Malaysia have also rested on ethnic foundations, namely Malay support for the Pan-Malaysian Islamic Party (Parti Islam SeMalaysia, PAS) and Chinese support for the Democratic Action Party (DAP).

The ethnic paradigm in Malaysian elections rests on certain assumptions and is a self-reinforcing dynamic. Voters are seen to prioritise their ethnicity over other features of their political identity, such as class or gender or even sub-ethnic identities. Moreover, they are believed to view their role as citizens along racial lines, for example to see politics as being about the rights of different ethnic communities who operate in an ethnically divided polity. Voters are also presumed to assess the performance of political parties by their ability to represent their respective community. These assumptions tie into different practices in electoral contests. Voters are categorised in constituencies along ethnic lines – with different ethnic rationales used to delineate seats – which in turn leads to a particularly ethnic-oriented contest. Ethnic-based issues such as language, education, affirmative action and religion closely intertwine with broader questions of ethnic representation and feature prominently in political campaigns. Finally, voters are believed to vote according to ethnic loyalties and patterns of mobilisation. Which comes first – ethnicity in the political identity of individuals, or in the way political parties engage with voters – is moot, as a perceived mutually reinforcing ethnic dynamic heightens this lens in analysing elections.

While scholars have rightly criticised the ethnic paradigm's use and dominance in electoral analyses (Loh and Saravanamuttu 2003), not least for its shallow understanding of ethnicity (Mandal 2004), the ethnic paradigm remains embedded in research and arguably in Malaysian voting behaviour itself. The significant patterns in voting behaviour along ethnic lines and continued use of ethnicity by political parties – prominent in GE13 (Welsh 2014) – make it impossible to dismiss ethnicity in understanding Malaysian elections.

In voting analyses, researchers have thus not surprisingly drawn attention to ethnic voting patterns (see, for example, Brown 2005; Welsh 2004; Chin and Wong 2009). This genre has run the gamut from heuristic studies based on culture to data-based analyses using detailed statistics on election results and polling. The main questions have generally revolved around two issues. Foremost is the 'loyalty' of the Chinese to the existing system. Traditionally, the Chinese community has been a swing group, moving away from the incumbent government in 1969, 1990, 2008 and 2013, and shoring up the incumbent coalition in elections such as 1995 and 1999. The issue of 'loyalty' of Malaysian Chinese is highly politicised in that Malay leaders in the dominant Malay party, UMNO, have regularly used the Chinese community as a target and labelled them as *orang pendatang* or 'foreigners' – despite many in the community having longer roots in Malaysia than other citizens. The Chinese, along with other ethnic minorities, are labelled as 'second-class' citizens. In 2013, Chinese Malaysians made up 24 percent of the population, a decrease from 36 percent at independence. Their 'loyalty' to the incumbent coalition is seen as decisive as it still can shape the final outcome in elections.

The second issue has been the level of unanimity of the Malay community. UMNO as a party draws its legitimacy from articulating the interest of the Malays, as they define it. Malays comprise 50.4 percent of the population currently (although with the other indigenous population of East Malaysia included, this increases to 67.4 percent). If the Malay community is split, or in other words, loyal to opposition parties, then the legitimacy of the ruling party is questioned. UMNO's greatest political challenge has come when it has lost ground in the Malay heartland of the country, namely the north and east (Kedah, Perak, Perlis, Kelantan, Terengganu and Pahang). Its greatest challenger has been the Islamist PAS, although since 1999, another party, now called the People's Justice Party or Parti Keadilan Rakyat, has also won considerable Malay support. Securing Malay support is portrayed as the legitimate marker of the right to hold onto power by those who conceive of political power as primarily ethnicity-driven. One of the ironies of UMNO in office is that it has set the terms of its own legitimacy, opening itself to challenge when it loses support among the Malay community.

While analysis has concentrated historically on the two largest ethnic communities, the Malays and the Chinese, with greater electoral competitiveness has come increased attention to smaller minorities. These groups are no less important in shaping political outcomes, as the minority groups are evaluated for their support for the incumbent government. Studies of East Malaysia are often subdivided to reflect the communities there – Malay/Melanau, Chinese, Kadazan, Dusun, Iban and more – highlighting the ethnic pluralism of Sabah and Sarawak. Over time, there have been increasing efforts to fit East Malaysia's ethnic communities into a peninsular-oriented framework of three different groups, a construct that does not reflect conditions on the ground. The use of the ethnic paradigm to understand voting has risen in prominence in East Malaysia as its role as a king-maker in national politics has increased (Chin 2013b).

The Indian community has also gleaned attention, although research on this community is hampered by its limited size – Indians currently comprise 7.3 percent of the population – and geographical dispersal. In 2008, the Indian community was highly mobilised over issues of religious freedom, forming a movement known as HINDRAF (Willford 2013; see also Anantha Raman Govindasamy, this volume). Their move away from the incumbent coalition is seen as one of the decisive factors that contributed to the BN's loss of its two-thirds majority in parliament that year. (The dominant coalition has held onto power in every election in

Malaysia, although it has fallen short of a two-thirds majority three times – 1969, 2008 and most recently, 2013.) In this ethnic approach, elections are seen to be determined by the support of different ethnic communities, with voters acting as unified race-based groups.

The ethnic heuristic tool is reinforced by the use of two other related social cleavages to understand voting. The first is an extension of the ethnicity rubric to include religion. The other is geography. Let us take each of these in turn. The synergy between religion and ethnicity has always been close. From Malaysia's early years, when the organisation that became PAS was formed in 1947 by a split over Islam within UMNO, to more recent mobilisation of religious minorities over religious freedom, a focus on religion simultaneously has been an outgrowth of, and reinforced, the ethnic voting paradigm. Religious issues have permeated political campaigns due to the link with morality, party identity and political mobilisation. How much actual voters are swayed by religion as opposed to other aspects of ethnic identity is challenging to distinguish because of the explicit linking of race with religion, especially among Muslims. How much voting is determined by religion alone is even more challenging, given the complexity of religious practice and Malaysia's religious pluralism. While a Malay, as defined in the Malaysian constitution, is a Muslim and lacks the freedom to choose another religion, there are differences within the Malay community in how Islam is practised, as is the case for all of Malaysia's religious communities for their respective faiths. Recent scholarship has drawn attention to how religious issues mobilise voters and how religiosity among both Muslims and Christians has shaped voting patterns (Hamayotsu 2013; see also Puyok and Liow and Afif, this volume). The findings do show that religion and religiosity, like race, help us understand voting behaviour, especially in recent polls. For example, among Malays, PAS continues to win over more religiously devout and conservative Muslims (Yahoo! News Malaysia 2013). We also find that religiously devout Christians are more inclined to support the opposition (Welsh 2014). This scholarship, however, is less rigorous in its empirical methodology than are other studies in the ethnicity paradigm that now rely on statistical analysis of local polling-station data as well as surveys.

Another analytical framework for understanding voting behaviour has been geography, or place. The urban–rural divide remains one of the most important political cleavages in Southeast Asia, including Malaysia. Studies of rural–urban differences have pointed to the impact of information, messaging and campaigning as underscoring why rural voters differ from their urban counterparts (Ockey 2004). Seen as less informed and more focused on parochial politics and personal patronage, rural voters are believed to be more conservative and usually to favour the incumbent. In Malaysia, as a result of the concentration of Chinese in cities and Malays in rural areas, at least before the 1980s, the ethnic paradigm has been conflated with the urban–rural lens. While there remains a higher concentration of Chinese in urban areas, especially in East Malaysia, the country as a whole is more than 70 percent urbanised, with Malays now on a par with or exceeding Chinese in number in many of the urban centres of Selangor and Penang. Studies through the 1980s continued to highlight this geographic divide, with more recent scholarship holding different views of urban–rural cleavages. In analyses of the 2013 results, for example, some scholars (Chin 2013a) argue this divide was decisive for the BN while others posit that both the cleavage itself (Thompson 2013; also Thompson, this volume) and actual voting patterns (except in East Malaysia) do not help us understand the results (Welsh 2014). The view that the government gets its support from the rural areas remains prominent (Lee 2013).

This emphasis on geography has extended to other regional patterns, focused around states and dynamics in particular regional governments. East Malaysia especially has regularly been singled out for its unique voting patterns, with the power of personality and local issues given greater explanatory importance (Chin 2013a; Welsh 2014). The use of place in politics has been a useful tool to interpret differences in voting patterns.

The contemporary use of socio-economic lenses to understand voters has moved from groups to individuals, bringing more complexity to research. Gender and generational factors are now meshed with ethnicity and place. Research shows that women generally favour the incumbent regime, except Chinese Malaysian women (Yahoo! News Malaysia 2013). We also find that young voters are decisive in electoral outcomes, and have been since 1999. This trend will likely continue as a result of Malaysia's young population. In 2008, young voters gave the opposition sufficient boost to break the two-thirds barrier, but in 2013, young voters were more split, leading to limited opposition electoral gains (Welsh 2014). Data collected from polling stations and surveys have been used to capture such voting patterns with increasing sophistication.

Of these lenses, one is noticeably missing – class. While there have been efforts to bring class into our understanding of voters – pointing to lower-class support for the opposition (Syed Husin 1984) and more recently, the effectiveness of the BN in winning over lower-class voters in 2013 (Welsh 2014) – the socio-economic positions of voters are often overlooked or ignored altogether. Ethnicity continues to trump all the other frameworks, even as our appreciation of the richness and diversity of the political identities of voters themselves has been enhanced.

From clients to citizens: voters in context

Despite a deeper understanding of voting patterns, questions continue to linger in our understanding of voters. Why exactly does a Malay vote as he or she does, for example? Socio-economic markers capture differences, but do not necessary help our understanding; we can identify patterns in our research, but are left grappling with the search for causes of voting behaviour. Rather than look at voters themselves, scholars searching for causation have turned to more interactive models that connect voters with the state or political campaigns. Malaysians are portrayed as voting in response to government efforts to win support through the provision of public services, economic performance and stability. In one of the earliest broad reflections on Malaysian elections, scholar Harold Crouch (1996) stressed the importance of the interaction between voters and the government, with elections serving to legitimise the government and simultaneously forcing the government to recalibrate its governance. The focus on the government was extended in the seminal works of Francis Loh (2002), who emphasised the impact of 'developmentalism', or the use of development resources and rhetoric, to hold onto power. Complementing such work are recent analyses of the populist use of government resources to woo support in the 2013 polls through 'commercialisation' (Welsh 2013). Looking at elections with attention to the state, through the lens of the actions of the government, allows us to understand better why voters may opt to maintain their loyalty to the BN.

Another interactive approach has involved a focus on campaigns. Traditionally, the discussion of campaigns has involved the three 'Ms' – media, machinery and money (with a fourth 'M' of Mahathir Mohamad, the country's fourth premier) (Mustafa 2004; George 2006). In each of these areas, the incumbent has been seen to have the edge, using its control over the mainstream media, large party organisation and access to resources to its advantage. Technological change and the use of the Internet and social media have levelled the playing field in media, although this rebalancing has not extended to mainstream media and analyses of the recent election reveal that the government was able to master new media, as well, although less well (Diamond 2010; Khoo 2010; Houghton 2013; Steele 2009; Tapsell 2013).

Contemporary campaigns in Malaysia are a hybrid, melding pre-modern forms of mobilisation in *ceramah* (public rallies) with post-modern practices of centralised planning and the use of professional consultants. They combine performance and theatre with policy-oriented public engagement (Lim and Ong 2006). The campaign itself has been seen as decisive in shaping outcomes, as occurred in 2008. In that contest, the government was on the defensive over issues of ethnic exclusion and perceptions of unfulfilled promises by then premier Abdullah Badawi. Besides drawing attention to the Internet and social media, contemporary research has helped us appreciate the effects of different types of messaging in campaigns – yet another 'M' – and their effectiveness (Ibrahim 2010). Polling and focus group analyses are now well integrated into campaign strategies. The central role of governance issues such as corruption and cost of living concerns reflects greater attention to the problems identified by voters themselves. Voters have had more impact on campaigns and in turn, campaigns have become more impactful. The interaction of campaigns and outcomes points to a further people-oriented trend in Malaysian elections: a greater attention to the needs of citizens in elections.

Citizens are also taking electoral politics into their own hands. In the last decade citizens have felt empowered at the ballot box. They know they can make a difference to the outcome. From the *reformasi* movement of 1999 that brought a generation into the streets, many of whom are now in parliament, to the political awakenings that have taken place in less politically active towns such as Bentong and Miri and states such as Johor and Perak since 2008, Malaysia's political life around elections has become energised and engaged. Elections remain the focal point for political life, but the political relationships forged during campaigning extend into everyday politics. There has been a political mobilisation of the electorate, with groups across the political spectrum making demands and contesting with each other. Ordinary citizens are no longer relying on elites and political parties for representation. Some citizens see too much 'politics' now in Malaysia, while others do not see the form and substance of contemporary politics, both its polarisation and its personalisation, to be constructive. Elections, however, have become less of a controlled arena of politics as described by Benedict Anderson (1996) in his characterisation of elections in the region. Rather, they are an extension of broader political engagement.

Contesting the rules: challenges of electoral reform

A central dimension of this citizen politics has been contestation over the electoral process. Dressed in yellow and marching for electoral reform, participants in the Bersih (Coalition for Clean and Fair Elections) movement catapulted the issue of electoral integrity onto the national stage. Since 2007, there have been intense discussions about how to make the rules and administrative processes governing elections fairer. Scholarship has similarly expanded to draw attention to electoral reform. Broadly, four major areas have come under scrutiny, all of which point to ways the system favours the incumbent party and negatively affects electoral integrity.

Foremost among these issues has been the conduct of the institutional bodies that administer and regulate the conduct of elections (Lim 2002, 2005). Complaints have repeatedly centred on the perceived bias and lack of professionalism of the main institution, the Election Commission (EC). This body is constituted by the prime minister and since 1962 has lost its ability to administer polls independently. The EC is comprised of senior civil servants, many of them lacking professional backgrounds in administering polls, and is seen to favour the incumbent party. That former and current commissioners have publicly claimed loyalty to UMNO has contributed to concerns about a lack of neutrality.

The institutional organisation of elections extends beyond the EC to include the Registrar of Societies (ROS) (who monitors political parties and their registration), the police (who regulate campaigns, while other branches provide intelligence reports to the incumbent party), as well as the judiciary. Concerns have been raised about the police for their support of the incumbent party and of the ROS for decades, as the party registration process has been seen as arbitrary and politically tainted. Recent complaints over the lack of a fair hearing in the over sixty electoral petitions that were filed in GE13, including measures that arbitrarily dismiss petitioners, have reinforced the view that even the judiciary's role in elections does not meet international standards of neutrality. Some reports go further, to suggest that administrators of Malaysia's polls fail adequately to ensure transparency in counting, secure and accurate ballots and the rule of law; such critiques move an assessment of the administration of Malaysia's polls away from one of non-neutrality, to suggest active participation in ensuring victory for the incumbent coalition (Pemantau 2013). While these matters remain highly contested, concerns over administrative neutrality point to a major weakness in Malaysia's electoral integrity.

These concerns are reinforced by evidence that points to exclusion and suspect practices in the management of voter registration. Malaysia has a higher voting age than the global average, twenty-one, thereby excluding millions of its young citizens from voting. The issue of exclusion goes beyond the voting age to involve the registration process itself. The EC has been seen as arbitrary in assessing when to include voters in the final electoral roll, as occurred in the competitive 1999 election, which excluded 100,000 newly registered voters from participating. While steps in recent years have allowed for online voter registration, the burden this administrative hurdle places on voters effectively excludes many citizens from voting. The exclusion is particularly acute in the more remote areas of East Malaysia, where voters are effectively registered through government civil servants as they often lack access to register otherwise. The opposite concern is also raised, with reports of non-citizens being allowed to vote. This is particularly common in Sabah, where hundreds of thousands of illegal migrants have been granted the right to vote since the 1980s, according to a recently concluded Royal Commission of Inquiry (Welsh 2013). While the EC rightly is not the sole organisation responsible for this practice and it lacks enforcement capacity to review questions of citizenship, the end result has been that elections in Malaysia have excluded citizens in the registration process, yet in some cases, included non-citizens. There is a perception that these non-citizens (some of whom are later granted citizenship) skew the electoral outcome in the incumbent party's favour.

The issue of who is included and excluded is tied to the integrity of the electoral roll itself. Recent audits of the electoral roll before GE13 identified significant problems in the composition of the list, with persistent 'phantom voters' reported, many of whom either lacked addresses or were listed all in one residence (MERAP 2013). Repeated calls to revamp the electoral roll have been effectively ignored by the EC; a cleaning exercise left many parties unsatisfied as the reported problems remained. Malaysia's judiciary has denied the ability of opposition political parties to question the electoral roll, despite reports and witnesses.

Concerns with the electoral roll are compounded by unexplained placements and transfers of voters among different constituencies. GE13 in particular saw an unprecedented rise in the share of new voters, including in some constituencies of senior leaders in the incumbent party. For instance, the remote rural constituency of Prime Minister Najib Tun Razak himself received over 30 percent new voters (Welsh 2014). Voters in the same household, including a husband and wife, have been assigned to different constituencies without explanation. The padding phenomenon for leaders, as well as strategic movement and placement of voters within constituencies, has occurred at regular intervals, especially in elections before delineation exercises, most recently in GE13, or in highly competitive contests such as in Terengganu in 2004. These practices are conducted by the EC and deepen concerns over electoral integrity.

A third area in which scholarship on elections has questioned the electoral playing field involves the conduct of the campaign. This area ties into the discussion of the 'Ms' noted above, especially money and the media. Financial resources have become more important in political campaigning with the move away from pre-modern campaigning to post-modern practices (Fernandez 2010; Gomez 1996). This shift has impacted the conduct of elections. The advantages of money have significantly benefited the incumbent government. Effectively unregulated campaign financing, vote buying and the abuse of state resources in campaigns have become the norm, although these practices are being challenged. The attention to money in campaigns for its favouring of the incumbent government parallels long-running complaints about control of mainstream media and obvious biases in reporting. Malaysia's mainstream media outlets are owned by companies linked to the government political parties (Mustafa 2004). There is a lack of access for opposition parties and skewed coverage during the campaign itself.

Finally, scholars have questioned the electoral framework, both the electoral system itself and organisation of constituencies, and the legal framework (Lim 2003; Das 2005; Rachagan 1980; A. Rahman 1994). In 2013, the incumbent government won 47.4 percent of the popular vote but obtained 59.9 percent of the seats (Ostwald 2013). This skew has extended the outcry over how the electoral framework advantages the incumbent. Malaysia's 'winner takes all' first-past-the-post electoral system has been criticised, with calls increasing for the introduction of a more inclusive proportional-representation system. Failure to meet international standards for constituency delineation has generated even more concern, including inconsistent use of standards, heavy malapportionment by creating seats in 'safe' areas, and lack of transparency in the delineation process itself. Malaysia has long stood out as an example that does not conform to the global trend of reducing discrimination and bias in drawing constituencies.

New understandings, persistent question

Greater scrutiny of voters, voting and the electoral process has brought increased appreciation of the complexity of elections and their importance. Scholars continue to flock to analyse elections and debates have flourished. Yet all these studies have yet to provide a clear answer to the question that has underscored much of the research: whether elections in Malaysia will serve as a means to change the government (Case 1993; Liow 1999). The BN now stands as the longest-serving government in the world. Many Malaysians believe that a change of government will open a path to new forms of governance and greater democracy. Others would like to hold onto what they know.

Contemporary studies of elections suggest that the obstacles to changing the government are high. They have been illuminated in the attention to electoral integrity and in efforts to gain a clearer sense of who constitutes the base of support for the incumbent government and why. Rather than providing a clear trajectory of trends ahead for electoral behaviour and outcomes, these contributions generally point to greater contestation and increasing confrontation over elections. Malaysia's electorate – as is the case in many parts of Southeast Asia – is polarised and this polarisation is widening. The electoral process itself is now also being contested.

Will this polarised pattern of voting change? What sort of campaign will allow the government to hold onto power? Will electoral reform move forward and how will this happen? Despite contributions to knowledge on elections, the answers to key questions of what motivates Malaysians to vote as they do and whether they can overcome the obstacles embedded in electoral rules remain elusive. If there is one certainty in our understanding of elections in Malaysia, it is that elections will continue to generate interest and debate.

Notes

1 GEs usually coincide with state legislative polls that determine the government in Malaysia's thirteen states, with the major exception of the East Malaysian states of Sabah and Sarawak, which have traditionally operated on different calendars. Malaysia has not held local elections since 1965, as they have been suspended. The opposition state government of Selangor introduced elections at the local level in some communities after they won power in 2008.

2 See Loh 2011 for an excellent review of the study of Malaysian elections. He makes the point that electoral analyses have been focused on ethnicity.

Bibliography

A. Rashid Rahman (1994) *The Conduct of Elections in Malaysia*, Kuala Lumpur: Berita Publishing.

Anderson, Benedict (1996) 'Elections in Southeast Asia', in R.H. Taylor (ed.), *The Politics of Elections in Southeast Asia*, Washington DC: Woodrow Wilson Center Press.

Brown, Graham (2005) Playing the (Non) Ethnic Card: The Electoral System and Ethnic Voting Patterns in Malaysia, CRISE Working Paper No. 21, Oxford: CRISE, University of Oxford.

Case, William (1993) 'Semi-democracy in Malaysia: withstanding the pressures for regime change', *Pacific Affairs*, 66(2): 183–205.

Case, William (2013) 'Post-GE13: any closer to ethnic harmony and democratic change?', *The Round Table: The Commonwealth Journal of International Affairs*, 102(6): 511–19.

Chin, James (2013a) 'So close and yet so far: strategies in the 13th Malaysian elections', *The Round Table: The Commonwealth Journal of International Affairs*, 102(6): 533–40.

Chin, James (2013b) 'Chinese tsunami or urban revolt? It is both actually', *The Round Table: The Commonwealth Journal of International Affairs*, 102(6): 499–501.

Chin, James and Wong Chin Huat (2009) 'Malaysia's electoral upheaval', *Journal of Democracy*, 20(3): 71–85.

Crouch, Harold (1996) 'Malaysia: do elections make a difference?', in R.H. Taylor (ed.), *The Politics of Elections in Southeast Asia*, Washington DC: Woodrow Wilson Center Press, pp. 114–35.

Das, Cyrus (2005) 'Election laws: compelling areas for reform', in Mavis Puthucheary and Norani Othman (eds), *Elections and Democracy in Malaysia*, Bangi: Penerbit UKM, pp. 372–82.

Diamond, Larry (2010) 'Liberation technology', *Journal of Democracy*, 21(3): 69–83.

Fernandez, Josie M. (ed.) (2010) *Reforming Political Financing in Malaysia*, Kuala Lumpur: Transparency International.

George, Cherian (2006) *Contentious Journalism and the Internet: Towards Democratic Discourse in Malaysia and Singapore*, Singapore: Singapore University Press and Seattle: University of Washington Press.

Gomez, Edmund T. (1996) 'Electoral funding of general, state and party elections in Malaysia', *Journal of Contemporary Asia*, 26(1): 81–99.

Hamayotsu, Kikue (2013) 'Towards a more democratic regime and society? The politics of faith and ethnicity in a transitional multi-ethnic Malaysia', *Journal of Current Southeast Asian Affairs*, 32(2): 61–88.

Houghton, Tessa J. (2013) *'Watching the Watchdog': Malaysian Media Coverage of GE13: Preliminary Results – Release 2*, 26 April, University of Nottingham Malaysia Campus and the Centre for Independent Journalism, available at http://pilihanraya.info/wp-content/uploads/2012/10/WtW.Release.1.2.pdf (accessed 6 May 2014).

Ibrahim, Suffian (2010) *Reflections of the 2008 Malaysian General Election: Role of the Internet in Political Communications*, Kuala Lumpur: Merdeka Center for Opinion Research.

Kee Thuan Chye (2013) *The Elections Bullshit*, Kuala Lumpur: SIRD.

Khoo Boo Teik (2010) Cyber-networks and Physical Coalitions in Malaysia: Realizing Dissent between Reformasi and the Tsunami, IDE Discussion Papers No. 244, Chiba: IDE-JETRO.

Khoo Boo Teik (ed.) (2013) 13th General Election in Malaysia: Issues, Outcomes and Implications, Interim Report 2013, Chiba: IDE-JETRO.

Lee Hock Guan (2013) 'Steadily amplified rural votes decide Malaysian elections', *ISEAS Perspective*, 34, 6 June.

Lim Hong Hai (2002) 'Electoral politics in Malaysia: "managing" elections in a plural society', in Auriel Croissant, Gabriele Bruns and Marie John (eds), *Electoral Politics in Southeast and East Asia*, Singapore: Friedrich Ebert Stiftung, pp. 101–48.

Lim Hong Hai (2003) 'The delineation of peninsular electoral constituencies: amplifying Malay and UMNO power', in Francis K.W. Loh and Johan Saravanamuttu (eds), *New Politics in Malaysia*, Singapore: Institute of Southeast Asian Studies, pp. 25–52.

Lim Hong Hai (2005) 'Making the system work: the election commission', in Mavis Puthucheary and Norani Othman (eds), *Elections and Democracy in Malaysia*, Bangi: Penerbit UKM, pp. 249–91.

Lim Hong Hai and Ong Kian Ming (2006) 'Electoral campaigning in Malaysia', in Christian Schafferer (ed.), *Electoral Campaigning in East and Southeast Asia*, Aldershot: Ashgate, pp. 55–78.

Liow, Joseph Chin Yong (1999) 'Crisis, choice and change: Malaysian electoral politics at the end of the 20th century', *Asian Journal of Political Science*, 7(2): 45–74.

Loh, Francis K.W. (2002) 'Developmentalism and the limits of democratic discourse', in Francis K.W. Loh and Khoo Boo Teik (eds), *Democracy in Malaysia: Discourses and Practice*, Richmond: Curzon, pp. 19–50.

Loh, Francis K.W. (2011) 'Studying elections and democracy in Malaysia: a survey and review', Keynote address for the Elections and Democracy Conference, UNIMAS, Sarawak, November. Unpublished.

Loh, Francis K.W. and Johan Saravanamuttu (eds) (2003) *New Politics in Malaysia*, Singapore: Institute of Southeast Asian Studies.

Malaysian Electoral Roll Analysis Project (MERAP) (2013) Available at http://malaysianelectoralroll-project.blogspot.sg/# (accessed 28 May 2014).

Mandal, Sumit K. (2004) 'Transethnic solidarities, racialization and social equality', in Edmund Terence Gomez (ed.), *The State of Malaysia: Ethnicity, Equity and Reform*, London: RoutledgeCurzon.

Merdeka Center Survey Release (2003) 3 May, available at www.merdeka.org (accessed 7 February 2014).

Mustafa K. Anuar (2004) 'Muzzled: the media in Mahathir's Malaysia', in Bridget Welsh (ed.), *Reflections: The Mahathir Years*, Washington DC: Johns Hopkins University Press, pp. 486–93.

Ockey, James (2004) *Making Democracy: Leadership, Class, Gender and Political Participation in Thailand*, Honolulu: University of Hawaii Press.

Ostwald, Kai (2013) 'How to win a lost election: malapportionment and Malaysia's 2013 general election', *The Round Table: The Commonwealth Journal of International Affairs*, 102(6): 521–32.

Pemantau Pilihan Raya Rakyat (2013) *Clean & Fair?: An Election Observation Report for GE13*, available at www.bersih.org/wp-content/uploads/2013/09/PEMANTAU-Report-FINAL-10-Sept-2013.pdf (accessed 6 May 2014).

Rachagan, Sothi (1980) 'The development of the electoral system', in Harold Crouch, Lee Kam Hing and Michael Ong (eds), *Malaysian Politics and the 1978 Elections*, Kuala Lumpur: Oxford University Press, pp. 255–92.

Ratnam, K.J. and R.S. Milne (1967) *The Malayan Parliamentary Election of 1964*, Kuala Lumpur: University of Malaya Press.

Steele, Janet (2009) 'Professionalism online: how Malaysiakini challenges authoritarianism', *The International Journal of Press/Politics*, 14(1): 91–111.

Syed Husin Ali (ed.) (1984) *Ethnicity, Class and Development, Malaysia*, Kuala Lumpur: Persatuan Sains Sosial Malaysia.

Tan Lee Ooi (2010) 'The emergence of a virtual civil society: transcending ethnic politics?', in Francis K.W. Loh (ed.), *Building Bridges, Crossing Boundaries: Everyday Forms of Inter-Ethnic Peace Building in Malaysia*, Kuala Lumpur: Persatuan Sains Sosial Malaysia and Jakarta: The Ford Foundation, pp. 273–96.

Tapsell, Ross (2013) 'Negotiating media "balance" in Malaysia's 2013 general election', *Journal of Current Southeast Asian Affairs*, 32(2): 39–60.

Thompson, Eric C. (2013) 'GE13 and the politics of urban chauvinism', *New Mandela*, 14 May, available at http://asiapacific.anu.edu.au/newmandala/2013/05/14/ge13-and-the-politics-of-urban-chauvinism/ (accessed 28 May 2014).

Ufen, Andreas (2013) 'Introduction: the 2013 Malaysian elections: business as usual or part of a protracted transition?', *Journal of Current Southeast Asian Affairs*, 32(2): 3–17.

Vasil, Raj (1972) *The Malaysian General Election of 1969*, Singapore: Oxford University Press.

Weiss, Meredith L. (ed.) (2013) *Electoral Dynamics in Malaysia: Findings from the Grassroots*, Singapore: Institute of Southeast Asian Studies and Petaling Jaya: SIRD.

Welsh, Bridget (2004) 'Real change? Electoral behavior in the reformasi era', in Edmund Terence Gomez (ed.), *The State of Malaysia: Ethnicity, Equity and Reform*, London: RoutledgeCurzon, pp. 162–93.

Welsh, Bridget (2013) 'Malaysian elections 2013: a step backward', *Journal of Democracy*, 23(4): 136–50.

Welsh, Bridget (2014, forthcoming) *Democracy Denied? Malaysia's GE13*, Singapore: Marshall Cavendish.

Willford, Andrew (2013) 'Every Indian is burning inside', in Bridget Welsh and James Chin (eds), *Awakening: The Abdullah Badawi Years in Malaysia*, Kuala Lumpur: SIRD.

Yahoo! News Malaysia (2013) 'Class, gender divide seen in GE13 voting trends, says Merdeka Center', Yahoo! News Malaysia, 16 May.

2
Malaysian political parties and coalitions

Ong Kian Ming

The purpose of this chapter is to provide an overview of political parties and coalitions in Malaysia in the context of existing political science theories with specific emphasis on features which are of interest from a comparative politics perspective. First, the nature of political party competition is discussed by placing the ruling coalition and the opposition along various dimensions of political party competition – the ethnic, local and emerging 'democracy' dimensions. Second, the challenges of building and maintaining political coalitions are discussed including the incentives and strategies used to sustain the ruling coalition and the absence of similar incentives for many short-lived opposition coalitions. The favourable circumstances underlying the formation and development of the most recent opposition coalition, Pakatan Rakyat, seem to indicate a consolidation of the two coalition system in Malaysia. Third, a brief overview in terms of the structures of the major political parties is given. Fourth and finally, a few words are offered with regard to possible developments in the political landscape in the future pertaining to political parties and coalitions.

Nature of political party competition

The nature of political competition in Malaysia determines the formation of new parties and coalitions, their configurations and reconfigurations, the manner in which they campaign and organise themselves and also the path by which they cease to exist. Understanding the various dimensions of political competition is key to understanding the nature of political parties and the coalitions to which they belong.

First dimension of political competition: dominant multiracial coalition in the centre, ethnic parties on either flank

Political competition in Malaysia has been, and continues to occur, largely along the ethnic dimension. Graphically, this has been represented by the coalition that has ruled Malaysia since independence, the Alliance Party and later the reconfigured National Front or Barisan Nasional (BN), occupying the political 'centre' with opposition parties 'flanking' the ruling coalition on either side (Horowitz 1985: 410–24). On one flank are parties representing the interests of the non-Malays, the most dominant being the Democratic Action Party (DAP), and on the other are parties representing the interests of the Malays, the most dominant being the Malaysian Islamic Party (Parti Islam seMalaysia, PAS) (Figure 2.1).

The formation of the Alliance coalition pre-independence was instrumental in shaping the nature of political competition post-independence. The success of the United Malays National Organisation (UMNO) and Malaysian Chinese Association (MCA) in contesting using a joint slate of candidates in the municipal elections in Kuala Lumpur in 1952 led to the formation of the Alliance, which included the Malaysian Indian Congress (MIC). The ability of the three parties to pool votes – to attract support from a majority of voters from the respective ethnic groups each party represented – allowed the Alliance to dominate the first pre-independence national elections in 1955 and post-independence elections in 1959 and 1964 (Horowitz 1985: 393–404; Ratnam and Milne 1967).

Even after the electoral setback in the 1969 general elections and the 13 May racial riots, the rewards from vote-pooling as well as the attraction of governing as part of a multiracial coalition enabled the expansion of the ruling coalition under a new name – BN – to include then opposition parties such as Parti Gerakan Rakyat Malaysia (GERAKAN), PPP and even PAS as well as a number of parties from East Malaysia. A strong 'centrifugal' force was set in motion by the electoral success of the Alliance that exists till today (Horowitz 1985: 439).

That is not to say that there were no other parties or coalitions vying for the centre along the ethnic dimension of political competition. But these parties and coalitions were not politically viable or sustainable as a result of the Alliance's and then later the BN's political dominance, the failure to find a unifying identity or cause, and government crackdown, especially against forces on the political left.

The All-Malaya Council of Joint Action (AMCJA) and the Pusat Tenaga Rakyat (PUTERA) or AMCJA–PUTERA Coalition – comprised mostly of non-Malay and Malay forces on the political left, respectively – established in 1946 as a pressure group against British

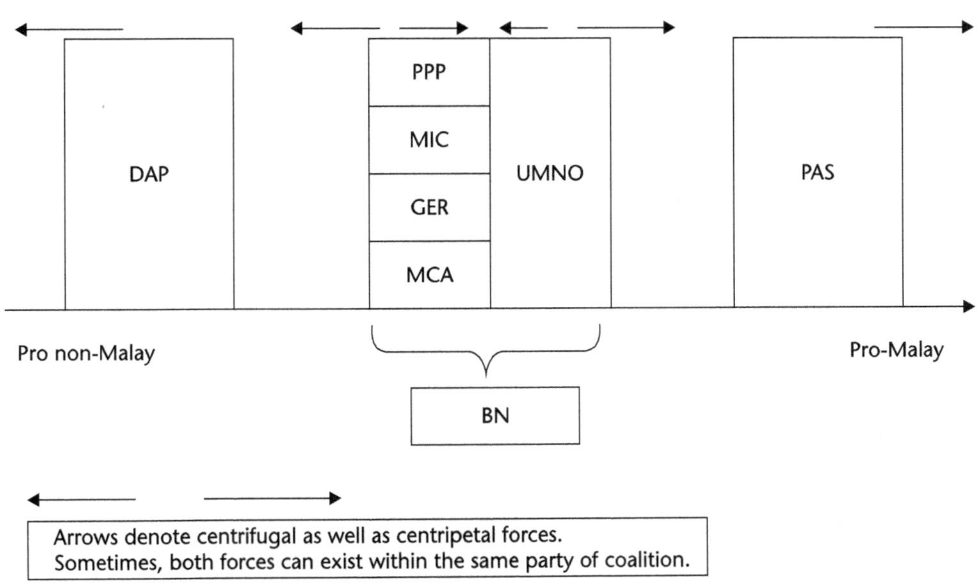

Figure 2.1 Centrifugal and centripetal forces of political competition in Malaysia

post-war policies in Malaya, was an early attempt at building a multiracial coalition. But it fell apart in 1948 when it failed to extract any concessions from the British (Oong 2000: 117) and when the Malayan Communist Party (MCP), a key component of the AMCJA, escalated its guerrilla activities as well as a result of the arrest of key members of PUTERA (Andaya and Andaya 2001: 269).

Onn Jaafar, the first president of UMNO, made two attempts at building a Malay-led multiracial party to challenge the Alliance. His first attempt, the Independence of Malaya Party (IMP), occurred as a result of his failure to open up UMNO to all races. But Onn abandoned the party after it succeeded in winning only two out of twelve seats in the KL municipal elections in 1952, losing out to the UMNO–MCA Alliance. Onn then went on to form Parti Negara (PN) in 1954. PN failed to win a single seat in the 1955 federal Legislative Council elections. It limped on by winning only one parliament seat in the 1959 general elections and went defunct after failing to win any seats in the 1964 general elections.

The Socialist Front (SF) – comprising the Chinese-dominated Labour Party (LP) and the Malay-led Parti Rakyat (PR) – won two parliamentary and eight state seats in the 1964 general elections and was gaining support among urban voters, especially non-Malays, in the lead-up to the 1969 general elections. However, the decision of the Labour Party to boycott the 1969 general elections saw many of the non-Malay voters switch their support to other non-Malay opposition parties such as the DAP and GERAKAN (Crouch 1996: 19). The racial riots on 13 May 1969 and the subsequent declaration of a state of emergency, coupled with the expansion of the ruling coalition to include nearly all the political parties in Malaysia, with the exception of the DAP, consequently led to the decrease in support for parties on the left, including the LP and PR.

Multiracial Malay-led parties such as the IMP and PN and more recently, Parti Keadilan Rakyat (PKR), inevitably face the challenge of assuring Malay voters that they can better protect their interests compared with the Malay-only UMNO, while at the same time being able to be inclusive enough to capture enough of the non-Malay vote (Mauzy 1983: 15–16). For multiracial coalitions, the challenges are similar. The coalition has to be led by a Malay-led or Malay-dominant party or parties in order to gain the votes of the majority group in Malaysia. And its non-Malay-led or -dominant party or parties have to gain sufficient credibility among non-Malay voters. AMCJA–PUTERA and the Socialist Front were not able to overcome the first hurdle in that they were both perceived to be dominated by the Chinese among the major component groups and parties.

The dominance of the Alliance in the political centre was strengthened with its expansion into the BN after the 1969 general elections. GERAKAN, which had a strong base in Penang, and the PPP, which had a strong base in Perak, especially in the city of Ipoh, joined the ruling coalition, as did PAS, although it would leave the ruling coalition in 1977. In Sarawak, the PBB and the Sarawak United Peoples' Party (SUPP) joined the BN. The Sabah Alliance comprising the United Sabah National Organization (USNO) and Sabah Chinese Association (SCA) also joined the BN.

BN's political dominance – helped by the manipulation of the electoral rules (Lim 2002), the use of repressive laws and a massive advantage in money, access to the media and machinery (Hwang 2003) – allowed it to win all thirteen post-independent elections. Until the twelfth general election in 2008, the BN had governed with at least two-thirds control of parliamentary seats, which gave the coalition power to amend the constitution unilaterally.[1]

BN's dominance in the centre meant that opposition parties could gain political representation only from occupying the ethnic flanks. With most of the major non-Malay parties joining the alliance, the non-Malay flank was quickly occupied by the DAP. PAS occupied the Malay flank after it left the BN. The DAP won most of its parliament and state seats in non-Malay majority urban areas in the west coast of Peninsular Malaysia while PAS won most of its seats in the majority non-urban areas in northern Peninsular Malaysia.

Interestingly, DAP and PAS dominance in their respective flanks meant that other smaller parties that wanted to contest in the flanks were also crowded out of the political marketplace. Smaller parties such as Parti Keadilan Masyarakat Malaysia (Pekemas) and subsequently the Malaysian Democratic Party (MDP), who were competing for the same non-Malay urban vote as the DAP, were not politically viable.

Second dimension of political competition: local competition at the state level in Sabah and Sarawak

The other salient dimension of political competition has been local competition at the state level in Sabah and Sarawak. Until the 1990s, most of the political parties which won seats in both states had been local parties in that they were present only in either Sabah or Sarawak. At the time of writing, all four parties in the ruling coalition in Sarawak are local parties – Parti Persaka Bumiputera Bersatu (PBB), Sarawak United Peoples' Party (SUPP), Sarawak Progressive Democratic Party (SPDP) and Parti Rakyat Sarawak (PRS). In Sabah, four out of six parties in the ruling coalition in Sabah are local parties – PBS, United Pasokmomogun Kadazandusun Murut Organisation (UPKO), Parti Bersatu Rakyat Sabah (PBRS) and the Liberal Democratic Party (LDP). UMNO made its entry into the Sabah political scene only after the then majority party in the BN, Parti Bersatu Sabah (PBS), left the ruling coalition. MCA only has one state seat and no parliamentary seats in Sabah.

The difference in the ethnic composition of Sabah and Sarawak compared with Peninsular Malaysia – Malays are a minority in both states; non-Muslim *bumiputera* are a majority in Sarawak and used to be a majority in Sabah – and the existence of local parties prior to the formation of Malaysia in 1963 – SUPP is the first political party in Sarawak (Chin 1997) – meant the creation of barriers to entry into both states for Peninsular-based political parties.

The same reasons for the presence and dominance of local parties within the BN in both states indicated that the most serious opposition would also come from locally based parties. Peninsular-based opposition parties were vulnerable to attack owing to not being able adequately to represent the interests of the voters in the respective states.

The Sarawak National Party (SNAP) left the Sarawak Alliance in 1966 after it lost the position of chief minister and was the main opposition party until it rejoined the ruling coalition in 1976. During this period, it performed credibly by playing on Iban sentiment regarding the ousting of Stephen Kalong Ningkan as the Iban chief minister and the subsequent appointment of Abdul Rahman Yaakub, with the approval of the federal government, as the first Malay/Melanau chief minister. SNAP won nine parliamentary seats (out of twenty-four) in the 1970 and 1974 parliamentary elections and eighteen (out of forty-eight) state seats in the 1974 Sarawak state elections.

The next serious opposition challenge in Sarawak came from Parti Bansa Dayak Sarawak (PBDS), a breakaway party from SNAP. PBDS, together with Persatuan Rakyat Malaysia Sarawak (PERMAS), a breakaway party from PBB, won a total of twenty out of twenty-eight state seats in the 1987 state elections, with PBDS winning fifteen and PERMAS winning five. However, by the end of 1988, eight of the fifteen PBDS state assembly representatives had defected to BN parties. In the 1991 state elections, PBDS managed to win only seven out of fifty-six state seats. Acknowledging its weakened position, PBDS applied to rejoin the BN and was readmitted in 1994 (Chin 1996). Interestingly, during its time as an opposition party, PBDS was still part of the ruling coalition at the federal level.

In Sabah, Parti Bersatu Rakyat Jelata Sabah (BERJAYA), a multi-ethnic party, was formed in 1975 to challenge the USNO-led Sabah Alliance. With the blessing of the federal government, BERJAYA went on to win twenty-eight out of forty-eight state seats in the 1976 state elections, thereby replacing USNO as the new state government. BERJAYA was accepted into the BN in 1976. USNO remained as part of the federal government but was in the opposition at the state level (Mauzy 1983: 112). BERJAYA's success came as a result of unhappiness with the excesses of Chief Minister Tun Mustapha (Sin 1979) that angered not only voters but also BN leaders in Kuala Lumpur. BERJAYA would go on to consolidate its position by winning forty-four out of forty-eight state seats in the 1981 state elections. USNO formed a multi-ethnic alliance with the Kadazan-based Pertubuhan Kebangsaan Nanukragong Bersatu (PASOK) and the Chinese-based Sabah Chinese Consolidated Party (SCCP), but this opposition coalition only managed to win four seats (Kalimuthu 1986).

The next opposition challenge in Sabah was to come from PBS, a breakaway party from BERJAYA that was formed just prior to the 1985 state elections. Relying on mostly Kadazan and Chinese support, PBS pulled off an upset result, winning twenty-five out of forty-eight state seats; USNO, having been expelled from the BN at the federal level in 1984, won another sixteen seats. BERJAYA managed only a measly six seats. Like BERJAYA before it, PBS would join the BN after the 1985 state elections. After only a year in office, the new chief minister, Joseph Pairin Kitingan, called for fresh elections. Having extended its influence beyond just its Kadazan and Chinese base, PBS was able to win thirty-four out of forty-eight state seats in the 1986 Sabah state elections, then thirty-six in 1990.

Growing frustration with the federal government, especially with regard to the issue of Filipino migrants into the state, among other issues, led PBS to leave the BN just prior to the 1990 general elections. This defection led to UMNO's expanding its wings into Sabah as well as the formation of new non-Muslim *bumiputera*-led parties within the BN, including Sabah Progressive Party (SAPP), LDP and AKAR (Parti Angkatan Keadilan Rakyat). The 1994 Sabah state elections were very close, with PBS winning twenty-five state seats and the BN winning twenty-three, eighteen of them by UMNO. The defection of a number of PBS state assembly representatives led to the fall of the short-lived PBS government and the addition of a number of new parties into the BN in Sabah, including Parti Demokratik Sabah (PDS) and PBRS (Chin 1994). Subsequently, having lost power at the state level, PBS experienced further electoral setbacks in the 1995 and 1999 general elections as well as the 1999 Sabah state elections, in which it won only seventeen out of forty-eight state seats. Realising that its chances of winning back power at the state level were all but nil, especially with the increase in Muslim *bumiputera* voters, PBS rejoined the BN in 2002.

Two features of local political competition in Sabah and Sarawak need to be noted. First, local opposition parties have successfully campaigned using states' rights and interference by the federal government as salient political issues. Even though this axis of political competition has an ethnic dimension – Iban disaffection in Sarawak and Kadazan as well as Chinese agitation in Sabah – the larger overarching political message of fighting for the rights of the state was the main message of the political campaign. Second, most of the local parties could not sustain themselves in opposition and would eventually join (or re-join) the ruling coalition as this would give them access to government resources at the state and federal levels. This meant that a strong and credible opposition at the local level in both states could not be sustained, especially by local parties. If any local party emerges as a possible contender against the ruling coalition, incentives will be offered to them to join the BN.

Emerging dimensions of political competition: justice, good governance and democracy

If the dominant dimension of political competition remained along the ethnic axis and if local competition in Sabah and Sarawak could not be sustained, it seems likely that the status quo of the BN's remaining dominant in the political centre, with little chance of being unseated, would stand firm. While the ethnic dimension of political competition still remains the most salient one, recent political developments have given rise to the emergence of a new dimension of political competition – one that emphasises good governance, anti-corruption, justice, free and fair elections, the protection of human rights and the promotion of democratic values. The rise of this non-ethnic dimension of political competition has allowed for the emergence of a stronger opposition, notably after the 2008 general elections.

A strong case can be made that this new dimension of political competition emerged as a result of the 1998 economic and political crisis. The *reformasi* movement which led to the formation of Keadilan, which included many civil society agents, and subsequently to the formation of the Barisan Alternatif (BA, Alternative Front) as a united opposition coalition gave rise to the possibility of campaigning on non-communal issues of 'justice' and 'democracy' (Weiss 2006: 184). Even the success of the BN's campaign in the 2004 general elections under Mr Clean – Abdullah Badawi – could be characterised as co-opting the *reformasi* message by the BN. The emergence of the Bersih movement – a campaign to advocate for free and fair elections – in 2007 was also crucial to shifting the political momentum in favour of the opposition prior to the 2008 general elections.

While the specific issues may change depending on their respective political salience, a non-ethnic dimension of political competition has undeniably emerged to contend with the still-salient ethnic dimension of political competition.

The building and maintenance of political coalitions

The Alliance/BN

The conditions that led to the formation of the Alliance have been discussed earlier. The ability of the ruling coalition to maintain itself is explained by the following: (1) access to the machinery, money and media that allow each component party to win seats and hold government positions as part of the ruling coalition; (2) the dominant position of UMNO as the anchor of the ruling coalition; and (3) flexibility in incorporating new members into the coalition.

Within the context of a dominant party authoritarian regime (Greene 2007; Magaloni 2006; Scheiner 2006), there is little chance of forming a government either at the state or federal level outside the ruling coalition. Hence, once a party is in the ruling coalition, there are many more incentives for it to stay within the coalition than to leave it. Furthermore, because of the advantages of vote-pooling in the context of a first-past-the-post, single-member constituency electoral system, parties within the coalition, especially those representing minority groups, know that their chances of winning seats are significantly reduced if they leave the coalition.

Malaysia's ruling coalition does not fulfil one important criterion of a consociational system (Lijphart 1968): there is no mutual veto within the coalition. One party, UMNO, stands dominant. Ironically, UMNO's dominant position within the ruling coalition has acted as a 'stabilisation' force within the party through its control of the position of prime minister who acts as the final arbiter on contentious political issues concerning race, religion and language and also in intra-coalition contestations over seats and positions.

The political dominance of UMNO within the ruling coalition can be seen by the number and percentage of parliamentary seats contested and won by the party in each election since 1959. UMNO has never contested fewer than 40 percent of parliament seats. This percentage increased to more than 50 percent after UMNO's entry into Sabah politics in 1990. The fact that UMNO wins, on average, eight out of ten of the seats it contests further accentuates its dominant position within the coalition. In fact, after the 2004 general elections, in which UMNO won 110 seats (out of a total of 219 parliament seats), it could have formed the government by itself (Table 2.1).

The ruling coalition has also demonstrated a great deal of flexibility in accepting new parties within its fold and designing new structures to incorporate these parties. The reconfiguration of the Alliance into the BN after the 1969 general elections was described earlier. In Sabah and Sarawak, the BN regularly accepts new entrants into the ruling coalition – BERJAYA, PBS, PDS, AKAR, UPKO, PBRS, LDP and SAPP in Sabah; SUPP and the PBDS in Sarawak. It also routinely accepts the return of parties that have previously left the ruling coalition – SNAP and PBDS in Sarawak, PBS in Sabah. In addition, the coalition manages intra-party splits by incorporating parties formed as a result of these splits into the BN. For example, it was quick to admit the PRS, formed after PBDS was deregistered, and SPDP, formed after SNAP was deregistered, into the BN in Sarawak. Even independent candidates who sometimes win seats in Sabah and Sarawak are quickly absorbed into one of the BN component parties.

The admission of these parties into the BN fulfils a dual strategic role. First, the inclusion of the mostly non-Malay and non-Muslim *bumiputera* parties strengthens the position of the dominant parties – UMNO at the national level, PBB in Sarawak – because the non-Malay and non-Muslim *bumiputera* seats are allocated among a larger number of parties. Second, it sends a strong signal, especially in Sabah and Sarawak, that the ruling coalition is 'the only

Table 2.1 Number and percentage of parliamentary constituencies contested and won by UMNO, 1959–2013

Year	*Contested*	*Total seats*	*% UMNO seats*	*Won*	*% won*	*UMNO seats as % of BN seats*
1959	71	104	68.3	53	74.6	51.0
1964	68	104	65.4	59	86.8	56.7
1969	68	144	47.2	53	77.9	36.8
1974	62	154	40.3	62	100.0	40.3
1978	75	154	48.7	69	92.0	44.8
1982	75	154	48.7	70	93.3	45.5
1986	85	172	49.4	84	98.8	48.8
1990	92	180	51.1	77	83.7	42.8
1995	105	192	54.7	90	85.7	46.9
1999	104	193	53.9	72	69.2	37.3
2004	117	219	53.4	110	94.0	50.2
2008	117	222	52.7	79	67.5	35.6
2013	121	222	54.5	88	72.7	39.6
Average			**52.9**		**84.3**	**44.3**

game in town', thus pre-empting the viability and sustainability of any credible opposition parties.

The BN also uses the once-in-a-decade delimitation exercise as part of the coalition management process. Parliamentary and state seats are added during these exercises and each member of the coalition receives some proportion of these new seats. The process is particularly useful when new parties are admitted (or in the case of PBS in 2002, readmitted) into the BN, as the coalition can allocate seats to them while minimising the disgruntlement of other parties which would otherwise have to yield seats to these new entrants.

Elite splits and opposition coalitions, 1990–2008

The nature of political competition illustrated in Figure 2.1 above seems to preclude the possibility of opposition coalitions, especially after the initial failures prior to the 1969 general elections. But examples from other dominant-party authoritarian regimes such as Mexico, Taiwan, Senegal and Paraguay show that a reconfiguration of political party competition could emerge as a result of elite splits. In all these cases, elite splits weakened the dominant party and subsequently extracted sufficient support away from the ruling regime to allow an opposition win to take place in presidential elections. This occurred in Mexico (Magaloni 2006; Greene 2007), Taiwan (Niou and Paolino 2003: 727), Senegal in 2000 (Vengroff and Magala 2001; Mozaffar and Vengroff 2002) and Paraguay in 2008 (Nickson 2009). It would also take elite splits within the ruling coalition in Malaysia to bring about new possibilities in political party competition. But unlike in the aforementioned countries, the parliamentary, first-past-the-post, constituency-based elections in Malaysia require defecting elites from the ruling coalition to work with opposition parties to build new opposition coalitions.

The first such attempt occurred prior to the 1990 general elections after a bitter UMNO party election in 1987 led to the formation of a new Malay party – Semangat '46 (Spirit of '46 or S46) – by Tengku Razaleigh, a former finance minister and failed challenger to Dr Mahathir for the UMNO presidency (Hwang 2003: 131). But because of ideological differences and fears of a political backlash, both flank parties – the DAP and PAS – could not join with S46 in a grand opposition alliance. Instead, S46 formed a Malay alliance with PAS and two other smaller Muslim/Malay parties (BERJASA and Hamim), and a separate alliance with DAP and two smaller non-Malay opposition parties (PRM and the IPF). The former was called Angkata Perpaduan Ummah (APU) or the Muslim Community Unity Movement and the latter was called Gagasan Rakyat (Gagasan for short) or the Malaysian People's Front. This two-pronged alliance was meant to unite the opposition, with S46 acting as the bridge that held together the two largest but ideologically incompatible opposition parties on either side of the ethnic divide, DAP and PAS. This was the first serious attempt by the opposition parties to form a united front against the BN at the national level (Jomo 1996: 101).

This opposition arrangement did not yield sufficient electoral dividends. While APU managed to wrest the Kelantan state government from the BN by winning thirty-eight out of the forty-eight state seats, S46 managed to win only eight parliamentary seats (out of a total of 180), not enough for it to emerge as even the largest opposition party. The failure of any of the opposition parties to win seats beyond their respective ethnic strongholds (in the northern states for APU and in the non-Malay majority-urban areas for the DAP) meant that the benefits of vote-pooling could not be reaped. S46's electoral performance worsened in 1995, when it managed to win only six parliamentary seats. With its status as the smallest opposition party and with no hope of displacing UMNO at the national level, S46 disbanded in 1996 and most of its members rejoined UMNO, including Tengku Razaleigh.

The second attempt to build an opposition coalition occurred as a result of the 1998 political and economic crisis. The sacking of then Deputy Prime Minister Anwar Ibrahim led to the formation of a new multiracial party, Keadilan, which provided the anchor to link both DAP and PAS in the first united opposition coalition, named the Alternative Front or Barisan Alternatif (BA). In the 1999 general elections, Keadilan managed to win only five parliamentary seats (out of a total of 199) and, like S46, it failed to emerge as the largest opposition party. PAS won twenty-seven parliamentary seats compared with DAP's ten and emerged as the leader of the opposition. PAS also won control of the Terengganu state legislature. The weak political position of Keadilan meant that it could not play the role of an effective moderator between PAS and the DAP. PAS's insistence on passing a *hudud* bill in 2001, despite protests from the DAP, and the 11 September terrorist attacks, created the conditions for the DAP to announce its departure from the BA just prior to the Sarawak state elections in 2001. The opposition coalition had lasted twenty-two months.

Elite splits at the state level also led to the formation of opposition coalitions in Sarawak and Sabah. Disagreements between then Chief Minister Taib Mahmud and his uncle, former Chief Minister Rahman Yaacub, led the latter to form PERMAS, which then teamed up with PBDS to challenge the BN in the 1987 Sarawak state elections (Chin 1996). The inability of this coalition to win power at the state level and subsequent defections among their elected representatives finally led to its collapse. PBDS would eventually rejoin the BN in 1994 (Chin 1996).

In Sabah, the PBS was able to maintain control of the state government after leaving the BN coalition just prior to the 1990 general elections because it had won the state elections earlier in the same year. It was also able to entice some members of its former political rival, USNO, to join forces to compete under its ticket in the 1994 state elections. Even though PBS won a small majority (twenty-five seats compared with BN's twenty-three), massive defections from its ranks to the BN cost it the state government (Chin 1994). PBS would eventually rejoin the BN in 2002.

The common challenge all the opposition coalitions described above face is precisely what sustains the BN as a coalition. These opposition coalitions were not able to (1) win access to power and share the rewards of political cooperation; (2) benefit from vote-pooling by winning a sufficient number of multi-ethnic seats; and (3) weather the bleak prospect of continuing in opposition – instead, many either defected as individuals or rejoined the BN as parties. This pattern changed after the 2008 general elections.

Emergence of a credible opposition coalition

The 2008 general elections led to the formation of a credible opposition coalition for the following reasons. First, all three opposition parties, even though they were not in a formal opposition coalition prior to the 2008 general elections, were able to pool votes because of an electoral pact to avoid three-cornered contests. As a result, all three parties were able to win seats outside their traditional strongholds, including in many ethnically heterogeneous seats. In fact, the opposition parties won eighty-two out of 222 seats (37 percent), thereby denying the BN a two-thirds majority in parliament. Importantly, PKR (formerly Keadilan) emerged as the largest opposition party by winning thirty-one parliament seats (DAP won twenty-eight while PAS won twenty-three). This meant that PKR, led by opposition leader and candidate for prime minister, Anwar Ibrahim, could effectively anchor the opposition coalition from a position of political strength and credibility. The Pakatan Rakyat or Pakatan coalition was formed soon after the results of the 2008 general election were announced to present a united opposition of increased strength in parliament and to form state governments in states where all three parties together held a majority of seats.

Second, the opposition managed to win control of five state legislatures. PAS had controlled Kelantan since 1990, but now the opposition also won control of the Kedah, Penang, Perak and Selangor state legislatures. Importantly, the configuration of seats won was such that the support of all three parties was needed in order to govern in all five states. This provided the electoral and political incentive for the formation and also maintenance of an opposition coalition. For example, PAS was the dominant party in Kedah but needed PKR's seats in order to form the state government. DAP was the dominant party in Penang but needed PKR's seats in order to form the state government. DAP needed both PAS's and PKR's seats to form the government in Perak, while PKR needed PAS's and DAP's seats in order to form the government in Selangor (Table 2.2).

Third, the electoral success of all three parties provided the possibility that an opposition coalition, if sustained, could offer itself as a credible alternative to the ruling coalition in forthcoming elections.

While Pakatan failed to win a majority of seats in the 2013 general election, it did succeed in winning more parliament seats (up from eighty-two to eighty-nine) and in winning 51 percent of the popular vote. It also managed to retain the state governments of Kelantan, Penang and Selangor, but failed to win back Kedah and Perak. The electoral incentives of governing at the state level in these three states and the increased prospect of winning power in the next general election seem, at this point in time, to provide sufficient incentives to sustain the Pakatan coalition, at least into the fourteenth general election.

Number and effective number of parties

The large number of parties that have contested in the parliament and state elections since independence seem to indicate a fragmented party system. But a closer inspection of the election results shows that the effective number of parties in Malaysia follows Duverger's law: that the first-past-the-post, single-member constituency system tends to create a two-party, or in the case of Malaysia, a two-coalition system.

According to Table 2.3, the effective number of parties would exceed five since 1969 if the vote shares for individual parties are used in Laakso and Taagepera's (1979) formula. If all the votes of the BN component parties are added together, then the effective number of parties is

Table 2.2 Number of state constituencies won by the opposition parties in opposition controlled states, 2008 general election

State	*PAS*	*DAP*	*PKR*	*Total*[a]
Kedah	16	1	5	22 (36)
Kelantan	37	0	1	38 (45)
Penang	1	19	9	29 (40)
Perak	6	18	7	31 (59)
Selangor	8	13	15	36 (56)

Source: Election Report (2008).

Note:

[a] Total state seats in parenthesis.

Table 2.3 Number and effective number of parties, 1959–2013 general elections

Year	*No. of parties*	*Separate parties*	*BN vs opposition separate parties*	*BN vs opposition coalition (starting from 1990)*	*Effective no. of parties at constituency level*
1959	8	4.49	3.80	NA[a]	2.09
1964	9	4.27	2.54	NA	2.03
1969	16	5.87	3.56	NA	2.18
1974	14	NA	2.42	NA	1.95
1978	22	5.20	2.47	NA	1.98
1982	18	5.47	2.48	NA	1.93
1986	17	5.09	2.50	NA	1.98
1990	15	6.41	3.18	NA	1.89
1995	17	5.36	2.32	NA	1.75
1999	21	6.11	2.70	2.08	1.88
2004	22	5.34	2.32	1.99	1.80
2008	21	5.49	2.64	1.89	2.01
2013	23	5.49	3.20	2.07	1.94
Average	**17.2**	**5.38**	**2.78**	**2.01**	**1.95**

Note:
[a] NA = not applicable.

reduced to an average of 2.78 since 1959. If the votes of all the opposition parties, starting from the 1990 opposition alliance, are tallied, the average effective number of parties reduces further to 2.01. The average effective number of parties reduces to 1.95 if the vote shares of individual parties are used at the constituency level.

Hence, even as new parties are formed and new coalitions are reconfigured – whether among the ruling coalition or the opposition – the underlying pattern of voting and party competition appears very stable, with two main contenders for each seat.

Structure of political parties

The formation and registration of any political party needs to be approved by the Registrar of Societies (RoS). There have been complaints in the past in regard to selective approvals on the part of the RoS for parties which are aligned to the BN, but much slower approval for parties which are pro-opposition. One of the most contentious approvals for the registration of a new party was that of UMNO Baru by factions aligned to Dr Mahathir after the old UMNO was deregistered by a court ruling declaring its 1987 party elections to be null and void. The RoS had rejected an earlier application from a faction that was aligned to Dr Mahathir's rival, Tengku Razaleigh, to register UMNO Malaysia (Crouch 1996: 120). The RoS reports to the minister of home affairs, who at that time happened to be Dr Mahathir. The minister of home affairs thus has a great deal of control over which applications to form political parties are approved.

The structure of each political party is governed by its constitution, including such aspects as membership, setting up of branches, the conduct of party elections at various levels, the composition and powers of the party leadership, disciplinary processes against members and the disclosure of accounts. Each party holds party elections at the national level once every two to three years. These party elections can be postponed for a period of time, usually on the basis that party elections held too close to an impending general election can be harmful to party unity and morale. Only delegates representing branches are eligible to vote in party elections at the national level, although recent reforms within UMNO and PKR have increased the number of eligible voters.

All the major political parties, with the exception of the DAP, hold direct elections for their top two positions, president and deputy president. All the major parties also have elected committees at the central leadership level comprising between fifteen and twenty-five members. The central leadership or the president of the major parties also has the power to appoint additional members to the ranks of the central leadership committee. For its part, the DAP holds elections for twenty committee members who then decide on the allocation of the various posts, including those of secretary general and chairman.

All the parties hold elections at the branch level for various positions, such as branch chairman, deputy chairman and treasurer. All the major parties also hold elections for at least some positions at the division level. A division is represented by a parliamentary constituency. DAP is the only party which holds elections at the state level. For the other major parties, the party president appoints state leaders.

The president of the major parties (with the exception of DAP, which does not have a directly elected president) possesses significant powers of appointment not just for leadership positions at the state level but also for heads of various political bureaus and other non-elected positions, such as secretary general.

All the major parties have youth wings and women's wings. The youth wings of MCA, DAP and PKR include both genders, whereas UMNO has separate male and female components (UMNO Youth and Puteri UMNO) and PAS has only a male youth wing.

The power to select candidates to be fielded in elections is very much in the hands of the central leadership of each party. While grassroots members have the right to nominate their preferred candidates, the central leadership has the power to overrule local preferences. It is not uncommon, especially among the opposition parties, to see candidates and incumbents being shifted from one constituency to another, or even one state to another, because of larger strategic concerns – to place a leader or candidate in a safe seat, to place a leader in a strategic seat to break new political ground, or to account for ethnic and gender quotas, for instance. This practice is less common in UMNO because of the entrenched nature of local leadership, more popularly known as local political 'warlords'. It is also much less common in Sabah and Sarawak because of local opposition toward candidates from other states or from Peninsular Malaysia.

Recent reforms have occurred within some of the major parties to make internal party politics more democratic. For example, MCA has introduced a three-term limit for its top leadership positions, including the presidency. DAP has also introduced a three-term limit for the position of secretary general. PKR held its first party elections in 2010 in which all members could vote for the top leadership positions, while in its 2013 party elections, UMNO expanded the number of eligible voters from approximately 2,000 to 150,000.

Political developments moving forward

The pattern of political competition and the major contending parties and coalitions, namely BN and Pakatan, look likely to remain until the fourteenth general election. The consolidation of the two-party system in Sabah and Sarawak, where local parties have steadily lost ground, as indicated in the 2008 and 2013 general election as well as the 2011 Sarawak state election, also seems likely to continue until the next Sarawak state election, due in 2016, and into the fourteenth general election.

A change in power at the federal level in the fourteenth general election may provide the impetus to change the configuration of political party competition. It would increase the chances of the BN coalition's fracturing, with some parties leaving its fold and perhaps joining PR. If this happens, UMNO may pull what is remaining within the BN into a flank opposition coalition. Non-Malay parties such as the MCA and GERAKAN may end up on the other flank if they leave the BN. It is also possible that some of the non-Malay parties – MCA, GERAKAN, SUPP – may unite in order to boost their electoral and political strength if the BN loses power.

The introduction of local elections (see Goh, this volume) may also introduce new parties and new dimensions of political competition, especially if a proportional representation electoral system is chosen. This would give rise to smaller parties competing on different issues – the environment, public safety, public transportation, and so forth – at the local level. But at the national level, the effective number of parties competing, especially at the constituency level, is likely to remain at two.

Note

1 The riots of 13 May immediately after the 1969 general elections led to the declaration of emergency rule. When emergency rule was lifted, the ruling coalition had invited a sufficient number of parties to join the newly configured BN to allow it two-thirds control of parliament.

Bibliography

Andaya, Barbara Watson and Leonard Y. Andaya (2001) *A History of Malaysia*, Honolulu: University of Hawaii Press.

Chin, James (1994) 'The Sabah state election of 1994: end of Kadazan unity', *Asian Survey*, 34(10): 904–15.

Chin, James (1996) 'PBDS and ethnicity in Sarawak politics', *Journal of Contemporary Asia*, 26(4): 512–26.

Chin, James (1997) 'Politics of federal intervention in Malaysia, with reference to Sarawak, Sabah and Kelantan', *Journal of Commonwealth and Comparative Politics*, 35(2): 96–120.

Crouch, Harold (1996) *Government and Society in Malaysia*, Ithaca: Cornell University Press.

Greene, Kenneth F. (2007) *Why Dominant Parties Lose: Mexico's Democratization in Comparative Perspective*, Cambridge: Cambridge University Press.

Han Sin Fong (1979) 'A constitutional coup d'état: an analysis of the birth and victory of the Berjaya Party in Sabah, Malaysia', *Asian Survey*, 19(4): 379–89.

Horowitz, Donald L. (1985) *Ethnic Groups in Conflict*, Berkeley: University of California Press.

Hwang In-Won (2003) *Personalized Politics: The Malaysian State under Mahathir*, Singapore: Institute of Southeast Asian Studies.

Jomo K.S. (1996) 'Deepening Malaysian democracy with more checks and balances', in Muhammad Ikmal Said and Zahid Emby (eds), *Malaysia: Critical Perspectives: Essays in Honour of Syed Husin Ali*, Petaling Jaya: Persatuan Sains Sosial Malaysia.

Kalimuthu, K. Ramanathan (1986) 'The Sabah state elections of April 1985', *Asian Survey*, 26(7): 815–37.

Laakso, Markku and Rein Taagepera (1979) '"Effective" number of parties: a measure with application to West Europe', *Comparative Political Studies*, 12(1): 3–27.

Lijphart, Arendt (1968) *The Politics of Accommodation: Pluralism and Democracy in the Netherlands*, Berkeley: University of California Press.

Lim Hong Hai (2002) 'Electoral politics in Malaysia: "managing" elections in a plural society', in Aurel Croissant, Gabrielle Bruns and Marei John (eds), *Electoral Politics in Southeast & East Asia*, Singapore: Fredriech Ebert Stiftung, pp. 101–48.

Magaloni, Beatriz (2006) *Voting for Autocracy: Hegemonic Party Survival and Its Demise in Mexico*, Cambridge: Cambridge University Press.

Mauzy, Diane K. (1983) *Barisan Nasional – Coalition Government in Malaysia*, Kuala Lumpur: Marican & Sons.

Mozaffar, Scarrit and Richard Vengroff (2002) 'A "whole system" approach to the choice of electoral rules in democratising countries: Senegal in comparative perspective', *Electoral Studies*, 21(4): 601–16.

Nickson, Andrew (2009) 'The general election in Paraguay, April 2008', *Electoral Studies*, 28(1): 145–49.

Niou, Emerson and Phillip Paolino (2003) 'The rise of the opposition party in Taiwan: explaining Chen Shui-Bian's victory in the 2000 Presidential Election', *Electoral Studies*, 22(4): 721–40.

Oong Hak Ching (2000) *Chinese Politics in Malaya 1942–55 – the Dynamics of British Policy*, Bangi: UKM Press.

Ratnam, K.J. and Robert S. Milne (1967) *The Malayan Parliamentary Election of 1964*, Kuala Lumpur: University of Malaya Press.

Scheiner, Ethan (2006) *Democracy without Competition in Japan: Opposition Failure in a One-Party Dominant State*, Cambridge: Cambridge University Press.

Vengroff, Richard and Michael Magala (2001) 'Democratic reform, transition and consolidation: evidence from Senegal's 2000 Presidential Election', *The Journal of Modern African Studies*, 39(1): 129–62.

Weiss, Meredith L. (2006) *Protest and Possibilities: Civil Society and Coalitions for Political Change in Malaysia*, Stanford: Stanford University Press.

3

Malaysia's *un*exceptionalism

Like elsewhere, elites are fractious

William Case

Most national elites in Southeast Asia must be understood as divided, skirmishing ceaselessly for factional advantage while surging periodically in epic warring. Thus, in countries like Thailand and the Philippines, regimes have been rocked by *autogolpes*, military coups, and social upheavals. In other cases, elites have mostly been contained, but coercively, whether by an enveloping executive as in Indonesia under Suharto or in Cambodia under Hun Sen; an absorptive single party system as in Vietnam and Laos, encrusted with revolutionary origins and ideology; or fearsome security apparatuses as in Myanmar during the generalship of Ne Win. But though regimes in these latter cases might avoid outright breakdown, relations between elites are punctuated still by purges, economic ruin, imprisonment, and exile. Such fractiousness is typical. Surveying elites around the world and across time, Higley and Burton (1989: 19) describe elite-level conflict as the 'modal condition'. And in focusing more closely on Southeast Asia, Dan Slater (2010: 10) concurs, writing that 'strong elite coalitions are extremely difficult to construct and consolidate at the national level. In most places and under most circumstances, elite politics is rife with factionalism and parochialism'.

But in Malaysia, elites have been evaluated differently. For reasons canvassed below, their relations have been cast by analysts as comparatively cohesive (see Lijphart 1977; Mauzy 1983; Zakaria 1989; Case 1995; Brownlee 2007). Attuned to sundry legacies, structural pressures, and institutional incentives, elites in Malaysia, though competing avidly for positions, resources, and constituencies, conduct their interactions in accord with rare codes of 'restrained partisanship' (Higley and Burton 1989). Hence, the 'strain points' in their relations that inevitably set in are depicted as stopping well short of the ruptures that occur in Thailand and the Philippines. Nor has even a posture of 'semi-loyalty' prevailed, characterised by Linz and Stepan (1996) as one wherein elites may bide their time, sometimes for long periods, but on first provocation or opportunity, finally defect and collate into factions, revealing that all along they had been quietly divided. The evident rivalries that simmer between the president and prime minister in Vietnam today, as well as the impatience of hard-lining generals with liberalising ministers in Myanmar, might be understood in this way, threatening finally to erupt in open warring if paramount leaders falter or institutions weaken. Hence, in stark contrast, elites in Malaysia are described as avoiding the open or delayed confrontations that mar relations between most other national elites in Southeast Asia. And hence, the political regime that they operate has long been regarded as one of the most stable in the region.

This account argues, however, that on closer inspection, elites in Malaysia and the regime that they operate have never been so exceptional. Little more than a decade after independence, reasonably even terms of coalescence between ethnic Malay and Chinese elites lost symmetry. And as conciliation gave way to greater Malay hegemony, even if still accommodative, the country's electoral democracy narrowed into electoral authoritarianism (Schedler 2006). Moreover, during the past decade-and-a-half, as both communal and intra-ethnic fractiousness between elites rose, a social reform movement and opposition coalition emerged, able to press for greater civil liberties and electoral uncertainty, therein recalibrating the regime into competitive authoritarianism (Levitsky and Way 2010). At this juncture, then, though the playing field remained uneven, an outright victory by the opposition in a general election grew imaginable. But more recently, Malay elites in government have regained their hegemony, then tightly excluded their Chinese rivals. Further, they have begun rolling back their regime once again to a posture of electoral authoritarianism, though this time even more heavily manipulated and coercively applied.

Accordingly, we can identify in Malaysia's record a sequencing in elite-level relations, tilting over time from coalescence to fractiousness and from a comparative evenness between ethnic communities to more overt Malay dominance. The political regime has changed commensurately, first from electoral democracy to electoral authoritarianism, then to competitive authoritarianism. More recently, it has contracted into electoral authoritarianism once again, though its disequilibrium now requires increasingly muscular enforcement. In addition, throughout this trajectory, relations between elites have bristled with factional battles, purges, and jailings, though so routinely that they fail even to register in regime changes. In blunt terms, then, elites in Malaysia have never been so cohesive, nor their regime so stable, as usually depicted.

In making this case, this account begins by briefly establishing that elites are a valid unit of analysis. Measurement problems abound when proposing indicators and thresholds for elite fractiousness and cohesion. Declaring the extent to which a regime is correspondingly unstable or stable is equally fraught. Next, some common explanations for a purported cohesion between elites in Malaysia are rehearsed. In doing this, we will see that the same sets of factors that are typically designated as encouraging cohesion have gradually promoted fractiousness. Throughout, the determinative pressures of ethnic identification in Malaysia, distinctive in Southeast Asia, are addressed, enabling us to chart changes in elite relations through isolable postures of coalescence, accommodative hegemony, a more symmetrical split, and renewed, though more exclusionary, hegemony.

The elite variable

Amid a decade-long resurgence of elite analysis and regime change during the 1980s–90s, elites were variously profiled as soft- and hardliners, swingmen and semi-loyalists, and minimalists and maximalists. Unveiling a New Elite Paradigm, John Higley and Michael Burton (1989: 18) defined elites as 'persons who are able, by virtue of their authoritative positions in powerful organizations and movements of whatever kind, to affect national political outcomes regularly and substantially'. Further, elites are described as cohesive (or in Higley and Burton's lexicon, 'consensually unified') to the extent that in competing for positions, resources, and organised constituencies, they adhere to

> rules and codes of political conduct amounting to 'restrained partisanship'. . . . [Elites] view decisional outcomes as a . . . 'politics-as-bargaining' game, rather than a . . . 'politics-as-war' game. . . . They consistently refrain from pushing their differences to the point of violent conflict.
>
> *(Higley and Burton 1989: 19)*

Conversely, elites are fractious (or 'disunified') when they break with the rules and norms that had restrained them, with factions pushing for ascendancy or paramount leadership. In doing this, they resort to ruthless strategies by which to run down the statuses of rival elites, including purges, expropriating resources, jailing, exile, and appropriating or crushing the constituencies arrayed against them. In this way, the regimes that they operate are destabilised, likely collapsing in executive or military coups or instigated social upheavals, hence paving the way for new types of regimes, though not necessarily of any greater stability.

To be sure, inconsistent statuses, uncertain autonomy, fluctuating and immeasurable relations, and a lack of independent referents for elite-level behaviours and regime outcomes seem to bedevil elite analysis, raising questions over rigour and tautology. Hence, in trying to avoid the uncertainty and contingency of leadership, many mainstream theorists have abandoned elites for large-*n* deductive methods. In brief, they seek to overcome the indecipherability of elite-level behaviours by averaging them out across many cases whose historical, social, and developmental features are more readily apprehended. But this is of little help when trying to understand a particular case like Malaysia, where even brief consideration of a counterfactual makes plain the impact of leadership: the country's political trajectory would doubtless have been quite different had its prime ministers, with their distinctive leadership styles, been reordered, with Tun Razak or Mahathir Mohamad having been leader at the time of independence, for example, or Abdullah Badawi during the developmentalist decades of the 1980s–90s.

Thus in accounts of regimes in particular cases, we must capture the impact that disproportionately empowered persons impose on regime types and change. In this analysis of Malaysia, elite statuses are limited to those holding high positions in top political parties and state agencies, Next, indicators of elite fractiousness include a confiscation of personal assets, often through partisan tax offices or regulatory bodies, an appropriation or marginalisation of rival constituencies, cultural humiliation, purges, jailing, assaults on elite persons and their family members, disappearance, and forced exile. When enumerated in this way, fractiousness can be understood as distinct from, and causally prior to, their regime's instability, easing our doubts over the measurability of elite statuses and relations, as well as the risks of tautology. Thus, while fashioned by Higley and Burton more than two decades ago, their paradigm offers a good platform upon which to address questions over elite statuses, relations, and regimes in Malaysia, offering both guidelines about how to proceed and a foil that invites refinement.

Accounting for elite relations in Malaysia

This section canvasses three sets of explanations for cohesion among elites, examining them in the Malaysian setting. We look first at the segmental 'pillarisation' and elite coalescence proposed by Arend Lijphart (1977), as well as the legacies of British colonial rule and a 'tutelary model' outlined by Myron Weiner (1987). Second, we turn to redistributive pressures and a pact of cohesion that features in recent work by Dan Slater (2010). Finally, we consider a single dominant party, investigated by Jason Brownlee (2007) through a historical-institutional approach, as well as the patronage distributions which, though assessed by Beatriz Magaloni and Kenneth Greene during the Institutional Revolutionary Party (PRI)'s tenure in Mexico, also characterise the functioning of the United Malays National Organisation (UMNO) in Malaysia. As we rehearse these explanations, we will see too that the factors that they identify have as readily promoted fractiousness among elites in Malaysia as the cohesion thought more often to prevail.

Segmental pillars and colonial legacies: elite coalescence

Arend Lijphart, in analysing elites and regimes in small multi-ethnic countries in central Europe, contended that in such plural settings, ethnic, religious, linguistic, cultural, and deep-seated ideological affiliations usually segmented society, therein posing grave challenges to elite relations and democratic stability. However, under some conditions, elites might still attain 'coalescence', enabling them to cooperate across segmental lines in order to perpetuate a 'consociational' form of democracy. Under this framework, a majoritarian, government-versus-opposition, winner-takes-all approach is avoided in order that the leaders of all societal segments might provide for their constituencies, a practice safeguarded in decisional committees by informal understandings, under-mobilisation of followers, and usage of a 'mutual veto'. Further, these features are reinforced through particular institutions of federalist power sharing, proportional representation in a parliamentary setting, a grand coalition and an 'oversized' cabinet.

In accounting for such cohesion among elites, Lijphart scoured the supportive structural features that plural societies might possess. He identified first the desirability of a 'balance of segmental power' with key social constituencies similar in size, therein deterring their leaders from striving for paramountcy. Lijphart also cited the helpfulness of distinct and 'isolated' segmental 'pillars', strengthening support for leaders, but also the need for crosscutting cleavages and overarching loyalties, therein helping to instil a crucial 'tradition of elite accommodation'. During the 1960s, then, in extending his gaze from Europe to some developing countries, Lijphart espied at least some of these features in Malaysia. They appeared to foster, then, a rare configuration of elite coalescence, hence underpinning what Lijphart (1977: 150) regarded as a 'reasonably successful consociational democracy in the Third World'.

Myron Weiner (1987: 20) developed these notions of elite cohesion further. Addressing countries that gained independence after World War II, he focused specifically on British colonial experience, in particular 'the British tradition of imposing limits on government, of establishing norms for the conduct of those who exercise power, and of creating procedures for the management of conflict'. In brief, the British offered in colonial settings what Weiner terms a 'model of tutelage' that involved recruiting local elites into bureaucratic structures and representative councils, then gradually introducing them to elections.

In developing an extractive economy in colonial Malaya, the British recruited labour from China, India, and elsewhere, therein articulating a deeply plural society. In this situation, Milton Esman (1972: 228) observed that 'seldom . . . have people with so little in common been fated to share the same territory and participate in the same political system'. But in addition to the ways identified by Lijphart through which segmental pillars might incentivise elites to cooperate, we see too how the British, while applying the tutelary model conceptualised by Weiner, purposively took additional steps to facilitate trust across ethnic lines. In brief, after dropping the Malayan Union proposal, the British encouraged accommodation by convening local elites in a series of committee meetings during 1949–50, seeking to lay the foundation for political independence and stable democracy. Known as the Communities

Liaison Committee (CLC), the British gathered six Malay representatives, six Chinese, and one member each from the Indian, Ceylonese, Eurasian, and European communities.

Malcolm McDonald, a former governor general of Malaya, mediated all the CLC sessions. He barred 'subelites' from UMNO and the newly formed Malaysian Chinese Association (MCA) from attending the meetings in order that discussion could be kept secret from mass constituencies. Only after elite agreements had been reached were proposals made to the Federal Legislative Council, then revealed publicly through press statements. Gordon Means (1976: 124) thus noted the CLC 'demonstrate[d] that significant communal compromise was more likely to emerge from semi-secret and "of-the-record" negotiations conducted by communal leaders'. Lijphart (1977: 155) further observed that the CLC 'provided valuable experience for the intersegmental bargaining of the Alliance a few years later'. And he concluded that

> [Malaysia's] segments are separated from each other by the mutually reinforcing cleavages of language, religion, culture, and race. The all-important consociational device of Malaysia is the Alliance, a grand coalition of the principle Malay, Chinese, and Indian political parties. . . . Proportionality [is evident] if the political and economic spheres are considered together . . . [with] political and government superiority for the Malays and continued economic hegemony for the Chinese.
>
> *(Lijphart 1977: 150–51)*

Thus, R.S. Milne (1967: 41) assessed, too, that 'when the whole scene is surveyed, in its social, economic, and political aspects, it becomes clear that a kind of short-term rough justice between the claims of the communities [was] in fact . . . attained'. Accordingly, 'the bargain' had been reached, seemingly providing Malaysia, made independent in 1957, with a propitious start in coalescent elite relations and democratic politics.

But where Lijphart and Weiner saw in Malaysia's social structure and historical legacies the basis for coalescent elites, other authors predicted ruptures and breakdown. Donald Horowitz (1985), in evaluating relations between the pre-eminent Malay and Chinese constituencies, found less balance in segmental power than a highly volatile bipolar faceoff. Rabushka and Shepsle (2009: 207) stated flatly that 'history shows that democratic stability and cultural diversity are often incompatible in the post-independence politics of many plural societies . . . [I]ntense ethnic conflict frequently erupts shortly after native peoples obtain their independence'.

Elites in UMNO, the MCA, and an ethnic Indian vehicle, the Malay(si)an Indian Congress (MIC), collaborated through the Alliance in contesting elections for more than a decade after independence. However, though forming a grand coalition and oversized cabinet, their sharing of state positions could hardly be characterised even at this stage as fully proportional. Put simply, Chinese elites accepted marked under-representation in the government, bureaucracy, and military in exchange for some economic assurances and minimal citizenship guarantees. Stephen Chee (1991: 63–66) observes also that in the Alliance Council and cabinet meetings, UMNO elites never conceded to the Chinese any power of mutual veto over what they held to be vital Malay interests. Additionally, UMNO elites refused to grant the Chinese even firm segmental autonomy over the latter's own cultural politics and concerns, especially 'as expressed in . . . demands for linguistic and education pluralism' (Chee 1991: 66). Thus, while elites in Malaysia appeared more cohesive than in some other Southeast Asian countries during the 1960s, the skewness in the terms of their relations boded poorly for coalescence over time.

What is more, this weakening of elite relations would remain unchecked by any hint of what Levitsky and Way (2012: 871) posit as a far more powerful source of elite cohesion in developing countries than tutelage and bargaining amid peaceful decolonisation. For them, lasting accommodation must be forged in violence, whether made manifest in wars of independence or revolutionary upheavals. It is through great risks and sacrifice, characteristic of 'sustained, violent, and ideationally driven struggle', that elites may forge the 'enduring partisan identities' and 'military-style internal discipline' that perpetuate their cohesion over time. In Malaysia, however, what political violence occurred during the decade prior to independence was hardly undertaken by local elites. Rather, it was waged by British colonial officials and Commonwealth troops against leftist insurgents in defence of local elites, a campaign known as the Emergency. Thus, with elites avoiding the violence that was waged on their behalf, their tradition of accommodation, derived from ethnic pillarisation, tutelage, and bargaining at independence, gradually faded.

Thus, little more than a decade after independence, the fears of Rabushka and Shepsle were borne out. In the election held in 1969, many Malays, discontented with UMNO's tolerance of free markets and skewed distributions, voted for PAS, while many Chinese, resentful over their 'second-class' citizenship, supported new, mostly ethnically Chinese opposition parties. Thus, with the UMNO-led Alliance gravely weakened, the frictions between segmental pillars were brought to the boil, finally erupting in ethnic rioting known locally as the 'May 13th incident' (Von Vorys 1975). Elites then reordered relations in ways that were more starkly asymmetrical, then reset their consociational democracy as electoral authoritarianism. In brief, elites in UMNO absorbed almost all opposition vehicles into their coalition, rechristened as Barisan Nasional (National Front), then vastly enhanced their own party's dominance. What is more, they used their increased state power to make deep inroads in the world of business and finance. Zakaria (1989: 372) once assured us that, despite this tilt, a hegemonic configuration persisted with accommodationist elements. But the strains in relations were declared by the shift in control over key economic ministries and bureaucratic agencies from the MCA to UMNO. It was shortly after this, too, that UMNO unveiled the New Economic Policy (NEP), systematising its assertion of state-owned enterprises and cross-ethnic transfers of private sector assets and positions. In this context, Ian Lustick (1979) observed that uneven relations between elites had grown so skewed that elite coalescence and consociationalism, if they had ever existed, were supplanted now by a 'control model'.

During the 1960s–70s, we find many more indicators of fractiousness among elites across ethnic lines. The enmity between Alliance leaders and Lee Kuan Yew, chief executive of Singapore, was exacerbated by the latter's political vehicle, the People's Action Party (PAP), audaciously contesting general elections in 1964. In mobilising Chinese voters over calls for a 'Malaysian Malaysia', Lee struck squarely at indigenous Malay privileges (Means 1976: 347). Further, after the election, the PAP joined with other opposition parties to form the Malaysian Solidarity Convention, invigorating debate in parliament and arousing the sentiments of Chinese constituents. Regarding this as betrayal, the UMNO prime minister, Tunku Abdul Rahman, summarily expelled Singapore from the Federation of Malaysia in 1965. And only after much debate did he permit a local successor to the PAP, the Democratic Action Party (DAP), to be registered in Malaysia.

Inter-ethnic tensions, straining relations between elites in UMNO and the MCA, continued to simmer during this period over political hegemony, economic redistribution, and the cultural role of Malay vernacular, now officially made the national language. But even more than this, fractiousness among Malay elites also began to intensify. Tunku Abdul Rahman, personally conciliatory in his conduct of ethnic relations, was purged as prime minister in 1971 by a faction of 'ultra Malays' led by his successor, Tun Abdul Razak, shortly before emergency rule was lifted and electoral authoritarianism installed. Further, an Islamist opposition vehicle, the Pan-Malaysian Islamic Party (PAS), which had broken from UMNO in 1951 (Funston 1980: 92–94), was lured into the Barisan in 1973. But soon afterward leaders of UMNO and PAS disagreed over who should become chief minister in the latter's bailiwick state of Kelantan. In a clear indicator of rising fractiousness, then, UMNO mobilised its followers in Kelantan, fomenting such confrontation that it was able to declare emergency rule yet again, then impose its candidate (Chin 1997). In 1978, PAS abandoned Barisan, returning to opposition. And throughout the 1980s, as PAS grew more Islamist in tenor, its rivalries with UMNO intensified over religiosity, precipitating rancorous disputes in which they accused one another of being *kafir* (infidels). In the late 1990s, the UMNO-led government arrested the son of the PAS chief minister of Kelantan for terrorism, detaining him and several party associates for long periods without trial under the country's notorious Internal Security Act (ISA). Imprisonment on such terms registers plainly the deepening fractiousness between elites, not only across ethnic lines but deep within the Malay segmental pillar. Indeed, as we will see below, factional warring would break out even within UMNO, sparking purges, jail sentences, and televised confessions, actions that culminated in the irregular seizures of executive power that Higley and Burton define as regime instability.

Redistributive pressures: accommodative hegemony

After recalling that elites in most national settings are fractious, Dan Slater next contends that they may overcome the collective action problems that inhibit cohesion when threatened sufficiently from below by redistributive pressures. These pressures involve, however, very specific combinations of mass-level sentiments, first made manifest in class-based demands, then ignited by communal resentments, so shaking elites from their lateral warring, usually waged in capital cities, that they come finally to acknowledge one another as elites, rather than as irksome pretenders or unworthy foes. In these circumstances, elites reorganise their relations in a 'pact of protection' through which to repress redistributive demands and safeguard their mutual statuses. Moreover, in doing this, elites now so empower and articulate the state with ruling parties, bureaucratic agencies, and security apparatuses that rather than installing a democracy, even a consociational one, they erect instead a sturdy authoritarian 'Leviathan'. In the Southeast Asian context, Slater cites Malaysia and Singapore, mighty in their tax collection and coercive capacity, as arch examples.

Slater is right that when class-based demands for redistribution appeared in Malaysia in the wake of World War II, cumulating in leftist insurgency, elites in UMNO, often aristocratic civil servants, and in the MCA, mainly business tycoons, discovered additional impetus for gathering together under the tutelage of the British. But when mass demands for redistribution gained a more avowedly communal tenor during the late 1960s–70s, the pact of protection, rather than gaining new affirmation, was at least partially shattered. Elites in UMNO, far from joining their counterparts in the MCA to quash redistributive demands, now led the way in heightening them among the Malay constituencies that they sought to re-energise. In brief, through measures collectively designated as the NEP, they introduced pro-Malay quotas on university placements, state enterprise formation and managerial recruitment, corporate hiring, and equity ownership (Jesudason 1989). These quotas were most intensely applied under the Industrial Coordination Act during the 1970s, cheering the Malays, but deepening resentments among the Chinese, to the point that many of those who possessed necessary resources migrated overseas in large numbers during this period. It is difficult to imagine any surer indicator than flight of eroded constituent loyalties and consequent tensions between elites.

What is more, when fractiousness erupted within UMNO, it seldom unfolded in ways that motivated elites to rekindle old ties to MCA leaders. To the contrary, factions in UMNO would more typically stoop to competing with one another by castigating the Chinese over their business activities, vernacular schools, and cultural displays. Thus, in a fracas canvassed more thoroughly below that erupted between 'teams' designated 'A' and 'B' over succession during the late 1980s, spiralling dynamics gave rise to shrill criticisms of the Chinese. Indeed, as pressures intensified, Najib Razak, associated with Team B, was prodded by factional supporters to lead a rally through which to re-energise Malay support. In view of banners, then, that depicted a Malay ceremonial dagger, the *kris*, and reading 'soak it in Chinese blood', Najib was driven to wave a long-bladed sword over his head, while burning an MCA flag and an effigy of the party's deputy president. The leader of Team A, Mahathir himself, countered finally by ordering a notorious security sweep known as Operation Lalang. Over the course of several weeks, some 106 politicians and activists were detained without trial under the ISA, including members of UMNO's Youth wing associated with Team B, but more glaringly, the DAP's secretary-general, Lim Kit Sang, and fifteen other DAP parliamentarians. PAS officials and Chinese educationists were also held, some for long periods.

During the 1990s, as Malaysia's economy and middle class grew swiftly, fractiousness among elites within UMNO and across ethnic lines subsided. Indeed, Mahathir, in estimating that amid the decade's buoyancy, the *korporat Melayu* (Malay entrepreneurs) that he had nurtured could now engage more fruitfully with Chinese tycoons, celebrated the convening of *bangsa Malaysia*, a new national identity that connoted 'people . . . able to identify themselves with the country, speak Bahasa Malaysia, and accept the Constitution' (*Asiaweek* 1995: 38). Even Lim Kit Siang, leading the DAP, was moved to reply: 'I concede that Mahathir's statement was courageous. His remarks are the most enlightened he has made on nation-building for some time' (*Asiaweek* 1995: 38).

Severe tensions among elites recurred across ethnic lines during the next decade, however. Mahathir's successor as prime minister and UMNO president, Abdullah Badawi, led his Barisan government to its mightiest electoral victory ever in 2004, drawing robust voter support from across the Malay and Chinese communities. But activists in UMNO, evidently made confident by this win that they had turned back a social reform movement and opposition coalition led by the former deputy prime minister, Anwar Ibrahim, calculated that it was timely now more vigorously to assert Malay special rights. In the next section, we will explore in more detail Anwar's expulsion from UMNO, his imprisonment, the rise of a social reform movement, and the implications for elite relations. What requires attention here is the renewed burst of communalism in UMNO that was unleashed, highlighted by its Youth leader and also Home Minister Hishammuddin Hussein's raising a *kris* at successive UMNO general assemblies on national television. Abdullah, while having campaigned on a promise to be 'a prime minister for all Malaysians', reacted to Hishammuddin's gestures languidly, remarking that 'the keris is a weapon, but it is a weapon to protect yourself and your friends' (*Malaysiakini* 2007).

As UMNO's communalism intensified, it reawakened the suspicions of the Chinese, driving them back into the arms of the opposition, hence eroding constituent support for MCA elites. Thus, when a general election was held in March 2008, Barisan leaders were stunned by the extent to which Chinese voters deserted to the opposition, with PAS, the DAP, and Anwar's new vehicle, the People's Justice Party (PKR) forging electoral agreements. UMNO elites were struck, too, by a swing of some 5 percent among Malay voters, principally members of the new urban middle class who were alienated over the government's incessant patronage flows. Accordingly, some elites in UMNO underwent a rare period of introspection, reflecting on their party's eroded popularity, while contemplating significant liberalising reforms.

Unrepentant factions, however, soon regained the upper hand. And in a sharp display of elite fractiousness, they steadily undermined Abdullah, then finally purged him as prime minister and UMNO leader in 2009, replacing him with Najib Razak. Over the next few years, Najib, rather like Abdullah, tried to steer a modest course of reform, easing authoritarian controls, liberalising the economy, and making overtures to the Chinese – promising new support for Chinese-language schools, for example, while campaigning under a banner of '1Malaysia' for the next election in 2013. Yet attitudes had so hardened that in this election the Chinese instead nearly completed their swing to the opposition, with PAS, the DAP, and PKR having drawn more closely together as Pakatan Rakyat (People's Alliance). The MCA fared badly, then, with Barisan collectively losing even more of the popular vote and parliamentary seats. UMNO, though, had its 'best election ever', winning eighty-eight seats, just one shy of Pakatan's total.

Afterward, Daim Zainuddin, a former finance minister, chastised Najib for his moderate campaigning, declaring that UMNO strategists had known all along 'that the Chinese majority areas were gone. Why waste time and money?' (Lim 2013). Even more assertively, A. Kadir Jasin, an influential editor-in-chief associated closely with UMNO, exclaimed, 'UMNO is particularly upset as we told Najib not to throw money at the Chinese as other constituencies needed the resources and the Chinese wouldn't vote for us anyway' (Berthelsen 2013). And a former Court of Appeal judge, Mohd Noor Abdullah, serving currently on the Malaysian Anti-Corruption Commission and the UMNO Disciplinary Committee, berated the Chinese for their 'betrayal', declaring that 'we gave them recognition and protection and eventually citizenship until they became rich. . . . [W]hen Malays are betrayed, there is a backlash and the Chinese must bear the consequences of a Malay backlash' (Aw 2013). A group of Islamic NGOs then demanded that the Malay community boycott Chinese-owned companies that had contributed to Pakatan's campaign (*Malaysiakini* 2013).

As relations worsened, Najib recoiled from his earlier moderation. He announced a new volley of redistributive measures benefiting the Malays, collectively labelled Bumiputera Economic Empowerment. They include formation of the Bumiputera New Entrepreneurs Start-Up Scheme (SUPERB), more vigorous use of the country's extensive set of Government Linked Corporations (GLCs) to procure goods from *bumiputera* vendors, and a second unit trust, Amanah Saham Bumiputera 2 (ASB2), more broadly advantaging 'middle' Malay shareowners with favourable returns. Plainly, the fissures between Malay and Chinese communities have widened, indeed so weakening the MCA's constituencies that the party, holding only seven seats in parliament and initially no ministerial positions in cabinet, is barely able today even to support elite statuses.

To sum up this section, redistributive pressures posed from below failed in Malaysia to inspire any lasting pact of protection through which elites might cooperatively react in defence of their interests. Instead, elites fractured across ethnic lines, with those in UMNO responding avidly to demands in order to re-energise their Malay supporters, but therein undermining the Chinese constituencies, and hence the standing, of their counterparts in the MCA. At the same time, a hardy authoritarian Leviathan was created in Malaysia, but along vectors that sharply depart from Slater's account. A powerful state apparatus was built by elites in UMNO, but then fused with their party in order to respond fully to redistributive demands, not to repress them, therein delivering the exclusivist benefits that accord with Malay special rights. To be sure, for some three decades after the introduction of the NEP, some level of elite cohesion was nonetheless perpetuated across ethnic lines, captured in a refrain of hegemony with accommodativeness. But after the election in 2004, as elites in UMNO asserted Malay special rights more vigorously, they inflamed resentments within the Chinese community. In addition, Abdullah's utter inability to contain the patronage flows in UMNO that coursed alongside the NEP's redistributions began to alienate some 'progressive' urban middle-class Malays. In these circumstances, a social reform movement and political opposition emerged which, by energising vast popular support, came even to threaten UMNO's hegemony and the regime's electoral authoritarianism. Thus, as elites in opposition scaled new heights, a configuration took shape that must be characterised as fractious, but marked by increasingly balanced multi-ethnic coalitions. Thus, for UMNO to recover, relations among its leaders required the renewal of historical-institutional legacies and codes, as well as the practised issuance of patronage, posing serious challenges to the party, to which we now turn.

Patronage and single-party dominance: from even splits to new hegemony

Dan Slater is mainly concerned with the ways in which elites reach cohesion through a pact of protection, then fashion a supportive array of authoritarian institutions. Other authors, however, stress what Slater labels a 'pact of provision', with single-dominant parties maintaining cohesion among elites by accessing and mediating flows of state patronage. Kenneth Greene (2007) and Beatriz Magaloni (2006), in developing respectively a 'resource theory . . . of hyper-incumbency' and a theory of 'hegemonic party survival', narrow their attention to the methods by which party leaders once extracted public sector resources and allocated them across elite-level persons and factions in ways that reproduced elite cohesion. As Magaloni (2006: 18) succinctly puts it, 'hegemonic parties must distribute ample spoils . . . so as to deter elites from splitting'.

Jason Brownlee (2007) extends this analysis to a variety of hegemonic parties in developing countries, including UMNO. Through his 'historical-institutional' approach, he traces the structural forces that first divide elites, the triumph of one set of elites over others (rather than any lasting bargain), and the installation of victorious elites based in a single dominant party. And steeled by historical legacies, this party then regulates reliably the allocation of patronage among elites, while energising constituent loyalties. Thus, while the spoils emphasised by Greene and Magaloni are important for maintaining dominance, Brownlee (2007: 203) argues that UMNO does more than meet material needs. By combining patronage streams with a communally arousing 'Malay agenda', it 'binds together otherwise fractious elites in [a] durable coalition that enable[s] individual advancement amid collective security'.

Accordingly, with its patronage distributions, historical resonance, mediating capacity, and structural grounding, UMNO is depicted by Brownlee as enabling elites to resolve episodic strains in their relations. But even if we acknowledge that relations between elites in UMNO and the MCA were eroded, permitting us to focus solely on UMNO, it is difficult to support a claim of unbroken cohesion between elites in even the latter vehicle. As we noted in the previous section, their dynamics have regularly bristled with upsurges in fractiousness.

Thus, even a brief recount of factional conflicts in UMNO shows that they can amount to much more than mere 'strain points', amenable to conciliation. As we have seen, Tunku Abdul Rahman and Abdullah Badawi, their party presidencies and ex officio prime ministerships supposedly sanctified by Malay cultural notions of authority and grounded institutionally in UMNO procedures, were respectively purged after setbacks in the 1969 and 2008 elections. Further, though the patronage resources said to help underpin elite cohesion swelled during the mid-1970s upon introduction of the NEP, ensuring that distribution was 'ample' and reliable, the chief minister of Selangor, Harun Idris, after challenging the UMNO president and prime minister, Hussein Onn, was sentenced to a lengthy jail term for corruption. Conversely, when patronage was depleted by local recession during the mid-1980s, factional warring again broke out, pitting the then prime minister, Mahathir, against his deputy, Musa Hitam.

Brownlee (2007: 138) writes that this episode 'began with a split', with Mahathir, evidently fretting over Musa's greater popularity, so berating his deputy that Musa suddenly resigned. And encouraged by more widespread grievances against the prime minister, a larger 'anti-Mahathir faction' soon formed, the leader of which, Tengku Razaleigh Hamzah, challenged Mahathir for the presidency of UMNO at the party's polls in 1987. Elites within UMNO then gathered into the teams mentioned previously, with 'Team A', led by Mahathir, and 'Team B', led by Razaleigh and Musa. More than a political clash between party factions, these teams were egged on by the sections of local, but immobile capital, now starved of patronage, with which they were respectively allied (Khoo 1992). In brief, Mahathir had championed the indigenous *korporat Melayu* mentioned above, showering them with state contracts, credit, and concessions. On the other side, Razaleigh, notwithstanding his family wealth, had promoted small and medium-sized Malay businessmen who, as contractors and suppliers, were more modest beneficiaries of the NEP.

Mahathir claimed victory in the party poll. However, the conduct of the election and the events that followed intimated none of the 'restrained partisanship' that hallmarks elite-level cohesion. Rather, with the vote count close, it triggered suspicions of cheating. Mahathir then purged his cabinet of ministers associated with Team B. Razaleigh retaliated by taking the fight over polling results outside UMNO's appeal mechanisms to the High Court. The judge, finding that some of UMNO's branch organisations had been improperly registered, ruled that UMNO was itself illegal and so ordered its deregistration. Mahathir then pressed bureaucratic officials furiously, besting Razaleigh in the race to re-register the party. This enabled Mahathir to gain leadership over what in its new guise was badged 'UMNO Baru' (i.e. New UMNO).

Razaleigh next took the fight over UMNO's 'name and assets' to the High Court. Mahathir feared that the court would favour Team B, driving him now to make heavy use of the attorney-general's chambers and even the king's royal offices to purge the body of most of its judges. Further, to silence the public outcry that followed, Mahathir arrested top opposition leaders through Operation Lalang, described above. In this way, Mahathir kept control over UMNO Baru, winning the approval of new judges whose installation he oversaw. Unable, then, to make headway, Razaleigh and key supporters in Team B broke with the party outright, registering a new vehicle, Semangat '46, named for the year in which UMNO had been founded.

A decade later, patronage again ran thin during the Asian financial crisis. Mahathir this time clashed with Anwar Ibrahim, his deputy at the time, producing momentous elite-level fractiousness. At the UMNO General Assembly in 1998, Anwar openly accused Mahathir of issuing state contracts to family members and cronies. Mahathir retaliated, with Anwar purged from the party, beaten by the police chief, and charged with sexual misconduct, leading to a lengthy jail sentence. Mahathir also purged elites in media organisations and state enterprises in order to deter more defection. But these behaviours again so violated Malay cultural expectations, specifically the sanctions against humiliating subordinates, that a social reform movement took shape, even inspiring opposition parties to coalesce across ethnic lines in order to contest the 1999 general elections. Thus, one of the conclusions that can be drawn from this episode is that whether patronage resources are plentiful or scarce, far from encouraging accommodation between elites, they may instigate the ruthlessness that characterises splits.

For Brownlee, though, patronage is only part of what keeps elites cohesive. Through his historical-institutional lenses, he observes the more crucial presence of legacies of struggle and ethnic solidarity, culminating in a mentality that enables dominant parties like UMNO to regulate competitions and perpetuate loyalties. But on this count, too, just as patronage flows might fuel fractiousness, ideological consensus has sometimes broken down. During the mid-1970s, as Tun Razak began to implement the NEP, distinct factions emerged of 'old guards' led by the Tunku, more communalist, but still traditional 'ultra-Malays' associated with Harun Idris, and a fresher cohort of modernising 'ultra-Malays', including Ghafar Baba, Tengku Razaleigh, and Mahathir Mohamad, better equipped with the technocratic skills that Tun Razak valued for state-driven ethnic redistributions.

Tun Razak died in 1976 and was succeeded by his deputy, Hussein Onn, who, in later choosing his own successor from among the new ultra-Malay cohort, selected Mahathir over Ghafar, Razaleigh, and the highly ambitious home minister, Ghazali Shafie. Harun Idris, his conviction having been stayed pending an appeal, then mounted a new leadership challenge, prompting Hussein to oust him from UMNO and the Selangor chief ministership, an action regarded by the old guards and old ultras as an 'abandonment of party traditions' (Case 1996: 126). These factions then responded, asserting that Hussein's government was riddled with communist agents, allegations made inflammatory against a backdrop of guerrilla bomb attacks in Kuala Lumpur and bitter recollections of the Emergency. Ghazali Shafie followed up by invoking the ISA, arresting some of Hussein's top advisors, then televising their confessions over sundry plots and schemes. But shortly afterward, Harun's conviction was upheld, and his jail term was increased from two to six years. Only at this point, then, did Hussein regain the upper hand, finally quelling the ideologically charged fractiousness between elites that had reverberated within UMNO despite, or even because of, the patronage resources, foundational mentalities, and institutional apparatus that the party possessed.

In short, the material, historical, and institutional features found by Brownlee to underpin a single dominant party can themselves become objects of struggle, therein threatening elite-level cohesion. Over time, fractiousness spread in Malaysia from inter-ethnic and intra-Malay arenas to infect even the internal dynamics of UMNO, rocking the party with epic and iterated warring during the late 1960s, the mid- to late 1970s, the mid- to late 1980s, the late 1990s to early 2000s and 2008 to 2009. Purges, beatings, forced confessions on television and other forms of humiliation, appropriation of constituencies, and long terms of imprisonment stand as ready indicators of fractiousness between elites in UMNO, undiminished by single-party dominance.

Conclusion

Malaysia is often viewed as distinctive in the cohesion between its elites, the stability of its regime, and the resilience of its dominant party. It has thus gained scrutiny for its avoidance of the military and executive coups, social upheavals, and incessant ethnic and separatist conflicts that have roiled Thailand, the Philippines, Cambodia, New Order Indonesia, and

Myanmar. Even so, Malaysia's record of elite relations and regime outcomes has fluctuated much more than simple notions of cohesion and stability convey.

Despite consociational and tutelary modelling, elite relations began first to slip on an ethnic plane, with the coalescence between Malay elites in UMNO and Chinese elites in the MCA upended by redistributive pressures from below. A new configuration thus emerged, marked by greater Malay hegemony and enhanced UMNO dominance, even if still accommodative. Accordingly, politics were commensurately truncated from electoral democracy to electoral authoritarianism. Next, with Chinese elites subordinated, fractiousness mounted among Malay elites, with UMNO confronting PAS and eventually Anwar's vehicle, PKR. Further, as PAS and PKR came to collaborate across ethnic lines with the DAP in order more effectively to contest elections, relations among elites changed yet again, with multi-ethnic coalitions in government and opposition, weighted increasingly evenly, standing starkly in confrontation. And when an election was held in 2008, the opposition made such gains that the regime was shown also to have shifted, with electoral authoritarianism widening into a far more competitive hybrid, therein reactivating fractiousness, long endemic, within UMNO.

However, after the most recent election in 2013, elites in UMNO seem to have regained much cohesion and single-party dominance. Yet while vigorously asserted, their unity remains brittle, driven by collective and utter defiance over their party's ebbing support. Indeed, they blame the shrinkage of their base on desertion by 'traitorous' Chinese and 'ungrateful' Malays. Further, in clinging to power atop a minority of voters, their regime is shown to have changed yet again, with the extent of social exclusion, electoral manipulation, and the attendant need for coercion now more plainly in view. Accordingly, Malaysia's politics appear to be nearing the completion of the progress foreshadowed long ago by Rabushka and Shepsle, contracting into a deeply exclusivist form of authoritarian rule. But whether this form will remain any more stable than what it has replaced is doubtful, for Malaysia's elites, in their fractiousness, are unexceptional.

Bibliography

Asiaweek (1995) 'One nation, one people: Mahathir lays the groundwork for stronger unity', available at www-cgi.cnn.com/ASIANOW/asiaweek/95/1006/nat4.html (accessed 7 May 2014).

Aw, Nigel (2013) 'Ex-judge warns Chinese of backlash for "betrayal"', *Malaysiakini*, 12 May, available at www.malaysiakini.com/news/229909 (accessed 7 May 2014).

Berthelsen, John (2013) 'Malaysia's deep divides', *Asia Sentinel*, 29 May, available at http://asiancorrespondent.com/108303/malaysia-divides-election-2013–ge13/ (accessed 7 May 2014).

Brownlee, Jason (2007) *Authoritarianism in an Age of Democratisation*, Cambridge: Cambridge University Press.

Case, William (1995) 'Malaysia: aspects and audiences of legitimacy', in Muthiah Alagappa (ed.), *Political Legitimacy in Southeast Asia: The Quest for Moral Authority*, Stanford: Stanford University Press, pp. 69–107.

Case, William (1996) *Elites and Regimes in Malaysia: Revisiting a Consociational Democracy*, Clayton, VIC: Monash Asia Institute.

Chee, Stephen (1991) 'Consociational political leadership and conflict regulation in Malaysia', in Stephen Chee (ed.), *Leadership and Security in Southeast Asia: Institutional Aspects*, Singapore: Institute of Southeast Asian Studies.

Chin, James (1997) 'Politics of federal intervention in Malaysia, with reference to Sarawak, Sabah and Kelantan', *Journal of Commonwealth and Comparative Politics*, 35(2): 96–120.

Esman, Milton J. (1972) 'Malaysia: communal coexistence and mutual deterrence', in Ernest Q. Campbell (ed.), *Racial Tensions and National Identity*, Nashville: Vanderbilt University Press.

Funston, John (1980) *Malay Politics in Malaysia: A Study of UMNO and PAS*, Petaling Jaya: Heinemann.

Greene, Kenneth (2007) *Why Dominant Parties Lose: Mexico's Democratisation in Comparative Perspective*, Cambridge: Cambridge University Press.

Higley, John and Michael G. Burton (1989) 'The elite variable in democratic transitions and breakdowns', *American Sociological Review*, 54(1): 17–32.

Horowitz, Donald (1985) *Ethnic Groups in Conflict*, Berkeley: University of California Press.

Jesudason, James V. (1989) *Ethnicity and the Economy: The State, Chinese Business, and Multinationals in Malaysia*, Singapore: Oxford University Press.

Khoo Kay Jin (1992) 'The grand vision: Mahathir and modernisation', in Joel Kahn and Francis Loh (eds), *Fragmented Vision: Culture and Politics in Contemporary Malaysia*, Honolulu: University of Hawaii Press.

Levitsky, Steven R. and Lucan A. Way (2010) *Competitive Authoritarianism: Hybrid Regimes After the Cold War*, Cambridge: Cambridge University Press.

Levitsky, Steven R. and Lucan A. Way (2012) 'Beyond patronage: violent struggle, ruling party cohesion, and authoritarian durability', *Perspectives on Politics*, 10(4): 869–89.

Lijphart, Arend (1977) *Democracy in Plural Societies: A Comparative Exploration*, New Haven: Yale University Press.

Lim, Ida (2013) 'Daim: BN lost votes due to wrong strategy, infighting', *Malaysian Insider*, 27 May, available at www.themalaysianinsider.com/malaysia/article/daim-bn-lost-votes-due-to-wrong-strategy-infighting (accessed 7 May 2014).

Linz, Juan J. (1996) 'Toward consolidated democracies', *Journal of Democracy*, 7(2): 14–33.

Linz, Juan J. and Alfred Stepan (1996) *Problems of Democratic Transition and Consolidation: Southern Europe, South America, and Post-Communist Europe*, Baltimore: Johns Hopkins University Press.

Lustick, Ian (1979) 'Stability in deeply divided societies: consociationalism versus control', *World Politics*, 33(3): 325–44.

Magaloni, Beatriz (2006) *Voting for Autocracy: Hegemonic Party Survival and its Demise in Mexico*, Cambridge: Cambridge University Press.

Malaysiakini (2007) 'PM defends keris at Umno assembly', *Malaysiakini*, 7 November, available at www.malaysiakini.com/news/74468 (accessed 7 May 2014).

Malaysiakini (2013) 'NGOs urge boycott of "Chinese Pro-Pakatan" firms', *Malaysiakini*, 14 May, available at www.malaysiakini.com/news/230085 (accessed 7 May 2014).

Mauzy, Diane (1983) *Barisan Nasional: Coalition Government in Malaysia*, Kuala Lumpur: Marican & Sons.

Means, Gordon P. (1976) [1970] *Malaysian Politics*, London: Hodder and Stoughton.

Milne, Robert S. (1967) *Government and Politics in Malaysia*, Boston: Houghton Mifflin.

Rabushka, Alvin and Kenneth A. Shepsle (2009) *Politics in Plural Societies: A Theory of Democratic Instability*, Columbus: Charles E. Merrill.

Schedler, Andreas (ed.) (2006) *Electoral Authoritarianism: The Dynamics of Unfree Competition*, Boulder: Lynne Rienner.

Slater, Dan (2010) *Ordering Power: Contentious Politics and Authoritarian Leviathans in Southeast Asia*, Cambridge: Cambridge University Press.

Von Vorys, Karl (1975) *Democracy Without Consensus: Communalism and Political Stability in Malaysia*, Princeton: Princeton University Press.

Weiner, Myron (1987) 'Empirical democratic theory', in Myron Weiner and Ergun Ozbudun (eds), *Competitive Elections in Developing Countries*, Durham: Duke University Press, pp. 3–34.

Zakaria Haji Ahmad (1989) 'Malaysia: quasi-democracy in a divided society', in Larry Diamond, Juan J. Linz and Seymour Martin Lipset (eds), *Democracy in Developing Countries: Asia*, Boulder: Lynne Rienner, pp. 347–81.

4

Islam, the state and politics in Malaysia

Joseph Chinyong Liow and Afif Pasuni

Muslims account for approximately 60 percent of the population of Malaysia. Among Malaysia's many ethnic groups, Malays are the largest followers of the Islamic faith. In fact, Malay identity is legally tied to Islam, for according to the Malaysian constitution, a 'Malay' is 'a person who professes the religion of Islam, habitually speaks the Malay language, conforms to Malay custom . . .'.[1]

The imbricated nature of religious and ethnic identity, and the persistence of the racial narrative in Malaysia's social, economic, and political spheres, has meant that the factor of Islam has enjoyed considerable influence and attention in Malaysian politics. This influence can be traced back to the rise of anti-colonialism in British Malaya, when Muslim groups such as Hizbul Muslimin played a significant role in mobilising opposition to the colonial administration after the Pacific War. Following decolonisation in 1957, Islamist forces formed the Pan-Malayan Islamic Party, which eventually morphed into Parti Islam Se-Malaysia, better known by its acronym, PAS. Since 1955, when PAS managed to secure the first opposition representation in the federal government dominated by UMNO (United Malays National Organisation) through the Alliance coalition, rivalry between UMNO (also a Malay-Muslim based party) and PAS has become a definitive (and mostly divisive) feature of politics in Muslim-majority Malaysia. At the same time, growing Islamic consciousness and piety among the Muslim population have also witnessed the emergence of a host of Islamic civil society movements that have further animated political Islam in Malaysia, thereby fuelling the intensification of Islamist discourse in the country. In Malaysia's federal system of government, matters of religion come under the jurisdiction of state authorities, and *shari'a* is accorded the foremost role in managing the personal affairs of Muslims. This has created controversy in recent years, however, as the scope of religious authority appears to have expanded at the expense of the constitutionally enshrined right to religious freedom.

The evolution of Islamism in post-colonial Malaysia

While 'Islamism' remains in some respects a contested term, there is broad consensus among social science scholars on one point: it is a political ideology premised on the primacy of Islam as an organising principle for government. In the case of Malaysia, Islamism is most profoundly expressed in political competition between key Malay-Muslim parties, UMNO and PAS, and more broadly, in the increasingly exclusivist social and political discourse in the country that has caused great consternation to the sizeable non-Muslim minority.

PAS was officially formed prior to Malaysian independence, on 24 November 1951.[2] Ironically, PAS was initially a part of UMNO, which was established in 1946 by the traditional Malay nationalist movement in an attempt to unite a hitherto disparate Malay-Muslim community in preparation for independence. The genesis of PAS came about when clerics, dissatisfied with the role that Islam was accorded by UMNO politicians of that generation, left the party to form another. Yet such was the close proximity between PAS and UMNO in PAS's formative years, its members enjoyed the privilege of holding dual party membership. It was only under its second president, Dr Abbas Alias, that PAS was officially registered as a political party on 31 May 1955 in order to contest federal elections, and ties with UMNO were officially severed. Once PAS became fully independent from UMNO, it intended to serve as a direct challenge for the Malay-Muslim vote bank (Funston 1976). From then on, the core objective of PAS, from which it has never wavered, is the creation of an Islamic governing structure in Malaysia by elevating what the party perceives to be the purely symbolic status of Islam accorded in the Malaysian Constitution to a more substantive and operational plane.[3] Put differently, PAS was the first proponent of the cause of the transformation of Malaysia into an Islamic state.[4]

In its formative years, PAS advocated the creation of an Islamic state in only the most general of terms. In addition to the religious aspects of its agenda, strong emphasis was initially placed on what former PAS president Burhanuddin al-Helmy described as 'Malay nationalism with Islamic ambitions' (Syed 2002: 85).[5] The ethno-nationalist ethos behind PAS's early Islamist discourse was driven by what the party perceived to be UMNO's selling out of Malay interests to the ethnic minorities, in particular the ethnic Chinese, in return for political power.

PAS's initial foray into mainstream politics was unimpressive – it won a solitary parliamentary seat in the first federal elections in July 1955. However, after that performance, the party's leadership concentrated attention on creating a more robust organisational structure, expanding the geographical reach of the party, increasing its number of members, exploiting new means for the dissemination of the party's agenda and message, and better integrating religious and nationalist agendas. This expanded focus resulted in PAS's first substantial electoral victory in the 1959 election, which saw the party gain control of the state assemblies in the north-eastern Peninsular Malaysian states of Kelantan and Terengganu – where the electorate was largely traditional, conservative, and Malay – as well as thirteen national parliamentary seats. With this election, PAS made history by becoming the first Islamist party to come to power (albeit as a state government in a federal system) by electoral means in Southeast Asia, and one of the first in the entire Muslim world. PAS met with mixed results in the 1964 general elections, when it lost the Terengganu state assembly even as it saw its share of the popular vote in the northern Malay states increase.[6]

The 1969 election yielded similar results despite the fact that PAS won almost half the Malay-Muslim popular vote nationally. The suspension of parliament from May 1969 until 1972 due to the rise of ethnic tensions, coupled with the highly personalised and authoritarian style of leadership under then PAS president Asri Muda, led PAS to join its rival UMNO and other parties in a coalition as a means of consolidating the political power of the Malay community. Prior to joining the coalition, there had been much debate within PAS about whether or not to cooperate with UMNO, given that many within PAS fundamentally disagreed with UMNO's secular approach to governance and politics. Under the leadership of Asri Muda, a staunch Malay ethno-nationalist, PAS's own agenda had begun drifting away from Islamism towards that of ethnic politics, which alienated the religious component of the party's traditional base of support. This alienation was further amplified by the rise of Islamic consciousness within the Malay-Muslim community as a whole, as a consequence of the global Islamic resurgence in the 1970s. Despite residual differences between UMNO and PAS, both sought accommodation for reasons of political expediency. For its part, PAS's leadership was able to justify compromise with its political rival after identifying its priorities (purportedly, Malay-Muslim unity) and possible areas of shared interests with UMNO.

While participation in the coalition brought some benefits, many of PAS's more substantive Islamic proposals, such as amendments to parts of the Constitution in order to make it more 'Islamic', were rejected outright by UMNO, leaving PAS dissatisfied with its role in the governing coalition (Liow 2009: 31–33). PAS's first power-sharing experiment unravelled in 1977 when it was unceremoniously ejected from the coalition by UMNO due to internal disagreements. The internal disagreements which forced PAS from the ruling coalition also caused a split within the party leadership, with many PAS leaders and members joining the ranks of a new, offshoot Malay-Muslim party, Berjasa, as well as UMNO. These factors contributed to the party's loss of Kelantan at the 1978 elections.

The loss of the party's Kelantan stronghold, which it had controlled since 1959, was a major psychological blow for PAS, and paved the way for a fundamental shift towards a more religious register when in 1982, Islamic clerics, inspired by the 1979 Iranian Revolution (despite deep-seated misgivings towards the Shi'a brand of Islam in Iraq), gained control of the party. At the same time, the controversial UMNO president, Mahathir Mohamad, took high office to begin twenty-two years as Malaysia's prime minister.

Mahathir's initial focus upon entering office was to defeat the political challenge posed by PAS. He sought to do this by beating the Islamist opposition at their own game by pursuing his own brand of modernist-developmentalist Islamic policies. To assist him in this endeavour, Mahathir enlisted the help of the charismatic Islamic youth movement leader Anwar Ibrahim – long considered to be a PAS sympathiser – through his UMNO ally, Suleiman Palestine, who was also Anwar's uncle. The successful co-option of Anwar allowed UMNO to contest actively for Islamic discursive space against the clerics of PAS. Anwar led the charge by overseeing a raft of policies and programmes perceived to be Islamic, including the creation of more Islamic education institutions up to tertiary levels, the introduction of Islamic finance, the inflation of the religious bureaucracy at both state and federal levels, greater tolerance for the practice of moral policing by state religious departments, and an active watch against Christian proselytisation in the country, especially among Malay-Muslim communities. This contestation ushered in what has come to be known in the Malaysian political lexicon as the UMNO–PAS 'Islamisation race'.

To be sure, this Islamisation race was not merely a consequence of Anwar's co-option. Since the early 1970s, Muslim civil society activism had been on the rise on the back of international events that had quickened the political consciousness of Muslim societies worldwide. In Malaysia, the Malaysian Islamic Youth Movement, ABIM (Angkatan Belia Islam Malaysia), which Anwar led in the mid-1970s, played a pivotal role as a pressure group that lobbied the Malaysian government to focus more on Islamic governance. ABIM soon provided the collective pool of politically socialised Muslim youths from which UMNO and PAS would draw a new generation of leaders. Indeed, even as Anwar joined UMNO, many of his ABIM peers and colleagues chose to join PAS. Among their numbers were Fadzil Noor and Abdul Hadi Awang, two future presidents of the Islamic party.

Islamist reformists

The latter half of the 1990s marked a major turning point in the fortunes of the Islamist opposition, when economic adversity and the removal of Mahathir's ambitious heir-apparent, Anwar Ibrahim, triggered a period of political ferment. As Mahathir's term in high office drew to a close, he was increasingly seen by many Malaysians as an authoritarian leader under whose leadership the Malaysian business–politics nexus was contaminated by chronic corruption. This was made strikingly clear when the Asian financial crisis struck the Malaysian economy and brought down several erstwhile high-profile and politically connected indigenous enterprises. Led then by the moderate reformist Fadzil Noor, PAS recognised the political opportunity presented by Mahathir's increasing unpopularity and began to refocus the party's mobilisation around themes of democracy, social justice, and transparency, while the hard-line Islamist rhetoric that had come to define the party was kept expediently on the backburner. Shortly after PAS embarked on this transition, popular Islamic activist and former deputy prime minister Anwar Ibrahim was arrested and incarcerated in 1999. This action on the part of the ruling government was met with widespread condemnation from all sectors of Malaysian society and led PAS to join forces with other opposition parties to launch the *reformasi*, or reform, movement.

As a member of the newly formed Barisan Alternatif (Alternative Front) opposition coalition, PAS secured its greatest election victory in 1999 when it recaptured the state assembly of Terengganu after having lost it in 1978 and secured a commendable twenty-seven parliamentary and ninety-eight state seats. Following this electoral success and the confidence gained from it, PAS once again began to press its Islamic agenda with renewed vigour, under the mistaken impression that the widespread support it had won on its anti-UMNO, anti-Mahathir platform was instead a sign that the population was prepared to accept its Islamic agenda. This shift is at least in part attributable to the sudden death of Fadzil Noor in 2002 and his succession by his deputy, the fiery orator Abdul Hadi Awang. Following this transition in leadership, the party released its Islamic State Document, which was thus far the most detailed articulation of the party's vision for Islamic government in Malaysia. What was striking about the document, which was originally the idea of Fadzil Noor, was the fact that its earlier iterations were comparatively moderate, inclusivist, and outward-looking in language and orientation. Controversial issues of *hudud* and *shari'a* were skirted and principles of democracy and sensitivity to Malaysia's multicultural social landscape were acknowledged, whereas the subsequent 'official' document stressed Islamic governance and included references to the controversial issue of *hudud*.[7] Not surprisingly, the move to formalise the document without consultation with party progressives was heavily criticised by the latter, who enjoyed a strong presence in the party's Central Working Committee but who at the time had little say in the Majlis Shura or Consultative Council.[8] With these disagreements, the seeds of internal discord were sown within the party.

Following Mahathir's retirement on 31 October 2003 after twenty-two years at the helm, his replacement, Abdullah Ahmad Badawi, sought to capitalise on his initial popularity by recasting UMNO's position on Islamic governance in order to regain support lost to PAS. To that end, the concept of Islam Hadhari (Civilisational, or Progressive, Islam) was introduced as a means of continuing UMNO's Islamisation of government and countering the political challenge posed by PAS. While criticised for its ambiguity and lack of substance, Islam Hadhari nevertheless provided a viable platform from which Abdullah sought to challenge PAS for the Malay-Muslim vote at the 2004 election. Under Abdullah's leadership, UMNO managed to regain the ground lost to PAS in 1999, with the new prime minister providing a much-needed breath of fresh air after twenty-two years of 'Mahathirism'.

PAS faced its 2004 electoral setback in the same way it has historically dealt with defeat: through self-examination and reform. In response to the debacle of 2004, the leadership began to craft a new strategy of moderation. Foremost in this strategy was the introduction of younger, reform-minded leaders into the party's leadership ranks. PAS initiated leadership changes during its 2005 Muktamar (general assembly), when younger, more progressive leaders were voted into key party leadership positions. Along with the changes in leadership, PAS advanced several additional policies to broaden its appeal and counteract the caricatures of the party in state-owned media as a party of religious Taliban-type fundamentalists. These steps included de-emphasising its agenda on an Islamic state, calling for enhanced civil liberties and freedoms of assembly and the press, building better relationships with the Chinese and other non-Muslim communities, and enhancing the role of women in the party. At the ballot box, PAS's shift to a more moderate and inclusivist register, including the creation of a non-Muslim PAS Supporters' Wing, paid dividends at the 2008 elections when the party joined together with opposition partners, the Democratic Action Party (DAP) and the People's Justice Party (PKR), to make significant inroads into the support base of the UMNO-led incumbent coalition. Yet the reality was that PAS's success was attributed to the non-Muslim support the party received at the election, as a consequence of its watering down of its traditional Islamist agenda in order to broaden its appeal. Paradoxically, the success of 2008 also presented the Islamists of PAS with an existential conundrum: whether PAS should remain on its current path and be accused of losing its core focus, or return to its Islamist fundamentals. This dilemma exercised the party for five years, from 2008–13, as it was pulled deeper into the opposition People's Alliance coalition.[9] During this period, small but not inconsequential segments within the party started voicing reservations towards the compromises that the party leadership were making, such as agreeing to support Anwar Ibrahim as the opposition's candidate for prime minister or endorsing the rights of non-Muslims to use the word 'Allah' in reference to their deity, and continuing to downplay what was hitherto the heart of the party's political agenda – the Islamic state.

PAS's conundrums were compounded by UMNO's own Islamisation agenda, which had gathered pace. The point has already been made that UMNO's Islamisation agenda was triggered by the resurgence of Islamic consciousness primarily in the Islamic heartland of the Middle East in the late 1960s, but also affecting Muslim communities from Europe to Asia. In Malaysia, this development took the form of a growing Muslim proselytisation movement, known as *dakwah*, which was driven by social activism of Islamic groups such as ABIM. Specific to the Malaysian context, this resurgence of Islamic identity and piety coincided with a shift in national discourse and policy to the advantage of the Malay-Muslim community when, after the race riots of 13 May 1969, Malaysian society was fundamentally reorganised with the introduction of affirmative action policies that favoured the Malay-Muslim community in the political, economic, and cultural spheres. It was in this climate that UMNO's Islamisation policy first took root in the form of greater emphasis on Islamic education. By the 1980s, the agenda extended beyond the cultural sphere to encompass economics, with the introduction of Islamic banking, the proliferation of Waqf (Islamic foundations), and Mahathir's (and Anwar's) attempt to engineer a Muslim work ethic to drive his industrialisation programme for the country. The agenda stretched to politics, too, particularly foreign policy, as Mahathir sought to position Malaysia as the vocal champion for Muslim causes globally, from Palestine to Bosnia, as well as governance, through an inflated religious bureaucracy.

Importantly, Mahathir's UMNO Islamisation agenda for Malaysia was pursued in tandem with the party's tightening grip on society through the incumbent government's control of various institutions of the state. Through prodigious use of institutions such as the Internal Security Act, created to defend the country against the subversive threat of communism and racial extremists but, under the Mahathir administration, increasingly used to silence political opponents, Mahathir proceeded to eliminate potential challengers and restrict alternatives to UMNO's Islamisation agenda. Concomitantly, fringe religious groups such as the Darul Arqam movement and followers of different Islamic traditions such as the Shi'a were demonised as 'deviants' by state religious authorities. PAS politicians were not spared either, with several purportedly running afoul of the UMNO-aligned state religious authorities and, where necessary, Malaysian government, because of acts interpreted as support for terrorism (see Farish 2003).

Issues

The prominence that Islamism has gained in recent years in Malaysian politics is best demonstrated in a number of controversial, high-profile issues. Two of particular note and interest for this chapter are the controversies over apostasy and perceived proprietary rights to the usage of the term 'Allah' (see also López, this volume, on interfaith issues).

Apostasy

Apostasy, specifically with reference to Malaysian Muslims who desire to leave the faith, is an issue that has reverberated across the Malaysian socio-political terrain at multiple levels, generating tension in Malaysia's multireligious fabric between Muslims and non-Muslims and escalating UMNO–PAS competition over the definition of *aqidah* (principles of the faith). The apostasy issue has also caused friction within UMNO and the government itself between those who favour hard-line fundamentalist positions on the issue and their more accommodating counterparts. UMNO parliamentarians have reproved the government for appearing to be crippled by the PAS charge that 'the UMNO-led Government provided no punishment for those who leave Islam, and yet would fine a citizen RM500 (US$132) just for throwing a cigarette butt on the market floor' (cited in Zainah 2003a).

On the other hand, PAS has been unequivocal in its position on the issue. In his capacity as menteri besar (chief minister) of Terengganu state in 1999, Abdul Hadi introduced a bill in parliament to make apostasy a categorical offence punishable by death. To him, the call for the death penalty was legitimate, for it was based on a *hadith* that called on believers to 'kill whomever changes his religion' (Norani 2003: 129).

Malaysian human rights activist Zainah Anwar makes the case that there are essentially three traditional juristic opinions on the punishment for apostasy. First is the orthodox view of death to all apostates; second is the opinion that prescribes the death penalty only in cases where apostasy is accompanied by rebellion against the community and its legitimate leadership; and third is the view that even though apostasy is a great sin, it is not a capital offence in Islam and hence warrants no punishment (Zainah 2003b). Under conservatives such as Abdul Hadi, PAS appears in this regard to subscribe to the most extreme juristic opinion: death to all who leave Islam.

The controversy over apostasy came to a head with the deceptively straightforward case of Lina Joy, which generated heated national debate. The case revolves around a woman formerly named Azalina Jailani, a convert to Christianity who changed her name to Lina Joy in 1998.

Since then, Joy has been attempting to remove the religious designation of 'Islam' from her personal identity card. Her application was rejected by the National Registration Department on the grounds that she had to furnish certification from the *Shari'a* Court that officially declared her an apostate before such a change could be made. The Federal Territories *Shari'a* Court, which she consulted on the issue, refused her request to leave the religion. Joy's appeal to the lower courts against the decision of the *Shari'a* Court in 2001 was likewise dismissed on grounds that civil courts had no jurisdiction over matters concerning religion. Joy appealed the *Shari'a* Court decision to the Federal Court on constitutional grounds, thereby setting the stage for a watershed decision with grave ramifications.

Predictably, the Lina Joy case elicited sharp responses from key political actors. The religious leadership of PAS maintained categorically that jurisdiction over this case lay squarely with the *Shari'a* Court, and moreover that the court should not grant apostate status, as that would entail the death penalty according to the Qur'an.[10] Privately, however, some *ulama* did say that given her insistence on changing her religion and her conversion to Christianity, Lina Joy's case was a moot point, as she was already 'lost to Islam'. Similarly, while some more orthodox UMNO *ulama* spoke equally stridently of the sanctity of the *Shari'a* Court, others have been more prepared to countenance Joy's act of leaving Islam as one of personal choice, albeit one that should remain in the private realm. They further intimate that apostates should refrain from using their case to challenge the delicate balance between the constitution and the *shari'a*.

On 30 May 2007 the Malaysian Federal Court finally made a much-awaited decision regarding the Lina Joy apostasy case. In a landmark pronouncement that will likely reverberate across the Malaysian socio-political landscape for a long time to come, the Federal Court ruled two to one to dismiss Lina Joy's appeal of the earlier High Court decision. The panel concluded that only an Islamic *shari'a* tribunal could certify her renunciation of Islam and the legitimacy of her conversion. In the eyes of the Malaysian judicial system, Lina Joy remains a Muslim despite her public renunciation of the faith (by virtue of her baptism into the Christian religion) many years ago. In addition, the decision established a legal precedent that apostasy matters lay in the jurisdiction of state *shari'a* courts.

The debate over apostasy lent itself to greater controversy because of the multicultural and multireligious nature of Malaysian society. Political expediency, coupled with a concern for the alleged proliferation of apostasy cases over the past few years, has forced the UMNO-led government's hand and pressured the state into engaging in this difficult debate. The Department of Islamic Development or JAKIM, the federal agency responsible for governing Islamic practice across the country, stood at the forefront of the state's response by suggesting the possibility of a parliamentary bill on apostasy in 1998, the contents of which remain to be fully fleshed out. Then legislation was enacted that levied punishment in the form of a RM5,000 fine or a three-year jail term, or both, for the Islamic offence of *murtad* (Norani 2003: 128). These laws also clarified Article 11(4) of the Federal Constitution, which forbade adherents of other faiths to proselytise to Muslims in Malaysia. In sum, this provision permits states to punish attempts by non-Muslims to proselytise to Muslims by outlawing the propagation of any non-Muslim religious doctrine or belief among persons professing the religion of Islam. In response to concerns raised by non-Muslims who were alarmed at the discriminatory tenor of the clause, the minister in charge of religious affairs, Abdul Hamid, described Article 11(4) as a 'preventive measure' against apostasy, intended less to punish than to rehabilitate. Privately, however, notable Islamic figures who supported apostasy laws have argued that their main purpose was to address the problems particularly surrounding Muslim converts – non-Malay Muslims who for various reasons revert to their previous religion or renounce Islam by way of a statutory declaration.

According to the legislation proposed by UMNO for the 'crime' of apostasy, those convicted would also be forced to undergo compulsory rehabilitation at specially created centres. Recalcitrant detainees at the end of the detention period will be officially declared *murtad* by the *Shari'a* Court and released from the faith. This rehabilitation programme has come under heavy criticism from civil society groups for undermining the constitutionally guaranteed right to freedom of religion. In the UMNO-controlled state of Perlis, matters were taken further when the Perlis state legislature passed the Islamiah Aqidah Protection (State of Perlis) Bill 2000 (alternatively known as the Islamic Faith Bill 2000). According to clause seven of the Bill, evidence of an attempt to change *aqidah* by a Muslim would be met by a summons to appear before the *Shari'a* Court (Norani 2003: 128). The Bill further allows for *shari'a* courts to prosecute deviationist Islamic teachers and detain offenders in *aqidah* rehabilitation centres for up to a year. Predictably, the Perlis bill caused considerable consternation among the Muslim community for how it evidently criminalised the act of religious conversion, and various petitions were submitted to the government-appointed Human Rights Commission as expressions of concern. In response, notwithstanding the fact that it was state law, the federal government announced that the legislation would be considered further before implementation.

The Allah issue

Another issue which has fuelled religious fervour in Malaysia in recent times was the court ruling over the permissibility of non-Muslims' use of the word 'Allah' in their publications. The issue began back in the 1980s when, in Mahathir's Islamisation era, certain words were reserved only for Malay-Muslim usage, such as 'Allah', 'Solat' and 'Rasul', which are the Arabic-based words for God, Prayers and Messenger respectively (Kairos Research Centre 2004: 51–52). However, the Catholic publication *The Herald* was still using the term 'Allah' until the Home Ministry prevented it from doing so in 2007. *The Herald* then opted to resolve the issue through legal channels. When the Malaysian court sided with *The Herald* in allowing 'Allah' to be used by the publication in December 2009, the Home Ministry appealed against the decision. In a ruling in October 2013, upheld by the Federal Court in June 2014, the appellate court overturned the earlier decision and upheld the Home Ministry's ban on *The Herald*'s usage of the word 'Allah' on grounds that non-Muslims' use of the term would create 'confusion' for Muslims.

The government's official position to restrict 'Allah' only for Muslims signalled UMNO's pertinacity and bolstered its position as the party that defends Malay-Muslim interests. This was a further demonstration of how UMNO's policies in recent times have indicated that the party has moved towards the right of the political spectrum, thereby risking the consociational relationship that underpins the governing coalition. Indeed, the consequence of this increasing conservatism within UMNO was evident at both the 2008 and 2013 elections, when non-Muslims abandoned UMNO's coalition partners in droves. Nevertheless, both gerrymandering (an advantage of incumbency) and a first-past-the-post electoral system ensure that UMNO has no incentive to move away from its conservatism. If anything, the opposite is true – UMNO need only appeal to a rural Malay-Muslim base with its mix of conservatism and access to largesse, the latter of which PAS is unable to provide, to cement its political position.

As for the other Malay-Muslim based party, PAS, it initially took a more conciliatory position and officially supported non-Muslims' use of 'Allah'. This 2010 decision came at a time when the Islamist party had been acquiescent on other key issues pertaining to its identity as an Islamist party, such as the goal of an Islamic state, and also on the controversial *hudud* issue. Although PAS's initial view on 'Allah' was based on religious texts, its opinion on the matter displayed the party's readiness to take the less popular decision involving Malay-Muslim issues. Its initial stance in 2010 was well accepted by its secular counterparts in the People's Alliance coalition. However, it resulted in PAS's being criticised in several religious circles as being too compliant with secular parties. In 2013, a few months before the general election, PAS rescinded its earlier position on the issue. The PAS *Shura* (Consultation) Council issued a statement clarifying that 'Allah' should not be used by non-Muslims except verbally. In changing its position, the party was clearly attempting to appease both the Malay-Muslim conservative bloc and Christians. Even so, this was a marked change from its original position in support of the right of non-Muslims to use the term 'Allah'.

Conclusion

This brief chapter has attempted to outline the contours of Islamist trends in Malaysia and to discuss how and why these contours have not only sharpened over the years, but have in fact expanded as well. In October 2013, during a visit to Malaysia, US Secretary of State John Kerry complimented Malaysia for being a model moderate Muslim-majority country. Several days later, the Malaysian courts declared that non-Muslims had no right to use the word 'Allah'. This dichotomy speaks to the contradictions inherent within Muslim society in Malaysia.

Religious issues in recent years have polarised political parties as well as voters. While it might prove detrimental to racial and religious relations in the country, the outcome has thus far galvanised Malay-Muslim support for UMNO, as it adopted and defended positions parallel to conservative public sentiment. These divisive religious overtones perpetuate a cycle of seeking political legitimacy through the brandishing of religious credentials. Yet in Malaysia, religious credentials are not confined to the endorsement of Islamic scholars. More than that, they are best secured through strident defence of the Islamic faith against any perceived attack, whether on Islam or Malay identity.

Notes

1 See Article 160 of the Malaysian Constitution. The full text of the Constitution is available at http://confinder.richmond.edu/admin/docs/malaysia.pdf (accessed 7 May 2014).
2 For a history of PAS, see Shafie 1981; Alias 1991, 1994; Farish 2004.
3 It is important to note that while PAS leaders today would make reference to the Islamic state, the formation of such a political entity was not an official objective of the party as reflected in its constitution (interview with Mustafa Ali, Kuala Lumpur, 2 March 2010).
4 Significantly, today, PAS cannot claim to be the 'only' proponent of the Islamic state as many within UMNO also share that view. In fact, two UMNO presidents, who were (and are) also prime ministers, Mahathir Mohamad and Najib Tun Razak, have openly declared that Malaysia is already an Islamic state.
5 For an analysis of Burhanuddin's political thought, see Ramlah 1996.
6 The political currents that influenced PAS's electoral fortunes are studied at length in Liow 2004.
7 For a detailed discussion of internal party debates surrounding the Islamic State document, see Liow 2009: 81–91.
8 This fact was revealed to the first author on condition of anonymity by a Central Working Committee member during an interview in Taman Melewar, Kuala Lumpur, 7 February 2004.
9 These internal party issues are discussed at length in Liow 2011a and 2011b.
10 Interview with PAS *ulama* and officials, Petaling Jaya, Malaysia, 15 August 2006.

Bibliography

Alias Mohamed (1991) *Malaysia's Islamic Opposition: Past, Present, and Future*, Kuala Lumpur: Gateway Publishing House.

Alias Mohamed (1994) *PAS' Platform: Development and Change 1951–1986*, Petaling Jaya: Gateway Publishing House.

Farish Ahmad Noor (2003) 'Blood, sweat, and Jihad: the radicalisation of the discourse of the Pan-Malaysian Islamic Party (PAS) from the 1980s to the present', *Contemporary Southeast Asia*, 25(2): 200–32.

Farish Ahmad Noor (2004) *Islam Embedded: The Historical Development of the Pan-Malaysian Islamic Party PAS, 1951–2003*, Kuala Lumpur: Malaysian Sociological Research Institute.

Funston, John N. (1976) 'The origins of Parti Islam Se Malaysia', *Journal of Southeast Asian Studies*, 7(1): 58–71.

Kairos Research Centre (2004) *Doing the Right Thing: A Practical Guide on Legal Matters for Churches in Malaysia*, Petaling Jaya: Kairos Research Centre.

Liow, Joseph Chinyong (2004) 'Exigency or expediency? Contextualising political Islam and the PAS challenge in Malaysian politics', *Third World Quarterly*, 25(2): 359–72.

Liow, Joseph Chinyong (2009) *Piety and Politics: Islamism in Contemporary Malaysia*, New York: Oxford University Press.

Liow, Joseph Chinyong (2011a) 'Creating cadres: mobilisation, activism, and the youth wing of the Pan-Malaysian Islamic Party, PAS', *Pacific Affairs*, 84(4): 665–86.

Liow, Joseph Chinyong (2011b) 'Islamist ambitions, political change, and the price of power: recent successes and challenges for the Pan-Malaysian Islamic Party, PAS', *Journal of Islamic Studies*, 22(3): 374–403.

Norani Othman (2003) 'Islamisation and democratisation in Malaysia in regional and global contexts', in Ariel Heryanto and Sumit K. Mandal (eds), *Challenging Authoritarianism in Southeast Asia: Comparing Indonesia and Malaysia*, London: RoutledgeCurzon.

Ramlah Adam (1996) *Burhanuddin al-Helmy: Suatu Kemelut Politik* [*Burhanuddin al-Helmy: A Political Crisis*], Petaling Jaya: Dewan Bahasa dan Pustaka.

Shafie Ibrahim (1981) *The Islamic Party of Malaysia: Its Formative Stages and Ideology*, Kota Bahru: Nuawi bin Ismail.

Syed Ahmad Hussein (2002) 'Muslim politics and the discourse on democracy', in Francis Loh Kok Wah and Khoo Boo Teik (eds), *Democracy in Malaysia: Discourses and Practices*, Richmond: Curzon Press, pp. 74–107.

Zainah Anwar (2003a) 'Islamisation and its impact on laws and the law making process in Malaysia', available at http://wrrc.wluml.org/sites/wluml.org/files/import/english/pubs/pdf/wsf/08.pdf (accessed 19 May 2014).

Zainah Anwar (2003b) 'Beyond the veil: rethinking gender, modernity and Islam', available at http://asialink.unimelb.edu.au/cpp/pdf/0912FinalAnwarTranscript.pdf (accessed 21 June 2007).

5

Rise of Christian political consciousness and mobilisation

Arnold Puyok

Malaysia is a multiracial and multireligious country of twenty-nine million people. In terms of racial background, Malays and other *bumiputera* (literally, sons of the soil)[1] make up the majority at 62 percent, followed by Chinese (22 percent) and Indians (7 percent). But this multiracial composition only tells a little about Malaysia's ethnic diversity. In East Malaysia – Sabah and Sarawak[2] – the racial composition is more complex. The Kadazandusun[3] and other indigenous people account for 37 percent of Sabah's 3.2 million population, followed by the Bajau, at 14 percent. In Sarawak, Iban comprise 29 percent of the population, followed by the Chinese and Malays (around 23 percent each), and the Bidayuh (14 percent).

Malaysia's multifaith society is also distinctive. Sixty-one percent of Malaysia's total population profess Islam, followed by Buddhism (20 percent), Christianity (9 percent), Hinduism (6 percent), and adherents to other religious beliefs (3 percent). Despite Islam's predominance in Peninsular Malaysia, Christianity is the largest religion in Sarawak and the second largest in Sabah. Of Sarawak's 2.4 million population, 43 percent are Christians, compared with 32 percent Muslims and 14 percent Buddhists. In Sabah, *bumiputera* Muslims account for 65 percent of the total population,[4] followed by Christians (27 percent) and Buddhists (6 percent).

Due to Malaysia's unique character, issues of race and religion have always been a focal point of debate. An ongoing dispute over who may use the term 'Allah', for instance, discussed below, has tested Malaysia's race relations, recalling the dark episode of 13 May 1969, of ethnic riots primarily between the politically dominant Malays and the economically dominant Chinese. The political conflict between the Alliance Party and the opposition then quickly turned into a serious ethno-religious issue, raising concerns about the prospects for race relations in Malaysia. Decades on, ethnic-religious conflict once again threatens peace and harmony in the country. Even though the Allah issue has been described by many people as a contest for power between UMNO (United Malays National Organisation) and PAS (Pan-Malaysian Islamic Party), the manner in which the issue has been debated has caused animosity between Muslims and non-Muslims.

The role of religion in politics is also often complicated by the ethnic factor. Political parties in Malaysia have typically formed along racial lines, to represent the interests of their respective ethnic communities. UMNO, for instance, was formed to protect the interests of the majority Malays, while the MCA (Malaysian Chinese Association) and the MIC (Malaysian Indian Congress) were established to fight for the rights of the Chinese and Indians, respectively. In Sabah and Sarawak, most political parties are also communal. However, compared with Peninsular Malaysia, the contest for political power in Sabah and Sarawak sometimes happens not at the inter-ethnic, but the intra-ethnic level. Furthermore, race and religious issues do not feature prominently in Sabah and Sarawak's electoral politics. The electorate in East Malaysia is more interested in raising regional issues such as state rights and autonomy (Chin and Puyok 2011: 219–35). Politics in East Malaysia is also dominated by the contest for power among different elite groups, who are driven by the desire more to control state resources than to pursue ethno-religious issues.

After the 2008 general election, racial and religious issues polarised Malaysian society. In 2008, the ruling BN (Barisan Nasional or National Front) failed to retain its customary two-thirds majority in parliament. It also lost a substantial share of votes from the Malays and Chinese. In the 2013 general election, a similar trend emerged: BN once again failed to win with a two-thirds majority and substantially lost Chinese electoral support. Regardless, BN, through UMNO, continued to assert its dominance in Malay-Muslim majority rural areas. Due to increasing Malay support for UMNO, the party maintained its hard-line stance at the expense of Prime Minister Najib Razak's '1Malaysia' policy and his calls for moderation. The issues raised in the subsequent UMNO General Assembly indicated that UMNO would continue with its conservative outlook, regardless of the reaction of non-Muslims.

The intensification of race and religious debates is further precipitated by the role of NGOs (non-governmental associations) such as Perkasa (Pertubuhan Pribumi Perkasa Malaysia or Malaysian Indigenous Empowerment Organisation) and ISMA (Ikatan Muslimin Malaysia, Malaysian Muslim Solidarity) – accused by many of helping UMNO to roil Malay sentiment. UMNO's growing dominance and the raising of ethno-religious issues by various Islamic NGOs met with strong opposition from non-Muslims. After the 2008 and 2013 elections, non-Muslims have become more critical in expressing their views. The Allah issue, UMNO dominance and the institutionalisation of the Islamic faith have all contributed to the rise of Christian political consciousness in Malaysia.

Politics and religion

The role of religion in politics is significant because it 'serves to create group solidarity, strengthening the ties between individuals and their society' (Driskell *et al.* 2008: 295). The Church, for instance, plays a role of 'instigator' 'for both political and social movements such as the civil rights movement' (Beyerlein and Hipp 2006, cited in Driskell *et al.* 2008: 296). Moreover, church leaders can send messages politically to influence their followers' electoral decisions (Guth *et al.* 2003, cited in Driskell *et al.* 2008: 296). In sum, 'religion provides ideological and organisational instruments by which affected communities can express their class interests' (Hamayotsu 2008: 181). For instance, the Republican Party in the US has long relied on evangelical movements for its successive electoral victories. The Catholic Church in the Philippines is so influential that former president Gloria Macapagal Arroyo had to abandon the government's family planning programmes due to lack of support from the church leaders. In Peru, the role of Protestant Christians was crucial in elevating Alberto Fujimori to the presidency in 1992. In Brazil, the Catholic Church has played an important role in the country's transition to democracy since the 1970s (Hamayotsu 2008). Religion 'without doubt continues to make its presence felt in the realm of politics across the globe' (Gill 2001: 118) and the role of religion in politics will remain an important subject of inquiry in the social sciences.

In the context of Malaysia, religion and politics are intertwined. As the largest ethnic group in Malaysia, the Malays identify themselves closely with Islam – the official religion of the federation. Article 160 of the Federal Constitution defines a Malay as 'a Muslim who habitually speaks Malay and follows Malay customs' (Syed Husin 2008: 2). So a Muslim Chinese, Muslim Indian or Muslim Kadazandusun is technically recognised as Malay even though many Muslim indigenous people in East Malaysia prefer to retain their unique cultural identities. Given the close connection of the Malay identity with Islam, UMNO, the largest component party in BN, regards it as its duty to protect the rights of the Malays and sanctity of Islam. Some UMNO leaders even suggest that non-Muslims should recognise the dominance of the Malays and the supremacy of Islam. In the 1970s in Sabah, Mustapha Harun of the Malay-Muslim dominated United Sabah National Organization (USNO) snubbed Sabah's multiracial and multifaith make-up by allowing Islamisation to take place through the works of USIA (United Sabah Islamic Association) and MUIS (Majlis Ugama Islam Sabah or Sabah Islamic Council). With support of the federal government, Mustapha launched his massive Islamisation programme throughout Sabah (Luping 1994). Mustapha believed that Sabah could be developed only under one culture (Malay), one language (Malay) and one religion (Islam) (Luping 1994).

However, the flagrant manipulation of religion in politics does not sit well with religious minorities, who claim that UMNO is misusing government machinery to promote Islam in order to strengthen its position among Malays. A case in point is enactments barring Christians from using 'Allah' and other Arabic words deemed exclusive to Muslims. Even though the government has argued that legislation pertaining to Islam will not affect Christians' religious freedom, the banning of words which can also be found in Christian scriptures has raised concerns about Islam's overriding influence over non-Muslims' religious practices.

In Malaysia, numerous studies have been conducted into the role of religion in politics. However, most focus on the role of Islam in the country's political development (for instance, Kessler 1978, or Liow and Afif, this volume). Few studies have examined the role other religious institutions, such as the Christian Church, have played in Malaysian politics. Examining the role of the Church and Christians' participation in the political process is crucial as Christianity accounts for 9 percent of Malaysia's total population and is the most populous religion in East Malaysia. Such a study is also critical as since 2008, Christians as a whole have been very vocal in airing their views publicly. The decision of church leaders to bring the Allah issue to court is an example of Christianity's growing influence in Malaysia's political landscape. Despite the ban on the word 'Allah' and Islamic religious groups' warning to Christians to stop raising the issue, Christian leaders continue to press the government to allow Christians to practise their religious beliefs freely. Church leaders are not the only 'instigators' responsible for raising sentiment against Islam's growing influence; Christian leaders from both sides of the political divide are equally responsible for encouraging Christians to engage proactively with the state. But within Malaysian churches, clergy, pastors, elders and lay leaders teach their followers to exercise their democratic rights dutifully and to speak against misuse of power. 'New religious ideas and interpretations of religious texts and doctrines' (Hamayotsu 2008: 194) have changed the way most Christians think about politics and their role as citizens in a democratic country. But before one can have a deeper understanding of the impact of Christianity in Malaysia's political development, it is necessary to briefly examine the factors contributing to the rise of Christian political consciousness.

Rise of political Islam

Political Islam is loosely referred to as the promotion of Islam and Islamic symbolism by political leaders and the institutionalisation of Islamic religious beliefs to justify the right of the Malay-Muslim population to power and dominance. Islam's influence in Malaysia can be traced to the twelfth century, when Muslim traders made their first contact with local inhabitants. At Malaya's independence in 1957, Islam was made the official religion of the federation. The decision was part of the concession given to UMNO by its partners in the Alliance coalition – MCA and MIC – as a symbolic recognition of the status of the majority Malays. However, it was not the intention of the Alliance leaders to turn Malaysia into an Islamic state and to deny the religious rights of non-Muslims. Rather, citing former Lord President Mohamed Suffian Hashim, Fernando (2006: 250) postulates that making Islam the official religion was 'primarily for ceremonial purposes, to enable prayers to be offered in the Islamic way on official public occasions, such as the installation or birthday of the Yang di-Pertuan Agong (King of Malaysia), independence day and similar occasions'. Other prominent legal figures argued that 'the term Islam in Article 3(1) [in the Federal Constitution] meant only such acts as relate to rituals and ceremonies' (cited in Fernando 2006: 250).

Despite the assurance Malaysia's founding fathers gave that Islam's official status would have no 'practical effect' on non-Muslims due to the secular nature of the Federal Constitution, political leaders from UMNO and PAS were quick to capitalise on the elevation of Islam to state religion for their own gains (Kessler 1978). When Malaysia's fourth prime minister, Mahathir Mohamad, assumed power, Islam was further embedded in the political system. Facing stiff competition from PAS, which accused UMNO of lacking the religious zeal to protect the interest of Muslims, Mahathir worked to strengthen the role of Islamic religious institutions such as the Federal Religious Council, the Office of Islamic Affairs and the Islamic Missionary Foundation. These institutions were used to accelerate a 'dakwah movement to harness the legitimising power of Islamic symbolism and discourse' (Moustafa 2013a: 10).

As part of Mahathir's attempt to deepen the role of Islam in the national political scene and arguably to increase his popularity among the Malays, the government ordered the banning of the Indonesian-language Alkitab (Bible) in 1981. Wielding the Internal Security Act (ISA), the government argued that the open sale and distribution of the Bible could lead to public disorder. In 1982, the ban was lifted after the intervention of the Christian Federation of Malaysia (CFM). In 1987, Operasi Lalang was launched to detain people deemed a threat to national security, including those who proselytised to Muslims. Among those arrested was Jamaluddin Othman, a Christian convert accused of propagating Christianity to Muslims. His right to convert was upheld on 6 October 1988 by the High Court, which ruled 'that Jamaluddin was free to follow his conscience and practice his newfound religion' (Walters 2007: 76).

The institutionalisation of Islamic religious beliefs intensified with the amendment of the Federal Constitution. The amendment involved the insertion of Clause (1A) into Article 121, which says that 'the High Courts of the Federation shall have no jurisdiction in any respect of any matter within the jurisdiction of the Syariah Courts' (Moustafa 2013b: 778). With the amendment, 'all matters pertaining to Islam should be handled by the Shariah Court' (Walters 2007: 77). Mahathir argued that the amendment was necessary 'to protect the jurisdiction of the Shariah courts vis-à-vis the federal civil courts' (Moustafa 2013b: 778). The amendment would later create far-reaching legal complications and dilemmas. For instance, Muslims who want to convert to other religions must first seek approval from the Syariah Court. A case in point is Lina Joy, who wanted to change her religious status from Islam to Christianity on her identity card. The National Registration Department (NRD) refused to grant her request, stating that changing religion is not the jurisdiction of the NRD, but of Islamic religious authorities. When Lina Joy brought her case to the court, the court concurred with the NRD, claiming that as a Muslim, she must first seek redress in the Syariah Court (Walters 2007).

In 1991, the government reiterated its stance on banning the word 'Allah' and other Arabic words deemed exclusive to Muslims. This decision caused discontentment among, and a huge setback for, Bahasa Malaysia-speaking Christians, especially in Sabah and Sarawak, who translate the English word 'God' to 'Allah'. Christians' fear of Islam's growing dominance was further compounded when Mahathir announced Malaysia as an Islamic state on 29 September 2001. The state interpreted Mahathir's support for an Islamic state as an endorsement of the use of the state apparatus to promote Islamic influence throughout the country. This included the inculcation of Islamic religious values and education in schools and higher learning institutions (Moustafa 2013a). Compounding restrictions in Christians' religious practices were allegations that Christians were being discriminated against in securing permits for places of worship and distribution of land for religious purposes (Walters 2007).

When Abdullah assumed power in 2002, he promised to reform the country through various reform initiatives, including promoting the concept of 'Islam Hadhari'. This concept represented Abdullah's attempt to promote a brand of Islam that 'is peaceful, moderate and just, and embraces all races and creeds' (cited in Walters 2007: 73), in contrast with Mahathir's 'inimical' form of Islam. Abdullah's Islam Hadhari also aimed at gaining back non-Muslims' support for the BN. The strategy worked. Abdullah won the 2004 general election with a resounding victory, sealing his popularity as a reform-minded leader, well liked by Malaysians of all races and religions.

Despite Abdullah's promising leadership, the country continued to be marred by ethnic-religious fissures. The trouble started when the Home Ministry banned the distribution of the Iban-language Bible, containing the words 'Allah Taala' – translated as 'God Almighty'. The Home Ministry argued that the word 'Allah' is exclusive to Muslims and its usage among non-Muslims could lead to confusion among Muslims. The Abdullah administration was also criticised for failing to act decisively in the demolition of churches by local authorities in the state of Johor. In this case, Orang Asli (indigenous people) clashed with local authorities over a piece of land on which the Orang Asli had built a church. The authorities charged that the church was illegally built on state land. Various Christian organisations voiced their disappointment with the manner in which the issue was handled. The Malaysian Consultative Council of Buddhism, Christianity, Hinduism and Sikhism (MCCBCHS) said the issue could have been solved amicably, had the authorities initiated dialogue and consultation with the Orang Asli community.

The change in leadership in 2008 provided little hope that Christians would be able to practise their religious rights freely. Like Abdullah's, Najib Razak's moderate approach was not wholly supported even by most UMNO members. The Allah issue once again came into the picture. This time, the government refused to allow the *Herald* bulletin to use the word 'Allah', on grounds of public order and national security, suggesting that Christians who have a different theological interpretation of Allah could mislead Muslims. The government reiterated its stance that the Arabic term 'Allah' is sacred to Islam and, in particular, to the Malays in Malaysia (Keyes 1996). The Catholic Church that published the bulletin defended the use of the word 'Allah', as the bulletin was only meant for its Bahasa Malaysia-speaking congregation.

The Catholic Church filed suit against the government and won in the High Court. The presiding judge, Lau Bee Lan, argued that the Home Ministry's ban was 'illegal, null and void . . . adding that all Malaysians had the right to use the word under the constitution which guarantees freedom of expression and religion' (*Al Jazeera* 2010). While waiting for the government to appeal the court's decision, Najib introduced a ten-point solution to address the confiscation and distribution of the aforementioned Bibles, as well as usage of the word 'Allah' by non-Muslims. The ten-point solution was introduced just before the 2011 Sarawak state election. One of its main tenets was that Christians are permitted 'to print and/or import the Alkitab (Bible) freely without any restriction or conditions' (NECF 2011).

In the meantime, the Home Ministry appealed to strike out the High Court's decision to allow the Catholic Church to use the word 'Allah' in its bulletin. As expected, the government won the appeal, on the grounds that 'Allah was not integral to the Christian faith' (*Malaysian Insider* 2014b). At the time of writing, the Catholic Church and the Home Ministry await the final decision of the Court of Appeal. Not long after the court's decision, the Jabatan Agama Islam Selangor (Selangor Islamic Religious Department, JAIS) raided the Bible Society of Malaysia and confiscated more than 300 Bibles, causing further unhappiness among Christians, who accused the government of reneging on its promise to uphold the ten-point solution. The raid was conducted after JAIS received a complaint that the Bibles contained the word 'Allah' and other prohibited Arabic words. In justifying its action, JAIS said that it was merely carrying out its duty in accordance with a state enactment preventing the propagation of Christianity to Muslims(*Star* 2014).[5]

As ethno-religious tension threatened to destabilise inter-ethnic harmony, a Christian family in Pitas – a remote area in the district of Kudat, Sabah – claimed they had been duped into converting to Islam by a Muslim group from Kuala Lumpur (*Daily Express* 2014). The alleged conversion of the indigenous people of Sabah to Islam is symptomatic of a bigger problem among Sabahans with Malay names. Many Sabahans complain that instead of seeking clarification, the NRD arbitrarily classifies Sabahans with Muslim names or those carrying 'bin' (son of) or 'binti' (daughter of) as Malay *bumiputera* Muslims. When they want to change the religious identity on their identification card, they have to go through numerous bureaucratic hurdles (*Malaysian Insider* 2012).

Christian response

Christians in Malaysia are generally politically apathetic. Church leaders are mostly conservative in their views of Christians' participation in politics. Most church leaders teach their followers to respect the rule of law and authority, based on their reading of Romans 13:1–2:

> everyone must submit himself to the governing authorities, for there is no authority except that which God has established. The authorities that exist have been established by God. Consequently, he who rebels against the authority is rebelling against what God has instituted, and those who do so will bring judgment on themselves.

But younger and progressive Christian leaders interpret Romans 13:1–2 differently, stating that the verses should be read together with complementary verses that talk about Christians' duty to initiate godly change.

A well-known Christian leader who was a former church elder and now serves as Sarawak Parti Keadilan Rakyat chief, Baru Bian, for instance, evoked the popular verses of 2 Timothy 1:7–8 which states that:

> for God did not give us the spirit of timidity but a spirit of power, of love and of self-discipline. So do not be ashamed to testify about our Lord or ashamed of me his prisoner. But join with me in suffering for the Gospel, by the power of God.

Christians are also encouraged 'to challenge the abuse of power and seek a level playing field in terms of power relations for the good of all' (Yapp 2011), and to be proactive in defending their religious rights. The president of the largest indigenous church in East Malaysia, the SIB (Sidang Injil Borneo or Borneo Evangelical Mission), Jerry Dusing, was quoted as saying that Christians are 'compelled to speak against . . . attempt[s] to undermine their religious freedom' (*Free Malaysia Today* 2013).

Apart from the role of church and Christian leaders, Christian political consciousness also rose rapidly after the 2008 election. The rise of participatory democracy and new media, coupled with rising educational attainment, contributed to Christians' increasing level of political awareness. Even though most church leaders did not declare their political affiliation publicly, they often talked about democracy, transparency and reforms in governance. They also encouraged their followers to support political leaders and parties sincerely committed to transforming the country and to ensuring that Malaysians are treated not according to their race or religion, but their constitutional rights. Coincidently, the message of change promoted by church leaders was identical to the one contained in the opposition parties' election manifesto. This reinforced the allegation that some church leaders were supporting the opposition covertly, with the aim of toppling the ruling party.

Another factor contributing to Christians' increasing participation in the political process is changes in the country's political climate since 2003, particularly after the end of the Mahathir era. Under the Mahathir regime, 'sensitive' issues of race and religion could not be discussed, let alone debated publicly. Those who disregarded this order were detained under the ISA. While rule of law was a hallmark of the Mahathir administration, the rights of communities on the periphery were often ignored. The lack of open and constructive dialogue during Mahathir's twenty-two years in power partly contributed to deepening mistrust among the different races in Malaysia.

Abdullah came to power with the promise of institutional reform and of greater freedom. His tolerant attitude towards open dialogue and direct criticism provided an opportunity for Christians to speak up and to demand greater religious freedom. However, Abdullah's policy of openness backfired due to his inability to accommodate the conflicting demands of Islamic religious groups and proponents for non-Muslims' religious rights. Christians' critical voices continued to fluster the Najib administration, which promised to transform Malaysia into a progressive nation through the implementation of the Government Transformation Plan (GTP) and the Economic Transformation Plan (ETP). Najib's decision to abolish the ISA and other repressive laws encouraged more Christians to take part in political activism without fear of retribution.

Of all the factors above, however, the single most important issue which motivated Christians to participate actively in the political process is the rise of political Islam. The institutionalisation of Islam which started during the Mahathir era and the spreading of Islamic religious values through various government apparatuses 'had [encouraged] Christians to [activate] their own organisations, mobilising their members, or forming their own societies in order to champion the cause of their co-religionists in the face of the Islamists' challenge'; (Abu Bakar 2001: 69–70, cited in Walters 2007: 71). Islam's overriding influence, as indicated in the Allah episode, disturbed and angered Christians in Malaysia (*Malaysian Insider* 2014a).

This Christian response to the rise of political Islam is noticeable in electoral politics. In the 2011 Sibu by-election,[6] the banning of the word 'Allah' in spite of Najib's '1Malaysia' assurance of tolerance proved decisive in causing BN component Sarawak United Peoples' Party (SUPP) to lose to the opposition Democratic Action Party (DAP) by 398 votes (Wong 2012: 142–43). Despite attempts by Sarawak BN to convince Christians in Sibu that religious freedom would be upheld, voters were given the impression that BN, and in particular UMNO, would continue to protect the interests of Malays and Islam at the expense of the rights of minorities in Sabah and Sarawak. As noted above, religious issues do not usually feature prominently in East Malaysia, but in the Sibu by-election, opposition leaders managed to play out the issue of religious freedom, to their advantage.

Another glaring example of religion's role in electoral politics is evident in the remote area of Ba' Kelalan constituency, where 90 percent of the electorate are staunch Christians. Ba' Kelalan was a 'hot seat' in the 2006 and 2011 state elections. Religion, along with land and development issues, had been key in shaping voting patterns there. In the 2006 by-election, BN promoted the issue of development, while the opposition promoted social justice and religious faith. BN's main challenger, Baru Bian, publicly proclaimed: 'our faith and principles must influence our politics and not politics influencing our faith and principles' (Puyok 2006: 212–28). Baru's religious credentials and close association with the SIB church earned him the respect and admiration of the Lun Bawang – the majority group in Ba' Kelalan. Despite losing in the Ba' Kelalan constituency, Baru managed to obtain a substantial number of votes, indicating his popularity among the Lun Bawang community.

Using the same strategy of raising religious sentiments, coupled with a marked improvement in his election strategies, Baru finally managed to defeat BN in the 2011 Sarawak state election, by 428 votes. Once again, religion played a central role. Baru knew how to mobilise SIB's vast rural networks to spread his campaign messages. Among his main campaign points was not accepting the government's ten-point solution, deeming it a political gimmick to pacify the Christian community. Even though Baru was not directly involved in the dissemination of text messages throughout the campaigning period, the short messages had a profound impact on the attitude of Ba' Kelalan voters towards the ruling party. One of the messages read:

> today the Council of Churches Malaysia has rejected the government's 10-point solution on the Alkitab. Vote against BN is a vote for Jesus. BN is an anti-christ agent. Christians are being discriminated and rights in constitution denied. Don't vote for BN. If you are a true Christian, send this message to all other Christians.

Opposition leaders also used the Allah issue in Kadazandusun-majority areas during the 2013 Sabah general election. For instance, in the remote area of Kota Marudu, opposition campaigners reminded voters that there would be no religious freedom in Malaysia if BN retained power, citing the banning of the word 'Allah' and confiscation of Christian publications as examples of restrictions in Christians' religious practices (Puyok 2014). In the also remote area of Keningau, supporters of the highly popular Kadazandusun and Christian leader, Jeffrey Kitingan, blamed BN and UMNO for the erosion of Kadazandusun and Christians' constitutional rights (Puyok 2014). The consequences of the Allah issue and restrictions on Christians' religious freedom were significant: of seventeen Kadazandusun-majority constituencies, five went to the opposition – which was significant, given the opposition's lack of resources and BN's well-oiled campaign machinery (Puyok 2014). There was also a marked decline in the popular votes obtained by BN Kadazandusun leaders.

Mobilisation of Christian political consciousness

There are four main agents responsible for mobilising Christian political consciousness: Christian umbrella associations, individual Christian churches, Christian religious leaders and Christian political leaders. Each of these agents works independently but with the same message of protecting the religious rights of Christians in accordance with the Federal Constitution. The CFM formed in 1985 in reaction to the state's rapid Islamisation. It represents 5,000 member churches, from most of the different Christian denominations in Malaysia (Walters 2007). The three main Christian groupings in CFM are Council of Churches of Malaysia (comprising mainly Protestant churches), National Evangelical Christian Fellowship (evangelicals) and Catholic Bishops' Conference of Malaysia (Roman Catholic). The CFM came under the spotlight for supporting the editor of the *Herald* bulletin, Father Andrew, who defended the use of the word 'Allah' by Christians despite the government's ban. As the CFM represents more than 90 percent of Christians in Malaysia, it represents a prominent voice for Christians to air their views on religious freedom.

The National Evangelical Christian Fellowship (NECF) was formed in 1983 amid the difficulties faced by Christians in exercising their religious freedom given laws limiting the distribution of Christian publications. Unlike the CFM, the NECF is more explicit in its desire to contribute to nation-building by urging its members to become 'agents of transformation in the various places and sphere of influence that God has placed and called each one to be in'.[7] The NECF also urges Christians to 'engage in intentional mission for the purpose of transforming society and the nation'. One of the NECF's strategies to engage with the state is through its 'transforming the nation programmes'. The NECF also formed a nation-building committee to address current issues affecting Christians. Due to Sabah's growing role in national politics, the NECF established the COSA (Commission of Sabah Affairs) on 2 April 2012. The COSA's formation was significant given the large number of SIB followers from Sabah.

Like the CFM, the NECF is also critical of growing Islamisation in Malaysia. In responding to the raid on the Bible Society of Malaysia, the NECF said Islamic religious authorities have no jurisdiction over non-Muslims and therefore Christians can deny religious officials entry into the premises they use for worship and activities (NECF 2014). In the run-up to the 2013 election, the NECF organised prayer rallies throughout the country and published numerous publications urging Christians to participate actively in the country's political process. For instance, one of NECF's well-read booklets, *Christians and the Ballot Box*, stated:

> the church today does not need to start from scratch. What needs to be done is to ensure that the governments correctly interpret and implement their constitutions . . . the least a Christian can do is to inform him or herself about the truth concerning his nation and his government and then vote with conscience.
>
> *(NECF 2012)*

The research arm of the Council of Churches, Catholic Research Centre, even produced a YouTube video, titled 'Responsible Stewardship and General Elections', aimed at educating Christians about their rights to vote and to vote contentiously in the 2013 election.

Individual churches from various denominations also play a crucial role in raising Christians' political awareness. One of the fastest-growing and most influential churches is the SIB, which has more than 500,000 members in East Malaysia, 'making it the largest Christian denomination in Malaysia next to the Roman Catholic Church'.[8] The SIB has also set up numerous branches throughout Peninsular Malaysia to cater for the spiritual needs of a growing Christian population there. The SIB's growing membership is due to its contemporary outlook and strategic missionary activities. It is one of the main litigants in the suit against the government over the Allah issue.

In rural East Malaysia, the SIB is part and parcel of the people's social life. The pastor is a respected figure in the SIB church. He or she is normally ordained and trained in theology before he or she can be officially accepted to lead a church. The pastor is assisted by a church council (or Majlis Sidang) whose members comprise people with influence and good moral standing. During the formative years of the SIB, the pastor and members of the church were required to have some basic theological training, and focused their duties on helping with the spiritual growth of church members. But now, there are a growing number of SIB pastors who are not trained theologically prior to being ordained. Most church council members come from various professional backgrounds – accountants, medical doctors, lawyers, professors and so on. Apart from being influential figures within their church, the pastor and members of the church council are also respected outside of the church. The growing interest of professional people in the SIB's vision and mission has gradually transformed the SIB from a conservative church, initially focused only on the spiritual aspect of its members, into a progressive church with influence in the political, economic and social spheres.

There are eight Christian government ministers in Najib's present cabinet. Notable among them is Idris Jala – the architect of the ten-point agreement on the word 'Allah' and distribution of Christian Bibles. Even though the decision was criticised due to its lack of legal clout, it helped pacify Christian discontent in the wake of the 2011 Sarawak state election. Other vocal pro-government Christian leaders who defended the use of the word 'Allah' by Christians are Bernard Dompok, a former federal cabinet minister and UPKO (United Pasok Momogun Kadazandusun Organisation) president, and Sarawak's minister of land development, PRS (Parti Rakyat Sarawak or Sarawak People's Party) president, James Masing. Masing even went to the extent of reminding the federal government to honour the Malaysia Agreement of 1963, which promised to protect the religious rights of Christians in East Malaysia. On the other side of the political divide, leaders such as Teresa Kok, Ong Kian Ming and Baru Bian have consistently called for the government to respect the religious rights of Christians.

Conclusion

Religion and politics in Malaysia are closely intertwined. Political leaders use religion not only to win support but also to maintain their power. Religion's role in Malaysian politics can be seen in the context of the rise of political Islam and the response of religious minority groups. The role of Islam in politics deepened during the reign of Mahathir, through the promotion of Islamic religious values and institutionalisation of Islam. Even after the end of the Mahathir era, Islam's dominance in the country remained intact. Abdullah and Najib tried to promote an all-encompassing and all-embracing Islam to win the support of moderate Malays and non-Muslims, but without much success, due to strong opposition from conservative Islamic religious groups. While the rise of political Islam is not the only factor contributing to the rise of Christian political consciousness, it has motivated Christians from various denominational backgrounds to assert their religious rights. Apart from a reaction to Islam's dominance, Christians' growing participation in the political process is also attributed to changes in the country's political climate, particularly after the end of the Mahathir era. Abdullah and Najib led a more open government, which tolerated criticisms and allowed the exchange of views on sensitive matters. This approach provided the opportunity for Christians to voice their grievances without the fear experienced by Christians during the Mahathir era. The progressive interpretation of religious texts and doctrines has also played a role in the rise of Christian political consciousness. Conservative church leaders teach their followers to respect the rule of law and authority. But a new generation of church leaders has broken with tradition, urging church followers to become agents of transformation not only in the spiritual, but also in the political, economic and social realms. Umbrella Christian organisations, and Christian leaders from various denominations, have worked independently to affirm Christians' rights to religious freedom. Their message to Christians is clear: it is high time for Christians to rise up and to protect their rights to freedom, as enshrined in the Federal Constitution of Malaysia.

Notes

1 The Sanskrit term *bumiputera* is generally used to refer to the original inhabitants of Malaysia. In Peninsular Malaysia, the two main *bumiputera* groups are the Malays and the Orang Asli (indigenous people). In Sabah and Sarawak, *bumiputera* peoples are numerous. They include the majority Kadazandusun in Sabah and the Iban in Sarawak, as well as other sub-ethnic groups.
2 Sabah and Sarawak were former British colonial territories. They became part of Malaysia in 1963. Sabah and Sarawak were accorded a greater degree of autonomy in managing their own affairs than the other states in Malaysia as a pre-condition for joining the federation.
3 The Kadazandusun people comprise two distinct ethnic groups: the Kadazans and the Dusuns. Even though different in name, they share linguistic and cultural traits. In the 1980s, Kadazan and Dusun leaders agreed to combine their ethnic names – hence, the Kadazandusun.
4 Before the formation of Malaysia in 1963, non-Muslims outnumbered Muslims in Sabah. But in the 1970s, the number of Muslims grew as a result of Mustapha Harun's rapid Islamisation policy and his government's tolerant attitude towards an influx of Muslim Filipinos from the neighbouring Philippines.
5 The Non-Islamic Religions (Controls of Propagation Among Muslims) Enactment 1988 was enacted to prevent proselytisation among Muslims.
6 The Sibu by-election was held following the death of Robert Lau, the SUPP incumbent. Sibu is a Chinese-majority constituency with a sizeable number of Iban. It also has a strong Christian presence, mainly from the Anglican, Methodist and SIB denominations.
7 See the NECF Malaysia website at www.necf.org.my (accessed 7 May 2014).
8 This figure is obtained from the SIB Kuala Lumpur official website at www.sibkl.org.my (accessed 7 May 2014).

Bibliography

Al Jazeera (2010) 'Malaysia Allah ban overturned', *Al Jazeera*, 1 January, available at www.aljazeera.com/news/asia-pacific/2010/01/20101114114404185.html (accessed 29 January 2014).

Chin, James and Arnold Puyok (2011) 'Going against the tide: Sabah and the 2008 Malaysian General Election', *Asian Politics and Policy*, 2(2): 219–35.

Daily Express (2014) 'Group claims tricked into joining another faith', *Daily Express*, 8 January, available at www.dailyexpress.com.my/news.cfm?NewsID=87882 (accessed 29 January 2014).

Driskell, Robyn, Elizabeth Embry and Larry Lyon (2008) 'Faith and politics: the influence of religious beliefs on political participation', *Social Science Quarterly*, 89(2): 294–314.

Fernando, Joseph M. (2006) 'The position of Islam in the Constitution of Malaysia', *Journal of Southeast Asian Studies*, 37(2): 249–66.

Free Malaysia Today (2013) 'Burn Bible call alarms Sabah Christians', *Free Malaysia Today*, 26 January, available at www.freemalaysiatoday.com/category/nation/2013/01/26/burn-bible-call-alarms-sabah-christians/ (accessed 29 January 2014).

Gill, Anthony (2001) 'Religion and comparative politics', *Annual Review of Political Science*, 4: 117–38.

Hamayotsu, Kikue (2008) 'Beyond doctrine and dogma: religion and politics in Southeast Asia', in Erik M. Kuhonta, Dan Slater and Tuong Vu (eds), *Southeast Asia in Political Science: Theory, Region, and Qualitative Analysis*, Stanford: Stanford University Press, pp. 171–98.

Kessler, Clive (1978) *Islam and Politics in a Malay State: Kelantan, 1838–1969*, Ithaca: Cornell University Press.

Keyes, Charles F. (1996) 'Being Protestant Christians in Southeast Asian worlds', *Journal of Southeast Asian Studies*, 27(2): 280–92.

Luping, Herman J. (1994) *Sabah's Dilemma: The Political History of Sabah, 1960–1994*, Kuala Lumpur: Magnum Books.

Malaysian Insider (2012) 'MyKad "Islamisation" of Sabah's Bumiputera Christians', *The Malaysian Insider*, 5 November, available at www.themalaysianinsider.com/sideviews/article/mykad-islamisation-of-sabahs-bumiputera-christians-bob-teoh (accessed 29 January 2014).

Malaysian Insider (2014a) '"Allah" row a non-issue, look at bigger picture, say experts', *The Malaysian Insider*, 11 January, available at www.themalaysianinsider.com/malaysia/article/allah-row-a-non-issue-look-at-bigger-picture-say-experts (accessed 29 January 2014).

Malaysian Insider (2014b) 'Resolve Allah issue quickly, former AG urges Federal Court', *The Malaysian Insider*, 7 January, available at www.themalaysianinsider.com/malaysia/article/resolve-allah-issue-quickly-former-ag-urges-federal-court (accessed 29 January 2014).

Moustafa, Tamir (2013a) 'Judging in God's name: state power, secularism, and the politics of Islamic Law in Malaysia', *Oxford Journal of Law and Religion*, 2: 1–16.

Moustafa, Tamir (2013b) 'Liberal rights versus Islamic Law? The construction of a binary in Malaysian politics', *Law & Society Review*, 47(4): 771–802.

NECF (2011) 'Response to the 10-point plan by the government', available at www.necf.org.my/newsmaster.cfm?&menuid=43&action=view&retrieveid=1285 (accessed 29 January 2013).

NECF (2012) *Christians and the Ballot Box*, Kuala Lumpur: NECF.

NECF (2014) 'Re: responding to possible action against churches for using "Allah"', available at www.necf.org.my/newsmaster.cfm?&menuid=43&action=view&retrieveid=1549 (accessed 29 January 2014).

Puyok, Arnold (2006) 'Voting pattern and issues in the 2006 Sarawak State Assembly Election in the Ba' Kelalan constituency', *Asian Journal of Political Science*, 14(2): 212–28.

Puyok, Arnold (2014) 'Kota Marudu and Keningau, Sabah: personality, patronage and parochial politics', in Meredith L. Weiss (ed.), *Electoral Dynamics in Malaysia: Findings from the Grassroots*, Petaling Jaya: SIRD and Singapore: ISEAS, pp. 181–96.

Star (2014) 'JAIS acted within non-Islamic religions enactment, says JAIS', *The Star*, 10 January, available at www.thestar.com.my/News/Nation/2014/01/10/Jais-acted-within-NonIslamic-Religions-Enactment-says-Mais/ (accessed 29 January 2014).

Syed Husin Ali (2008) *The Malays: Their Problems and Future*, Petaling Jaya: The Other Press.

Walters, Albert Sundararaj (2007) 'Issues in Christian–Muslim relations: a Malaysian Christian perspective', *Islam & Christian–Muslim Relations*, 18(1): 67–83.

Wong Chin Huat (2010) 'P212 Sibu, Sarawak', in Wong Chin Huat and Soon Li Tsin (eds), *Democracy at Stake? Examining 16 By-elections in Malaysia, 2008–2011*, Petaling Jaya: SIRD, pp. 141–62.

Woo, Joshua and Tan Soo-Inn (2011) *The Bible and the Ballot*, Singapore: Friends in Conversation and Graceworks Private Limited.

Yapp, Eugene (2011) 'The Christian and politics', available at www.Kairos-Malaysia.org (accessed 29 January 2014).

6

Centralised federalism in Malaysia

Is change in the offing?

Francis Loh Kok Wah

In the keenly contested thirteenth general election (GE13) held on 5 May 2013, the Barisan Nasional (BN) coalition emerged victorious, for the thirteenth time. Thanks to the first-past-the-post electoral system used in Malaysia, it won 133 of 222 parliamentary seats at stake, although it garnered only 47.5 percent of the popular vote (down from 51.4 percent in the previous polls in 2008). The opposition coalition Pakatan Rakyat (PR), which polled 50.9 percent of the popular vote (up from 47.5 percent in 2008), won only 89 of the 222 parliamentary seats. However, the PR's performance was enough to deny the BN a two-thirds majority in parliament, for the second successive general election. As well, the PR defeated the BN again in the states of Kelantan, Penang and Selangor. It also came close to winning two other state legislative assemblies. To a large extent, the electoral results are a reflection of the outcome of the previous (twelfth) general election (GE12) held on 8 March 2008.

Then, the BN lost not only its two-thirds majority in parliament; it also lost an unprecedented five of the thirteen states to the PR. There occurred various dramatic developments thereafter. Former prime minister Dr Mahathir Mohamad, who had handed power to Abdullah Badawi, soon launched an assault on his former deputy which resulted in Abdullah's retirement. There were also soul-searching reviews by the United Malays National Organisation (UMNO), and the other BN component parties on why they had fared so poorly. There were even reformist initiatives by the new prime minister, Najib Tun Razak.

Less anticipated were the tensions that arose between the BN federal government and the PR-led states. Whereas the academic and public discourses on BN's political dominance since independence in 1957 had previously focused on how the executive had accumulated power at the expense of the legislature and the judiciary, and how the BN state had penetrated deep into the sinews of the everyday lives of ordinary citizens in Malaysia's multi-ethnic society, post-GE12 discourse on centralisation also focused on the central government's domination over the state and local governments.

This chapter focuses on the structure and design of Malaysia's federalism, which has been described as 'highly centralized' (Anderson 2008: 69). Another analyst has stated that 'the concentration of functions within the Federal Government has been carried so far that, in respect of the states of Malaya, one could almost question whether there is any justification to speak of a federation at all' (Holzhausen 1974: 178). The origins of Malaysia's federal system and the factors that have shaped Malaysia's centralised federalism will be discussed first. The second part of the chapter elaborates on major aspects of federal–state relations during 1957–2007. The final part highlights the controversies and the ferment that have occurred in federal–state relations since 2008; however, a formal restructuring of federal–state ties will probably require a change of government at the centre first.

Origins of the federal system

Malaysia's federalism is not derived from the demographic distribution of ethnic groups, for the major ethnic groups are distributed unevenly all over the peninsula. If anything, the Chinese and Indians tend to reside more in urban areas while the Malays predominate in rural areas. It is only in Sabah and in Sarawak that there reside large concentrations of regional 'native' minorities, namely the Kadazandusun in Sabah and the Dayak in Sarawak.

Nor is the origin of Malaysia's federalism to be found in the principle of 'subsidiarity', since Malaysia is a small country.[1] Rather, the origin lies in the peninsula's historical legacy. Prior to colonialism, the territory comprised distinct Malay states, each ruled by a Malay sultan. British colonisation reinforced these divisions by recognising these states as separate legal entities in the late nineteenth and early twentieth centuries. Although the British attempted to centralise administration in the 1930s, the attempt proved unsuccessful, due to strong objections by the Malay rulers. In this regard it is significant that early civil society organisations, including those which advocated popular political participation, were state-based entities too.

It was only after World War II that pan-Malaya political organisations and movements emerged. In 1946, the returning British colonialists proposed the establishment of the Malayan Union (MU) which would have done away with the separate Malay states and centralised administration over British Malaya. The MU proposal also offered citizenship rights quite liberally to all then domiciled in British Malaya, an offer that would have benefited the immigrant Chinese and Indians. Significantly, the British succeeded in pressuring the Malay rulers, who had collaborated with the Japanese during the war, to support the MU proposal. However, the Malay aristocrats, as distinct from the rulers, opposed the MU proposal and mobilised ordinary Malays against it, paving the way to the formation of UMNO. Although UMNO comprised numerous state-based organisations initially, it evolved into a pan-Malaya ethno-nationalist party, ultimately transcending state loyalties and appeal. Hence the rejection of the MU proposal and its replacement by the Federation of Malaya Agreement in 1948 emblemised continuity with the past on the one hand, but also reinforced the claim by UMNO ethno-nationalists of Malay pre-eminence on the other.

As for non-Malay immigrants, for whom state loyalty had little meaning in the first instance, the state order was not useful for defending their interests either. The resulting counter-mobilisation, and the political parties that non-Malays formed, were also pan-Malayan in nature. Little priority was given to endowing the states with wide powers, and with commensurate revenue and other resources.

Centralised constitutional design

Hence the 1957 Federal Constitution is decidedly top-heavy. This is evident in Part VI of the Constitution, which discusses federal–state relations. The Ninth Schedule of the Federal Constitution further details the distribution of legislative powers and responsibilities between the federal and state governments. The federal list is a long one and includes the areas of 'high politics' – internal security, law and order, foreign affairs, defence, administration of justice and citizenship; the macro-economic functions of trade, finance, commerce, industry, communication, energy, transport, surveys and research; and welfare functions and social development like education,[2] health, labour, social security, and fire prevention and extinguishment. By contrast, the state list is short. The only important areas are lands and mines, Muslim affairs and customs, agriculture and forestry, local government, local public services, and state works and water. The concurrent list covers social welfare, scholarships, town and country planning, drainage and irrigation, housing, culture and sports, fire safety measures, animal husbandry and public health.

State powers are qualified by granting legislative powers to the federal parliament for the purpose of ensuring uniformity of laws across states. In cases of conflict or inconsistency, federal legislation enjoys precedence. Federal laws on local government and most important matters related to land do not even require adoption or passage by the state legislatures. In the event of an emergency, the federal government is allowed to legislate on all state matters; however, residual powers remain with the states (Mohd Salleh bin Abbas 1978: 163–91; Watts 2008: 39).

These provisions in the 1957 Constitution defined the scope of federal–state relations for the peninsular states, and after amendment in line with the Federation of Malaya Act 1963, for the Borneo states of Sabah and Sarawak, too. Although the two Borneo states had proposed that a new constitution be drawn up to accommodate their special interests, their proposal was not realised due to the exigencies of the Cold War period, when Malaya was threatened by a 'Confrontation' from a then left-leaning Indonesia.

In the event, more rights and grants are accorded to Sabah and Sarawak than to the original eleven peninsular states. Indeed, Sabah and Sarawak political leaders considered the status of their states to be different. For them, Sabah or Sarawak was 'one of three' signatories to the London Agreement which paved the way for the formation of Malaysia in 1963. Some fifty years later, most of these rights have been whittled away through a series of constitutional amendments, resulting in Sabah and Sarawak's looking more like 'one of the thirteen' states (Loh 2009b: 144–53). Hence, due to its separate history, a different demographic pattern, plus the special rights and autonomy granted to them in the 1963 Constitutional amendments, a greater sense of regionalism prevails in each of these two states.

The Tenth Schedule of the Federal Constitution elaborates on revenue assignment based on the division of jurisdictions spelt out in the Ninth Schedule. Hence it is heavily skewed in favour of the central government. In the Tenth Schedule, income taxes, property and capital gains taxes, international trade taxes, as well as production and consumption taxes, are all assigned to the federal government. The state government is allowed to collect only natural resource-related taxes, such as revenue from lands and mines, as well as from forests.

Significantly, under the Petroleum Development Act (PDA) 1974, all states give up their rights to petroleum resources found within their states. Ownership and control of petroleum and gas, though natural resources, are transferred to the federal-owned company, Petronas, tasked with exploiting and mining the resource. Petronas pays the state and federal governments 5 percent royalty each (Petronas receives 49 percent while the producer company receives the remaining 41 percent) of the gross value of petroleum production. The federal government taxes the producer company (Sarawak Shell, Sabah Shell or Esso). Consequently, the federal government receives more revenue from petroleum than do the petroleum-producing states. However, should the petroleum resources be located beyond the state's three-mile territorial waters, the federal government can choose to deny this royalty to the state government (Nambiar 2007: 186).

The undemocratic political process

Second, apart from the federal bias in the constitutional design, the *political process* that has seen a single political party, the BN, controlling the central government and most of the thirteen states for fifty-plus years has furthered centralised federalism.

In fact, centralised federalism is only one part of the semi-authoritarian political system. For although a Westminster parliamentary system was adopted in 1957, the BN has ruled with a wide array of coercive laws passed by parliament which allowed for preventive detention as well as strict control over civil society organisations, publications and printing, trade unions, universities and colleges, peaceful assembly, access to so-called 'official secrets', and so on. The roots of this domination of the political process go back to the pre-independence era, when a communist uprising, euphemistically called the Emergency (1948–60), occurred. With the end of the uprising, emergency powers were incorporated into the 1957 Constitution and other laws passed by parliament. Through use of these coercive laws, the BN executive ensured uninterrupted control of Malaysian politics.

A related consequence was a politicised bureaucracy, already very centralised by design. Serving under the same BN government for over fifty years, the federal, state and local government bureaucracies became extensions of the BN. The flip side to this was that they became uncooperative, and sometimes hostile, towards the opposition. This attitude persisted even after the opposition took control of several state governments after GE12. The common complaint was that the state secretaries, state development officers, state legal officers, state financial officers, local authority chiefs, district officers, and even heads of the departments of Lands and Mines and Islamic Affairs, the last two falling under the purview of the state governments, were biased against the elected PR governments.

Moreover, as a result of the politicisation of the bureaucracy, incompetence, if not corruption, also crept into the workings of the entire bureaucracy. Not surprisingly, therefore, the displacement of the BN in Penang and Selangor, for instance, did not evidently result in more 'competent, accountable and transparent', or CAT, governments, their common proclaimed goal.

The development process and the NEP

Third, the *development process*, underscored by the implementation of the New Economic Policy (NEP, 1971–90), also contributed to the expansion and consolidation of the federal government.

The Constitution stipulates that the federal government is obliged to provide two major grants to the state governments, namely, a capitation grant, which is based on population size,[3] and a state road grant, which helps the states to maintain their network of roads, but is in effect a grant that takes into consideration the geographical size of the state. Apart from these two grants, there are about ten other tax-sharing taxes and levies that the state is allowed to collect or for which the federal government has to reimburse the state. The petroleum royalty is one such case. At any rate, the federal government has sole jurisdiction and discretion over the disbursement of development funds to the state and local governments (Wee 2006).

States that have little land and forest, and no petroleum or mineral resources can raise enough revenue for operations, but not enough for development. A study of the Penang state budget shows that the state's annual budget has been shrinking. A major explanation was that federal grants to the two local authorities in the state were transferred to them directly, bypassing the state government altogether after 2008 (Narayanan *et al.* 2010: 199).

An economist from the Malaysian Institute of Economic Research has observed that the total consolidated state government revenues (in absolute terms) for all the states has been rising from 1985 to the present. From 1995 to 2000, the average annual rate of growth of state government revenue was about 4.9 percent. However, the average rate of growth of consolidated state government revenue from 2000 to 2005 declined to approximately 2.5 percent, indicating that the state governments' capacity for revenue collection had diminished. Meanwhile, the average annual growth of federal government revenue rose from about 4.4 percent for 1995–2000 to 14.4 percent for 2000–05. Accordingly, the researcher concluded:

> the state and federal governments are not subject to the same kind of circumstances. The trend seems to indicate that those sources of revenue open to the federal government are growing, while those sources of revenue that the state governments can resort to are declining.
>
> *(Nambiar 2007: 190)*

Following the 1997–98 regional financial crisis, the federal government was further enhanced, for not only fiscal policy, but also budgetary allocations 'were concentrated in the hands of the centre' (Nambiar 2007: 187). Consequently, the central government grew stronger and the state governments weaker, further widening the original design of vertical imbalance.

Additionally, in pursuit of the affirmative-action NEP, the federal government established numerous statutory bodies and government-linked companies (GLCs) to promote *bumiputera* commercial and industrial interests. Implementation and monitoring of the NEP required the expansion of the public sector and tight control by the central authorities, which shifted even more power from the states to the federal authorities. A case in point is the Commercial Vehicles Licensing Board (CVLB), a federal authority charged with promoting *bumiputera* participation in the transportation industry. The licensing of taxis and buses, and even the routing of buses in the states, came under the purview of the CVLB. Although the CVLB has been replaced by the Land Public Transport Commission (SPAD), such regulatory control by the federal government over transport matters in the states and local areas persists.

Bullying the states into submission in the 1990s

BN machinations to bypass the PR-led state governments mirrored how the coalition had dealt with opposition-led states previously. In 1991, the federal government redirected development allocations under the Sixth Malaysia Plan 1991–95 away from opposition-controlled governments under the Parti Bersatu Sabah (PBS) in Sabah and under Parti Islam SeMalaysia (PAS) in Kelantan, towards newly established Federal Development Offices in those states. Only grants duly specified in the Constitution were provided directly to the state governments. Development allocations for the two states were also cut in the Mid-Term Review of the Sixth Malaysia Plan, ostensibly because of 'constraints in the implementation capacity in these states' (EPU 1993: 49). Yet BN-controlled states which had lower rates of project implementation had their allocations increased, instead.

During this period, the chief ministers of Sabah and Kelantan were no longer automatically invited to meetings on development matters involving executives of the state governments, either. In Sabah's case, the federal government also imposed a ban on the export of timber logs, ostensibly to promote the development of local wood-based industries. Sabah, which derived almost 50 percent of state revenue from forestry earnings, was severely affected. In part because of such financial constraints, Sabah's economic performance turned sluggish under the PBS (Loh 1996: 77–81).[4] Finally, during the early 1990s, several PBS leaders calling for greater autonomy for Sabah were detained without trial on grounds of fostering secession.

One would have thought that the BN federal government would not try to bully the five PR-led states in the same manner it had dealt with Sabah and Kelantan in the 1990s. After all, in Kelantan at least, the voters had continued to vote for the opposition. Moreover, Selangor and Penang, unlike Kelantan and Sabah, are not poor states and are much less dependent on federal funds. In fact, Selangor and Penang are part of the nation's industrial heartland, much incorporated into the global economy, and are capable of sustaining themselves even if there were federal funding cuts.[5] In the event, the PR-led states refused to be bullied by the central government. The immediate result was a stand-off of sorts.

Controversies over development projects

The discussion below elaborates some of the major federal–state controversies in the states of Penang and Selangor in the realm of development in particular, but also over issues of democratisation.[6]

A major controversy pitted the new Penang chief minister, Lim Guan Eng, against the Penang State Development Officer (SDO), a federal appointee. Lim alleged that the SDO had threatened to withdraw a RM7 million federal allocation for a Penang Botanic Gardens expansion project, which had run into a roadblock when a number of hawkers refused to relocate to a new site and a group of environmentalists complained about destruction of the gardens. Lim highlighted that the project was 'a federal one involving federal contractors' and that he was in the dark about the plans. He feared that the 'hiccup' in the plans would be used by the federal government to deny the state its share of funds under the Tenth Malaysia Plan (Loh 2010: 137). In response to Lim's 'insinuations', the SDO revealed that RM7.6 billion had been allocated to Penang under the Ninth Malaysia Plan and another RM278 million under the Economic Stimulus Package Phases I and II for 2009 and 2010 (Loh 2010: 137). Inadvertently, he also revealed that these allocations were put under the SDO's charge; the SDO answered to the Implementation Coordination Unit (ICU) of the Prime Minister's Department.

Another controversial issue concerned the worsening public transport problem in the island state. As mentioned earlier, the CVLB, now restructured as SPAD, a federal agency, monopolises land public transport licensing and approvals for routing. Consequently, the hands of the Penang state and local governments are tied. One of the Penang state government's proposals was to expand and construct more roads (which provoked the wrath of Penang environmentalists). But it also launched 'non-commercial' bus services (therefore outside the purview of SPAD) across the bridge and in the inner city in order to remove congestion on the streets and bridge. In fact, it offered the federal government-linked Rapid Penang bus company a RM10 million contract to provide free bus services for Penangites during rush hour, a proposal to which Rapid Penang still had not responded after more than a year.

Of course, the issue is a political one. In the run-up to GE13, the Penang BN announced in its electoral manifesto that it would build a monorail system in Penang should it take over the state. Presumably, federal funds would be forthcoming. In the event, the PR was returned to power and the BN has not talked about such a monorail system since.

As well, there were disputes over the control and management of Penang Port, which the federal cabinet, reportedly, has privatised to a tycoon closely associated with the BN federal government. The Penang state government has called upon the federal cabinet to privatise the port to the state government instead. Indeed, it has argued that its takeover of the port would allow it to synergise regular dredging of the port, which is nowadays plagued with a siltation problem, and more efficient running of the ferry services currently under the control of the Penang Port Commission – yet another federal agency, despite its name's perhaps suggesting otherwise. Thus far, the state government as well as the public remain in the dark about the future development of the port and related services (Emmanuel and Bahari 2011).

Meanwhile, Selangor Menteri Besar Tan Sri Khalid Ibrahim has repeatedly criticised the federal government for not providing adequate finance to develop his state. In 2009, he declared, 'Although RM16 billion in taxes are paid to the federal government by Selangor, the state only got RM400 million for development. This amount allocated by the federal government . . . was peanuts' (Loh 2010: 138).

Controversy over Selangor's water treatment and supply has hogged the headlines most since GE12. In 2006, the federal government decided to take over the supply and treatment of water throughout the peninsula and to privatise water services. In Selangor's case, three concessionaires closely related to the BN were offered what the Selangor Menteri Besar has termed overly generous terms. Subsequent to GE12, the Selangor government attempted to take back control over water treatment and supply; however, the concessionaires repeatedly rejected offers the state government considered fair. After GE13, it tried once again to push through a new deal, which two of the concessionaires accepted. However, the major concessionaire did not. In early 2014, the Selangor government pulled out of further negotiations and requested the federal water regulating authority to resolve the matter. Although the public has generally sided with the Selangor government in this controversy, the concessionaires are backed by the federal government, by the banks and by investors in the concessionaire companies. This problem highlights how difficult it is to reverse the centralising (and privatisation) process, even when a popularly elected state government desires to reverse that process (Yeoh 2012: 57–62).

Yet another move by the Selangor government was a call to revamp the operations of the federal Malaysian Anti-Corruption Commission (MACC). This matter had arisen because of the death of a Selangor state official after he was interrogated (Loh 2010: 138).

Another intervention on the part of the Selangor and Penang governments has been to declassify information considered 'secret' under the Official Secrets Act (OSA) in order to expose follies by the previous BN state governments. This was followed by the passage of Freedom of Information enactments in both state assemblies (Teh 2011; *The Sun* 2011).

Meanwhile, in Kelantan, the PAS-led government has written officially to the federal government seeking RM1 billion in oil royalty, backdated to 2004. It argues that this payment is in accordance with the Petroleum Development Act 1974. Sabah, Sarawak and Terengganu have all received 5 percent royalty payments, but Kelantan, also a petroleum-producing state, has been denied its equivalent. The PR pressed on with the issue and set up a parliamentary caucus to pursue the matter. Subsequently, the matter was taken to the Courts (Razak 2012).

These episodes highlighted the BN federal government's attempt to prevent power and financial resources from being transferred from the centre to the states, despite the outcome of the GE12 and GE13. In effect, the BN federal government refused to acknowledge the necessary distinction in federal systems between *(federal) government-to-(state) government ties* and *party-to-party ties*. In federal systems all over the world, the norm is to anticipate and expect a mix of different parties coming to power at the different levels of government, to recognise the rights of both the central and the lower order of governments, and to share power and funds accordingly, *regardless of party affiliation*.

Emerging controversies

The contradictions of centralised federalism have been pushed centre-stage as a result of the changes in several state governments after GE12 and GE13. However, some of the controversies that have emerged or are emerging are not related whatsoever to the rise of PR-led state governments. For instance, a major controversy is in the offing in the area of primary and secondary school education. Academic standards have been declining, discipline is worsening and the curriculum has been politicised. There have been volte-faces in policies – for example, for the teaching of science and mathematics in Malay, then in English, and recently, back to Malay again. Worse, many of the graduates from local public universities have found it difficult to find employment.[7]

It is not an understatement to say that there is widespread distrust of the education system in Malaysia on account of how it has been politicised and centralised (Loh 2014). In federal countries like Canada, Australia, Switzerland and Germany, as well as in developing ones with federal structures, like India, South Africa, Brazil and Ethiopia, primary and secondary schools fall under the ambit of state and even local governments; tertiary education is often the shared responsibility of central, state and sometimes local governments, too (Watts 2008: Appendix A). Not so in Malaysia!

This is the crux of the matter: our bureaucracy, including the ministry of education and individual teachers, has become very politicised and centralised after rule by a single party – the UMNO-dominated BN – for more than fifty-five years. Regardless of whether state and district education offices are located in BN- or PR-led states, these lower-level officers and teachers take orders from the federal ministry of education. An organisation which employs some 420,000 teachers and another 32,000-odd officers at the federal, state and district levels cannot be expected to function efficiently. Worse, it has been used by power-crazed politicians and officials for political ends.

Another area concerns the privatisation of utilities and the regulatory function that the federal government has assumed from the state and sometimes local authorities. The issue of water supply and treatment was earlier discussed. Here the focus is on cleansing and waste-collecting services, which have been privatised to only three contractors in the peninsula: Env Idaman Sdn Bhd in the north, Alam Flora Sdn Bhd in the centre, and Southern Waste Management Sdn Bhd in the south. Except in the states of Selangor, Perak and Penang (which opted out of the arrangement), the three contractors share an oligopoly over the provision of these services throughout the peninsula. Although it should be obvious that a local firm rather than a big-time company based elsewhere would be more familiar with local problems pertaining to cleaning and waste collection (as well as water treatment and supply), federalisation of these services was legislated for and passed in parliament, then the services were subsequently privatised. In tandem with these changes, a federal regulatory body was also set up. Almost immediately after privatisation, complaints over poor delivery of services were voiced. In the run-up to GE13, a local authority in the BN-led state of Perlis terminated the services of Env Idaman, whereupon the authority was informed by the federal regulator that termination of services could only be made by the federal authority, not the local authority Env Idaman served poorly. It further came to light that Env Idaman had been given a '22-year contract'!

These two examples illustrate that federal–state controversies do not necessarily arise as a result of the opposition-led state governments. Rather, most of these problems pertain to the centralisation of power and resources that have gone unchecked under more than fifty years of one-party rule, which has furthered the original central bias in Malaysia's constitutional design.

As these controversies have raged on, BN members of parliament from Sabah and Sarawak have seized the opportunity to flex their electoral muscles, too. In the 2008 polls, the Sarawak BN won thirty of thirty-one parliamentary seats, while the Sabah BN won twenty-four of twenty-five seats. Without these states' contribution of fifty-four seats, the BN would not have been able to claim victory. The results of GE13 further confirmed the importance of the BN in the two states. The BN won twenty-five of thirty-one seats in Sarawak and twenty-two of twenty-five seats in 2013. Accordingly, the Sabah and Sarawak BN have pressed their own demands. First, they have pressed for and been granted more cabinet representation as well as the positions of speaker and deputy speaker in parliament. The federal government promised and subsequently set up a Royal Commission of Inquiry to look into the question of illegal immigrants in Sabah who, at 610,000, made up one-sixth of the state's entire population – an issue for which most Sabahans, regardless of ethnic background or party affiliation, have demanded redress for more than two decades.

Second, the Sabah BN also called for the closure of the Federal Development Office in Kota Kinabalu, which was first established when PBS (then in opposition, where it sat from 1985–94) ruled the state. This was acceded to in early 2009. A RM1 billion allocation for rural development to reduce poverty was also approved, as was an East Malaysia Economic Growth corridor to coordinate regional development in the two states.

Finally, the prime minister proclaimed 16 September, the day Malaysia was formed, as a public holiday. This had been a demand by the Sabahans and Sarawakians for a long time. Significantly, the PR had also promised that it would recognise the importance of 16 September upon coming to power. In this regard, the prime minister stole the PR's thunder (Loh 2010: 139).

A Sabah leader had likened the BN Sabah to the coalition's 'fixed deposit', warning that 'if the interest rate offered was not good enough, we can put the deposit elsewhere'. A former Sabah chief minister has unequivocally called for 'greater autonomy' for Sabah, especially with regard to the selection of its own chief minister, who is now nominated almost unilaterally by UMNO federal leaders (Loh 2010: 139). Hence, it appears that the struggles between the PR-led states and federal governments have also paid dividends for Sabah and Sarawak, although they are currently under BN-led governments.

Conclusion

This survey of federal–state relations in Malaysia shows that there is considerable ferment in the matter. Although the constitutional design as expressed in the Ninth Schedule of the Federal Constitution has not been addressed directly, the ascendancy of the PR in five states (now reduced to four) has interrupted the one-party-dominant political process that has prevailed for more than fifty years, and which has facilitated not just BN domination at the centre, but its penetration and control into the state and local authority levels as well. The discussion above indicates that the PR-led states of Selangor and Penang, in particular, have challenged federal domination as never before. They have rejected the BN's bullying ways of the past, when it dealt with weaker and poorer opposition-led states. More than that, the new balance of federal–state relations has allowed the BN-led states of Sabah and Sarawak to press for more development funds, for attention to the problems they face, and for decentralisation in decision-making, too.

Similarly, although the Tenth Schedule of the Federal Constitution, which elaborates upon the sharing of financial resources, has not been amended, nonetheless, due to the controversies that have emerged between the BN federal government and the PR-led state governments, the federal government has been forced to continue providing development funds to the constituent states, and to take their particular interests into consideration. Hence in spite of the absence of constitutional reforms vis-à-vis federal–state relations, it appears that some restructuring of those relations is underway. However, the continued occurrence of silly spats and controversies over development projects, as well as demands for democratisation, suggest that Malaysia has still not transitioned from a centralised federalism to a more cooperative one yet. The PR government has declared in its electoral manifesto that it intends to conduct those reforms if and when it comes to power. This transfer of power did not occur in GE13. Might it occur in GE14?

Notes

1 The principle of subsidiarity asserts that taxing, spending and regulatory functions should be performed by the lowest level of authority capable of performing the tasks competently, unless a convincing case can be made to assign these to higher orders of government.
2 In federal systems, sectors like primary and secondary school education, public transport (apart from railways), and health are often under the state's rather than the central government's purview. See Watts 2008: Appendix A.
3 The capitation grant is calculated on the basis of a state's population as recorded in the last census. In 2013, the formula used provided for RM72.00 each for the first 100,000 residents; RM10.20 each for the next 500,000 residents; RM10.80 each for the following 500,000 residents; and RM11.40 each for residents beyond that. The latest version of the formula was passed via Act of Parliament 622 in July 2002. The grants are given in January and June for each year. In 2007, Selangor, the state with the largest population, received RM67,661,987; Perlis, with the smallest population, received RM8,389,573. Penang received RM22,417,694 (Dewan Rakyat 2008). See Wee 2006: 76–77 for capitation transfers during the early 1990s.
4 On the other hand, relations between the BN federal government and BN state governments were very cordial, in spite of various administrative irregularities. See Lim 2008: 81–97 on the Berjaya administration in Sabah from 1976 to 1985. However, during the 1970s, two UMNO MBs who questioned or disobeyed their federal leaders were put into political limbo (Loh 2009b: 121–53).
5 For instance, in mid-2009, citing federal government data, the Penang state government announced that 151 foreign investment projects totalling RM10.16 billion had been approved in 2008, and another RM1.1 billion worth of projects were in the process of being approved in early 2009 (Loh 2010: 136). In Selangor, the state owned several Kuala Lumpur Stock Exchange (KLSE) listed companies. At any rate, it would be foolhardy for the federal government to jeopardise Selangor's economy, which accounts for 17 percent of the national GDP (Shanmugam and Siow 2008).
6 A useful source on these controversies is Yeoh 2012.
7 A recent survey of these problems and the related problem of over-centralisation of the education system can be found in Loh 2014: 2–10.

Bibliography

Anderson, George (2008) *Federalism: An Introduction*, Oxford and Ottawa: Oxford University Press and Forum of Federations.

Dewan Rakyat (2008) Question No 61. Answer by Finance Minister to Y.B. Dr Mohamad Hayati Othman, Press release, 27 May.

Economic Planning Unit (EPU) (1993) *Mid-Term Review of the Sixth Malaysia Plan 1991–1995*, Kuala Lumpur: Government Printers.

Emmanuel, Marina and Bilqis Bahari (2011) 'Government decision on privatisation of Penang Port soon?', *Business Times*, 12 December, available at www.btimes.com.my/Current_News/BTIMES/articles/pinang (accessed 12 December 2011).

Holzhausen, Walter (1974) *Federal Finance in Malaysia*, Kuala Lumpur: University of Malaya Press.

Kitingan, Jeffrey G. (1997) 'Thorny issues in federal–state relations', in Tan Chee Beng (ed.), *Reflections on the Malaysian Constitution*, Penang: Aliran, pp. 149–68.

Lim, Regina (2008) *Federal–State Relations in Sabah, Malaysia: The Berjaya Administration*, Singapore: Institute of Southeast Asian Studies.
Loh Kok Wah, Francis (1996) 'A "new Sabah" and the spell of development: resolving federal–state relations in Malaysia', *South East Asia Research*, 4(1): 63–84.
Loh Kok Wah, Francis (ed.) (1997) *Sabah and Sarawak: The Politics of Development and Federalism*, Penang: Universiti Sains Malaysia.
Loh Kok Wah, Francis (2009a) 'Federation of Malaysia', in Hans Michelmann (ed.), *Foreign Relations in Federal Countries*, Montreal and Kingston: McGill-Queen's University Press, pp. 189–208.
Loh Kok Wah, Francis (2009b) *Old vs New Politics in Malaysia*, Petaling Jaya: SIRD.
Loh Kok Wah, Francis (2010) 'Restructuring federal–state relations in Malaysia: from centralised to co-operative federalism?', *The Round Table*, 99(407): 131–40.
Loh Kok Wah, Francis (2014) 'Political parties, stay out of our schools', *Aliran Monthly*, 33(8): 2–10.
Mohamad Agus Yusoff (2006) *Malaysian Federalism: Conflict or Consensus*, Bangi: Penerbit Universiti Kebangsaan Malaysia.
Mohamed Salleh bin Abas (1978) 'Federalism in Malaysia – changes in the first twenty years', in Mohammed Suffian, H.P. Lee and Francis A. Trindade (eds), *The Constitution of Malaysia: Its Development 1957–1977*, Kuala Lumpur: Oxford University Press, pp. 163–91.
Nambiar, Shankaran (2007) 'The practice of fiscal federalism in Malaysia', in Anwar Shah (ed.), *The Practice of Fiscal Federalism: Comparative Studies*, Montreal and Kingston: McGill-Queen's University Press, pp. 178–203.
Narayanan, Suresh, Lim Mah Hui and Ong Wooi Leng (2010) 'Re-examining Penang state finances and governance', in Ooi Kee Beng and Goh Ban Lee (eds), *Pilot Studies for a New Penang*, Singapore: Institute of Southeast Asian Studies, pp. 189–222.
Ng, Cecilia (2012) 'Gender and governance: the politics of federalism in Malaysia', *Kajian Malaysia*, 30(2): 1–26.
Razak, Radzi (2012) 'Federal Court grants Kelantan's appeal', *The Sun*, 2 October, p. 3.
Shanmugam, N. and Siow Chen Ming (2008) 'Funding the opposition state', *The Edge Malaysia*, 17 March, pp. 72–77.
The Sun (2011) 'Revised FOI Bill open for scrutiny', *The Sun*, 2 June, p. 11.
Teh Eng Hock (2011) 'Selangor passes freedom of information bill', *The Star*, 2 April, p. 6.
Watts, Ronald (2008) [1996] *Comparing Federal Systems*, Montreal and Kingston: McGill-Queen's University Press.
Wee Chong Hui (2006) *Regional Disparities and Federalism in Malaysia*, Kuala Lumpur: University of Malaya Press.
Yeoh, Tricia (2012) *States of Reform: Governing Selangor and Penang*, Penang: Penang Institute.

7

Exporting the BN/UMNO model

Politics in Sabah and Sarawak

James Chin

In terms of history, culture and demography, there was nothing in common between the peoples of the Malayan peninsula and Borneo, other than that all were once part of the British Empire. When Malaysia was established as the successor state to the peninsular Federation of Malaya in 1963, Sabah and Sarawak (which together comprise East Malaysia) were included to ensure that the total *bumiputera* population of the new federation would be numerically superior to that of non-*bumiputera*.[1] This chapter reviews political developments in Sabah and Sarawak since independence and argues that the common theme since independence has been an attempt to export the Barisan Nasional (BN)/United Malays National Organisation (UMNO) model of government to East Malaysia. The model is essentially based on a Muslim-led coalition government with Ketuanan Melayu (Malay Supremacy), and in more recent times, Ketuanan Islam (Muslim Supremacy), as its ideological core. After half a century of independence in the Malaysian federation, the indigenous non-Muslim *bumiputera* in both Sabah and Sarawak, who led their respective states at the time of independence, are politically marginalised, with little hope of getting back into power.

Sabah

The key political players in Sabah are the Muslim *bumiputera*, non-Muslim *bumiputera* (read Kadazandusun Murut, KDM) and Chinese community. The key to understanding Sabah politics is its changing demography. From 1970–2010, Sabah's population increased by 390 percent, making Sabah a Muslim-majority state by the early 1990s. This growth has completely changed the dynamics of Sabah politics.

The ten-year curse era

Locals often refer to the first three decades of Sabah politics as the 'ten-year curse' era. This moniker refers to a change in government in every decade.

From 1963–75, two men dominated Sabah politics: Mustapha Harun and Donald Stephens. Stephens, a Roman Catholic,[2] represented the KDM, the largest indigenous group in Sabah, while Mustapha represented the Muslims. When the Sabah Alliance formed the first post-independence state government, Stephens became chief minister and Mustapha became governor. Their political differences paralysed the state government and in 1965 the federal government intervened directly by appointing Stephens the federal minister for Sabah affairs, completely removing him from the state to Kuala Lumpur. Peter Lo was appointed interim chief minister until 1967, when Mustapha became chief minister. To ensure federal dominance of Sabah affairs, the federal government sent Syed Kechik, a peninsular Malay businessman with strong UMNO connections, to 'assist' Mustapha. Although Syed Kechik held no political post, he often ran the state when Mustapha was away (Ross-Larson 1976). Mustapha spent long periods overseas, often gambling (Hunter 1976).

This state of affairs lasted until 1975, when the federal government became increasingly alarmed by reports that Mustapha was contemplating Sabah's secession from the federation. Within a week a new political party, Bersatu Rakyat Jelata Sabah (Berjaya), had been established with federal help. Stephens was appointed party leader. In the April 1976 state election, Mustapha was decisively defeated and Stephens became the chief minister. Unfortunately, Stephens died in a plane crash a week later and Harris Salleh took his place (Raffaele 1986; Lim 2008).

Harris Salleh and his Berjaya government ruled Sabah from 1976 until 1985. In 1985, Joseph Pairin Kitingan, the *huguan siou* (paramount chief) of the KDM, formed Parti Bersatu Sabah (PBS or Sabah United Party). The KDM community were increasingly unhappy with the Harris Salleh state government. Salleh was accused of being 'too federal', especially when he transferred the sovereignty of Labuan Island, a small island off the west coast of Sabah, to Kuala Lumpur. Harris was also accused of trying to convert the KDM community to Islam and pursuing a policy of forced Islamisation, breaching a guarantee enshrined in the Twenty Points, constitutional safeguards under which Sabah and Sarawak agreed to join Malaysia in 1963, that all religions in Sabah would be protected.[3] He was also accused of discriminating against non-Muslim Sabahans in the civil service and working with the federal government to increase the Muslim population by way of Muslim migrants from Indonesia and the Southern Philippines.

In 1985, Harris Salleh called for a snap election, hoping to defeat the newly established PBS. To the surprise of many, PBS won twenty-five of the forty-eight seats in the state assembly. Immediately after PBS took power, a series of explosions rocked Kota Kinabalu, Sabah's capital. Muslim elements purportedly wanted to create chaos so that emergency rule could be imposed and PBS could be replaced by a Muslim-led government. At the same time, Kuala Lumpur was pressuring Pairin to form a 'unity government' with Muslim parties. Pairin, a Roman Catholic, refused and instead called a snap election in May 1986. This time the PBS increased its majority in the state assembly to thirty-five seats. Mahathir had little choice but to accept the new PBS administration, at least for the time being. Mahathir even allowed PBS to join the BN (Kahin 1992).

The tense relationship between the Muslim UMNO-led federal government and the Christian PBS-led state government was to fracture on the eve of the 1990 parliamentary election. A few days before polling, Pairin announced that PBS would leave the BN coalition and support Tengku Razaleigh Hamzah, Mahathir's political arch-rival. PBS said Razaleigh promised to review the Twenty Points if he should win the election. Unfortunately for PBS and Razaleigh, Mahathir's BN easily won the parliamentary election. Mahathir immediately announced that UMNO and other BN parties (hitherto confined to the peninsula) would move into Sabah to challenge PBS (Chin 1999). Jeffrey Kitingan, Pairin's younger brother and his political adviser, was detained under the Internal Security Act. In the 1994 Sabah state election, Kuala Lumpur mobilised all its massive resources to ensure a BN victory, but PBS won narrowly. PBS took twenty-five seats to BN's twenty-three. Before the state assembly could hold its first sitting, PBS had lost its slim majority when a dozen newly elected PBS Assemblymen defected to BN. The 'ten-year curse' persists, as PBS was in power from 1985–94 (Chin 1994).

Breaking the spell, 1994–2003

In the decade 1994–2003, Sabah was placed under what the BN called the 'rotation system': the post of chief minister rotated every two years among the three politically significant groups, the Christian KDM, the Muslim *bumiputera* and the Chinese (Table 7.1). UMNO calculated correctly that this provision was the easiest way to win support from the non-Muslims, for the time being. It is interesting to note that under the rotation system, the KDM was able to acquire the chief minister's office only once, and KDM Chief Minister Bernard Dompok served for only ten months, whereas both the Muslim and the Chinese communities were able to serve out their two-year terms. In 2002, after twelve years in opposition, PBS was readmitted into the BN, signalling its total capitulation. Pairin was made a deputy chief minister, but he had little or no power in the state administration. The Muslim-led UMNO state government was clearly in control.

Project IC and Muslim hegemony

On 27 March 2003, Musa Aman from UMNO was sworn in as Sabah's thirteenth chief minister. A year later, the rotation system was scrapped, apparently because, according to UMNO, Sabah was 'ungovernable' with the chief ministership changing every two years (*Malaysiakini* 2004). UMNO's Musa Aman has been in power since and the ten-year curse appears to have been finally broken by UMNO. As of 2014, BN has been in power for twenty years.

It is clear that opposition among the non-Muslims, especially the KDM community, to the scrapping of the rotation system will not make much of a difference, given the reality of electoral politics. By the late 1990s, Sabah's population and electoral system had dramatically changed, from a non-Muslim majority state to a Muslim-majority one. This process was effected via 'Project IC'. The origins and rationale for Project IC were simple. Throughout the 1980s and 1990s, the PBS-led KDM community caused political problems by challenging the Muslim-led UMNO federal government. By increasing the number of Muslims in Sabah, Kuala Lumpur could permanently alter the voting balance in the state. The Muslim population was allegedly increased by issuing Malaysian identity cards (ICs – hence the name,

Table 7.1 Chief ministers of Sabah under the rotation system

Name of chief minister	*Period*		*Party*
Sakaran Dandai, Salleh Said Keruak	March 17, 1994	May 28, 1996	BN–UMNO
Yong Teck Lee	May 28, 1996	May 28, 1998	BN–SAPP
Bernard Dompok	May 28, 1998	March 14, 1999	BN–UPKO
Osu Sukam	March 14, 1999	March 27, 2001	BN–UMNO
Chong Kah Kiat	March 27, 2001	March 27, 2003	BN–LDP

Source: Sabah Government website.

Table 7.2 Sabah: state constituencies by main voting groups

	1976	*%*	*2008*	*%*	*Change*
NMB[a]/KDM	22	45.8	13	21.6	−24.2
Muslim	18	37.5	36	60	+22.5
Chinese	8	16.6	6	10	−6.6
Mixed[b]	–		5	0.83	+0.83
Total	**48**	**100**	**60**	**100**	

Source: Chin (2012: 118).

Notes:

[a] NMB = Non-Muslim *bumiputera*.

[b] Mixed = Where no single ethnic group constitutes more than 50 percent of the voters.

'Project IC') to illegal Muslim migrants from the Southern Philippines and Indonesia Borneo. This process only could have been done by the federal government, since citizenship is a federal matter. A Royal Commission of Inquiry (RCI) in 2013–14 heard evidence of staff members in the National Registration Department in the federal Ministry of Home Affairs – directly under the control of then Prime Minister Mahathir, who was concurrently Home Minister – issuing Malaysian ICs to entire villages of illegal migrants. A special 'task-force' was even established to issue these ICs to Muslims (Sario 2013).[4] One witness, a civil servant who took part in the operation, bluntly told the RCI he saw it as his duty to ensure Muslim dominance (Murib 2013). A doctoral study in 2003 confirmed that there had been a systematic attempt to increase the number of Muslims in Sabah using migrants from the Southern Philippines and Indonesia (Sadiq 2003).

The net effect of these instant Sabahans has been a dramatic shift in electoral power among the three political groupings (Table 7.2). In 1976, before 'Project IC', there were only eighteen Muslim-majority seats (37.5 percent). In 2008, this share had gone up to thirty-six seats, or 60 percent of all state seats. This meant that if all the Muslims in Sabah supported UMNO, the party could win outright. In three decades, Muslims have become an absolute majority in terms of electoral politics. The Chinese, on the other hand, have seen their share of seats drop by about 7–10 percent. The KDM have suffered the most, as they saw their representation plunge from 45.8 percent of state seats to a mere 21.6 percent (Chin 2012). It is clear that Project IC was an unqualified success in eliminating the political threat from the KDM, or any non-Muslim grouping. Ketuanan Islam became an electoral reality.

Sarawak

Unlike Sabah politics, politics in Sarawak has been remarkably stable for over forty years. Essentially the state has been ruled by a single Melanau-Muslim family since 1970. In fact, the longest-serving chief minister in Malaysia is Taib Mahmud, Sarawak's chief minister for the past thirty-three years (1981–2014). He is easily Malaysia's most powerful state politician and probably the richest as well. The key political players in Sarawak are the Melanau-Muslim, the mainly Christian indigenous Dayak (Iban) and the Chinese community. Both the Melanau-Muslim and the Dayak are officially classified as *bumiputera*.

The Iban era

From 1963–70, both of Sarawak's chief ministers were Iban Christians. In 1966, the Sarawak Alliance government under Stephen Kalong Ningkan, from the Sarawak National Party (SNAP), fell as a direct result of federal government intervention. Ningkan had earlier ignored local Muslim political opposition over new legislation that would permit non-natives (read, Chinese) to buy land. Kuala Lumpur was sympathetic to these objections, as it wanted a Muslim-led state government. It was, moreover, unhappy with Ningkan over his strict interpretation of the Twenty Points in refusing to use the Malay national language and his not promoting more natives to replace expatriates in the civil service.

In May 1966, Ningkan's opponents had enough votes in the Council Negri (Sarawak legislative assembly) to unseat the chief minister. Kuala Lumpur then demanded Ningkan's resignation, citing his minority support in the Council Negri. Ningkan refused to resign and the federal government dispatched the federal minister of Home Affairs, the inspector general of police (IGP) and the federal attorney-general to convince the Sarawak governor to use his reserve powers to dismiss Ningkan and appoint a weak Iban politician, Tawi Sli, as chief minister. Instead of accepting his 'dismissal', Ningkan sought redress through the High Court, which found that he had been unconstitutionally replaced; the Court ruled that the governor did not have the power to remove a sitting chief minister until a proper no-confidence motion had been passed in the Council Negri.

Before Ningkan could be reinstated, Kuala Lumpur declared a state of emergency in Sarawak and amended the federal and Sarawak constitutions. The amendment gave the governor the power to call for a special sitting of the Council Negri; one was quickly convened and a vote of no confidence was passed, thus legally ending Ningkan's tenure as chief minister. Tawi Sli was reappointed chief minister, but real power lay with two Melanau-Muslim politicians with strong UMNO connections, Abdul Rahman Yakub and his nephew, Abdul Taib Mahmud from Parti Bumiputera. Rahman Yakub was the federal minister of education while Taib Mahmud was a state minister (Leigh 1973: 106).

The Melanau-Muslim era

After the July 1970 general elections, it was clear that no single party had a working majority; the Muslim-dominated Parti Bumiputera had twelve seats; the opposition Iban-based SNAP and Chinese-based SUPP also had twelve seats each; while the Iban-based Pesaka party had eight. Twenty-five seats in the forty-eight-seat Council Negri were needed to form a simple majority, so a coalition government was inevitable. Although SNAP and SUPP were much more compatible in terms of political outlook, SUPP decided to form a coalition government with Parti Bumiputera. The then deputy prime minister of Malaysia, Abdul Razak, made it clear that the federal government would not lift the state of emergency in Sarawak unless Parti Bumiputera were part of the state government. Parti Bumiputera's leader, Abdul Rahman Yakub, was a Melanu-Muslim. Rahman Yakub was to serve as chief minister from 1970 until 1981. Taib Mahmud, his nephew and hand-picked successor, then took over as chief minister (Chin U.H. 1996).

In 1987, the Iban-led Parti Bansa Dayak Sarawak (PBDS) tried to get rid of Taib Mahmud. It had the support Abdul Rahman Yakub, who turned against his nephew in a squabble over control of Sarawak's natural resources. PBDS, formed by a breakaway group from SNAP, claimed that it had majority support in the Council Negri and asked Taib to resign. Instead, Taib dissolved the Council Negri and called a snap election. In the campaign, PBDS claimed to be fighting for Dayakism and said it was time for an Iban to be a 'general' again, that is, to hold the chief minister's post. While there was strong Dayak support for PBDS, Muslim and Chinese voters decided to back Taib and he won the state elections narrowly. The Sarawak BN won twenty-eight out of forty-eight seats, then later received another eight assemblymen who defected from PBDS. PBDS remained in the opposition until it was readmitted into Sarawak BN in 1994 (J. Chin 1996).

The rise of Taib Mahmud

Since the Dayak-led 1987 putsch, the Dayak polity has been deliberately fractured to weaken it politically. In 2002, a SNAP breakaway group established the Sarawak Progressive Democratic Party (SPDP). Earlier in 2001, a power struggle had broken out in PBDS. Two years later, in 2003, the factions held separate party elections, resulting in PBDS's having two of everything, from two party presidents to two supreme councils. On 5 December 2003, PBDS was deregistered. One faction registered a new political party, Parti Rakyat Sarawak (PRS) (Chin 2004). Less than a decade later, in 2012, a power struggle in PRS led to the launch of a new political party, Sarawak Workers Party (SWP). All these parties – SNAP, PBDS, SPDP, PRS and SWP – seek to represent the Dayak community. With so many different parties seeking to represent them, Dayak political unity is impossible. Thus, mounting a challenge against the Melanau-Muslim government is almost impossible.

Besides political divisions in the Dayak community, there are three other key reasons why Taib has been able to maintain tight control over Sarawak: his massive wealth, his keeping UMNO out of Sarawak politics and consolidation of the Muslim vote.

Sarawak Report (www.sarawakreport.com), a website run out of London by journalist Clare Rewcastle Brown, a British investigative journalist, started in 2010 with the sole aim of exposing Taib Mahmud's corruption. Using documents from the Sarawak Land and Survey Department, Companies Commission of Malaysia and international NGOs, it has exposed massive land grabs by Taib's family and his family's extensive property holdings overseas. These properties, easily worth more than a billion dollars, are found in the US, Canada, Australia and the UK. In Sarawak, Taib's family are the majority shareholders of Cahya Mata Sarawak (CMS), a leading conglomerate listed on the Malaysian stock exchange, Bursa Malaysia (Aeria 2002). A Swiss NGO estimates that Taib's family is worth at least USD21 billion (BMF 2012). A court document filed by his daughter-in-law shows that just one of Taib's sons is worth more than a billion ringgit (Jong 2013). Global Witness, an international NGO based in London, produced a video, 'Inside Malaysia's Shadow State',[5] which shows how Taib's nieces tried to sell leases to plantation land worth millions to a foreign investor, openly declaring that 'cousin Taib' granted them the land's lease. Another part of the video shows a Chinese business associate claiming that Taib receives a share of the proceeds from the sale of the lease.

Wealth notwithstanding, it is highly unlikely that Taib would have been able to rule Sarawak as his personal fiefdom if UMNO were in Sarawak. Early on in his rule, he managed to reach a written agreement with then Prime Minister Mahathir, who was also UMNO president, that UMNO will not enter Sarawak so long as either is in power (Chin 2004a). This has meant that UMNO's key coalition partners in the peninsula, MCA and Gerakan, are absent from Sarawak, as well. Without UMNO, the Sarawak BN is highly autonomous. Taib's PBB plays the role locally that UMNO plays in the federal BN.

As in Sabah, one of the ways to consolidate Muslim control in Sarawak has been to increase the percentage of Muslim-majority seats in the state (Table 7.3). In 1969, a year before the

Table 7.3 Sarawak: state constituencies by main voting groups

	1969	*%*	*2008*	*%*	*Change*
Dayak	28	58.3	29	40.8	−18%
Muslim	12	25.0	27	38.0	+13%
Chinese	8	16.7	12	16.9	0%
Mixed	–	–	3	4.2	+4%
Total	**48**		**71**		

Source: Chin (2012: 112).

Rahman Yakub/Taib Mahmud Melanau family took control, Muslim-majority seats accounted for a quarter of the Council Negri. By 2008, this share had increased to 38 percent. The major losers were the Dayak community, whose share of state seats declined by 18 percent. Taib has also made sure that his PBB party has always been in a position to take power alone. In the two most recent state elections (2006 and 2011), PBB won thirty-five seats and needed just one defector to form the state government on its own.

The rise of East Malaysia

The 2008 general election was a game-changer for East Malaysia. In the 2008 general election, the BN lost its two-thirds majority in the 222-seat Malaysian parliament for the first time in half a century. The BN won 140 seats, to the opposition Pakatan Rakyat's 82. The same occurred in the 2013 general election. This time BN won 133 seats to Pakatan's 89. But the really important number is the number of members of parliament (MPs) Sabah and Sarawak BN contributed to the BN's national total.

East Malaysia provided fifty-five BN MPs in 2008 and forty-seven in 2013. In the 2013 general election, the BN margin of victory was twenty-one seats. Sarawak BN alone contributed twenty-five seats. In other words, without Sarawak BN, Najib and the federal BN would have lost power. In 2013, the forty-seven East Malaysian MPs made up 35 percent of all Barisan MPs. When Prime Minister Najib announced his post-election cabinet, more than twenty federal cabinet ministers and deputy ministers came from East Malaysia. The speaker of the Malaysian parliament and his two deputies were also from East Malaysia. Najib also declared an additional public holiday on 16 September as 'Malaysia Day', to commemorate the formation of Malaysia (Chin 2013). The rise of East Malaysia will have important implications for East Malaysian politics. With many Sabah and Sarawak MPs helming federal ministries, they will likely channel more federal development money to East Malaysia. More alarmingly, they will likely bring even more of the BN/UMNO style of politics to Sabah and Sarawak.

The BN/UMNO model

When the BN was established in 1973, it was clear that its aim was a government of national unity (Mauzy 1983). All parties, including all opposition parties, were invited to join the coalition. In fact, the leading opposition Islamic party, Parti Islam SeMalaysia (PAS), joined the BN before it was expelled in 1977. Only DAP refused to join the BN. From 1981 onwards, the coalition underwent significant changes to its internal dynamics. Mahathir, the newly elected UMNO president and prime minister, believed strongly in centralising power in the hands of the prime minister and UMNO (Hwang 2003). UMNO became the lynchpin of the BN and, in practice, UMNO was BN and BN was UMNO. The other component parties did not have any real power at the federal level. The unwritten norm of BN is 'Malay-first' in all government policies. In the past decade, Ketuanan Islam has also become an all-encompassing norm in the highest levels of government.

In Sabah and Sarawak, the Malays are minorities. Malays constitute about 10 percent of Sabah's population and about 20 percent in Sarawak. The BN/UMNO model was thus forced to compromise – in East Malaysia, it became a 'Muslims-first' model. UMNO was willing to accept a Muslim leader from East Malaysia, rather than insisting on a Malay leader. This was accepted easily because in the Malaysian constitution, a 'Malay' person is defined in cultural terms. Any person can be 'Malay' if he or she professes to be a Muslim, habitually speaks the Malay language, adheres to Malay customs and is domiciled in Malaysia or Singapore. Thus, although Taib is a Melanau in Sarawak, he can qualify as 'Malay'. Although Musa Aman comes from a mixed Pashtun–Dusun background, he, too, can be constitutionally defined as 'Malay' (Selvaraja 2012). Consequently, when one converts to Islam, the act is commonly referred to as *masuk Melayu* (becoming a Malay). This often means that the convert will have to ditch his or her cultural heritage and adopt Malay culture. Muslim converts can actually become 'Malay' in official documents and access the extensive government benefits given to the Malay community. It is a bureaucratic norm to register the children of Muslim converts as Malays at birth. One of the big fears among the KDM in Sabah and the Dayak in Sarawak is the loss of their cultural heritage as more and more indigenous peoples convert to Islam. This fear is not unfounded. In 2013, the mufti of Sabah, the highest Islamic official in the state, proposed a programme to '*meMelayukan*' (make Malay) all indigenous Sabahans (Zurairi 2013).

The BN/UMNO model of always backing a Muslim as chief minister of both states means that the largely non-Muslim KDM and Dayak population are automatically shut out of the chief minister's post, despite their status as the largest indigenous grouping in their respective states. It also means that the Christian population, made up largely of KDM and Dayak, are indirectly told that their Christian faith is a problem. This is best illustrated by the Kalimah Allah issue. In the 1980s, the federal government banned the use of the word 'Allah' and other Islamic terms by non-Muslims in Malaysia. Radical Islamic groups claimed that non-Muslims wanted to use the word 'Allah' to convert Muslims into Christians. In October 2013, the court of appeal ruled that the word 'Allah' is exclusive to Muslims in Malaysia. There was a strong reaction from the Christian community in East Malaysia because they have always used the word 'Allah' in their church service (conducted entirely in the local Dayak and Malay language). The KDM in Sabah and the Dayak in Sarawak are predominantly Christian. The issue of Ketuanan Islam will pose the major conflict between the Muslim and non-Muslim *bumiputera* of East Malaysia and Peninsular Malaysia in the coming years and will replace ethnicity as the main political divide in East Malaysia.

Conclusion

However little the peoples of peninsular Malaya and Borneo had in common in the colonial era, apart from British rule, Sabah and Sarawak experienced little ethnic or religious tension at the time. Since then, the UMNO-led federal government has intentionally tried to impose its BN-dominated framework, essentially an UMNO-led, Malay-first political system. This pattern can be seen in the direct federal intervention to ensure that the post of chief minister in both states has been held by Muslims. At the state level, Muslim leaders have worked to marginalise indigenous non-Muslim *bumiputera*. In Sabah, Project IC ensured that the largely Christian KDM lost their numerical majority. In Sarawak, the Dayak are hopelessly divided into a half-dozen political parties. The electoral system has also been used to ensure a Muslim majority in the state assembly. The Chinese community do not matter politically after fifty years of independence.

The largely non-indigenous KDM in Sabah and the Dayak in Sarawak are increasingly frustrated at their inability to stop or hinder the mirroring of UMNO-led BN power politics in East Malaysia. The KDM fought against the BN/UMNO model for most the 1980s and 1990s but they were defeated by 'instant' Sabahans. In neighbouring Sarawak, the Dayak tried in 1987, but failed, to unseat Taib Mahmud. Since then, they have been systematically divided into different political parties with little hope of coming together under a single party to mount a political challenge to the Muslims.

There is a sense that the non-Muslim indigenous peoples will never be able to assume political power under the BN/UMNO model. They are worried that Islam-first policies will lead to the destruction of their cultural heritage and divide the state along religious lines. The big fear among East Malaysians is that after half a century of federation, their entire socio-political environment is mirroring what is happening in Malaya. Prior to independence, East Malaysia had highly plural populations, with little or no religious tensions.

In reality, however, the boat has sailed. It is too late for the KDM and Dayak leadership to do anything substantial to slow the advance of Muslim hegemony in both states. The only difference between the domestic politics of Sabah and Sarawak is the presence of UMNO in Sabah politics. In Sarawak, it can be argued that while Taib has kept UMNO out, his style of kleptocracy is no better. Moreover, it is almost certain that UMNO will enter Sarawak now that Taib is retiring.

Change can happen only when BN/UMNO loses power at the federal level. Even then, there is no stopping the slow but steady march towards Islamisation of politics in Sabah and Sarawak.

Notes

1 Originally Brunei was to be included, but it pulled out at the last minute and only became independent in 1984.
2 He was later converted by Mustapha to Islam and became known as Muhammad Fuad Stephens. See Granville-Edge and Davadason 1999.
3 The main features of the 'Twenty Points' are:

   (a) Islam's status as a national religion was not applicable to Sarawak and Sabah.
   (b) Immigration control was vested in the state governments of Sabah and Sarawak.
   (c) Borneanisation of the civil service should proceed as quickly as possible.
   (d) No amendments or modification of the safeguards granted under the Twenty Points could be made by the federal government without the agreement of the Sabah and Sarawak state governments.
   (e) There would be no right to secede from the federation.
   (f) The indigenous peoples of both Sarawak and Sabah will be equal to the Malay community in Malaya.
   (g) Sabah and Sarawak were to be given a high degree of autonomy over their financial affairs.

4 Mahathir's involvement in the process led some to call the secret plan 'Project M' instead of 'Project IC'.
5 Global Witness, www.globalwitness.org/insideshadowstate/ (accessed 8 May 2014).

Bibliography

Aeria, Andrew Charles Bernard (2002) Politics, Business, the State and Development in Sarawak, 1970–2000, PhD Dissertation, London School of Economics and Political Science.

Bruno Manser Fund (BMF) (2012) *The Taib Timber Mafia: Facts and Figures on Politically Exposed Persons (PEPs) from Sarawak, Malaysia*, Basel: Bruno Manser Fund.

Chin, James (1994) 'Sabah state election of 1994: end of Kadazan unity', *Asian Survey: A Bimonthly Review of Contemporary Asian Affairs*, 34(10): 904–15

Chin, James (1996) 'PBDS and ethnicity in Sarawak politics', *Journal of Contemporary Asia*, 26(4): 512–26.

Chin, James (1999) 'Going east: UMNO's entry into Sabah politics', *Asian Journal of Political Science*, 7(1): 20–40.

Chin, James (2004a) 'Autonomy: politics in Sarawak', in Bridget Welsh (ed.), *Reflections: The Mahathir Years*, Washington DC: Johns Hopkins University Press, pp. 240–51.

Chin, James (2004b) 'The more things change, the more they remain the same', in Chin Kin Wah and Daljit Singh (eds), *South East Asian Affairs 2004*, Singapore: Institute of Southeast Asian Studies.

Chin, James (2012) 'Forced to the periphery: recent Chinese politics in East Malaysia', in Leo Suryadinata and Lee Hock Guan (eds), *Malaysian Chinese: Recent Developments and Prospects*, Singapore: Institute of Southeast Asian Studies, pp. 109–24.

Chin, James (2013) 'East Malaysia rising in political power', *The Straits Times*, 29 May.

Chin Ung Ho (1996) *Chinese Politics in Sarawak: A Study of the Sarawak United People's Party (SUPP)*, Kuala Lumpur: Oxford University Press.

Fonds, Bruno Manser (2012) *The Taib Timber Mafia: Facts and Figures on Politically Exposed Persons from Sarawak, Malaysia*, Basel: BMF.

Granville-Edge, P.J. and Rajen Davadason (1999) *The Sabahan: The Life & Death of Tun Fuad Stephens*, Family of the Late Tun Fuad Stephens.

Hunter, Ed (1976) *Misdeeds of Tun Mustapha: A Brief History of the Dictatorial Rule of Tun Mustapha Under the Guiding Hand of Datuk Syed Kechik, 1967–1976*, Hong Kong: Ed Hunter Enterprises.

Hwang In-Won (2003) *Personalized Politics: The Malaysian State under Mahathir*, Singapore: Institute of Southeast Asian Studies.

Jong, Rita (2013) 'Taib's son has more than RM2 billion in various bank accounts, says ex-wife', *The Malaysian Insider*, 2 September.

Kahin, Audrey R. (1992) 'Crisis on the periphery: the rift between Kuala Lumpur and Sabah', *Pacific Affairs*, 65(1): 30–49.

Leigh, Michael (1973) *The Rising Moon*, Sydney: Sydney University Press.

Lim, Regina (2008) *Federal–State Relations in Sabah, Malaysia: The Berjaya Administration, 1976–85*, Singapore: Institute of Southeast Asian Studies.

Malaysiakini (2004) 'Rotation system for Sabah CM scrapped', *Malaysiakini*, 27 March.

Mauzy, Diane K. (1983) *Barisan Nasional: Coalition Government in Malaysia*, Kuala Lumpur: Marican & Sons.

Murib Morpi (2013) 'PBS government side-lined Muslim natives, claims Hassnar', *The Borneo Post*, 17 August.

Raffaele, Paul (1986) *Harris Salleh of Sabah*, Kota Kinabalu: Condor.

Ross-Larson, Bruce Clifford (1976) *The Politics of Federalism: Syed Kechik in East Malaysia*, Singapore: Ross-Larson.

Sadiq, Kamal (2003) Redefining Citizenship: Illegal Immigrants as Voters in India and Malaysia, PhD Dissertation, University of Chicago.

Sario, Ruben (2013) '"Secret" taskforce entrusted from 1970s with issuing ICs to Sabah immigrants, Anwar tells RCI', *The Star*, 19 September.

Selvaraja Somiah (2012) 'The politics in Sabah: Aman Brothers Inc and the Suluk Filipinos', *The Star*, 12 April.

Zurairi, A.R. (2013) 'Citing unity, mufti wants Sabah's Bumiputera Muslims made Malay', *The Malay Mail Online*, 28 September.

8

Local government in urban Malaysia

Goh Ban Lee

Like most countries, Malaysia has three levels of government, namely the federal government, state governments, and local governments or local authorities. Unlike most democratic countries, only the first two tiers are elected. Local authorities in Malaysia are not elected by the people.

This chapter is an account of the unique system of urban governance in Malaysia. The chapter begins with a brief description of the roles of the federal and state governments in local government, the types and number of local authorities and their diminishing roles. It next describes the appointments of mayors or presidents and councillors and the roles of the local authorities. The chapter then discusses the effectiveness of the local authorities and the areas that need improvement.

Roles of the federal government and state governments

The Local Government Act (LGA) 1976 (Malaysia 1976a), the most important document in the workings of local governments, was passed by the federal government. So were other important laws, including the Town and Country Planning Act 1976 (Malaysia 1976b), the Street, Building and Drainage Act 1974 and the Uniform Building By-laws 1984. The East Malaysian states of Sabah and Sarawak have their own local government legislation. For Sabah, the relevant law is the Local Government Ordinance 1961 (Sabah No. 11 of 1991) and for Sarawak, it is the Law of Sarawak Chapter 20 Local Authority Ordinance 1996.

The highest body involved in local government matters is the National Council for Local Government (NCLG). Its role is to facilitate consultation between the federal government and the state governments and among state governments themselves in matters related to local government. Although the chairman can be any minister in the federal government, in practice the post is traditionally held by the deputy prime minister. Its members are made up of a maximum of ten ministers and the eleven menteri besar, or chief ministers, in Peninsular Malaysia. Although the number of ministers is one less than those representing the state governments, the federal government is still in control of the NCLG. The chairman is in control of the agenda. More importantly, he or she has the right to vote and also casts a vote in case of stalemate. Sarawak and Sabah are not members of NCLG, but they can send observers to its meetings. The Malaysian Constitution states that if Sabah and Sarawak become full members of the body, the number of federal ministers in the council will also increase by two.

There is a Ministry of Urban Wellbeing, Housing and Local Government (MUHLG) in the federal government and, within it, a Local Government Department. Both the ministry and the department play little direct role in the workings of the local authorities; however, they do provide grants to local authorities for special projects. The ministry also routinely gives annual grants to local authorities equivalent to the amount the federal government would have to pay if federal buildings were to be rated and the owners were required to pay, just as every property owner has to do. Also, the federal government has an important role in the number and grades of local government officers as it pays their pensions.

The federal government has direct control over three federal territories, namely Kuala Lumpur, Putrajaya and Labuan. Kuala Lumpur is the biggest city in the country and the hub of commercial, cultural and social activities. Putrajaya is the administrative centre of the federal government, while Labuan, which is located off the coast of Sabah, is an off-shore financial centre.

Although Malaysia is a federation of states, the state governments have very limited roles. One of the very few matters in which they have significant roles is local government. State governments play the main role in the creation of local authorities and the appointment of mayors or council presidents, councillors and municipal secretaries. The laws also enable state governments to pass policies which must be followed by local authorities. All by-laws passed by the local authorities and their annual budgets have to be approved by the respective state government. The same provision applies to the sale of land and renaming of roads.

Every state government has a state executive councillor in charge of local government. As the LGA and other acts related to local government make no mention of the role of state executive councillors in charge of local government, their role in the workings of the local council largely depends on their ability, knowledge and commitment. Their relationship with fellow members of the state executive council, especially the menteri besar or chief minister, is also crucial.

State governments have wide power over the development policies of the local authorities. For instance, the Town and Country Planning Act, which empowers the local authorities to undertake development control measures, also allows the State Planning Committee (SPC) to pass development policies that must be followed by local authorities. The SPC is chaired by the menteri besar or chief minister, with members of the state executive council and senior state officers as members.

Apart from appointing mayors or presidents and councillors, the menteri besar or chief ministers have a very limited direct role in the workings of local authorities. The only specific instance where they have a direct role is when there is a deadlock between the councillors and the presidents or mayors. In such an instance, the matter can be taken to the menteri besar or chief minister. His or her decision is final.

Number and types of local authorities

There are 150 local authorities in Malaysia, made up of nine city councils, three city halls, forty municipal councils and ninety-eight district councils. The numbers do not include the bodies that govern Putrajaya, the administrative centre of Malaysia, and Labuan, an island off Sabah. Malaysian local authorities cover very large areas, with many having jurisdiction over areas of more than 500 square kilometres. For example, Seberang Perai Municipal Council covers about 740 square kilometres.

There are official guidelines for the elevation of district councils to municipal councils and of municipal councils to city councils or city halls. Elevation from municipal council to city council or city hall requires the consent of the king, with the support of the federal government. However, the guidelines have not been strictly followed.

There is a difference between city councils and city halls. The former have mayors and councillors while the latter have only mayors. The city halls are Kuala Lumpur, Kota Kinabalu and Kuching North. They have advisers, but the mayor need not follow their advice.

Roles and responsibilities of local authorities

Generally, local authorities manage public spaces, regulate the preparation and sale of food, operate wet markets, control sanitation, regulate activities that may cause public nuisances and control the pollution level of streams. The law also enables the local authorities to manage cemeteries that do not belong to associations or religious bodies. Local authorities are given the responsibility and power to make local plans and control town planning and land development projects. They also manage free trade zones. In order to carry out their roles, the local authorities have the power to pass by-laws.

Unlike the federal government and state governments, local authorities are not sovereign bodies. They are infra-sovereign entities, meaning that they are created by their respective state governments in consultation with the minister of wellbeing, housing and local government. As such, they can be mutated or even dissolved.

A common misconception of local authorities is that they can do anything they choose. They cannot. They do not have 'general competence', meaning that they can only do things that they are legally allowed to do. Doing things that are not specifically provided for by law can render the actions null and void. This restriction is in contrast to the situation in the Scandinavian countries, where local authorities can do everything except those items that are specifically excluded.

It is also wrong for state governments to treat the local authorities as if they were their own departments. Local authorities are not departments of state government. As a result, it is wrong for menteri besar or chief ministers or state executive councillors in charge of local government to direct local authorities to carry out certain activities or to refrain from taking action against illegal activities. Making things worse, municipal presidents or mayors and councillors seem to believe that they must follow the instructions of state government leaders.

The blurring of the line between the power of state governments vis-à-vis that of local authorities is largely the result of the abolition of local government elections. As local councillors and presidents or mayors are appointed by the state governments, there is a tendency to treat state government leaders as their superior officers.

Diminishing roles

The role of local authorities has been diminishing over time. For example, from 1957 to the 1960s, apart from the responsibilities that local authorities have today, George Town City Council was also in charge of fire brigades, public transportation, mother and child clinics, piped water supply and sewage. It also ran public buses and provided electricity for Penang Island. These activities have been taken away from the Penang Island Municipal Council, which covers the territories under the jurisdictions of George Town City Council and the Penang Island District Council.

In fact, the federal government has continued to take over roles that were traditionally carried out by local authorities. In most states, solid waste management has been taken over by Solid Waste Management Corporation, an agency of the federal government. The Penang state government has resisted the federal government's taking over solid waste management. Its two municipalities continue to manage the disposal of solid wastes. Following the change of the Selangor state government in 2008, local authorities in this state have also terminated the services of the consortium engaged by Solid Waste Management Corporation. Today, solid waste management in Selangor is the responsibility of individual local councils.

The role of the councils in development control has also diminished. From 1976 to the 1980s, local authorities prepared and implemented both local plans and structure plans. Today, the State Town and Country Planning Department, under the supervision of the State Planning Committee (SPC), has taken over the preparation and implementation of structure plans.

The roles of local councillors in development control have also been reduced. Until 2008, the approval of applications to undertake land development was the responsibility of the Town Planning and Development Committee, which was made up of the municipal president and thirteen or fourteen councillors. The power to approve applications to undertake land development has been taken from this committee. It was placed under the One Stop Centre (OSC) in 2008. There are only four councillors in the OSC. Although the chairman is still the president of the council, the committee members are largely made up of technical officers from the council, state departments and federal departments.

In 2010, Pemandu, the organisation created by the federal government to design and implement 'transformation programmes', introduced a 'New Economic Model'. Among other things, it calls for the devolution of roles to the local authorities. But nothing concrete has been done so far.

Mayors and councillors

The heads of city councils or city halls are addressed as 'mayors', while those of municipal councils or district councils are termed 'presidents'. Mayors or presidents of local authorities in each state are appointed by the state government. The laws governing local government do not require any minimum academic qualifications to become mayors or presidents. In practice, they are appointed from among senior government officers. There have been cases in which politicians have been appointed mayors or presidents, but such appointments are rare.

The LGA allows the state government to appoint a maximum of twenty-four councillors. According to Section 10 of the Act,

> Councillors of the local authority shall be appointed from amongst persons the majority of whom shall be persons ordinarily resident in the local authority area who, in the opinion of the State Authority, have wide experience in local government affairs or who have achieved distinction in any profession, commerce or industry, or are otherwise capable of representing the interests of their communities in the local authority area.
>
> *(Malaysia 1976a)*

The requirements are so general that almost anyone, unless he or she is a convicted felon or bankrupt, is eligible to be appointed. Most local councillors have a minimum of nine years of schooling. Many have university degrees and professional qualifications.

Most councillors are members of the political parties that form the state government. For instance, in Penang, which is under the control of Pakatan Rakyat (PR), the councillors in the two municipal councils are from its component parties, namely DAP, PKR and PAS. In Perak, which is controlled by Barisan Nasional (BN), the councillors are from UMNO, MCA, MIC, Gerakan and PPP, the BN's component parties.

The tendency to appoint ruling party members was foreseen as early as the 1960s. The Royal Commission of Enquiry to investigate into the Workings of Local Authorities in West Malaysia, better known as the Athi Nahappan Commission of Enquiry, predicted that there would always be a tendency to appoint people who were politically connected. As the Commission warned,

> Even if there were legal provisions governing the principle of nomination, it is common knowledge that the Government of the day usually favours and appoints its own party members or supporters and not always the best persons available. The legal provisions are often conveniently circumvented by the appointing authority. Nomination therefore is a much abused system.
>
> *(Athi Nahappan 1968: 99)*

Although the law allows the state government to appoint a councillor for a term of three years, in practice the tenure of councillors is one to two years. Many councillors are reappointed. There have been councillors who serve for more than ten years. The Selangor State Government has decided that the maximum length of service of councillors will be two two-year terms.

Performance of local authorities

It is very difficult to judge whether a government is very good, good, bad or very bad. It is easier if the performance of the local authorities is compared with those of others in the region or the world. As a general rule, the living conditions in Malaysian cities and towns are better than in most urban areas of developing countries. One only has to visit the towns and cities of the Philippines, Vietnam or Indonesia to realise that things could be much worse. Malaysian urban areas are also more liveable than those in India and China.

According to the ECA International Quality of Living study, which is used to assist multinational corporations to establish expatriate allowances to compensate staff for difficulties in adapting to living in their assigned locations, Asian expatriates have consistently ranked George Town and Kuala Lumpur relatively high among Asian cities in terms of the quality of living. In the 2012 ranking, George Town was ranked eighth while Kuala Lumpur was ranked tenth, with Singapore ranked number one among Asian cities.

However, considering the economic status of the country, the quality of life in Malaysian towns and cities should be better than what it is today. Many towns and cities have traffic jams, flash floods, squatter settlements and poorly maintained apartment complexes. In many instances, pleasant neighbourhoods have been allowed to deteriorate due to incompatible development or illegal changes of land use and building use. Lately, there has been a growing fear that the towns and cities are not safe, with daily reports of snatch thefts, robberies and even murders. The fear of crime has led to the rapid growth of gated communities, especially in the Klang Valley. Making things worse, residents of normal residential areas have installed gates in their housing enclaves, thus causing problems of access to nearby residents and visitors from other towns and cities.

The road to better quality of urban life

For Malaysian towns and cities to be attractive places, they must be safe, efficient and pleasant. They must be clean and have well-maintained parks, squares and marketplaces. The built environment must have human-scale architecture and mixed land use for shops, houses, outdoor cafes and space for community festivals to promote civic engagement. The towns and cities must be equipped with efficient telecommunication services and good public transportation with safe and efficient pedestrian walkways and bicycle paths. The bigger towns and cities must have heritage sites, museums and art galleries, convention halls, iconic built environments, and facilities for sports, fine arts and cultural activities.

Safe cities do not mean more gated communities. Safety comes from proper arrangement of the built environment, augmented by effective urban management. 'Fixing Broken Windows' (Kelling and Coles 1995) should be the mantra of urban management in the local authorities.

Managing Malaysian towns and cities is no walk in the park, in view of the diversity of Malaysia's interest groups, rapid urbanisation and shortage of funds. The situation is made worse because many Malaysians are afflicted with the malaise of a 'Third World mentality'. Too many cannot be bothered about the consequences of their actions, such as discarding rubbish indiscriminately or parking their cars anywhere they like. No local council, no matter how committed its leaders are, can make their cities pleasant and efficient under such conditions (Goh 2002).

Yet while many urban problems are caused by the people, the local authorities should also share the blame. The general consensus is that the performance of the local authorities can and should be improved.

Good urban governance

Accountability

One of the main weaknesses of Malaysian local authorities is the lack of accountability. The councillors and mayors or presidents are not elected by the people. As appointees, they are not representatives of the people. As pointed out by the Athi Nahappan Commission,

> Nominated advisers cannot effectively voice the interests of the ratepayers because they are not answerable to them. Nomination is no real substitute for elective representation. If anything, nomination is an anachronism and a relic of colonialism. It is antithetic to democracy.
>
> *(Athi Nahappan 1968: 99)*

What the report warned of has come to pass.

In states that are governed by Barisan Nasional (BN), the councillors are appointed from amongst its component parties. As a general rule, UMNO members dominate the councils. In the district councils, government officers are routinely appointed councillors. In Selangor, Penang and Kelantan, where the state governments are under the Pakatan Rakyat (PR), most of the councillors are also members of the component parties ruling those states, with only a small number of representatives from non-governmental organisations.

The lack of accountability is also caused by poor documentation of the workings of local authorities. Minutes of meetings are not kept verbatim. Only decisions or resolutions are recorded, without proper recording of the reasons for the approvals or rejections.

The lack of written records on enforcement work also leads to lack of accountability on the part of those responsible for enforcing the law. It is usually not possible to ascertain the person or persons responsible when an illegal hawker is allowed to continue for years, for instance. The agent responsible could be the area inspector, director of the licensing department, municipal secretary, municipal president, a member of the state executive council or even the chief minister or menteri besar.

All acts of non-compliance with rules and standards must be recorded. Enforcement officers, such as field inspectors, must report all cases of non-compliance. These must be brought to the attention of the officers' superiors and documented. If follow-up action is not taken, the reasons must also be recorded. All cases of interference in enforcement actions must be recorded, including the names of the persons who interfere. The annual report of each department must contain all cases of non-compliance. The names of those who interfere in the workings of a department must also be stated. The heads of departments should be responsible for explaining why actions have not been taken.

Transparency

The workings of the local councils are too opaque. Part of the blame lies in the LGA. Only full council meetings are open to the public. Most meetings are classified as committee meetings and therefore not accessible to the public. Almost all important issues are discussed and debated in closed meetings and the decisions of the committee meetings are endorsed in the full council meetings. As a result, rate-payers have very little idea of the workings of the local authorities and the justifications for certain policies and actions.

Making things worse, some local authorities have made it difficult for members of the public to attend full council meetings. In some local councils, rate-payers are required to obtain permission from the municipal secretary. The Subang Jaya Municipal Council once adopted this practice, during the days when Selangor was ruled by the BN.

Local government issues involve matters of everyday life, such as cleanliness, parking, wet markets, food handling and development control. There is no need for secrecy in the decision-making process in local councils. However, as there may be occasions when potentially emotional issues, such as the erection of religious buildings, are on the agenda, the council should have the power to pass a resolution to hold certain meetings behind closed doors.

The OSC meetings, which decide on applications by developers to undertake land development, should be open to the public and the mass media. Development projects should not be treated as national secrets that need to be decided in closed-door meetings. As new development projects can change the character of neighbourhoods, the process of approving or rejecting a project should be public knowledge. Both the developers and people whose welfare might be affected by development projects should be allowed to be present when the councillors and officers make decisions.

All procurements of goods and services should be transparent. Justification for tender decisions must be made public by displaying them on notice boards and on websites.

Rule of law

Acts of non-compliance are ubiquitous. These include littering and indiscriminate disposal of waste, illegal change of land or building use, illegal extensions to houses, illegal parking and illegal hawking. A sizeable number of Malaysians see no wrong in parking their cars in prohibited places or discarding solid waste into the drains. Despite the establishment of the Malaysian Integrity Institute, the 'Third World mentality' syndrome is still abundantly evident.

The main reason for numerous acts of non-compliance is the inability or unwillingness of the local councils to enforce the law. A detailed discussion on this topic has been given in *Non-compliance – A Neglected Agenda in Urban Governance* (Goh 2002). It is sufficient to reiterate that the lack of action against the culprits is due to inadequate enforcement manpower, cumbersome processes in enforcement actions and corruption among officers. The biggest obstacle to enforcement by the local councils is interference by politicians, especially by state assemblymen and members of parliament.

Local councils must enforce all laws and gazetted development plans. Heads of department must be held accountable for non-enforcement. They, in turn, must hold their subordinate officers accountable for their actions or non-action in cases of non-compliance. Interference from the higher-ups must be put on record.

Efforts to enforce compliance with the law must be preceded by an exercise to ensure that all rules and regulations in the book are updated and can be complied with without huge sacrifices. This is especially important when there is great disparity of income within society, since most laws and standards cater to the middle-income earners and the dominant socio-cultural groups. There is legitimacy in the concept of 'weapons of the weak' when the poor and the disenfranchised break the law in order to have a stake in the towns and cities.

Reviewing and restructuring local authorities

It has been about forty years since the present system of local government was established. The country has undergone tremendous changes, economically and spatially. The population has increased considerably. More significantly, there has been an influx of population to the towns and cities. The demand for factories, shops and houses has increased tremendously. Furthermore, as Malaysians become richer, they generate more waste. As a result, there is a demand for better governance in the local authorities.

A review of local government administration in Malaysia is long overdue. An important area that needs review is the size of the local authorities. There is a need to scale down the geographical size of the councils while ensuring that each will be able to sustain itself. At present, many local authorities are too big to allow good urban governance. As a result, councillors and senior officers are not familiar with their towns and villages. They have to depend on complaints from affected residents. It is useful to note that in the 1950s and 1960s, there were 390 local authorities in Peninsular Malaysia (Athi Nahappan 1968: 21).

The responsibilities of the local authorities should also be reviewed. Compared with the elected state governments, local councils have more responsibilities. This is why state leaders interfere in the workings of the local councils. The presidents or mayors of the local authorities have been made the Commissioners of Building following the enactment of the Building and Common Properties (Maintenance and Management) Act 2007. This was and still is a mistake. The heads of local authorities already have their hands full implementing the Local Government Act and other responsibilities, including development control.

Local government elections

There is a serious need to bring back local government elections. Although elected local councils by themselves do not necessarily lead to efficiency and effectiveness, it is a fact that all reputable liveable cities have elected local governments. Elected councillors and mayors or presidents are more accountable to the rate-payers than are appointed ones.

As a matter of principle, government leaders in democratic societies are elected by the people. The councillors and mayors or presidents should be elected. Besides, since the local councils collect taxes in the form of assessment rates, the people who decide how the money is to be spent must be elected on the principle of 'no taxation without representation'.

Local government elections will also ensure that the councillors and mayors or presidents are known to the rate-payers. They not only have to tell the voters their positions on issues such as wet markets, hillside development and hawkers, but also advertise themselves during election campaigns. The present system makes it difficult to meet the mayors or presidents of local authorities. Being government servants, they do not have service centres. There is no doubt that if the mayors or presidents were elected, they would be more accessible because they would have service centres, which would be open at convenient hours for the rate-payers.

An elected local council would also give the councillors and mayors or presidents a sense of power in their own right. Accordingly, they would not tolerate interference from members of parliament or state assemblymen, including those who are state executive councillors.

Conclusion

Seen in the context of Asian cities, Malaysian towns and cities are in enviable positions. But it is fair to say that the quality of life in these towns and cities has not been getting better, even though most Malaysians have become financially richer in the last few decades.

Local authorities play very important roles in the quality of life. But their performance has not been successful. There is a serious and urgent need to improve the workings of the local authorities. Bringing back local elections is an important step. But it is also important to improve urban governance.

Bibliography

Anthony, James (1971) Urban Politics in Malaysia – A Study of Kuala Lumpur, PhD dissertation, Australian National University.

Athi Nahappan (1968) *Report of the Royal Commission of Inquiry to Investigate into the Workings of Local Authorities in West Malaysia*, Kuala Lumpur: Penchetak Kerajaan.

City Council of George Town (1966) *Penang – Past and Present, 1786–1963*, Penang: City Council of George Town.

Goh Ban Lee (2002) *Non-compliance – A Neglected Agenda in Urban Governance*, Skudai: Institut Sultan Iskandar.

Goh Ban Lee (2005) 'The demise of local government elections and urban politics', in Mavis Puthucheary and Norani Othman (eds), *Elections and Democracy in Malaysia*, Bangi: Penerbit Universiti Kebangsaan Malaysia.

Goh Ban Lee (2007) *Counselling Local Councils*, Petaling Jaya: FOMCA.

Goh Ban Lee (2012) 'Governance and accountability in Southeast Asian cities', in Yap Kioe Sheng and Moe Thuzar (eds), *Urbanisation in Southeast Asia – Issues and Impacts*, Singapore: Institute of Southeast Asian Studies.

Kelling, George L. and Catherine M. Coles (1996) *Fixing Broken Windows: Restoring Order and Reducing Crime in our Communities*, New York: Touchstone.

Lim Kit Siang (1978) *Time Bombs in Malaysia*, Petaling Jaya: Democratic Action Party.

Malaysia (1974) *Street, Drainage and Building Act*, Kuala Lumpur: Di-Chetak oleh Penshetak Kerajaan.

Malaysia (1976a) *Local Government Act (Act 171)*, Kuala Lumpur: Ketua Pengarah Percetakan.

Malaysia (1976b) *Town and Country Planning Act (Act 172)*, Kuala Lumpur: Ketua Pengarah Percetakan.

Mohamed Afandi (1989) 'Local government restructuring in Peninsular Malaysia: a review of the local authority function and capacity', *Planning and Administration*, 16(2).

Norris, Malcolm W. (1980) *Local Government in Peninsular Malaysia*, Farnborough: Gower.

Tennant, Paul (1973a) 'The abolition of elective local government in Penang', *Journal of Southeast Asian Studies*, 4(1): 72–87.

Tennant, Paul (1973b) 'The decline of elective local government in Malaysia', *Asian Survey*, 13(4): 347–65.

UNESCAP (n.d.) *Country Paper: Malaysia, in Local Government in Asia and the Pacific, A Comparative Study*, Bangkok: United Nations Economic and Social Commission for Asia and the Pacific.

9

Public administration in Malaysia

Origins, influence and assessment

Norma Mansor and Raja Noriza Raja Ariffin

The public administration's primary function is to execute government policies at all levels (federal, state and local) of the nation's administration. Malaysia's public administration has its origins in the British colonial administration. The history and the socio-political makeup of the country have shaped its public administration since Malaysia gained independence in 1957, although reforms have been made to institutions, procedures and work processes to accommodate new roles and functions. The neoliberal stance of international lending institutions, such as the International Monetary Fund and the World Bank, influenced thinking especially in the 1980s and had an impact on reforms made in the Malaysian public bureaucracy. Nevertheless, as stipulated in the Federal Constitution, public administration very much embodies the history, culture and religion of the country.

Two earlier authors succinctly described the nature of its character. Tilman (1964a) argued that contemporary Malayan bureaucracy must be viewed as a product of the total Malayan environment, for its development has been influenced by the culture, history and politics of Hinduism and Islamic, colonial and independent Malaya. And the work of Puthucheary (1978) clearly describes the post-independence bureaucracy, which she argues is paradoxically highly professional, without any political interference in its recruitment, but so culturally embedded that it is a microcosm of the Malaysian society at large.

The purpose of this chapter is to review some of the key developments of public administration in Malaysia and to contrast these with key values in public administration. Malaysia's public administration will be analysed against successive theories of public administration, namely the colonial bureaucratic model, development administration and institution building, and particularly the advent of a neoliberal stance toward government administration via new public management (NPM), including how some elements of NPM have been incorporated into the Malaysian public administration. Issues arising from public debates on public administration and the Malaysian bureaucracy over the last four decades will be explored, highlighting some of the reforms made in response to changes in the political landscape, citizens' expectations and public opinions, especially as the arrival of information technology in recent years has enabled a more vociferous public opinion.

Definition of scope

Public administration refers to government institutions performing public service. In Malaysia, the public service as defined in Article 132 of the Federal Constitution includes the entire government administration – essentially, the federal and state general public service, the joint public services, the education service, the health service, the police force, the judiciary and the legal service and the armed forces.

For the purpose of this chapter, however, the Malaysian public administration, or the bureaucracy, refers to the general federal, state and local administration. The size of personnel in this group in 2013 was 455,587, representing about 32 percent of Malaysian public sector employment of 1.4 million (PSD 2013). Derivatives of the Malayan Civil Service organised by British administrators, who then made major decisions in the administration of the colony (Puthucheary 1978), the administrative and diplomatic services remain dominant until today.

History and development

Theories of public administration suggest that Malaysian public administration can be divided into four main trajectories. We adapt Haque's (2007) typology of the stages of bureaucratic development, as well as Esman (1967) and North (1984, 1992), with some modifications, to suggest that the development of the Malaysian public administration has gone through four phases. These can be broadly described as: (1) a traditional bureaucratic model during the colonial period; (2) development administration and institution building during the postcolonial era (development administration was more pronounced from the 1970s into the early 1980s); (3) new public management (NPM) in the mid-1980s; and (4) a second phase of institution building after 2010.

Western Weberian bureaucracy

When the British arrived in Malaya, there was a system of government, the Malay Sultanate, which operated with a simple hierarchical framework, in some states right down to the village level (Mansor 1980). The Sultan collected revenue and taxes in exchange for protection. The system was based on lineage and kinship and typically ascriptive in nature. The legal system, too, was based on customary law. To secure British strategic economic interests in the region – linking the two big economies of Asia, China and India – a western style of administration was introduced, beginning with the Straits Settlements and continuing with the Federated Malay States and the Unfederated Malay States. The Colonial Office appointed the best men to represent British interests in the colony, performing both political and administrative roles (Puthucheary 1978).

The colonies were administered based on a similar strategy to that which brought about economic development in the United Kingdom and Western Europe: reliance on the free market economy. Suffice it to say that the colonial power was less interested in development goals than in maintaining law and order at the lowest cost possible and in ensuring a balanced, and as low as possible, budget. Under no circumstances could a budget deficit be tolerated.

The immediate post-independence bureaucracy continued on the same principles. The earliest significant event in the history of the post-independence Malaysian administration was the Malayanisation of the bureaucracy, which began in 1956 and was fully completed by 1965. The bureaucracy was organised per the Weberian doctrine of legal-rational administration, however, with very clear, prescribed rules and procedures, hierarchical authority structures, merit-based appointment, and a formal nature to holding office, very much separated from personal life. The neutrality of the service was maintained and the service was highly regarded as being very competent and technically efficient. This was made possible by the establishment of a separate entity for selection and recruitment, the Public Service Commission (PSC), and management of the personnel in the civil service by the Public Service Department. This structure has been maintained until today. Hence, at the time of independence, relative to the political and private institutions, the civil service was the most developed institution.

Development administration and institution building

A decade on after independence, whilst Malaysia, like many developing countries, started to embark on the developmental model path (Haque 2007), it was also working on strengthening institutions, including rules and procedures (North 1984, 1992), and establishing organisations to support a new role of the public bureaucracy as a change agent (Esman 1967). Institution building is described as adopting a process or strategy that helps practitioners to introduce change (Esman 1967).

The political slogan of nationalism for independence was replaced by the demands of socio-economic progress and nation building. Ethnic tension that erupted in violence on 13 May 1969 led the government to rethink and to redesign its past policies. Distribution became a goal, with growth targets written in the Second Malaysia Plan: 'a state has been reached in the nation's economic and social development where greater emphasis must be placed on social integration and more equitable distribution of income and opportunities for national unity and progress' (EPU 1971: 1).

The New Economic Policy (NEP, 1970–90) was a departure from past policies in that the government played a more active role in the economy, especially in distributive functions. The strategy of development through industrialisation, urbanisation and agricultural development, together with the spread of education and the general political awakening of the population, all lent added momentum to the new functions of the government. The new goals of the government thus expanded, and grew more diverse and complex in nature – or as Gayl Ness wrote, 'The goals of the Malaysian Government changed from custody to development' (Ness 1967).

The government's approach changed from a laissez-faire economy to a mixed one, with central planning, whilst local entrepreneurs, the indigenous financial sector and foreign industrial concerns still played major roles in the economy. Ness best described the system's characteristics when he wrote:

1. There was a change from an emphasis on a balanced budget to an emphasis on an expanding economy.
2. There was a change from an unstated emphasis on urban development, or development for the modern sector, to a stated and actual emphasis on rural development [the contentious disparity between the five urban cities and other parts of the country], or development largely for the uplift of the Malays in the traditional sector.
3. Social services, especially education, moved from a position of low priority to one of high priority, and were partially redefined as elements of investment rather than consumption.
4. There was an increased demand for, and finally the creation of, new organizations competent to plan for and stimulate the development of the economy.

(Ness 1967: 89–90)

This period also witnessed the proliferation of public enterprises in the main sectors of the economy. The role of the administration fundamentally changed from that of an administrator to a change agent. Certain elements in the Weberian structure became a hindrance to that new role. Friedrich (1952) argued that at least six elements had to be altered: centralisation of control and supervision; differentiation of functions; qualifications for office; objectivity; behaviour, including precision and continuity; and secrecy or discretion. The bureaucratic structure was conducive towards efficiency in general but towards inefficiency in specific cases. This feature seemed to inhibit the Malaysian Civil Service because the majority of top administrators had the tendency to inhibit change and there seemed to be no room for the development of innovational tendencies among the top administrators (Tilman 1964a).

The then deputy prime minister, who was also the minister of rural development, realised that the institutions to support development planning and implementation were inherently inappropriate within the existing structure. New planning and implementation approaches for the Malaysian public bureaucracy had their origins in the new state's first development plan. In the first Malaya Plan (1956–60), about 50 percent of the money spent on roads and bridges, utilities, telecommunications and social services was spent on the rural sector. Thus, approximately half of every five-year plan was allocated to rural development. The effective utilisation of rural funds, however, faced some structural problems within the federal framework. Poor coordination between the federal government and the state governments slowed down the process for a majority of the development projects.

Faced with these structural problems after that first development plan, the government had two alternatives. First, it could conceivably change the structure of government and create a unitary state, so that massive economic development programmes could be rushed through from the centre, without interference from local or provincial authorities. Alternatively – and this was the path the government chose – it could utilise the structure and personnel of the existing bureaucracy, within the existing political framework, and make marginal improvements in the system with the hope that these improvements would, in due course, have some effect on the civil service.

The new development administration technique was introduced in the early 1960s. The approach essentially used four main mechanisms aimed at standardising and decentralising at the local level or the district level: the committee room, the operations room, Rural Economic Development (RED) book plans, and the briefing method and field inspections.

(a) Committee system: The committee system followed closely the pattern of war executive committees and started with the implementation of the Second Malaysia Plan. A directive was issued to streamline and strengthen the basic structure of development administration. In accordance with this directive, a National Action Council and National Security Council were established. Both these councils are under the chairmanship of the prime minister himself. A new unit was also established in the Prime Minister's Department to serve as secretariat, particularly for the National Action Council. The committee is chaired by the minister for national and rural development at the national level. And to ensure participation at the lowest level, village committees were also set up, each chaired by the village headman, who was elected, as were the representatives in the committee.
(b) Operations rooms: All heads of departments at the state level were required to attend meetings of state action and development committees six times a month, while at the district level, heads of departments had to attend at least twelve meetings a month held at the operations room, tracking development progress in the area.

(c) RED book plans: It was during the period of the Second Malaya Plan that the government began to realise the need for active participation of the people as an integral part of the plan itself. In the previous plan, the economic secretariat compiled projects submitted by the various ministries and departments. Its goals tended to be long-term objectives, such as raising the level of productivity, increasing employment opportunities or eradicating poverty. With this new plan, it needed to provide for the involvement of the people not only at the implementation level, but also at the stage of planning and policy formulation, so that the best interests of the people could be fulfilled. The RED book system was aimed at gathering ideas from the people and consolidating them in respect of planning for development and coordinating development at the village, district, state and national levels, as well as reviewing the progress of implementation, based on quick and direct feedback from the people. It was through the RED book system and development committees at all levels that development planning and programme formulation ceased to be a concern merely of government, but became also that of the people as a whole. This method ceased to be utilised after the mid-1960s.
(d) Briefing method and field inspections: Briefings of the National Development Committee are held monthly at the National Operations Room, where the minister for national and rural development meets all the heads of ministries and public corporations, together with advisers from the Economic Planning Unit, the Treasury and from his own ministry. At the briefing, the ministry is kept informed of progress, identifies problems, finds solutions and in general effects greater coordination.

Government leaders felt that that despite these improvements to the existing structure of the Malaysian Civil Service, however, the administration was still caught up with administrative barriers in the form of organisational and structural obstacles, not to mention the 'silo mentality' mentioned by Razak as among 'the deadly sins of bureaucracy'. Hence in 1965, a team of professors led by Professors Montgomery and Esman was invited to assess the Malaysian Civil Service. The Montgomery–Esman report, named after the two American professors, was accepted by the government and led to the establishment of the Development Administration Unit (DAU) in the Prime Minister's Department, with specific terms of reference. The proposal was comprehensive, covering the planning, budgeting and financial management system of the federal government; personnel management and the civil service system at the federal level; organisation structures and management methods pertaining to government ministries and operating agencies; and the land and local government administration at the state level. The DAU undertook several studies and introduced a number of reforms under the concept of development administration within its terms of reference. In later years, however, lack of support from central agencies and capacity limitations prevented the unit from making more inroads in the area of administrative reform. The unit later evolved into the Implementation Coordination and Development Administration Unit (ICDAU) in 1972, and five years later, became the present Malaysian Administrative and Modernisation and Manpower Planning (MAMPU).

During this period, existing institutions were strengthened and several new institutions were added to improve development planning and implementation. The planning function of the public bureaucracy started with the long-term plan called the Outline Perspective Plan (OPP) and the five-year development plans. This approach was coordinated at the highest level by a National Development Planning Committee (NDPC) chaired by the chief secretary to the government.

New public management

New public management entails the adoption of private sector principles in public bureaucracy. Disillusionment with government, fear of government encroaching onto the daily lives of citizens, and a perceived threat to free markets gave rise to new thinking in public administration. Ideologically influenced by neoliberal economics, the private business model started to gain traction in public administration. Its mantras were rolling back the public sector, 'lean and mean' organisation and being customer-focused. Though the NPM paradigm started in Western countries like the United States, UK, Canada and Australia, the ideas were adopted by many developing countries, including Malaysia.

The period of expansion of the developmental state with the implementation of Malaysia's New Economic Policy (NEP; see Hwok-Aun Lee, this volume) from 1970–90, particularly with the proliferation of public enterprises financed through external borrowings, contributed to a twin deficit problem of the 1980s. Malaysia had both a government budget deficit and a current account deficit due to heavy government investments in unproductive infrastructure projects and public investment in heavy industries through public enterprises; the need to pay for large imports caused an imbalance in the current account. With the global oil crisis, the Malaysian economy experienced an unprecedented recession in 1985.

Malaysia had voluntarily undertaken structural adjustment by privatising public enterprises and by making rules and regulations under the NEP more flexible. A technocrat in his approach to administration, Dr Mahathir Mohamad, the fourth prime minister, embraced NPM. Public bureaucracy reform was essentially geared towards the development of an efficient and professional managerial administration. Unlike his predecessors, he had no civil service background, hence he had no attachment to the bureaucratic, rule-bound model of administration. Among his early initiatives were the introduction of manuals of work procedures and desk files which aimed to improve work systems and procedures, and quality control circles (QCCs), which focused on efforts to enhance productivity in public sector agencies. The adoption of internationally recognised ISO 9000 standards and total quality management (TQM), as well as a client charter and various client-oriented counter service measures, was seen as part of a programme to improve the quality of the public service. The Malaysia Incorporated Policy and the Look East Policy were to change the orientation of the British legacy of a detached civil service (the regulator) from the private sector (the regulatee). This shift also led to the formation of the Malaysian Business Council, which was later replaced by the National Economic Action Council (NEAC).

Mahathir's successor as prime minister, Abdullah Ahmad Badawi, continued these efforts when he established PEMUDAH (Pasukan Petugas Khas Pemudahcara Perniagaan, Special Task Force to Facilitate Business). Reporting directly to the prime minister, the team comprised representatives from the private and public sectors, co-chaired by the secretary to the government and the president of the federation of Malaysian manufacturers. With regard to conducting business, the public bureaucracy showed positive results, as shown in Figure 9.1, which displays government effectiveness as surveyed by the World Bank, measuring governance.

These efforts to improve performance, however, were not conceived of as part of overall institutional reforms instituted to serve the nation. Some rules and procedures, especially at the local authority level, dated back to pre-independence days. Numerous permits and licences introduced under the NEP were not reviewed. A report by the World Bank on doing business (2005) suggests that Malaysia took the most number of days in the region – 143 days – to register a property. Cumbersome rules and procedures did not help, as Malaysia was faced with growing competition from other emerging investment destinations. Figure 9.2

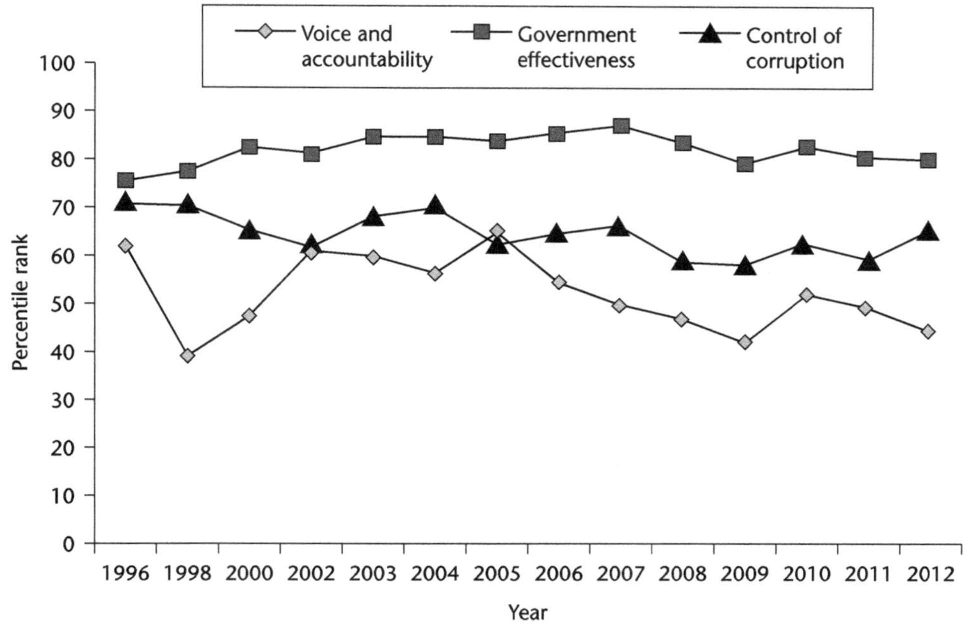

Figure 9.1 Voice and accountability, government effectiveness and control of corruption, 1996–2012

Source: Adapted from World Bank (n.d.).

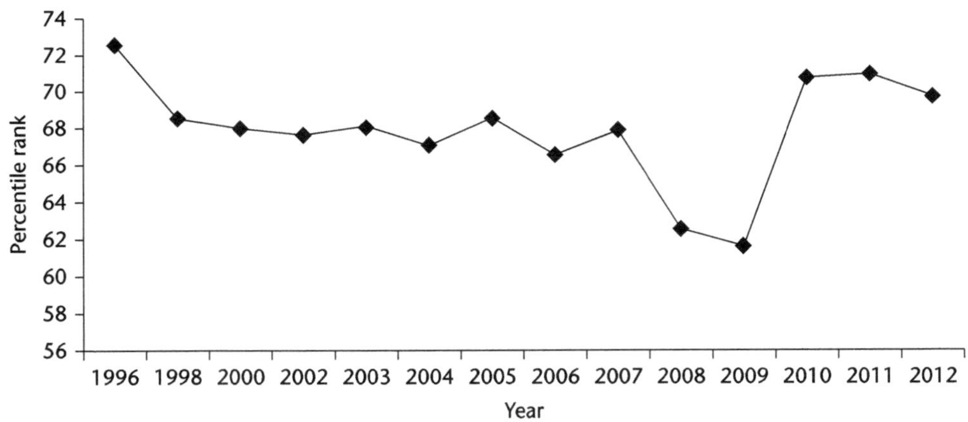

Figure 9.2 Regulatory quality in Malaysia, 1996–2012

Source: World Bank (n.d.).

depicts performance over the years in quality of regulation. The survey aimed at measuring investors' perception of the government's ability to create an eco-system for investment, such as policies and regulations that permit and promote private sector development (World Bank 2009). After the 1997 Asian financial crisis, a factor often cited as one of the obstacles for private investment was the array of and procedures. As shown by the survey, perceptions had not improved a decade post-crisis. The existence of the Official Secrets Act (OSA) 1972, as well as cumbersome and numerous licences and permits, led to red tape and abuse of power. If the perception of corruption index of public officials by Transparency International (2005) was any indication, Malaysia fared very poorly, at about 5–5.28 for the ten years 1995–2005 (ratings are 1: low through 10: high). Also as shown in Figure 9.1, perceptions on corruption did not show much improvement.

The reforms of the NPM period did not address the rigid structure of the civil service. That structure is based on the 1967 Suffian Salaries Commission, which strictly defined grades and promotion based purely on seniority. The 1992 New Remuneration System (NRS) applied some revisions to grades and salaries by simplifying the grades into two: managerial and professional and a support group. The NRS's attempts at strengthening the promotion system to be based on performance did not, however, improve the situation, as there was no clarity in criteria, hence managers often tended to fall back on seniority. Perceptions of slow promotion and relatively less attractive compensation packages (compared with the private sector and alternatives abroad) during good economic conditions (1987–97) made the civil service less attractive. Therefore, the civil service was not able to attract the best talent.

The Malaysian economy was buoyant and GDP growth peaked at 9.7 percent for the period 1987–97. In mid-1997, the Asian region was struck by the Asian financial crisis. As a measure to address and overcome this financial crisis, the government established an advisory council, known as the National Economic Action Council (NEAC), on 7 January 1998. The NEAC's recommendations had three prongs: (1) strengthen government delivery systems with regard to licences; (2) redesign the government's interface with the public, based on clear rules and transparent procedures; and (3) improve the quality of information and data available to the government.

In terms of this last domain, there have been some improvements in the process of administration largely enabled by the digital wave of information and communications technology (ICT). E-government was one of seven flagships under the aegis of Malaysia's Multimedia Super Corridor (MSC) project, established in 1996 as a primary vehicle for the infusion of ideas and research in ICT and multimedia. The e-Procurement system, Electronic Budget Planning and Control System (e-SPKB), e-Land system and Project Management System II (SPPII) gained momentum. One achievement worth mentioning, however, is the introduction of assigning a single reference number for dealings between individuals and government agencies through the MyID initiative.

To overcome cumbersome bureaucratic red tape and reduce burdens on potential investors, one-stop centres were established to handle all clearances and queries. Under this programme, all necessary services pertaining to issuance of licences and permits were to be provided from a single point. The improvements achieved are reflected in the ease of doing business survey in Figure 9.3. Institutions continued to work in silos, however; what Razak highlighted in the 1970s as one of 'the deadly sins of the bureaucracy' is still prevalent today.

Second wave of institution building

After the ruling party, the National Front, suffered an unprecedented loss of its two-thirds majority in parliament, Najib Tun Razak, Malaysia's sixth prime minister, was forced to re-evaluate the role of the state in the economy. He established a matrix structure in his administration by forming a project management office reporting directly to him, known as the Performance Management Delivery Unit (PEMANDU). To spearhead his ideas on reforms he started the Government Transformation Programme (GTP), which continued the reform of the public bureaucracy by measuring outcomes or indicators through key performance indicators. At the launch of his New Economic Model (NEM) in 2010, he remarked, 'gone were the days when the government knows best' (Razak 2010) and asserted the government's intent to be inclusive in policy-making.

The NEM, which covers a ten-year period, proposes eight structural, cross-cutting reforms. At its core is an effort to re-engineer public institutions to enable Malaysia to grow to the next level of development. Malaysia had created good institutions, including rules and regulations, to implement the development policies of the 1970s and 1980s, but some of these institutions are dated and have become obstacles to new innovation and ideas. The relevance of central agencies needs to be reassessed. Also, there are overlapping functions among some of the public institutions which require rationalisation. The NEM calls for a re-examination of the relationship among the functions of federal, state and local government. Outdated and cumbersome rules, procedures and regulations are to be simplified.

The government has started implementing the NEM with regard to rules and regulations. The Malaysian Productivity Council (MPC) has started to work with several states and the local authorities within those states to streamline rules, regulations and permits. The Ministry of Finance, for instance, is working on rationalising its numerous treasury circulars and replacing them with one all-encompassing circular. This has augured well with investors, as shown in Figure 9.2, which shows investors' positive sentiment towards the quality of regulations in Malaysia with the introduction of the NEM.

ICT has enabled the government to improve service delivery. A Business Process Re-engineering (BPR) Manual was started in 1991 and further improved in 1993. The concept of BPR fundamentally shifted the approach, thinking and structure of work processes towards a more pragmatic framework. Each work procedure was scrutinised under the BPR initiative to reduce redundancies and overlap, while adopting a clear governance structure to ensure effective execution and compliance. Based on intensive BPR initiatives, eighty-two public agencies, in consultation with MAMPU, have transformed the number of work processes from an initial 932 to a newly re-engineered 545. Another success of BPR was to expedite business licensing processes via a Business Licensing Electronic Support System (BLESS).

Businesses can access eight ministries involved with thirty-nine types of business licence. This portal, BLESS, has been visited by more than 265,000 visitors since its inception and has assisted almost 7,000 users. In 2011, 599 businesses were registered via BLESS. This number doubled to 1,201 in 2012 and in 2013, 5,112 businesses were registered in the first half of the year alone. Figure 9.3 shows improvement in assessments of the ease of doing business post-NEM.

As noted above, improving access to good-quality data and information was identified as one of the three core strategies to improve the public sector after the 1997 crisis. One very important set of data is on poverty. A National Poverty Databank termed eKasih was developed in mid-2000. Eradication of extreme poverty was highlighted as a goal in the Ninth Malaysia Plan (2005–10). To facilitate this effort, eKasih served as a single database for everything from individual profiles, to assistance rendered to households, to new applications. Redundancies and overlapping functions were reduced through the existence of a single comprehensive database. The database should enable the government to map and monitor welfare support. As of mid-2013, eKasih included 442,000 entries, with the greatest results thus far in Sarawak.

Year	2006	2007	2008	2009	2010	2011	2012	2013
Malaysia	21	25	25	21	23	21	18	12

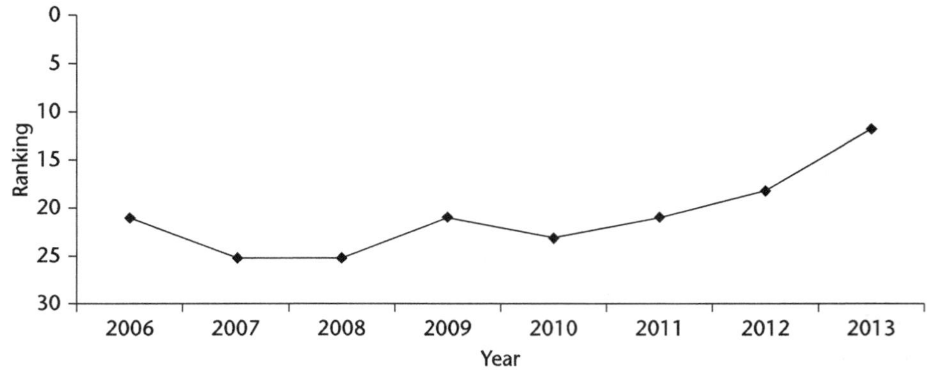

Figure 9.3 Ease of doing business, 2006–13
Source: World Bank (various years).

Malaysian public bureaucracy has over the years lost the representative character of a public bureaucracy. Part of that shift is due to the decade of rapid growth from 1987 to 1997, when the best and the brightest of new graduates chose to work in the private sector. This was true for all ethnic groups, but especially among ethnic Chinese and Indians. Relatively less attractive remuneration packages and slow career development in the public sector were among the reasons given for young people's avoiding public sector employment. In 2002, the Malaysian Remunerations System (MRS) was adopted, salaries were revised and regular performance assessment was strengthened; however, these efforts did not meet with much success. Najib further strengthened the recruitment process for the public service by establishing a search committee led by the Public Service Commission as well as a joint committee led by the Public Service Department. The search committee is responsible for assisting the government in the recruitment of human resource specialists into the Public Service Commission, to address the quality of hired civil servants. Specialist service commissioners are expected to institutionalise better selection criteria, to attract the best into the service from all ethnic groups, genders and regions. The programme started only in 2012; it is too soon to gauge its success. Attempts have been made to bring talent at higher levels to the civil service, too, but there have been too few cases thus far.

Whilst the ease of doing business has improved, much more has to be done with public institutions. As suggested by institutional economists such as North (1992), good institutions reduce transaction costs. The problem with developing countries is that these institutions, or the software of development, are still lacking. Notwithstanding other factors affecting transaction costs in Malaysia (Schwab 2013), the inefficient bureaucracy and corruption are still quoted as two main problematic areas for doing business (Table 9.1).

Strengthening some of Malaysia's planning and implementation institutions would help to address some of these problems. Reviving the National Development Planning Committee (NDPC), where projects were thoroughly discussed at the highest level of the bureaucracy, would avoid the approval of projects on an ad hoc basis. Development projects could be

Table 9.1 Inefficient government bureaucracy and corruption, 2010–13

Year	*Inefficient government bureaucracy (%)*	*Corruption (%)*
2010	13.0	8.0
2011	12.9	9.6
2012	13.8	12.7
2013	14.7	14.4

Source: Schwab (2013).

scrutinised before reaching the cabinet. With the full implementation of the Outcome Based Budget (OBB), different ministries' projects could be viewed in a more holistic manner.

The OBB has been implemented in five main ministries at the pilot stage. The OBB is to address the weak linkages among policy formulations, the budgeting process, project implementation and evaluation. The move towards outcome-based planning, implementation and monitoring was initially featured in the Ninth Malaysia Plan (2005–10). The OBB will integrate both development and operating expenditures towards achieving efficient allocation of resources and effective implementation of programmes. Programmes that involve more than one ministry or agency can now be strategically linked through the OBB process. Outcomes will be identified through the alignment of a series of key result areas. Outcomes will be measured against key performance indicators to evaluate the effectiveness of programmes and projects implemented by ministries and agencies. The OBB approach aims to eliminate redundancies and ensure value for money, while providing flexibility to review programmes and projects that do not contribute to expected outcomes. The OBB is expected to streamline and integrate the planning, implementation, monitoring and evaluation of policies and programmes to be more outcome-based.

Conclusion

Public administration is at the core of any government, therefore it contributes to the quality of a government – the way a government discharges its functions. Malaysia started well with developing good public institutions after independence. Institutions mirror society and its history, but after many decades, there had been no effort to rationalise institutions to adapt to new changes in society. What Malaysia did was borrow good practices from outside, without trying to make fundamental changes, especially to the structure of public administration. Prime Minister Mahathir embraced NPM by focusing on the professionalism of the public administration. A matrix structure was created to include new players in policy-making. Engagement and consultation were further diversified by the establishment of numerous private think-tanks where policy issues were discussed. The private sector and business gained dominance during the NPM era.

Having said that, to change an institution that is culturally embedded is a mammoth task. Public bureaucracy tends to reproduce its values, especially within a closed system like Malaysia. Promotion from within further isolates the bureaucracy from new ideas. The relative success of the second wave of institution building under the comprehensive transformation agenda is too early to assess. It will need a strong political will on the part of the government to develop Malaysia's public bureaucracy to become responsive, accountable and effective.

Bibliography

Abdullah Sanusi Ahmad, Norma Mansor and Abdul Kuddus Ahmad (2003) *The Malaysian Bureaucracy: Four Decades of Development*, Petaling Jaya, Selangor: Pearson Prentice Hall.

Brewer, Gene A., Yujing Choi and Richard M. Walker (2007) 'Accountability, corruption and government effectiveness in Asia: an exploration of World Bank governance indicators', *International Public Management Review*, 8(2): 200–19, available at www3.imp.unisg.ch/org/idt/ipmr.nsf/ac4c1079924cf935c1256c76004ba1a6/fa561face1283fe2c1257380004ff8f6/$FILE/Brewer.Choi.Walker_IPMR_Volume%208_Issue%202.pdf (accessed 8 May 2014).

Economic Planning Unit (EPU) (1971) *The Second Malaysia Plan 1971–1975*, Kuala Lumpur: Government Press, Prime Minister's Department.

Esman, Milton J. (1967) *The Institution Building Concepts, an Interim Appraisal*. Inter-University Research Program in Institution Building, Pittsburgh: University of Pittsburgh, Graduate School of Public and International Affairs, available at http://pdf.usaid.gov/pdf_docs/PNAAD226.pdf (accessed 8 May 2014).

Friedrich, Carl J. (1952) 'Some observations on Weber's analysis of bureaucracy', in Robert K. Merton *et al.* (eds), *Reader in Bureaucracy*, New York: Free Press, pp. 27–33.

Global Development Network (2013) *Varieties of Governance: Effective Public Service Delivery*, available at www.gdn.int/admin/uploads/editor/files/GDN%20Governance%20Concept%20Note.pdf (accessed 14 October 2013).

Haque, M. Shamsul (2007) 'Theory and practice of public administration in Southeast Asia: traditions, directions, and impacts', *International Journal of Public Administration*, 30(12–14): 1297–326.

Kambayashi, Ryo (2013) 'The role of public employment services in a developing country: the case of Japan in the twentieth century', *PRIMCED Discussion Paper Series No. 40*, Institute of Economic Research, Hitotsubashi University, available at http://hermes-ir.lib.hit-u.ac.jp/rs/bitstream/10086/25645/1/No40-dp.pdf (accessed 8 May 2014).

Mansor, Norma (1980) Kelantan State Civil Service, undergraduate graduation exercise, University of Malaya.

Mansor, Norma (2013) 'Making reform happen in Malaysia: overview', *The Proceedings of 2013 MRH Policy Workshop of KRI@UNSW and CID@KDI*, Siem Reap.

Matsuura, Miki, Joanna Watkins and William Dorotinsky (2010) *Overview of Public Sector Performance Assessment Processes in Japan*, Washington DC: World Bank, available at https://openknowledge.worldbank.org/handle/10986/10477 (accessed 8 May 2014).

Milne, R.S. and Diane K. Mauzy (1978) *Governments and Politics in Malaysia*, Singapore: Federal Publications.

Najib Tun Razak (2010) Speech at the launch of the New Economic Model (NEM) at Invest Malaysia, Kuala Lumpur, 30–31 March.

Nakamura, Etsuhiro (2013) 'Governance reform in Japanese local governments', available at www.cpsa-acsp.ca/papers–2013/Nakamura.pdf (accessed 8 May 2014).

National Economic Action Council (NEAC) (2010) *New Economic Model for Malaysia Part 1*, Kuala Lumpur: Percetakan Nasional Malaysia Berhad.

Ness, Gayl D. (1967) *Bureaucracy and Rural Development in Malaysia*, Berkeley and Los Angeles: University of California Press.

Noore Alam Siddiquee (2006) 'Public management reform in Malaysia: recent initiatives and experiences', *International Journal of Public Sector Management*, 19(4): 339–58.

North, Douglass C. (1984) 'Transaction costs, institutions, and economic history', *Zeitschrift für die gesamte Staatswissenschaft* [*Journal of Institutional and Theoretical Economics*], 140(1): 7–17.

North, Douglass C. (1992) *Transaction Costs, Institutions, and Economic Performance*, San Francisco: International Centre for Economic Growth.

Public Service Department (PSD) (2011) *Annual Report*, Putrajaya: Public Service Department.

Public Service Department (PSD) (2013) *Status of Education of Public Bureaucracy*, Putrajaya: Public Service Department.

Puthucheary, Mavis (1978) *The Politics of Administration: The Malaysian Experience*, Kuala Lumpur: Oxford University Press.

Rajkumar, Andrew Sunil and Vinaya Swaroop (2008) 'Public spending and outcomes: does governance matter?', *Journal of Development Economics*, 86: 96–111, available at http://www.unicef.org/socialpolicy/files/Public_spending_and_outcomes_governance.pdf (accessed 8 May 2014).

Santiso, Carlos (2001) 'Good governance and aid effectiveness: the World Bank and conditionality', *The Georgetown Public Policy Review*, 7(1): 1–22, available at www.sti.ch/fileadmin/user_upload/Pdfs/swap/swap108.pdf (accessed 8 May 2014).
Schwab, Klaus (2010) *The Global Competitiveness Report 2010–2011*, Geneva: World Economic Forum.
Schwab, Klaus (2011) *The Global Competitiveness Report 2011–2012*, Geneva: World Economic Forum.
Schwab, Klaus (2012) *The Global Competitiveness Report 2012–2013*, Geneva: World Economic Forum.
Schwab, Klaus (2013) *The Global Competitiveness Report 2013–2014*, Geneva: World Economic Forum.
Simon-Davies, Joanne (2010) *How Many Are Employed in the Commonwealth Public Sector?*, Statistics and Mapping Section, Department of Parliamentary Services, Parliament of Australia, available at http://parlinfo.aph.gov.au/parlInfo/download/library/prspub/388683/upload_binary/388683.pdf (accessed 8 May 2014).
Siti Nabiha Abdul Khalid (2008) 'New public management in Malaysia: in search of an efficient and effective service delivery', *International Journal of Management Studies*, 15: 69–90.
Tilman, Robert O. (1964a) *Bureaucratic Transition in Malaya*, Durham: Duke University Press.
Tilman, Robert O. (1964b) *Incentives to Encourage Private Sectors Mentioned Earlier: Bureaucratic Transition in Malaya*, Durham: Duke University Press.
Transparency International (2005) *Corruption Perceptions Index 2005*, Berlin: Transparency International.
World Bank (2005) *Doing Business in 2005: Removing Obstacles to Growth*, Washington DC: World Bank, The International Finance Corporation and Oxford University Press.
World Bank (2009) *Doing Business 2010: Reforming through Difficult Times*, Washington DC: World Bank, IFC and Palgrave Macmillan.
World Bank (2013) *Indicators*, available at http://data.worldbank.org/indicator (accessed 21 August 2013).
World Bank (n.d.) 'Country data report for Malaysia, 1996–2012', *Worldwide Governance Indicators*, available at http://info.worldbank.org/governance/wgi/pdf/c155.pdf (accessed 21 August 2013).

10

Social movements in contemporary Malaysia

The cases of BERSIH, HINDRAF and Perkasa

Anantha Raman Govindasamy

The emergence of civil society movements like Gabungan Pilihanraya Bersih dan Adil (BERSIH, Coalition for Clean and Fair Elections), Hindu Rights Action Force (HINDRAF) and Pertubuhan Pribumi Perkasa Malaysia (Perkasa, Malaysian Indigenous Empowerment Organisation) has been among the fundamental forces behind a changing political landscape in Malaysia. In breaking away from past traditions, these movements have brought about new, vibrant, politically engaged activism, often 'confrontational' with the state and radical in achieving its objectives. The emergence of these movements has also created a sense of political awareness that has successfully mobilised Malaysians. Although these movements are deeply rooted in issues of ethnic discontent (in particular HINDRAF and Perkasa), BERSIH's successful multi-ethnic mobilisation has set a promising precedent in Malaysian politics. In fact, had it not been for BERSIH and HINDRAF rallies, it would arguably have been impossible for the Malaysian opposition political parties to gain a more secure foothold in Malaysian politics. On the other hand, Perkasa has showcased Malay race-supremacy debates more openly than ever.

Past studies have indicated that social movement activism in Malaysia is very ethnic-oriented and hence has failed to influence political outcomes. As a matter of fact, the nature of social movement advocacy is mainly related to the welfare of ethnic or religious groups. For instance, various Islamic *dakwah* movements emerged in the late 1960s and 1970s, like Angkatan Belia Islam Malaysia (ABIM, Malaysian Islamic Youth Movement), which promoted and supported Islamic revivalism in Malaysia (Kessler 1983: 8). Tan (1997) notes that Chinese educationist movements such as Dongjiaozong have fiercely defended the right to Chinese mother-tongue education in Malaysia since the 1950s. To stop such advocacy efforts, the government used legislative enactments, including the Universities and University College (Amendment) Act 1975, to crush Muslim students' activism, and detained many leaders, for promoting Chinese mother-tongue education in the 1980s (Collins 2006).

As Weiss and Saliha (2003) note, the *reformasi* movement which was created in the late 1990s, right after the sacking of then Deputy Prime Minister Anwar Ibrahim, can be considered as a turning point in Malaysia's politically related civil society activism. In a study on the *reformasi* movement's failure, Brown (2004) argues that in an ethnically divided society like Malaysia, differences between ethnic groups have blocked effective mobilisation of social movements. His observation was based on Malay-Muslim domination of the *reformasi* movement. He further notes that the slippage between a multi-ethnic civil society and the ethnic bases of movement mobilisation in Malaysia has hampered the emergence of an effective opposition to the state in Malaysia (Brown 2004: iv).

By analysing the activism of BERSIH, HINDRAF and Perkasa, this study argues that in contemporary Malaysia, while ethnic issues are still central, BERSIH's advocacy suggests greater potential for effective, multi-ethnic social movements in Malaysian politics, particularly since 2008. In tracing such changes, the first section of this chapter focuses on BERSIH's multi-ethnic mobilisation, the second section primarily focuses on HINDRAF's working-class Indians' rally, and the third section explores Perkasa's Malay supremacy in Malaysian politics. The chapter concludes by considering these social movements' meaning and implications for Malaysian politics and civil society.

BERSIH's multi-ethnic mobilisation

BERSIH is an electoral reform movement which became a household name in Malaysia in late 2000. It was officially launched on 23 November 2006. Prior to that, BERSIH was a small joint action committee that pushed for meaningful electoral reforms in Malaysia, supported by more than eighty non-governmental organisations (Tan 2011: 2–3). In 2010, BERSIH was relaunched as BERSIH 2.0 and came under the multi-ethnic co-leadership of Ambiga Sreenevasan (former Malaysian Bar Council President) and A. Samad Said (Malaysian National Laureate). Since its formation, BERSIH has mobilised Malaysians irrespective of race, religion or political affiliation. BERSIH also has global solidarity movements, or international chapters, which have been supported by the Malaysian diaspora in at least nine countries. Though BERSIH maintains its stance as non-partisan, its prime backers are the three main Malaysian opposition political parties – Pan-Malaysian Islamic party (PAS), Parti Keadilan Rakyat (PKR) and Democratic Action Party (DAP), which together form the Pakatan Rakyat. In fact, it can be argued that without Pakatan Rakyat, BERSIH's success at multi-ethnic mobilisation for various rallies would have been highly questionable.

Pakatan Rakyat's support for BERSIH activism is due to their common understanding that the Malaysian electoral system is highly corrupted. That such issues have become a serious impediment to Malaysian democracy and that Barisan Nasional's corrupt electoral practice has denied the opposition advancement in Malaysian politics have prompted the coming together of both Pakatan Rakyat and BERSIH. In fact, the impetus for the creation of BERSIH was the 2004 Malaysian general elections. SUARAM, an NGO, oversaw those elections and later noted that vote buying, phantom voters, multiple voting, rampant abuse of postal votes and prevention of equal access to media and coverage of political parties have been the main hurdles preventing free and fair elections in the country (Lim 2011). In addition, Loh (2004) notes that the very independence of the Malaysian Election Commission can be questioned, as there is a growing perception that the Election Commission is highly influenced by the government. He further argues that the ruling Barisan Nasional's landslide victory in 2004 was the outcome of amendments to the Election Act and Election Offences Act in April 2002, which had reduced the Election Commission's autonomy, as well as the redrawing of election boundaries. Both were an advantage to the ruling Barisan Nasional in the 2004 general elections (Loh 2009: 84–86).

In fact, the objective of BERSIH – to campaign for and create public awareness on the issue of clean and fair elections in Malaysia – was very similar to Pakatan Rakyat's demand for electoral reform. In a memorandum submitted in 2007, BERSIH had put forward four electoral reform demands: (1) usage of indelible ink to indicate who had already voted; (2) a clean-up of the registered voters list; (3) abolition of postal votes; and (4) providing access for all political parties to government controlled print and electronic media. With the relaunch of BERSIH in 2010, eight specific demands were proposed: (1) a clean electoral roll; (2) reform of postal ballots; (3) use of indelible ink; (4) minimum twenty-one days' campaign period; (5) free and fair access to media; (6) strengthening of public institutions; (7) stopping corruption; and (8) stopping dirty politics.[1]

From 2007–12, BERSIH organised three important rallies, which comprised an important part of its activism. A closer observation, however, reveals that the majority of BERSIH supporters who turned up for these rallies were also Pakatan Rakyat members. In fact, prior to these rallies, Pakatan Rakyat leaders like Abdul Hadi Awang (PAS), Anwar Ibrahim (PKR) and Lim Kit Siang (DAP) openly endorsed their support of BERSIH and galvanised their party supporters to attend such rallies. The close relationship between BERSIH and Pakatan Rakyat contributed to the significance of the series of public rallies, which had an important impact in the 2008 and 2013 Malaysian general elections, in which Pakatan Rakyat emerged as a solid opposition force in Malaysian politics.

The first BERSIH rally was organised on 10 November 2007. It was historic: for the first time, a social movement managed to mobilise somewhere between 10,000 and 40,000 Malaysians. BERSIH used non-governmental organisations, online media and blogs as tools for mobilisation, and also invited the ruling Barisan Nasional component parties to join the rally; however, a majority of the supporters for the BERSIH rally were mobilised by PAS, DAP and PKR. In fact, PAS's president, Abdul Hadi Awang, DAP's Lim Kit Siang and PKR's Anwar Ibrahim were on the scene, actively involved in encouraging their supporters to march to the Istana (Palace) in the 2007 BERSIH rally.

On the day of the rally, the country's capital city, Kuala Lumpur, came under a heavy police cordon, and major roads leading to the city centre were closed. Nevertheless, BERSIH supporters, mainly Malays, managed to gather at three important locations, namely, Sogo Shopping Complex, Masjid India and Masjid Negara. The supporters were stopped halfway and forced to disperse when the police open fired with tear gas and water cannons. Later, several dozen BERSIH supporters – most of them were opposition supporters – were detained for various reasons. The most noticeable arrest was of the then PAS Deputy President Mohammad Sabu and PKR's Tian Chua (*Star* 2012). Later that day, when BERSIH submitted its four-point memorandum to the Istana, the three opposition parties' leaders were present, highlighting the importance of this BERSIH rally to the Malaysian opposition.

The second BERSIH rally, famously dubbed BERSIH 2.0, was a walk for democracy on 9 July 2011. This time around, BERSIH rallies were also held simultaneously in at least nine countries around the world by overseas Malaysian communities. The rally was a follow-up to the 2007 rally, as the coalition's demands had not been properly addressed by the Malaysian government. BERSIH co-chairperson Ambiga Sreenivasan noted that the Election Commission had totally rejected the movement's call for electoral reform (Boo 2011). As a result, BERSIH put forward its eight-point solution to clean up the Malaysian electoral system.

The government under Prime Minister Najib Razak pointed out that BERSIH's public rally could not be allowed as it would only create chaos; the government's priority was maintaining the public's safety. The government also pointed out that groups like Perkasa and the youth wing of United Malays National Organisation (UMNO) were planning to counter the BERSIH rally. BERSIH co-chairperson Ambiga Sreenivasan secured an audience with the Malaysian head of state. In the ensuing days, coalition leaders issued a statement agreeing to hold the rally indoors in the historic Merdeka Stadium (Syed 2011).

The government, however, rejected the use of Merdeka Stadium. BERSIH was adamant it would proceed with its plan to use the stadium and accused the Malaysian government of not being in favour of even indoor rallies. On 9 July 2011, 10,000–20,000 people gathered in various locations in Kuala Lumpur and began to march to the stadium. The police stopped their progress by firing heavy tear gas and water cannon. In the aftermath of this rally, one supporter was killed and more than 1,000 BERSIH supporters were arrested, including the BERSIH chairperson and six opposition politicians, under the Emergency Ordinance (Shazwan 2011).

Again in 2012, BERSIH organised another rally on 28 April, called BERSIH 3.0, following the government's failure to include BERSIH demands in a Parliamentary Select Committee which was formed to give recommendations on issues of election reform in Malaysia. Once again, the rally was strongly supported by the opposition, Pakatan Rakyat. The government felt that the BERSIH rally was being used by the opposition to overthrow the ruling Barisan Nasional. Due to this, BERSIH's initial proposal to hold the rally in Dataran Merdeka (Independence Square) was rejected, but eventually the government suggested the use of stadiums. This time, the stadium plan was rejected by the organiser.

The rally, however, was the biggest in Malaysian history; it was recorded that more than 80,000 people turned up in support, although government-controlled media put the figure at around 25,000 (Alibeyouglu 2012). The use of force by the police and violent retaliation from supporters overshadowed the rally's success (Shazwan 2012). In fact, several journalists covering the event were detained or had their cameras destroyed by the police. On a more positive note compared with the 2011 rally, the number of people arrested by police decreased to 388 (Ariffin 2012).

It can be said that BERSIH's multi-ethnic mobilisation for clean and fair elections would be impossible without support from the opposition, that is, Pakatan Rakyat. To a large extent, the success of BERSIH rallies in mobilising thousands of Malaysians could be attributed to Pakatan Rakyat. Conversely, Pakatan's support for the BERSIH movement was based on the assumption that a clean electoral system would increase the chances of the opposition's forming the next government.

HINDRAF's working-class Indian rally

HINDRAF was formed in January 2006 as an ad hoc committee comprising thirty Indian-based non-governmental organisations. The aim was to create a discursive forum among hitherto divided Indian organisations in the interest of the minority ethnic Indians.[2] HINDRAF became famous after a 2007 rally which saw thousands of working-class Indians take to the streets in various parts of Kuala Lumpur. In the aftermath of the rally, the government labelled this movement as radical, racist and terrorist. HINDRAF's activism was very much restricted to working-class ethnic Indian issues and failed to get continuous support from opposition parties. It should be noted, however, that the emergence of HINDRAF and its November 2007 rally significantly changed working-class Indians' perceptions towards the Malaysian Indian Congress (MIC) and the ruling Barisan Nasional in Malaysian politics.

It is important to note that HINDRAF did not set out to become a major force. It had no symbol, membership, organisational chart or ideology, and initially had no anti-government agenda. In fact, many of the thirty organisations that originally signed up to HINDRAF were avowedly pro-government (Govindasamy 2009). Yet, it was in the nature of even this limited brief that HINDRAF would clash with the government. Soon after its formation, many organisations that had initially been associated with HINDRAF left or became inactive, largely in response to HINDRAF's continuous criticism of the MIC and the government. In the wake of these departures, HINDRAF changed its character: it came to be dominated by a small group centred around the energetic and charismatic Ponnusamy brothers. Wathayamoorty Ponnusamy became the president and his brother, Uthayakumar Ponnusamy, became the main legal adviser and de facto leader. Even before the formation of HINDRAF, both brothers were known for their activist orientation, especially Uthayakumar. The brothers also handled other Indian cases such as those concerning issues of birth certificates and the plight of Tamil schools.

Although HINDRAF was famously known for defending Hindu temples in Malaysia, the real impetus for the creation of HINDRAF dated back to an episode that occurred in December 2005. When Maniam Moorthy – a Malaysian Indian who was famous as a hero who had climbed Mount Everest – died on 20 December 2005, the nation witnessed an extraordinary tussle over his body between his wife, Kaliammal, and the state religious authorities. She claimed her husband was Hindu but the Islamic religious authorities, including the Syariah Court, rejected her claim, saying that Moorthy had converted to Islam and the body should be buried according to Islamic rites. The Malaysian High Court decided that it had no jurisdiction over the case because the Syariah Court had already ruled and ordered Moorthy's body to be buried according to the ruling of the Court (Fauwas 2005). This episode sparked the coming together of the thirty non-governmental Indian organisations that formed HINDRAF to address the socio-religious interests of Malaysian Indians. Although many of these NGOs left when HINDRAF became increasingly critical of state policies pertaining to Indians, HINDRAF stayed on, hence becoming the sole participant representing the community against the Malaysian government.

This history notwithstanding, the issue of defending Hindu temples from demolition made HINDRAF popular among working-class Indians in Malaysia. In 2006, several incidents highlighted the fact that local governments in states like Selangor had taken aggressive stands against temples built 'illegally' in public and private land by working-class Indians. In some cases, these temples had been built when the land was still under British plantation estates. MIC, the sole Indian representative in the ruling Barisan Nasional, had pleaded several times to stop such exercises of temple demolition, but had failed to get a positive response from then Prime Minister Abdullah Badawi (*Malaysiakini* 2006).

MIC's failure and continued temple demolition exercises gave HINDRAF a valid reason to emerge as the voice of marginalised working-class Indians. In fact, from 2006, HINDRAF had been sending various memorandums to the government on the issue of temple demolition, which had become a sensitive one to the working-class Indian community. When this strategy failed, it turned to small-scale rallies, normally held near the demolished temple. At the same time, HINDRAF also organised various public forums throughout peninsular Malaysia to explain to the Indian community about the MIC's failure to protect Indians' rights in Malaysia, as part of its drive to mobilise Indians. The government, however, ignored HINDRAF's requests; it maintained its stand that any issues pertaining to Malaysian Indians' would be dealt with only by the MIC.

The second stage of HINDRAF activism was with the intent to internationalise the issue of Indian marginalisation in Malaysia, in order to put pressure on the Malaysian government. The continuous refusal of the Malaysian government under Prime Minister Abdullah Badawi to negotiate and find amicable solutions, particularly regarding the issue of temple demolition, forced HINDRAF to stress the issue on a global scale. For instance, in 2007, on the fiftieth anniversary of Malaysia's independence from the British, lawyers representing

HINDRAF filed a class action lawsuit against the government of the United Kingdom for US$4 trillion as compensation for transporting Indians from the mainland, who presently form the majority of the Malaysian Indian community, and leaving them unprotected, at the mercy of Malays, in Malaysia. Later, to create awareness, HINDRAF also organised a '100,000 signature' campaign throughout Malaysia to explain the class action lawsuit and gain financial support for its course among the Malaysian Indian community.

One week before Deepavali (the Hindu festival of lights) in 2007, a temple in the working-class area of Padang Jawa was demolished by local authorities, sparking major outrage among Malaysian Indians (Lee 2008: 190). HINDRAF used this incident to organise a peaceful rally on 10 November 2007 to submit a petition to the British High Commissioner in Kuala Lumpur. One of the key points in the petition, which was addressed to then Prime Minister of the United Kingdom Gordon Brown, was the accusation of 'ethnic cleansing' of Indians in Malaysia (Vinood 2007). On the day of the rally, clashes were reported in various places between HINDRAF supporters and police; the most notable one was around the famous Hindu temple in Batu Caves and a large crowd also gathered around the iconic Petronas Twin Towers, considered symbols of a modern, vibrant and progressive multi-ethnic Malaysian society. The government responded by sending nearly 5,000 armed police to disperse the crowd. This action, however, failed to stop the Malaysian Indians from showing their support for HINDRAF. It was reported that nearly 20,000–50,000, mostly working-class ethnic Tamils turned up in various parts of Kuala Lumpur – the biggest ever Indian rally against the government in Malaysian history (Lee 2008: 190).

In the aftermath of this rally, nearly 200 HINDRAF supporters were detained. Furthermore, the organisation was accused of having links with the Liberation Tamil Tigers of Elam (LTTE) in Sri Lanka and was later declared to be a terrorist organisation. The government also accused HINDRAF of distorting the actual picture of Malaysian Indians to the international community and planning to create racial unrest in Malaysia. Later, its five main leaders, namely, Uthayakumar, Manoharan, Kenghadharan, Ganabatirau and Vasanthakumar, were detained under the Internal Security Act (ISA) (Yeng 2007).

The Malaysian government felt the impact of HINDRAF in 2008, when working-class Indians largely deserted the MIC and the ruling Barisan Nasional government lost its two-thirds majority in parliament. Since then, the government has taken various measures to win Malaysian Indians' support, such as releasing the leaders who were detained under ISA in May 2008, as well as recognising various splinter groups of HINDRAF, such as the Makkal Sakthi Movement. And just before the 2013 general elections, the Malaysian government formally recognised one such splinter group, known as Persatuan HINDRAF Malaysia, and signed a memorandum of understanding to improve the socio-economic position of Malaysian Indians (Ng 2013).

In the case of HINDRAF, it can be concluded that its activism primarily focused on working-class ethnic Indian issues in Malaysia. HINDRAF's November 2007 rally was the first and last of its kind and played an important part in changing working-class Indians' perceptions of MIC and the ruling Barisan Nasional. Among the majority Malays, this movement's method of activism, which questioned Malays' special privileges and demanded equal rights, seemed radical for Malaysia.

Perkasa's Malay supremacy

Perkasa was formed in the aftermath of the 2008 general elections. It was officially registered under the Malaysian Registrar of Societies on 12 September 2008. Perkasa is a conservative, extreme-right-wing Malay movement. The core of Perkasa's ideology is to protect and defend *bumiputera*, in particular the majority Malays and their rights as stipulated in the Malaysian Constitution. This movement is famously known for its critical view of non-Malays and the Malaysian opposition coalition, Pakatan Rakyat (Teo 2011). The movement's current president is Ibrahim Ali; former Malaysian Prime Minister Mahathir Mohammad is its adviser. Perkasa is the radical face of UMNO. Its core members are UMNO supporters and it was formed to win back the Malays' support UMNO lost in the 2008 general elections.

In the aftermath of the 2008 general elections, Perkasa gained popularity mainly among Malays for defending the Malays' socio-economic and political rights in Malaysia. Perkasa has argued that it is not a racist organisation, claiming that it is only demanding the rights of the Malays and *bumiputera* in Malaysia. As a matter of fact, Ibrahim Ali has noted that the welfare of the Malays, who comprise 60 percent of the Malaysian population, should be taken care of in order to maintain security and political stability in Malaysia. He further claimed that should Malays remain poor economically, the possibility of a 'fresh' race riot will be very high in Malaysia (Anbalagan 2013).

This organisation also argued that since 2008, the Malaysian government has tolerated and given in too much to minority demands. When Najib Razak took over as prime minister, one of his main strategies was to win back Chinese and Indian support for the ruling Barisan Nasional. Toward that end, the government was even willing to negotiate with radical Chinese and Indian organisations. In fact, prior to the 2013 general elections, the government held negotiations with 'radical minority groups' such as Dong Zong (United Chinese School Committees Association) and signed a memorandum of understanding with HINDRAF splinter group Persatuan HINDRAF Malaysia (Ding 2013).

Such governmental actions and poor support from minority groups for the ruling Barisan Nasional in the 2013 general elections made Perkasa question minority Chinese's and Indians' loyalty and sincerity to the government. The group demanded the Malaysian government immediately stop giving handouts to minorities and focus on Malays, who are the main supporters of the government. Right after the 2013 elections, Perkasa's youth wing chief told Prime Minister Najib Razak to step down if he continued to support minorities and failed to prioritise the Malays (Mohd 2013). Most Perkasa members, who number over 500,000, are also UMNO members, and their main aim is to maintain UMNO's status quo in Malaysian politics (Anbalagan and Awang Chik 2013).

Since its formation in 2009, Perkasa's activism has been mainly linked to mobilising for, creating awareness of, fighting for and defending Malay rights in Malaysia. The central part of Perkasa's activism is to monitor, identify and counter any statements or action by organisations or minority groups which are interpreted as questioning Malay rights in Malaysia. In this process, Perkasa has been actively involved in issuing various radical-racist statements, which underline the Malay supremacy that undermines minority ethnic groups. Perkasa has also organised counter-demonstrations against any organisations which are deemed as opposing Malay rights in Malaysia. Unlike BERSIH's and HINDRAF's activism, Perkasa's activism has enjoyed wide coverage in government-controlled media, and authorities' responses to its more radical-racist statements have been lukewarm.

For instance, Perkasa was one of the key organisations which promoted a ban on the Malay-language Bible in Malaysia (Athi 2013). In January 2013, its president, Ibrahim Ali, issued a statement asking Muslims to seize and burn copies of Bibles that contain the word 'Allah' as the only way to stop non-Malays from using the term, and hence protecting the sanctity of Islam in Malaysia. Again in October 2013, he issued another statement asking the government to ban the Malay Bible, called Alkitab in the East Malaysian states of Sabah and Sarawak, which have used Malay Bibles for centuries (Netto 2013; see also Puyok, this volume). In March 2013, Perkasa's vice president insulted Malaysian Hindus by mocking their religious practice. Although these actions conflicted with Prime Minister Najib's '1Malaysia' slogan, which glorifies ethnic and religious diversity in Malaysia, the government has maintained its silence on these issues.

In December 2012, Perkasa reminded the Malay community that the Chinese-dominated DAP's growing political influence in Malaysia since 2008 could turn out to be a national security threat. Perkasa argued that given their strong economic background, the Malaysian Chinese's increasing influence in politics would lead to the reoccurrence of the 13 May incident, which saw a race riot mainly between Chinese and Malays (Hoi 2012). Perkasa also noted that Malaysian Chinese are not sensitive towards the majority Malays and told Malays to put aside their political differences in order to unite to protect their rights in Malaysia. For example, the case of Lim Guan Eng, who has successfully defended his post as the chief minister of Penang for the second consecutive term, reflects the growing dominance of the DAP in Malaysian politics. Perkasa has frequently accused Lim of discriminating against the Malays in Penang in not safeguarding their socio-economic interests, such as through business tenders and public housing.

Perkasa is also actively involved in countering various accusations against the government from non-governmental organisations and opposition political parties. For instance, when BERSIH organised its rally in 2011 for clean and fair elections, Perkasa threatened to organise a counter-rally and warned BERSIH supporters to stay away from the rally, as demanded by the Malaysian government. In another incident, Perkasa strongly supported the government's position on lesbian, gay, bisexual and transsexual (LGBT) issues, accusing non-governmental organisations like SUARAM of conspiring with foreign countries to undermine Malaysian Muslims' faith (*Malaysiakini* 2012).

Unlike BERSIH and HINDRAF, Perkasa has generally enjoyed a warm relationship with UMNO. This nexus was evident in the last Malaysian general elections, in 2013. Its president contested as an independent candidate when the Barisan Nasional candidate, from UMNO, withdrew from the competition. Perkasa's vice president, Zulkifli Nordin, stood as an UMNO candidate under the Barisan Nasional banner. In fact, UMNO supporters, including the former prime minister, Mahathir Mohammad, campaigned for these Perkasa candidates.

It can be concluded that Perkasa, which was formed right after the 2008 Malaysian elections, was designed to engage Malay supremacy debates more openly in order to win Malay support back for UMNO. In fact, UMNO leaders have given silent approval for Perkasa's radical approach in championing Malay rights in Malaysia. It can also be said that UMNO has overcome the limitations it faces on being too radical as a race-based component party in Barisan Nasional through Perkasa; to an extent, Perkasa is the radical face of UMNO.

Conclusion

BERSIH, HINDRAF and Perkasa have significantly contributed to the changing political landscape in Malaysia. These social movements and their activism have quite substantially impacted Malaysian politics, which, in turn, has provided the impetus for future debates regarding the role of civil society in strengthening democracy and race relations in an ethnically divided country like Malaysia. In fact, it cannot be denied that had it not been for BERSIH and HINDRAF, it would be highly unlikely that PKR, PAS and the DAP could have denied the Barisan Nasional government its two-thirds majority in parliament. Meanwhile, Perkasa, since its formation right after the 2008 elections, has made the Barisan

Nasional more exclusively Malay-centric than ever, setting the stage for the return of race supremacy discourse in Malaysian politics.

Unusually in Malaysian history, these social movements managed to successfully mobilise the peoples of the country for their respective causes. BERSIH, through vigorous activism, managed to mobilise thousands of Malaysians, irrespective of race, in 2007, 2008 and 2012, through illegal rallies against the state for clean and fair elections in Malaysia. Likewise, HINDRAF managed to mobilise thousands of working-class Malaysian Indians in its 2007 rally, changing their perceptions forever towards the MIC and Barisan Nasional. Perkasa's consistent radical-racist approach toward non-Malays, particularly after the 2008 general elections, has mobilised rural Malays to some extent to return to UMNO.

The state's responses to the demands outlined by these social movements underline the significance of the latter. In the case of BERSIH and HINDRAF, although the government initially reacted harshly by using police force and detaining leaders under draconian state laws, it eventually incorporated numerous demands that these social movements stipulated into its decision-making process. These provisions include the use of indelible ink during elections and the creation of a unit in the Prime Minister's Department specifically to oversee Indians' welfare. By the same token, the government's launch of a new Bumiputera Economic Empowerment (BEE) initiative in 2013 is a direct result of Perkasa's constant demand for the extension of national economic policies favouring *bumiputera* (Lee 2013).

As a whole, these three social movements' origin, development and activism have set a promising new stage in civil societal discourse in Malaysia. These movements have not only successfully mobilised Malaysians, but have also managed to influence the government's decision-making process as never before in Malaysian politics.

Notes

1 BERSIH's Memorandum to the Election Commission on Immediate Electoral Reforms in Malaysia, 9 July 2011.

2 The early information on HINDRAF was obtained from interviews conducted with Datuk Vaithalingam, the former president of Malaysian Consultative Council of Buddhism, Christianity, Hinduism, Sikhism and Taoism.

Bibliography

Alibeyouglu, Ayse (2012) 'Police violence marks Malaysia reform rally', *Al Jazeera*, available at www.aljazeera.com/news/asia-pacific/2012/04/20124286221449574.html (accessed 10 October 2013).

Anbalagan, V. (2013) 'Perkasa chief warns of fresh race riot if Malays not helped economically', *The Malaysian Insider*, available at www.themalaysianinsider.com/malaysia/article/Perkasa-chief-warns-of-fresh-race-riot-if-malays-not-helped-economically (accessed 6 October 2013).

Anbalagan, V. and Hasbullah Awang Chik (2013) 'Ku Li to open Perkasa meeting in the hope of turning right-wing Malay group around', *The Malaysian Insider*, available at www.themalaysianinsider.com/malaysia/article/ku-li-to-open-perkasa-meeting-in-the-hope-of-turning-right-wing-malay-group (accessed 6 February 2014).

Ariffin, Lisa J. (2012) '388 arrested at Bersih Rally', *The Malaysian Insider*, available at www.themalaysianinsider.com/malaysia/article/at-least-100-arrested-at-BERSIH-rally (accessed 10 October 2013).

Athi Sankar (2013) 'Burn "Allah" Bibles Perkasa chief to Muslims', *Free Malaysia Today*, available at www.freemalaysiatoday.com/category/nation/2013/01/19/burn-allah-bibles-Perkasa-chief-tells-muslims (accessed 10 October 2013).

Boo Su Lyn (2011) 'Ambiga asks politicians to join Bersih rally', *The Malaysian Insider*, available at www.themalaysianinsider.com/malaysia/article/ambiga-asks-politicians-to-join-BERSIH-rally (accessed 6 October 2013).

Brown, Graham K. (2004) Civil Society and Social Movements in an Ethnically Divided Society: The Case of Malaysia, 1981–2001, PhD Dissertation, University of Nottingham.

Collins, Alan (2006) 'Chinese educationalists in Malaysia: defenders of Chinese identity', *Asian Survey*, 46(2): 298–318.

Ding, Emily (2013) 'Hindraf sacks Waythamoorthy just days after pact with BN', *The Malaysian Insider*, available at www.themalaysianinsider.com/malaysia/article/hindraf-sacks-waythamoorthy-just-days-after-pact-with-bn (accessed 6 February 2014).

Fauwas Abdul Aziz (2005) 'Heavy security at Everest hero's burial', *Malaysiakini*, available at www.malaysiakini.com/news/45075 (accessed 10 September 2013).

Govindasamy, Anantha Raman (2009) From Submission to Assertion: A Study of Peninsular Malaysian Indians' Responses to Marginalisation, PhD thesis, Flinders University.

Hoi, Clara (2012) 'Growing Chinese clout may cause new May 13', *The Malaysian Insider*, available at www.themalaysianinsider.com/malaysia/article/growing-chinese-clout-may-cause-new-may-13-says-ibrahim-ali (accessed 10 October 2013).

Kessler, Clive (1983) 'Malaysia: Islamic revivalism and potential disaffection in a divided society', *Southeast Asia Chronicle*, 75: 3–11.

Lee Hock Guan (2008) 'Malaysia in 2007: Abdullah administration under siege', *Southeast Asian Affairs*, 1: 185–206.

Lee Long Hui (2013) 'Dr M: BEE not a return to favouring the bumiputeras', *Malaysiakini*, available at www.malaysiakini.com/news/243483 (accessed 10 October 2013).

Lim Teck Ghee (2011) 'Academic consensus on unfair elections: reinforcing the case for Bersih's march', Centre for Policy Initiatives, available at http://english.cpiasia.net/index.php?option=com_content&view=article&id=2201:academic-consensus-on-unfair-elections-reinforcing-the-case-for-bersihs-march&catid=141:lim-teck-ghees-contribution&Itemid=93 (accessed 6 October 2013).

Loh Kok Wah, Francis (2004) 'Understanding the 2004 General Election: looking beyond the Pak Lah factor', *Aliran Monthly*, 3, available at http://aliran.com/archives/monthly/2004a/3g.html (accessed 8 October 2013).

Loh Kok Wah, Francis (2009) *Old vs New Politics in Malaysia*, Kuala Lumpur: SIRD and Aliran Publications.

Malaysiakini (2006) 'Protest against Hindu temple demolition', *Malaysiakini*, available at www.malaysiakini.com/news/59827 (accessed 6 February 2013).

Malaysiakini (2012) 'Perkasa: Suaram funders also behind LGBT programmes', *Malaysiakini*, available at www.malaysiakini.com/news/209048 (accessed 10 October 2013).

Mohd Farhan Darwis (2013) 'Perkasa rap youth chief for telling Najib to quit', *The Malaysian Insider*, available at www.themalaysianinsider.com/malaysia/article/Perkasa-to-rap-youth-chief-for-telling-najib-to-quit? (accessed 6 October 2013).

Netto, Terence (2013) 'Bishop demands to repudiate "Ban Al-kitab" call', *Malaysiakini*, available at www.malaysiakini.com/news/244250 (accessed 10 October 2013).

Ng, Eileen (2013) '100 days on, HINDRAF dismayed with Putrajaya deal', *The Malaysian Insider*, available at www.themalaysianinsider.com/malaysia/article/100-days-on-HINDRAF-dismayed-with-putrajaya-deal (accessed 10 October 2013).

Shazwan Mustafa Kamal (2011) 'Cops not responsible for Bersih man's death', *The Malaysian Insider*, available at www.themalaysianinsider.com/malaysia/article/cops-not-responsible-for-BERSIH-mans-death-says-najib/ (accessed 6 October 2013).

Shazwan Mustafa Kamal (2012) 'Police brutality more widespread during Bersih 3.0, says bar council', *The Malaysian Insider*, available at www.themalaysianinsider.com/malaysia/article/police-brutality-more-widespread-during-BERSIH-3.0-says-bar-council/ (accessed 10 October 2013).

Star (2012) 'Mat Sabu, Tian Chua to enter defence over 2007 Bersih rally', *The Star Online*, available at www.thestar.com.my/News/Nation/2012/03/01/Mat-Sabu-Tian-Chua-to-enter-defence-over-2007-Bersih-rally.aspx (accessed 9 May 2014).

Syed Muaz Syed Putra (2011) 'Ambiga: Bersih to rally in stadium, not on streets', *The Malaysian Insider*, available at www.themalaysianinsider.com/malaysia/article/ambiga-BERSIH-to-rally-in-stadium-not-on-streets/ (accessed 6 October 2013).

Tan Liok Ee (1997) *The Politics of Chinese Education in Malaya, 1945–1961*, Kuala Lumpur: Oxford University Press.

Tan, Nathaniel (2011) *9 July 2011: What Really Happened*, Kuala Lumpur: Kinibooks.

Teo, Shannon (2011) 'Curb "fascist" Perkasa, Rahim Noor, Pakatan MPs tell Najib', *The Malaysian Insider*, available at www.themalaysianinsider.com/malaysia/article/curb-fascist-Perkasa-rahim-noor-pakatan-mps-tell-najib/ (accessed 6 October 2013).

Vinood, G. (2007) 'HINDRAF submits "racism" memo to UN', *Free Malaysia Today*, available at www.freemalaysiatoday.com/category/nation/2012/03/21/HINDRAF-submits-racism-memo-to-un (accessed 10 October 2013).

Vinood, G. (2013) 'Govt lifts ban on HINDRAF', *Free Malaysia Today*, available at www.freemalaysiatoday.com/category/nation/2013/01/26/govt-lifts-ban-on-HINDRAF/ (accessed 6 October 2013).

Weiss, Meredith L. and Saliha Hassan (eds) (2003) *Social Movements in Malaysia: From Moral Communities to NGOs*, London: RoutledgeCurzon.

Yeng Ai Chun (2007) 'Abdullah slams genocide claim', *The Star*, 7 December, p. 3.

Part II
Economics

Overview

Meredith L. Weiss

The Malaysian economy presents a variable mix of state management and free market activity, and of consistent growth (with the occasional notable downturn) and areas of chronic inefficiency. Both priorities and constraints have shifted over time, from ethnic equilibration, to rent-seeking/distribution, to upwardly mobile competitiveness. A predominantly agricultural society, with a clear congruence between ethnicity and occupational sector and a high level of foreign ownership, Malaysia is now over two-thirds urban, with a large and growing multiracial middle class. However, Malaysia struggles with issues of distribution, of sustainability (environmental and otherwise), and of balancing economic rationality, social desirability and partisan exigency, given the government's heavy reliance on redistributive policies and performance legitimacy.

Greg Felker kicks off the section by exploring the paradoxes of Malaysian economic development: liberalism mixed with state direction, targeting both efficient growth and politically expedient distributional rules. He details a seemingly 'gyroscopic' pattern of vacillating between openness and intervention, which reveals short-term, partial responses to crises layered atop an underlying continuity. The common thread since the early days of independence, Felker suggests, has been a pattern of selective intervention to channel benefits in such a way as to consolidate political dominance, largely through ethnic-oriented disbursements, but also per broader clientelist networks. Felker characterises this approach as one of 'distribution-through-growth', in which these potentially competing objectives are approached symbiotically and in tandem.

Xiaoye She traces this same tension in her discussion of fiscal and monetary policies. In both policy domains, the state has been challenged to adjust in light of overarching economic and institutional changes, as well as domestic and global financial crises and other shocks. Throughout, monetary policy, managed by the largely independent Bank Negara Malaysia (Malaysia's central bank), has been easier to reform than politically volatile fiscal policy, although neither domain is immune to political influence.

Hwok-Aun Lee homes in on those political imperatives with his careful assessment of the bases for, progress of, and strengths and weaknesses of affirmative action policies in Malaysia. However warranted and valuable as part of a broader programme of socio-economic development and transformation, Lee argues that these policies may easily drift – and arguably have drifted – off-course, as by missing the mark in improving education such that all may achieve the same standard, or by skewing employment patterns and equity ownership in sub-par directions. Most importantly, he suggests, the policies should aim at achieving their own superfluity, as the surest indicator of success, yet Malaysia's seem securely entrenched.

Among the goals of affirmative action was creation of a Malay middle class. Abdul Rahman Embong notes that this class has indeed expanded, although not just among any one ethnic group. He situates the Malaysian middle class within a larger, global phenomenon of middle-class growth, especially across Asia. To a large extent, this class status is defined in terms of consumption, in terms of producers' perspective on a burgeoning market and of members' aspirations, alike. Yet both the size and the economic security – and hence, class stability – of this population segment may be overstated. Given unaffordable (or inadequate affordable) housing, rising debt, decreased subsidies and impending new taxes, reaching, maintaining and reproducing a middle-class lifestyle has become all the more difficult in Malaysia. Household debt in particular, already at unsustainable levels, is rising and of especial concern, given the centrality of consumption to the middle-class way of life.

Yet the Malaysian state has more than one set of tools at its disposal to stave off discontent. Helena Varkkey characterises Malaysia as a rentier state, which uses rents from abundant natural resources (palm oil, timber, petroleum, etc.) to stabilise politics by 'buying off' both elites and masses. The result is sustained Barisan Nasional (BN, National Front coalition) dominance and avoidance of the destabilising 'resource curse', as well as reasonably widely distributed economic advantage (for instance, via the programmes Lee details to help the rural Malay poor), but also the coalition's real dependence on these resources as founts of patronage for currying support and precluding potential challenges.

Indeed, there may be a fine line between redistribution and buying (or selling) favour. In his chapter, Jeff Tan explores the multiple meanings of, and distinctions between, rent-seeking and money politics. While commonly approached in terms of individual actors, these phenomena have fundamentally political bases. Spanning state–business relations as well as electoral dimensions, the distribution and capture of rents distort political decision-making on all sides, in ways more complex than conventional discussions suggest: class and cronyism overlay seemingly ethnic patterns, for instance, and dynamics of state capture (e.g. by businesses in search of rents) cross-cut efforts at political capture by bureaucrats and politicians. A nuanced analysis of rent-seeking and money politics, Tan suggests, including political capacity or will to address sources of inefficiency or skew, requires attention to underlying social relations (particularly class analysis), the relative power of patrons and clients, state capacity, and the sequence of policy initiatives.

Amarjit Kaur brings us back to more concrete, but still politicised, policy processes with her discussion of labour migration. Ethnic and nationalist concerns have prompted restrictions on immigration since independence, even as the need for workers forces relaxation; stringency on paper has not always held up, given irregular flows and ad hoc arrangements. Policies on labour and migration have shifted with changing economic conditions, international precedents and security concerns, but include guidelines for recruitment of both skilled expatriates and low-skilled migrants, and at least some level of regulation of working conditions (both contract terms and living arrangements) for migrant workers, with enforcement through both government and quasi-governmental channels. Meanwhile, labour broadly has been expected and pressured to accede to larger development, security, stability objectives; downward wage pressure and similar effects have arguably pushed Malaysian trade unionists to find common cause between domestic and migrant labour.

Adnan A. Hezri suggests that Malaysia's record on environmental sustainability has been perhaps less erratic and politicised, though still falling short. Starting with forest management under the colonial administration and continuing through ever more comprehensive structures and policies, Malaysia has a record of striving for sustainable development. However, more needs to be done in terms of renewable energy, enforcement of environmental impact assessments and generally adapting to the reality that Malaysia is no longer so resource-abundant as it once was. More broadly, he suggests, Malaysia must develop a more comprehensive policy framework and institutional infrastructure if it is effectively to combat climate change, build a green economy, and incorporate environmental concerns in all domains.

The final two chapters in the section focus in on rural and urban development, respectively. Eric Thompson leads off by painting a picture of rural transformation that extends well beyond agriculture, to encompass economic, political, and social change against a backdrop of (or as part of) overall urbanisation and an increasing urban bias. His chapter offers both an overview of prevailing dynamics and a trenchant critique of a literature that focuses overly much on the Malay community, on the one hand, neglecting Orang Asli, Chinese, Indian, and immigrant populations, and on only certain dimensions of rural life (for instance, giving politics noticeably short shrift in recent years), on the other hand. A range of government schemes to extend land ownership and support or extend cultivation of particular food or cash crops (e.g. rice, palm oil), as well as the more general expansion of education, public sector employment, and information and communications technology (ICT) penetration, have had generally positive effects in terms of alleviating poverty and fostering social and geographic mobility. The results for income inequality, however, are more mixed.

Yeoh Seng Guan takes the other side of this coin, exploring Malaysia's rapidly growing urban population. Affirmative action programmes promoting especially Malay social, economic, and geographic mobility since the 1970s, as well as initiatives to promote inter-ethnic cohesion and both Western and non-Western (e.g. Islamist) cultural flows, have transformed the urban landscape. Adding to that remaking have been both conscious government policies to develop new areas, as with the Iskandar Malaysia project in Johor, or to develop specific urban and other zones (as articulated in periodic Malaysia Plans and other enactments), and less planned, more organic shifts. Among the latter, too, have been ideational and cultural flows, including towards new spatial hierarchies or differentiation, as consumption, production, and residential habits shift.

11

Malaysia's development strategies

Governing distribution-through-growth

Greg Felker

Malaysia's economy grew at an average annual rate of almost 6.5 percent from 1961 to 2011. With sustained growth came profound structural change, transforming a post-colonial commodity exporter into one of Asia's newly industrialised countries (NICs) (Table 11.1). Yet, Malaysia fits uneasily into the conceptual terms that inform much of the literature on comparative development strategies. The country's heavy reliance on trade and foreign investment appears exemplary of a broadly liberal, outward-oriented economic regime, yet the government has intervened extensively to direct the course of growth. Economic policies have promoted private sector competitiveness while simultaneously pursuing a far-reaching programme of inter-ethnic socio-economic redistribution. Finally, despite extraordinary continuity in political leadership since independence, the focus of development policy has changed dramatically several times in response to major political or economic crises.

What explains Malaysia's seemingly paradoxical development trajectory – state interventionism amidst deep integration into global markets, growth-focused policies permeated by distributional politics, and sustained growth across multiple policy shifts? Katzenstein (1985: 29–30) famously argued that the economic policies of small states are best understood as efforts to satisfy, simultaneously, the demands of international economic competitiveness and domestic political legitimation. At several junctures in Malaysia's history, external shocks have induced downturns that precipitated reforms aimed at reviving growth momentum (Figure 11.1). Domestic political pressures have likewise motivated far-reaching policy

Table 11.1 Structure of GDP by sector, 1961–2010 (value-added, %)

Sector	*1961*	*1970*	*1980*	*1990*	*2000*	*2010*
Agriculture	36	29	23	15	9	10
Industry	21	27	41	42	48	41
Manufacturing	8	12	22	24	31	25
Services	43	43	36	43	43	48

Source: World Bank, *World Development Indicators*, http://data.worldbank.org/data-catalog/world-development-indicators.

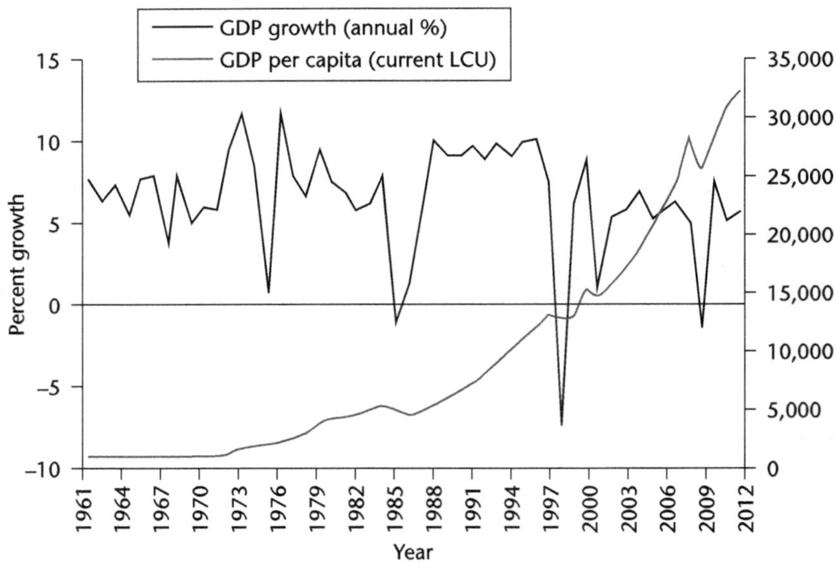

Figure 11.1 GDP per capita and annual growth, 1961–2011

interventions to shape the economy's distributional outcomes. The metaphor of a pendulum swinging between market-driven liberalisation and politically motivated interventions captures important aspects of the crisis-and-recalibration dynamic that recurs across Malaysia's economic history. What the image does not explain is why and how Malaysia has managed the relationship between growth and distributional imperatives more or less successfully over five decades.

The proximate reasons for that 'gyroscopic' proclivity are two-fold. First are Malaysian leaders' political incentives and capacities to re-equilibrate the balance of development goals when disruptions put them into short-term conflict. Just as important, though, are the ways that development strategies per se have reconciled growth and distributional imperatives, and even rendered them complementary over time, in a pattern of 'distribution-through-growth'. The country's political regime, organised around a hegemonic Malay party with an attendant coalition of other ethnic parties, fostered among governing elites a relatively encompassing and long-term interest in the economy. Thus, the constant factor amidst Malaysia's shifting development strategies has been efforts to foster growth in ways that preserve the state's central governance role to superintend the distribution of economic advantages.

Development strategy from independence to New Economic Policy

Gereffi (1990) compares NICs' development trajectories in terms of sequential choices among strategic options defined by their focus on particular leading industries or sectors, as well as on either domestic or export markets. The most successful East Asian NICs, such as South Korea and Taiwan, used protectionist policies to launch industrialisation that focused temporarily on serving the domestic market (import-substitution industrialisation, ISI), but soon compelled those industries to venture into export markets, or export-oriented industrialisation (EOI) (thus moving from primary ISI to primary EOI). This quasi-mercantilist cycle was later repeated with more capital-intensive and high-technology goods (a move from secondary ISI to secondary EOI), and eventually with information-intensive services.

Many surveys of Malaysian development follow similar chronological schema by dividing the country's economic history into discrete phases marked by changes in the focus of development policy.[1] The dozen years following independence in 1957 are often described as an era of laissez-faire policy, during which Malaysia's growth continued to depend upon the activities that had made it one of the British Empire's most profitable colonies, notably the export of commodities like rubber and tin. Primary product exports accounted for 85 percent of total exports and 40 percent of GDP upon independence in 1957, and remained high, at almost 80 percent and 30 percent, respectively, by 1970. Macroeconomic policy likewise remained conservative in the 1960s. Independent Malaya opted to retain a currency board system inherited from the colonial state up through 1967, when the link to the British pound was replaced with a US dollar peg. Controls on foreign investment were minimal, and foreign corporations continued to dominate the plantation sector. Public expenditures rose with a steadily growing development budget, but fiscal balance remained a hallmark of economic policy-making, especially as new streams of revenue were derived from export taxes. Both foreign enterprises and businesses owned by ethnic Chinese Malayans were allowed to prosper with minimal attempts to control their growth.

The newly independent government did, of course, make certain adjustments to the colonial-era policy framework in an effort to advance development. A primary import-substitution industrialisation programme was launched following the advice of a 1955 World Bank mission, and comprehensive development planning in a five-year cycle began in 1966. In comparative perspective, though, these measures were decidedly modest, especially when compared with the statist-nationalist and socialist programmes pursued across much of the developing world during the same period. The 1957 Pioneer Industrial Ordinance, for example, rejected broad-front tariff protection as the means to nurture new manufacturing industries, and instead relied on tax holidays to induce investment. Effective rates of protection did rise across a number of consumer products and other manufacturing industries which relied on imported inputs for final assembly, yet overall tariff protection remained lower than in other developing economies (Lim 1992). Moreover, the chief beneficiaries of primary ISI were, yet again, foreign-owned and ethnic-Chinese Malayan businesses.[2]

That Malaya's ruling elites sought to build upon, rather than dismantle, the colonial-era commodity-export economy owed less to liberal ideology, however, than to the constraints of domestic and external political-economy factors. As part of the country's negotiated independence from Britain, local elites forged a consociational political arrangement that enshrined Malay political pre-eminence and in exchange pledged to maintain the broadly free-enterprise economic system in which ethnic Chinese businesses accounted for the bulk of domestically owned capital (Jesudason 1989; Bowie 1991). This essentially conservative political settlement was motivated in large part by challenges to the state-in-formation from the non-violent left and the Malayan Communist Party's armed insurrection (Slater 2010: 74–93). External pressures and actors were equally important in precluding a decisive break with colonial-era economic policies. So long as the survival of the new state hinged on its continued protection by the former colonial power, any broad effort to displace British and other foreign investment interests was unlikely. Asia's wider Cold War conflicts also provided an economic inducement to policy continuity. The Korean War boosted rubber and tin prices through the mid-1950s, fuelling both economic expansion in Malaya and, in particular, rapid growth in public revenue from export taxes (Stubbs 2005: 78–82).

The first major turning point in Malaysia's development history came in the wake of the 13 May 1969 ethnic riots. A reconstituted ruling coalition promulgated the New Economic Policy (NEP) as a two-decade long project of national social engineering, with the over-arching goals of alleviating absolute poverty and eliminating the identification of socio-economic status and occupation with ethnicity or race. These goals were to be realised amidst an expanding economy, with the focus of growth policy shifting from agriculture to the manufacturing and commercial sectors. Manufacturing grew swiftly, at rates of 25 percent per annum during the 1970s. However, rising prices in global commodities markets, together with ongoing diversification into oil palm and petroleum, spurred a simultaneous expansion of the primary sector, which accounted for over 60 percent of exports through the early 1980s (Table 11.2).

Federal and state governments expanded agencies charged with fostering *bumiputera* entry into commerce and industry through contracting and franchising programmes. The flagship of this effort was Perbadanan Nasional (Pernas) and, subsequently, Permodalan Nasional (PNB), which pooled Malay investment capital to acquire and develop new *bumiputera* commercial enterprises. Also backing the growth of state-owned enterprises (SOEs) was the rise of government-owned banks and finance companies to dominant positions in the financial sector.

The NEP's inter-ethnic restructuring mission, and the expansion of the government's economic role that accompanied it, were responses to powerful domestic political pressures arising from a changing Malaysian social structure. Throughout the 1950s and 1960s, income disparities between the major ethnic groups rose, despite the national economy's steady growth. Malay out-migration to urban centres and the rapid expansion of education resulted in growing urban unemployment, and generated pressure on the government to increase opportunities for the ethnic majority in commerce and manufacturing. Bumiputera Economic Congresses in 1965 and 1968 gave voice to these demands, and following the 1969–71 state of emergency, the Second Malaysia Plan 1971–75 articulated the goal of using state intervention to ensure Malay participation in the 'modern' urban and corporate sectors.

While domestic politics drove expanded state intervention, external factors also exerted an important influence on NEP-era development strategy. In a delayed echo of earlier nationalisations throughout the post-colonial world, the government soon moved to Malaysianise the largest plantation and mining corporations through targeted share acquisitions. The Petroleum Development Act 1974 mandated partial foreign divestment and shared managerial control over petroleum exploration and extraction with the national oil company, Petronas. Despite this pressure on foreign enterprises in the primary sector, though, rising state activism did not mark a broad turn towards a more inward-looking or nationalist development strategy.

Table 11.2 Structure of merchandise exports by sector, 1965–2010 (%)

	1965	*1980*	*1995*	*2010*
Agricultural raw materials	50	31	6	3
Food	11	15	10	12
Fuel	5	25	7	16
Manufactures	5	19	75	67
Ores and metals	29	10	1	2

Source: World Bank, *World Development Indicators*, http://data.worldbank.org/data-catalog/world-development-indicators.

Rather, new sources of externally driven growth bolstered the push for domestic economic and social restructuring. Booming commodity-export revenues, including new oil production, fuelled the expansion of public budgets devoted to the creation of a *bumiputera* commercial and industrial community.

Equally significant, however, was the rapid growth of export-oriented industrialisation, a development thrust first signalled in the Investment Incentives Act 1968. Though the NEP's planners did not initially regard export-focused foreign direct investment (FDI) as central to the new development agenda, the sector's growth gained momentum following the Free Trade Zone (FTZ) Act 1971 and successful experimentation with FTZs in Penang, Malacca, and Johor. The influx of FDI in labour-intensive industries like textiles and semiconductor assembly enabled the rapid expansion of Malay manufacturing employment envisioned by the NEP. Khoo (2012a: 34–6) observes that the emergence of a new global division of labour in manufacturing occasioned a coincidence of interests between Malaysia's newly activist state and international capital, as large corporations from the US, Japan and Europe sought low-cost locations for labour-intensive assembly and re-export.

The Mahathir era: strategic shifts on the road to 'NIC-hood'

Official development strategy took two sharp turns during the 1980s. Upon becoming prime minister at the beginning of the decade, Mahathir Mohamad launched an ambitious secondary import-substitution industrialisation programme. He and many observers believed that, despite continued growth, import-dependent, low-value-added FTZ-based export-processing industries could not lead a genuine industrial transformation. Impressed with the development strategies of Asia's first-generation NICs, Mahathir proclaimed that Malaysia would 'Look East' and emulate Japan and South Korea by forging state–business corporatism under the banner of a 'Malaysia, Inc.' policy. He directed a state-owned Heavy Industries Corporation of Malaysia (HICOM) to launch large, capital-intensive projects in cement, fertiliser, steel, petrochemicals, and most famously, production of a national automobile, Proton (Jomo 1994). Most of these projects took the form of joint ventures with Japanese partners who supplied technology, and were supported with subsidised credit and significant tariff protection. The second oil shock of 1979 provided new revenues to finance the large investment budget, but commodity prices soon levelled off, and external public debt more than quadrupled from 1979 to 1984.

In 1985, moreover, a sharp drop in oil and other commodity prices combined with a cyclical downturn in electronics to throw Malaysia into recession. GDP shrank by 1.1 percent, a negative turnaround of 8.9 percentage points from the previous year's 7.8 percent growth rate. With balance of payments and fiscal deficits climbing, Mahathir was compelled to seek renewed private investment. On the domestic front, his administration relaxed enforcement of the NEP's equity-sharing provisions, and heavy industry projects were scaled back and their management teams replaced with foreign and local private sector figures. Meanwhile, the government signalled a renewed commitment to export-led manufacturing growth in the Promotion of Investments Act 1986, which extended the liberal ownership and tax provisions of the FTZs across the manufacturing economy.[3] Rather than moving Malaysia toward higher value-added 'secondary EOI', the Act (together with a significant currency depreciation) aimed at drawing more investment into existing assembly-based export industries.

Though initially something of a strategic retreat to 'primary EOI', the new investment policies nonetheless met with striking success. In the wake of the 1985 Plaza Accord between the United States and Japan, which led the Japanese yen to appreciate sharply, a tide of FDI from Japan and other East Asian NICs, as well as North America and Europe, washed into Malaysia. In the leading electronics sector, major investments in consumer and industrial production augmented the upgrading and expansion of established semiconductor test and assembly operations. By the mid-1990s, successive years of nearly 9 percent GDP growth seemed to ensure Malaysia's transition to NIC status. The economy was hailed internationally as an exemplar of a pro-globalisation development model organised around the pursuit of systematic national competitiveness through private investment-led growth (World Bank 1993: 310–11). Mahathir codified the new national strategy in 1991 in a manifesto titled 'Vision 2020', which projected a two-decade pathway to status as a fully developed economy fuelled, aspirationally, by the growth of national entrepreneurship and technological innovation.

As Khoo (2006, 2012b), Gomez and Jomo (1997), and Jomo (2003) detail, the vicissitudes of economic policy in Mahathir's first decade in power were closely linked to domestic politics. His development strategies arose largely from his own complex vision of a capitalist transformation that would instil the discipline necessary to empower the *bumiputera* community while simultaneously cultivating a broader Malaysian nationalism (Case 2000). Yet, their implementation also involved an effort to marginalise a rival faction of the ruling party with support in the branches of the state bureaucracy that had expanded to administer NEP programmes. While investing in new state-backed industrial projects, Mahathir simultaneously sought to cull the sprawling population of state and federal SOEs through privatisation and the corporatisation of the state's infrastructural agencies. Private business, involving prominent figures from the country's major ethnic groups, was encouraged to grow through a range of formal consultation bodies as well as through networks of exchange that dealt in contracts, share allocations, and political finance (Gomez 2002).

Mahathir's ideological and political ambitions moulded Malaysia's boom era, but external forces played a crucial role in shaping his development thrusts. As Khoo (2006: 46) noted of the mid-1980s pivot, 'At one time FDI was enlisted in support of the NEP's objectives; this time a sacrifice of (some features of) the NEP's restructuring drew FDI in order to combat recession.' The strategy that emerged entailed a growth pattern that Jayasuriya (2003) termed 'embedded mercantilism': a foreign-dominated, internationally competitive export sector married to a domestic political economy in which non-tradeable sectors (finance, construction, infrastructure, property development) were shaped by quasi-corporatist or clientelist interventions. This growth pattern was enabled by the unexpected dynamism of the previously shallow and low-value added manufactured export sector. Finding Malaysia a conducive site in which to produce for global markets, multinationals upgraded their technology through process automation, invested selectively in deepening production of components and sub-assemblies, and engaged in limited production-related design.

A decade of rapid expansion came to a spectacular end in late 1997, when the Asian Financial Crisis (AFC) drove Malaysia into recession along with other regional economies. Though less exposed to foreign creditors than Thailand or Indonesia, Malaysia's private financial sector had run up considerable leverage via the liberalised stock market while major corporations had taken on high debt loads to finance government-sponsored infrastructure mega-projects. As the prospect of a financial collapse loomed, the government initially and inconsistently experimented with austerity measures, but in a decisive and controversial move, Mahathir imposed controls on the capital account on 1 September 1998. Insulated from further capital flight, the government used monetary and fiscal policy tools to reflate the economy (see She, this volume), and set lending targets to pressure the banking system to assist corporate debt restructuring and finance continued consumption spending. Special-purpose government entities bought bad debts from major corporations and banks, injected capital into the financial system, and renationalised major failing conglomerates, including some of those privatised to *bumiputera* investors just a few years before.

Many observers viewed Malaysia's heterodox crisis response as the beginning of a new, more inward-focused, even 'semi-autarchic' development strategy (Khoo 2006: 186–89). Just as with the NEP era's interventions, however, Mahathir's post-AFC policies sought not to withdraw Malaysia from its engagement with global investors and markets, but to restructure the domestic economy while selectively recalibrating its international linkages. Even as Malaysia's financial system was temporarily quarantined, foreign export manufacturers were exempted from the restrictions on foreign currency transactions. In fact, the government removed remaining restrictions on foreign equity ownership in the manufacturing sector. Moreover, just as in the crisis of the mid-1980s, measures to refresh FDI-led EOI led to a quick recovery via another cyclical boom in global electronics markets.

That same cycle's downturn in 2001, however, together with China's rise as the premier host for export-oriented manufacturing, prompted a new round of alarmed projections that Malaysia's FDI-led model would lose steam in the new millennium. Even before the crisis, Mahathir had launched efforts to prompt a new transition in Malaysia's growth strategy, this time focused on information technology, spearheaded by a high-profile Multimedia Super Corridor project. Following his retirement, the succeeding Abdullah and Najib administrations broadened efforts to nurture new growth sectors. These included information technology industries like software, media production, and business-process outsourcing; biotechnology and green technology that could add new value to old primary sector output; and value-added service industries such as Islamic banking, international education, healthcare, and tourism. Though large sums have been invested, these strategic policies have met with mixed or incremental results; meanwhile, FDI-led export manufacturing remains the pillar of Malaysia's development. Fears that Malaysia would see a sharp fall-off in FDI in the face of regional competition have proved unfounded, as multinational corporations have built production networks integrating Malaysian operations with affiliates in China, Vietnam, and other locations. Though reasonably steady, however, foreign investment has arrived at lower average levels in the new millennium than in the boom years.

Growth, distribution, and governance – pendulum swings and gyroscopic continuity

As the history narrated above shows, Malaysia's development features a pattern in which recurrent political and economic crises prompt sudden shifts in development priorities. Its record is thus hard to portray in terms of a coherent strategic sequence, much less as a singular development 'model'. Though rapid growth has often followed policy change, this often seemed less the result of technocratic foresight than of the partly fortuitous coincidence of international economic forces and shifting domestic political exigencies. Alongside sustained growth, moreover, is a record of costly policy failures (Gomez and Jomo 1997; Gomez 2012). Nonetheless, the fact that Malaysia's policy-makers have proved able, over nearly six decades, to respond to crises, adapt to changing international constraints and opportunities, and find new growth formulae points to important continuities in the political economy of the nation's development.

Hal Hill's (2012) comprehensive survey argues that the oscillations of official development agendas should not obscure the continual importance of competent macroeconomic management and relative international openness. In his assessment (2012: 13), 'openness has always placed a discipline on political excess and policy error . . . The presence of a large export sector with a fundamental imperative of international competitiveness . . . requires at least reasonably efficient government operations, infrastructure and financial services'. Yet, the history recounted above suggests that the reverse causation was at least as important, as Malaysia's successive development strategies provided the policy and political conditions for FDI-led EOI to flourish.

In this regard, the adaptive capacity underpinning Malaysia's development is the product of political factors more than the discipline of market forces, whether external or domestic. A general precondition is the Malaysian state apparatus's relative capacity or strength, something often noted in comparative studies of Southeast Asia (Slater 2010: 7–10). Abdul Rahman (2008, 2012) analyses the sources of the Malaysian government's relative proficiency in formulating and executing development policy, highlighting its institutional mechanisms for mobilising revenue, executing detailed planning, and implementing funding and regulation of growth priorities via a relatively competent civil service. Though the bureaucracy as a whole has been suffused with the NEP's inter-ethnic restructuring mission, key economic policy institutions have been reformed periodically to check inefficiency and upgrade their technical capacity. At the same time, the efficacy of state institutions and developmental interventions has been subject to persistent and trenchant criticism (Hill 2012: 27–31).

A broader point concerns the relationship among politics, institutions, and development strategy. Many of the turning points in Malaysia's development policies have involved simultaneous introduction of new policy-making institutions, from the Department of National Unity that formulated the NEP and the various state economic agencies that implemented it, to Mahathir's HICOM and public–private consultative councils, to the supra-ministerial National Economic Action Council that devised the heterodox response to the AFC, to Najib's vesting a Special Task Force to Facilitate Business (PEMUDAH) with power over his signature development initiatives.

Malaysian development as 'distribution-through-growth'

The focus of explanation must therefore go beyond institutions as necessary factors to the strategic imperatives animating Malaysia's political leadership. A key starting point is the recognition that, more than a question of economic policy, development strategies have been central to the political regime's legitimation, and specifically to the maintenance of the hegemony of the ruling coalition and its dominant party, UMNO. That political project explains the state's pervasive and detailed efforts to manage the distribution of wealth, income, and professional opportunity in Malaysian society. In this vein, many excellent studies of Malaysia's political economy emphasise the effects on economic policy of one or both of two forms of distributional politics. First are the ethno-nationalist motivations for the NEP and its successor policies, and second is the way that practices of patronage and rent-seeking, which have played a growing role in maintaining UMNO rule, have shaped economic policy. The salience of these distributional pressures has often been cited as the chief reason for the failures of Malaysian industrial policies (Jesudason 1989; Hasli and Jomo 2007; Rasiah and Schmidt 2010: 9; Lee 2012).

The question then becomes why and how Malaysia's leaders have restored a balance between these imperatives when crisis has put them into seemingly intractable conflict. A common approach frames this question as one of managing the contradictions between the two imperatives, with policy priorities oscillating between them, pendulum-like, over time.

In this telling, the shift from early post-independence liberalism to the NEP era's socio-economic restructuring reflected the rise of ethno-nationalist politics, which demanded a focus on previously neglected distributional problems that growth had not ameliorated (Khoo 2006: 175). Likewise, the policy turns of the 1980s represented Mahathir's effort to rebalance priorities towards growth, first via an East Asian-style interventionist strategy and subsequently by liberalisation in line with the prevailing forces of globalisation (Stafford 1997). In the crucible of the AFC, the pendulum swung yet again towards distributional goals, this time the maintenance of the state's ability to distribute patronage to favoured business clients as a foundation of UMNO's power and legitimation as the defender of inter-ethnic equity (Khoo 2006: 189–91). Current debates explicitly posit that preoccupations with inter-ethnic wealth distribution inhibit the reforms of governance, educational institutions and service sector industries that are needed if Malaysia is to enhance its competitiveness and escape from the 'middle-income trap' (Henderson and Phillips 2007; Woo 2009; World Bank 2011; Nelson 2012).

While tension between growth and distributional goals is evident in each of the crisis turning-points in Malaysia's development history, the 'pendulum' pattern is less an explanation than a restatement of the question of why and how Malaysia's rulers have harmonised these ostensibly conflictual imperatives across several decades and major policy shifts. This 'gyroscopic' quality of Malaysia's development has much to do with the extraordinary continuity in political leadership across nearly six post-independence decades. A hegemonic party-state regime like Malaysia's creates political incentives for leaders to pursue 'distribution-through-growth', rather than to maximise either short-term distributional pay-offs or growth-promoting liberalisation that would limit the state's discretionary power to shape the economy's distributional patterns.

Three interrelated themes emerge as this analysis is applied to Malaysia's development history. The first is that economic policy-making has not simply balanced specific growth-promoting policies, state agencies, and economic sectors against other policies and industries that serve ethnic or patronage distributional politics, a pattern seen in 'bifurcated states' (Doner and Ramsay 1997: 249). Rather, Malaysia's interventionist state has crafted development strategies in which growth and distributional purposes are inextricably intertwined and simultaneously pursued. Second, the disjunctures in Malaysia's development history have typically involved a selective layering of new policies onto old ones, rather than clean breaks with prior strategies. Crisis-response measures have been abrupt and politically fraught, yet most significant reforms have been implemented in a comparatively selective or incremental way, often by applying new policies to particular sectors or new projects while exempting established interests temporarily. Third, and following on these points, changes in economic strategy have not been matched with deep changes in governance, with periods of market-based reforms aimed at restoring growth alternating with interventions focused wholly on redistributing wealth or income. Instead, government leaders have maintained the state's superintending role in national development throughout the country's history, even while shifting the specific forms and tools of policy intervention.

Thus, for example, while the early post-independence period is usually described as involving a laissez-faire economic strategy, the ruling Alliance in fact used strategic developmental interventions to consolidate the coalition's political position. Tun Razak, as minister of national and rural development, substantially revamped the institutional mechanisms for Malay rural development that had been instituted in the late colonial period. The development of FELDA estates, which packaged infrastructure and credit facilities for smallholder agricultural development, presaged the NEP's expansion of bureaucratic regulation in the commercial, petty manufacturing, and construction sectors. The Rural and Industrial Development Authority, forerunner to MARA (Majlis Amanah Rakyat, Council of Trust for Indigenous People), expanded its programmes into urban areas starting in 1959, focusing on providing loans to Malay contractors and small enterprises, and on business training. The growth of Maybank during the 1960s reflected government efforts to integrate the Malay community into the modern financial sector, a mission even more overtly espoused by the establishment of Bank Bumiputera in 1965. The pattern of political–business patronage later blamed on NEP-era statism was also evident in the Alliance period (White 2004: 392–98). Thus, economic policy during the Alliance period was imbued with developmental and distributional logics, even if these took a quite different form than the more expansive statist-nationalist programmes prevailing across the contemporaneous developing world.

The post-1969 reconfiguration of Malaysia's political regime – from an inter-ethnic elite partnership to 'coercive consociationalism' (Mauzy 1993) – indisputably reflected ethno-nationalist pressures; these found expression in the NEP's state-led socio-economic restructuring agenda. Jesudason (1989: 117–23) argues that the Malaysian state quickly became 'overburdened' by its distributional commitments. Against the backdrop of ethno-populist pressure, however, the government's efforts to maintain high growth rates become analytically important. The NEP's signature documents, especially the Mid-Term Review of the Second Malaysia Plan, explicitly framed social restructuring within a context of a new commitment to growth. The controversial Industrial Coordination Act and Petroleum Development Act were both amended within a few years when negative impacts on investment rates became clear. Most importantly, as noted above, the NEP's interventionist mission was matched by the embrace of FDI-led export-production, initially segmented in the FTZs in order to protect established industries serving the domestic market (Stafford 1997).

A similar pattern of policy layering and recalibration of state interventionism is evident across the Mahathir era's major strategic shifts. Though the heavy industries thrust was ostensibly an emulation of East Asian statist-nationalism, the pillars of Malaysia's prior development strategy – FDI-reliance and the promotion of *bumiputera* enterprise – were reconfigured rather than jettisoned. Notably, the heavy industry projects relied on joint-venture partnerships between state-enterprise and multinational business, with communal political motives evident in the exclusion of domestic ethnic-Chinese capital (Bowie 1991). The sudden near-bankruptcy of state-led development in 1985–86, however, appeared to place Malaysia's rulers in a terrible bind between the demands of ethno-nationalist legitimation and the need to revive private sector investment. The government announced the 'temporary abeyance' of the NEP's restructuring goals in 1986, with Mahathir observing that, '[t]he government will slow the redistribution of wealth whether we like it or not, now that there is no growth at all.'[4]

Many accounts heralded a turn towards the market and a new priority on growth at the expense of state-orchestrated distributional politics (Stafford 1997; Bowie and Unger 1997: 93–4). While symbolically significant, though, the 1986 liberalisation measures remained incremental and selective, and did not herald a broad-front 'retreat of the state' from efforts to shape the pattern of investment and distribution of wealth. The SOEs of the heavy industries programme were revamped rather than abandoned, while government-linked companies in telecommunications, finance, transportation, and property development took on new service-provision roles supporting the booming foreign-dominated export sector. FDI policy itself deployed new incentives and infrastructure, in the form of high-technology parks and skills-development agencies, targeted at encouraging more capital- and technology-intensive production (Felker and Jomo 2007). Mahathir's privatisation policy became the means of cementing networks between top state and party officials and a class of established and new business tycoons (Jomo 1995). In short, Malaysia's boom-era commitment to globalisation and private sector-led growth involved a layering of new policies on old in pursuit of the long-standing commitment to 'distribution-through-growth'.

The power of the state's distributional role became suddenly more obvious to international observers in the wake of the AFC. Mahathir's bold, market-defying response was widely regarded as a hard swing of the policy pendulum, with distributional politics now paramount at the expense of the systemic liberalisation required for restoring growth. Notwithstanding the prime minister's acid condemnation of global financial investors, however, it soon became clear that the government's post-crisis strategy involved incremental change rather than a decisive break in the established pro-globalisation growth model. The National Economic Recovery Action Plan of 1998 resisted a 'fire sale' approach that would liquidate entire swathes of the insolvent corporate establishment, yet the government did broker the sale of several major industrial projects. Even as capital controls impinged on global portfolio investors, the government opened new opportunities for FDI in a range of service industries. Meanwhile, ethnic share-holding quotas were relaxed to permit ethnic-Chinese Malaysian investors' acquisition of major *bumiputera* corporations, while other major Malay-owned conglomerates were renationalised by the Finance Ministry's investment arm. These measures belied a widely held view that the state's *bumiputera* corporate clients had effectively captured the policy agenda and hobbled the prospects for growth-seeking reforms.

Upon taking the reins of government in 2003, the Abdullah administration initially signalled a departure. He cancelled several infrastructure 'mega-projects' and pledged to subject the roster of government-linked corporations to performance-based management discipline as a prelude to gradual privatisation. Yet, the promised retrenchment of the government's economic role failed to arrive (Case 2005). Rather, Abdullah's development programme simply reorganised the pattern of government intervention to orchestrate infrastructure investment in support of FDI-led growth, primarily through new public authorities' administration of investment incentives and infrastructure development in regional 'economic corridors'.

A similar policy dynamic unfolded after the 2009 leadership transition. Najib Razak's signature initiatives pledged broad economic liberalisation and government reform in order to complete Mahathir's Vision 2020 project of elevating Malaysia to high-income status. The Government Transformation Programme (GTP) pledged to revive the efficiency and responsiveness of public services, while the Economic Transformation Programme (ETP) aimed to stimulate private investment by privatising government-backed corporations, ensuring fairer competition, and refocusing the development budget on investments in skills and technology. Through consultations with the business sector, the ETP identified a large number of specific investment projects aimed at upgrading Malaysia's key industries. Much like the policies issued in earlier phases of Malaysia's development, however, these plans comprise an array of selective interventions to be implemented at the state's discretion. Calls for broader changes to NEP-inspired *bumiputera* preferences met with opposition from within the ranks of the ruling party, UMNO. By the 2013 election, the two headline development programmes themselves had become objects of political controversy. The ruling coalition's diminished electoral support suggested that efforts to harness the new development thrusts to bolster regime legitimacy had not paid dividends. The response from international observers and investors was mixed. Malaysia sustained inflows of FDI during a downward global trend after the Great Recession of 2008 (though capital outflows grew even faster), and the country's position in international indexes of competitiveness and governance quality ticked upwards.

Conclusion

Malaysia's changing development strategies reflect adaptive responses to changing domestic politics and international conditions, rather than unique strategic foresight or nimble policy sequencing. Yet, neither these strategies' content, nor their implementation successes and failures were predetermined by crisis exigencies. Key to Malaysia's development record has been the government's ability to shift its economic policies to restore growth while preserving its powers and practices of discretionary intervention. That ability relied on the state's relatively strong institutions and policy capacity, which have enabled Malaysia's leaders not only to adopt new strategies, but to do so selectively.

Despite change over time, therefore, Malaysia's development strategies reflect an enduring political logic by which policy-makers have integrated growth and distributional goals. Even in the context of a pluralistic society in which politics revolves around representing and responding to the demands of societal interests, the drive to maintain the ruling coalition's quasi-monopoly over a semi-democratic regime has given Malaysia's leaders comparatively encompassing and long-term interests in economic affairs. Alongside more prosaic and short-term distributional politics, therefore, the promise of development and claims of credit for its achievement have remained vital to the perennial quest for legitimation. This imperative, rather than either the demands of market competition or the rise of liberalising social coalitions, explains the 'gyroscopic' quality of Malaysia's efforts to find new growth formulae in the wake of successive crises while preserving an interventionist governance system in which state agencies actively shape investment opportunities and rewards.

Whether the Malaysian state's adaptive capacity can engineer a new round of growth, by escaping the middle-income trap, is the focus of vigorous academic and policy debates. According to many observers, the need to shift from production- to innovation-based growth holds profound implications for Malaysia's development strategies in general and its system of economic governance in particular (Nelson 2012). From a liberal perspective, only a reduction in the state's overbearing economic presence and an increased role for free competition can stimulate gains in economic efficiency needed for Malaysia's next stage of development (Hill 2012; Lee 2012; Menon 2012).

The development pattern recounted in this chapter, however, cautions against any hasty conclusion that Malaysia has reached a juncture at which incremental policy layering is insufficient to sustain growth. Some observers thus argue that the missing element in Southeast Asian NICs' upgrading agenda is not freer and more competitive markets, but more effective state policy interventions and institutions to support the growth of innovation capabilities among local industry (Doner 2009; Rasiah 2010: 90). In Malaysia, the Najib administration's policy agenda signals an effort to undertake this latter route, reforming the public sector and liberalising selectively while continuing to assert the state's central role in guiding development through new strategic investments. Apart from the merits of its content, therefore, the approach itself suggests instead that the Malaysian state retains its ambition to manage 'distribution-through-growth' (Gomez 2012: 78–80).

Finally, though, Malaysia's current strategy is being pursued in a political environment far different from that of earlier programmes. Today, a more assertive civil society and a more sceptical private sector mean that the *credibility* of government initiatives is more directly important to their success. In this view, the Economic Transformation Programme confronts a central paradox in pledging to trim the state's role in favour of private sector leadership, but relying on detailed, centrally coordinated projects to engineer a new growth model. Asia's other industrialising economies have seen a variety of reform trajectories, some involving the retreat of state interventionism and others its renovation (Walter and Zhang 2012; D'Costa 2012). In Malaysia, contestation surrounding the political regime and the quality of governance has overshadowed the specifics of initiatives to reform the public sector and prompt industrial upgrading. As in several of Asia's most successful NICs, then, the emergence of a new democratic dispensation may be integral to the Malaysian state's effort to reinvigorate its governance capacity, and thereby enable novel strategies to address emergent development challenges and opportunities (Nelson 2012: 56).

Notes

1 Edited volumes offering historical overviews of Malaysia's economic development strategies include Hill *et al.* 2012; Jomo 1993, 2007; ISIS 2011; Khoo 2012b; Nelson *et al.* 2008. Monographs include Ariff 1991; Bowie 1991; Gomez and Jomo 1997; Jesudason 1989; Jomo 1990; Rasiah 1995; Searle 1999. Chapter-length overviews include Hill 2012; Khoo 2006, 2012a; Lim 2011; Ishak 2003.

2 Jesudason (1989: 56) writes that 'Malaysia was among the few newly independent countries to keep intact the large Western stake in the economy and to solicit foreign capital to enter into the anticipated growth sector, manufacturing.'

3 The act initially allowed 100 percent foreign ownership in projects exporting more than 80 percent of their output, and that qualifying ratio was later relaxed.

4 *Asian Wall Street Journal*, 22 September 1986, quoted in Jesudason 1989: 122.

Bibliography

Abdul Rahman Embong (2008) 'Developmentalist state in Malaysia: its origins, nature, and contemporary transformation', in Joan M. Nelson, Jacob Meerman and Abdul Raman Embong (eds), *Globalization & National Autonomy: The Experience of Malaysia*, Bangi: Institute of Malaysian and International Studies, Universiti Kebangsaan Malaysia, pp. 27–58.

Abdul Rahman Embong (2012) 'Developmental state capacity and institutional reform', in Khoo Boo Teik (ed.), *Policy Regimes and the Political Economy of Poverty Reduction in Malaysia*, New York: Palgrave Macmillan, pp. 217–50.

Athukoralge, Prema-chandra (2001) *Crisis and Recovery in Malaysia: The Role of Capital Controls*, Cheltenham: Edward Elgar.

Bowie, Alasdair (1991) *Crossing the Industrial Divide: State, Society, and the Politics of Economic Transformation in Malaysia*, New York: Columbia University Press.

Bowie, Alasdair and Daniel Unger (1997) *The Politics of Open Economies*, New York: Cambridge University Press.

Case, William F. (2000) 'The new Malaysian nationalism: infirm beginnings, crashing finale', *Asian Ethnicity*, 1(2): 131–47.

Case, William F. (2005) 'Malaysia: new reforms, old continuities, tense ambiguities', *Journal of Development Studies*, 41(2): 284–309.

D'Costa, Anthony P. (2012) 'Capitalism and economic nationalism: Asian state activism in the world economy', in Anthony P. D'Costa (ed.), *Globalization and Economic Nationalism in Asia*, Oxford: Oxford University Press, pp. 1–32.

Doner, Richard F. (2009) *The Politics of Uneven Development: Thailand's Economic Growth in Comparative Perspective*, New York: Cambridge University Press.

Doner, Richard F. and Ansil Ramsay (1997) 'Competitive clientelism and economic governance: the case of Thailand', in Sylvia Maxfield and Ben Ross Schneider (eds), *Business and the State in Developing Countries*, Ithaca: Cornell University Press, pp. 237–76.

Felker, Greg and Jomo K.S. (2007) 'Investment policy in Malaysia', in Jomo K.S. (ed.), *Malaysian Industrial Policy*, Singapore: Singapore University Press, pp. 56–81.

Gereffi, Gary (1990) 'Paths of industrialization: an overview', in Gary Gereffi and Donald L. Wyman (eds), *Manufacturing Miracles: Paths of Industrialization in Latin America and East Asia*, Princeton: Princeton University Press, pp. 3–31.

Gomez, Edmund Terence (2002) 'Political business in Malaysia: party factionalism, corporate development, and economic crisis', in Edmund Terence Gomez (ed.), *Political Business in East Asia*, London: Routledge, pp. 82–114.
Gomez, Edmund Terence (2012) 'State–business linkages in Southeast Asia: the developmental state, neo-liberalism, and enterprise development', in Andrew Walter and Zhang Xiaoke (eds), *East Asian Capitalism: Diversity, Continuity, and Change*, Oxford: Oxford University Press, pp. 68–88.
Gomez, Edmund Terence and Jomo K.S. (1997) *Malaysia's Political Economy: Politics, Patronage, and Profits*, Cambridge: Cambridge University Press.
Hasli Hasan and Jomo K.S. (2007) 'Rent-seeking and industrial policy in Malaysia', in Jomo K.S. (ed.), *Malaysian Industrial Policy*, Singapore: Singapore University Press, pp. 157–78.
Henderson, Jeffrey and Richard Phillips (2007) 'Unintended consequences: social policy, state institutions and the "stalling" of the Malaysian industrialization project', *Economy and Society*, 36(1): 78–102.
Hill, Hal (2012) 'Malaysian economic development: looking backward and forward', in Hal Hill, Tham Siew Yean and Ragayah Mat Zin (eds), *Malaysia's Development Challenges: Graduating from the Middle*, New York: Routledge, pp. 1–42.
Hill, Hal, Tham Siew Yean and Ragayah Mat Zin (eds) (2012) *Malaysia's Development Challenges: Graduating from the Middle*, New York: Routledge.
Institute of Strategic and International Studies (ISIS) (2011) *Malaysia: Policies and Issues in Economic Development*, Kuala Lumpur: Institute of Strategic and International Studies Malaysia.
Ishak Shari (2003) 'Economic growth and social development in Malaysia, 1971–98', in Martin Andersson and Christer Gunnarsson (eds), *Development and Structural Change in Asia-Pacific: Globalising Miracles or End of a Model?*, London: RoutledgeCurzon, pp. 108–24.
Jayasuriya, Kanishika (2003) 'Embedded mercantilism and open regionalism: the crisis of a regional political project', *Third World Quarterly*, 24(2): 339–55.
Jesudason, James V. (1989) *Ethnicity and the Economy: The State, Chinese Business, and Multinationals in Malaysia*, Singapore: Oxford University Press.
Jomo K.S. (1990) *Growth and Structural Change in the Malaysian Economy*, Basingstoke: Macmillan.
Jomo K.S. (ed.) (1993) *Industrialising Malaysia: Policy, Performance, Prospects*, London: Routledge & Kegan Paul.
Jomo K.S. (1994) 'The PROTON saga: Malaysian car, Mitsubishi gain', in K.S. Jomo (ed.), *Japan and Malaysian Development: In the Shadow of the Rising Sun*, London: Routledge, pp. 263–90.
Jomo K.S. (ed.) (1995) *Privatizing Malaysia: Rents, Rhetoric, and Reality*, Boulder: Westview Press.
Jomo K.S. (2003) *M-way: Mahathir's Economic Legacy*, Kuala Lumpur: Forum.
Jomo K.S. (ed.) (2007) *Malaysian Industrial Policy*, Singapore: Singapore University Press.
Katzenstein, Peter J. (1985) *Small States in World Markets: Industrial Policy in Europe*, Ithaca: Cornell University Press.
Khoo Boo Teik (2006) 'Malaysia: balancing development and power', in Garry Rodan, Kevin Hewison and Richard Robinson (eds), *The Political Economy of South-East Asia: Markets, Power and Contestation*, 3rd edn, New York: Oxford University Press, pp. 170–96.
Khoo Boo Teik (2012a) 'Development strategies and poverty reduction', in Khoo Boo Teik (ed.), *Policy Regimes and the Political Economy of Poverty Reduction in Malaysia*, New York: Palgrave Macmillan, pp. 28–63.
Khoo Boo Teik (ed.) (2012b) *Policy Regimes and the Political Economy of Poverty Reduction in Malaysia*, New York: Palgrave Macmillan.
Lee, Cassey H. (2012) 'Microeconomic reform in Malaysia', in Hal Hill, Tham Siew Yean and Ragayah Mat Zin (eds), *Malaysia's Development Challenges: Graduating from the Middle*, New York: Routledge, pp. 155–73.
Lim, David (1992) 'The dynamics of economic policy-making: a study of Malaysian trade policies and performance', in A. MacIntyre and K. Jayasuriya (eds), *The Dynamics of Economic Policy Reform in South-east Asia and the South-west Pacific*, Singapore: Oxford University Press, pp. 94–114.
Lim, David (2011) 'Economic development: a historical survey', in Institution of Strategic and International Strategies (ed.), *Malaysia: Policies and Issues in Economic Development*, Kuala Lumpur: Institution of Strategic and International Strategies Malaysia, pp. 1–38.
Mauzy, D. (1993) 'Malaysia: Malay political hegemony and "coercive consociationalism"', in J. McGarry and B. O'Leary (eds), *The Politics of Ethnic Conflict Regulation*, London and New York: Routledge, pp. 106–27.

Menon, Jayant (2012) 'Growth without private investment: what happened in Malaysia and can it be fixed?', *ADB Economic Working Papers*, Manila: Asian Development Bank.

Mohammad Ariff (1991) *The Malaysian Economy: Pacific Connections*, Singapore: Oxford University Press.

Nelson, Joan M. (2012) 'Political challenges in economic upgrading: Malaysia compared with South Korea and Taiwan', in Hal Hill, Tham Siew Yean and Ragayah Mat Zin (eds), *Malaysia's Development Challenges: Graduating from the Middle*, New York: Routledge, pp. 43–62.

Nelson, Joan M., Jacob Meerman and Abdul Rahman Embong (eds) (2008) *Globalization and National Autonomy: The Experience of Malaysia*, Bangi: Institute of Malaysian and International Studies, Universiti Kebangsaan Malaysia.

Rasiah, Rajah (1995) *Foreign Capital and Industrialization in Malaysia*, New York: St Martin's Press.

Rasiah, Rajah (2010) 'Industrialization in the second-tier NIEs', in Rajah Rasiah and Johannes Dragsbaek Schmidt (eds), *The New Political Economy of Southeast Asia*, Cheltenham and Northampton: Edward Elgar, pp. 44–102.

Rasiah, Rajah and Johannes Dragsbaek Schmidt (2010) 'Introduction', in Rajah Rasiah and Johannes Dragsbaek Schmidt (eds), *The New Political Economy of Southeast Asia*, Cheltenham and Northampton: Edward Elgar, pp. 1–43.

Searle, Peter (1999) *The Riddle of Malaysian Capitalism*, Sydney: Allen & Unwin.

Slater, Dan (2010) *Ordering Power: Contentious Politics and Authoritarian Leviathans in Southeast Asia*, Cambridge and New York: Cambridge University Press.

Stafford, D. Geoffrey S.D. (1997) 'Malaysia's new economic policy and the global economy: the evolution of ethnic accommodation', *Pacific Review*, 10(4): 556–80.

Stubbs, Richard (2005) *Rethinking Asia's Economic Miracle: The Political Economy of War, Prosperity and Crisis*, Houndmills: Palgrave Macmillan.

Walter, Andrew and Zhang Xiaoke (2012) 'Debating East Asian capitalism: issues and themes', in Andrew Walter and Zhang Xiaoke (eds), *East Asian Capitalism: Diversity, Continuity, and Change*, Oxford: Oxford University Press, pp. 3–26.

White, Nicholas J. (2004) 'The beginnings of crony capitalism: business, politics and economic development in Malaysia, *c.* 1955–70', *Modern Asian Studies*, 38(2): 389–417.

Woo Wing Thye (2009) Getting Malaysia Out of the Middle Income Trap, PhD Dissertation, University of California, Davis.

World Bank (1993) *The East Asian Miracle: Economic Growth and Public Policy*, Washington DC: World Bank.

World Bank (2011) 'Brain drain', *Malaysia Economic Monitor*, Washington DC: World Bank.

12

Fiscal and monetary policy in Malaysia

Juggling economic imperatives and political reality

Xiaoye She

Since its independence, Malaysia has achieved rapid economic growth and significant poverty reduction, while keeping a relatively successful record of curbing inflation in comparison to other developing countries. Fiscal and monetary policy play major roles in guiding investment and spending behaviour to meet development and stabilisation goals in both the public and private sectors. This chapter provides an overview of fiscal and monetary policy in Malaysia, with attention to institutional foundations, the role of economic and political determinants in policy formulation and implementation, as well as interrelations among crises, economic restructuring and policy reforms. While political influence cannot be ignored in either policy area, recognition of the unsustainability of fiscal deficits as well as continued commitment to a balanced-risk approach in central banking may serve as important first steps in reorienting macroeconomic policies toward supporting private sector development and structural reforms.

Fiscal policy in Malaysia: institutions, history and the issue of fiscal deficits

Fiscal policy in Malaysia is designed to serve both stabilisation and development goals in meeting key objectives such as growth, equity, macroeconomic stability, reform and restructuring, as well as pursuing sectorial and regional development. The federal constitution provides the fundamental institutional structure for fiscal policy in Malaysia, as it grants the federal government revenue-raising power, via most important taxes, and the power to expend operating and development allocations. State and local governments are responsible for providing essential services, however; intergovernmental transfers and loans from the federal government supplement their relatively small and inelastic revenue base. Public finance accounts are divided into operating and development accounts, with the size of the budget for each determined by revenues and the government's capacity to raise non-inflationary financing, respectively (IMF 1999). Various statutory bodies and non-financial public enterprises (NFPEs)[1] share these operating and development expenditures in pursuing government objectives (IMF 1999).

Within the federal government, the Economic Planning Unit (EPU) under the Prime Minister's Office performs the most important role in formulating and implementing development policies that directly impact upon fiscal policy, including drafting five-year Malaysia Plans. The ministry of finance (MOF) serves as the main centre for drafting, implementing and executing year-to-year budget plans, upon consultation with EPU and other federal ministries (IMF 1999; Hassan *et al.* 2012). The longer time horizon of Malaysia Plans complements budget plans in spelling out major policy directions and changes, as well as detailing new tax proposals and yearly expenditures.

Adherence to the principle of fiscal conservatism inspires tight budgetary control over operating expenditures, which are required to not exceed current revenues (Meesook 2001). This commitment has allowed the Malaysian government to maintain a current surplus, defined as current revenues less operating expenditures, in most years since 1970. In addition, the majority of borrowings used to finance development expenditures come from non-inflationary domestic sources, with explicit debt ceilings specified by the External Loan Act 1963 and other legislation. Nonetheless, fiscal discretion exists and contributes to a persistent overall fiscal deficit, reflected mostly in development expenditures and off-budget activities. Figure 12.1 presents a synopsis of the government's overall financial position, revealing a fiscal deficit in most years except the brief period of 1993–97.

New Economic Policy and thereafter: the role of fiscal policy

As Doraisami (2011: 9) argues, fiscal policy in Malaysia has been intimately linked to the New Economic Policy (NEP) since its commencement in 1970. The pre-NEP era, 1956–70, was marked by import-substitution industrialisation (ISI) and a relatively laissez-faire approach towards the domestic private sector, which failed to promote significant economic development (Hassan *et al.* 2012; Ritchie 2004). While the government promoted ISI through tax exemptions under the Pioneer Industries Ordinance 1958, state intervention was much less pervasive and lacked a significant ethnic dimension compared with the NEP's focus on macroeconomic stabilisation, infrastructure, social services and labour market conditions (Schätzl 1988: 46). During this period, rural poverty and unemployment rates both rose dramatically, due to drops in primary commodity prices in international markets (Ritchie 2004).

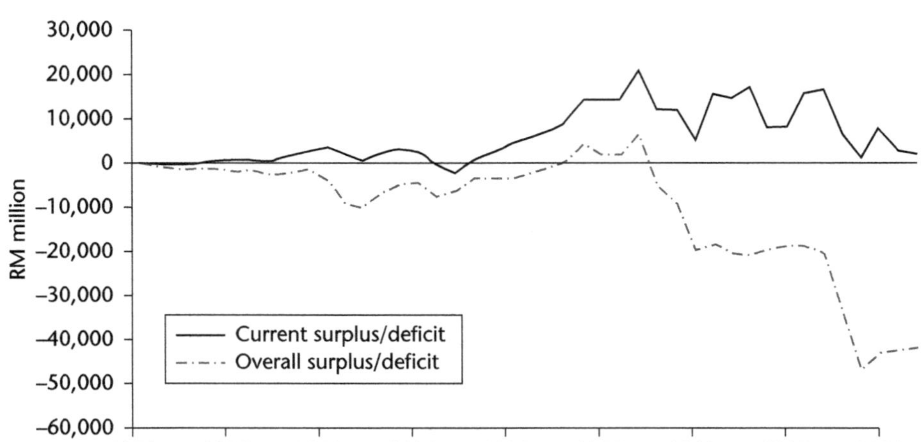

Figure 12.1 Government financial position in Malaysia, 1970–2012
Source: Ministry of Finance, Time Series: Public Finance.

The ethnic dimension in rising economic inequality triggered political and social unrest in 1969 and induced the design and implementation of the NEP (see Hwok-Aun Lee, this volume). Towards meeting the NEP's goals of restructuring the economy and reducing inequality between ethnic groups, fiscal policy helped inject tax and other sources of revenues to fuel policy thrusts, while creating incentives and disincentives that guided private investment and employment behaviour. Massive government expenditure and heavy government intervention in the economy were supported by newly discovered petroleum reserves, which prevented a dramatic increase in debt in the short term (Doraisami 2011: 9).

Introduced under the premiership of Tun Abdul Razak Hussein, these highly interventionist economic strategies flourished under Mahathir Mohammad, prime minister from 1982 to 2003, who adopted an extreme pro-Malay position and nationalist 'Look East' policy, marked by a combination of government subsidies and tariff protection (Ritchie 2004). As earlier, these fiscal incentives were supported by rising income from petroleum sales and expanding exports from foreign multinationals (Ritchie 2004). Nonetheless, with moderation of federal revenue growth over 1980–83 and a decline in internal sources of saving, this expansionary fiscal policy was no longer sustainable without over-relying on foreign borrowing (Narayanan 1996).[2] Resulting twin deficits in fiscal position and balance of payments forced the Malaysian government to implement comprehensive structural reform programmes, with the aim of reducing spending and reordering national objectives to be more consistent with domestic resource availability (Vijayaledchumy 2003: 173).

Daim Zainuddin, finance minister in the mid-1980s, moved to cut development spending and curb current expenditures, while pushing for major privatisation initiatives in national industries such as airlines, telecommunications, shipping, electricity and heavy industry (Narayanan 1996). The remaining NFPEs also increasingly operated along commercial principles (IMF 1999). While these moves resulted in improvements in the federal budget and better external debt conditions, privatisation moves during this period were not only small and selective, but also arguably helped transfer state-controlled assets to private *bumiputera* entrepreneurs with close government ties (Adam and Cavendish 1995; Ritchie 2004).

Anwar Ibrahim, Daim's successor as finance minister, continued Daim's pro-private initiatives and maintained the fiscal line on curbing current expenditures, while introducing new measures to reduce income and corporate taxes. On the other hand, Anwar chose to shelve Daim's proposal for a value-added tax (VAT) and did little to curb development spending, the majority of which went to infrastructure projects (Narayanan 1996). While some view Anwar as a rational politician who was unwilling to make a politically unpopular decision, others argue that he had little power to implement broader fiscal reform, as most oversight power resided with the EPU (Narayanan 1996; Ritchie 2004).

Although a fiscal surplus was achieved between 1993 and 1997 (see Figure 12.1), a deficit reappeared in 1998 and was maintained thereafter. Prolonged fiscal expansion after 1997 indicates that the crisis of that year might have served as a trigger and justification for increased spending. However, unsustainably high government expenditures, including massive infrastructural upgrading, counterbalanced by unstable petroleum levies, predated the crisis (Narayanan 1996).

Fiscal deficit: economic and political perspectives

Persistent fiscal deficits in Malaysia raise important theoretical and policy debates over both the nature and sources of those deficits, including issues of fiscal discretion, counter-cyclicality versus pro-cyclicality, reliance on petroleum-generated revenues, and the impact of political interests and institutions.

In analysing fiscal deficits in Malaysia, Narayanan (2007) finds these have been higher than in neighbouring countries as a result of lack of fiscal discipline.[3] While Malaysia maintains an official commitment to counter-cyclical fiscal policies, that preference has not been borne out in reality. For example, Rafiq (2013) discovers that fiscal policy in Malaysia has been increasingly pro-cyclical over the last twenty-five years, as revealed by a strong positive correlation between changes in government spending and domestic economic conditions.

Other scholars have raised the issue of over-reliance on oil wealth or other natural resources as a major revenue source. Eifert *et al.*'s (2003) analysis of oil wealth and fiscal policy shows that the extent to which a country benefits from oil wealth is often unclear, limited or even negative. In Malaysia, reliance on natural resources as a revenue source has increased in recent decades, with the share of non-tax revenues from PETRONAS and petroleum and gas royalties exceeding 20 percent of non-tax revenue in 2007–10. As Narayanan (1996) points out, the future of fiscal management in Malaysia may depend on how well the country can reverse its current reliance on petroleum and tap into new and reliable sources of revenue.

Political interests and institutions may also serve as important factors in determining the direction of fiscal policy in Malaysia. Doraisami (2011) finds that Malaysia has the highest ratio of public servants to overall population among neighbouring countries, with wages and salaries of public servants as the largest line-item by function in annual budgets. Others suggest that coalition politics drive illiberal government intervention, noting a strong influence of political business cycles on the magnitude of expansionary fiscal policies (Ritchie 2004; Pepinsky 2007). Finally, there has been a lack of consistent commitment to liberalisation and privatisation, as fiscal and other economic policies have often been introduced to maximise coalition support for political and economic interests (Ritchie 2004; Narayanan 1996; Jomo and Hamilton-Hart 2001).

Monetary policy in Malaysia: institutions, history and central bank independence

Since its establishment, Bank Negara Malaysia (BNM) has served as the most important monetary policy-making body in Malaysia. Governed by a board of directors, BNM is tasked with multiple mandates, including maintaining price stability, sustainable economic growth and financial stability. In recent years, BNM has increasingly emphasised balancing risks to growth and inflation whenever a policy decision is made (Zeti 2009). BNM also oversees other financial authorities, such as Labuan Financial Services Authority, the Securities Commission of Malaysia, and the Malaysian Deposit Insurance Corporation (BNM 2013b).

BNM implements its commitment to price stability without an explicit inflation-targeting framework (McCauley 2006: 172). In reality, exchange rate stability represents another key monetary policy objective (McCauley 2006). In tackling competing imperatives, BNM claims that the key issue is the maintenance of a flexible exchange rate and monetary independence in the face of increasingly volatile capital flows (Ooi 2009).

Policy communication has been strengthened in recent years through regular release of policy announcements and frequent signalling through policy rates and monetary operations. Previously, monetary targets such as monetary aggregates were often kept as informal targets and not formally announced to the public (Cheong 2005: 209). Since 2004, a newly established monetary policy committee has met at least six times a year, issuing monetary policy statements on the same day (BNM 2013c). With the implementation of a new interest framework, the overnight policy rate (OPR) has become the main indicator of monetary policy stance, with moderate adjustments usually between 25 and 50 base points to signal changes in monetary policy directions. Initially set at 2.70 in 2004, the policy rate was raised incrementally to 3.50 by 2008 to combat inflationary pressure, then gradually reduced to avoid curbing growth; it has remained at 3.00 since May 2011 (BNM 2013c).

The framework for monetary operations and liquidity management comprises instruments for both conventional and Islamic interbank money markets, as well as monetary operations on the foreign exchange market. BNM has taken efforts to widen the range of available monetary policy instruments on the domestic money market. Current monetary instruments on the conventional money market include uncollateralised money market borrowings, repo borrowings, BNM monetary notes and several others, whereas the introduction of Islamic monetary instruments based on *shari'a* concepts is intended to increase the effectiveness of monetary transmission mechanisms on the Islamic money market (BNM 2012, 2013a).

On the foreign exchange market, sterilised intervention is BNM's major instrument, although it tends to work more effectively in combination with capital controls (McCauley 2006). While Malaysia abandoned its official commitment to bilateral exchange rate stability in 2005, sterilised intervention is still used to influence the level and volatility of exchange rates on a regular basis. On the other hand, the shutdown of the offshore market for ringgit in 1998 marked the beginning of de-internationalisation of the ringgit, which barred its international convertibility and forced foreign holders of ringgit assets to repatriate their assets (Pepinsky 2007: 149). Despite the development of a non-deliverable off-shore market in 2005, the reinternationalisation of the ringgit is still a topic under discussion, possibly to be pursued, cautiously and progressively, in the future (McCauley 2006; BNM 2013a).

Balancing growth and inflation: from monetary targeting to interest rate targeting

On 26 January 1959, BNM opened its doors as the central bank of Malaysia. In its early days, BNM focused on liquidity management in the financial system, primarily through prescriptions of interest rates and portfolio restrictions, which included ceilings on lending (BNM 2009). Similar to other central banks, BNM's monetary policy often reflects its reaction to prevailing economic conditions, in particular when facing external shocks (Shaari 2008).

BNM's commitment to price stability faced major challenges in the two global oil shocks in the early and late 1970s. Annual inflation in consumer prices reached a historical high of 17.3 percent in 1974, then spiked again to 9.7 percent in 1981 (World Bank 2013). Facing destabilising international monetary conditions, BNM focused during this period primarily on maintaining price stability and ensuring a stable currency (Shaari 2008: 12). By the mid-1980s, a sharp decline in global commodity prices brought the Malaysian economy and fiscal position again into trouble, and BNM stepped in to ease monetary policy, allowing the ringgit to depreciate. These steps worked in tandem with steps toward privatisation and liberalisation in fiscal and other macroeconomic policies to boost both domestic and export markets in a relatively short time.

The economy recovered with a growth rate of 5.4 percent in 1987, marking the beginning of a decade of economic expansion, with an average growth rate of 9.3 percent until the Asian financial crisis (World Bank 2013). Monetary management during this period focused on dealing with steadily growing inflationary pressures. The tight monetary policy stance signalled by the rise of domestic interest rates, however, juxtaposed against the general perception of an undervalued ringgit,[4] attracted substantial inflows of short-term foreign capital, which caused excess liquidity in the banking system and created a dilemma for monetary policy-making (Shaari 2008). Since sterilised intervention operations failed to constrain the inflow of short-term capital, BNM was forced to implement several temporary exchange control measures in early 1994 (BNM 1999; Shaari 2008).

Prior to the mid-1990s, the major strategy for monetary policy was thus based on targeting monetary aggregates (Cheong 2005).[5] The increasing volatility of capital inflows in the early 1990s indicated that monetary aggregates were no longer stable targets, so a shift to interest-rate targeting was considered necessary to improve effective transmission of monetary policies (Cheong 2005). As Cheong (2005: 211) points out, the move was preconditioned by the liberalisation of interest rates since the 1970s, gradual financial deregulation, and a shift in financing patterns towards a more interest-sensitive market since the 1980s.

Central bank independence in Malaysia: a political economy perspective

An interesting comparison between fiscal and monetary policy in Malaysia is that monetary policy formulation and implementation have enjoyed higher levels of institutional and behavioural independence, coupled with an explicit mandate on major policy objectives (Byun 2006; Hamilton-Hart 2002; McCauley 2006). As Eijffinger and De Haan (1996) indicate, these provisions are important institutional devices for maintaining price stability, which provides a potential explanation for the relatively low inflation levels in Malaysian economic history. Furthermore, Malaysia has comparatively infrequent turnovers in the position of central bank governor; in Malaysia, terms average 6.6 years, compared with 3.2 years in neighbouring Thailand, for instance, which may indicate a higher level of behavioural autonomy (Cukierman and Webb 1995; McCauley 2006).[6]

In a comparison between Malaysia and South Korea, Byun (2006: 168) argues that BNM has seldom made use of interest rate controls or credit incentives to support industrial policy. Similarly, Hamilton-Hart (2002: 107) points out that the UMNO-led government's most interventionist financial policies did not involve Malaysia's central bankers, either. The behavioural independence BNM has enjoyed may have been usefully strengthened by significant legal guarantees (McCauley 2006). The original Central Bank Act 1958 (CBA 1958), revised in 1994, spelled out the major functions of BNM and provided the legal foundation for this behavioural independence; a new CBA in 2009 further strengthened BNM's power through institutionalising everyday practices and expanding macro-prudential power (Zeti 2009).[7]

Nonetheless, some argue that this relative independence can be subject to informal political pressures and may be compromised at times. A review of central bank history in the 1980s by Byun (2006: 169) points out that the resignation of the third BNM governor may have had to do with a disagreement with then Finance Minister Daim Zainuddin, who removed the Capital Issues Committee from BNM control to push capital-intensive industrial deepening. In classifying central bank autonomy into political and economic dimensions, Arnone *et al.* (2008) find that BNM enjoyed a relatively lower level of political autonomy in comparison to economic autonomy in terms of daily operations on credit facilities and setting interest rates.[8]

From this perspective, strengthened policy coordination between BNM and MOF during and after the recent global financial crisis may become a double-edged sword. A comparison between BNM annual reports in 2008 and 2009 indicates an implicit attitudinal change, from emphasising the limits of monetary policy as a demand management tool, towards stressing policy coordination between BNM and the rest of the government (BNM 2009,

2011a). On the one hand, there is a consensus among central bankers that strengthened coordination between fiscal and monetary policy can improve policy effectiveness on both sides and avoid conflicting goals.[9] On the other hand, a joint report of the IMF and World Bank warned against potential intervention by MOF and advised BNM to stay independent and provide legal protection for its staff (IMF 2013).

Crisis, recovery and reform: the role of fiscal and monetary policy

Although economic crises always pose significant challenges, they sometimes create windows of opportunity for long-term macroeconomic policy and structural reform. Malaysia has implemented significant reform measures after both the Asian financial crisis (AFC) and the recent global financial crisis (GFC). Nonetheless, the pace and magnitude of reform in fiscal policy and monetary policy differ significantly.

After a decade of economic boom, the AFC's strike to the Malaysian economy in 1998 was somewhat unexpected to international observers. Large capital inflows into the region before the crisis, mostly from offshore borrowing by banks and the private sector, created increasingly fragile economic and financial growth (Radelet and Sachs 2000: 117). The scenario was somewhat different in Malaysia, with net portfolio inflows often small or negative during the years before the crisis (Radelet and Sachs 2000: 117). Nonetheless, bank and corporate failures, juxtaposed with political uncertainties, in some countries in the region created contagion effects for countries with relatively sound economic fundamentals, such as Malaysia (Radelet and Sachs 2000: 136).

The withdrawal of foreign funds triggered a chain reaction both across countries and domestically, from one sector to another. In Malaysia, the evolution from currency crisis to fully-fledged financial economic crisis took place in a relatively short period: the ringgit depreciated by almost 40 percent at its nadir, the stock market collapsed, and the economy deteriorated from a 7.3 percent growth rate in 1997 to a 7.4 percent contraction in 1998 (BNM 1999; Zeti 2009; World Bank 2013). While BNM mentioned the IMF view that the AFC reflected domestic policy weaknesses in its 1998 annual report, it attributed the quick domestic contagion primarily to the rapid accumulation of short-term debt in the domestic private sector (BNM 1999).

Another surprise came when Mahathir and policy-makers in Malaysia chose to implement a distinct policy package that significantly differed from prescriptions offered by the IMF, with an expansionary fiscal and monetary stance in conjunction with the implementation of capital controls and a fixed exchange rate. The structural reforms conducted after the crisis primarily occurred in the financial sector, while an expansionary stance was maintained in fiscal policy. The IMF package implemented in other Asian countries, by contrast, provided rescue funds under strict conditions of fiscal contraction, immediate restructuring of the bank sector, tight domestic credit and immediate debt repayment (Radelet and Sachs 2000: 141). In criticising this approach, the Malaysian government argued that this prescription was based on a set of ideal assumptions of a perfect, self-equilibrating market system, which made it fundamentally flawed for facing volatile global markets and irrational collective sentiments (Mustapa 1999).

In comparison to the AFC, the impact of the recent GFC on the Malaysian economy has been more ephemeral and less significant in its magnitude. Table 12.1 provides a comparison of selected economic indicators in the two crises. As a small, export-oriented economy, Malaysia experienced its most significant economic downturn in early 2009, when the economy contracted by 6.2 percent amidst major declines in major exports and imports as

Table 12.1 Selected economic indicators, 1997–2000 and 2007–10

Year	*GDP growth (annual %)*	*Inflation*[a] *(annual %)*	*External balance*[b] *(US$ million)*	*Official exchange rate*[c] *(per US$)*	*Central government debt (% of GDP)*	*Total reserves (% of external debt)*
Before and after Asian financial crisis						
1997	7.3	2.7	0.9	2.8	NA	45.5
1998	–7.4	5.3	22.0	3.9	NA	61.9
1999	6.1	2.7	25.1	3.8	NA	73.7
2000	8.9	1.5	19.2	3.8	NA	68.3
Before and after global financial crisis						
2007	6.3	2.0	19.9	3.4	40.1	161.7
2008	4.8	5.4	22.3	3.3	39.8	136.2
2009	–1.5	0.6	20.3	3.5	50.8	138.6
2010	7.2	1.7	17.2	3.2	51.2	125.1

Source: World Bank, *World Development Indicators* (various years).

Notes:

[a] Consumer prices.

[b] Goods and services.

[c] Period average.

NA = Not available.

well as gross fixed investment (Doraisami 2011). However, the economy quickly rebounded in late 2009 and throughout 2010.

In a keynote address, BNM's deputy governor attributed the quick recovery to sound counter-cyclical fiscal and monetary policy as well as previously successful financial restructuring and deepening (Ooi 2009). The fiscal packages came with a stronger emphasis on private sector recovery and development, in comparison to fiscal responses during and after the AFC, which focused on boosting public sector investment. On the other hand, unlike earlier unconventional measures on the foreign exchange market, Malaysia's monetary policy responses to the GFC primarily focused on conventional measures such as adjustments to policy rates and statutory reserve requirements, and targeting monetary operations.

Fiscal policy: responses to crises and proposals for reform

Fiscal reform in Malaysia has moved at a much slower pace than have monetary policy reform and financial restructuring. Malaysia's initial fiscal policy stance during the AFC was in fact similar to IMF recommendations, with a tightened operational budget aimed at reducing the current account deficit and countering inflationary pressures arising from the ringgit's depreciation (Vijayaledchumy 2003). However, as the situation continued to deteriorate, the administration's fiscal policy stance shifted quickly from contractionary to expansionary. A stimulus package of RM7 billion was issued in 1998 along with an announcement of a target federal deficit of 25 percent of GDP (Vijayaledchumy 2003). As a result of these fiscal moves, fiscal deficit re-emerged after five consecutive years of surpluses.

In claiming that the economy has fallen into a vicious cycle, the Malaysian government asserted that a tight fiscal stance would intensify rather than alleviate the crisis. In addition, an expansionary fiscal policy with a focus on public sector investment was viewed as necessary given that the private sector was considered more a problem rather than the solution (BNM 1999; Mustapa 1999). Interestingly, actual fiscal contributions failed to meet planned targets and accounted for only 1.5 percent of GDP in 1998, which in the IMF's view, was the result of a relative lack of automatic stabilisers in both tax and expenditure systems (IMF 1999).

Rather than showing concern for re-emerging fiscal deficits and implementation issues in its fiscal stimulus package, however, the Malaysian government maintained an expansionary fiscal stance between 1999 and 2003, which continued to be justified in terms of the lacklustre performance of the private sector and as counter-cyclical and pre-emptive responses to a global economic slowdown (EPU 2013a). At the same time, the government took few measures in the post-AFC period to correct over-reliance on petroleum-related revenues, which continued to expand in the 2000s.

In this regard, the GFC provoked a fiscal policy response that differed in both magnitude and effectiveness, with an explicit concern over fiscal sustainability. In the early stages of the external shock, the finance minister introduced an initial stimulus package of RM7 million, financed from savings accumulated from a reduction in fuel subsidies earlier in the year (BNM 2009). A second stimulus package was introduced in 2009, with expansionary measures emphasising strong resumption of private consumption and investment, as well as enhancing the role of the private sector as the engine of economic growth (BNM 2011a). While there were still many components in the stimulus package that were for the benefit of the public sector and civil servants, the expansionary fiscal stance was altered in 2010, in contrast to the continued growth of deficits following the AFC.

The introduction of the New Economic Model (NEM) in 2010 aimed to transform Malaysia into a high-income economy without falling into the middle-income trap, and put the private sector at centre-stage for economic upgrading (Ahmad 2009; EPU 2013b). While political stability was considered as a necessary component, the model also emphasised restoration of Malaysia's fiscal position to a more sustainable level, as well as recalibration of subsidy distributions and the gradual dismantling of the open-ended protection of certain industries (Ahmad 2009; EPU 2013b). Fiscal consolidation was thus considered imperative, as the EPU expressed concern over investor attitudes towards unsustainable sovereign debt levels as well as a projected decline in domestic petroleum production (EPU 2013b).

Proposals for a VAT also re-emerged as MOF announced its plan to introduce a new goods and service tax (GST) in the coming years, which would serve to streamline the current tax structure and improve its transparency, while broadening the tax base (MOF 2013a).[10] As mentioned before, Daim Zainuddin's VAT proposal was shelved due to political unpopularity in the 1980s. While the new tax system may provide a more neutral structure across certain industries, supplies for agriculture, exports and public sector products are considered as either zero-rated or exempt categories (MOF 2013a). The effectiveness of the new tax system in improving transparency and neutrality, as well as providing a stable source of revenue, is thus yet to be tested. On the other hand, the establishment of a Fiscal Policy Committee chaired by the prime minister and a Fiscal Policy Office within the MOF signalled further centralisation and coordination of policy-making (MOF 2013a). Nonetheless, the political implications of these institutional reforms are unclear, as they may well provide new venues for political intervention in fiscal policy formulation and implementation.

Monetary policy: responses to crises and continued modernisation

Compared with fiscal reform, which began to take shape only in recent years, monetary policy modernisation proceeded relatively smoothly after the AFC, although a selective and progressive approach was emphasised for certain liberalisation and reform measures, such as on the foreign exchange market. While policy coordination and stronger intervention by the Prime Minister's Office and MOF are often seen in crisis periods, the overall balanced-risk approach between growth and inflation has not been compromised and monetary policy has quickly normalised after the crises.

During the AFC, volatile short-term capital flows and exchange rate volatility undermined the ability of BNM to influence domestic interest rates through regular monetary transmission mechanisms. With the implementation of selective exchange rate controls and a fixed exchange rate, BNM claimed that a greater degree of monetary autonomy was temporarily achieved to avoid the impossible trinity of flexible exchange rates, free capital flows and independent monetary policy (Cheong 2005). In its annual report for 1998, BNM indicated that monetary operations in dealing with the crisis were targeted at managing liquidity to maintain interest rates at levels that were sufficient to promote economic activity, while ensuring a positive return to depositors (BNM 1999).

As the economy started to recover, the Malaysian government and BNM took measures to restructure the financial sector, with plans to consolidate domestic financial institutions and improve balance sheets and corporate governance, as well as to liberalise price determination in the service sector (Cheong 2005; Zeti 2009). A new monetary policy framework was a natural step following strengthened financial risk management and a more market-based price determination framework (Cheong 2005). The introduction of the OPR as the new interest rate target for monetary policy, as well as regular announcements of target rates, allowed for greater clarity in policy communication, and thus increased the role of expectations in monetary policy-making (BNM 2009).

Since effective transmission of policy signals such as changes in policy rates depends on the effectiveness of relevant mechanisms, BNM also took further measures to adapt its monetary instruments to correspond to the changing domestic and external financial environment (Ooi 2008). While the conventional banking system remains the major source of financing for the private sector, BNM has expanded its monetary instruments to incorporate capital-based and Islamic monetary instruments (Ooi 2008).

When the GFC hit the Malaysian economy in 2009, the financial system was relatively sound, with improved balance sheets, while BNM had matured its practice using OPRs in both conventional and Islamic financial markets. Instead of resorting to AFC measures such as capital controls and fixed exchange rates, BNM chose to rely on a more conventional approach, using interest rate and monetary operations, while preserving previous liberalisation measures on foreign exchange administration (BNM 2009, 2011a, 2011b).

At the beginning of the crisis, BNM adopted a balanced-risk approach for growth and inflation, as usual. The OPR remained unchanged until November 2008, when it was clear that the downturn in the economy greatly outweighed inflationary pressures (BNM 2009, 2011a). Even so, BNM emphasised in its 2008 annual report that monetary policy has its limits when it comes to demand management (BNM 2009). That tone changed in the 2009 report, in which BNM explained its more comprehensive measures to reduce policy rates and statutory reserve requirements much further, as well as to increase coordination between BNM and other government machinery (BNM 2011a, 2011b). In some way, this change of tone signalled that the relatively autonomous decision-making by BNM in the earlier crisis period would be less the case as this crisis deepened.

Despite the softening of BNM positions during the crisis, normalisation of monetary policy practices also began quickly once the growth–inflation balance changed. By early 2010, BNM had raised the policy rate repeatedly, given concerns that a low rate over an extended period could encourage risk-taking behaviour and excessive credit growth (BNM 2011a, 2011b). Liberalisation of foreign exchange administration rules continued after the crisis, with increasingly relaxed conditions for domestic corporations, Islamic banks and residents (BNM 2014). Finally, the integration of major financial service laws into the Financial Services Act 2013 and the Islamic Financial Services Act 2013 empowered BNM to further specify standards and issue directions to operators on both the conventional and Islamic financial markets (BNM 2013b).

Conclusion

Macroeconomic policy in Malaysia is designed to balance among key objectives such as growth, stability and equity. While both fiscal and monetary policy serve development and stabilisation goals, fiscal policy-making in Malaysia involves a more significant ethnic and political dimension, while monetary policy has been largely focused on ensuring price and financial stability. Although MOF often serves as the main physical centre for fiscal policy formulation and implementation, actual decision-making power resides more with the Prime Minister's Office. The NEP and the 'Look East' policy created opportunities for the government to adopt a highly interventionist approach favouring *bumiputera* entrepreneurs with strong government ties and establishing an alliance with foreign capital (Narayanan 1996). Fiscal deficits have been the norm except in the early 1990s and continued to expand until 2009.

The unsustainability of this trend forced the Malaysian government eventually to begin to adjust its fiscal policy orientation and to call for reducing the 'dependency syndrome' of *bumiputera* entrepreneurs (Ahmad 2009). Proposals on reforming the tax structure as well as for fiscal consolidation may help alleviate the current fiscal imbalance, although the directions and effectiveness of these proposals are not yet clear, given potential political influence and room for policy discretion.

While fiscal reform is yet to take shape, BNM has used its relative behavioural independence to institutionalise its practices and to modernise Malaysia's monetary policy framework. It has seldom abandoned a balanced-risk approach, weighing growth and inflation, even when facing external shocks and economic downturns. Efforts to implement a new interest rate framework and to improve monetary transmission mechanisms may complement moves for further financial deepening in conventional and Islamic financial markets, as well as the gradual liberalisation of the foreign exchange market, with the ultimate goal of reinternationalising the ringgit. Nevertheless, the influence of political factors has not completely faded, especially during crisis periods, while an informal commitment to exchange rate stability may create policy dilemmas when facing future external shocks.

Notes

1 NFPEs are public enterprises in which 50 percent or more of equity is held either directly by the government or indirectly through other public enterprises. Reforms in recent decades allow NFPEs to operate on an increasingly commercial basis (IMF 1999).

2 From 1980 to 1983, net foreign borrowing as a source of government finance increased dramatically, from RM310 million to RM4,569 million.
3 Yet cognate issues arise, too, in other developing countries; see Fatás and Mihov 2003; Manasse 2006.
4 An IMF estimate shows that the ringgit faced sustained upward pressure, and gradually strengthened by about 15 percent in real effective terms, between 1990 and 1997 (IMF 1999: 28).
5 Monetary aggregates are classified into M1 (currency in circulation and demand deposits), M2 (M1 plus narrow quasi-money, defined as the sum of deposits or interest-bearing instruments) and M3 (M2 plus deposits placed with other banking institutions) (BNM 2013d).
6 According to Cukierman and Webb (1995), political influence on the central bank can be measured by the probability of a central bank governor's being replaced shortly after a political change of government.
7 For example, the 2009 CBA charged BNM with the tasks of obtaining information for risk management purposes and taking early actions to avert and manage crises (BNM 2009).
8 Following Grilli *et al.* (1991), Arnone *et al.* (2008: 7) define political autonomy in terms of the ability of central banks to select the final objectives of monetary policy, including considerations of appointments of key personnel, as well as legal obligations and provisions. Economic autonomy is defined in terms of operational autonomy, such as constraints on government access to credit facilities at the central bank and the central bank's ability to set the policy rate.
9 See, for example, a discussion by Nordhaus *et al.* (1994), which indicates that separation of powers in monetary and fiscal policy-making, as occurs in many large countries, often results in conflicting policy objectives, as indicated by high fiscal deficits and tight monetary policy with overly high interest rates.
10 The new GST is a broad-based consumption tax and will replace the current sales and service tax introduced in the 1970s, with distinctions among zero-rated, exempt and standard-rated supplies (MOF 2013).

Bibliography

Adam, Christopher and William Cavendish (1995) 'Early privatizations', in Jomo K.S. (ed.), *Privatizing Malaysia – Rents, Rhetoric, Realities*, Boulder: Westview Press, pp. 219–35.

Ahmad Husni Hanadzlah (2009) 'Address and official opening', *National Economic Outlook Conference 2010–2011*, Kuala Lumpur: Ministry of Finance Malaysia.

Arnone, Marco, Bernard J, Laurens, Jean-François Segalotto and Martin Sommer (2008) 'Central bank autonomy: lessons from global trends', *IMF Staff Papers*, 56(2): 263–96.

Bank Negara Malaysia (BNM) (1999) *Annual Report 1998*, Kuala Lumpur: Bank Negara Malaysia.

Bank Negara Malaysia (BNM) (2009) *Annual Report 2008*, Kuala Lumpur: Bank Negara Malaysia.

Bank Negara Malaysia (BNM) (2011a) *Annual Report 2009*, Kuala Lumpur: Bank Negara Malaysia.

Bank Negara Malaysia (BNM) (2011b) *Annual Report 2010*, Kuala Lumpur: Bank Negara Malaysia.

Bank Negara Malaysia (BNM) (2012) *Annual Report 2011*, Kuala Lumpur: Bank Negara Malaysia.

Bank Negara Malaysia (BNM) (2013a) *Annual Report 2012*, Kuala Lumpur: Bank Negara Malaysia.

Bank Negara Malaysia (BNM) (2013b) *Legislative Powers to Enforce Supervisory and Regulatory Functions*, Bank Negara Malaysia, available at www.bnm.gov.my/index.php?ch=fs_ovr&pg=fs_ovr_legislative&lang=en (accessed 12 May 2013).

Bank Negara Malaysia (BNM) (2013c) *Monetary Stability: Overnight Policy Rate Decision and Statement*, available at www.bnm.gov.my/index.php?ch=mone&pg=mone_opr_stmt&lang=en (accessed 12 May 2013).

Bank Negara Malaysia (BNM) (2013d) *Monthly Statistical Bulletin*, Kuala Lumpur: Bank Negara Malaysia.

Bank Negara Malaysia (BNM) (2014) *BNM Foreign Exchange Administration: Overview and Summary of Rules*, available at www.bnm.gov.my/index.php?lang=en&ch=en_newfea&pg=en_newfea_overview&ac=355&eid=box1 (accessed 11 February 2014).

Byun Young Hark (2006) Choosing Coalition Partners: The Politics of Central Bank Independence in Korea and Taiwan, PhD Dissertation, University of Texas at Austin.

Cheong, Latifah Merican (2005) 'Globalisation and the operation of monetary policy in Malaysia', in *Globalization and Monetary Policy in Emerging Markets*, BIS Papers 23, Basel: Bank for International Settlements, pp. 209–15.

Cukierman, Alex and Steven B. Webb (1995) 'Political influence on the central bank: international evidence', *The World Bank Economic Review*, 9: 397–423.

Doraisami, Anita (2011) The Global Financial Crisis: Countercyclical Fiscal Policy Issues and Challenges in Malaysia, Indonesia, the Philippines, and Singapore, ADBI Working Paper.

Economic Planning Unit Malaysia (EPU) (2013a) *Eighth Malaysia Plan 2001–2005*, Kuala Lumpur: Economic Planning Unit Malaysia, available at www.epu.gov.my/en/eighth-malaysia-plan-2001-2005 (accessed 23 November 2013).

Economic Planning Unit Malaysia (EPU) (2013b) *New Economic Model*, Kuala Lumpur: Economic Planning Unit Malaysia, available at www.epu.gov.my/en/new-economic-model (accessed 25 November 2013).

Eifert, Benn, Alan Gelb and Nils Borje Tallroth (2003) 'The political economy of fiscal policy and economic management in oil-exporting countries', *Fiscal Policy Formulation and Implementation in Oil-producing Countries*, Washington DC: International Monetary Fund.

Eijffinger, Sylvester C.W. and Jakob De Haan (1996) 'The political economy of central-bank independence', *Special Papers in International Economics*, 19(May), available at www.researchgate.net/ (accessed 10 May 2014).

Fatás, Antonio and Ilian Mihov (2003) 'The case for restricting fiscal policy discretion', *The Quarterly Journal of Economics*, 118(4): 1419–47.

Grilli, Vittorio, Donato Masciandaro and Guido Tabellini (1991) 'Political and monetary institutions and public financial policies in the industrial countries', *Economic Policy*, 6(13): 342–92.

Hamilton-Hart, Natasha (2002) *Asian States, Asian Bankers: Central Banking in Southeast Asia*, Ithaca: Cornell University Press.

Hassan, Gulam, Mohamed Aslam and Yee Shin Tan (2012) 'Political economy of the budgetary process in Malaysia', MPRA Paper, available at http://mpra.ub.uni-muenchen.de/id/eprint/37873 (accessed 10 May 2014).

International Monetary Fund (IMF) (1999) *Malaysia – Selected Issues*, Washington DC: International Monetary Fund.

International Monetary Fund (IMF) (2013) 'Malaysia: financial sector stability assessment', IMF Country Report, Washington DC: International Monetary Fund.

Jomo K.S. (1995) *Privatizing Malaysia: Rents, Rhetoric, Realities*, Boulder: Westview Press.

Jomo K.S. and Natasha Hamilton-Hart (2001) 'Financial regulation, crisis and policy response', in Jomo K.S. (ed.), *Malaysian Eclipse: Economic Crisis and Recovery*, London: Zed.

McCauley, Robert Neil (2006) 'Understanding monetary policy in Malaysia and Thailand: objectives, instruments and independence', in *Monetary Policy in Asia: Approaches and Implementation*, BIS Papers 31, Basel: Bank for International Settlements, pp. 172–98.

Manasse, Paolo (2006) Procyclical Fiscal Policy: Shocks, Rules, and Institutions – A View from Mars, IMF Working Paper, Washington DC: International Monetary Fund.

Meesook, Kanitta (2001) *Malaysia: From Crisis to Recovery*, Washington DC: International Monetary Fund.

Ministry of Finance Malaysia (MOF) (2013a) *Economic Report 2013/2014*, Kuala Lumpur: Ministry of Finance Malaysia.

Ministry of Finance Malaysia (MOF) (2013b) *Time Series: Public Finance*, Kuala Lumpur: Ministry of Finance Malaysia.

Mustapa Mohamad (1999) 'Keynote address by Minister of Finance II', *Strategies for Economic Recovery in Conjunction with the 54 Anniversary of the Formation of the United Nations*, Kuala Lumpur: Ministry of Finance Malaysia.

Narayanan, Suresh (1996) 'Fiscal reform in Malaysia: behind a successful experience', *Asian Survey*, 36(9): 869–81.

Narayanan, Suresh (2007) 'The challenges of raising revenues and restructuring subsidies in Malaysia', *Kajian Malaysia*, 25(2): 1–28.

Nordhaus, William D., Charles L. Schultze and Stanley Fischer (1994) 'Policy games: coordination and independence in monetary and fiscal policies', *Brookings Papers on Economic Activity*, 2: 139–216.

Ooi Sang Kuang (2008) 'The monetary transmission mechanism in Malaysia: current developments and issues', in *Transmission Mechanisms for Monetary Policy in Emerging Market Economies*, BIS Papers 35, Basel: Bank for International Settlements, pp. 345–62.

Ooi Sang Kuang (2009) 'BNM Deputy Governor keynote address', National Economic Outlook Conference 2010–2011, Kuala Lumpur.

Pepinsky, Thomas (2007) 'Autocracy, elections, and fiscal policy: evidence from Malaysia', *Studies in Comparative International Development*, 42(1/2): 136–63.

Radelet, Steven and Jeffrey D. Sachs (2000) 'The onset of the East Asian Financial Crisis', in Paul R. Krugman (ed.), *Currency Crises*, Chicago: University of Chicago Press, pp. 105–53.

Rafiq, Sohrab (2013) *The Growth and Stabilization Properties of Fiscal Policy in Malaysia*, Washington DC: International Monetary Fund.

Ritchie, Brian K. (2004) Politics and Economic Reform in Malaysia, William Davidson Institute Working Paper, Ann Arbor: William Davidson Institute.

Schätzl, Ludwig H. (1988) *Growth and Spatial Equity in West Malaysia*, ASEAN Economic Research Unit, Institute of Southeast Asian Studies.

Shaari, Mohamad Hasni (2008) *Analysing Bank Negara Malaysia's Behaviour in Formulating Monetary Policy: An Empirical Approach*, Canberra: Australian National University.

Vijayaledchumy, Veluppilai (2003) 'Fiscal policy in Malaysia', in *Fiscal Issues and Central Banking in Emerging Economies*, BIS Papers 20, Basel: Bank for International Settlements, pp. 173–79.

World Bank (2013) *World Development Indicators: Malaysia*, New York: World Bank.

Zeti Akhtar Aziz (2009) 'BNM Governor's keynote address: 50 years of central banking – stability and sustainability', Ceremony for the 50th Anniversary of Bank Negara Malaysia, Kuala Lumpur, Malaysia.

13

Affirmative action

Hefty measures, mixed outcomes, muddled thinking

Hwok-Aun Lee

Few Malaysian issues are as complicated and consequential – and at the same time, as inflamed and muddled – as affirmative action. To help us gain an informed, systematic and critical understanding of affirmative action, we need to dwell on the policy's basis, the specific objectives and programmes under its banner, and the results of pursuing its broad range of interventions. Toward these ends, this chapter will:

- define affirmative action and clearly articulate its policy objectives and instruments;
- explain constitutional and socio-political factors underpinning its conception, in particular, Article 153 and the New Economic Policy;
- outline specific programmes and outcomes, with a focus on contemporary developments and challenges; and
- consider policy implications.

What is affirmative action?

While there is no canonical definition of affirmative action, policies falling under this banner can be distinguished by assessing the principal problem being resolved and the methods employed. To conceptualise affirmative action in a way that is broadly applicable, yet specific to the Malaysian context, we glean insights from international literature, the Malaysian Federal Constitution's Article 153 and the New Economic Policy.

Affirmative action can be defined as preferential policies to redress the under-representation of a disadvantaged population group in socially esteemed and economically influential positions (Weisskopf 2004; ILO 2007; Fryer and Loury 2005). These policies address a specific problem: under-representation of a population group – categorised by race, ethnicity, gender, disability, region, and so on – in socio-economic positions that affect the collective esteem and stature of the group. A group that is conspicuously and persistently absent among university students, doctors, lawyers, managers or business owners may be perceived or stereotyped negatively, discouraged from gaining upward mobility and continually excluded over the long term. This situation is further characterised by various disadvantages that the group on average may face – inferior schooling, shortage of work experience, and lack of capital ownership or access to credit – and compounded by barriers to entry into these positions – university entry grades, higher education qualifications for professional jobs, work experience and network connections for managerial positions.

Focusing on these specific problems and obstacles clarifies the key role of preferential treatment. Affirmative action rests on a premise that conventional criteria of need, formal qualifications or 'merit' will not sufficiently facilitate upward educational and occupational mobility or capital ownership. It is plain to see – but perhaps hard to admit – that persons of a disadvantaged group will severely struggle to qualify for positions targeted by affirmative action unless conferred some degree of preference based on their identity with that group. Because affirmative action inherently grants preference based on identity, it is imperative that such policies be productive, dynamic and impermanent.

Undeniably, the policy is contentious and involves both benefits and costs to economy and society, of which the salient ones are worth outlining briefly. As noted above, increased upward mobility of members of a disadvantaged group can raise the collective position and esteem of the group as a whole, and attenuate stereotype, stigma, discrimination or other adverse effects of persistent absence in esteemed and influential positions. Increased proportionality in group representation also can foster cross-cultural interaction and integration, which is especially important among those in decision-making ranks. Conversely, affirmative action, by granting preferential access to the beneficiary group, potentially generates inefficiencies from selection based on identity instead of pure ability, alienates qualified non-beneficiaries, creates dependency of beneficiaries on state support while devaluing the achievements of members of the beneficiary group who qualify on their merits, and reinforces group differences, thereby fragmenting society.

Affirmative action cross-cuts broader aspirations, chiefly national unity and multicultural integration. However, such aspirations are contingent on myriad other factors – cultural policy, basic schooling, education curricula, political discourse – and the role of affirmative action is indirect and supplementary. For greater clarity and coherence in understanding affirmative action, and in view of space limitations of this chapter, we focus on the principal policy objective and instruments, as well as immediately relevant empirical outcomes.

The approach here is also temporal and institutional, in recognising the constitutional basis, policy precedents and path dependencies, and political difficulties in reforming affirmative action. Regardless of one's position towards its purpose and impact, affirmative action was established, has become entrenched in Malaysia and cannot be simply discarded.

Consequently, the more pressing questions for the present concern the efficacy of affirmative action and the preconditions and prospects for coherent, viable reforms. It is less pertinent whether the policy should have been conceived in the first place, and less helpful to press for instant abolition or to pronounce reform rhetoric that does not actually chart any passage away from the current affirmative action system.

Policy basis and alternatives

Article 153

Malaysia's Constitution clearly provides for affirmative action – not as a perpetual obligation but as possible action contingent on necessity. Article 8, setting out basic rights, includes the proviso that equality of persons is safeguarded and discrimination is prohibited, 'except as expressly authorized by this Constitution'. Article 153 provides express authorisation to discriminate in favour of the *bumiputera*, and it is helpful to reproduce the pertinent section:

> the Yang Di-Pertuan Agong [king] shall exercise his functions under this Constitution and federal law *in such manner as may be necessary* to safeguard the special position of the Malays and natives of any of the States of Sabah and Sarawak and to ensure the reservation for Malays and natives of any of the States of Sabah and Sarawak of such proportion as he may deem reasonable of positions in the public service, . . . scholarships, . . . [and permits and licences].
>
> *(my emphasis)*

Article 153 does not confer an absolute mandate or indefinite term for ethnic reservations and quotas, but establishes those possibilities 'in such manner as may be necessary'. In other words, the Constitution does not stipulate that quotas *must* be enforced regardless of circumstances, but quotas *may* be instituted *if* necessary. Ethnic quotas and reservations are contingent on evaluating whether such extraordinary measures are needed, implying that they may be unnecessary as the *bumiputera* increasingly gain upward mobility. The specification of higher education, public sector employment and permits and licences also signals that interventions should be grounded in productive activity and learning instead of wealth acquisition.

New Economic Policy

The New Economic Policy (NEP) is most tightly associated with affirmative action, largely due to the fact that *bumiputera* preferential policies massively expanded and transformed Malaysia's economy and society since the NEP's inception in 1971. The close connections, however, should not lead us to conflate the poverty alleviation and affirmative action mainstays of the NEP.

The NEP sagaciously articulated two prongs. The first sought to eradicate poverty *irrespective of race*. The second purposed to *accelerate social restructuring* to reduce and eventually eliminate the identification of race with economic function. The second prong concisely identified the problems targeted by affirmative action policies. The severe disproportionate under-representation of *bumiputera* in universities and among professionals and managers, and their concurrent over-representation among farmers and agricultural workers, was deemed an unacceptable and unsustainable ethnic division of labour. Furthermore, this structure would persist, although some change could be expected over time, as increased provision of basic education and economic growth widened the scope for *bumiputera* upward mobility.

Nonetheless, while social restructuring may happen as an indirect result of general development policies, for it to occur at a more accelerated pace – arguably, in line with sociopolitical pressures and expectations – direct and proactive interventions were deemed necessary. Accordingly, ensuing interventions required conferring preference on *bumiputera*, who were on the whole disadvantaged in their capacity to gain upward mobility and capital ownership.

The NEP also emerged from a convergence of economic, social and political developments that compelled state action. The key factors, of course, had strong ethnic dimensions. From Malayan independence through the 1960s, the Malay community remained largely in poverty, residing in rural areas and engaged in agriculture. An ethnic division of labour, disparities in opportunity and income, and lack of social interaction generated fissures and tensions in Malaysian society and polity (Andaya and Andaya 2001). Most pertinent to affirmative action, Malay upward mobility in the educational and occupational ladder, and in access to credit and ownership of capital, were severely constrained.[1] The 1960s, a period of relatively limited state intervention, had also in the latter part of the decade seen increasing calls for more policies favouring a *bumiputera* capitalist class. The 13 May 1969 inter-ethnic violence and social upheavals swept Malaysia onto a different political and policy path, characterised by consolidation of Malay power, assertion of Malay primacy, centralisation of state power and dominance of the executive (Ooi 2013). These factors have shaped affirmative action since the start of the NEP, in the form of discretionary exercise of executive power, ethnic quotas or *bumiputera*-exclusive programmes, and highly centralised administration.

'Need-based affirmative action': a flawed alternative

The ethnicity-basis of affirmative action and various problems associated with its implementation in Malaysia have raised questions on alternatives – specifically, the utilisation of policies that target assistance on the basis of need. It is worth reiterating that the need-based policies of the NEP's poverty alleviation prong and the ethnicity-based policies of the affirmative action prong are fundamentally separate – with slight overlap. The nature of the relationship must be clarified in discourses on the subject. Affirmative action, as a preferential system targeting beneficiaries based on population grouping and not socio-economic status, can be complemented by need-based considerations, but cannot be systematically substituted for by 'need-based affirmative action'. Malaysia's existing, specific and entrenched pro-*bumiputera* programmes cannot be simply replaced with pro-poor preferential selection.

This point warrants exposition, in view of popular and muddled contemporary views on the subject. Since 2008, both federal government and opposition alliances have articulated reform platforms that ostensibly replace ethnicity-based affirmative action with need-based affirmative action.[2] The argument is appealing but flawed. It holds that focusing on socio-economic need is all that matters. *Bumiputera* will be helped the most if help is targeted based on need, since the community constitutes an overwhelming majority of the poor. Hence, targeting based on ethnicity can be abolished and replaced with targeting based on need, hence avoiding troublesome and unpopular ethnic categorisations. While removing ethnicity from the picture can make pro-poor programmes more fair and equitable, upon closer examination, the argument poses little relevance to affirmative action.

Need-based and ethnicity-based policies – respectively, preferential programmes favouring the poor versus programmes favouring an ethnic group – correspond with the NEP's two prongs, which pursue different objectives through different instruments. Poverty alleviation programmes principally deliver basic needs such as schooling, healthcare and social assistance. *Bumiputera* will undoubtedly heavily benefit in proportion to their representation among the poor, but they will benefit predominantly and directly in the form of poverty alleviation, not upward mobility. There are steep limits to the extent that need-based policies can have an impact on the goals associated with affirmative action. The possible effects of improved rural schooling on *bumiputera* participation among lawyers and managers, for instance, are too remote for promotion of basic rural schooling to be a coherent and effective policy for cultivating lawyers and managers.

Need-based considerations can complement affirmative action in some spheres, and reinforce the progressiveness of outcomes. It is desirable and legitimate that those with greater socio-economic need within the *bumiputera* community receive more help. This principle is not applicable in all areas, however. In higher education, the case for conferring preference in university admissions and scholarships based on socio-economic background is clearest, since the disadvantages borne by such young beneficiaries are primarily due to circumstances outside of their control. It is also viable; family background can reasonably and practically be taken into account in selection into university. The limits and downsides of such a programme must also be recognised, however, most consequentially the fact that students from lower socio-economic backgrounds are on average less equipped for university-level study.

In other spheres of affirmative action, need-based preferential selection presents exceedingly limited policy alternatives. In public sector employment, the implication of need-based preference in employment is that persons from lower-income backgrounds should be given priority. This is plainly unworkable; we cannot expect parental income to be considered in recruitment or promotion. Conferring preference on those from lower socio-economic rungs in public procurement, licensing or any right to produce goods and services also potentially imperils quality of delivery, for this entails privileging poorer-earning or lower-performing companies. Policy discourses, therefore, will do well to avoid the notion of need-based preferential treatment *as a systemic alternative* for ethnicity-based affirmative action.

Affirmative action programmes

A systematic conceptualisation of affirmative action, such as the one offered here, helps identify Malaysia's salient affirmative action programmes. Based on the key criteria – preferential selection in strategic areas of *bumiputera* under-representation – major interventions in four main spheres are outlined next and summarised in Table 13.1.

Education

At the secondary level, MARA (Majlis Amanah Rakyat, or Council of Trust for the People) junior science colleges (MRSM) provide quality instruction and superior facilities to *bumiputera* students, especially from rural communities. At the post-secondary level, matriculation colleges offer a one-year preparatory course prior to university entry, a shorter and evidently easier path compared with the two-year Malaysian Higher School Certificate (Sijil Tinggi Pelajaran Malaysia, STPM). These institutions were exclusively for *bumiputera* students until the recent introduction of 10 percent non-*bumiputera* quotas.

In higher or tertiary level education, university admissions abided by ethnic quotas – reportedly 55 percent *bumiputera* – centrally administered by the federal government (Aihara 2009; Faridah 2003). MARA's technical institute, recently upgraded to University Technology MARA (UiTM), has maintained 100 percent *bumiputera* enrolment, and MARA scholarships are also solely for *bumiputera*. Government-sponsored scholarships have also operated as an instrument of affirmative action, with the vast bulk of awards to *bumiputera*. Since 2002, a portion of Public Service Department scholarships has been reserved for *bumiputera*, and another portion is open for competitive, merit-based selection.

High-level occupations

The NEP pronounced that 'employment patterns at all levels and in all sectors . . . must reflect the racial composition of the population' (Malaysia 1971: 42). In practice, affirmative action has operated consistently and substantively in the public sector and state-owned enterprises. For the most part these institutions have facilitated *bumiputera* entry to professional and managerial positions without a particular code of practice, over time acquiring an inertia that

Table 13.1 Malaysia's affirmative action system: spheres, programmes and notable features

Sphere	*Programmes/agencies*	*Notable features*
Education	• MARA junior science colleges (MRSM)	• Exclusively *bumiputera* until 10 percent non-*bumiputera* quota from 2000
	• Post-secondary matriculation colleges	• Exclusively *bumiputera*, until 10 percent non-*bumiputera* quota from 2002. From late 1990s, predominant route for *bumiputera* university entry
	• MARA University of Technology (UiTM); MARA scholarships	• Exclusively *bumiputera*
	• Public university admissions quotas	• Centrally administered by federal government. Since 2002, 'meritocracy' declared, but questionable in view of differences in duration and difficulty of matriculation and Higher Education School Certificate (STPM) examinations
	• Government scholarship quotas	• Ethnic allocations publicised from mid-2000s
High-level occupations	• *Bumiputera* representation among professionals and management	• De facto quota in public sector, though largely ad hoc in implementation
Managerial and enterprise development	• Bumiputera Commercial and Industrial Community (BCIC)	• Agencies engaged in direct employment of *bumiputera* and enterprise support through upstream/downstream linkages, predominantly large and medium scale: state economic development corporations (SEDCs) (since 1970s); Petronas, national petroleum agency (since mid-1970s); takeover of previously foreign companies through government investment agencies (since late 1970s); heavy industries (1980s); privatisation (1980s until 1997–98 Asian financial crisis); government-linked companies (GLCs) – renationalised privatisation entities, corporations held through government investment agencies
	• Government investment agencies	• Financial and advisory support for government-linked companies
	• Public procurement/contracting and licensing	• Small contracts reserved for *bumiputera* contractors; price handicaps favouring *bumiputera* contractors, for medium to large contracts
	• Small enterprises	• Loans and business support by MARA, PUNB and other agencies
Equity and wealth ownership	• Industrial Coordination Act (ICA) 1975	• 30 percent *bumiputera* allotment in new and existing medium to large manufacturing firms; waiver to export-oriented firms. Conditions relaxed over time; ended by 2004
	• Foreign Investment Committee regulations	• 30 percent *bumiputera* requirement in public listing and foreign investment. FIC closure, investment liberalisation, reduced public listing requirements in 2009
	• Government investment funds	• *Bumiputera* quotas
	• Privatisation	• Massive transfer of previously state-owned assets, creation of new rights

obviated the need for *bumiputera* preferential measures, as the number of non-*bumiputera* entrants and employees has severely dwindled.[3] Conspicuous absence of non-*bumiputera* in top administrative posts, saliently in public universities, suggests a significant exercise of group reservation. Senior officials in the public sector have also transitioned to high-level positions in state-owned enterprises.

Managerial and enterprise development

Malaysia has devoted enormous attention and resources to this sphere of affirmative action. Unlike in public administration, *bumiputera* participation here involves the commercial production of market goods and services, and overlaps widely with promotion of *bumiputera* ownership. As outlined in Table 13.1, Malaysia has employed various instruments, some of which are sector-specific (petroleum) or periodic (heavy industries and privatisation), while the roles of state economic development corporations (SEDCs) and government-linked companies (GLCs) have featured more continuously since the 1970s. We should note that a number of major GLCs were reconfigurations of privatised entities that collapsed during the Asian financial crisis (AFC), thus ownership structure changed more than productive capacity.

Government investment agencies, such as Khazanah Nasional, Permodalan Nasional (National Corporation) and Ministry of Finance, Inc., hold sizeable stakes in GLCs, which are tasked to support the Bumiputera Commercial and Industrial Community (BCIC), while the recently created Ekuinas and Teraju schemes aim to cultivate new *bumiputera* ventures. Public procurement or contracting and licensing constitute other major channels for promoting *bumiputera* industrial participation. Policies are more clearly stipulated in public procurement, with the smallest class of contracts reserved for *bumiputera* contractors, while medium to large contracts (except for the largest category) offer price handicaps. Toward promoting *bumiputera* small businesses, financial and advisory assistance is made available through MARA, PUNB (Perbadanan Usahawan Nasional, the National Entrepreneurial Corporation) and other agencies.

Equity and wealth ownership

The Industrial Coordination Act (ICA) 1975 marked the start of major efforts to promote *bumiputera* equity ownership. The ICA required medium- to large-scale manufacturing establishments to allocate at least 30 percent of existing and new equity to *bumiputera* hands. In response to fervent protests, the requirement was waived for export-oriented firms and enforcement rules were revised over time to exempt more domestic, predominantly Chinese-owned, companies. Terms were further liberalised in response to the mid-1980s recession and the 1997–98 AFC; by 2004, equity requirements in manufacturing were effectively nullified. Foreign investments in general, as well as mergers and acquisitions, property purchases and public listings, have also been subjected to *bumiputera* preferential conditions administered by the Foreign Investment Committee, following the conventional benchmark of 30 percent *bumiputera* holdings. These regulations were mostly rescinded in 2009.

Privatisation has played a dual role of transferring managerial control and ownership to individual *bumiputera* capitalists. Government investment funds, notably unit trusts managed by Permodalan Nasional, have continually contributed to bolstering *bumiputera* ownership, both for equity participation and wealth accumulation, with offerings in part or whole reserved for *bumiputera* investors. From the late 2000s, more emphasis has been placed on active equity participation as well as commercial property ownership.

Outcomes and implications

The importance of maintaining focus on the objectives and instruments of affirmative action extends to evaluations of policy outcomes. In the literature, commentary on affirmative action, for the most part, has been woven into overviews of the NEP and Malaysia's development achievements in general, including economic growth and structural change, poverty reduction and narrowing of inter-ethnic disparities (Faaland *et al.* 1990; Snodgrass *et al.* 2003; Chakravarty and Roslan 2005; Faridah 2003; Gomez and Jomo 1999; Kamal and Zainal 1989; Jomo 2004). A few works have specifically probed affirmative action outcomes (Lee 2005; Lee 2012; Zainal 2013; Gomez and Saravanamuttu 2013).

As emphasised in this chapter, affirmative action constitutes one distinct element of the NEP, and warrants specific empirical analyses consistent with its chief objectives and mechanisms: increasing *bumiputera* representation in specified areas, through preferential selection. Poverty and household income are undoubtedly interconnected, since *bumiputera* upward mobility presumably raises incomes and reduces poverty – but are more germane to broader appraisals of Malaysia's development than to affirmative action in particular. This chapter analyses direct policy outcomes and immediate implications, engaging with contemporary issues and synthesising current, available data.

Education

Malaysia's extensive affirmative action programmes have rapidly raised the academic profile of the *bumiputera* population. *Bumiputera* proportions of public university student bodies increased from 40 percent in 1970 to 63 percent by 1985, and stabilised at that level until 2003 (Khoo 2005; Sato 2005). Current data on ethnic composition of university enrolment have not been reported, but affirmative action in public universities undeniably sustains *bumiputera* representation. In 2009, UiTM, solely reserved for *bumiputera* students, enrolled 140,000 out of a total 590,000 in the public university system.

Entry into university has been facilitated by continual expansion of secondary and post-secondary programmes. MRSMs have maintained their role, and recently enjoyed curricular and instructional upgrades. The contribution of MRSMs and MARA overseas scholarships towards intergenerational mobility, however, has been reduced by these opportunities increasingly becoming the domain of Malay middle and upper classes (Lee 2013). For the vast majority of *bumiputera* students, matriculation colleges have become the pathway to university. Enrolment in these institutions grew from about 15,000 in 1995 to over 55,000 in 2005.

On the whole, *bumiputera* have continually gained upward educational mobility. Labour force data shed light on changes over time in academic attainment, as shown in Figure 13.1. Indeed, by 2010, the Malay labour force registered the highest share with tertiary (degree, diploma or certificate) qualifications. Importantly, Malays exceed all other groups in this respect, while non-Malay *bumiputera* lag considerably. However, other evidence points to quality shortfalls and policy flaws. The official 'meritocracy' policy, in practice since 2002, commits false equivalence by considering matriculation grades on par with the STPM, further compounding the disparity in standards. Matriculation's lighter programme is evidenced by the lesser preparedness of its graduates for university study (Tan and Raman 2009). This seemingly ethnicity-blind policy is thus illusory and, by paving easier paths instead of adequately equipping students for university, ultimately does a disservice to the *bumiputera* community. It also compromises the potential for post-secondary programmes

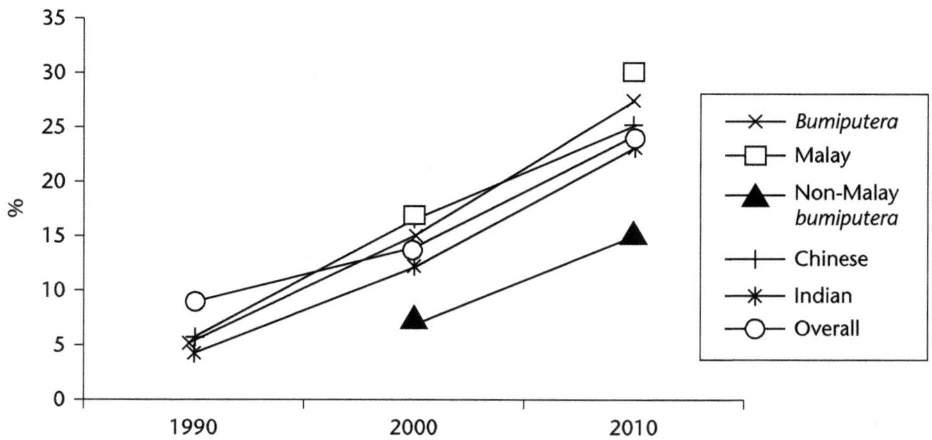

Figure 13.1 Share of labour force with tertiary education, by ethnic group
Source: *Labour Force Survey Report* (various years).

to narrow primary and secondary schooling gaps, since the matriculation colleges, being residential institutes, relocate vast numbers of students from socio-economically disadvantaged settings.

Shortcomings at pre-university extend to the post-university stage, where *bumiputera* graduates experience steeper challenges in labour market entry. *Bumiputera* graduates of public universities are much more dependent on public sector employment. This tendency partly captures voluntary choice, but also suggests shortfalls in achieving the affirmative action objective of equipping beneficiaries for mobility across public and private sector labour markets (Lee 2012). The Malaysian government's considerable efforts to provide basic technical and interpersonal skills and enhance *bumiputera* graduates' employability also reflect the deficiencies of affirmative action in public higher education.[4]

High-level occupations

Bumiputera representation in high-level occupations rose over the 1970s toward the 1990s. Since about the mid-1990s, however, the momentum of progress has waned, indicated by flatter increases in *bumiputera* proportions in professional and managerial positions (Figure 13.2). It should be noted that *bumiputera* representation among registered professionals varies across fields, with higher shares among lawyers and lower shares among engineers. The public sector has been instrumental in fostering upward mobility and building a Malay middle class, particularly over the 1970s and 1980s (Torii 2003; Abdul Rahman 1996). *Bumiputera*, especially Malays, are heavily over-represented in the bureaucracy; dependency on public sector employment persists (Lim 2013).[5] In 2005, the share of teachers and lecturers (predominantly in the public sector) among total professionals was 52.5 percent for *bumiputera*, 22.4 percent for Chinese and 30.8 percent for Indians.[6]

Bumiputera representation in high-level occupations across all sectors, especially in private organisations, depends on the mobility of tertiary qualified participants. Shortcomings in *bumiputera* empowerment through education, discussed above, have thus extended to the employment sphere, although perceptions of *bumiputera*, especially Malay, graduates and possible biases against them also perpetuate schisms between the private and public sectors.

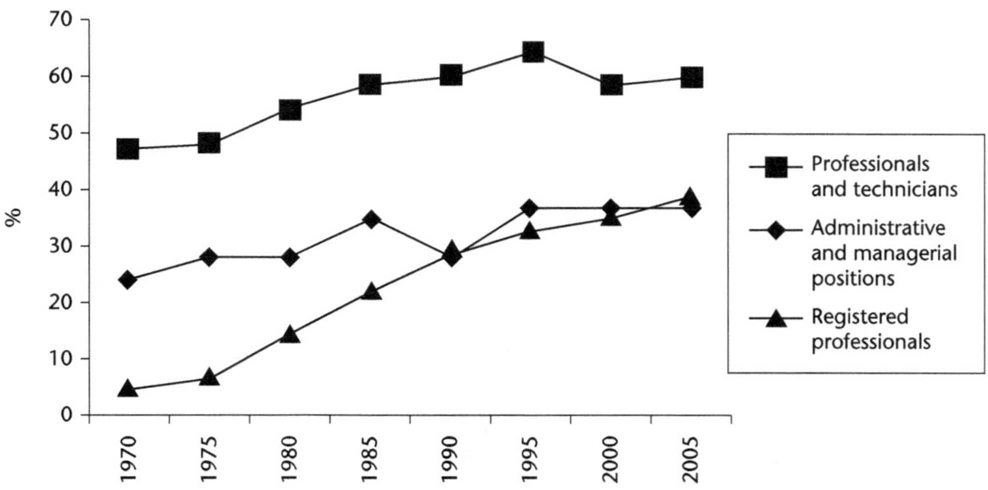

Figure 13.2 Share of *bumiputera* in high-level occupations in Malaysia
Source: *Malaysia Plans* (various years).
Notes:
1970 and 1975 for Peninsula only.
Occupational classifications changed in 1980 and 2000.

Managerial and enterprise development

Bumiputera representation is consistently lower in managerial positions, more so in private companies, given the dominance of *bumiputera* in administrative positions in the public sector (Figure 13.2). This is to be expected; the barriers to entry are substantially higher. At the same time, policies in this regard have garnered a chequered record. State-owned enterprises performed poorly over the 1970s and 1980s (Jesudason 1989). Nonetheless, in particular sectors, notably finance and banking, plantations and mining, a significant Malay presence has prevailed since the 1980s (Kamal and Zainal 1989). Privatisation in the 1990s massively propelled the BCIC and catapulted Malays into management of corporations across many sectors, but widespread collapse of these entities in the aftermath of the AFC thoroughly restructured the government–business nexus, shifting the locus of the BCIC back to renationalised state-owned, renamed government-linked companies.

In the contemporary context, GLCs are instrumental in carrying out the BCIC agenda, but progress in building a corps of dynamic and independent *bumiputera* companies, especially SMEs in manufacturing, remains sluggish (Gomez and Saravanamuttu 2013). Affirmative action through public procurement, contracting and licensing has continually fallen short, beset by poor selection, ineffective monitoring for efficiency and technical progress, and deficient checks against corruption, political patronage and cronyism.

Equity and wealth ownership

Bumiputera equity ownership has been the most vigorously targeted and tracked affirmative action outcome, ever since the 30 percent target was set under the NEP. The official estimates show demonstrable gains in the *bumiputera* share over the 1970–90 era, but slow

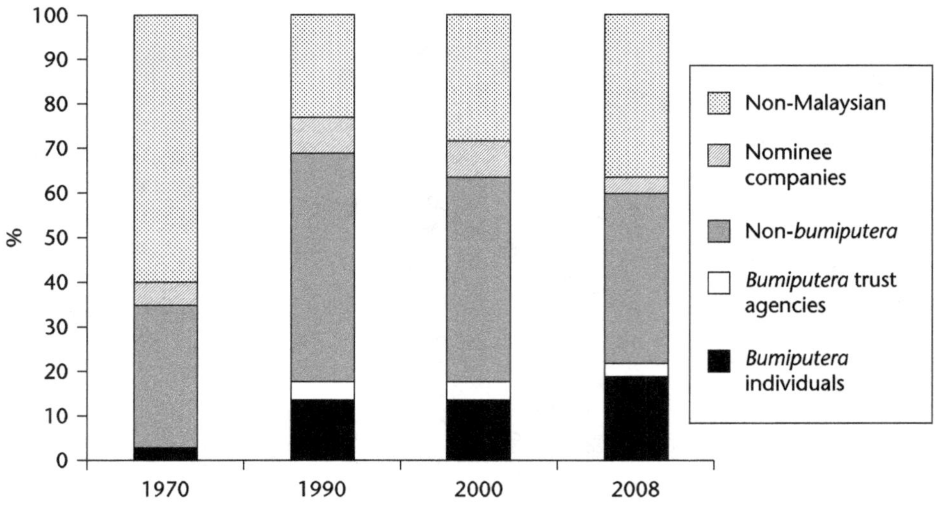

Figure 13.3 Equity ownership (at par value), percentage of total
Source: *Malaysia Plans* (various years).

progress since 1990 (Figure 13.3). The data are disputable, on grounds of the opacity of shares held through nominees, the application of par value instead of market value, and the omission of government ownership (Jomo 2004; CPPS 2006). Alternative estimates have obtained significantly higher figures, but have been ignored or dismissed, spurred by vested interests for estimation methods that show low *bumiputera* ownership to legitimise continuity of privileged access.[7]

While these debates remain unresolved, evidence highlights pervasive profiteering and rent-seeking, compounded by Malaysia's poor track record in disciplining recipients of state largesse (Gomez and Jomo 1999). Mandated equity allocations have overwhelmingly been sold off for profit. Additionally, related patterns of ownership indicate that the vast majority of *bumiputera* have scarcely been impacted by pro-*bumiputera* wealth redistribution measures. Ownership of the Amanah Saham Bumiputera unit trust is exceedingly skewed, and recent issues have been undersubscribed. In sum, these developments warrant a return to basics of developing capabilities and earnings capacity.

Looking ahead

We have considered the objectives and instruments of affirmative action, the policy's constitutional and historical context, and its specific programmes and outcomes. Malaysia is at a crossroads, having achieved various numerical outcomes but floundered in the ultimate goal of cultivating capability, confidence and self-reliance, towards genuinely and effectively redressing *bumiputera* socio-economic disadvantage. The implications are too numerous and complex to be fully expounded here. In the contemporary context, three basic and vital questions help us to look ahead:

- How should we think about affirmative action?
- How do Malaysia's accomplishments and shortfalls inform future policy?
- How might the nation transition away from the current system?

It is crucial to maintain clarity and specificity in thinking about the key objectives and instruments of affirmative action. The policy is in principle transitory, unravelling as it progresses. Adverse consequences and abuses of the policy, a source of discontent in Malaysia, underscore its unsustainability and the need for reforms. At the same time, as discussed above, the objectives and instruments of affirmative action have been and remain structured around ethnic group representation and preferential treatment, and cannot be replaced systemically with poverty alleviation programmes and need-based selection. Conferring preference on those from low-income backgrounds can facilitate intergenerational upward mobility and thus reinforce the ultimate goal of redressing socio-economic disadvantage. However, this is applicable almost exclusively in education – and not without adverse consequences – but not in the other spheres of affirmative action.

Empirical evidence of policy outcomes demonstrates that affirmative action programmes have steadily bolstered *bumiputera* tertiary education qualifications and *bumiputera* representation at professional and managerial levels, but preferential treatment has not been adequately reinforced with robust development of capabilities, mobility across sectors and the intended transition to self-reliance. Dependency on public institutions and preferential access remains high. Efforts to promote enterprises and transfer wealth have fluctuated in outcome, and are more prone to corruption and abuse. Disparities in upward mobility between Malays and non-Malay *bumiputera* constitute another major area of concern.

Malaysia's passage away from the current ethnicity-based and quota-structured affirmative action system involves making programmes more effective again, consolidating *bumiputera* capability and confidence, before any scaling down of quotas and systemic policy reforms can realistically be contemplated. The adverse political ramifications of drastic reforms must also be factored into policy discourses. Assertions of pure 'meritocracy', usually without acknowledgement of the likely ensuing decline in *bumiputera* representation, have continually and unsurprisingly failed to move reform agendas forward.

Consideration of policy reforms also needs to account for variations across the spheres of intervention. In education, arguably the most positively impacting sphere, due to its productive – and non-acquisitive – orientation and the scale of beneficiaries, reforms to raise standards in pre-university programmes will be needed to narrow gaps in standards and achievements, before moving ultimately to some common university entry requirements. Whether this shift eventually takes the form of a standardised national examination in place of matriculation and STPM or of universities setting their own yardsticks, uniformly applied across all applicants, and how the balance settles between group representation and academic qualification, are broader issues that demand national deliberation.

Disproportionate ethnic representation in the public sector generally draws less discontent than university entry and education-related issues, but over the long term, preferential selection and severe under-representation of non-Malays in governmental decision-making positions is unwholesome for all groups. Efforts to increase diversity will have to overcome big hurdles; two constructive components of a reform package are worth noting here. First, fair employment legislation and concomitant parameters for what constitute unfair employment practices provide a needed legal framework on issues of discrimination – and must be applied across both private and public sectors. Second, in view of the inadequacy of prohibiting discrimination towards fostering diversity, initiatives to promote diversity can help moderate anxieties that arise from the dilution of quotas in the public sector. Increasing employment of non-*bumiputera* in the public sector will likely need to be accompanied by efforts to increase *bumiputera* presence in the private sector.

Enterprise development and equity ownership, the spheres where affirmative action has pronouncedly fallen short, pose massive challenges for reform. Selection and monitoring processes in public procurement, GLC operations and the gamut of enterprise development programmes must be increasingly stringent and prudent – and executed with a clear long-term plan for scaling down outright *bumiputera* quotas and privileged access. Existing highly skewed ownership arising from *bumiputera* wealth distribution calls for restraint in further implementation of such programmes.

The breadth, complexity and seeming intractability of affirmative action pervade the obvious difficulties in rendering it, as originally intended and as provided in the Constitution, successful and thus unnecessary. Contemporary Malaysia faces urgent and deep challenges to a shift away from affirmative action, particularly in the form of ethnic quotas and reservations, towards policies and institutions that more effectively attain productive and equitable outcomes. Proceeding with coherence and efficacy requires conceptual clarity, critical policy analysis, and judicious consideration of possible change and reform.

Notes

1 In 1957, the poverty rate among Malays was 70.5 percent, compared with 27.4 percent for Chinese and 35.7 percent for Indians. The disparity persisted through 1970, as poverty remained considerably higher for Malays (64.8 percent) than for Chinese (26.0 percent) and Indians (39.2 percent) (Leete 2007). In Peninsular Malaysia in 1967, the Chinese to Malay household income ratio was recorded at 2.47, and 1.95 for Indian to Malay households (Anand 1981).

2 Under the headline, 'Need-based Affirmative Action', *Pakatan Rakyat Policies*, released in December 2009, resolved to provide economic assistance and fair distribution to all races based on need, to avail scholarships based on need and merit, and to utilise savings from curbing corruption towards poverty alleviation. Soon after, Barisan Nasional's (BN) New Economic Model (Part 1) declared in April 2010 the continuation and revamp of affirmative action, to remove rent-seeking and market-distorting features, and to 'consider all ethnic groups fairly and equally as long as they are in the low income forty percent of households' (NEAC 2009).

3 Puthucheary (1978) notes that, in post-independence Malaya, four-fifths of positions in the Malayan civil service were reserved for Malays (cited in Khoo 2005).

4 The government spent RM415 million over 2001–05 to retrain 40,000, preponderantly *bumiputera*, graduates (Cheong *et al.* 2011).

5 In 2009, Malays comprised 79 percent of top management and 75 percent of professional and management positions (Lim 2013).

6 Author's calculations from Malaysia 2006.

7 Fazilah (2002) concluded that the 30 percent threshold had been reached by 1997. The Centre for Public Policy Studies (2006) traced 45 percent of equity in 2005 as *bumiputera*-owned – assigning 70 percent of omitted government holdings as representing *bumiputera* interest.

Bibliography

Abdul Rahman Embong (1996) 'Social transformation, the state and the middle classes in post-independence Malaysia', *Southeast Asian Studies*, 34(3): 56–79.

Aihara, Akihito (2009) 'Paradoxes of higher education reforms: implications on the Malaysian middle class', *International Journal of Asia-Pacific Studies*, 5(1): 81–113.

Anand, Sudhir (1981) *Inequality and Poverty in Malaysia: Measurement and Decomposition*, Oxford: Oxford University Press.

Andaya, Barbara Watson and Leonard Y. Andaya (2001) *A History of Malaysia*, Honolulu: University of Hawai'i Press.

Centre for Public Policy Studies (CPPS) (2006) *Corporate Equity Distribution: Past Trends and Future Policy*, Kuala Lumpur: Centre for Public Policy Studies.

Chakravarty, Shanti P. and Roslan Abdul-Hakim (2005) 'Ethnic nationalism and income distribution in Malaysia', *The European Journal of Development Research*, 17(2): 270–88.

Cheong Kee-Cheok, Viswanathan Selvaratnam and Goh Kim-Leng (2011) 'Education and human capital formation', in Rajah Rasiah (ed.), *Malaysian Economy: Unfolding Growth and Social Change*, Shah Alam: Oxford University Press, pp. 159–84.

Department of Statistics (various years) *Labour Force Survey Report*, Kuala Lumpur: Government Printer.

Faaland, J., J.R. Parkinson and R. Saniman (1990) *Growth and Ethnic Inequality: Malaysia's New Economic Policy*, London: Hurst.

Faridah Jamaludin (2003) 'Malaysia's new economic policy: has it been a success?', in William Darity and Ashwin Deshpande (eds), *Boundaries of Clan and Color: Transnational Comparisons of Inter-Group Disparity*, London and New York: Routledge, pp. 152–74.

M. Fazilah Abu Samad (2002) *Bumiputeras in the Corporate Sector: Three Decades of Performance, 1970–2000*, CEDER Research Reports Series 1, Kuala Lumpur: CEDER, University of Malaya.

Fryer, Roland G., Jr. and Glenn C. Loury (2005) 'Affirmative action and its mythology', *Journal of Economic Perspectives*, 19(3): 147–62.

Gomez, Edmund Terence and Jomo K.S. (1999) *Malaysia's Political Economy: Power, Profits, Patronage*, Cambridge: Cambridge University Press.

Gomez, Edmund Terence and Johan Saravanamuttu (eds) (2013) *The New Economic Policy in Malaysia: Affirmative Action, Ethnic Inequalities and Social Justice*, Singapore and Petaling Jaya: NUS Press, Institute of Southeast Asian Studies and SIRD.

International Labour Organization (ILO) (2007) *Equality at Work: Tackling the Challenges*, ILO Conference 96th Session, Report I(B), Geneva: International Labour Organization.

Jesudason, James V. (1989) *Ethnicity and the Economy*, Singapore: Oxford University Press.

Jomo K.S. (2004) *The New Economic Policy and Interethnic Relations in Malaysia*, Identities, Conflict and Cohesion Programme Paper 7, Geneva: United Nations Research Institute for Social Development.

Kamal Salih and Zainal Aznam Yusof (1989) 'Overview of the NEP and framework for a post-1990 economic policy', *Malaysian Management Review*, 24: 13–61.

Khoo Boo Teik (2005) *Ethnic Structure, Inequality and Governance in the Public Sector: Malaysian Experiences*, Democracy, Governance and Human Rights Programme Paper 20, Geneva: United Nations Research Institute for Social Development.

Lee Hock Guan (2005) 'Affirmative action in Malaysia', in Institute of Southeast Asian Studies (ed.), *Southeast Asian Affairs 2005*, Singapore: Institute of Southeast Asian Studies, pp. 211–28.

Lee Hock Guan (2013) 'Racial citizenship and higher education in Malaysia', in Edmund Terence Gomez and Johan Saravanamuttu (eds), *The New Economic Policy in Malaysia: Affirmative Action, Ethnic Inequalities and Social Justice*, Singapore: Institute of Southeast Asian Studies, pp. 235–61.

Lee Hwok-Aun (2012) 'Affirmative action in Malaysia: education and employment outcomes since the 1990s', *Journal of Contemporary Asia*, 42(2): 230–54.

Leete, Richard (2007) *From Kampung to Twin Towers: 50 Years of Economic and Social Development*, Petaling Jaya: Oxford Fajar.

Lim Hong Hai (2013) 'Public service and ethnic restructuring under the New Economic Policy', in Edmund Terence Gomez and Johan Saravanamuttu (eds), *The New Economic Policy in Malaysia: Affirmative Action, Ethnic Inequalities and Social Justice*, Singapore: Institute of Southeast Asian Studies, pp. 175–203.

Malaysia (1971) *The Second Malaysia Plan, 1971–75*, Kuala Lumpur: Government Printer.

Malaysia (1996) *Seventh Malaysia Plan, 1996–2000*, Kuala Lumpur: Government Printer.

Malaysia (2001) *Eighth Malaysia Plan, 2001–2005*, Kuala Lumpur: Government Printer.

Malaysia (2006) *Ninth Malaysia Plan, 2006–2010*, Kuala Lumpur: Government Printer.

Malaysia (2010) *Tenth Malaysia Plan, 2011–2015*, Kuala Lumpur: Government Printer.

National Economic Advisory Council (NEAC) (2009) *New Economic Model – Part 1*, Putrajaya: National Economic Advisory Council.

Ooi Kee Beng (2013) 'The new economic policy and the centralisation of power', in Edmund Terence Gomez and Johan Saravanamuttu (eds), *The New Economic Policy in Malaysia: Affirmative Action, Ethnic Inequalities and Social Justice*, Singapore: Institute of Southeast Asian Studies, pp. 317–34.

Puthucheary, Mavis (1978) *The Politics of Administration: The Malaysian Experience*, Kuala Lumpur: Oxford University Press.

Sato, M. (2005) 'Education, ethnicity and economics: higher education reforms in Malaysia, 1957–2003', *NUCB Journal of Language Culture and Communication*, 7(1): 73–88.

Snodgrass, Donald, Zainal Aznam Yusof and Ishak Shari (2003) *Managing Economic Growth and Ethnic Diversity: Malaysia, 1970–1990*, Cambridge, MA: Harvard Institute for International Development.

Tan, Jeff (2008) *Privatization in Malaysia: Regulation, Rent-seeking and Policy Failure*, London and New York: Routledge.

Tan Yao Sua and Santhiram R. Raman (2009) *The Transformation from Elitist to Mass Higher Education in Malaysia: Problems and Challenges*, CenPRIS Working Paper 101/09, Pulau Pinang: Universiti Sains Malaysia.

Torii, Takashi (2003) 'The mechanism for state-led creation of Malaysia's middle classes', *The Developing Economies*, 41(2), pp. 221–42.

Weisskopf, T.E. (2004) *Affirmative Action in the United States and India: A Comparative Perspective*, London: Routledge.

Zainal Aznam Yusof (2012) 'Affirmative action in Malaysia: an overview of progress and limitations', in Graham Brown, Francis Stewart and Arnim Langer (eds), *Affirmative Action in Plural Societies: International Experiences*, Basingstoke: Palgrave Macmillan, pp. 128–50.

14

The middle class in Malaysia

Market expansion, consumption and vulnerabilities

Abdul Rahman Embong

The middle class has become a very important social force influencing the direction of social and political change, as well as the consumer industry. Looking at the growth and expansion of the middle class historically, it can be said that the middle class has undergone three phases of emergence and expansion, the first phase being in Europe after the Industrial Revolution around 1800, while the second was also in Europe, North America and Japan after World War II. Today, it is argued that we are witnessing the third phase of expansion, with the so-called 'emerging markets' – namely, Asia – being the centre of growth (Ernst & Young 2013: 1). While some scholars aptly regarded the twentieth century as 'the century of the middle class' (Fujimura 2000), the twenty-first century, which is witnessing the third phase of middle-class growth, is characterised by an unparalleled expansion of this class across the globe, thereby shifting the base of consumption from the West to the East, as will be shown below.

Market analysts and researchers on the middle class and its huge appetite for consumption of new products are almost in unison in their excitement and jubilation about the expansion of the middle class in the twenty-first century and its impact upon the consumer industry. A leading global bank, HSBC, in a report prepared by its Global Economics Research Team on the rise of the middle class in 'emerging markets', argues that such an unprecedented middle-class expansion will result in 'transforming demand in sectors from clothing to travel, and IT to financial services' (HSBC 2012: front cover). Estimates on the size of the middle class vary. Using the World Bank criterion of US$6,000 per capita gross national income (GNI) as the cut-off point for the middle class in selected developing countries, an economist from the University of Minnesota, Professor Benjamin Senauer, estimated that by the beginning of this century, 93 percent of households in South Korea, 46 percent in Malaysia and Mexico, 45 percent in Russia, 35 percent in Brazil, 23 percent in China and 9 percent in India were already middle class (Senauer and Goetz 2003). Although the percentages may be lower in China and India, the absolute figures are huge given the size of their population, with the middle class estimated to be in the region of 290 million in China and over 90 million in India.[1]

Appearing a decade after the Minnesota study, the HSBC report is more jubilant. It argues that

> a global consumer revolution is in the offing – and it will be driven by an unprecedented expansion of the world's middle class. Almost three billion people – more than 40% of today's population – will join the middle classes by 2050 and these entrants are to be found almost exclusively in today's emerging markets.
>
> *(HSBC 2012: 2)*

The report projects that emerging market consumption, which makes up about one-third of global consumption today, will increase dramatically to almost two-thirds of global consumption by 2050. The report sees this as an opportunity 'for businesses . . . to capture this rising tide of middle-class spenders. Tastes and habits are not yet as firmly established as in other societies, offering opportunities to reposition brands and build entirely new markets' (HSBC 2012: 26).

Per the data in the HSBC report, some of the top 'emerging markets', like Argentina and Brazil, already had a high proportion of middle class in their population by the end of 2010, with Argentina registering 70 percent (26 million people) while Brazil had some 40 percent (78 million). In China, the middle class constituted 30 percent of the population (404 million) in 2011 compared with 23 percent (290 million) in 2000, while India also showed an increase from 9 percent (90 million) in 2000 to 10 percent (121 million) in 2011. Based on these developments, some analysts suggest that by 2030, of the 4.9 billion middle class globally, 64 percent will be in Asia, accounting for over 40 percent of global middle-class consumption. In other words, Asia will have the largest proportion of the global middle class in two decades to come.

A study by Kharas and Gertz argues that there is a cross-over from West to East in the products, fashions, tastes, and designs oriented to the middle class. They estimate that

> by 2015, for the first time in 300 years, the number of Asian middle class consumers will equal the number in Europe and North America. By 2021, on present trends, there could be more than 2 billion Asians in middle class households.
>
> *(Kharas and Gertz 2010: 33)*

In another study, Kharas highlights that while in 2000, Asia (excluding Japan) accounted for only 10 percent of global middle-class spending,

> by 2040, this could reach 40 per cent, and it could continue to rise to almost 60 per cent in the long-term. The steep increase in Asian demand, and the replacement of US demand by Asian demand, is clearly seen as a trend that accelerates in the coming decade.
>
> *(Kharas 2010: 28)*

What is important in this expansion, from the perspective of the market, is the increased purchasing power and spending of this class. An OECD estimate indicates 'global middle class spending [is] increasing from $21 trillion to $56 trillion by 2030, in constant 2005 dollars' (Calamos 2012: 1). According to a report by the London-based professional services firm Ernst & Young (2013: 1), 'companies accustomed to serving the middle-income brackets of the old Western democracies' will have to re-strategise in order to capture the middle-class market in Asia, Africa and Latin America. The report further asserts that from a business perspective, focused on purchasing power, only those earning between US$10 and US$100 per day – thus having effective disposable income – can be considered as belonging to the category of the global middle class.[2]

While figures may vary depending on the definition, the various studies cited above seem to concur that the middle class is undergoing an unprecedented global expansion in the twenty-first century, and that the Asian middle class is fast becoming the largest component in the global middle class. These studies also imply that the global expansion of the middle class – especially in Asia, with its penchant for consumption of goods and services, especially of multinational corporations – means that another consumerist revolution is in the making. The above discussion also shows how sensitive market researchers and strategists are to these developments, and their advice to corporations on the need to strategise and expand their businesses in the coming decades to benefit from the global middle-class expansion.

The Malaysian middle class as part of the global middle-class expansion

For the purposes of this chapter, what is relevant and significant is that the Malaysian middle class is recognised as being part and parcel of this historic global middle-class expansion and is seen as a potential market for the products of multinational corporations. While in absolute terms, the size of the middle class in Malaysia may be small compared with those of its bigger neighbours, as a proportion, the middle class is already more than half of the population – whether analysed by using income criteria as above or by using an occupational definition.[3] The dramatic rise of the middle class in Malaysia took place during the era of the state-led modernisation under the New Economic Policy from the 1970s onwards, becoming a clearly visible social force since the 1980s and 1990s. Using the occupational definition (Abdul Rahman 2002: 41), the middle class in Malaysia constituted about 19.8 percent of households in 1957, 23.9 percent in 1970, 28.5 percent in 1980 and 38.3 percent in 1990. By 2000, it had expanded to 43.2 percent, and today, more than a decade later, the middle class is estimated to be about 51 percent, that is, slightly more than half the population. This seems to tally with the income-based estimates mentioned above.

Much of the discussion on this class in Malaysia has been on the rise and expansion of the middle class, especially its Malay component, its socio-economic characteristics, consumption patterns, family, cultural and religious orientations, as well as its political participation in democratisation processes and civil society movements (Saravanamuttu 1989, 2001; Kahn 1991, 1992, 1996; Abdul Rahman 1995, 1996, 2001, 2002, 2006, 2013). There are also a few studies on the second-generation middle class, but these studies are still few and far between (see Abdul Rahman 2006; Noraini 2014). While there has been some discussion on the consumption of the middle class (for example, Fischer 2008; Abdul Rahman 2002, 2013), the critical question of the sustainability of their status and the economic and financial challenges faced by the middle class in light of changing economic and financial scenarios inside the country and internationally needs more detailed examination. Such an analysis needs to take into account the onslaught of market expansionism, as indicated above, and persistent mesmerising efforts by corporations to ensure the middle class remains a captive market for their products – or in the words of the HSBC report (2012: 26), 'to capture this rising tide of middle-class spenders'.

Several questions merit analysis: is the mass of the middle class in Malaysia financially strong and stable? Or have they placed themselves in a vulnerable situation as a result of their consumption patterns, on the one hand, and their dependence on loans and the hire-purchase system, coupled with the rising cost of living, on the other? Have some sections of the middle class become a vulnerable group subject to changes in economic fortunes, and if so, to what extent are they vulnerable?

This chapter attempts to discuss these interrelated questions in brief.[4] It will first discuss the financial strength of the middle class by examining their income, followed by a discussion of middle-class lifestyles and social reproduction in the face of the rising cost of living and household debts, and the implications of these. Finally, in the concluding section, the chapter will assess the vulnerability of this class.

Income of the middle class

As indicated in the literature, the middle class is basically a class of salaried workers, or the salariat. As their main source of income is their salaries and/or wages, its increase will depend upon increments in salaries and wages over the years, but their purchasing power depends upon the value of the currency as well as inflation. In Malaysia, the main source of data which gives us an idea of the income of employees is supplied by the regular surveys conducted once every five years by the Malaysian Department of Statistics. However, the survey covers only employees, who today represent 74.4 percent of the total workforce in the country. It does not include employers, who make up about 3.9 percent, the self-employed (17.2 percent) and unpaid family workers, who constitute the remaining 4.5 percent (Malaysia 2012a).

According to the survey, of the 9.09 million employed persons in the country in 2012 (see Table 14.1), 16.6 percent were aged 15–24 years old, 33.6 percent aged 25–34, and 23.9 percent aged 35 to 44. This means that half (50.2 percent) of the employed persons in Malaysia are young persons below 35; 74.1 percent are below 45. Those aged 45 to 54 consist of some 18.1 percent while those in the 55–64 year old age bracket, i.e., at the end of their career, make up a small proportion of 7.8 percent.

As shown in Table 14.1, the new middle class of administrators, managers, professionals, as well as technicians and associate professionals, currently makes up 28.9 percent of employees, while the lower middle class (clerical and half of service and sales workers) comprise some 21.7 percent. This means that middle-class employees, that is, the new middle class and the lower middle class, comprise 50.6 percent of the employed workforce in Malaysia. In terms of pay, the mean monthly income for the administrators and managers category is RM5,213 per month (US$1,580, or US$52 per day)[5] and for professionals, RM3,807 (US$1,154, or US$38.50 per day), while technicians and associate professionals

Table 14.1 Mean and median monthly salaries and wages by occupation, Malaysia, 2012

	Occupation	*Number ('000)*	*Mean income (RM)*	*Median income (RM)*
1	Managerial and administrative	302.0 (3.3%)	5,213.00	4,000.00
2	Professional	1134.7 (12.5%)	3,807.00	3,440.00
3	Technicians and associate professionals	1,188.6 (13.1%)	2,435.00	2,200.00
4	Clerical support workers	1,136.5 (12.5%)	1,718.00	1,500.00
5	Services and sales workers	1,685.3 (18.5%)	1,299.00	1,000.00
6	Craft and related trades workers	133.6 (1.5%)	1,283.00	1,100.00
7	Plant and machine operators, and assemblers	950.0 (10.4%)	1,216.00	1,000.00
8	Skilled agricultural, forestry, and fishery workers	1,389.9 (15.3%)	1,065.00	860.00
9	Elementary occupations	1,167.9 (12.8%)	959.00	810.00
	Total	**9,088.6 (100%)**	**1,881.00**	**1,400.00**

Source: Malaysia (2012a).

average RM2,435 per month (US$738, or US$24.60 per day). The lower middle class, that is, the clerical support workers category, earn, on average, RM1,718 per month (US$520, or US$17.30 per day) and those in the sales and service category earn RM1,299 (US$394, or US$13.10 per day). Actual pay, of course, varies depending on the post as well as length of service. Some of those in the administrative, managerial and professional categories, for example, earn as much as RM10,000–30,000 a month or more, while some of those in other categories can earn between RM2,000 and RM4,000 a month. The income disparity between the new middle class and the lower middle class can be in the range of a factor of five to ten.

The above figures, however, provide only the income of employees, and not household incomes, which would reflect more accurately the financial strength or weakness of Malaysian households of all classes, including the middle class. The data from another survey indicate that about two-thirds of all households in Malaysia have less than RM5,000 a month, while almost 40 percent earn less than RM3,000. Only 9.7 percent of all Malaysian households have a monthly income of RM10,000 and above (Malaysia 2012b). This means that members of the middle class, especially those on the middle and lower rungs, have a relatively weak financial position, especially in light of the rising cost of living, while only a minority – those in the new middle class of administrators, managers and professionals – enjoy a higher income level.

Maintaining and reproducing a middle-class lifestyle

As noted in an earlier paper, a major concern among the middle and lower classes in Malaysia

> is the rising cost of living, as seen in rising prices of food items, housing, fuel, motor vehicles and other durables as well as education and healthcare. Being salaried and highly dependent on their take-home pay, members of the middle class find that prices of commodities especially houses and other types of property as well as cars have increased manifold while wages have not been able to keep pace with price increases.
>
> *(Abdul Rahman 2013: 70)*

As part of the middle-class lifestyle, they require decent homes, cars, various modern household gadgets, good foods, clothing, jewellery, proper childcare facilities in the neighbourhood, good schooling and higher education for their children, domestic maids, modern medical and healthcare, health and life insurance, entertainment, overseas travel, investment in financial instruments, savings for retirement, and so on. Indeed, as one commentator put it, 'middle-class Malaysians today have become used to spending on far too many things compared with the previous generations' (Yap 2013). Middle-class families also pay special attention to social reproduction through providing education and other means to ensure their children enjoy the same class position and status as the parents. All these involve financial costs, which incur a heavy burden for middle-class families. With all these competing goals, maintaining a middle-class lifestyle and social reproduction for the family under prevailing economic conditions is a big challenge.

For a middle class so used to spending sprees during earlier periods of economic growth and a whole array of subsidies, to face a new situation in the second decade of the twenty-first century under the spectre of inflation, rising prices and weakening currency is quite a big shock. Since the end of the twentieth century, the Malaysian government has been under great pressure to liberalise and restructure the economy to ensure the country's global competitiveness, and one of the ways of doing so is to reduce subsidies and the dependency syndrome (Abdul Rahman and Tham 2011; Idris 2013). Despite its promise during the thirteenth general elections in May 2013 not to raise prices, the Malaysian government later in the year announced a slew of subsidy cuts to be enforced with immediate effect, and the introduction of a 6 percent goods and services tax (GST) by 1 April 2015. These moves further fuelled inflationary pressures, especially with the removal of subsidies for strategic items – sugar, petrol and diesel – and a promise of other cuts, thus causing a domino effect on prices of various items, with an immediate impact on people's livelihood. The official consumer price index (CPI) rose 3.2 percent in December 2013, more than double the 1.2 percent a year earlier, but consumers – especially the educated middle class – felt that the CPI did not fully reflect the stark reality on the ground. With the subsidy cuts, a Bloomberg report (Chong 2014) noted an immediate 14 percent increase in sugar prices, 11 percent jump for gasoline, and an average of a 15.0–16.9 percent hike in monthly electricity bills from the beginning of 2014. Moreover, a weakened ringgit against the US dollar not only affected prices of imported goods by making them more expensive, but rendered overseas travel and education outside of Malaysia, such as in Australia, the US and Europe, more expensive and beyond the reach of many children of the middle class.

The effect on the middle-class spending and psychology has been quite dramatic and telling. To illustrate an example, media reports showed how a project engineer with two preschool-aged children reacted. He conceded that 'Definitely it's difficult . . . My kids will be without toys, no more vacation, no new cars and we must be very wise on spending money.' Another member of the middle class, a freelance writer, who had elderly parents to support, said that with the rising cost of living, her focus was to save money to put sufficient food on the table, and cut out purchases of personal items such as clothes, shoes, bags and so on. Frustrated with the rising cost of living, she said, 'The government is strangling us. We are now scared to read the daily newspaper because every day, the price of something is going up' (quoted in Chong 2014). In sum, with shrinking purchasing power, particularly among middle-class households, economists and market analysts expect the decline of private consumption growth will impact Malaysia's GDP growth for 2014 and probably beyond (Rochan 2014).

Owning a decent home and possibly having a second home is a crucial component of the middle-class lifestyle and dream. This is a major concern of the middle class. What is the situation regarding house ownership among Malaysian households, including the middle class? Table 14.2 on house ownership status shows that 74.5 percent of all households in Malaysia in 2012 own houses, with the proportion higher in rural areas (84.0 percent) and lower in urban areas (70.9 percent). Households that have to rent their accommodation constitute some 20.2 percent, the highest rate being in urban areas, at 24.8 percent, while others stay in living quarters provided by their employers. Although the data show that the majority of households throughout the country own houses, especially in rural areas, they do show that about 30 percent of all households are without their own homes, and that housing remains a major issue for both the middle and lower classes, especially in major cities such as Kuala Lumpur, Penang and Johor Bharu. As shown in the table, in Kuala Lumpur, only 50.8 percent of households own houses, while almost half stay in rented accommodation (43 percent) or in quarters (6.2 percent). In highly urbanised states such as Selangor, Johor and Penang, the percentage of urban households living in rented accommodation is 29.3 percent, 26.2 percent and 20.9 percent, respectively. In Putrajaya, the administrative capital of Malaysia, which is inhabited by the administrative middle class, the overwhelming majority of households (88.3 percent) live in government quarters, while some 7.4 percent

Table 14.2 Percentage distribution of households by types of ownership of housing, Malaysia 2012 (selected states)

	Owned			*Rented*		
	Total (%)	*Urban (%)*	*Rural (%)*	*Total (%)*	*Urban (%)*	*Rural (%)*
Malaysia	74.5	70.9	84.0	20.2	24.8	8.3
Johor	74.3	72.5	80.0	22.4	26.2	11.0
Melaka	80.6	79.5	85.7	16.5	17.7	10.6
Negri Sembilan	78.1	75.6	82.1	14.7	20.2	6.0
Penang	79.0	78.3	82.1	19.9	20.9	15.4
Perak	81.6	81.3	82.0	14.0	15.7	10.9
Selangor	69.4	68.6	77.7	28.7	29.3	21.5
Kuala Lumpur	50.8	50.8	–	42.7	42.7	–
Putrajaya	4.3	4.3	–	7.4	7.4	–

Source: Malaysia 2012a (computed from Table 3.1).

Note:
Data on 'quarters' as a form of housing status are not included in the table.

live in rented apartments or houses, and the remaining 4.3 percent live in their own houses. It is not clear whether those staying in government quarters own houses elsewhere, but the fact remains that they do not own the premises in which they currently live.

Demand for housing is not only strong among those without their own houses, but also among house owners who may want better houses and locations than their present ones. While in the past the demand was largely for low-cost housing for the poor, today it is affordable housing for the middle class (Abdul Rahman 2013). But as has been pointed out by various media reports, housing prices keep surging, especially in major cities and their satellite towns. To address this, the government set up Perbadanan Program Perumahan 1Malaysia (PR1MA) (1Malaysia Housing Programme Corporation), which launched a housing programme – dubbed as 'affordable housing' – in July 2012. PR1MA is responsible for planning, developing, building and maintaining housing for the middle class or middle-income groups in major cities in Malaysia. For purposes of the housing programme, the middle-income group is defined as households with a monthly income of between RM2,500.00 and RM7,500.00. Houses built by PR1MA carry a price range of RM100,000–400,000. Malaysians aged 21 years and above and not owning more than one property are eligible to apply. Allocations are done through an open balloting process, and successful applicants are required to live in the houses, which cannot be sold within the locked-in period of ten years (www.pr1ma.my/en/eligibility).

While PR1MA is a good programme, the number of applicants far outnumbers the available units as demand well exceeds supply. According to media reports, PR1MA plans to build 500,000 houses by 2018, and for the first phase, it announced thirty housing projects of 38,000 houses throughout the country. However, by August 2013, there were already 250,000 applicants, and the number was increasing (Lee 2013). For PR1MA's first project, located in Putrajaya, for example, while it planned for 560 housing units, the number of applicants was more than 7,000, which meant demand exceeded supply by 12 times. It should be noted that in its 2013 election manifesto, the Barisan Nasional promised to build an average of 200,000 housing units a year. Real Estate and Housing Developers' Association Malaysia (REHDA) President Michael Yam deemed this target impractical, suggesting 100,000 houses per year would be more realistic. This means that the waiting time for middle-class prospective house buyers under this programme would be long – at least about three years – before they could be given the key to their 'dream homes'.

Houses built by private developers meant for the middle class are often more expensive, depending on the location and type of house. As shown elsewhere (Abdul Rahman 2013), houses priced at RM380,000 in 2008 would fetch up to RM600,000 or more today. While part of the price hike is due to property speculation, which is still rampant despite attempts to control it (Goh 2013), it does mean that there is a huge demand for housing within this price range among the middle class.

A nagging question remains: is the PR1MA housing programme – dubbed as 'affordable housing' – really affordable to the majority of middle-class households? What about the houses offered by private developers – are they within the financial reach of the majority of middle-class buyers? These questions will be taken up in the next section on the middle class and private debts.

Middle-class household debts

Analysts are concerned about rising debt levels in Malaysia and the debt levels of middle-class households. As an analyst writing for the financial weekly *The Edge* (Yap 2013) puts it in a cover story, what is being witnessed today is 'Malaysia's debt mountain'. Although the 'debt mountain' metaphor may be rather harsh, the reality is that all three types of debt – government, corporate and household – are on the rise, constituting a huge proportion of the GDP. While the government debt, for example, stood at 35.3 percent in 2001, it increased sharply in just four years to 45.7 percent in 2005. Debt levels peaked in 2010, at 55.4 percent of GDP, declining in 2013 to 53.1 percent, just slightly below the statutory ceiling of 55 percent. Besides government debt, corporate debt has also been rising, from 79.9 percent of GDP in 2007 to 95.8 percent in 2013, which is very high.

What is the situation regarding household debt? Just like for government and corporate debts, the overall trend has been a steady climb in the last decade. Based on statistics released by Malaysia's central bank, Bank Negara Malaysia (BNM), we can see that while household debt stood at 69.0 percent of GDP in 2006, it increased to 76.0 percent in 2010, and climbed sharply further to 83.0 percent in 2013, one of the highest levels in Asia. While there is no breakdown of the income or socio-economic background of indebted households, it is safe to assume that the overwhelming majority are middle-class households who take up loans from banks, finance companies and other institutions for various purposes. According to BNM, purchase of residential properties and non-residential properties took up 56 percent of loans by consumers in 2012 (Joseph 2013). According to estimates by the Consumers Association of Penang (CAP), housing loan repayment alone takes up about 45 percent of income, while the rest goes to pay off car loans, personal loans (17 percent), credit cards, and so on.

It should be noted that the growth in private consumption has been generated by debts, rather than by increases in income. Pay increases have been slow, especially in the private sector, and have not kept pace with rising prices. Despite all this, private consumption, especially by middle-class households, has been growing faster than GDP, and this is worrying. Data show that between 2005 and 2009, private consumption grew at 7.7 percent per annum, resulting in household debt growth of 7.1 percent, much higher than the GDP growth rate of 5.4 percent during the same period. In 2010, the GDP grew faster, reaching 7.2 percent, but household debt grew at a much higher rate of 12.5 percent.

What is the level of exposure of households in terms of debt? The evidence indicates that household debt in Malaysia is 140 percent higher than household disposable income (*The Edge*, 22 November 2010). This means that the amount of loans taken by households, on average, is 1.4 times higher than the income at their disposal to service the loans (household disposable income consists of the balance after deducting expenditures for food items, clothing, transportation, health, education, savings, etc.). When examined from this perspective, the situation faced by Malaysian households, namely the middle class, is far more serious than in some other countries. In Singapore, for example, the ratio of household debt to disposable income is much lower, at 105 percent; in the US it is 123 percent; South Korea, 101 percent; Thailand, 53 percent; and Indonesia, 36 percent.

Figures show that the proportion of income spent on loan repayments has hence tended to increase over the years. In 2006, some 39.1 percent of income was used to pay back loans, but this increased to 41.1 percent in 2007. Although that figure decreased to 39.5 percent the following year, it was back up to 49.0 percent in 2009 and 47.8 percent in 2010. In short, almost half of monthly household income has been used to service loans in the last several years (*The Edge*, 22 November 2010), with not much of a balance left for other expenditures. From the perspective of banks and other lending institutions, this ratio is considered still 'healthy', but from the perspective of indebted households, this is risky and dangerous.

Conclusion

Based on the analysis above, it would seem that the mass of the middle class in Malaysia is financially vulnerable in the face of a rising cost of living and inflation, though the nature and causes of their vulnerability may in some ways differ from those of the lower classes. Indebted middle-class households in particular may face a difficult situation. Their exposure to debt makes them vulnerable, especially in times of economic or financial crisis, or when they are struck by personal crises, such as the death or illness of the family's breadwinner. It would be instructive to draw some comparisons with experiences of the middle class in rapidly growing economies such as Brazil, Russia, Mexico, Turkey and India. The middle class in these countries, especially Brazil, is in trouble. A report in the *Wall Street Journal* by Chao and Lyons (2013) argues that

> Brazil's troubles offer a warning to emerging markets caught up in one of the most enticing economic stories of the past decade: the rise of middle-class consumers in the developing world. From Brazil to Indonesia to South Africa, faster growth rates lifted millions from poverty in the last 10 years, bringing more people into the middle class and introducing many of them to credit for the first time. But . . . the case of Brazil shows how middle-class growth can also be knocked off track by too much debt. . . . [C]onsumer-debt worries have prompted a rethink on how far Brazil's new middle class will climb, and how fast. The percentage of household income that goes to pay off debts is unusually high: In Brazil, it is more than a fifth of household income compared with 10% in the U.S., according to both countries' central banks.
>
> *(Chao and Lyons 2013)*

As indicated above, in Brazil one-fifth, or 20 percent, of household income is used to pay off debts, and this is considered already 'off-track'. If this is the yardstick, then the situation in Malaysia, where the proportion of income used to pay off debt is almost 50 percent, is certainly far worse. The implication of this is that indebted middle-class households might default on loans, leading them into deeper trouble. In Brazil, the middle-class loan default rate is 5.6 percent, higher than that in Russia, South Africa, Mexico, Turkey and India (Durden 2013).

Malaysian middle-class household debt is a cause for worry. Though exact figures are not readily available, many have defaulted on loans and been declared bankrupt. Looking at the situation as a whole, it can be said that a substantial section of the middle class has become a vulnerable group in a specific sense, namely, that they have fallen for the persuasions of banks and other lending institutions to take up loans that sometimes are beyond their means to pay off. Their economic and financial situation is not strong, except for those in the upper echelons of the new middle class. But, as consumption is part of their lifestyle, they may not be able to resist the market blitz and temptations of new products emerging in the market. While this attraction may be a boon to business, it is a bane to middle-class households that have multiple loans to service and personal consumption to sustain. As the prospects of containing the rising cost of living and raising household incomes do not look promising in the near future, many indebted Malaysian middle-class households may have to 'slave' for the banks for the rest of their working lives in order to rid themselves of debt shackles.

Notes

1 As explained in the paper, 'The size of the emerging middle class in eleven countries is estimated with a cut-off level of $6,000 using the World Bank data . . . for GNI per capita, converted into US dollars using purchasing power parity (PPP) and the percentage shares of income or consumption by quintile and for the top 10 percent of the population' (Senauer and Goetz 2003: 4).

2 The Ernst & Young report disagrees with the World Bank's definition of the middle class. It argues that 'The World Bank's definition . . . is a useful way of ascertaining how many people have been lifted out of poverty – and the numbers who have moved into this bracket in the developing world is something to be applauded. But this definition is not very helpful for companies dependent on sales to those with large disposable incomes; they require a more realistic estimation of the number of people entering their target markets. For most businesses, a much more useful definition of middle class is people earning between US$10 and US$100 per day. At this level, consumers start having the kind of disposable incomes that will allow them to buy the cars, televisions and other goods that have been the staples of bourgeois life in the West for 60 years. People in this income bracket can be considered a "global middle class" – middle class by the standards of any country' (Ernst & Young 2013: 3).

3 Using occupation as the criterion, the middle class consists of the following categories: managerial and administrative, professionals, technician and associate professionals, as well as clerical, sales and about half of service workers. Those in the managerial, administrative, professional, associate professional and technical categories are defined as the 'new middle class', while the rest constitute the lower middle class (for details see Saravanamuttu 1989; Abdul Rahman 2002).

4 I have briefly discussed in an earlier paper the consumption and challenges to the living standards of the middle class and dilemmas they face (see Abdul Rahman 2013). The present paper takes up some of the issues in the earlier paper, but goes beyond it by raising critical questions on the economic vulnerability of the middle class today.

5 At prevailing exchange rate of US$1.00 to RM3.30.

Bibliography

Abdul Rahman Embong (1995) 'Malaysian middle classes: some preliminary observations', *Jurnal Antropologi dan Sosiologi*, 22: 31–54.

Abdul Rahman Embong (1996) 'Social transformation, the state and the middle classes in post-independence Malaysia', *Southeast Asian Studies*, 34(3): 56–79.

Abdul Rahman Embong (2001) 'Beyond the crisis: the paradox of the Malaysian middle class', in Abdul Rahman Embong (ed.), *Southeast Asian Middle Classes: Prospects for Social Change and Democratisation*, Bangi, Malaysia: Penerbit Universiti Kebangsaan Malaysia, pp. 80–102.

Abdul Rahman Embong (2002) *State-led Modernization and the New Middle Class in Malaysia*, Houndmills: Palgrave Macmillan.

Abdul Rahman Embong (2006) 'Between optimism, contestation and caution: the second generation middle classes in Malaysia', in Michael Hsiao (ed.), *The Changing Faces of the Middle Classes in Asia-Pacific*, Taipei: Center for Asia-Pacific Area Studies, Academia Sinica, pp. 133–54.

Abdul Rahman Embong (2013) 'Responding to globalization and the state: negotiations and contestations by the middle class in Malaysia', in C. Tazreiter and Tham Siew Yean (eds), *Globalization and Social Transformation in the Asia-Pacific: The Australian and Malaysian Experience*, Houndmills: Palgrave Macmillan, pp. 63–77.

Abdul Rahman Embong and Tham Siew Yean (eds) (2011) *Malaysia at a Crossroads: Can We Make the Transition?*, Bangi: Penerbit Universiti Kebangsaan Malaysia.

Calamos Advisors LLC (2012) *Growth of the Global Middle Class*, Calamos Thematic Update, July, Naperville, IL: Calamos Investments LLC.

Chao, Loretta and John Lyons (2013) 'Bill comes due for Brazil's middle class: debt woes help explain why the country's once-dazzling growth has fizzled', *Wall Street Journal*, 8 October.

Chong Pooi Koon (2014) 'Malaysians seen curbing spending as living costs surge', *Bloomberg News*, 7 January, available at www.bloomberg.com/news/2014-01-07/ (accessed 10 January 2014).

Durden, Tyler (2013) 'How Brazil's middle class dream became a debt-fuelled nightmare', available at www.zerohedge.com/news/2013-10-09 (accessed 15 January 2014).

Ernst & Young (2013) *Hitting the Sweet Spot: The Growth of the Middle Class in Emerging Markets*, n.p.: Ernst & Young.

Fischer, J. (2008) *Proper Islamic Consumption: Shopping among the Malays in Modern Malaysia*, Honolulu: University of Hawai'i Press.

Fujimura, M. (2000) 'The welfare state, the middle class, and the welfare society', *Review of Population and Social Policy*, 9: 1–23.

Goh Ban Lee (2013) 'Make property speculation costly', *The Sun Daily*, 26 August.

HSBC (2012) *Consumer in 2050: The Rise of the EM Middle Class*, London: HSBC Global Research.

Idris Jala (2013) 'The way forward for the middle class is increasing incomes and cutting living costs', *The Star*, 2 December.

Joseph, Samantha (2013) 'Necessary loans: a house, a car and spare change', *Kinibiz*, 20 August.

Kahn, J.S. (1991) 'Constructing culture: towards an anthropology of the middle classes in Southeast Asia', *Asian Studies Review*, 15(2): 50–57.

Kahn, J.S. (1992) 'Class, ethnicity and diversity: some remarks on Malay Culture in Malaysia', in J.S. Kahn and Francis Loh Kok Wah (eds), *Fragmented Vision: Culture and Politics in Contemporary Malaysia*, Sydney: Allen & Unwin.

Kahn, J.S. (1996) 'The middle class as a field of ethnological study', in Muhammad Ikmal Said and Zahid Emby (eds), *Critical Perspectives: Essays in Honour of Syed Husin Ali*, Kuala Lumpur: Malaysian Social Science Association, pp. 12–33.

Kharas, Homi (2010) The Emerging Middle Class in Developing Countries. Working Paper 285 (January), Paris: OECD Development Centre.

Kharas, Homi and Geoffrey Gertz (2010) 'The new global middle class: a crossover from west to east', in Cheng Li (ed.), *China's Emerging Middle Class: Beyond Economic Transformation*, Washington DC: Brookings Institution Press, pp. 32–51.

Lee Long Hui (2013) 'PR1MA unlikely to meet demand', *Malaysiakini*, 29 December.

Malaysia (2012a) *Household Income and Amenities Survey Report*, Putrajaya: Department of Statistics.

Malaysia (2012b) *Labour Force Survey Report*, Putrajaya: Department of Statistics.

Norani Dhiauddin (2014) 'Reproduksi Sosial dalam Keluarga Kelas Menengah Melayu: Satu Kajian Kes Di Sekitar Lembah Kelang' [Social reproduction among the Malay middle class family: a case study in the Kelang Valley], in Chin Yee Whah, Nor Hayati Sa'at and Sity Daud (eds), *Sains Sosial dan Kajian Pembangunan* [Social Science and Development Studies], Kajang: Malaysian Social Science Association, pp. 301–15.

Perbadanan PR1MA Malaysia, available at www.pr1ma.my/en/eligibility (accessed 10 January 2014).

Rochan, M. (2014) 'Middle-class spending curbs may hit Malaysia's GDP growth', *International Business Times*, 7 January, available at www.ibtimes.co.uk (accessed 10 January 2014).

Saravanamuttu, Johan (1989) ‘Kelas Menengah dalam Politik Malaysia: Tonjolan Perkauman atau Kepentingan Kelas?’ [Middle class in Malaysian politics: communalism or class interests?], *Kajian Malaysia*, 7(1–2): 106–26.
Saravanamuttu, Johan (2001) ‘Is there a politics of the middle class?’, in Abdul Rahman Embong (ed.), *Southeast Asian Middle Classes: Prospects for Social Change and Democratisation*, Bangi: Penerbit UKM, pp. 103–18.
Senauer, Benjamin and Linde Goetz (2003) The Growing Middle Class in Developing Countries and the Market for High-value Food Products, Working Paper 03–02, Minnesota: University of Minnesota, Food Industry Centre.
Yap, Cindy (2013) ‘Malaysia’s debt mountain’, *The Edge*, 2 October.
Yap Ming Hui (2013) ‘Financial realities of the middle class’, *The Star*, 17 April.

15

Natural resource extraction and political dependency

Malaysia as a rentier state

Helena Varkkey

Natural resources are materials or substances like petroleum, minerals, forests, water and fertile land that occur in nature and can be used for economic gain (Chichilnisky 1996: 136). The two main schools of thought on the relationship between natural resource wealth and political stability are the 'resource curse' school and that of the 'rentier state'. Proponents of the resource curse hypothesis claim that states with an abundance of natural resources have a tendency towards political instability, and this will most likely result in in civil war. With such an abundance of natural resources, there is both a motive and opportunity for conflict. This may thus indirectly create instability as a result of institutional or economic factors (Basedau and Lay 2009: 757).

On the other hand, the theory of the rentier state suggests that natural resource wealth may contribute to the consolidation of political control and stability (Dunning 2005: 452). In a rentier state, the economy is dominated by rents from abroad, earned mainly through the exporting of natural resources. In such states, the presence of natural resources offers a valuable political opportunity (Sloane-White and Beaulieu 2010: 389). The theory of the rentier state argues that in a rentier economy, the state's main role is to distribute rents. In such regimes, states use the revenue from abundant resources to 'buy off' peace. This is done through several methods, namely, repression, external support, patronage and large-scale distributive policies. Hence, it would be likely that these rentier regimes would be comparatively more politically stable and less inclined to conflict (Basedau and Lay 2009: 757–61).

Malaysia is blessed with an abundance of natural resources: ground rich with ore, vast deposits of oil and gas underground, tropical forests lush with valuable timber, and soils fertile for agricultural production. Hence, resources like tin, rubber, palm oil, oil and gas, and timber have over the years remained crucial to Malaysian economic performance (Sloane-White and Beaulieu 2010: 381–89; Ahm. Mustain 2005: 704). Post-independence, Malaysia's resource abundance and its associated wealth, complemented further by comparatively inexpensive labour costs, allowed the state to sustain high levels of production of primary agriculture, timber and mineral products for export (Jomo 2003: 16; Hirsch and Warren 1998: 6; Roberti 1989: 54–56). At its highest, raw resource exports contributed up to 40 percent of Malaysian GDP (Suraya 2003). The 1970s onwards saw Malaysia pursuing manufacturing and industrialisation policies that added value to its natural resources before export (Lim and Stern 2003: 33–35; Naguib and Smucker 2009: 100–10; Sumiani *et al.* 2007: 896–98). Supported by the revenue generated by these raw exports (Hurst 1987: 170–71), the government encouraged modernisation of the economy by promoting the development of natural resource processing industries, like petroleum and palm oil refining, and processing timber. Malaysia experienced massive and sustained economic growth as a result, becoming one of the 'East Asian miracle' economies (Raman 2006: 38–40).

At the same time, Malaysia has enjoyed uncommonly high levels of political stability since its independence in 1957. The ruling coalition, Barisan Nasional, has retained its majority in the political landscape of Malaysia for more than fifty years. Malaysia remains one of the least seismic of the Southeast Asian nations and has never experienced *coups d'état*, revolutions, political assassinations or any other serious threat to its political institutions (Sloane-White and Beaulieu 2010: 381–89). Barisan Nasional remains the only ruling party the country has ever known.

Sloane-White and Beaulieu (2010: 382) argue that the reason for this political stability is Malaysia's rentier-based economy that exploits natural resource wealth to consolidate political control over the population. This chapter uses and extends these arguments of Malaysia as a rentier state. It proposes that Malaysia displays two of the four motives to 'buy off' peace in a rentier state system, namely, patronage (to 'buy off' the elite) and large-scale distributive policies (to 'buy off' the masses). This chapter thus argues that the choices that the Malaysian ruling elite has made on the distribution of its rents have contributed to the consolidation and continuation of political control in the hands of the ruling coalition since independence. At the end of the chapter, the rentier state framework is applied to the Malaysian palm oil sector to explain the ruling elite's political dependency on natural resources in an updated context.

The politicisation of the natural resource sector

While the economy of pre-colonial Malay kingdoms was based largely on subsistence agriculture, this changed with the advent of British colonial rule. British rule triggered the systematic exploitation of natural resources, by placing large tracts of land under state 'ownership', introducing forestry and agriculture departments, and bringing in new technologies for harvesting and natural resource extraction (Suparb and Lebel 2000: 18; Hurst 1987: 170). Many British investors established mining companies and plantation estates in Malaya to exploit these resources. They converted massive swathes of forests into arable land, and as a result Malaya's agricultural area increased fivefold between 1900 and 1950 (Hezri and Hasan 2006: 37–47). In this way, Malayan natural resources were incorporated into world markets (Sutton 2001: 90–94).

When the British granted independence to Malaya in 1957, many of these foreign companies continued their economic activities in Malaya. Therefore, resource extraction and export continued to drive the Malayan economy; however, Malayan society was not well integrated into this sector. The Chinese worked in the tin mines (and also dominated the local economies in the cities) and Indians worked on the estates. The Malays, who made up the majority of the population, were largely poor subsistence farmers and fishermen living in rural villages. This racially imbalanced economy fuelled tensions among the races, which culminated in bloody post-election riots in 1969. Following this conflagration, the Malay-dominated government[1] attempted to alleviate racial tensions by better integrating the Malay population into the economy. This was a major objective of the New Economic Policy (NEP), which intended to diminish the identification of race with economic function and geographical location (Lim and Stern 2003: 33–35; Naguib and Smucker 2009: 100–10). Natural resource exploitation was seen as a key avenue to facilitate this shift, being a sector that involved comparatively low start-up costs and knowledge (Hurst 1987: 170). Therefore, the pursuit of economic growth and development, fuelled by easy access to natural resources, has been the credo of national unity in an ethnically divided Malaysia since the 1970s (Hezri 2004: 358–63).

A major strategy under the NEP was 'market nationalisation', which involved the government's facilitating stock purchases of private, resource-based companies (mostly British companies mentioned above) and converting them into state-owned enterprises (Lim and Stern 2003: 33–35; Naguib and Smucker 2009: 100–10). This strategy was promoted as a patriotic cause of 'reclaiming Malaysian control over Malaysian resources' from foreign investors who were part of the colonial legacy (Pletcher 1991: 624–33). In this way, Malaysia was able to inherit sector-specific knowledge from these companies. Permodalan Nasional Berhad (PNB, the national capitalisation agency) was one agency established for such purposes. The Malaysian government initiated PNB's takeover of London-based tin miner Malaysia Mining Corporation in 1976 (Mohanlall 2012: 114). It also facilitated PNB's purchase of almost eight million shares of Guthrie Corporation, a major British plantation company, and acquisition overnight of over 80,645 hectares of Malaysian estate land (Gellert 2005: 1346), in what was known as the 'Guthrie Dawn Raid' (Yacob 2010: 919).

Opportunities for patronage

Rentier state elites tend to distribute rents selectively. This results in the creation of patron–client networks that benefit only the leaders of politically important groups.[2] Since personal ties with state elites are important in gaining access to such resource revenues, these networks limit the distribution of revenues to a comparatively tiny portion of the populace (Basedau and Lay 2009: 761–62). The NEP aimed to achieve 'a wider and more effective representation and participation of the Bumiputera[3] community in modern and commercial agriculture, agribusiness and trade' (Murad *et al.* 2010: 406–14). Hence, to increase wealth among the Malay population, the government proceeded to transfer control of the recently nationalised companies to Malays (or *bumiputera*) who were well connected to the ruling elite, creating 'government-linked' companies (GLCs). These GLCs were given priority access to permits, licences and government contracts (Mariati and Kamarulzaman 2005: 31–45; Lim and Stern 2003: 33–35). This was further complemented by the provision of additional subsidies, training, advisory assistance and credit facilities for these priority companies (Naguib and Smucker 2009: 100–10; Cheema 1978: 48).

This process planted the roots of the patronage dynamics in the Malaysian natural resource sector.[4] For example, in the state of Pahang on the peninsula, timber licences were awarded to selected Malays, especially in the run-up to elections. This included the Pahang royal family, other dignitaries, *penghulu* (village headmen), former prominent members of the armed forces, and non-ranking members of political support groups (Cooke 1997: 220–21). With this transfer of wealth to select Malays, the government was able to achieve the political goal of somewhat reducing racial economic disparity within Malaysian society, while at the same time channelling resources for the benefit of itself and its clients (Gunes-Ayata 1994: 21–26).

As a result, these hand-picked Malay entrepreneurs became extremely wealthy, but because of their indebtedness to their patrons, they were expected to assist the government in times of need. For example, in 2001, noted Malay entrepreneur Syed Mokhtar AlBukhary, a beneficiary of the NEP initiatives, was called upon by the then Prime Minister Mahathir Mohamed to 'rescue' the government's debt- and scandal-ridden Perbadanan Nasional Berhad

(Pernas) by absorbing it under his corporation, Tradewinds. In his 2012 biography, AlBukhary details how taking over Pernas was a private bail-out, which he undertook at a cost of RM1.4 billion. In his own words, AlBukhary viewed this exercise as 'helping the hand that once fed him' (Mohanlall 2012: 117–22).

But rather than being criticised by less well-connected Malays for their unfair access to the rewards of the rentier state, these well-connected Malays were publicly valorised as paragons of Malay entrepreneurial modernity. The pro-Malay government's promise that it will always safeguard Malays' special rights (as part of its strategy to 'buy off' the masses) fed into the belief that these successful Malays would always look after, uplift, and assist other Malays. And, due to inclusionary ethnic ideology, some members of the Malay middle class also believed they could collaborate with the elite, perhaps even to become elites themselves, with access to the rentier state (Sloane-White and Beaulieu 2010: 393–97).

Patronage is also useful in accommodating potential political rivals to reduce threats to power (Basedau and Lay 2009: 761–62). To further integrate Malays into the economy, the NEP placed restrictions upon non-Malay enterprises, shutting them out of many business opportunities. However, the Chinese community was traditionally more experienced with business than were these newly minted Malay entrepreneurs, therefore an opportunity arose to accommodate the Chinese, as potential political rivals due to their economic power, into these patronage networks. A situation of mutual dependency arose: Chinese businessmen needed Malay entrepreneurs to obtain contracts, and the Malays needed the Chinese to carry out the projects efficiently. Hence, another layer of patron–client relationships developed (Lim and Stern 2003: 33–35), producing what were called 'Ali-Baba' arrangements. A Chinese businessperson ('Baba') gained access to business opportunities through subcontracting, or by buying over rights given to a Malay ('Ali') (Naguib and Smucker 2009: 100–10; Mariati and Kamarulzaman 2005: 31–45).

For example, in Sarawak in the years after independence, political elites distributed access to Sarawak's timber to a hand-picked minority (political supporters, friends and family) to ensure loyalty and support. They in turn usually contracted these licences out to a few major timber and logging tycoons, often Chinese, in the typical 'Ali-Baba' fashion (Raman 2006: 38–40). As a result, in Sarawak, around six Malaysian–Chinese companies essentially controlled timber extraction (Dauvergne 1995: 192–212).

These well-connected companies often paid monthly salaries to local headmen, to keep them 'on side', to allow for the smooth continuation not only of their resource exploitation activities, but also of activities of the government in office (Leigh 1998: 94–101). In the spirit of mutual dependency, part of the earnings of these private businesses was often channelled to ensure the awarding party's return to power in elections (Naguib and Smucker 2009: 100–10; Mariati and Kamarulzaman 2005: 31–45). This included paying off headmen to influence their villagers' voting, buying votes and swaying the allegiance of potential political rivals. Such funds were also helpful for politicians to reach a dispersed electorate (Dauvergne 1995: 194–99). For example, during the campaign period for the 1991 elections, the ruling party enjoyed access to a fleet of helicopters and seemingly unlimited funds to reach voters deep within the jungles of Sabah and Sarawak (Cooke 1997: 218–35). These patronage relationships established at the elite level clearly transcended ethnicity, especially with the Ali-Baba arrangements; however, at the popular level, ethnic differences were emphasised to hold the loyalty of the constituents (Leigh 1998: 94–101).

This close reciprocal association between the government and private interests has led to some criticisms of lack of transparency, coordination and competitiveness, little motivation to be cost-conscious or sales-driven, duplication of functions, and corruption. A major reason why such a relationship-based system did work, however, is because it was fundamentally self-governing. Patrons and clients could be expected to honour the spirit of agreements, often in spite of the lack of written contracts. This is because they would be determined to preserve these precious 'connections' to guarantee a constant supply of future dealings from within the same network (Naguib and Smucker 2009: 100–10; Mariati and Kamarulzaman 2005: 31–45; Cheema 1978: 51–52). In short, 'the objective of productive and optimal resource allocation within the economy was met' (Mariati and Kamarulzaman 2005: 43).

Large-scale distribution policies

The chapter now turns to the methods by which the Malaysian rentier state has at the same time been able to 'buy off' the larger population. Rentier states may employ large-scale distributive or 'populist' policies, including increasing public sector employment, apportioning subsidies, or providing free education and healthcare. As a result, potential opposition leaders may be discouraged, or may have problems recruiting supporters (Basedau and Lay 2009: 761). Indeed, for the last twenty years, Malaysia's level of public expenditure as a percentage of GDP has been the highest in Southeast Asia, and higher than in most developing countries. Malaysia's distributive strategies have focused on free primary and secondary education and basic healthcare, as well as building a mostly competent bureaucracy of significant size (Sloane-White and Beaulieu 2010: 388–90). Furthermore, to live up to its promise to safeguard Malays' special rights, the government established targeted programmes for poorer Malays, including the economic modernisation of the rural sector, providing Malays with exclusive facilities for higher education and shifting rural Malays to urban areas (Cheema 1978: 47).

Distribution policies have also concentrated on creating multiple public institutions and companies to address national and public well-being. This strategy can be seen in two crucial natural resource sectors: agriculture, and oil and gas. The institutions the government established within these sectors were of great political and developmentalist help to the Malaysian rentier state (Sloane-White and Beaulieu 2010: 388–91), and hence were often promoted by the government as national saviours (Cooke 1997: 218–35).

The government focused on modernising agriculture by providing supplies like new seeds and fertilisers, and by developing infrastructure and welfare facilities in the rural areas. The underlying assumption was that this focus on the rural agricultural sector would benefit the Malay masses, in particular, since the Malays made up the majority of the rural populace. Towards that end, the government established the Ministry of Rural and Regional Development to oversee other newly established specialised institutions like the Federal Land Development Authority (FELDA), the Federal Agriculture Marketing Authority (FAMA, to coordinate public and private marketing), and the Malaysian Agricultural Research and Development Institute (MARDI, to improve agricultural research and extension services). Furthermore, to improve upon existing institutional weaknesses, cooperative societies and farmers' associations were also established (Cheema 1978: 44–45).

The government established FELDA in 1965 as a statutory body designed to eradicate rural poverty (Sloane-White and Beaulieu 2010: 384; Dauvergne 1994: 505). It was promoted as a 'catch up' vehicle for rural communities, especially poorer Malay and *bumiputera* communities (Cooke 1997: 218–35), who were given preferential treatment (Cheema 1978: 44). FELDA's main role was opening up vast amounts of commercial agricultural land, while providing landless peasants the opportunity to be smallholders (Sloane-White and Beaulieu

2010: 388–90). Indeed, FELDA has been credited for playing an important role in reducing poverty in Malaysia from 49.3 percent in 1970 to 5.1 percent in 2002 (Abdullah and Hezri 2008: 913). A strong element of political co-option also was observable, as a criterion of political loyalty to Barisan Nasional was used to select settlers (Pletcher 1991: 624–33). FELDA has thus been an important institution for retaining the support of rural Malays (Sloane-White and Beaulieu 2010: 388–90), with funds officially set aside to be given to these settlers as a 'reward' during festive seasons. Rulers often reiterate that the support of more than 100,000 FELDA settler families nationwide was important to maintain political stability in the country (Benjamin and Gasper 2001).

In the oil and gas sector, the national oil company, Petroliam Nasional Berhad (PETRONAS), was created in 1974. It is a state-owned corporation holding exclusive ownership of and rights to all oil and gas in Malaysia. This exclusive right means that any foreign and private oil and gas companies are allowed to operate in Malaysia only through production-sharing contracts with PETRONAS. PETRONAS has also contributed towards the Malaysian strategy of developing a labour-intensive export industrialisation sector to absorb poor workers. It now employs over 30,000 people. PETRONAS contributes substantially to the national budget, paying high taxes and dividends. Indeed, since the mid-1980s, more than 25 percent of government revenue has come from activities related to oil and gas. This influx has been useful for the government in administering its generous populist redistributive policies, balancing public finances, avoiding external debt, and dodging inflation crises (Sloane-White and Beaulieu 2010: 388–91).

Like many other Malaysian GLCs and federal agencies, both PETRONAS and FELDA also act as instruments of political patronage. For example, when FELDA was privatised in what was Asia's biggest initial public offering in 2012, a significant percentage of its shares was allocated to unnamed *bumiputera* investors (Grant 2013). And while PETRONAS is known as a well-run and professional organisation, its operations are allowed to be generally opaque (Hill *et al.* 2012: 1708). In return, PETRONAS provides the state with access to its immense profits. For example, PETRONAS was called upon twice in the 1980s to financially 'rescue' Bank Bumiputera Malaysia Berhad (now CIMB Bank). PETRONAS was also often called upon to finance 'national causes' by undertaking economically risky but strategically attractive projects (Tay 2003: 51–53), like erecting the Petronas Twin Towers in the 1990s (Jomo and Gomez 2000: 280).

In these ways, these institutions, together with the private companies discussed in the previous section, helped build modern Malaysia. Therefore, this sector has been viewed as a valuable, yet expendable resource, useful primarily in its ability to generate foreign exchange to fund other developmental goals and populist policies. Such high-value public services generate broad economic satisfaction among the citizenry. Thus, the Malaysian rentier state has retained its resilience by delivering the material conditions the population expects (Dauvergne 1994: 506–07; Sloane-White and Beaulieu 2010: 388–90). This has also resulted in a low level of government dependency on public taxation, and thus a low tax burden upon Malaysian citizens, with personal income tax representing only around 10 percent of the government's revenue. In fact, for the fiscal year of 1998, after the Asian financial crisis, the government was easily able to afford to declare a year free of personal income tax for all citizens and residents of the country. Indeed, the populace may not feel such a strong urge to protest against a government that does not levy high taxes (Basedau and Lay 2009: 761).

Hence, the Malaysian state distributes more revenues *to* than it extracts revenues *from* its population (Sloane-White and Beaulieu 2010: 389–90). This tendency becomes especially pronounced during election seasons, when the need to 'buy off' the masses is highest. For example, in the run-up to the 2013 elections, the incumbent government implemented a variety of populist handouts targeted to its traditional political base, like raising salaries for civil servants, instituting a cash transfer programme known as Bantuan Rakyat 1Malaysia (BR1M, or 1Malaysia People's Assistance Programme) (Welsh 2013: 13), establishing health clinics in poor areas, and creating a chain of government-subsidised general stores dubbed Kedai Rakyat 1Malaysia (KR1M, or 1Malaysia People's Store) (Brown 2013: 162). In these ways, Malaysia's low-taxation policy and redistributive activity are weapons of the strong. They result in Malaysian citizens demanding little participation or political representation, as they are highly rewarded for their quiescence, effectively demobilising entire segments of the population (Sloane-White and Beaulieu 2010: 383–97).

Extraction and dependency within the palm oil sector

Natural resources (mainly mining and agriculture) continue to play an important part in the Malaysian economy. Raw natural resources contribute about 11 percent of Malaysia's GDP, while industry and manufacturing (mainly of said natural resources) contribute around 40 percent of Malaysia's GDP. Hence, natural resources and their derivatives contribute almost half the Malaysian GDP today (Asan Ali 2004: 130; CIA 2012), with Malaysia being a major exporter of palm oil, oil and gas (Sloane-White and Beaulieu 2010: 388).

In recent times, palm oil has been an important export commodity for Malaysia, and thus a main source of rent from abroad. Malaysia is the world's second-largest producer of palm oil (Md. Wahid *et al.* 2004: 1–8; McCarthy 2010: 822–44). It currently accounts for 39 percent of world palm oil production and 44 percent of world exports (MPOC 2013). Oil palm plantations in Malaysia now occupy more than 12 percent of total land mass (Tan *et al.* 2009: 423; Basiron 2007: 289–95; Wahid *et al.* 2004: 1–8). The local palm oil industry is an important driver of economic growth (Bernama 2010), steadily contributing 5–6 percent of the country's GDP (MPOB 2011), and brings in annual foreign exchange earnings of over US$80 billion (Basiron 2007: 289–95). Similarly to what is detailed above, the Malaysian state can be observed to distribute rents from this sector to the elite through patronage, and to the masses through large-scale distributive policies. In this way, the palm oil sector today represents an important avenue for the consolidation of political stability.

As mentioned above, the Guthrie Dawn Raid and similar activities brought all major plantation land in Malaysia under the control of government-owned agencies in the mid-1980s (Pletcher 1991: 624–33). Much of these plantation lands were later distributed to companies spearheaded by prominent Malays or *bumiputera*. These companies continued to maintain close association with the ruling elite, while the government often retained a substantial controlling stake in them. For example, Sime Darby, the world's largest oil palm plantation company in terms of its land bank (Oetomo and Sandianto 2011: 5), has a prolific Malay, Datuk Mohd Bakke Salleh, as its CEO. Salleh is also chairman of another GLC, Bank Islam (Adnan 2010), which has been an important financier for Sime Darby and other Malaysian plantation companies. Its board of directors is made up of former Malaysian politicians like the former deputy prime minister, Tun Musa Hitam, and the former chief secretary to the Malaysian government, Tan Sri Samsudin Osman. PNB, the Employee Provident Fund (EPF) and Amanah Saham Trustee Berhad are its major shareholders (Sime Darby 2011).

Besides providing its clients with preferential treatment in terms of land and other permits, the Malaysian government has also set up several agencies to uphold the economic interests of these firms. The most prominent among these is the Malaysian Palm Oil Council (MPOC), a government-legislated company tasked with the promotion and expansion of the palm oil market for Malaysian companies operating in Malaysia and overseas. The MPOC works 'to enhance the image of palm oil and create better acceptance of palm oil through awareness of its various technological and economic advantages and environmental sustainability' (MPOC 2011). The MPOC works closely with the Malaysian Ministry of Plantation Industries and Commodities (Basiron 2010), and is funded both by the government and by a 'cess' (special tax) from the sale of palm oil. It invests heavily in lobbying and advertising on behalf of Malaysian palm oil companies (Md. Wahid *et al.* 2004: 1–8) and also functions as a watchdog for the industry. The MPOC has been especially active in countering allegations of Malaysian palm oil companies' supposed involvement in a range of environmentally unfriendly activities, like illegal burning, habitat destruction and human rights abuses. It is also often the first agency that identifies trade barriers against palm oil and undertakes appropriate counter-actions. For example, the MPOC appeared before a public hearing of the Australian House Standing Committee on Economics in August 2011 (Basiron 2011: 10) and was successful in convincing the parliament to repeal a bill that would have made palm oil the only vegetable oil to be distinctly labelled on Australian products.

In return, these companies have also been prepared to come to the assistance of the Malaysian government when needed (Cheema 1978: 48; Tay 2003: 51–53). For example, in 1987, when the government agency overseeing plantation development in Sarawak, Sarawak Land Development Board (SLDB), was suffering from serious losses and carried major liabilities, Sime Darby stepped in to assist the state government. It bought over the management of SLDB including all its plantation assets, which accumulated to over 24,000 hectares of oil palm in thirteen estates (McCarthy and Cramb 2009: 113–19). And, as part of the Pernas rescue exercise discussed above, AlBukhary Johor Tenggara Oil Palm Berhad (now Tradewinds Plantation Berhad) was injected into Pernas's ailing plantation assets in 2001 (Mohanlall 2012: 121).

These companies also complement the government's large-scale distributive policies. Palm oil in Malaysia is primarily produced on estates owned by these large companies (Pletcher 1991: 624–33; Basiron 2007: 289–95). The estates provide employment for the local communities, both directly through employment on the plantations and indirectly through the 'nucleus and plasma' arrangement, through which surrounding small farmers with varying sizes of oil palm holdings sell their fruit bunches by contract to company-owned mills for extraction. The companies also often build hospitals, schools and religious buildings for use by the local communities. In this way, the sector has become one of the biggest employers in Malaysia, and expansion of the sector has been seen as an important strategy for poverty alleviation and development among rural communities (Basiron 2007: 289–95; Hurst 1987: 170). In these ways, rents from the sector are distributed to the masses as well. This has not only contributed to the steady growth of the sector, but also towards the larger political stability of the country, as the sector is seen to bring jobs and developmental benefits to rural communities. Indeed, rural communities continue to demand little participation or political representation (Sloane-White and Beaulieu 2010: 383–97), and continue to be a stronghold of support for the ruling Barisan Nasional government.

Conclusion

This chapter has explained how, since independence, natural resource extraction has been an important means to 'buy off' peace in Malaysia's rentier state system. Being a country that is naturally rich in resources, the extraction and exploitation of said resources has been an easily accessible strategy to obtain rents that can then be distributed back to various levels of society.

The Malaysian government has seen the presence of natural resources as a valuable political opportunity, and has developed its rentier-based economy to favour the many, not only the elite few. Hence, while ruling elites have used revenue from these resources to enrich themselves and their inner circle, they have also appeased the masses through large-scale distribution policies. In these ways, the rentier state has been able to 'buy off' peace and political stability. Thus, choices that the ruling elite has made on the distribution of natural resource rents have successfully avoided the instability-prone 'resource curse', and instead further consolidate their standing as the only ruling party that Malaysia has ever known. Hence, the political dependency of the Malaysian ruling elite on this sector will likely spell the continued exploitation of the country's natural resources for political interests.

Notes

1 Malaysia's ruling coalition, Barisan Nasional, is made up of mostly race-based political parties. The major parties within this coalition are the United Malays National Front (UMNO), which holds the majority of seats, the Malaysian Chinese Association (MCA) and the Malaysian Indian Congress (MIC).
2 For more detailed discussion on the literature of patronage and on patronage linkages within the Malaysian palm oil sector, see my earlier publication, Varkkey 2013a.
3 Literally 'sons of the soil'. *Bumiputera* commonly refers to citizens of Malaysia, excluding Chinese and Indian 'immigrants' who generally arrived in Malaysia during the British occupation to work on mines and plantations. Malays are a subset of *bumiputera*, and *bumiputera* indigenous groups make up the majority of the citizens of the East Malaysian states of Sabah and Sarawak.
4 For more detailed discussion of the intensification and institutionalization of the Malaysian natural resources sector, see my earlier publication, Varkkey 2013a.

Bibliography

Ahm. Mustain Billah (2005) 'Measuring the economic sustainability: a case of forest extraction in Malaysia', *Indian Journal of Agricultural Economics*, 60(4): 698–708.

Asan Ali Golam Hassan (2004) *Growth, Structural Change, and Regional Inequality in Malaysia*, Burlington: Ashgate.

Basedau, Matthias and Jann Lay (2009) 'Resource curse or rentier peace? The ambiguous effects of oil wealth and oil dependence on violent conflict', *Journal of Peace Research*, 46(6): 757–76.

Basiron, Yusof (2007) 'Palm oil production through sustainable plantations', *European Journal of Lipid Science and Technology*, 109(4): 289–95.

Basiron, Yusof (2010) 'Testimony of Dr. Yusuf Basiron Chief Executive Officer of the Malaysian Palm Oil Council (MPOC) to the Hearing of the Senate Community Affairs Committee (Truth in Labelling – Palm Oil) Bill 2010', in *Australia Hearing Testimony* (ed.), Canberra: Malaysian Palm Oil Council.

Basiron, Yusof (2011) '"Truth" held hostage', *Global Oils & Fats*, 8(3): 10–12.

Benjamin, Nelson and Desiree Tresa Gasper (2011) 'Don't fall for Opposition's gimmicks, Felda settlers told', *The Star*, 15 August.

Bernama (2010) 'Palm oil sector to become larger contributor to GDP', Bernama *Daily Malaysian News*, 30 March.

Brown, Graham K. (2013) 'Malaysia in 2012: promises of reform; promises met?', in Institute of Southeast Asian Studies (ed.), *Southeast Asian Affairs 2013*, Singapore: Institute of Southeast Asian Studies, pp. 153–67.

Cheema, G. Shabbir (1978) 'Malaysia's development strategy: the dilemma of redistribution with growth', *Studies in Comparative International Development*, 13(2): 40–55.

Chichilnisky, Graciela (1996) 'The economic value of the Earth's resources', *Trends in Economy & Evolution*, 11(3): 135–40.

CIA (2012) *The World Factbook*, Washington DC: Central Intelligence Agency, available at www.cia.gov/library/publications/the-world-factbook/fields/2012.html (accessed 2 August 2012).

Cooke, Fadzilah Majid (1997) 'The politics of "sustainability" in Sarawak', *Journal of Contemporary Asia*, 27(2): 217–41.

Dauvergne, Peter (1994) 'The politics of deforestation in Indonesia', *Pacific Affairs*, 66(4): 497–518.

Dauvergne, Peter (1995) Shadows in the Forest: Japan and the Politics of Timber in Southeast Asia, PhD Dissertation, University of British Columbia.

Dunning, Thad (2005) 'Resource dependence, economic performance, and political stability', *The Journal of Conflict Resolution*, 49(4): 451–82.

Gellert, Paul K. (2005) 'The shifting natures of "development": growth, crisis and recovery in Indonesia's forests', *World Development*, 33(8): 1345–64.

Grant, Jeremy (2013) 'Climate for change: Malaysia', *Financial Times*, 3 May, p. 11.

Gunes-Ayata, Ayse (1994) 'Clientelism: premodern, modern, postmodern', in Luis Roniger and Ayse Gunes-Ayata (eds), *Democracy, Clientelism, and Civil Society*, London: Lynne Rienner Publishers, pp. 19–28.

Hanim Adnan (2010) 'Sime's Bakke has vast expertise', *The Star*, 15 June.

Hezri, Adnan A. (2004) 'Sustainability indicator system and policy processes in Malaysia: a framework for utilization and learning', *Journal of Environmental Management*, 73: 357–71.

Hezri, Adnan A. and Mohd. Nordin Hasan (2006) 'Towards sustainable development? The evolution of environmental policy in Malaysia', *Natural Resources Forum*, 30(1): 37–50.

Hal, Hill, Tham S. Yean and Ragayah H.M. Zin (2012) 'Malaysia: a success story stuck in the middle?', *The World Economy*, 35(12): 1687–711.

Hirsch, Philip and Carol Warren (1998) 'Introduction: through the environmental looking glass', Philip Hirsch and Carol Warren (eds), *The Politics of Environment in Southeast Asia: Resources and Resistance*, Abingdon: Routledge, pp. 1–25.

Hurst, Philip (1987) 'Forest destruction in South East Asia', *Ecologist*, 17: 170–74.

Jomo K.S. (2003) 'Reforming East Asia for sustainable development', *Asian Business & Management*, 3: 7–38.

Jomo K.S. and Edmund Terence Gomez (2000) 'The Malaysian development dilemma', in Mushtaq H. Khan (ed.), *Rents, Rent-Seeking and Economic Development: Theory and Evidence in Asia*, New York: Cambridge University Press, pp. 274–303.

Leigh, Michael (1998) 'Political economy of logging in Sarawak, Malaysia', in Philip Hirsch and Carol Warren (eds), *The Politics of Environment in Southeast Asia: Resources and Resistance*, Abingdon: Routledge, pp. 93–106.

Lim, Linda Y.C. and Aaron Stern (2003) 'State power and private profit: the political economy of corruption in Southeast Asia', *Asian-Pacific Economic Literature*, 16(2): 18–52.

McCarthy, John F. (2010) 'Process of inclusion and adverse incorporation: oil palm and agrarian change in Sumatra, Indonesia', *The Journal of Peasant Studies*, 37(4): 821–50.

McCarthy, John F. and R.A. Cramb (2009) 'Policy narratives, landholder engagement, and oil palm expansion on the Malaysian and Indonesian frontiers', *The Geographical Journal*, 175(2): 112–23.

Mohanlall, Premilla (2012) *Syed Mokhtar AlBukhary: A Biography*, Selangor: pVm communications.

Malaysian Palm Oil Board (MPOB) (2011) *Sustainable Palm Oil*, Kuala Lumpur: Malaysian Palm Oil Board, available at www.palmoilworld.org/sustainability.html (accessed 22 July 2013).

Malaysian Palm Oil Council (2011) *About MPOC*, Kuala Lumpur: Malaysian Palm Oil Council, available at www.mpoc.org.my/Corporate_Profile.aspx (accessed 13 December 2011).

Malaysian Palm Oil Council (MPOC) (2013) *Malaysian Palm Oil Industry*, Kuala Lumpur: Malaysian Palm Oil Council, available at www.mpoc.org.my/Malaysian_Palm_Oil_Industry.aspx (accessed 22 July 2013).

Mariati Norhashim and Kamarulzaman Ab. Aziz (2005) 'Smart partnership or cronyism? A Malaysian perspective', *International Journal of Sociology and Social Policy*, 25(8): 31–48.

Md. Wahid Murad, Rafiqul Islam Molla, Mazlin Bin Mokhtar and Md. Abdur Raquib (2010) 'Climate change and agricultural growth: an examination of the link in Malaysia', *International Journal of Climate Change Strategies and Management*, 2(4): 403–17.

Mohd. Basri Wahid, Siti Nor Akmar Abdullah and I.E. Henson (2004) 'Oil palm – achievements and potential', in R.A. Fischer (ed.), *New Directions for a Diverse Planet*, Proceedings of the 4th International Crop Science Congress, Brisbane.

Naguib, Rabia and Joseph Smucker (2009) 'When economic growth rhymes with social development: the Malaysia experience', *Journal of Business Ethics*, 89(2): 99–113.

Oetomo, Teddy and Agus Sandianto (2011) *New Forestry Ministerial Decree: Indonesia Palm Oil Sector*, Jakarta: Credit Suisse.

Pletcher, James (1991) 'Regulation with growth: the political economy of palm oil in Malaysia', *World Development*, 19(6): 623–36.

Raman, Meenakshi (2006) 'Environmental struggles in Malaysia', *Development*, 49: 38–42.

Roberti, M. (1989) 'Agribusiness: Asia's next economic miracle', *Asian Finance*, 15(7): 54–56.

Saiful Arif Abdullah and Adnan A. Hezri (2008) 'From forest landscape to agricultural landscape in the developing tropical country of Malaysia: pattern, process and their significance on policy', *Environmental Management*, 42(5): 907–17.

Sime Darby (2011) *Annual Report*, Kuala Lumpur: Sime Darby.

Sloane-White, Patricia and Isabelle Beaulieu (2010) 'Beyond 50 years of political stability in Malaysia: rent and the weapons of the power elite', *Canadian Journal of Development Studies*, 30(3–4): 381–402.

Sumiani Y., Y. Haslinda and G. Lehman (2007) 'Environmental reporting in a developing country: a case study on status and implementation in Malaysia', *Journal of Cleaner Production*, 15: 895–901.

Suparb Pas-ong and Louis Lebel (2000) 'Political transformation and the environment in Southeast Asia', *Environment*, 42(8): 8–19.

Suraya Izad (2003) *Malaysian Economy: Development of the Agricultural Sector*, Kuala Lumpur: Department of Agriculture.

Sutton, Keith (2001) 'Agribusiness on a grand scale – Felda's Sahabat complex in East Malaysia', *Singapore Journal of Tropical Geography*, 22(1): 90–105.

Tan Kok Tat, K.T. Lee, A.R. Mohamed and S. Bhatia (2009) 'Palm oil: addressing issues and towards sustainable development', *Renewable and Sustainable Energy Reviews*, 13(2): 420–27.

Tay, Simon (2003) 'Corruption after the crisis: governance, Asian values, and international instruments', in Simon Tay and Maria Seda (eds), *The Enemy Within: Combating Corruption in Asia*, Singapore: Eastern University Press, pp. 37–63.

Varkkey, Helena (2013a) 'Malaysian investors in the Indonesian oil palm plantation sector: home state facilitation and transboundary haze', *Asia Pacific Business Review*, 19(3): 381–401.

Varkkey, Helena (2013b) 'Patronage politics and natural resources: a historical case study of Malaysia and Singapore', *Asian Profile*, 41(4): 319–30.

Wahid, M.B., Abdullah, S.N.A. and Henson, I.E. (2004) 'Oil palm – achievements and potential', *New Directions for a Diverse Planet*, Proceedings of the 4th International Crop Science Congress, Symposia Papers, 12, Brisbane: Australian Agronomy Conference.

Welsh, Bridget (2013) 'Divided or together?: Southeast Asia in 2012', *Southeast Asian Affairs*, 2013: 1–16.

Yacob, Shakila (2010) 'The "unfinished business" of Malaysia's decolonization: the origins of the Guthrie "Dawn Raid"', *Modern Asian Studies*, 44: 919–60.

16

Rent-seeking and money politics in Malaysia

Ethnicity, cronyism and class

Jeff Tan

This chapter raises three questions: what is the relationship between rent-seeking and money politics? What drives rent-seeking and money politics? How do these drivers affect the contestation for, and allocation of, rents? To answer these questions we first examine the meaning of, and relationship between, rent-seeking and money politics, and how both are manifested in Malaysia. We then critically review the dominant discourses on rent-seeking and money politics in Malaysia, which centre on ethnicity, cronyism (political patronage) and political business. These approaches offer insights into the practice of rent-seeking and money politics based on political capture by state bureaucrats or politicians, and focus on the relationship between patrons and their clients. However, the idea of political capture is centred on individual (political) actors and does not clearly identify the political basis of power or underlying changes in wider social relations which shape the allocation of rents, and which are manifested in ethnic politics and cronyism. An analysis of class and changing social relations draws from, and builds on, insights offered in the wider literature to offer an alternative explanation of rent-seeking and money politics in Malaysia. This analysis centres on changes in class formations and social relations related to the Malay middle class which led to the introduction of the New Economic Policy (NEP) and privatisation as the main vehicles for rent distribution and hence capital (wealth) accumulation.

Rent-seeking and money politics

Both rent-seeking and money politics broadly involve the use of money to influence political decisions. Rent-seeking generally refers to business seeking to secure the state allocation of economic rents through legal (e.g. lobbying) or illegal (e.g. bribery) means. 'Rents' are typically defined as excess returns or windfall gains otherwise absent in competitive markets. Money politics is described as 'the use of money in the political arena to secure control over the state in order to influence the distribution of state-generated economic rents', with the focus usually on political funding by business (Gomez 2002a: 3; 1991). The terms 'rent-seeking' and 'money politics' may thus describe the process of state capture by business, and the subsequent redistribution of resources to favoured individuals usually through patronage relationships or patron–client networks. As money politics also refers to the electoral process, in the form of 'vote-buying with funds raised from the private sector' (Gomez 2002a: 15), we need to distinguish between rents for votes (in elections or political party leadership contests) and rents for business.

'Money politics' in Malaysia covers 'a range of practices whereby the benefits of State economic sponsorship and protection are channeled to individuals, groups and private companies associated with the ruling political parties, in particular UMNO [the United Malays National Organisation]' (Loh and Kahn 1992: 2). However, rather than powerful economic interests typically seeking to influence the allocation of rents through state capture, money politics in Malaysia refers to the political capture of the state by politicians and bureaucrats, with the allocation of rents initially controlled by an autonomous state, and subsequently by political parties and individual political leaders. In other words, money politics in Malaysia is distinct from rent-seeking conceptually and in terms of the direction of influence. From the literature we can identify three dominant discourses on rent-seeking and money politics in Malaysia. These centre on the overlapping categories of ethnicity (ethnic politics), cronyism (political patronage) and political business.

Ethnicity

The ethnic politics approach attributes policy changes (and failure) to changes in the balance of power between ethnic groups. Here, the breakdown of the 'consociational' framework (Jesudason 1989) or changes in the 'communal settlement' (Bowie 1991) provide one ethnic group with the upper hand, leaving the state unconstrained to act. Thus, the threat to the 'communal bargain' and Malay 'special rights' led to 'race riots' in 1969 and increased state intervention under the NEP in 1971. Although its aim was to eradicate poverty irrespective of race and restructure society to eliminate the identification of race with economic function, the NEP is mainly associated with the second objective, and in particular the creation of Malay capitalists or a Bumiputera Commercial and Industrial Community (BCIC).

Rents to this end included licences, contracts, concessions, preferential lending (at low interest rates) and share allotments (at below market prices), and guaranteed high-return investments (see e.g. Jesudason 1989; Jomo 1995; Searle 1999; Chin and Jomo 2000). In the (interim) absence of Malay capitalists, the government created state enterprises and acquired shares in well-managed, profitable companies to facilitate Malay ownership and provide managerial training. Rents here took the form of state protection from competition, the socialisation of risks, easy access to finance and unconditional subsidies (Jesudason 1989; Gomez and Jomo 1997).

An 'ethnic imperative' to increase group 'capacity' and economic control entailed an efficiency trade-off, constraining rational economic policies and economic growth (see e.g. Lim 1985; Bowie 1988, 1991; Jesudason 1989; Bruton 1992). As a result, the NEP is associated with public and private sector inefficiency, rentier behaviour, Malay dependence on the state, an inefficient and fragile Malay bourgeoisie, business failure and more generally, the failure of Malaysia's import-substituting industrialisation (ISI) policies (Jesudason 1989; Kamal 1989; Bowie 1990; Bruton 1992; Khoo 1995; Rasiah 1998). The state was able to ignore rational economic responses as it was unconstrained by social forces, including the weak private sector, and financed by its considerable resources, in particular oil revenues (Jesudason 1989).

We can identify several related problems with the ethnic analysis of rent-seeking and money politics. First, the approach views the state as inherently predatory, with bureaucrats and politicians acting in their own interests, especially when unchecked by the private sector.

As the state is unconstrained and free to act, there is no rent-seeking (i.e. state capture), with the starting point being political capture. This premise is associated with the predatory state model and based on public choice theory assumptions about 'politically autonomous state elites [extracting] surplus from society in order to enrich themselves and their supporters' (Felker 1998: 88). As such, it assumes rather than explains state motivation.

Without an analysis of the state itself, the ethnic approach is unable to answer the question: political capture by whom and why? State motivation cannot be understood without an examination of the state's relationship with society, given that power does not exist in a vacuum and state power must be grounded in its connections with society. In the case of an ethnic imperative, this analysis would at least entail examining the relationship between the state (in this case, bureaucrats and politicians) and the Malay community on whose behalf the state was acting. Second, as the creation of Malay capitalists under the NEP favoured certain individuals and segments of the Malay community over others, ethnic redistribution invariably involved cronyism (political patronage), which serves to dilute ethnicity as the primary reason for rent allocation under the NEP.

This brings us to the third problem: the conflation of appearance with underlying cause. Ethnic discontent can be seen as a manifestation of class interests (Singh 2001), where the Malay ruling class promotes 'its own class interests as the common interest of all Malays' (Lian and Appudurai 2011: 64; Jomo 2004). Thus the impatience and anger of emerging Malay businessmen 'manifested itself within UMNO and was expressed in communalist terms' (Azeem 2012: 2). Class interests can be identified from the demands and threats of political instability made at the 1965 and 1968 Bumiputera Economic Congress (Puthucheary 1984; Lim 1985; Ho 1988; Jesudason 1989), and confrontation in UMNO between 'liberal accommodationists' and hardliners (or 'Young Turks' and 'ultras') over direct state intervention (Heng 1997). Ethnic identity and conflict are thus intricately linked to the survival and displacement of elites (Singh 2001), with the NEP allowing UMNO to re-energise Malay support (Case 2009) following the electoral setback which precipitated the 1969 riots.

Cronyism

The political patronage approach expands on ethnic politics by examining the influence of political factors on rent allocation and identifying the main beneficiaries of ethnic redistributive rents through cronyism and money politics. Money politics is associated with political capture, which forms the starting point of the analysis. As with the ethnic politics approach, patrons (politicians and bureaucrats) hold the balance of power over clients (business) in the allocation of rents, with political power used to create a capitalist class (Hirschman 1998). Under the NEP, the government was able to centralise redistribution without state capture due to a unified party elite under a strong leadership which had the support of a large Malay middle class and rural populace (as a result of bureaucratic expansion and rural development) (Leong 1991, cited in Felker 1998: 90). This centralised patronage allowed UMNO to control resources, providing benefits to its supporters and strengthening party loyalty (Jesudason 1989; Crouch 1992; Khoo 1992; Felker 1998). The government was also able to strengthen and insulate the state's planning and economic agencies (such as the Economic Planning Unit), with bureaucrats controlling resources through the management of state assets, initially with minimal private business influence on economic policies (Felker 1998; Leong 1991, cited in Felker 1998: 90).

As a result, almost all Malay businessmen, regardless of type, were created either by the state or with crucial state support (Jomo 1993b). The literature identifies two types of Malay businessmen emerging from the NEP: those connected with the state, and those created by the state and supported through state patronage. While the latter were heavily dependent on the state, which remained in control (Ho 1988), the former comprised a small but powerful Malay 'bureaucratic-capitalist elite' (or bureaucratic trustees), which emerged to capture rents and create distributional coalitions and opportunities for self-enrichment, and which exercised considerable influence over policy (Jomo 1986; Mehmet 1988; Bowie 1991; Bruton 1992; Jomo and Tan 1999).

The nature and beneficiaries of patron–client relationships changed with the introduction of privatisation and the replacement of centralised rent allocation with personalised patronage. Privatisation served as the main vehicle for the allocation of rents 'by which former state managers and senior bureaucrats made the transition to the private sector' (Doraisami 2005: 253), benefiting a group of big businessmen and former state-owned enterprise managers closely connected to the new political leadership. Most new Malay capitalists also continued to 'retain, cultivate and ultimately rely on their connections with top UMNO leaders to secure continued patronage while, in turn, providing financial and other backing for their political patrons' (Jomo and Gomez 2000: 296). Clientelism here was thus 'symbiotic or reciprocal, with both businesses and the state elite (powerful politicians and bureaucrats) serving as patrons as well as clients to the other depending on the matter concerned' (Jomo and Gomez 2000: 296).

Privatisation provided captive markets for large state and privatised enterprises, while Malay contractors and smaller businessmen benefited from a range of contracts and licences mainly centred on construction and infrastructure privatisation (see e.g. Rasiah 1998; Tan 2008, 2012). Government contracts or tenders (known as 'Class F' projects) were restricted to Malay contractors and businesses while 'approved permits' (licences to import cars) were issued only to Malay businessmen (Chin 2009). As was the case with ethnic politics, these rents offered protection from market competition, which minimised risks and diluted incentives, while the speed of asset acquisition undermined learning-by-doing (Jesudason 1989; Gomez and Jomo 1997). In this case, the failure of indigenous entrepreneurship and import-substitution industrialisation policies is associated with ersatz or crony capitalism (see e.g. Yoshihara 1988; Rasiah 1998, 2001; Jomo and Gomez 2000; Chin and Jomo 2000, 2001; Jomo and Hamilton-Hart 2001).

The political patronage approach shares the same analytical starting point, assumptions and problems with the ethnic analysis approach. In both cases, political capture by bureaucrats and politicians remains largely under-theorised and divorced from an analysis of state–society and wider social relations. As such, the basis of power underpinning political capture is largely assumed rather than explained, with the political process of rent-seeking and money politics reduced to an elite-level, individual-centred analysis.

Political business

This brings us to the political business model, which examines the links between politics and business through the 'exchange relationship between a ruling party or politicians and specific business interests' (Wedeman 2002: 36). The model seeks to elaborate on and refine the cronyism argument by focusing on the expansion of political party involvement in business and the machinations within the political system, including leader motivation (Gomez 2002a). The aim is to identify the changing pattern of ownership and control of politically well-connected companies and explain the presence of growth policies alongside patronage, unproductive rents and corruption, thereby providing an alternative account to developmental state theories which centre on the relationship between state (bureaucracy) and capital (Gomez 2002a).

The underlying explanation focuses on state–business linkages through political party ownership or control of major enterprises, with politicians distributing rents through the state, and where political funding by business is central in influencing the distribution of rents through factions loosely based around political leaders (Gomez 2002a). Money politics is manifested in: (1) the use of UMNO's easy access to funds from business by influential leaders to consolidate their power; and (2) the considerable increase in the number of politicians entering business as a result of access to state rents (Gomez 2002a: 10). The political business model thus reinforces the idea of political capture centred on UMNO's hegemony, where 'politicians still have an inordinate influence over the corporate sector' and where 'capital is still very subservient to the state' (Gomez 2002a: 10; 2002b).

This model is represented in a flow chart with political capture as the starting point. The control by political leaders over government and the state provides rents for clients. These rents are typically used for unproductive wealth accumulation (such as share-for-assets swaps, reverse takeovers, and mergers and acquisitions), creating a politically linked 'new rich' with access to substantial funds, some of which are channelled back as political funds to government (Gomez 2002a: 4). A central feature of political business here is a conglomerate-style business expansion, facilitated by the capture of financial sector rents through the banking system and government promotion of the stock market (Gomez 2002a; see also Rasiah 1998; Chin and Jomo 2001).

The political business model then seeks to explain a shift in rent allocation related to the high degree of autonomy of the political leadership, which allowed Prime Minister Mahathir Mohamad to 'selectively distribute government-created rents' by picking winners (Gomez 2002b: 83). This ability

> contributed to a change in the nature of political business, from a form that was institutionalized, involving a state-sanctioned policy of developing and distributing rents to the indigenous community, to one conducted through government leaders on a personalized basis to select individuals.
>
> *(Gomez 2002b: 83)*

The result was heightened party factionalism, the increased use of rents to cultivate party grassroots support, and the use of money to secure votes in UMNO elections, which further increased the ties between business and politics. Rents for grassroots support typically involved development funds for various road-building and renovation projects distributed among Malay 'Class F' contractors, with mid-ranking UMNO office-bearers given priority (Case 2008).

The roots of political business can be traced back to the establishment of the three main ethnic-based political parties – UMNO, the Malaysian Chinese Association (MCA) and the Malaysian Indian Congress (MIC) – and their involvement in business to increase membership. Political party involvement in business, in particular UMNO, increased considerably from the 1970s through the ownership and control of major private and public-listed companies (Gomez 1991, 2002b). UMNO incorporated Fleet Holdings in 1972 as the party's own holding company to establish its financial independence from its Chinese-based coalition-partner, MCA (see e.g. Yusoff 1990; Bowie 1991). This development shaped the nature of patronage, which centred on party needs as well as the interests of individual leaders (Gomez 2002b). UMNO's expansion into business thus aimed to establish the party's economic dominance and finance intra-party/leadership contests by securing votes through the allocation of contracts to supporters.

With growing intra-party conflict, control of UMNO's corporate assets subsequently shifted from the party to individual UMNO leaders through proxies (see Gomez 1991). The combined effects of the NEP and UMNO's political dominance also transformed wider rent-seeking and money politics. Malay businessmen began capturing key posts in the UMNO hierarchy as a means to secure positions in government for greater access to state rents, while Chinese businessmen bypassed MCA to cultivate direct links with individual UMNO leaders in order to secure state rents (Gomez 2002a, 2002b). The latter was also in response to Malay competition, as a result of the NEP and privatisation rents, in sectors of traditional Chinese dominance (construction, transportation, distribution and retail trade) (Heng 1997).

The political business model tells us about the nature of rent-seeking and money politics in Malaysia, and how these are characterised by the relationship between politics (namely, politicians) and business. However, the model largely describes the mechanisms of rent-seeking and money politics rather than providing an explanation of the underlying factors driving these processes. The problem here is that the term 'political business' is not concisely defined or distinguished. The term is used to describe and discriminate between different forms of state–business relations, which vary depending on context, and is therefore not fundamentally different from the concepts of political patronage or money politics upon which the model is based. This is reflected in the model of political business itself, which generally elaborates on the process of political capture and patronage.

The focus on political capture in the political business model offers an individual-centred analysis of a social problem, leaving the question of the political basis of power largely unanswered. Although the influence of individual political leaders is analysed, the nature of the patron–client relationship and balance of power between patron and client are assumed rather than explained. The corresponding individual-centred solutions based on 'political will and independence from capital' (Gomez 2002a: 18; see also Jomo and Hamilton-Hart 2001; Teh 2002) imply that clients (businesses) do exert influence over patrons (political leaders). The balance of power is thus unclear given that access to rents depends on the influence of the leader (Gomez 2002a: 7–8), but political funding by business is central in influencing the distribution of rents through factions and by capturing key UMNO posts (Gomez 2002b). This circular reasoning may arise from an ambiguity in the wider literature on the direction of influence between patron and client (see e.g. Jomo and Gomez 2000) related to a lack of clarity about the different types of clients and, hence, their different relationships to patrons.

The underlying concern about patronage, unproductive rents and corruption associated with political business reveals a misreading of the development process and specifically the process of capital accumulation, where the emergence of a capitalist class has historically involved the creation and transfer of economic rents through political patronage (see e.g. Tan 2010, 2011). The issue, then, is less about the existence of policies promoting growth alongside patronage, unproductive rents and corruption, but rather, the factors that drive the creation and allocation of productive and unproductive rents. In the case of Malaysia, the threat of political instability necessitated rents for an emerging Malay middle class. These rents included both productive (learning) rents and unproductive rents (e.g. political transfers). The analysis of the political drivers of rent-seeking and money politics which moves beyond individual explanations and solutions necessitates an analysis of underlying social forces and social relations.

Class

A class analysis seeks to identify the drivers behind rents, rent-seeking and money politics by examining how changes in class formations and social relations influence policy. It locates the issue of political power associated with political capture by individual politicians within an analysis centred on class (social relations), of which ethnic politics, political patronage and political business are manifestations. It thus incorporates insights offered in the ethnic, political patronage, political business and wider literature into a framework centred on class interests. Central to this analysis is the state, whose motivation can neither be examined outside of society nor reduced to individual politicians or leaders. Rather, state motivation will depend on the nature of the state's relationship with society, and in particular the balance of power between the state and segments of society to which it is connected. At the same time, state survival will invariably entail policies to promote growth which also maximise returns to state elites. This 'growth imperative' necessary for capital accumulation will often be in contrast to a 'redistributive imperative' required for political stability (and manifested in a variety of ways, including ethnic claims). Both imperatives involve rents, and the balance between growth and redistribution invariably shapes the type of rents, their distribution, and their impact.

The discourse on state–society relations is not new and is central to the idea of state capacity in the statist literature on the developmental state. Unlike public choice theory, the statist literature views learning rents (e.g. subsidies, protection) as necessary for technological catching-up, with the state assumed to be benevolent or developmental and the problem being state capture rather than political capture. State capacity to implement long-term policies promoting economic growth is thus equated with state autonomy and insulation from private vested interests, to avoid state capture (Haggard 1990; White and Wade 1988; Johnson 1982). The idea of the state being (completely) autonomous from society is, however, neither realistic nor desirable. The concept of 'embedded autonomy' is a rudimentary attempt to address this by stipulating the importance of an autonomous bureaucracy, insulated enough to be able independently to formulate and implement policy, but also connected to productive groups in society (Evans 1995).

A more sophisticated elaboration of state–society relations is offered by the neo-institutionalist approach which views political insulation as 'an obstacle to effective policy making' as it 'prevents the exchange of information necessary to design and monitor policies effectively' and 'raises business uncertainty about future government policy' (Felker 1998: 87–88). Networks or linkages between state and business actors thus 'allow state and business elites to negotiate consensus on goals, foster business confidence by lowering the perceived risks of predation or arbitrary policy changes and generate pressures for accountability on personalistic patronage networks' (Felker 1998: 88). However, this approach largely avoids the politics and asymmetric power relations in patron–client relationships which affect the types and allocation of rents, and pattern of rent-seeking.

A more instructive approach is to examine how the relationship between patrons and clients shapes state–society relations and hence state motivations and policies. The nature of patron–client relationships (in terms of its influence on economic decisions) depends on: the objectives and ideologies of the patrons and clients; the number of potential clients and their degree of organisation; the homogeneity of clients; and the institutions through which patrons and clients interact, including their degree of fragmentation (Khan 1998). The direction of influence between patron and client in Malaysia can be clarified by distinguishing among different types of client and, hence, their potential relationships with patrons.

From the literature, we can identify three potential types of clients: Type A businessmen seeking rents through patronage; Type B businessmen who join UMNO at different levels to access state rents; and Type C bureaucrats and politicians who enter into business. Each type of client will have a different relationship to the patron and some may even act as both patron and client. Type A businessmen represent typical business clients pursuing rents. The direction of influence here will depend on the size of the political contribution to the patron and the patron's financial dependence on the client, amongst other factors. The influence of Type B businessmen will depend on their position in the party hierarchy, the degree of contestation for party positions, and related to this, their ability to mobilise political support (and funds) for their patron in exchange for rents. Type B businessmen may thus act both as client and as patron to smaller clients whom they reward financially or economically.

Type C businessmen represent both the early generation NEP 'bureaucratic-capitalist elite' and subsequent politician-in-business that characterised the privatisation period. The former included state enterprise managers and 'administocrats' (administrator-aristocrats), whose influence depended in part on their positions within UMNO and their relationships with the political leadership (see e.g. Popenoe 1970). The latter group were the product of the NEP and included former NEP-trained state-owned enterprise managers who emerged either as outright businessmen or UMNO trustees whose support in leadership contests was crucial. Invariably, these three typologies are somewhat crude, as they are often fluid and likely to overlap: a businessman may start as a Type A client, then decide to contest UMNO elections, thereby evolving into Type B. Nonetheless, this simple typology of clients provides a framework to understand the direction of influence between patron and client and thus the nature of rent-seeking and money politics.

More importantly, patron–client relationships can only be properly understood in the wider social context, namely, the increase in the size, organisation and influence of the Malay business class, itself the outcome of a growing Malay middle class since independence (e.g. teachers, religious figures, lower civil servants, businessmen, and politicians in business) (Neuman 1971; Lim 1981; Jomo 1999). Demands for economic redistribution were made through the Associated Malay Chambers of Commerce, Kuala Lumpur Petty Traders Association, and UMNO, and at the 1965 and 1968 Bumiputra Economic Congress (Toh and Jomo 1981, cited in Puthucheary 1984; Tan 1982; Lim 1985; Ho 1988; Jesudason 1989; Searle 1999). The Alliance Party's failure to secure a two-thirds parliamentary majority in the 1969 elections provided UMNO with the tactical mobility and strength to introduce the NEP with the crucial support of UMNO MPs and legislators now comprising Malay vernacular teachers, former government clerks, local party cadre, and small businessmen (Neuman 1971; Goh 1971; Ahmad 1985). Not surprisingly, the NEP incorporated the very same demands made by the Malay middle class and specifically by Malay businessmen (see Tan 2008).

Corporate restructuring under the NEP to increase Malay share ownership, along with state efforts to control the 'commanding heights' of the economy, such as plantations and tin mines, fostered a growing number of Malay businessmen and a powerful group of former state managers increasingly active in business (Jesudason 1989). The late 1970s saw the emergence and transformation of the Malay bourgeoisie from primarily directors – not owners – of large corporations (before the mid-1970s) to Malay millionaires (Lim 1985). By the 1980s, Malay businessmen – including professional and trustee Malay executive directors – were an increasingly important element in the Malay political elite (Searle 1999). This shift reflected the changing composition of UMNO leaders, from politicians and 'administocrats' to a combination of politicians and businessmen (Ho 1988; Leigh 1992), and UMNO membership from schoolteachers and other local leaders to businessmen and university-educated professionals produced by the NEP (Crouch 1992; Searle 1999). 'Middle-class elements', including a younger, more professionally trained managerial cadre, were able to completely take over UMNO by the early 1980s (Jomo 1999; Milne and Mauzy 1999).

The changing composition of the Malay middle class, and changing patron–client relationships, reshaped the internal politics within UMNO local branches. Increasing economic patronage changed the nature of the patron–client relationship, transforming local UMNO representatives into political patrons. Elected members of parliament who were previously political patrons, providing political support in return for economic benefits, greatly increased their control of the district development machinery, allowing them to distribute development benefits and purchase continued support (Shamsul 1986). Malay businessmen became an important force in the internal politics of UMNO through the party's extensive patronage network (Khoo 1992; Crouch 1992; Aziz 1997), increasing bitter factional struggles for nomination, and outbreaks of violence at UMNO branch and division meetings after 1984 (Shamsul 1986). Although factions were already present in all levels of UMNO (Ahmad 1985), the rise of money politics was closely related to, if not a direct result of, the NEP (Shamsul 1986).

The conflict was between two factions and over the choice of the NEP or privatisation as the vehicle to redistribute rents. The NEP faction comprised small and medium Malay businessmen, and the 'bureaucratic class', concentrated primarily at the branch level of UMNO and within various Malay chambers of commerce. This group was heavily dependent on access to patronage and favoured continued state intervention under the NEP. It was thus the most affected by the government's response to the 1980s recession, which included the tightening of credit, austerity measures, centralisation of assets, and the suspension, restructuring or shelving of state enterprises (see e.g. Malek 1986; Searle 1999).

The privatisation faction involved a coalition of political and business elites and included an NEP-trained 'Malay rentier-business cadre' who stood to benefit disproportionately from greater business opportunities afforded by privatisation, and whose political support was crucial (Jomo 1993b; Felker 1993). These rents included significant implicit subsidies in privatisation contracts which were difficult to capture under the NEP where state ownership and bureaucratic control restricted rents mainly to broad-based subsidies and cheap credit (Tan 2008). Privatisation provided this faction with opportunities for rent capture, at the expense of the NEP faction, through its close connections with the political leadership. Privatisation thus presented a segment of the political leadership with opportunities to reward its supporters and secure support at party elections (see Gomez 1990, 1991).

This analysis of changing social relations suggests that the state allocation of rents depends largely on its capacity, which is shaped by the nature of patron–client networks and the relative power of patrons and clients. This analysis of state capacity allows us to examine another aspect of rent-seeking related to the wider process of late industrialisation and state attempts to create a BCIC. The statist literature on Malaysia highlights the poor quality of state intervention, with rent management characterised by the absence of objectives, performance standards and disciplinary mechanisms (enforcement) (see e.g. Rasiah 1998, 2001; Alavi 1998, 1999; Felker 1998, 1999; Chin and Jomo 2000, 2001: 102, 129; Jomo and Hamilton-Hart 2001: 83; Jomo and Gomez 2000; Rasiah and Ishak 2001). This approach usually equates state autonomy with state capacity, where the efficacy of rents is compromised by state capture or political capture (see Gomez 1991).

In the absence of an analysis of social forces, however, the solutions to weak rent management and rent-seeking tend to be largely institutional and technical (Alavi 1998; Felker 1998, 1999; Rasiah 2011). Ethnic and crony explanations are similarly inadequate, given government attempts to discipline bureaucrats and inefficient state enterprises (Tan 1984; Bruton 1992; Felker 1993, 1999). These policy adjustments became more difficult after the early 1970s with the emergence of state bureaucrats who entrenched themselves and resisted discipline (Bruton 1992). Despite official recommendations to halve levels of protection to improve efficiency and international competitiveness, the government continued to provide high levels of protection for inefficient import-substituting industries and even increased protection, irrespective of productive capabilities and without performance conditions (Bruton 1992; Alavi 1996, 1998; Jomo and Tan 1999; Jomo and Edwards 1993; Rasiah and Ishak 2001).

Privatisation in this context represented the political leadership's attempts to shift power away from the bureaucracy by centralising economic authority in the Prime Minister's Department and elevating links between political and select business leaders (Leigh 1992; Felker 1999). The support of the privatisation faction facilitated the shift to narrow and personalistic policy networks in order to bypass formal bureaucratic channels, enabling politicians to take over control of state-held assets from technocrats and bureaucrats (Shamsul 1986; Felker 1999; see also Gomez 2002a, 2002b). It also allowed the government to rein in state enterprises and streamline regulation, and to discipline the bureaucracy for greater efficiency, particularly in economic regulation (Felker 1999).

New forms of state intervention, including re-regulation, aimed to achieve different industrial (and technology) policy objectives (Jomo and Tan 1999), with economic liberalisation allowing 'political elites to de-bureaucratise policy-making and draw business into greater consultation within clientelist channels at the apex of the political party and government system' (Felker 1999: 104). The government was thus increasingly unwilling to subsidise broadly, focusing more narrowly on a small group of entrepreneurs through the management of key government-linked projects to overcome distributional constraints and inefficiencies (Felker 1993).

Despite this, privatisation failed to improve the government's disciplinary capacity (Tan 2008), with business exercising increasing political leverage over government controls as a result of increasing involvement of the Malay elite in business (McVey 1995). Here, the personalisation of patronage and centralisation of authority was itself an outcome as well as a driver of changing patterns of rent-seeking associated with changing social relations. Personalised patron–client relationships involving vested party and individual interests led to moral hazard, making it difficult to discipline clients, particularly given the degree of competition and conflict in UMNO. The more intense the competition, the more dependent the patron was on the client for support, and the more personalised the patron–client relationship became. Mahathir's increasing authoritarianism to reassert central control may thus also be seen as a reflection of political weakness rather than strength.

Conclusion

By incorporating the insights from the literature centred on ethnicity, political patronage and political business, a class analysis allows us to better answer the three questions posed at the start of this chapter about the relationship between rent-seeking and money politics in Malaysia, the drivers of rent-seeking and money politics, and the impact of these on the contestation for, and allocation of, rents. The dominant discourse here is premised on a definition of money politics as the political capture of the state by politicians and bureaucrats. Rather than focus on individual actors to explain social processes, a class analysis examines the wider social and political context to help explain the actions of both patrons and clients.

This approach entails distinguishing between different types of client – regular businessmen, businessmen in politics, and politicians/bureaucrats in business – in order to identify the nature of their relationship with patrons and hence the direction of influence which determines whether state capture or political capture occurs. This will be shaped by various factors, most notably the degree of political contestation related to changes in class formations and social relations.

Here, an emergent Malay middle class pushed for, and benefited from, rents under the NEP. The subsequent rapid growth of, and differentiation within, this class increased competition for, and heightened conflict over, the distribution of rents, resulting in changes in the nature of patronage, pattern of rent-seeking, and ultimately, the introduction of privatisation as a vehicle for rent distribution and capital accumulation which favoured a new Malay business class. The difficulties the government faced in promoting a BCIC can be traced back to these social changes which constrained the state's disciplinary capacity needed to manage rents effectively. While unproductive (redistributive) rents (e.g. in captive markets or non-tradeable sectors) may have been necessary to ensure political stability, even potentially productive rents for learning were dissipated as political leaders were unable or unwilling to discipline those on whose support they depended. In this context, competition and liberalisation only pushed the private sector, including previously productive firms, into other unproductive sectors related to construction, real estate and finance, which provided rents in relatively captive markets.

Bibliography

Ahmad Atory Hussain (1985) *Pembentukan Dasar Awam Malaysia* [Malaysia's Public Policy Formation], Kuala Lumpur: Utusan Publications.

Alavi, R. (1996) *Industrialisation in Malaysia: Import Substitution and Infant Industry Performance*, London: Routledge.

Alavi, R. (1998) 'Management of protection policy: lessons from Malaysian experience', in Ishak Yussof and Abdul Ghafar Ismail (eds), *Malaysian Industrialisation: Governance and the Technical Change*, Bangi: Penerbit Universiti Kebangsaan Malaysia.

Alavi, R. (1999) 'Rents, technological innovation and firm competitiveness in a Bumiputra Malaysian firm', in Jomo K.S., Greg Felker and Rajah Rasiah (eds), *Industrial Technology Development in Malaysia: Industry and Firm Studies*, London: Routledge.

Azeem Fazwan Ahmad Farouk (2012) 'State and entrepreneurship: the failure to create a Bumiputera Commercial and Industrial Community (BCIC) in Penang, Malaysia', *Kajian Malaysia*, 30(1): 1–20.

Aziz Zariza Ahmad (1997) *Mahathir's Paradigm Shift*, Taiping: Firma.

Bowie, Alasdair (1988) 'Redistribution with growth? The dilemmas of state-sponsored economic development in Malaysia', in John Ravenhill (ed.), *Singapore, Indonesia, Malaysia, the Philippines and Thailand*, vol. I, Aldershot: Edward Elgar Publishing.

Bowie, Alasdair (1991) *Crossing the Industrial Divide: State, Society and the Politics of Economic Transformation in Malaysia*, New York: Columbia University Press.

Bruton, Henry J. (1992) *Sri Lanka and Malaysia*, Washington DC: Oxford University Press.

Case, William (2008) 'Malaysia in 2007: high corruption and low opposition', *Asian Survey*, 48(1): 47–54.

Case, William (2009) 'Electoral authoritarianism in Malaysia: trajectory shift', *The Pacific Review*, 22(3): 311–33.

Chin, J. (2009) 'The Malaysian Chinese dilemma: the Never Ending Policy (NEP)', *Chinese Southern Diaspora Studies*, 3: 167–82.

Chin Kok Fay and Jomo K.S. (2000) 'Financial sector rents in Malaysia', in Mushtaq H. Khan and Jomo K.S. (eds), *Rents, Rent Seeking and Economic Development*, Cambridge: Cambridge University Press.

Chin Kok Fay and Jomo K.S. (2001) 'Financial liberalisation and system vulnerability', in Jomo K.S. (ed.), *Malaysian Eclipse: Economic Crisis and Recovery*, London: Zed Books.

Crouch, Harold (1992) 'Authoritarian trends, the UMNO split and limits to state power', in Joel S. Kahn and Francis Loh Kok Wah (eds), *Fragmented Vision: Culture and Politics in Contemporary Malaysia*, Sydney: Allen & Unwin.

Doraisami, Anita (2005) 'The political economy of capital flows and capital controls in Malaysia', *Journal of Contemporary Asia*, 35(2): 249–63.

Evans, Peter B. (1995) *Embedded Autonomy*, Princeton: Princeton University Press.

Felker, Greg (1993) 'Political economy and Malaysian technology policy', in Jomo K.S. (ed.), *Industrialising Malaysia: Policy, Performance, Prospects*, London: Routledge.

Felker, Greg (1998) 'Political economy and Malaysian technology policy', in Ishak Yussof and Abdul Ghafar Ismail (eds), *Malaysian Industrialisation: Governance and the Technical Change*, Bangi: Penerbit Universiti Kebangsaan Malaysia.

Felker, Greg (1999) 'Malaysia's innovation system', in Jomo K.S. and Greg Felker (eds), *Technology, Competitiveness and The State: Malaysia's Industrial Technology Policies*, London: Routledge.

Goh Cheng Teik (1971) *The May Thirteenth Incident*, Kuala Lumpur: Oxford University Press.

Gomez, Edmund Terence (1990) *Politics in Business: UMNO's Corporate Investments*, Kuala Lumpur: Forum.

Gomez, Edmund Terence (1991) *Money Politics in the Barisan Nasional*, Kuala Lumpur: Forum.

Gomez, Edmund Terence (2002a) 'Introduction: political business in East Asia', in Edmund Terence Gomez (ed.), *Political Business in East Asia*, London: Routledge.

Gomez, Edmund Terence (2002b) 'Political business in Malaysia: part factionalism, corporate development, and economic crisis', in Edmund Terence Gomez (ed.), *Political Business in East Asia*, London: Routledge.

Gomez, Edmund Terence and Jomo K.S. (1997) *Malaysia's Political Economy: Politics, Patronage and Profits*, Cambridge: Cambridge University Press.

Haggard, Steven (1990) *Pathways from the Periphery: The Politics of Growth in the Newly Industrializing Countries*, Ithaca: Cornell University Press.

Heng Pek Koon (1997) 'The new economic policy and the Chinese community in Peninsular Malaysia', *The Developing Economies*, 35(3): 262–92.

Hirschman, Charles (1998) 'Ownership and control of the Malaysian economy revisited: a review of research in the 25 years since the publication of J.J. Puthucheary's classic', in Dominic Puthucheary and Jomo K.S. (eds), *No Cowardly Past: James J. Puthucheary Writings, Poems and Commentaries*, Kuala Lumpur: INSAN.

Ho Khai Leong (1988) Indigenizing the State: The NEP and the Bumiputra State in Peninsular Malaysia, PhD Dissertation, Ohio State University.

Jesudason, James V. (1989) *Ethnicity and the Economy: The State, Chinese Business, and Multinationals in Malaysia*, Singapore: Oxford University Press.

Johnson, Chalmers A. (1982) *MITI and the Japanese Miracle*, Stanford: Stanford University Press.

Jomo K.S. (1986) *A Question of Class: Capital, the State and Uneven Development in Malaya*, Singapore: Oxford University Press.

Jomo K.S. (1993a) 'Prospects for Malaysian industrialisation in light of East Asian NIC experiences', in Jomo K.S. (ed.), *Industrializing Malaysia: Policy, Performance, Prospects*, London: Routledge.

Jomo K.S. (1993b) *The Way Forward?: The Political Economy of Development Policy Reform in Malaysia*, Kuala Lumpur: University of Malaya.

Jomo K.S. (1995) *Privatizing Malaysia: Rents, Rhetoric, Realities*, London: Westview Press.

Jomo K.S. (1999) 'A Malaysian middle class?: Some preliminary analytical considerations', in Jomo K.S. (ed.), *Rethinking Malaysia*, Hong Kong: Asia 2000.

Jomo K.S. (2004) 'The New Economic Policy and ethnic relations in Malaysia', *Identities, Conflict and Cohesion Programme Paper No. 7*, Geneva: United Nations Research Institute for Social Development.

Jomo K.S. and Chris Edwards (1993) 'Malaysian industrialisation in historical perspective', in Jomo K.S. (ed.), *Industrializing Malaysia: Policy, Performance, Prospects*, London: Routledge.

Jomo K.S. and Tan Kock Wah (1999) *Industrial Policy in East Asia: Lessons for Malaysia*, Kuala Lumpur: University of Malaya Press.

Jomo K.S. and Edmund Terence Gomez (2000) 'The Malaysian development dilemma', in Mushtaq H. Khan and Jomo K.S. (eds), *Rents, Rent Seeking and Economic Development*, Cambridge: Cambridge University Press.

Jomo K.S. and Natasha Hamilton-Hart (2001) 'Financial regulation, crisis and policy response', in Jomo K.S. (ed.), *Malaysian Eclipse: Economic Crisis and Recovery*, London: Zed Books.

Kamal Salih (1989) The Malaysian Economy in the 1990s: The Alternative Scenarios, MIER [Malaysia Institute of Economic Research] Discussion Paper 27.

Khan, Mushtaq H. (1998) 'Patron–client networks and the economic effects of corruption in Asia', *European Journal of Development Research*, 10(1): 15–39.

Khoo Boo Teik (1995) *Paradoxes of Mahathirism*, Kuala Lumpur: Oxford University Press.

Khoo Kay Jin (1992) 'The grand vision: Mahathir and modernisation', in Joel S. Kahn and Francis Loh Kok Wah (eds), *Fragmented Vision: Culture and Politics in Contemporary Malaysia*, Sydney: Allen & Unwin.

Leigh, Michael (1992) 'Politics, bureaucracy, and business in Malaysia: realigning the eternal triangle', in Andrew J. McIntyre and Kanishka Jayasuriya (eds), *The Dynamics of Economic Policy Reform in Southeast Asia and South West Pacific*, Singapore: Oxford University Press.

Lian Kwen Fee and Jayanath Appudurai (2011) 'Race, class and politics in peninsular Malaysia: the general election of 2008', *Asian Studies Review*, 35(1): 63–82.

Lim Mah Hui (1981) *Ownership and Control of the 100 Largest Corporations in Malaysia*, Singapore: Oxford University Press.

Lim Mah Hui (1985) 'Contradictions in the development of Malay capital: state, accumulation and legitimation', *Journal of Contemporary Asia*, 15(1): 37–63.

Loh Kok Wah, Francis and Joel S. Kahn (1992) 'Introduction: fragmented vision', in Joel S. Kahn and Francis Loh Kok Wah (eds), *Fragmented Vision: Culture and Politics in Contemporary Malaysia*, Sydney: Allen & Unwin.

McVey, Ruth (1995) 'The Southeast Asian entrepreneur', in John Ravenhill (ed.), *Singapore, Indonesia, Malaysia, the Philippines and Thailand*, vol. I, Aldershot: Edward Elgar Publishing.

Malek Merican (1986) 'Review of the NEP from a private sector perspective', paper presented at GEMAPUTRA, Kuala Lumpur, Malaysia.

Mehmet, Ozay (1988) *Development in Malaysia: Poverty, Wealth and Trusteeship*, Kuala Lumpur: Insan.

Milne, R.S. and Diane K. Mauzy (1999) *Malaysian Politics Under Mahathir*, London: Routledge.

Neuman, Stephanie G. (1971) The Malay Political Elite: An Analysis of 134 Malay Legislators, Their Social Backgrounds and Attitudes, PhD Dissertation, New York University.

Popenoe, Oliver (1970) Malay Enterprises: An Analysis of the Social Backgrounds, Careers and Attitudes of the Leading Malay Businessmen in Western Malaysia, PhD Dissertation, London School of Economics.

Puthucheary, Mavis (1984) 'The political economy of public enterprise in Malaysia', in Lim Lin Lean and Chee Peng Lim (eds), *The Malaysian Economy at the Crossroads: Policy Adjustment or Structural Transformation*, Kuala Lumpur: Malaysian Economic Association and Organisational Resources.

Rasiah, Rajah (1998) 'Capital expansion, cronyism and contraction', *Journal of the Asia Pacific Economy*, 3(3): 358–78.

Rasiah, Rajah (2001) 'Pre-crisis economic weaknesses and vulnerability', in Jomo K.S. (ed.), *Malaysian Eclipse: Economic Crisis and Recovery*, London: Zed Books.

Rasiah, Rajah (2011) 'Is Malaysia facing negative deindustrialization?', *Pacific Affairs*, 84(4): 715–36.

Rasiah, Rajah and Ishak Shari (2001) 'Market, government and Malaysia's New Economic Policy', *Cambridge Journal of Economics*, 25: 57–78.

Searle, Peter (1999) *The Riddle of Malaysian Capitalism*, Honolulu: Allen & Unwin and University of Hawai'i Press.

Shamsul Amri Baharuddin (1986) *From British to Bumiputra Rule*, Singapore: Institute of Southeast Asian Studies.

Singh, Hari (2001) 'Ethnic conflict in Malaysia revisited', *Commonwealth & Comparative Politics*, 39(1): 42–65.

Tan Chee Khoon (1984) *Without Fear or Favour*, Petaling Jaya: Eastern Universities Press.

Tan, Jeff (2008) *Privatization in Malaysia: Regulation, Rent-Seeking and Policy Failure*, London: Routledge.

Tan, Jeff (2010) 'Can the East Asian developmental state be replicated? The case of Malaysia', in Robert Springborg (ed.), *Development Models in Muslim Contexts*, Edinburgh: Edinburgh University Press.

Tan, Jeff (2011) 'Conceptualising entrepreneurship, innovation and late industrialisation: the state creation of entrepreneurs in Malaysia', *International Journal of Management Concepts and Philosophy*, 5(2): 38–158.

Tan, Jeff (2012) 'The pitfalls of water privatization: failure and reform in Malaysia', *World Development*, 40(12): 2552–63.

Tan Tat Wai (1982) *Income Distribution and Determination in West Malaysia*, Kuala Lumpur: Oxford University Press.
Teh Yik Koon (2002) 'Money politics in Malaysia', *Journal of Contemporary Asia*, 32(3): 338–45.
Wedeman, Andrew (2002) 'Development and corruption: the East Asian paradox', in Edmund Terence Gomez (ed.), *Political Business in East Asia*, London: Routledge.
White, W. and Robert Wade (1988) 'Developmental states and markets in East Asia', in Gordon White (ed.), *Developmental States in East Asia*, Sussex: Institute of Development Studies.
Yoshihara, Kunio (1988) *The Rise of Ersatz Capitalism in Southeast Asia*, New York: Oxford University Press.
Yusoff, Marina (1990) *Time for Change*, Kuala Lumpur: The Champ.

17

Labour in Malaysia

Flexibility, policy-making and regulated borders

Amarjit Kaur

Labour migration has been a significant policy issue in Malaysian history since the late nineteenth century and continues to dominate policy-making, security concerns and migration management. Immigration played a pivotal role in the growth of wage labour and shaped labour practices and regimes in various sectors. Crucially, it led to major demographic changes and transformed Malaysia into an immigrant nation.

Two major labour migration surges may be identified since the late nineteenth century. The first was in the 1870s, when the British colonial administration established pathways for the primarily unrestricted circular migration of Chinese and Indian workers to Malaya. These labour movements were consistent with industrialisation in the West, the pursuit of tropical commodities by European firms and the need for cheap labour. Migration led to labour force growth in the country, facilitating the expansion of the tin and rubber industries and advancing the economic interests of the colonial administration and European investors. After independence, the national government halted low-skilled labour migration and thousands of Indian and Chinese 'foreign citizens' were repatriated to their homelands. Concurrently, the government implemented a new immigration policy directed at recruitment of skilled migrants with abilities needed by the newly independent country.

In the mid-1980s, Malaysia made an about-turn in its low-skilled labour migration policy. In common with the United States and the European Union, Malaysia implemented a new labour policy focusing on temporary or guest worker programmes. This policy change marked a second stage in foreign labour employment, consistent with Malaysia's new growth strategies and increasing demand for workers for the agricultural, manufacturing, construction and domestic work sectors. The new migration processes for guest workers hinged on two policy domains, circular migration and border control. The state also gradually increased its immigrant detention centres and instigated regular deportation exercises for irregular migrants. Additionally, Malaysia embraced biometric identification systems for controlling the movement of guest workers and reducing irregular migration flows. Nevertheless, like the US and EU, Malaysia also began to rely on the regularisation of irregular migrants as a policy instrument, extending legal status to undocumented economic migrants.

Meanwhile, the government's state-driven programmes for recruitment of highly skilled professionals mirror Malaysia's aspiration to achieve developed nation status by 2020. Like

Singapore, therefore, Malaysia has amended its immigration infrastructure to capitalise upon the mobility of highly skilled individuals by offering them pathways to permanent residence and citizenship. Focusing on this second migration surge, this chapter examines Malaysia's evolving migration management frameworks and policies in light of changing migration realities in the country. It then appraises Malaysia's border-control system and its impact on migrant workers' human rights.

Initial migration policy and border management after 1957

Malaysia's national migration policy after independence has to be viewed from the perspective of political transitions and competing ethnic aspirations. Under the terms of the 1948 Federation of Malaya Agreement, Malays were granted federal citizenship while Chinese and Indians could acquire citizenship only by fulfilling residency qualifications; however, most Chinese and Indians did not have documentation confirming their residency status in the country. Following this agreement, the Malay-dominated government's indigenisation efforts and hostility towards further Indian and Chinese low-skilled immigration dominated policy regarding Malaya's future national, racial and economic borders. In 1957, the Malayan government enacted new legislation that effectively ended Chinese and Indian immigrants' access to the labour market. The subsequent Immigration Act 1959 put in place a tough new policy that denied citizenship rights to Chinese and Indian residents and forced them to leave, despite their earlier connections to and residence in the country. This legislation also included a clause that reinforced right-of-entry rules under the section on reunification of families. Thus, wives and children of Chinese and Indians living separately from their husbands or fathers for a continuous period of five years after December 1954 were denied admission into Malaya.

In 1968, the government approved new legislation – the Employment Restriction Act – against the backdrop of worsening economic conditions in the country. This legislation resonated with the colonial government's Immigration Ordinance 1953 that restricted permanent admission to migrants possessing 'specialised services' and who could contribute 'to the expansion of commerce and industry' (Kaur 2008; Saw 1988: 17). The 1968 legislation further enshrined specific eligibility criteria based on applicants' expertise for recruitment as foreign workers. Simultaneously, less-skilled foreigners were denied right of entry into Malaysia. Nevertheless, the state surreptitiously allowed low-skilled Indonesian migrants to work in the plantation sector following the departure of Indian plantation workers.

Following the 1969 racial riots in Malaysia and a change in leadership, the government espoused state-led economic growth and launched the New Economic Policy, aimed at promoting economic growth through industrialisation. The state's export-oriented industrialisation strategy was associated with Japan's post-World War II ascendency in the international economy and the new international division of labour. Its economic strategies included large-scale infrastructure development projects, public sector expansion, and agricultural growth and diversification. Poverty reduction and income redistribution schemes for Malays were also begun while agricultural development centred on resettlement of Malays who either owned small plots of land or were landless. The government further approved the development of large blocks of land by public agencies such as the Federal Land Development Authority (FELDA). All these projects, as well as a construction boom in the urban areas, had a predictable impact on labour supply, creating labour shortages and disruption in several sectors.

According to the World Bank (1995: 58), 14 million new jobs were created in 1987–93, for an annual labour market growth rate of 3.9 percent. The domestic labour force grew an average of 3.1 percent per year during the same period. Job creation in the public sector and expansion of government projects also attracted large numbers of rural Malays to the towns, for government jobs. These circumstances foreshadowed changes in Malaysia's official labour immigration policy, leading to a new phase in foreign labour recruitment. The policy was designed to meet a skills shortage (highly skilled workers) and also meet labour force growth (less-skilled workers).

Policy-making, migration management and border control since the 1980s

New migration frameworks

Malaysian labour policies enacted after the 1980s focused on international labour migrants; the colonial administration had already laid the basis for labour laws and labour rights for Malayan workers in the 1940s and 1950s. In 1940, for example, the British approved the Trades Union Ordinance in Malaya, stipulating compulsory registration of unions and emphasising conciliation procedures. Nevertheless, workers were denied the right to picket and prohibited from carrying out political and sympathy strikes. Then, after World War II, Britain supported the creation of trade unions in the colonies, establishing two important principles of law relating to labour contracts. The first was associated with security of tenure, while the second emphasised individual employment rights (Kaur 2004: ch.7; Morgan 1977: 153; Ramasamy 2001). As discussed later in the chapter, Malaysia reintroduced 'indirect' labour relations and reinstated the contract labour system in 2006 to manage the evolving migration situation and reduce labour costs.

In the early 1980s, policies on hiring less-skilled migrant workers in labour-intensive sectors were devised on an ad hoc basis to meet enterprises' 'urgent' labour needs and Malaysia turned a blind eye to the recruitment of 'irregular' workers from Indonesia and Thailand. As incomes rose in Malaysia in the 1980s, demand for seasonal labour in agriculture and domestic work also increased. Against the backdrop of labour shortages, employers utilised their social networks and relied on private labour brokers or intermediaries to recruit Indonesian and Thai workers clandestinely for the construction, plantation and domestic work sectors (Kassim 1987: 267–68). The employer-driven system and lack of a legal policy framework and channels for labour recruitment resulted in the illegal recruitment of large numbers of mostly Indonesian migrants to fill labour market gaps. According to Jones (2000: 15), citing Indonesian Ministry of Manpower records, estimates of irregular Indonesian migrant workers in Malaysia ranged from 200,000 to 700,000 in the early 1980s. These labour movements reflected Malaysia's attraction as an immigrant destination, and, as Andreas (2011) notes, 'increases in the flows of cross-border illicit goods . . . and migrants . . . [were] a natural consequence of increased globalization'.

Despite opposition from trade union officials, Malaysia saw foreign labour recruitment as a tool for economic competitiveness. The initial legal framework focused on labour accords with neighbouring labour-sending countries. In 1984, Malaysia signed the Medan Agreement with Indonesia for the supply of Indonesian workers for the plantation and domestic work sectors. Next, in 1985, Malaysia approved a labour accord with the Philippines for the recruitment of domestic workers. Labour accords were subsequently also signed with Bangladesh and Thailand for employment of workers for the plantation and construction sectors. These labour accords both permitted the employment of foreign workers in low-wage jobs and dealt proactively with those living in Malaysia.

In 1991, Malaysia adjusted its initial position on low-skilled labour immigration and established a cabinet committee on foreign workers to develop new strategies and procedures for labour recruitment for the economy. A new policy, the Comprehensive Policy on the

Recruitment of Foreign Workers, was adopted to ensure coordination on foreign labour employment. A separate committee was also set up in the Ministry of Human Resources to deal with the comprehensive management of foreign workers. These committees were tasked with developing a policy framework for admitting immigrants and ensuring cooperation among relevant government departments. The bureaucratic frameworks also set numerical limits on annual work permits to manage immigration. Importantly, the regulatory process included three policy instruments: the Immigration Act, the Employment of Foreign Workers Act (including the Employment Agencies Act) and the Penal Code.

Malaysia subsequently introduced an annual levy on migrant workers in the 1991/92 federal budget to deter excessive dependence on foreign workers. The levy charged was consistent with the sector and migrants' skill categories (general, semi-skilled and unskilled) and could be paid by either employers or workers. Predictably, employers insisted that workers pay the levy. Levies were increased in subsequent years, correlating with global economic conditions and demand for Malaysian commodities. These developments institutionalised cooperation among relevant departments, emphasising increased scrutiny of eligibility criteria, recruitment, employer sponsorship and visa conditions of foreign labour.

Concurrently, against the backdrop of a new geography of migration, neoliberal globalisation and capital's shifting national and supranational boundaries, Malaysia readily embraced the principles underpinning the relocation of foreign labour-intensive manufacturing industries to the country. Thus in 1995, the government offered incentives to Malaysian and foreign investors to set up industries such as electronics, automated manufacturing, biotechnology and information technology in Malaysia. These industries were seen as critical to attaining developed country status by 2020 and necessitated further amendments to the migration management apparatus. Malaysia subsequently authorised foreign labour schemes for employment of professionals and skilled workers alongside the hiring of low-skilled workers. A Special Task Force on Foreign Labour was also established to take control of foreign labour recruitment (excepting domestic workers and shop assistants). The task force and official guidelines for foreign labour recruitment streamlined Malaysia's immigration processes.

The task force subsequently took over the Immigration Department's job of processing foreign workers' work applications. Malaysia also pursued greater cross-border cooperation with labour-sending states through memoranda of understanding (MoU), signing MoUs on recruitment and employment of low-skilled workers with major labour-sending states, including Indonesia, Bangladesh, Pakistan, Sri Lanka, Thailand and Vietnam. The Immigration Department's role also expanded to include better regulation of foreign labour, identifying 'appropriate' labour-source countries, and monitoring the eligibility of sectors and firms applying for foreign workers.

Malaysia thus created institutional capacity for immigration policy-making, instituted a border-control system and implemented legal channels for admission of migrants who met broader policy-defined goals to boost economic growth. Subsequently, various sorts of inequalities among workers became apparent, such as between local and migrant workers, between men and women, among different ethnic groups and employment sectors, and in who received training on the job. The recruitment of a docile foreign workforce was also designed to undermine the influence of trade unions and the existing low-skilled labour force, comprising mostly Malaysian Indians and Chinese. Malaysia also utilised new migration policies to manipulate race-based politics in Malaysia.

Malaysia's foreign labour policy involved off-shore recruitment procedures and included guidelines on such issues as assisted passages for workers and repayment of travel costs and other advances through salary deductions. Workers' employment was prearranged with a specific employer; it included fixed-term employment and obligatory return to the country of origin upon completion of the contract (Kaur 2006: 23–51). Not long afterwards, the Asian financial crisis of 1997–98 triggered an economic and financial crisis in Malaysia, resulting in the addition of further legal frameworks, a greater emphasis on security issues and a prohibition on further recruitment of foreign workers. Nevertheless, the manufacturing and service/hospitality sectors were exempted from this policy decision. Malaysia then disbanded the foreign labour task force in March 1997 and transferred recruitment matters to the Foreign Workers Division of the Immigration Department.

After economic conditions improved towards the end of 1998, foreign labour recruitment recommenced. Additionally, Malaysia established a new committee to administer the admission of professionals and skilled workers (known as expatriates), and the government permitted foreign multinationals and Malaysian companies to sponsor the recruitment of expatriates to meet Malaysia's changing labour needs. Like the US and EU, Malaysia relied on salary thresholds to identify professionals and highly skilled workers. This policy was essential to reduce the amount of discretion held by immigration officials. A brief description of the two categories of immigrant workers is necessary to understand public discourse on the different visa streams and policy frameworks.

Expatriates

Skilled, managerial, professional and technical foreign workers who earn a monthly salary of at least RM3,000 are classified as expatriates. The government's increasing emphasis on knowledge-based industries has meant that expatriates are allowed to work in almost all sectors (except those relating to national security). Expatriates could be people sponsored by Malaysian employers or who are self-employed (Kaur 2008). They are admitted on an Employment Pass visa if their employment contracts are for at least two years. Expatriates admitted on short-term contracts (under one year) are issued a Visit Pass for Professional Employment. Married expatriates hired on employment pass visas are allowed to have their dependents accompany them to Malaysia. The initial employment pass visas were for two years (later extended to five years) and in 2011, Malaysia created channels to allow expatriates to stay on for longer periods. For instance, the Residence Pass for Talent (RP-T) is a ten-year work visa that allows expatriates to work in the country and also change jobs without having to renew their employment pass. A further amendment has permitted expatriates to apply for permanent residence if they satisfy the criteria of a points-based system that include age, education, work experience, language skills and ties with Malaysians (see Talent Corp n.d.). Similar to Singapore, Malaysia has also devised regulations that include longer periods of stay, incorporate other forms of social protection and allow expatriates to secure Malaysian citizenship (World Bank 2013).

Guest workers

Semi-skilled and less-skilled workers are classified as migrant workers and issued a Visit Pass for Temporary Employment for jobs in the manufacturing, construction, plantation and services sectors (excluding domestic work). These guest workers comprise about 98 percent of foreign workers in Malaysia. Guest workers were previously recruited on one-year work permit visas that could be renewed for a further five years; they were paid on a daily basis until recently (see below). There are age restrictions in their service conditions and their dependents cannot accompany them to Malaysia. They may now work for up to ten years in some sectors (*New Straits Times*, 16 April 2008); however, they are required to return to their countries after a five-year period and undergo the application process again. Their remuneration was officially fixed at below RM2,500 per month (now below RM3,000), but few actually earned/earn this amount. According to reports, 34 percent of the 1.3 million guest workers earned under RM700 in 2009, when the official poverty line income was RM800 (Alyaa 2014).

In addition, annual levies, ranging from RM410 to RM1,850, are designed to reduce dependence on these workers (Kaur 2013a). The government has vacillated with regard to the levy imposed. For example, in 2009, Malaysia made it obligatory for employers to pay the levy, following adverse criticism by national and international NGO groups. This policy amendment was short-lived. In 2013 (an election year), the government backtracked on this issue and currently allows employers to deduct the levy from their foreign employees' wages.

The government also introduced detailed recruitment criteria for the allocation of a specific number of work permits to enterprises and employers, based on factors such as categorisation of the industry, whether of export or non-export orientation, paid-up capital and sales value, and ratio of local workers to foreign workers employed. The details of this legal framework are presented in Table 17.1.

Table 17.1 Malaysia: criteria for employment of foreign workers in selected sectors

MANUFACTURING SECTOR

1. Export-oriented companies

Eligibility criteria

a. Minimum export value: RM50 million
b. Eligibility ratio of local workers to foreign workers 1:3

2. Non-export-oriented companies

Eligibility criteria

a. Minimum paid-up capital: RM100,000
b. Sales value RM2 million
c. Eligibility ratio of local workers to foreign workers 1:1

3. Companies in the electrical and electronic sectors

Eligibility criteria

a. None
b. Eligibility ratio of local workers to foreign workers is 1:2, irrespective of whether the company is designated 'export-oriented' or 'non-export-oriented'

PLANTATION SECTOR

Eligibility criteria: owner of plantation or lessee
Type of cultivation or nursery: oil palm, rubber, cocoa, teak and other species of forest
Approval criteria depend on two factors:
a. Land area
b. Number of existing workers (local and foreign)
(i) for every 8 hectares of oil palm: 1 foreign worker
(ii) for every 4 hectares of rubber: 1 foreign worker

CONSTRUCTION SECTOR

a. For construction workers < 50
Employer needs to get approval from the Construction Labour Exchange Centre
b. For construction workers > 50
Employer needs to get approval from Ministry of Home Affairs

Source: Adapted from Shamsuddin (2006).

It is doubtful whether the government-established 'dependency ceiling', defined as the maximum share of foreign workers in a firm's total employment, is in fact supported by employers. It is also generally known that employers and investors prefer hiring foreign labour over local labour since they are able to manipulate workers' working conditions, compel them to work overtime and pay them lower wages (Kaur 2013a; Devadason and Chan 2014). According to a Malaysian labour activist, not only have the state's safeguards, such as the levy system, employer-provided housing and recruitment quotas, all been ignored by employers, but guest workers' working conditions are abysmal. They have to work about eleven to twelve hours daily (including rest days and public holidays) and factories have two twelve-hour shifts (Hector 2014).

Guest workers are recruited from sixteen countries, namely, Indonesia, Bangladesh, Pakistan, India, Laos, Nepal, Vietnam, Cambodia, Philippines, China, Sri Lanka, Thailand, Burma, Turkmenistan, Kazakhstan and Uzbekistan. Originally, there were no official regulations stipulating provision of accommodation for migrant workers. Migrants hired by construction companies had to build their own shacks at their worksites, while employers of domestic workers had to accommodate their domestic workers (this was implicit since domestic workers are hired on an 'always on call' basis). Foreign workers employed in urban areas reside in sub-standard housing. Most live in crowded apartment blocks or squatter settlements while those employed in restaurants are usually housed in rooms on the premises.

Plantation companies have been obliged to provide accommodation for their workers under the Workers' Minimum Housing Standards and Amenities Act 1990. This regulation is consistent with the important position of palm oil exports in Malaysia's export economy and was implemented following foreign and local reports on forced labour on plantations (see US Government Department of Labor 2012; Kaur 2014). Employer-provided housing has also enabled greater employer supervision over workers, since a significant number of foreign workers situated in rural areas have frequently absconded to urban centres in order to earn higher wages. According to newspaper reports, 38,000 'legal' workers had 'illegally' changed jobs by 2011 (Letchumanan and Gaspar 2011).

The percentage share of foreign labour in the major economic sectors in the period 1985 to 2010 is listed in Table 17.2. In 2010, Malaysia employed approximately 1.9 million foreign workers in the main economic sectors. Indonesians comprised the largest group (50.9 percent),

Table 17.2 Malaysia: distribution of migrant workers in main economic sectors, 1985–2010 (%)

Sector	*1985*	*1990*	*2000*	*2005*	*2009*	*2010*
Agriculture[a]	50.1	37.7	24.8	26.0	26.1	20
Manufacturing	6.9	8.8	38.1	32.1	34.6	39
Construction	15.0	34.4	8.5	15.5	15.6	19
Services (non-domestic)	20.3[b]	19.1	6.7	8.8	10.6	10
Domestic services	–	–	22	17.6	13.1	12
Total (%)	95.3	99.5	100	100	100	100
Total ('000)	**212**	**441**	**807**	**1,815**	**1,918**	**1,900**

Sources: [1985–2009] Devadason and Chan (2011); [2010] Asrul (2011).

Notes:

[a] Includes forestry, fishing, mining and plantations.

[b] Includes domestic service.

followed by Bangladeshis (17.5 percent), Nepalese (9.7 percent), Burmese (7.8 percent) and Indians (6.3 percent). It was also estimated that there were an equal number of irregular migrants in the country (Asrul 2010).

Initially, the growing number of irregular immigrants (including workers who had run away from unbearable workplaces) led to changes in Malaysia's migration policy processes. In 2002 Malaysia amended the Immigration Act 2002 and introduced several new rulings that affected irregular workers. These included fines of up to RM10,000; five-year incarceration periods; and 'six strokes of the cane' (Sreenevasan 2006). A succession of events then took place whereby the government initially took measures to control the influx of irregular migrants by implementing a freeze on new admissions, then rounded up irregular migrants, and subsequently, authorised amnesty-cum-regularisation programmes (see IOM 2008: 55). This approach became a regular occurrence in Malaysia; the labour outsourcing system (discussed below) was a major contributing factor.

The government's labour outsourcing recruitment system was introduced in 2005 to attract further investment into the country. Briefly, against the background of affirmative action policies and race-based politics, Chinese investors had been deterred from investing in larger corporations. Consequently, many decided to elect for small and medium enterprises because these were 'below the size threshold' at which Malaysia's Industrial Coordination Act's employment quota (a prerequisite of 30 percent for Malays) was applicable (see Hill *et al.* 2012: ch.1). The government subsequently relaxed its tough foreign worker recruitment quotas to encourage further private sector investment, since Malaysia's share of Southeast Asian FDI flows had been dropping. Both situations facilitated irregular migration.

The labour outsourcing system encouraged employers to circumvent regulations on upper limits for foreign worker recruitment, since workers recruited under the system were not counted in the allocations established for the various sectors. Significantly, contract workers are required to 'pay' for the privilege of recruitment. Additionally, although labour-hire firms are legally obliged to provide jobs for the workers, they behave like speculative labour contractors, moving workers around to get the best deal for their enterprises. Thus, the right to a guaranteed employment relationship between workers and employers until retirement age has been replaced with short-term or limited-duration contracts (Hector 2011). It has also been alleged that the outsourcing system has transformed migrant workers into 'bonded' labour. The NGO Tenaganita has published accounts of their exploitation by employers (Tenaganita 2007).

Growing foreign labour recruitment and development of new forms of employment in Malaysia have also corresponded with the undermining of the previous industrial relations system and the trade union movement (Ayadurai 1993: 65–68; Kaur 2004: ch. 10). Earlier, rather than legislate better wages and working conditions for Malaysian workers, Malaysia condoned the entry of cheap foreign labour to undermine the position of Malaysian workers. This policy subsequently resulted in rising youth unemployment, increased crime rates and greater social unrest (see, for example, Rasiah 2014). Significantly, the Malaysian Trades Union Congress (MTUC), which was initially 'hostile' to migrant workers and considered them a possible threat to the working conditions of Malaysian workers, has in recent decades championed foreign workers' rights. The International Labour Organization (ILO), Malaysian civil society organisations, and trade unions from labour-sending states have also been influential in persuading the MTUC to address migrants' rights in the context of international human rights standards. The MTUC has thus been influential, together with civil society groups, in persuading the government to allow migrant workers to join the MTUC (though foreign workers cannot hold any posts in the union) and obtaining a weekly day off for domestic workers in 2011.

Significantly, demands for improved wages for all workers were realised when in January 2013 the Malaysian government announced the raising of the minimum wage for low-skilled (including foreign) workers to RM900 a month for Peninsular Malaysia and RM800 for Sabah and Sarawak (*Migration News* 2013). All employers were required to comply with the Minimum Wages Order 2012, with effect from 1 January 2014. This wage policy, nevertheless, was criticised by some politicians who preferred to attract foreign investment by promoting the availability of 'cheap' labour.

Border management and security

As noted above, Malaysia has put in place legal frameworks to cooperate with sending countries, monitored irregular immigration and also instigated specific strategies to defend its borders. Cooperation with sending countries and Malaysia's security apparatus have primarily been mediated via bilateral arrangements with labour-sending states (labour accords and MoUs), regional cooperation and partnerships through the Association of Southeast Asian Nations (ASEAN); and regional diplomacy via the Bali Process on People Smuggling, Trafficking in Persons and Related Transnational Crime. Importantly, Malaysia has adopted new migration governance through the deployment of a non-state actor, the Ikatan Relawan Rakyat Malaysia (RELA) or People's Voluntary Corps, and employment of a great number of police and military personnel to patrol the state's borders. Malaysia has also established immigration detention camps (IDCs), created better databases, and utilised biometric hardware to monitor and manage foreign labour movements.

One of the earliest border-management strategies was the adoption of an off-shore recruitment process alongside a circular migration policy. This allowed the state to gather data on potential immigrant workers and benefit from cheap and mobile foreign labour. The enlistment of RELA has further enabled Malaysia to monitor and discourage settlement of foreign workers. RELA's remit includes the right to 'stop, search and demand documents, arrest without a warrant, and enter houses or premises believed to house irregular migrants' (FIDH and Suaram 2007: 11). As an inducement, RELA recruits were initially given bounties for captured irregular migrants (Suaram 2006: 120–21) and were 'immune from prosecution in relation to their conduct' (FIDH and Suaram 2007: 12). The bounty system has since been dropped because it allegedly led to acts of violence against irregular migrants (Kaur 2013a).

Biometric information systems and mobile immigration enforcement teams have also been utilised to assist the state in the corroboration of the status of 'legal' foreign workers and assist with repatriation of undocumented workers (*Migration News* 2008; *New Straits Times*, 4 November 2008). Malaysia's Home Ministry has supplied colour-coded identity cards to migrant workers, thus ensuring that workers are objectified on the basis of their occupational qualities (*Star*, 17 January 2008). Malaysian authorities also regularly administer physical punishment and subject irregular migrants to public humiliation prior to detaining them in IDCs. Special law courts have also been set up in IDCs to try migrants. In 2011, there were fifteen IDCs (numbers have varied) and other temporary detention centres, mirroring the government's tough new policies on irregular migration. Importantly, irregular migrants have to pay for their deportation expenses (Kaur 2013b), although the workers' employers and their embassies are expected to defray the costs of the exercise.

The latest round-up/amnesty/regularisation of irregular migrants exercise (2011–13) was labelled the '6P' operation and included six fundamentals: *pendaftaran* [registration], *pemutihan* [legalisation], *pengusiran* [deportation], *pemantauan* [monitoring], *penguatkuasaan* [enforcement] and *pengampunan* [amnesty]. A second phase in this exercise, which has involved 10,000 enforcement officials, commenced in January 2014. It has been alleged that 'an estimated 2.3 million' undocumented migrants were targeted (*Malaysia Chronicle* 2014). Additionally, 'offenders' were swiftly deported, despite the fact that some had photocopies of their employment documents (Reuters 2014).

Malaysia is party to twenty-eight ILO conventions, including the Migration for Employment Convention (Revised) 1949 (C97) regarding equal treatment of migrant workers. Malaysia's ratification of this convention means it should 'apply treatment no less favourable than that which applies to their own nationals in respect to a number of matters, including conditions of employment, freedom of association and social security', as stated in the convention. Notwithstanding this, Malaysia's management of its urban spaces for irregular migrants, whether they are refugees or trafficked individuals, is judged to be the worst in the region (Department of State 2012).

Challenges and opportunities for Malaysia?

From an economic viewpoint, Malaysia's immigration policy has some fundamental drawbacks. The state's easy access to and excessive reliance on cheap labour in key industries has discouraged innovation and upgrading in the country. The race-based quota system governing enrolment in universities and employment in the public sector has also led to emigration of talent. Thus, although Malaysia has actively promoted its services sector (including medical tourism), it is finding it difficult to compete with neighbouring countries like Singapore, despite programmes to lure Malaysian talent from overseas. Crucially, crackdowns on irregular immigrants are also straining Malaysia's finances and affecting the budget deficit. In January 2014, the Home Ministry estimated that 'administrative costs for housing 68,000 undocumented foreign workers total[led] about RM2.4 million', excluding medical expenses (Gangopadhyay 2014). Finally, Malaysia has misplaced its priorities. Instead of directing such inordinate amounts of energy to controlling and regulating migrant workers' movements, it could and should ensure these workers' rights under international conventions, echoed in Malaysian law.

Bibliography

Alyaa Alhadjri (2014) '68,000 undocumented migrants detained in 10 detention depots nationwide as at 6/1/2014?', *Network of Action for Migrants in Malaysia (NAMM)*, 22 January, available at http://networkofactionformigrantsnamm.blogspot.com.au/2014/01/68000-undocumented-migrants-detained-in.html (accessed 23 January 2014).

Andreas, P. (2001) 'Illicit globalization: myths, misconceptions, and historical lessons', *Political Science Quarterly*, 126(1): 403–25.

Asrul Hadi Abdullah Sani (2010) 'Foreign worker levy hike in 2011', *Malaysian Insider*, 20 May, available at www.themalaysianinsider.com/malaysia/article/foreign-worker-levy-hike-in-2011/ (accessed 12 May 2014).

Ayadurai, Dunston (1993) 'Malaysia', in Stephen Deery and Richard J. Mitchell (eds), *Labour Law and Industrial Relations in Asia: Eight Country Studies*, Melbourne: Longman Cheshire, pp. 61–95.

Department of State (2012) 'Malaysia (Tier 2 Watch List)', pp. 234–38, available at http://www.state.gov/documents/organization/192596.pdf (accessed 22 May 2014).

Devadason, Evelyn Shyamala and Chan Wai Meng (2011) 'A critical appraisal of policies and laws regulating migrant workers in Malaysia', available at www.wbiconpro.com/210-DEVADASON.pdf (accessed 12 May 2014).

Devadason, Evelyn Shyamala and Chan Wai Meng (2014) 'Policies and laws regulating migrant workers in Malaysia: a critical appraisal', *Journal of Contemporary Asia*, 44(1): 19–35.

Economic Times (2011) 'Over 2 million register with Malaysia's immigration office', *Economic Times*, 1 December, available at http://articles.economictimes.indiatimes.com/2011-12-01/news/30463178_1_amnesty-programme-illegal-immigrants-illegal-workers (accessed 23 November 2010).

Fernandez, Irene (2008) 'Recruitment and placement of migrant workers in Malaysia', paper presented at the Malaysian Bar Council Conference on Developing a Comprehensive Policy Framework for Migrant Labour, 18–19 February, Kuala Lumpur (typescript).

FIDH and Suaram (2008) *Undocumented Migrants and Refugees in Malaysia: Raids, Detention and Discrimination*, March, no. 489(2), Paris: FIDH and Kuala Lumpur: Suaram, available at www.fidh.org/IMG/pdf/MalaisieCONJ489eng.pdf (accessed 23 November 2010).

Gangopadhyay, Abhrajit (2014) 'Crackdown on illegal immigrants strains Malaysian finances', *Wall Street Journal*, 8 January.

Hector, Charles (2011) 'Migrant workers (documented) 2010 – 1,817,817 from Indonesia, Bangladesh, Nepal, Burma . . .', 5 August, available at http://charleshector.blogspot.com/2011/08/migrant-workersdocumented-2010-1817817.html (accessed 23 November 2011).

Hector, Charles (2014) 'Guan Eng's proposed discrimination of migrant workers disappointing', 6 January, available at http://charleshector.blogspot.com.au/2014/01/guan-engs-proposed-discrimination-of.html (accessed 12 May 2014).

Hill, Hal, Tham Siew Yean and Ragayah Haji Mat Zin (eds) (2012) *Malaysia's Development Challenges: Graduating from the Middle*, Abingdon: Routledge.

International Organization for Migration (IOM) (2008) *World Migration Report 2008 – Managing Labour Mobility in the Evolving Global Economy*, Geneva: International Organization for Migration, available at http://publications.iom.int/bookstore/free/WMR_1.pdf (accessed 22 May 2014).

Jones, Sidney (2000) *Making Money off Migrants: The Indonesian Exodus to Malaysia*, Wollongong: Asia Ltd and Center for Asia-Pacific Transformation Studies, University of Wollongong.

Kassim, A. (1987) 'The unwelcome guests: Indonesian immigrants and Malaysian public responses', *Southeast Asian Studies*, 25(2): 265–78.

Kaur, Amarjit (2004) *Wage Labour in Southeast Asia Since 1840: Globalisation, The International Division of Labour and Labour Transformations*, Basingstoke: Palgrave Macmillan.

Kaur, Amarjit (2006) 'Order (and disorder) at the border: mobility, international labour migration and border controls in Southeast Asia', in A. Kaur and Ian Metcalfe (eds), *Mobility, Labour Migration and Border Controls in Asia*, Basingstoke: Palgrave Macmillan, pp. 23–51

Kaur, Amarjit (2007) 'Migration matters in the Asia-Pacific region: immigration frameworks, knowledge workers and national policies', *International Journal on Multicultural Societies (IJMS)*, 9(2): 135–37.

Kaur, Amarjit (2008) 'International migration and governance in Malaysia: policy and performance', UNE Asia Centre referred e-publication, 22(2008): 4–18.

Kaur, Amarjit (2010) 'Labour migration trends and policy challenges in Southeast Asia', *Policy and Society*, 29: 385–97.

Kaur, Amarjit (2013a) 'International labour migration dynamics in Southeast Asia: migration and inequality', in Tanja Bastia (ed.), *Migration and Inequality*, London: Routledge, pp. 65–92.

Kaur, Amarjit (2013b) 'Migration and the refugee regime in Malaysia: implications for a regional solution', in Angus Francis and Rowena Maguire (eds), *Protection of Refugees and Displaced Persons in the Asia-Pacific Region*, Farnham: Ashgate, pp. 95–116.

Kaur, Amarjit (2014) 'Plantation systems, labour regimes and the state in Malaysia, 1900–2012', *Journal of Agrarian Change*, 14(2): 190–213.

Letchumanan, A. and Desiree Tresa Gasper (2011) '7000 workers registered in first three days', *The Star*, 16 July.

Malaysia Chronicle (2014) 'Crackdown on illegal immigrants begins', *Malaysia Chronicle*, 21 January.

Migration News (2008) 'Southeast Asia', 15(4), October, available at https://migration.ucdavis.edu/mn/more.php?id=3445_0_3_0 (accessed 22 May 2014).

Migration News (2013) 'Southeast Asia', 20(1), January, available at https://migration.ucdavis.edu/mn/more.php?id=3814_0_3_0 (accessed 22 May 2014).

Morgan, M. (1977) 'The rise and fall of Malayan trade unionism, 1945–50', in Mohamed Amin and Malcolm Caldwell (eds), *Malaya: The Making of a Neo-colony*, London: Spokesman.

Nah, Alice M. (2012) 'Globalisation, sovereignty and immigration control: the hierarchy of rights for migrant workers in Malaysia', *Asian Journal of Social Science*, 40(4): 486–508.

Ramasamy, P. (2001) 'Union of discord', *The Star*, 17 September.

Rani Rasiah (2014) 'CM's myopic view of migrant workers', *Free Malaysia Today*, 6 January, available at www.freemalaysiatoday.com/category/opinion/2014/01/06/cms-myopic-view-of-migrant-workers/ (accessed 8 January 2014).

Reuters (2014) 'Crackdown on illegal migrant workers in Malaysia', available at www.reuters.com/video/2014/01/21/crackdown-on-illegal-migrant-workers-in?videoId=276510367 (accessed 12 May 2014).

Saw Swee-Hock (1988) *The Population of Peninsular Malaysia*, Singapore: Singapore University Press.

Shamsuddin Barden, Haji (2006) 'Terms and conditions of employment (foreign workers)/unionism', paper presented at the LAWASIA Labour Law Conference, Kuala Lumpur, 10–11 August (typescript).

Sreenevasan, A. (2006) 'Obligations of labour contractors and agents', unpublished paper presented at the LAWASIA Labour Law Conference on Labour Migration: International and National Progress, Kuala Lumpur, August.

Suaram (Suara Rakyat Malaysia) (2006) *Malaysia Human Rights Report 2005 Civil and Political Rights*, Petaling Jaya: Suaram.

Talent Corp Malaysia (n.d.) 'Residence Pass for Talent (RP-T)', available at www.talentcorp.com.my/expatriates/residence-pass/ (accessed 12 May 2014).

Tenaganita (2007) Fact Finding Report: Outsourcing in Labour or Trafficking in Migrant Labour, April–May (typescript).

US Government Department of Labor (2012) '2012 response to allegations of forced labour in the oil palm and textile industries. Act 1957', February 2012, retrieved from www.dol.gov/ilab/programs/ocft/tvpra/20120203.pdf (accessed 10 April 2013).

World Bank (1995) *Malaysia: Meeting Labor Needs, More Workers and Better Skills*, Washington DC: World Bank.

World Bank (2013) 'Immigration in Malaysia: assessment of its economic effects and a review of the policy and system', available at www.knomad.org/Annex/immigration-in-Malaysia (accessed 20 June 2013).

18

Mainstreaming environment and sustainable development policies

Adnan A. Hezri

As a policy problem, sustainable development (or sustainability) is complex, unstructured and multilayered. It seeks to reconcile the ecological, social and economic dimensions of development, now and into the future. As such, the task of implementing sustainable development is somehow more comprehensive and demanding, and therefore more challenging, than implementing conventional development models.

Malaysia is no exception to the difficulty of implementing development from such a holistic framework. Over the last five decades, Malaysia has undergone rapid economic and social change, a process which is still continuing. While impressive economic achievement has advanced human development and reduced poverty, the pursuit of socio-economic progress has been accompanied by an unprecedented rate of change in the natural environment (Aiken and Leigh 1992; Kathirithamby-Wells 2005; Vincent and Ali 1997). This chapter describes Malaysia's approach in confronting the multifaceted challenges of sustainable development by surveying four thematic policy objectives. These are conserving the environment, merging environment and development, combating climate change, and building a green economy.

Conserving the environment

The earliest environmentalist thought revolved around forests and their preservation (Barton 2002). The forests are considered a wilderness area whose conservation is deemed important for scientific, aesthetic and economic values. The push for conservation was mainly sparked by rapid forest clearance for industrialisation in both the developed and developing countries in the early twentieth century.

By the late 1960s, the issue of environmental pollution and waste arising from industrial processes made the dramatic leap to the top of the political agenda in industrialised and industrialising countries. This shift set in motion the enactment of pollution control legislation to manage the release of chemicals into the natural environment. Malaysia has responded to calls both for nature protection and for pollution control.

Forests and wildlife protection

Until well into the nineteenth century, almost the whole of the Malay Peninsula, Sabah and Sarawak was covered in tropical forests (Aiken and Leigh 1992). These forests are a reservoir of biological diversity of rich flora and fauna (Shuttleworth 1981; Whitmore 1984), with more than 25,000 plant species (van Steenis 1971). Apart from serving as a habitat for wildlife, Malaysia's rainforests are a source of timber and other products – such as rattan and medicinal plants – that support the livelihoods of numerous communities. In view of its exceptional species diversity and richness, Malaysia is currently recognised as one of the world's twelve mega-diverse countries, where special attention is needed to arrest habitat loss (Myers 1988).

The country's rich natural endowment gives it a unique position on the global map of sustainable development discourse. Oftentimes, its rich biodiversity creates tension between conservation and development. The rapid loss of Malaysian rainforests over the past century has been closely linked to economic development. Not only were large areas of forested land cleared to make way for agriculture and rubber and oil palm plantations, but logging intensified in response to increasing demand for timber from overseas markets, especially after the 1970s. The area of arable land increased fivefold between 1900 and 1950 as forested land gave way to agriculture and rubber plantations, especially during the rubber boom of the early 1900s (UNEP 2002). New roads, tracks and settlements accompanied the development of plantations, which by 1940 covered 11 percent of Peninsular Malaysia (Aiken and Leigh 1992: 55). By the mid-1950s, rural development was being pursued with new vigour, involving ever larger conversions of forest.

The British colonial government established a professional forest service in 1901 with the creation of the Forestry Department. The Department was tasked to manage commercial forestry and to administer forest reservation areas for future timber production. The first wildlife reserve in Peninsular Malaysia was the Chior Wildlife Reserve in Kuala Kangsar, Perak, established in 1903 under the Wild Animals and Protection Enactment for the state of Perak. These policy instruments were put in place to control the rapid loss of forests in the early twentieth century. Following independence, the federal government established the National Forestry Council (NFC) in 1971 to coordinate development of the forestry sector in all the states. The National Forestry Policy was formulated and endorsed by the NFC and the National Land Council in August 1977. In 1972, the government passed legislation for fauna protection, the Protection of Wildlife Act. The Act had identified 700 mammals and bird species under 'totally protected' and 'protected' categories. This was an important decision because wildlife was increasingly being seen as pests by planters and therefore hunted and killed indiscriminately. The Act empowers the Department of Wildlife and National Parks (DWNP) to be responsible for the management and protection of Wildlife Reserves gazetted by the state governments under the Act, as well as those created under previous state ordinances, and to promote fauna protection on public as well as private land.

Despite legal and administrative consolidations in the 1970s, the magnitude of environmental impacts continued to worsen. Inevitably, the tension between short-term economic gains and conservation strategies for long-term productivity became clearer. As a result, civil society organisations began to voice their concerns nationally and internationally, marking the start of the non-governmental environmental movement and 'environmentalism' in Malaysia (see Consumer's Association of Penang 1978; Sham 1993; Singh 1979).

Pollution control

Apart from timber resources, the forests also provide ecosystem services, such as maintaining a steady supply of fresh water, protecting soil from erosion and nutrient loss, regulating local climates and serving as carbon sinks. The ecological effects of forest clearing include high sediment loads in rivers from soil erosion and the pollution of river systems with effluent discharged from rubber and palm oil mills. These pollutants have a high organic content, and have been estimated to account for 90 percent of the total industrial pollution load of local rivers (Abdullah 1995).

Guided by the idea of limits, the federal government formulated a legal framework for pollution control, the Environmental Quality Act (EQA) 1974. This statutory provision was supported by the following actions: the creation of a national environmental agency, the Department of Environment, and a council of environmental experts, the Environmental Quality Council, in 1975; and the establishment of an environment portfolio in 1976. By global comparison then, Malaysia can be considered as one of the pioneers in environmental policy institutionalisation (see Hezri and Hasan 2006).

From late 1977, in response to a growing pollution load, the Environmental Quality Act 1974 was amended several times, to provide more specific regulations for the implementation of its general framework. These amendments included sectoral command-and-control regulations for prevalent pollutants and discharge fees, applied since 1978 to contain water pollution from palm oil mills (Panayotou 1994). Regulation remained the main policy instrument under the EQA, amplified with, for instance, controls on noise pollution in 1988, scheduled toxic wastes in 1989 and marine pollution in 1993.

Despite its laudable efforts, the effectiveness of the DOE in enforcing the EQA was curtailed by its small operational budget, limited human and technical resources (only nine officers in 1977) and poor support from outside the bureaucracy. By 1985, however, the number of professionals had grown to fifty-five (Sharp 1983) and in recent years, it has grown to over one thousand. Enforcement has been complicated by the fact that while federal standards are set and water quality monitored by the DOE, enforcement has been left mostly to the states (Lowry and Carpenter 1985). Nevertheless, despite such shortcomings, some pollution problems have been satisfactorily curbed. Revenue figures from 'polluters pay principle' licensing indicate a decline in effluent discharge of 88 percent within twelve years for palm oil wastes, and 44 percent within ten years for rubber wastes (Sham 1997: 21).

Merging environment and development

The publication of *Our Common Future*[1] by the World Commission on Environment and Development (WCED) in 1987 resulted in sustainable development's becoming a powerful concept in public and political discussions. Even though lacking 'any official status' (Pallemaerts 2003: 279), the Report had more 'influence on global policy-making than the formal outcome of its consideration by an international process within the United Nations Environment Program, Governing Council and the United Nations General Assembly' (Pallemaerts 2003: 279).

Following the Report, the focus of environmentalism across the world shifted from crisis to a reform agenda for sustainable development. The Report suggested that economic growth can continue with a reduced impact on the environment. Decoupling development and environmental impact was then launched as a policy focus especially in terms of ecological modernisation. The prescription is widely known, that is, sustainable development demands better policy integration. Malaysia has been trying since the 1980s to integrate principles of sustainability into its form and function of government.

Environmental impact assessment

One of the most widely accepted and integrated tools for evaluating physical development projects is the environmental impact assessment (EIA) mechanism. EIA reports offer predictions of how the environment is expected to change if certain alternative actions are implemented. After many years of discussions, the requirement of conducting EIA reports in Malaysia was legally recognised in Section 34A of the Environmental Quality Act 1974, Amendment 1985. Prior to this amendment, thirty-nine EIA reports were submitted to the DOE on a voluntary basis (Malaysia 1986). Detailing the specifications for nineteen categories of activities requiring mandatory EIA, the EIA Order 1987 was gazetted and came into effect in April 1988. Between 1988 and 1995, it was reported that a total of 1,705 projects requiring EIA were monitored by the EIA Unit in the DOE (Vun and Latiff 1999). Even though the EIA process was introduced as a preventive approach to environmental management, its efficacy as a tool in actual practice is somewhat questionable. Problems associated with its implementation include (Memon 2000; Nor 1991): inaccuracy of predictions, lack of follow-up audits, ineffective devolution to state governments, tending to accommodate projects already approved rather than force changes in engineering plans and designs, and limited accessibility of EIA reports to allow public scrutiny.

More importantly, the input of ecological knowledge in many of these EIA reports has been inadequate and in many cases, inaccurate, as shown in a study of EIA for coastal resort development projects (Vun *et al.* 2004). Only 27 percent of the EIA reports reviewed were found to be satisfactory in their methods and emphasis given to studies of the ecology of the local area and areas adjacent to the project location. In addition, few EIAs have been prepared for large-scale logging, with only two out of 160 EIAs received between April 1988 and December 1990 originating from the forestry sector (Cooke 1999).

Environmental policy integration

Broadly, environmental policy integration entails the incorporation of environmental objectives into non-environmental policy sectors. Lafferty and Hovden (2003: 8–9) defined environmental policy integration from two dimensions. The first involves the 'incorporation of environmental objectives into all stages of policymaking in non-environmental policy sectors'. Such development is observable in Malaysia with the incorporation of environmental objectives in sectoral policies and plans such as the National Spatial Policy, National Mineral Policy, and Third National Agriculture Policy. The incorporation of environmental objectives into non-environmental agencies and organisations has also flourished. The Department of Irrigation and Drainage, for example, expanded its focus on concepts such as integrated water resource management (Sharizaila *et al.* 2003).

The second dimension of environmental policy integration necessitates an attempt 'to minimise contradictions between environmental and sectoral policies but with greater priority granted to environmental objectives' (Lafferty and Hovden 2003: 9). This dimension is yet to become evident as a high priority for Malaysia. The Third Outline Perspective Plan (2001–2010) maintains that the nation will pursue 'environmentally sustainable development to reinforce long term growth' (Malaysia 2001). As in many countries, economic growth is still the overarching policy goal.

A major cabinet reshuffle in March 2004 revived the imperative of policy integration. The new Ministry of Natural Resources and Environment (NRE) was established as an outcome of a comprehensive reform by the then new Prime Minister Abdullah Badawi to deliver better services for the population. Compared with the former set-up of the Ministry of Science, Technology and the Environment, the NRE tackles policy fragmentation by combining more environmental portfolios under one ministry: forest management; irrigation and drainage management; wildlife management; minerals management; environmental conservation; marine park management; land management and administration; land surveying; and mapping processing.

In recent years, a number of integrated policy statements have been released, marking a step in the right direction of policy integration. The integrated sectoral policies include the National Biodiversity Policy (1998), National Policy on Climate Change (2010) and National Water Resources Policy (2012). Together, these policies underpin the choice of policy tools, such as voluntary approaches, information and awareness and tools, economic instruments, direct government expenditure and command-and-control mechanisms.

While efforts have been made to integrate the three pillars of sustainable development as well as to translate the international agenda into the local context, there is still insufficient convergence among various policy frameworks, both between levels of governments as well as among sectors. Indeed, there is a lack of clarity regarding what sustainable development actually means for government policy. This lack of clarity can mean that it is not apparent where the responsibility for sustainable development resides.

Combating climate change

By the turn of the century, stronger evidence of global warming had been made available by scientists and international organisations. Average global warming of more than 2°C from preindustrial levels could have dangerous climatic consequences (Schellnhuber *et al.* 2006). Soon after, climate change became firmly established as a critical global concern. Scientists argue that climate change could impede nations' abilities to find and achieve sustainable development pathways (Robinson *et al.* 2006). The needed solution is to mitigate greenhouse gas emissions to adapt to the inevitable impacts of climate change.

On the 2010 Climate Change Performance Index, which rates the emission levels, emission trends and climate policies of the world's fifty-seven largest carbon dioxide emitters, Malaysia appeared in the bottom-ranked group of countries, alongside countries like Canada, Australia, the United States and Saudi Arabia (Burck *et al.* 2009).

Climate change will affect all economic sectors and levels of society in Malaysia, and will also have a multiplier effect exacerbating environmental problems. As such, the country needs to embark on a path of climate-resilient development, both to respond to these impacts and to reduce Malaysia's contribution to greenhouse gas emissions. Disaster risk reduction, ensuring adaptation and meeting the economic and social costs of increasing risks will be major challenges for the future.

Energy issues occupy a central place in the debate on climate change and sustainable development (Najam and Cleveland 2003). Malaysia has been introducing incremental reforms in its energy policy to respond to the sustainability principles. The Five Fuel Policy was formulated under the 8th Malaysia Plan (2001–2005) to encourage the utilisation of renewable resources such as biomass, solar, mini hydro, etc. as an additional source for electricity generation. This policy was introduced in 2001 to encourage the utilisation of renewable energy (RE) resources for power generation. To fast-track the implementation of the Five Fuel

Policy, the Small Renewable Energy Power Program (SREP) was introduced in the same year. This programme allowed utilisation of all types of RE sources, including biomass, biogas, municipal solid waste, solar, mini hydro and wind. The low take-up rate[2] of RE development under the SREP, however, led to the formulation of the Renewable Energy Act 2010 which provides for the establishment and implementation of a Feed-in-Tariff (FiT) system to catalyse the generation of renewable energy. The FiT scheme encourages adoption of RE sources by bridging the gap between the cost of fossil fuel and renewable sources. The Act ensures participants have guaranteed access to the grid, through long-term contracts to sell electricity to power distributors. A new agency, the Sustainable Energy Development Authority (SEDA), was established to administer the Act.

In 2009, at the Climate Change Conference in Copenhagen (or COP 15), Prime Minister Najib Razak announced a conditional voluntary target of 40 percent reduction in the emissions intensity of Malaysia's Real GDP by 2020, measured against a 2005 baseline. Achieving this aspirational target in a rapidly developing society like Malaysia will require deeper energy reforms in the structure and operations of its institutions. Apart from diversifying the fuel mix to include alternative energy, Malaysia needs policy measures that include improving demand management and rationalising energy pricing and subsidy structures. Malaysia is studying the option of adding 2 gigawatts of nuclear capacity on the peninsula in 2021 or after. This quantity amounts to less than 10 percent of Malaysia's total generation capacity in 2008; as such, this addition would not drastically improve energy diversity at the national level.

In addition, there is a need to make major improvements in energy efficiency and conservation, in both the supply and demand sectors. Initiatives that have been undertaken to improve energy efficiency are categorised into three sectors, namely, industry, commercial and residential. For the industry sector, enforcement of the Efficient Management of Electrical Energy Regulations 2008 under the Electricity Supply Act will ensure that any installation which consumes more than 3 million units (kWh) of electricity over a period of six months will be required to engage an electrical energy manager responsible for efficient utilisation of energy in the installation. As for the commercial sector, the government of Malaysia has taken several proactive measures in promoting energy efficiency through the construction and operation of low-energy buildings, such as the Low Energy Office (LEO) building of the Ministry of Energy, Green Technology and Water, opened in 2004, and the Green Energy Office (GEO) of Malaysia Green Technology Corporation (MGTC) in 2008. In the residential sector, EE initiatives include the introduction of 'Star Labelling' in 2002, with five-star products being the most efficient and one-star being the least efficient. Finally, the Malaysian government seeks to mitigate demand growth by gradually moving towards market pricing for oil and gas supply by 2016. According to a recent simulation, the liberalisation of gas pricing would increase gas prices by 30 percent above the regulated price by 2020 and another 4 percent by 2030; it would also reduce demand by 4 percent (compared with demand projection absent price liberalisation).

Building a green economy

The green economy or green growth model is largely a reaction to the 'Triple F' crises (fuel, food and finance) which struck the globe from 2006 to 2009. It demands a sharp reduction in carbon intensity in order to revitalise the ailing world economy on a more sustainable basis. Across the developed world, there is increased public investment not only in energy conservation, but also in urban public transport, housing rehabilitation and organic agriculture

(United Nations 2011). The United Nations Environment Programme report *Towards a Green Economy* (UNEP 2011: 2) presents a working definition of a green economy 'as one that results in improved human well-being and social equity, while significantly reducing environmental risks and ecological scarcities'. For UNEP, a green economy is 'one which is low carbon, resource efficient and socially inclusive'.

Consistent with international trends, Malaysia has also introduced a systemic architecture to respond to the green economy agenda. This action was necessary largely because Malaysia's per capita carbon dioxide emissions from fuel combustion had increased by 32 percent from 2000 to 2006 (United Nations Country Team 2011). This figure is higher than those for Indonesia, the Philippines and Thailand, although lower than for some developed economies. Since 2009, a hotchpotch of policy statements and instruments has been introduced to loosely constitute Malaysia's green economy objectives and the means to achieve them.

In line with international trends, the country has embraced the goal of a low-carbon economy, which is dependent on the development of green technology and its adoption across all spheres of life. In 2009, Malaysia established the basic architecture for responding to a low-carbon agenda by incorporating the green technology portfolio into a newly established Ministry of Energy, Green Technology and Water. The central role of green technology was emphasised by the release shortly afterwards of a National Green Technology Policy and the restructuring of the National Energy Centre as the Malaysian Green Technology Corporation, tasked to implement the new policy area. The administration of Prime Minister Najib Tun Razak clearly aims to create a policy environment that will attract innovators and users of green technology. The policy was launched within one hundred days of the ministry's being established.

Also in 2009, Malaysia announced a new development policy framework called the New Economic Model (NEM). It outlined the three-pronged goals of inclusiveness, high income and sustainability in powering the nation to graduate to high-income status by 2020. Green technology is earmarked as an important driver for the twin goals of high income and sustainability. Evidence of convergence among the three goals includes Malaysia's success in attracting US$4 billion worth of foreign direct investment to the solar photovoltaic industry (MEGTW 2011). The emphasis on green technology is expected to increase the GDP contribution from green business from the current 2 percent to 8 percent by 2020. This growth would involve the creation of about 500,000 green jobs by 2020, from 95,000 green jobs in 2009 (Hezri and Ghazali 2011).

Conclusion

By addressing the objectives of combating climate change and building a green economy, Malaysia is acting as a responsible citizen of the planet. More urgent, however, is that Malaysia put more effort into dealing with the policy challenge of conserving the environment. Urbanisation, population and industrialisation pressures continue to threaten the remaining natural areas and environmental quality in Malaysia. In 2011, the Department of Environment reported that thirty-nine rivers were polluted, 3,177 open burning cases had been lodged, and about twelve illegal disposals of scheduled wastes had still been committed by unscrupulous offenders (DOE 2012). Throughout 2012 and 2013, environmental degradation received wide press coverage in mainstream news outlets in Malaysia.

Despite the government's constellation of policies and programmes on the environment, in reality it is extremely hard to bridge the gap between stated policy goals and practical strategies to achieve those goals. Inevitably, the gap had allowed environmental degradation to persist against the background of increasing land scarcity. In response to the increasing number of threatened forests, a coalition of twenty-four non-governmental organisations (NGOs) jointly released *Eco-Manifesto 2013: Forests, People and Sustainability in Malaysia* (Transparency International-Malaysia 2013). This manifesto, which declared a national deforestation and forest degradation 'eco-emergency', was launched before Malaysia's thirteenth General Election in May 2013, in the presence of both ruling and opposition political parties.

Scholars and scientists alike echo the sense of urgency to address regressive environmental conditions with new policy instruments (Aiken and Leigh 2011; Chan 2012; Anuar 2012; Khalid *et al.* 2013). For them, residual natural areas should be considered as the 'critical natural capital' essential for the functioning of life-support systems, and for that reason must be duly protected. To accommodate concurrent demands for human settlements, industries and conservation, scarce land resources require a better trade-off mechanism whose foundation is one of perception – that Malaysia is no longer the resource-abundant nation that it once was.

To deal with the situation of 'new scarcity', a new institutional design is needed, one which is based on integrated policy- and decision-making. At the risk of stating the obvious, policy formulation alone will not help in prompting institutional change. It is imperative to move from articulation of policy statements to an implementation stage which is backed up by adequate resources.

Notes

1 Also known as the Brundtland Report after the WCED's chairperson, Gro Harlem Brundtland.
2 After almost nine years since its launch, only ten SREP projects are in operation, amounting to 56.7 MW install capacity.

Bibliography

Abdul Rani Abdullah (1995) 'Environmental pollution in Malaysia: trends and prospects', *Trends in Analytical Chemistry*, 14(5): 191–98.

Aiken, S. Robert and Colin H. Leigh (1992) *Vanishing Rain Forests: The Ecological Transition in Malaysia*, New York: Oxford University Press.

Aiken, S. Robert and Colin H. Leigh (2011) 'In the way of development: indigenous land-rights issues in Malaysia', *The Geographical Review*, 101(4): 471–96

Anuar, Mustafa K. (2012) 'Reporting the environment: human rights, development, and journalism in Malaysia', *Asia Pacific Media Educator*, 22(2): 253–62.

Barton, Gregory Allen (2002) *Empire Forestry and the Origins of Environmentalism*, Cambridge: Cambridge University Press.

Burck, Jan, Christoph Bals and Verena Rossow (2009) *The Climate Change Performance Index: Results 2010*, Bonn and Brussels: Germanwatch and Climate Action Network.

Chan Ngai Weng (2012) 'Managing urban rivers and water quality in Malaysia for sustainable water resources', *International Journal of Water Resources Development*, 28(2): 343–54.

Consumer's Association of Penang (1978) *The Malaysian Environment in Crisis: Selections from Press Cuttings*, Penang: Consumer's Association of Penang.

Cooke, Fadzilah Majid (1999) *The Challenge of Sustainable Forests: Forest Resource Policy in Malaysia, 1970–1995*, Sydney: Allen & Unwin.

Department of Environment (DOE) (2012) *Environmental Quality Report 2011*, Kuala Lumpur: Department of Environment Malaysia.

Hezri, Adnan A. and Hasan Mohd Nordin (2006) 'Towards sustainable development? The evolution of environmental policy in Malaysia', *Natural Resources Forum*, 30(1): 37–50.

Hezri, Adnan A. and Rospidah Ghazali (2011) *A Fair Green Economy? Studies of Agriculture, Energy, and Waste Initiatives in Malaysia*, Occasional Paper 2 Social Dimensions of Green Economy and Sustainable Development, Geneva: United Nations Research Institute for Social Development.

Kathirithamby-Wells, Jayamalar (2005) *Nature and Nation: Forests and Development in Peninsular Malaysia*, Honolulu: University of Hawai'i Press.

Lafferty, Illiam M. and Eivind Hovden (2003) 'Environmental policy integration: towards an analytical framework', *Environmental Politics*, 12(3): 1–22.

Lowry, Kem and Richard A. Carpenter (1985) 'Institutionalizing sustainable development: experiences in five countries', *Environment Impact Assessment Review*, 5(3): 239–54.

Malaysia (1986) *The Fifth Malaysia Plan, 1986–1990*, Kuala Lumpur: National Printing Department.

Malaysia (2001) *The Third Outline Perspective Plan, 2001–2010*, Kuala Lumpur: Government Printer.

Memon, Ali (2000) 'Devolution of environmental regulation: environmental impact assessment in Malaysia', *Impact Assessment and Project Appraisal*, 18: 283–93.

Ministry of Energy, Green Technology and Water (MEGTW) (2011) *Green Impact: Low Carbon Green Growth*, Putrajaya: Ministry of Energy, Green Technology and Water.

Myers, Norman (1988) 'Threatened biotas: "hot spots" in tropical forests', *The Environmentalist*, 8(3): 187–208.

Najam, Adil and Cutler J. Cleveland (2003) 'Energy and sustainable development at global environmental summits: an evolving agenda', *Environment, Development and Sustainability*, 5(1–2): 117–38.

Nor, Y.M. (1991) 'Environmental policy making: problems and perspectives in Malaysia', *Environment Impact Assessment Review*, 11: 129–42.

Pallemaerts, Mark (2003) 'Is multilateralism the future? Sustainable development or globalisation as a "comprehensive vision of the future of humanity"', *Environment, Development and Sustainability*, 5: 275–95.

Panayotou, Theodore (1994) *Economic Instruments for Environmental Management and Sustainable Development*, United Nations Environmental Programme's Consultative Expert Group Meeting on the Use and Application of Economic Policy Instruments for Environmental Management and Sustainable Development, Nairobi.

Rasyikah Md Khalid, Suhaimi Ab Rahman and Mazlin Mokhtar (2013) 'Legal perspectives on development policies for sustainability of water in Malaysia', *Sustainable Development*, 21(3): 144–51.

Robinson, John, M. Bradley, P. Busby, D. Connor, A. Murray, B. Sampson and W. Soper (2006) 'Climate change and sustainable development: realising the opportunity', *Ambio*, 35(1): 2–8.

Schellnhuber, Hans Joachim, Wolfgang Cramer, Nebojsa Nakicenovic, Tom Wigley and Gary Yohe (eds) (2006) *Avoiding Dangerous Climate Change*, New York: Cambridge University Press.

Sham Sani (1993) 'Economic development and environmental management in Malaysia', *New Zealand Geographer*, 49(2): 64–68.

Sham Sani (1997) *Environmental Quality Act 1974: Then and Now*, Kuala Lumpur: Lestari.

Sharizaila, A., Low Kwai Sim and S. Zakaria (eds) (2003) *Capacity Building for Integrated Water Resources Management in Southeast Asia*, Kuala Lumpur: Department of Irrigation and Drainage.

Sharp, T. (1983) 'Malaysia's environment in danger', *Ambio*, 12: 275–76.

Shuttleworth, Charles (1981) *Malaysia's Green and Timeless World: An Account of the Flora, Fauna and Indigenous Peoples of the Forests of Malaysia*, Kuala Lumpur: Heinemann Asia.

Singh, Gurmit (1979) 'Some environmental threats in Malaysia', *Environmental Conservation*, 6(3): 242–43.

Transparency International–Malaysia (2013) *Eco-Manifesto 2013: Forests, People and Sustainability in Malaysia*, Petaling Jaya: TI–M.

United Nations (2011) *World Economic and Social Survey 2011: The Great Green Technological Transformation*, New York: United Nations Department of Economic and Social Affairs.

United Nations Country Team (2011) *Malaysia: The Millennium Development Goals at 2010*, Kuala Lumpur: UN Country Team and Economic Planning Unit, Prime Minister's Department.

United Nations Environment Programme (UNEP) (2002) *Global Environment Outlook 3*, New York: United Nations Environmental Programme.

United Nations Environment Programme (UNEP) (2011) *Towards a Green Economy: Pathways to Sustainable Development and Poverty Eradication, A Synthesis for Policy Makers*, New York: United Nations Environmental Programme.

van Steenis, C. (1971) 'Plant conservation in Malaysia', *Bulletin du Jardin Botanique National Belge*, 41: 189–202.

Vincent, Jeffrey R. and Rozali M. Ali (1997) *Environment and Development in a Resource-Rich Economy: Malaysia Under the New Economic Policy*, Cambridge: Harvard University Press.

Vun, L.W. and A. Latiff (1999) 'Preliminary ecological impact assessment and environmental impact assessment for coastal resort development in Malaysia', *Impact Assessment and Project Appraisal*, 17: 133–40.

Vun Leong-Wan, Abdul Latiff and Mohd Nordin (2004) 'Review of ecological input in preliminary EIAs for coastal resort development projects in Malaysia', *Journal of Environmental Assessment Policy and Management*, 6(3): 385–401.

Whitmore, Timothy Charles (1984) *Tropical Rainforests of the Far East*, London: Oxford University Press, available at www.unep.org/greeneconomy (accessed 27 September 2011).

19

Rural transformations

Eric C. Thompson[1]

As Malaysia has rapidly developed and urbanised over the past fifty years, so has rural Malaysia seen rapid transformations. These changes involve all aspects of rural Malaysia – economic, political, social and others. This chapter provides an overview of these rural transformations, particularly with respect to the changing topics of rural-based research conducted by social scientists.

In the mid-twentieth century, a great deal of attention was given to rural development, in keeping with a broader context of a development paradigm in Malaysia and elsewhere in the post-colonial, developing and so-called 'third' world. Rural development and transformation were primarily understood in terms of agricultural development (Sivalingam 1993). More recently, rural-based research has moved away from development and toward paradigms of rural transformation and agrarian transition. Again, these shifts parallel and fall within broader changes in and beyond Malaysia.

The first section of this chapter addresses the need to broaden considerations of rural Malaysia beyond those concerned with Malay society alone. The Malay *kampung* (village) has provided the archetype for rurality in Malaysia for a century or more of social science scholarship. Yet, rural society encompasses a broad range of Malays, non-Malays and increasingly non-Malaysians. A view of rural transformations needs to bring these communities into the account.

Subsequent sections turn to considerations of the economic, social and political transformations taking place in rural Malaysia. While a reasonable body of research exists, particularly from decades around the mid-twentieth century, attention to rural society in Malaysia has to some extent dwindled. Although a few excellent studies provided us with insights into contemporary rural Malaysia, there are significant gaps in our knowledge, particularly with respect to local, rural social change and the dynamics of local, rural politics.

Rural society: Malay and non-Malay

As Zawawi Ibrahim has argued, research on rural society in Malaysia has been dominated by attention to rural Malay society (Zawawi 1996). Malay *kampung* are the archetype of traditional rurality in Malaysia (Thompson 2007). Traditional and transitional Malay rural society has been examined from a variety of political, economic and sociological perspectives in twentieth-century social science literature. Non-Malay rural dwellers in Malaysia, with some exception for those in Sarawak and Sabah, have often been marginal to and represented in the social science literature and in popular imagination through relatively narrow, one-dimensional perspectives. As Zawawi (1996) argues, until recently, research on Orang Asli (the most common term for indigenous non-Malays on the Peninsula) has been cast in terms of primitive culture, analysed in terms of 'tribal' rather than 'agrarian' issues, thus excluding them from significant theorisation of rural, agrarian transformations. Similarly, other non-Malays have been at the periphery of studies of agrarian transformations in Malaysia, including Indians and Chinese as well as newer immigrants from Indonesia, Thailand, Myanmar, the Philippines and elsewhere.

In many places, Orang Asli on the Peninsula and various groups in Sarawak and Sabah have been subject to resettlement schemes, both to encourage settlement of formerly mobile, swidden-farming populations as well as to move them off land claimed for other purposes (Rusaslina 2013: 279–81; Zawawi 1996: 187–96). The most high profile of the latter cases include resettlement of Iban villages to make way for the controversial Bakun Dam in Sarawak and the displacement of Orang Asli villages for construction of the new Kuala Lumpur International Airport (Bunnell and Nah 2004). Eighty-five percent of Orang Asli live in rural areas, and more than other groups, they have been left behind in Malaysia's economic development projects (Rusaslina 2013: 267). Orang Asli have been treated as much as problems of administration and governance as they have as a set of citizens on whose behalf the government should function (Rusaslina 2013: 278–81). In the 1950s and 1960s, managing Orang Asli populations was treated as a security concern, as they were considered possible recruits for the Malayan Communist Party. From the 1970s onward, the main thrust of government and non-governmental interventions has been toward assimilation and Islamisation (ibid.; Nobuta 2009).

Beyond Orang Asli on the Peninsula and other indigenous groups in Sarawak and Sabah, even less attention has been given to rural Indians, Chinese and others. Malaysia's population of Indian origin traces largely to migrants who came under the aegis of British colonial authorities, as plantation workers and colonial civil servants, creating a split between working-class 'estate' (plantation) Indians and urban-based professionals, which continues to resonate into the present. Research on Indian communities in Malaysia, which is less common than scholarship on the Malay or Chinese populations, has largely been urban-based (e.g. Willford 2006; Baxstrom 2008).

Chinese are also largely absent from rural-based scholarship. In part, this bias reflects the extensive resettlement of Chinese out of rural areas and into towns during the 1950s and 1960s in an effort to cut off Chinese support to the Malayan Communist Party operating in the jungles and countryside. While Chinese are important traders and brokers of agricultural commodities, they are largely otherwise absent from the agrarian economy and rural society outside of small market towns. De Koninck and Ahmat (2012: 58) note, though, that with the scaling up and gradual consolidation of agriculture in areas such as the Kedah rice belt, some Chinese entrepreneurs have become more directly involved in agriculture as relatively large-scale farm operators.

Perhaps the most neglected population, at least with respect to research on rural social change, has been newer immigrants from Indonesia, southern Thailand, Myanmar, the Philippines and elsewhere. De Koninck and Ahmat (2012: 65–66) argue that these groups constitute the new rural poor in Malaysia, doing the labour and underwriting the profits of Malay family farms, whose owners and family members are engaged in more lucrative, urban-based employment elsewhere. Their presence is essential, yet economically and socially underappreciated with respect to both large- and small-scale rural projects.

Despite the increasing sophistication of social science analysis and research, by local and foreign researchers alike, greater integration of analysis of rural transformations across non-Malay and Malay communities would be desirable. The following sections of this chapter turn to a review of the work that has been done in terms of economy, society and politics in rural Malaysia in the more than five decades since the country's independence from British colonialism. While most of the work has focused on the transformation of rural Malay society, as argued here, it is important to be aware that non-Malays have been subject to and involved in many of the same forces and changes (see De Koninck *et al.* 2011; Ishikawa 2010; Lunkapis 2013; Zawawi 2001, 2008; Zawawi and NoorShah 2012).

Economics: agrarian transition

Into the mid-twentieth century, analysis of rural economics tended to focus on village-level subsistence agriculture and smallholder cash-cropping. Anthropologists and sociologists produced numerous monographs on kinship-oriented agrarian production (e.g. Bailey 1983; Banks 1983; Carsten 1997; Firth 1946; Firth 1966; Kuchiba *et al.* 1979; Peletz 1988; Scott 1985; Tsubouchi 2001), small-scale rural industries (Maznah 1996), rural development (Wilder 1982; Wilson 1967) and agrarian transitions to capitalism (De Koninck 1992; Guinness 1992; Halim 1992; Jomo 1986; Rutten 2003; Wan 1988; Wong 1987; Zawawi 1998). Scholarly interest in detailed attention to local, rural economic relations of production and consumption seems to have greatly declined if not altogether disappeared, accompanying a general decline of the peasantry in Malaysia and elsewhere in Southeast Asia (Elson 1997).

Up to the mid-twentieth century, rural Malaysia was predominantly marked by peasant economies of agricultural smallholders, most of whom were Malay. The high-colonial period of the late nineteenth and early twentieth centuries also saw the rise of large-scale plantation or 'estate' agriculture (Overton 1994). Such estate agriculture, cultivating cash crops, especially palm oil and rubber, remains a significant part of the rural landscape. Palm oil in particular is cultivated on a vast scale. These estates were successfully nationalised in the process of decolonialisation. Rather than nationalising these ventures through force or political seizure, in the late 1970s and 1980s Malaysian government-backed concerns bought out the British companies. In at least one case, this was done through a hostile, though market-authorised take-over. By the early 2000s, the major British concerns of Guthrie, Sime Darby and Golden Hope had been consolidated under a single, Malaysian-owned conglomerate.

Peasant agriculture, oriented toward subsistence and based primarily on rice cultivation, dramatically declined if not altogether disappeared over the course of the late twentieth century. From the early 1970s onward, under the New Economic Policy (NEP), sustained efforts were made to reduce poverty, which has been seen as mainly a rural phenomenon in Malaysia (Ragayah 2013: 35). Across Malaysia, absolute poverty has fallen dramatically, from 52.4 percent in 1970 to 3.8 percent in 2009 (ibid.: 33–35). In a recent review, Ragayah (2013) argues that while the focus of government efforts was on *in situ* rural development, urban employment was more effective in reducing rural poverty than were government rural development programmes. While the latter did have a positive impact in reducing absolute poverty in rural areas, they frequently if inadvertently exacerbated relative poverty and income inequality (ibid.: 56).

Government-led rural development programmes, nevertheless, have had a sustained and transformative effect on rural modes of production. Major agrarian land development took place under the Federal Land Development Authority (FELDA) and significant land consolidation under the Federal Land Consolidation and Rehabilitation Authority (FELCRA) (ibid.: 40–42). FELDA, in particular, was responsible for opening up land and resettling landless Malay villagers. At the beginning of NEP, large estates were turning to more lucrative palm oil and rubber was increasingly the domain of smallholders. Yet another government initiative, the Rubber Industry Smallholders Development Authority (RISDA), established in 1972, was initiated to sustain and protect the interests of smallholders through consolidation and regulation of rubber production and markets (Ragayah 2013: 43). A resettlement scheme, RPS (Rancangan Pengumpulan Semula), somewhat parallel to FELDA, has targeted Orang Asli groups. But in contrast to FELDA, it has led largely to dispossession and displacement rather than expansion of Orang Asli landholdings (Zawawi 1996). Overall, under the NEP, government programmes saw a relative neglect of rural 'estate' Indians and Orang Asli as well as rural Malays in areas that did not support the central Barisan Nasional government (Ragayah 2013: 56–57).

The government has also intervened extensively in the rice sector, with a substantial paddy support policy (Ragayah 2013: 47–51). The policy led to a skewed distribution, such that farmers sold rice at a subsidised price and bought it back from the market for their own consumption, a situation that indicated the thorough commodification of peasant-farmers' most basic staple. In Ragayah's assessment (ibid.: 49–51), rice policy led to an economic subsidy trap, benefited wealthy farmers more than poor farmers, and while reducing absolute poverty, at the same time increased income inequality. Overall the rice policy was less effective in redistribution favouring the poor than was FELDA, which fostered greater land ownership among landless Malay farmers. But by the 1990s, FELDA had ceased opening new smallholder settlements and evolved into a diversified business conglomerate (ibid.: 46).

Although rural development programmes increased income inequality, this was at least partially mitigated by remittances from urban employed migrants. Importantly, as Ragayah (2013: 54) points out, incomes among the urban working poor and lowest-level civil servants grew more rapidly than did incomes of the urban upper middle class; and many of those in the lower socio-economic strata of the urban economy were rural-to-urban migrants who at the same time were supporting rural kin with remittances. Ragayah and others (e.g. Ariffin 1994; De Koninck and Ahmat 2012; Thompson 2004, 2007) point to the significance of near-universal primary and secondary education and the absorption of educated rural poor, especially women, into urban, industrial employment.

De Koninck and Ahmat's 2009 restudy of villages originally surveyed in 1972 in the Kedah rice belt is particularly instructive in demonstrating the more general agrarian transformations taking place in Malaysia through the late twentieth and early twenty-first centuries (De Koninck and Ahmat 2012). From the 1970s to the 1980s, rice farming became increasingly mechanised, and labour-intensive farming methods largely disappeared in the Kedah rice belt (ibid.: 57–58). The same period saw nearly universal improvement in access to education by poor and rich rural families alike, coupled with a decline in household size and in the frequency of extended families living under one roof from 1986 to 2009 (ibid.: 58–60). These trends mirror the 'urbanisation' of *kampung* society observed by Thompson in a mixed rubber-tapping and paddy-planting village away from the Kedah Plain (Thompson 2004, 2007).

In the 1970s and 1980s, land consolidation in the Kedah Plain took place operationally but not in terms of land ownership. In other words, smallholders maintained ownership of small parcels of land, but increasingly leased these to larger operators rather than farming the land themselves (De Koninck and Ahmat 2012: 60). Some moderate consolidation of ownership appeared in evidence in the 1990s and 2000s (ibid.). It remains an open question whether this trend will accelerate as younger generations with weaker agrarian roots take possession from older generations.

Rice agriculture has expanded – in the sense that yields and the total amount of rice produced have increased substantially since the Green Revolution of the 1970s – but farming as an economic activity has been dramatically marginalised, particularly for smallholders and labourers. By the 2000s, De Koninck and Ahmat (2012: 62) observe that rice cultivation has become thoroughly industrialised and highly mechanised and agricultural labour has declined sharply. Furthermore, the involvement of women in agriculture has become insignificant and exchange of labour between farming households has disappeared altogether. The agricultural labour that remains is done almost entirely by men who operate the farming machinery.

Among villagers, agricultural labour has been overwhelmingly displaced by non-agricultural labour (ibid.: 62–65; Zahid 2003). Moreover, in the villages these authors studied, there is extensive use of foreign labour (Thai, Burmese and Indonesian) in the agricultural sector and local owners do little manual labour (De Koninck and Ahmat 2012: 65–66). The rural poor, especially the poorest of the poor, are for the most part no longer rural Malays, but rather, immigrant and often undocumented foreign workers from Southern Thailand, Myanmar, Indonesia and the Philippines, in the case of Sabah. An important and still under-examined issue is how well these immigrants will be integrated into Malaysian and Malay society, particularly those from Indonesia, in comparison to the long history of such migrations (see Tugby 1977).

Recent research has given some attention to rural economic diversification, especially into non-agricultural industries. With the possible or partial exception of some remote areas, particularly in East Malaysia, subsistence economies have largely disappeared in Malaysia. In their place, agricultural cash cropping and non-agricultural economic pursuits have led to a diversified economy in rural areas, which, like other aspects of rural life, has only been studied in a piecemeal fashion in recent scholarship. One area of the diversified economy that has received some attention in research has been the growth of a rural tourist economy, and in particular, the rapid proliferation of 'homestays' in rural areas (Liu 2006; Lo *et al.* n.d.; Pusiran and Xiao 2013). The impact of these activities in terms of rural economies and rural society remains to be seen.

Society: rural urbanisation

Along with economic transformation and diversification, rural Malaysia has seen dramatic social change over the past fifty years or more. Earlier research on rural society in Malaysia focused largely on *kampung* society (Firth 1946; Firth 1966; Kuchiba *et al.* 1979; Swift 1965; Wilson 1967) and on kinship in particular (e.g. Banks 1983; Carsten 1997; Peletz 1988). In the 1960s, Provencher (1971) drew sharp distinctions between Malay styles of social interaction in rural and urban settings. The major trend of the past fifty years has been the overwhelming influences of rural to urban migration, both in Peninsular and East Malaysia (Cramb 2012; Dalhan 1989; Gomes 2004; Thompson 2003, 2007; Wilder 1989).

With few exceptions (more so in Sarawak and Sabah than in Peninsular Malaysia), once 'remote' villages and city centres are in close, regular and frequent contact, through telecommunications and mobility of people and commodities. On the Peninsula, it would be difficult to find any place of human habitation that is not within a day's travel or less from Kuala Lumpur and other major urban centres. The upshot is that as much as any other country in Asia (excepting small city-states such as Singapore), Malaysia has been subject to what Gavin Jones describes as 'thoroughgoing urbanization' (Jones 1997).

Not only has this shifted the orientation of Malay society from rural *kampung* to urban society for the migrants, rural *kampung* have transformed in the process. Urban transformation within and on the periphery of cities, or peri-urban outskirts, has been widely noted (e.g. Brookfield *et al.* 1991; Ghazali 2013; Lockard 1987; McTaggart and McEachern 1972). Social relations within rural *kampung* have been extensively reorganised and reoriented as well, such that the substantive urban–rural distinction observed by Provencher (1971) no longer typifies the urban–rural divide (Thompson 2004, 2007).

One of the most noted changes has to do with gender relations and the status and role of women in Malay society (e.g. Karim 1992; Rudie 1994; Stivens 1996, 2013; Stivens *et al.* 1994; Strange 1981; cf. Thambiah 1999). From the late 1970s into the early 1990s, particular attention was given to the transition from farming to factory work and other urban-oriented occupations among women (Ackerman 1991; Ariffin 1994; Fatimah 1985; Hing 1984; Lie and Lund 1994; Maimunah 2001; Ong 1987, 1990; Stivens 2013). This attention largely displaced earlier ethnographic research on women's roles in rural village society (e.g. Firth 1966; Laderman 1983). By the 1990s, much of the moral panic around the subject had dissipated and factory work among rural women had become normalised (Thompson 2004, 2007). Although research in the 1970s and 1980s argued that substantial changes were taking place in terms of power and economic relationships within families, between women and men and across generations, little if any substantial rural-based research since the 1990s has followed up on or traced these issues into the present (cf. Peletz 1996; Stivens 2013).

In keeping with a broader interest in information and communications technology (ICT) that has been fostered through prominent attention to projects such as Cyberjaya and discourse surrounding the intended transition to a 'knowledge economy' since the 1990s, a number of studies have been done on rural ICT development. Most of these have focused on various sorts of Internet use (e.g. Alias 2013; Rohaya *et al.* 2013; Suhaida *et al.* 2013). Internet use has certainly penetrated into rural areas, particularly through the establishment of government sponsored Rural Internet Centres (Alias 2013). However, the much more extensive and rapid proliferation of mobile phones has almost certainly had a more profound effect on social relations and economic activity in rural Malaysia than has Internet use. While the appearance of mobile phones in rural Malaysia has been noted by some scholars (e.g. Preston and Ngah 2012: 355–56), an extensive and theoretically informed analysis of how this ICT has influenced rural sociality remains to be done (see Qui and Thompson 2007; Thompson 2009). New, proliferating ICTs such as the Internet and mobile phones are just one part of an extensive expansion of infrastructure that have brought cities and countryside closer together throughout much of Malaysia.

The idea of rural *kampung*, marked by close social relations and mutual self-help (*gotong-royong*) remains a powerful one in everyday discourse (Thompson 2002, 2007, 2013a). Scholars have also noted the significance of an often commodified nostalgia for rural *kampung* among the urbanised Malay middle class (Kahn 1992; Kessler 1992). Such nostalgia notwithstanding, researchers working in rural *kampung* have observed that rural sociality has changed significantly, reflecting forms of sociality typically thought of as urban rather than rural (Thompson 2004, 2007). Significant disagreements remain over whether or not rural Malay social life is best seen as undergoing dissolution (Maznah 2013) or regrounding (Preston and

Ngah 2012). A problem with the general lack of attention to rural-based research at present as compared with fifty years ago is that our basis for making empirically grounded arguments and for analysis of these changing social relations and processes is relatively thin. This weakness is even more the case when it comes to rural politics.

Politics: from local to national

Singularly lacking in social science research of the past two decades is analysis of local, rural politics. Prior to the 1980s or 1990s, scholars of Malaysia produced numerous important monographs and reports on rural, village-level politics. Among these were Syed Husin Ali's classic study of village leadership (Husin Ali 1975), Shamsul A.B.'s analysis of the transition from colonial to local rule (Shamsul 1986), James Scott's political-economic analysis of village-level class relations (Scott 1985) and numerous other monographs (e.g. Kessler 1978; Nash 1974; Ness 1967; Rogers 1993; Shamsul 1982–83, 1991). Historical studies of rural and village-level politics also reached an apex in the mid-twentieth century (e.g. Kratoska 1984; Lim 1977; Nonini 1992). This tradition of scholarship has largely vanished, and to a greater degree than elsewhere in Southeast Asia. In neighbouring Thailand, for example, works such as Andrew Walker's (2012) *Political Peasants* or Yoshinori Nishizaki's (2011) *Political Authority and Provincial Identity in Thailand* count among the most important recent works in scholarship on Thailand.

In part, the decline in the study of local, rural politics can be attributed to the general shift in focus from rural- to urban-based research. The lack of detailed, local-level analysis of rural politics may also in part be attributed to the chilling effect of government attitudes toward social science research. Foreign researchers are formally and informally warned to avoid 'sensitive issues' and 'political elements'. Local researchers are likewise subject to similar implicit and explicit restrictions. Whereas insightful analysis of on-the-ground rural politics has flourished in neighbouring countries such as Indonesia, Thailand, the Philippines and elsewhere over past decades, the tradition of empirically grounded, careful studies of rural politics pioneered by Malaysian and foreign academics of the mid-twentieth century mentioned above has dwindled, if not entirely died off, since the 1970s or 1980s.

Insofar as political analysis has had much to say about rural politics over the past couple of decades, it has been with respect to the role of rural voters and constituencies in terms of national, electoral politics. While the rural-biased gerrymandering of parliamentary constituencies has long been pointed out, the issue has become more prominent in the wake of the hotly contested twelfth and thirteenth general elections, held in 2008 and 2013, respectively. In 2008, the ruling Barisan Nasional (BN) coalition unexpectedly lost its long-held two-thirds majority in the federal parliament as well as losing outright in five state-level assemblies (Kedah, Kelantan, Penang, Perak and Selangor). This result raised opposition expectations in the lead-up to the thirteenth general election. Despite losing the popular vote in 2013, the BN was able to maintain a solid majority of seats in the federal parliament and form a new government.

In the wake of these results and the bitter disappointment of many opposition supporters (including many academics), renewed attention was given to the rural-biased skewing of constituencies and the rural–urban divide in voting patterns. Numerous academic and other commentators laid blame for the opposition's loss and BN's win at the feet of rural voters, and attributed support for the BN to those voters' lack of education, backwardness and responsiveness to vote-buying (Chin 2013; *Malaysiakini* 2013; Mohamed Nawab 2013). Problematically, however, in the absence of sophisticated or in-depth on-the-ground research into the motivations or dynamics of rural voting patterns, such analysis remains largely speculative and laced with no small amount of urbanite contempt for rural citizens (Thompson 2013a, 2013b).

Conclusion

In a recent review, Preston and Ngah (2012) argue for a view of rural society in Malaysia that focuses on processes of broadening, deepening and regrounding. In contrast to dystopic perceptions of rural social dissolution (e.g. Maznah 2013), Preston and Ngah see strength rather than weakness in the reconstitution of contemporary rurality in Malaysia. Their intervention usefully outlines a positive prescription for understanding contemporary rural change as well as pointing to areas for further and ongoing research.

While rural villages cannot be usefully studied in isolation from wider, and largely urban-oriented Malaysian society, neither should they be ignored economically, socially or politically. With regard to economics, both agricultural and non-agricultural activities need to be studied from an on-the-ground perspective rather than only through macro-economic data. Open questions remain as to whether such activities as rural tourism, rural industrialisation or various forms of cash crops are sustainable and whether or not the benefits of such activities will be widespread.

With regard to social issues, the trend in scholarship has been away from holistic ethnography and toward issue-oriented analysis, of concerns such as divorce, substance abuse, unemployment, health, nutrition, and the like (e.g. Cooper 2013; Rohaya *et al.* 2013). While such issue-oriented research is useful, it would be at least as, if not more, valuable if more studies could address the issue of rural social change at a more holistic level. Among other benefits, it would be valuable to return attention to issues of kinship, drawing on the past, rich ethnographic record to study how family and kinship are transforming in the present. Cramb (2012), for example, provides an intriguing view of the urban and transnational extensions of Iban longhouse-oriented society in rural Sarawak.

In the political arena, insofar as restrictions on research within Malaysia allow, a keen attention to the on-the-ground dynamics of local, rural politics could go a long way to moving scholarship and broader public discourse beyond stereotypes of incompetent rural voters and toward a better understanding of the ideas and interests of rural constituencies that have fed into the apparent urban–rural divide in the Malaysian electorate. Earlier work, such as Shamsul A.B.'s (1986) study of the transition from colonial to national rule, have shown that for many decades, local politics in rural Malaysia has been tied into broader national trends and interests. But that does not lessen the significance of local, rural political dynamics. Moreover, those dynamics have surely changed since studies such as Syed Husin Ali's (1975) examination of peasant leadership. Among other issues worth exploring is the role of return rural-to-urban migrants and of rural residents' attitudes toward Malaysia's changing political landscape.

Finally, studies of rural change in Malaysia have moved, and should continue to move, away from imagining the rural as typified by Malay *kampung* society. While Malay *kampung*, albeit transformed, continue to be a vital part of Malaysia's rural landscape, a broader view of rural transformation is called for, including studies that take more serious account of urban and national engagement with 'nature' (e.g. Kathirithamby-Wells 2005), environmental concerns and the range of non-Malay rural inhabitants. There is little to suggest that the demographic and scholarly trends in Malaysia toward urbanisation and urban issues are likely to abate any time soon. Nevertheless, a substantial portion of Malaysia's population continue to make their home outside of cities, and as Preston and Ngah (2012) argue, city-dwellers themselves appear increasingly inclined to desire a return to, or at least a reconnection with, the countryside.

Note

1 The author's research on rural Malaysia has been funded by NUS Academic Research Grant R-111-000-120-112 Circular Migration and Rural Gentrification.

Bibliography

Ackerman, Susan E. (1991) 'Dakwah and Minah Karan: class formation and ideological conflict in Malay society', *Bijdragen tot de Taal-, Land- en Volkenkund*, 147(2–3): 193–215.

Alias, Nor Aziah (2013) *ICT Development for Social and Rural Connectedness*, Dordrecht: Springer.

Ariffin, Jamilah (ed.) (1994) *From Kampung to Urban Factories: Findings of the HAWA Study*, Kuala Lumpur: University of Malaya Press.

Bailey, Conner (1983) *The Sociology of Production in Rural Malay Society*, Kuala Lumpur, Oxford, New York and Melbourne: Oxford University Press.

Banks, David J. (1983) *Malay Kinship*, Philadelphia: Institute for the Study of Human Issues.

Baxstrom, Richard (2008) *Houses in Motion: The Experience of Place and the Problem of Belief in Urban Malaysia*, Stanford: Stanford University Press.

Brookfield, Harold, Abdul Samad Hadi and Zaharah Mahmud (1991) *The City in the Village: The In-Situ Urbanization of Villages, Villagers and Their Land around Kuala Lumpur, Malaysia*, Singapore, Oxford and New York: Oxford University Press.

Bunnell, Tim and Alice Nah (2004) 'Counter-global cases for place: contesting displacement in globalising Kuala Lumpur metropolitan area', *Urban Studies*, 41(12): 2447–67.

Carsten, Janet (1997) *The Heat of the Hearth: The Process of Kinship in a Malay Fishing Community*, Oxford and New York: Oxford University Press.

Chin, James (2013) 'UMNO relies increasingly on rural Malay support', *The Straits Times*, available at www.straitstimes.com/the-big-story/asia-report/malaysia-elections/opinion-blogs/story/umno-relies-increasingly-rural-mala (accessed 12 May 2014).

Cooper, Elizabeth Elliott (2013) 'Evaluating household food insecurity: applications and insights from rural Malaysia', *Ecology of Food and Nutrition*, 52(4): 294–316.

Cramb, Rob A. (2012) 'Beyond the longhouse: Iban shifting cultivators come to town', in Jonathan Rigg and Peter Vandergeest (eds), *Revisiting Rural Places: Pathways to Poverty and Prosperity in Southeast Asia*, Singapore: NUS Press, pp. 68–87.

Dahlan, H.M. (1989) *Urbanization in Sabah: Probing into the Urban Social Mind*, Kota Kinabalu: Institute for Development Studies Sabah.

De Koninck, Rodolphe (1992) *Malay Peasants Coping with the World: Breaking the Community Circle?*, Singapore: Institute for Southeast Asian Studies.

De Koninck, Rodolphe and Raiha Ahmat (2012) 'A state-orchestrated agrarian transition on the Kedah Plain of Peninsular Malaysia, 1972–2009', in Jonathan Rigg and Peter Vandergeest (eds), *Revisiting Rural Places: Pathways to Poverty and Prosperity in Southeast Asia*, Singapore: NUS Press, pp. 52–67.

De Koninck, Rodolphe, Stéphane Bernard and Jean-François Bissonnette (eds) (2011) *Borneo Transformed: Agricultural Expansion on the Southeast Asian Frontier*, Singapore: NUS Press.

Elson, Robert Edward (1997) *The End of the Peasantry in Southeast Asia: A Social and Economic History of Peasant Livelihood, 1800–1990*, New York: St Martin's Press.

Fatimah Daud (1985) *'Minah Karan': The Truth about Malaysian Factory Girls*, Kuala Lumpur: Berita Publishing.

Firth, Raymond (1946) *Malay Fishermen: Their Peasant Economy*, London: Kegan Paul, Trench, Trubner.

Firth, Rosemary (1966) [1943] *Housekeeping among Malay Peasants*, London: Athlone Press.

Ghazali, Suriati (2013) 'Sense of place and the politics of "insider-ness" in villages undergoing transition: the case of City *Kampung* on Penang Island', in Tim Bunnell, D. Parthasarathy and Eric C. Thompson (eds), *Cleavage, Connection and Conflict in Rural, Urban and Contemporary Asia*, Dordrecht: Springer, pp. 117–42.

Gomes, Alberto G. (2004) *Looking for Money: Capitalism and Modernity in an Orang Asli Village*, Subang Jaya: Center for Orang Asli Concerns.

Guinness, Patrick (1992) *On the Margin of Capitalism: People and Development in Mukim Plentong, Johor, Malaysia*, Singapore, Oxford and New York: Oxford University Press.

Halim Salleh (1992) 'Peasants, proletarianization, and the state: FELDA settlers in Pahang', in Joel S. Kahn and Francis Loh Kok Wah (eds), *Fragmented Vision: Culture and Politics in Contemporary Malaysia*, North Sydney: Allen & Unwin.

Hing Ai Yun (1984) 'Women and work in West Malaysia', *Journal of Contemporary Asia*, 14(2): 204–18.

Husin Ali, Syed (1975) *Malay Peasant Society and Leadership*, Kuala Lumpur, London, New York and Melbourne: Oxford University Press.

Ishikawa, Noboru (2010) *Between Frontiers: Nation and Identity in a Southeast Asian Borderland*, Singapore: NUS Press.

Jomo K.S. (1986) *A Question of Class: Capital, State and Uneven Development in Malaya*, Singapore: Oxford University Press.

Jones, Gavin W. (1997) 'The thoroughgoing urbanisation of East and Southeast Asia', *Asia-Pacific Viewpoint*, 38(3): 237–49.

Kahn, Joel S. (1992) 'Class, ethnicity and diversity: some remarks on Malay culture in Malaysia', in Joel S. Kahn and Francis Loh Kok Wah (eds), *Fragmented Vision: Culture and Politics in Contemporary Malaysia*, North Sydney: Allen & Unwin.

Karim, Wazir Jahan (1992) *Women and Culture: Between Malay Adat and Islam*, Boulder: Westview Press.

Kathirithamby-Wells, Jeyamalar (2005) *Nature and Nation: Forests and Development in Peninsular Malaysia*, Singapore: NUS Press.

Kessler, Clive S. (1978) *Islam and Politics in a Malay State: Kelantan, 1838–1969*, Ithaca: Cornell University Press.

Kessler, Clive S. (1992) 'Archaism and modernity: contemporary Malay political culture', in Joel S. Kahn and Francis Loh Kok Wah (eds), *Fragmented Vision: Culture and Politics in Contemporary Malaysia*, North Sydney: Allen & Unwin, pp. 133–57.

Kratoska, Paul H. (1984) 'Penghulus in Perak and Selangor: the rationalization and decline of a traditional Malay office', *Journal of the Malayan Branch of the Royal Asiatic Society*, 57(2): 31–59.

Kuchiba, Masuo, Yoshihiro Tsubouchi and Narifumi Maeda (1979) *Three Malay Villages: A Sociology of Paddy Growers in West Malaysia*, Honolulu: University of Hawai'i Press.

Laderman, Carol (1983) *Wives and Midwives: Childbirth and Nutrition in Rural Malaysia*, Berkeley: University of California Press.

Lie, Merete and Ragnhild Lund (1994) *Renegotiating Local Values: Working Women and Foreign Industry in Malaysia*, Richmond: Curzon Press.

Lim Teck Ghee (1977) *Peasants and Their Agricultural Economy in Colonial Malaysia 1874–1941*, Kuala Lumpur: Oxford University Press.

Liu, Abby (2006) 'Tourism in rural areas: Kedah, Malaysia', *Tourism Management*, 27: 878–89.

Lo May Chiun, Peter Songan, T. Ramayah, Alvin W. Yeo and Vikneswaran Nair (2013) 'Rural tourism development: industry's perspective on sustainable tourism', DOI: 10.7763/IPEDR, 65(3).

Lockard, Craig A. (1987) *From Kampung to City: A Social History of Kuching, Malaysia 1820–1970*, Athens, OH: Ohio University Center for Southeast Asian Studies.

Lunkapis, Gaim James (2013) 'Confusion over land rights and development opportunities through communal titles in Sabah, Malaysia', *Asia Pacific Viewpoint*, 54(2): 198–205.

McTaggart, W. Donald and R. McEachern (1972) 'Kampong Pandan: a study of a Malay kampong in Kuala Lumpur', in Denis John Dwyer (ed.), *The City as a Centre of Change in Asia*, Hong Kong: Hong Kong University Press, pp. 125–40.

Maimunah Ismail (2001) *Malaysian Women in Rural Development and Entrepreneurship: From Rural Producers to Urban Entrepreneurs*, London: ASEAN Academic Press.

Malaysiakini (2013) 'More than half of Malaysians have rejected BN', *YOURSAY*, available at http://m.malaysiakini.com/news/229273 (accessed 12 May 2014).

Maznah Mohamad (1996) *The Malay Handloom Weavers: A Study of the Rise and Decline of Traditional Manufacture*, Singapore: Institute for Southeast Asian Studies.

Maznah Mohamad (2013) 'The New Economic Policy and poverty at the margins: family dislocation, dispossession and dystopia in Kelantan', in Edmund T. Gomez and Johan Saravanamuttu (eds), *The New Economic Policy: Affirmative Action, Ethnic Inequalities and Social Justice*, Singapore: NUS Press, pp. 61–83.

Mohamed Nawab Mohamed Osman (2013) 'Whither Malaysia: rethinking ethnic politics', *RSIS Commentaries*, 091/2013, available at www.rsis.edu.sg/publications/Perspective/RSIS0912013.pdf (accessed 12 May 2014).

Nash, Manning (1974) *Peasant Citizens: Politics, Religion, and Modernization in Kelantan, Malaysia*, Athens, OH: Ohio University Center for Southeast Asian Studies.

Ness, Gayl D. (1967) *Bureaucracy and Rural Development in Malaysia: A Study of Complex Organization in Stimulating Economic Development in New States*, Berkeley: University of California Press.

Nishizaki, Yoshinori (2011) *Political Authority and Provincial Identity in Thailand: The Making of Banharn-buri*, Ithaca: Cornell University Southeast Asia Studies Program.

Nobuta Toshihiro (2009) *Living on the Periphery: Development and Islamization among the Orang Asli*, Subang Jaya: Center for Orang Asli Concerns.

Nonini, Donald M. (1992) *British Colonial Rule and Resistance of the Malay Peasantry, 1900–1957*, New Haven: Yale University Southeast Asian Studies.

Ong, Aihwa (1987) *Spirits of Resistance and Capitalist Discipline: Factory Women in Malaysia*, Albany: State University of New York Press.

Ong, Aihwa (1990) 'Japanese factories, Malay workers: class and sexual metaphors in West Malaysia', in Jane Monnig Atkinson and Shelly Errington (eds), *Power and Difference: Gender in Island Southeast Asia*, Stanford: Stanford University Press, pp. 395–422.

Overton, John (1994) 'Agriculture and industry in colonial Malaya', in Harold Brookfield (ed.), *Transformation with Industrialization in Peninsular Malaysia*, Kuala Lumpur, Oxford, Singapore and New York: Oxford University Press, pp. 35–48.

Peletz, Michael G. (1988) *A Share of the Harvest: Kinship, Property, and Social History among the Malays of Rembau*, Berkeley, Los Angeles and London: University of California Press.

Peletz, Michael G. (1996) *Reason and Passion: Representations of Gender in a Malay Society*, Berkeley: University of California Press.

Preston, David and Ibrahim Ngah (2012) 'Interpreting rural change in Malaysia', *Singapore Journal of Tropical Geography*, 33: 351–64.

Provencher, Ronald (1971) *Two Malay Worlds: Interaction in Urban and Rural Settings*, Berkeley: Center for South and Southeast Asia Studies, University of California.

Pusiran, Arif Kamisan and Xiao Honggen (2013) 'Challenges and community development: a case study of homestay in Malaysia', *Asian Social Science*, 9(5): 1–17.

Qui, Jack L. and Eric C. Thompson (2007) 'Editorial: mobile communications and Asian modernities', *New Media and Society*, 9(6): 895–901.

Ragayah Haji Mat Zin (2013) 'The New Economic Policy and poverty eradication in Malaysia', in Edmund T. Gomez and Johan Saravanamuttu (eds), *The New Economic Policy: Affirmative Action, Ethnic Inequalities and Social Justice*, Singapore: NUS Press, pp. 31–59.

Rohaya Mohd-Nor, Teddy Edwin Chapun and Constance Rinen Justin Wah (2013) 'Malaysian rural community as consumer of health information and their use of ICT', *Malaysian Journal of Communication*, 29(1): 1–27.

Rogers, Marvin L. (1993) *Local Politics in Rural Malaysia: Patterns of Change in Sungai Raya*, Kuala Lumpur: S. Abdul Majeed and Company.

Rudie, Ingrid (1994) *Visible Women in East Coast Malay Society*, Oslo: Scandinavian University Press.

Rusaslina Idris (2013) 'Left behind: the Orang Asli under the New Economic Policy', in Edmund T. Gomez and Johan Saravanamuttu (eds), *The New Economic Policy: Affirmative Action, Ethnic Inequalities and Social Justice*, Singapore: NUS Press, pp. 265–91.

Rutten, Mario (2003) *Rural Capitalists in Asia: A Comparative Analysis of India, Indonesia and Malaysia*, London and New York: RoutledgeCurzon.

Scott, James C. (1985) *Weapons of the Weak: Everyday Forms of Peasant Resistance*, New Haven and London: Yale University Press.

Shamsul Amri Baharuddin (1982–1983) 'Malay village politics: some past observations', *Jurnal Anthropologi dan Sosiologi*, 11 & 12: 75–89.

Shamsul Amri Baharuddin (1986) *From British to Bumiputera Rule: Local Politics and Rural Development in Peninsular Malaysia*, Singapore: Institute of Southeast Asian Studies.

Shamsul Amri Baharuddin (1989) Village: The Imposed Social Construct in Malaysia's Development Initiative, Working Paper 115, Bielefeld: Southeast Asia Program, Faculty of Sociology, University of Bielefeld.

Shamsul Amri Baharuddin (1991) Formal Organization in a Malay 'Administrative Village'; An Ethnographic Portrait, Occasional Papers 15, Kent: Centre for South-East Asian Studies, University of Kent at Canterbury

Sivalingam, G. (1993) *Malaysia's Agricultural Transformation*, Petaling Jaya: Pelanduk Publications.

Stivens, Maila (1996) *Matriliny and Modernity: Sexual Politics and Social Change in Rural Malaysia*, St Leonards: Allen & Unwin.

Stivens, Maila (2013) 'Gender and the interplay of rural and urban: a Malaysian case', in Tim Bunnell, D. Parthasarathy and Eric C. Thompson (eds), *Cleavage, Connection and Conflict in Rural, Urban and Contemporary Asia*, Dordrecht: Springer, pp. 143–60.

Stivens, Maila, Cecilia Ng, Jomo Kwame Sundaram and Jahara Bee (1994) *Malay Peasant Women and the Land*, London and Atlantic Highlands, NJ: Zed Books.

Strange, Heather (1981) *Rural Malay Women in Tradition and Transition*, New York: Praeger Publishers.

Suhaida, M.A., M.S. Nurulhuda and Su-Fei Yap (2013) 'Access to ICT as moderating factor to women's participation in the labor force: a conceptual framework', *International Journal of Trade, Economics and Finance*, 4(4): 197–201.

Swift, Michael (1965) *Malay Peasant Society in Jelebu*, London: Athlone Press.

Thambiah, Shanthi (1999) 'Orang Asli women and men in transition', in Jomo Kwame Sundaram (ed.), *Rethinking Malaysia*, Kuala Lumpur: Malaysian Social Science Association, pp. 267–92.

Thompson, Eric C. (2002) 'Migrant subjectivities and narratives of the *Kampung* in Malaysia', *Sojourn*, 17(1): 52–75.

Thompson, Eric C. (2003) 'Malay male migrants: negotiating contested identities in Malaysia', *American Ethnologist*, 30(3): 418–38.

Thompson, Eric C. (2004) 'Rural villages as socially urban spaces in Malaysia', *Urban Studies*, 41(12): 2358–76.

Thompson, Eric C. (2007) *Unsettling Absences: Urbanism in Rural Malaysia*, Singapore: NUS Press.

Thompson, Eric C. (2009) 'Mobile phones, community and social networks among foreign workers in Singapore', *Global Networks*, 9(3): 359–80.

Thompson, Eric C. (2013a) 'Urban cosmopolitan chauvinism and the politics of rural identity', in Tim Bunnell, D. Parthasarathy and Eric C. Thompson (eds), *Cleavage, Connection and Conflict in Rural, Urban and Contemporary Asia*, Dordrecht: Springer, pp. 161–79.

Thompson, Eric C. (2013b) 'GE13 and the politics of urban chauvinism', *New Mandala*, 14 May, available at http://asiapacific.anu.edu.au/newmandala/2013/05/14/ge13-and-the-politics-of-urban-chauvinism/ (accessed 12 May 2014).

Tsubouchi Yoshihiro (2001) *One Malay Village: A Thirty-Year Community Study*, Kyoto: Kyoto University Press.

Tugby, Donald (1977) *Cultural Change and Identity: Mandailing Immigrants in West Malaysia*, St Lucia: University of Queensland Press.

Walker, Andrew (2012) *Political Peasants: Power in the Modern Rural Economy*, Madison: University of Wisconsin Press.

Wan Hashim (1988) *Peasants under Peripheral Capitalism*, Bangi: Penerbit UKM.

Wilder, William D. (1982) *Communication, Social Structure and Development in Rural Malaysia*, London: Athlone Press.

Wilder, William D. (1989) 'The peasant–urban interface in Malaysia', *Sojourn*, 4(1): 75–88.

Willford, Andrew (2006) *Cage of Freedom: Tamil Identity and Ethnic Fetish in Malaysia*, Ann Arbor: University of Michigan Press.

Wilson, Peter J. (1967) *A Malay Village in Malaysia: Social Values and Rural Development*, New Haven: HRAF Press.

Wong, Diana (1987) *Peasants in the Making: Malaysia's Green Revolution*, Singapore: Institute of Southeast Asian Studies.

Zahid Emby (2003) 'Changing occupations as a strategy for survival: case study of a Malay village in Peninsular Malaysia', in Donovan Storey, John D. Overton and Barbara Nowak (eds), *Contesting Development: Pathways to Better Practice*, Palmerton North: Massey University.

Zawawi Ibrahim (1996) 'Regional development in rural Malaysia and the "tribal question"', in Muhammad Ikmal Said and Zahid Emby (eds), *Malaysia: Critical Perspectives, Essays in Honour of Syed Husin Ali*, Petaling Jaya: Persatuan Sains Sosial Malaysia, pp. 171–207.

Zawawi Ibrahim (1998) *The Malay Labourer: By the Window of Capitalism*, Singapore: Institute of Southeast Asian Studies.

Zawawi Ibrahim (2001) *Voices of the Crocker Range Indigenous Communities of Sabah: Social Narratives of Transition in Tambuan and Its Neighbours*, Kota Samarahan: The Institute of East Asian Studies, University Malaysia Sarawak.

Zawawi Ibrahim (ed.) (2008) *Representation, Identity and Multiculturalism in Sarawak*, Kajang: Persatuan Sains Sosial Malaysia.

Zawawi Ibrahim (2010) 'The anthropology of the Malay peasantry: critical reflections on colonial and indigenous scholarship', *Asian Journal of Social Science*, 38(1): 5–36.

Zawawi Ibrahim and NoorShah M.S. (eds) (2012) *Masyarakat Penan dan Impian Pembangunan: Satu Himpunan Naratif Keterpinggiran dan Jatidiri*, Petaling Jaya: Strategic Information and Research Development Centre.

20

The great transformation

Urbanisation and urbanism in Malaysia

Yeoh Seng Guan

The census exercise of 2010 reported that the population of Malaysia stands at 28.3 million, an increase from 23.3 million in 2000.[1] About 80 percent of the population currently resides in Peninsular Malaysia and the rest in the East Malaysian territories of Labuan, Sabah and Sarawak. The average growth rate of 2 percent for the period 2000–10 was lower than that of the previous censal period (1991–2000) of 2.6 percent, and indicates an overall decline in fertility and international migration rates. The age structure of the population also points toward an ageing population. Per the present trajectory, it is projected that by 2021, the population aged 65 years and over will have reached 7.1 percent, an increase of 2.1 percent from the 2010 level. This points to a trend faced by many developed nations, of the working age (15–64 years) population's having to support an increasing old-age population.

The share of urban population has continued to increase as well, reaching 71 percent in 2010, compared with 62 percent in 2000 and 50.7 percent in 1991. The federal territories of Kuala Lumpur and Putrajaya both recorded 100 percent urbanisation. States with high levels of urbanisation include Selangor (91.4 percent), Pulau Pinang (90.8 percent) and Melaka (86.5 percent). Conversely, low urbanisation levels are found in Kelantan (42.4 percent), Pahang (50.5 percent) and Perlis (51.4 percent). Selangor continues to be the most populated state, with 5.4 million residents (19.3 percent of the country's population), followed by Johor with 3.3 million and Sabah at 3.2 million. Putrajaya had the highest population growth, increasing by 17.8 percent between 2000 and 2010.

These demographic shifts reflect and drive changing patterns of settlement, with attendant political, social and cultural implications. While urban development in Malaysia is a comparatively recent phenomenon, it has not been monochromatic or unidirectional. This chapter considers both the evolution of forms of urban settlement in Malaysia and the policies and programmes that have most shaped life within.

Urbanisation in British Malaya

As elsewhere in the former outposts of European empires in Southeast Asia, the genesis of Malaysia's long road to modernist urbanisation can be traced back to the advent of British colonial rule (e.g. Evers and Korff 2000; Rimmer and Dick 2009). Human settlements in the pre-colonial milieu were predominantly coastal, riverine or port cities, of which the most prominent was Melaka (Malacca) during the Age of Commerce (Reid 1988). Swamps, dense tropical vegetation and the diverse variety of parasites these landscapes harbour were inhospitable to the forging of large settlements in the interior.

As British administrators progressively expanded their hold into the hinterland, they reconfigured indigenous land tenure practices in order to facilitate the opening up of 'empty land' for food cultivation and cash crop plantations (Jackson 1968; Lim 1977; Wong 1975) and large-scale tin mining. For these varied enterprises, a liberal migration policy was crafted in tandem to attract waves of cheap and skilled labour as well as an array of entrepreneurs and petty capitalists to support wealth extraction. These diverse migrants originated largely from various regions and provinces of China, India and Indonesia, and contributed to laying the demographic template for what colonial scholar-administrator John Furnivall has famously characterised as a 'plural society', premised on putative racial differences.

The British administrators also built an infrastructural network of transportation links, both rail and roads, to facilitate the creation of trading and commercial centres that were skewed along the west coast of Peninsular Malaysia (Kaur 1985; Lim 1978). The polychromatic 'plural society' described by Furnivall was most salient in large towns where various material, social and cultural imprints of Western modernity – like urban planning, architecture, education, entertainment, dressing, and so forth – took root and produced diasporic varieties of cosmopolitan aesthetics and sensibilities. In most cases, these thriving urban centres were demographically and commercially dominated by the Chinese, Indians and British, while the overwhelming majority of local and migrant Malays, as well as indigenous peoples (collectively grouped as the 'Orang Asli' by the British) resided in rural smallholdings and forested areas (see Kahn 2006). In places where these two modes of settlement co-existed spatially, royal centres, personified by sultans, were weakened, if not displaced by an emergent modernist urbanism. Before the advent of World War II, many of these towns were already thriving because of a buoyant trade in tin, rubber and other agricultural commodities;[2] however, the ravages of war saw a significant temporary depopulation of many towns, as residents fled to the jungle, plantations and countryside for refuge and to escape Japanese atrocities.

Before independence in 1957, the largest urban population growth rate occurred between 1947 and 1957, when the government forcibly resettled around 600,000 persons – comprising mostly Chinese peasants – into hastily built, perimeter-fenced settlements situated close to existing towns in order to cut off the supply chain to an insurgent Communist Party intent on wresting control from the British through armed guerrilla conflict. Euphemistically called 'New Villages', these settlements, initiated under the Briggs Plan, resulted in a significant numerical jump in urban centres, then defined as gazetted localities with a population of 1,000 persons or more.[3] A related effect was the migration of several thousand others to small towns to escape these securitised hamlets. Finding insufficient or unsuitable lodgings for their families, many turned to residing in existing or new squatter settlements on vacant private and public lands in and around town centres. Until recently, these illegitimate 'squatter *kampung*' or 'urban villages' have been an enduring feature of the Malaysian city/townscape.

Post-colonial urbanism and national development

Since independence in 1957, this residual colonial legacy of the geography, morphology and demographic growth of towns and villages has remained largely intact. In particular, the spatial duality engendered between Malay and non-Malay citizens, and the socio-economic inequities this disparity embodies, has been a recurring narrative for post-colonial corrective social engineering.

In particular, two watershed policies have transformed the demographic and social fabric of urban centres in Malaysia. The first arose in the aftermath of the traumatic events of the 'race riots' of 13 May 1969, which erupted largely in various parts of Kuala Lumpur. In line with the interventionist 'growth with distribution' thrust of the New Economy Policy (NEP, 1971–90) and periodic Outline Perspective Plans (OPPs), the government exponentially stepped up its involvement in restructuring and managing the country's economy, with the express purpose of increasing Malay economic and corporate interests, especially in the areas of private sector employment, business, mining and manufacturing.[4] Moreover, Malays were encouraged to 'modernise' by seeking out better education, employment and business opportunities offered in the towns and cities, especially in the Klang Valley encompassing Kuala Lumpur. This push accelerated a rural–urban migratory pattern that had already begun since 1957 (Aitken and Leigh 1975: 548; see also Rimmer and Cho 1981).

The second watershed policy was promulgated after the formal end of the New Economic Policy in 1991. Although affirmative action policies for ethnic Malays and other *bumiputera* were not discarded, as NEP targets had not yet been realised, what was additionally introduced was an enticing trans-ethnic imaginary. With the catchphrase of Wawasan 2020 ('Vision 2020'), Prime Minister Mahathir Mohamad outlined a grand narrative of arriving at the status of a 'fully developed' and self-sufficient industrialised nation by the year 2020, via an intensification of key economic and social activities. For this collective goal to be achieved, Mahathir counselled the need for a more convivial inter-ethnic (and even trans-ethnic) cohesiveness, as suggested in the moniker 'Bangsa Malaysia' (Malaysian race), to address deteriorating inter-ethnic relations. At various urban centres, particularly in and around Kuala Lumpur, these disparate initiatives manifested themselves through several major infrastructural and mega-construction projects as well as populist appropriations of these slogans in local marketing strategies and everyday discourse.

Other trends have also impinged on the social and political character of contemporary urbanism in Malaysia. Beside flows of Western cultural forms, the phenomenon of Islamic revivalism in the oil-rich Middle East has tracked the rapid urbanisation of Malay-Muslims. That development has contributed to innovation in Islamic beliefs and practices, not all of them perceived to be theologically orthodox by state authorities. Many of the resultant sects and movements have been found in urban or semi-urban settings, and essentially seek to alleviate, if not provide alternatives to, the alienation of a putative secularised developmental path promoted by the state. The unsettling potential of some of these sects was recognised early by state authorities. Over the years, both repression and various counter-measures have been adopted. In particular, during the long tenure of Prime Minister Mahathir (1981–2003), a number of interlocking policy initiatives were developed to 'Islamise government machinery' as well as 'Islamise Malaysian society', through the establishment of an integrated network of legal, judiciary, financial and educational institutions operating in towns and cities throughout the country. Mahathir essentially believed that an Islamic modernism in the mould of Sunni orthodoxy was possible, and that returning to a 'correctly understood Islam', devoid of superstition and fatalism, would help Malay-Muslims address dilemmas of poverty and political subjugation (Schottmann 2013; cf. Peletz 2002).

In sum, the figure or persona of the 'New Malay' has been given particular traction since the advent of Wawasan 2020 (see Barker *et al.* 2014). At least two generations of urbanised Malay-Muslims of different social classes imbibing and articulating new 'structures of feeling'

(Williams 1981) have emerged and are distinctively different from their rural and semi-urban forebears (e.g. Abdul Rahman 2001; Hoffstaedter 2011; cf. Thompson 2007). For some, however, especially non-Malay-Muslims, these varied but interlocking policies and trends have been perceived as supporting an ideology of triumphalist Malay-Muslim exceptionalism. They have also engendered, in response, a heightened sense of defensive or alternative cosmopolitan identity politics, especially salient in urban settings (e.g. DeBernardi 2004; Lee and Ackerman 1997; Mandal 2004; Willford 2006; Yeoh 2009).

Wawasan 2020 and socio-spatial planning

Since 1991, the constant refrain of achieving the coveted 'fully developed' nation status by the year 2020 has infused all subsequent Malaysia Plans. This discourse runs alongside older nation-building aspirations of balancing social and economic development across states and regions, and raising the standard of living and quality of life of citizens.

Even as recently as the Ninth Malaysia Plan (9MP, 2006–10), however, it was conceded that while all states had recorded economic growth and there was material improvement in both rural and urban areas, little headway had been made in achieving this objective. Regional disparities had, in fact, widened further. As a corrective, the strategy of developing trans-border areas across states was emphasised, in addition to giving attention to existing growth centres within states. These growth centres included not only specified urban conurbations, but also rural growth centres.

Consequently, the overall rate of urbanisation throughout Malaysia proceeded at a rapid pace, albeit unevenly, in the first decade of the new millennium (Table 20.1). The Central Region – comprising the states of Melaka, Negri Sembilan, Selangor and the Federal Territory of Kuala Lumpur – has generally experienced the highest rates. Discounting Kuala Lumpur, which has been fully urbanised since much earlier, the adjoining state of Selangor has drawn in the largest numbers of local migrants – including foreign workers – because of spillover opportunities derived from its proximity to the capital city of Malaysia (e.g. Azizah 2011). The contiguity of Kuala Lumpur and Selangor also accounts for the metropolitan sprawl extending in all directions from the former (e.g. Lee 1997; Brookfield 1994; Brookfield *et al.* 1991). In the Northern Region, Pulau Pinang continues to be the most urbanised state while the other states of Kedah, Perak, and Perlis lag far behind. The only state in the Southern Region, Johor, is expected to experience an acceleration of urbanisation with the ongoing development of the extensive Iskandar Malaysia (see below). Although the Federal Territory of Labuan in Sabah has a comparatively high rate of urbanisation, its land area and population are small. The island has attracted significant in-migration largely because of deep-sea gas and oil economic-based activities.

As noted above, by 2010, already 71 percent of the total population of Malaysia were estimated to reside in urban centres. Cognisant of this trend, the Eighth Malaysia Plan (8MP, 2001–05) had mooted the formulation of a comprehensive urbanisation policy. This proposal was reiterated in the 9MP. Subsequently, the National Urbanisation Policy (NUP) for Peninsular Malaysia was launched in 2006. Essentially, the NUP – and the broader, five-yearly National Physical Plan (NPP) launched the previous year – adopts a socio-spatial planning perspective, premised on the proposition that cities and urban centres play an optimal role as engines of economic growth in an era of capitalist globalisation (Sassen 1994; cf. Lefebvre 1991). It provides a basic framework for all subsequent development plans, enumerating six key thrusts and thirty policies covering various aspects of planning development, urban governance and management of townships. The key thrusts identified are:

- an efficient and sustainable urban development;
- development of an urban economy that is resilient, dynamic and competitive;
- an integrated and efficient urban transportation system;
- provision of quality urban services, infrastructure and utilities;
- creation of a conducive liveable urban environment with identity; and
- effective urban governance.

The NUP also advocates for a rational urban hierarchy, so that the provision and distribution of facilities and infrastructure will be more efficient, with minimal wastage of national resources. The urban hierarchy comprises five distinct levels that correlate with current population sizes, zones extending beyond existing city/town administrative boundaries, and commuting times, with growth patterns over the past decade, namely, a National Growth Conurbation (Kuala Lumpur), three Regional Growth Conurbations (Georgetown, Johore and Kuantan), Sub-regional Growth Conurbations (Ipoh, Seremban), State Growth Conurbations and District Growth Conurbations.[5]

Table 20.1 Population and urbanisation rate by state, 2000–10

State	*Population[a] (million)*			*Urbanisation rate (%)*			*Average annual growth rate of urban population (%)*	
	2000	*2005*	*2010*	*2000*	*2005*	*2010*	*8MP*	*9MP*
Northern region								
Kedah	1.67	1.85	2.04	39.1	39.8	40.3	2.4	2.2
Perak	2.09	2.28	2.44	59.1	59.3	59.3	1.6	1.6
Perlis	0.21	0.23	0.25	34.0	35.1	35.9	2.2	2.2
Pulau Pinang	1.33	1.50	1.60	79.7	79.8	80.0	2	1.9
Central region								
Melaka	0.65	0.72	0.79	67.5	70.6	73.4	2.9	2.7
Negeri Sembilan	0.87	0.96	1.03	54.9	56.3	57.4	2.3	2.1
Selangor[b]	4.19	4.87	5.31	87.7	88.4	89.1	2.7	2.4
Wilayah Persekutuan Kuala Lumpur	1.42	1.62	1.70	100.0	100.0	100.0	1.9	1.5
Southern region								
Johor	2.76	3.17	3.46	64.8	66.5	67.7	2.9	2.6
Eastern region								
Kelantan	1.36	1.51	1.67	33.5	33.4	33.3	2	2.1
Pahang	1.30	1.45	1.57	42.0	43.5	44.6	2.7	2.5
Terengganu	0.90	1.02	1.12	49.4	49.8	50.3	2.6	2.6
Sabah	2.60	3.13	3.33	48.1	49.8	51.6	3.1	2.9
Wilayah Persekutuan Labuan	0.08	0.09	0.09	76.3	77.6	78.6	2.2	1.8
Sarawak	2.07	2.34	2.56	48.1	49.5	50.6	2.8	2.4
Malaysia	**23.49**	**26.75**	**28.96**	**62.0**	**63.0**	**63.8**	**2.5**	**2.3**

Source: Ninth Malaysian Plan, Table 17–5 (data from Economic Planning Unit and Department of Statistics).

Notes:

[a] Population data refer to mid-year population.

[b] Includes Wilayah Persekutuan Putrajaya.

To address perennial concerns with narrowing the rural–urban divide and promoting balanced regional development, earlier, private sector-led initiatives for developing growth corridors, regions and triangles, transcending state and national boundaries, were continued. For the first time, the Ninth Malaysia Plan also enabled the setting up of Regional Development Authorities in Sabah and Sarawak.

To date, the single largest development venture since the construction of the new urban centres of Putrajaya and Cyberjaya (King 2008; Bunnell 2006), and the first of its kind in the country, is the Iskandar Malaysia project, situated at the southern tip of peninsular Malaysia and close to important shipping lanes. Launched during the 9MP, the planned metropolis comprises five flagship development zones having a total area three times the size of neighbouring Singapore. Iskandar Malaysia is anticipated to be significantly financed by the private sector and foreign investments, drawn in by the multi-faceted infrastructural and lifestyle features of a master plan implemented by a single coordinating authority. In years to come, the scale and scope of this project promise to reconfigure urbanisation and investment patterns in the country.

The marked entrepreneurial thrust discernible in the making of Iskandar Malaysia metropolis is similarly salient in the Tenth Malaysia Plan (10MP, 2011–15). Moreover, in comparison to previous Malaysia Plans, the neo-liberal, globalist and urbanist aura of the 10MP is quite distinctive. Indeed, in the foreword to the plan, Prime Minster Najib Abdul Razak proposes that a 'new approach, new enthusiasm and a new determination driven by the 1Malaysia spirit' is needed to take the country to the next stage of development (Government of Malaysia 2010a: iii). The trope of 'transformation' is given prominence in the New Economic Model (NEM), which warns that despite being economically successful in the past, Malaysia is at risk of being 'caught in the middle-income trap' and overtaken by other countries because of increased competition (Government of Malaysia 2010a: 5). To transition to high-income status, it is proposed that the structure of the country's economy be substantially altered. This translates to developing far more investor-friendly policies and shifting away from ethnic-based to merit-based affirmative action policies. The NEM has two interlocking prongs. The Government Transformation Programme (GTP) aims at morphing the Malaysian government into an efficient and *rakyat* (people)-centred institution, via the delivery of measurable outcomes in the shape of National Key Result Areas (NKRAs) – reducing crime, fighting inflation, improving urban public transport, improving student outcomes, and so forth.[6] By comparison, the Economic Transformation Programme (ETP) outlines a road map to double the current gross national income per capita, to around US$15,000 by 2020, largely through attracting US$444 billion in investments and creating 3.3 million new jobs.[7] Repeatedly, the private sector has been identified as a major engine of growth for the national economy.

Greater Kuala Lumpur/Klang Valley and urban complexity

As noted earlier, the 9MP created economic development corridors. An innovation under the 10MP was to channel more resources to specific clusters, like cities and towns within these corridors. In this futuristic scenario, Greater Kuala Lumpur/Klang Valley (Greater KL/KV), covering ten municipalities, has been identified as being the only geographically specific National Key Economic Area (NKEA) of the ETP. The remaining eleven NKEAs are in the shape of sectors – namely, oil and gas, palm oil and related products, wholesale and retail sales, tourism, information and communications technology, education, electrical and electronics, business services, private healthcare, and agriculture. Greater KL/KV is geographically smaller than the Kuala Lumpur Conurbation identified in the NUP, as it concentrates on high-density economic agglomerations, including important sites like the Kuala Lumpur International Airport. In 2010, it was estimated that Greater KL/KV comprised about 20 percent of the national population, generated 30 percent of the nation's gross national income and contributed about eight times the gross domestic product of any other geographic cluster in the country (Figure 20.1).

Since the launch of the 10MP and ETP, there has been a discernible beehive of activities unleashed in the capital city. Most visible have been construction works on the public transportation system of the city ('a *rakyat*-centric public transportation system'), in order to improve connectivity and mobility as well as reduce traffic congestion woes stemming from heavy private vehicular usage. An entity, 'InvestKL', has been created to focus specifically on attracting substantive foreign investment to transform the city into a financial services centre of global repute. Human capital is also seen as crucial to this venture. In competing for highly skilled foreign talent, the aesthetic discourse of a world-class, artistically vibrant and liveable city has increasingly been foregrounded. Tourism remains a significant source of revenue. Besides shopping, the usual itinerary includes visits to iconic sites in and around Kuala Lumpur. The logic of the tourist gaze and place marketing have seen hitherto ethnically mixed places in well-established parts of the city rebranded into easily recognisable heritage enclaves (see Yeoh 2009). Moreover, leveraging on a tourist marketing slogan popularised

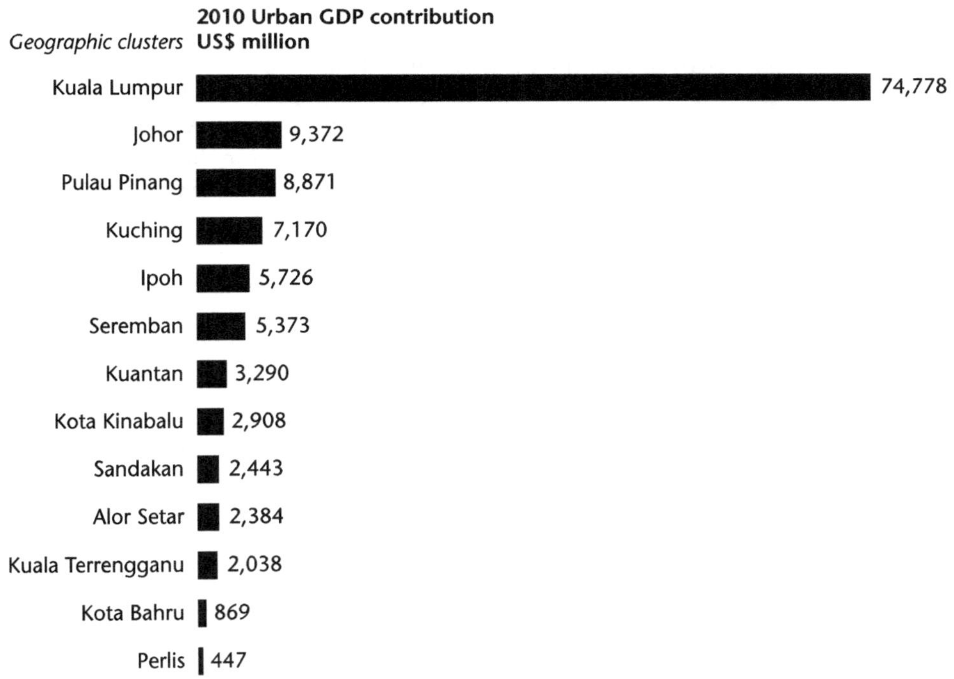

Figure 20.1 Kuala Lumpur contributes eight times the GDP of any other geographic cluster in Malaysia

Source: Tenth Malaysian Plan, Chart 3–19 (data from World Gazeteer, Department of Statistics Malaysia).

Note:

Population for Kuala Lumpur includes FT Kuala Lumpur, Klang, Petaling Jaya, Ampang Jaya, Shah Alam, Cheras and Kajang.

since 1999, a 'Malaysia, Truly Asia Centre' themed attraction park, controversially sited on one of the few remaining green spaces of the city, is being planned.[8]

Arguably, much of the aforementioned activity is an extension and consolidation of earlier spatial cleansing, beautification and gentrification initiatives during Mahathir's premiership, with the large-scale clearance of long-established squatter *kampong*, the acquisition of private land for urban redevelopment and the construction of several impressive and iconic structures like the Bukit Jalil Sports Complex and the Petronas Twin Towers in order to position Kuala Lumpur (and by extension, Malaysia) prominently on the global map (Yeoh 2014a; cf. Roy and Ong 2011).[9] Subsequently, smaller-scale versions of this urban planning discourse have been imitated and replicated in urban centres throughout the country. These ventures have been especially lauded by investors and property developers as desirable signs of 'development' and 'progress'.

Like other Asian metropoles, Kuala Lumpur offers the promise of greater freedom and upward mobility. Nevertheless, for many, it is also a place where these hopes have not readily materialised and, instead, where social and economic inequities have further deepened. This is because, as is implicit in all the plans discussed, modernist urbanisation is essentially characterised by its residents being segregated and dispersed according to rationalised social relations of production and consumption, resulting in urban spaces being differentiated by a social and economic hierarchy (e.g. Lefebvre 1991). At an architectural level, this is reflected by the once comparatively bare Kuala Lumpur skyline increasingly being marked by monolithic, high-density skyscrapers priced on a graduated scale based on location, floor space, quality of design, construction materials and range of in-house services available. Consumption habits and shopping lifestyles have similarly morphed. Expansive shopping malls and precincts featuring foreign cuisine, chain stores, health spas and entertainment are the preferred leisure destinations for an expanding middle class (see also Abdul Rahman, this volume). Ironically, where they exist, local cuisines are rebranded in a nostalgic register in these complexes. The staff servicing the customers are typically foreign migrant workers hailing from the Southeast Asian and South Asian regions.

Among those who have had to make way for these structures or are not able to partake of these luxuries, feelings toward 'development' are understandably more ambivalent. For instance, demolishing long-established squatter *kampung* and relocating their residents into high-rise and cramped, public or private, low-cost housing has not automatically alleviated urban poverty. Instead, by contrast to middle-class and elite condominiums, the sub-standard construction quality and poor maintenance of many of these structures have meant that living conditions in them often approximate the ambience of vertical slums. Moreover, for a city that boasts of having 'First World' facilities, detractors also decry the ubiquitous sight of homeless people, many of whom are aged or have children, sleeping rough under elevated highways and on sidewalks. Several humanitarian civil society and religious groups have responded by setting up soup kitchens and night hostels to supplement the local government's efforts. For underclass youths, the increasing costs of city life, lack of job opportunities, material deprivation and sense of discrimination have also inclined them to join gangs engaged in street crimes, burglaries, extortion, human trafficking and illegal money-lending. Although police statistics claim otherwise, reports of bag snatching, hold-ups and robberies of automated teller machines at banks have become staple everyday news.

Ethno-religious demographic shifts in Kuala Lumpur have altered the texture of cosmopolitan urbanism. Although Kuala Lumpur has been labelled as a 'Chinese town' ever since its genesis in the middle of the nineteenth century, the 2010 census indicates that Malays (44.7 percent) have now slightly overtaken Chinese (43.2 percent) as the majority ethnic group in the city. This has meant that more *surau* (Muslim prayer rooms) and mosques have been built to cater to Muslims' religious and spiritual needs. The periodic *azan* (call to worship) now punctuates city soundscapes, even in religiously mixed areas. Conversely, there have been incidents of fractious debates (especially over the Internet) when Muslim residents have objected to 'religious noise' produced by non-Muslims during temple festivities held in mixed neighbourhoods. In accordance with Syariah laws, Islamic religious authorities have conducted regular moral policing raids to weed out Muslims suspected of practising *haram* (religiously not permissible) activities like consuming alcohol or being in close physical proximity with a person of the opposite sex who is not one's spouse (*khalwat*) (e.g. Lee 2010). More recently, Muslims have also been advised by *fatwa* (learned opinions) from some *ulama* (religious teachers) not to observe Valentine's Day or practise yoga because of the non-Muslim origins and putative hostility to Islam of both (e.g. Yeoh 2014b). The intensity of surveillance activities, however, does suggest that urbanised Malay-Muslims in Kuala Lumpur (and by extension, other major cities) are not a homogeneous or easily manageable political entity. This finding is corroborated by voting patterns in the general election of May 2013. Among other reasons, it is evident that the face-to-face experience of living in an ethno-religiously complex, cosmopolitan and globalised city space like Kuala Lumpur produces emergent Malay-Muslim subject positions.

Conclusion

Unlike for extant ancient cities in the Southeast Asian region, urbanisation in Malaysia is of comparatively recent vintage. The creation and maintenance of towns during the colonial period was premised on the political economy of wealth extraction for the metropolitan centre. In the post-colonial milieu, these same centres and their hinterlands have been re-mapped and recalibrated in terms of achieving a 'balanced regional development' for the sake of 'national harmony' and 'progress'. In the context of deeper regional and global connectivity wrought by transnational capitalist expansion over the last three or four decades, however, these aspirations are being challenged and mediated by contemporary urbanisation (and urbanist) trends that are tightly tethered to trans-local forms, flows and processes. Rather than having to urbanise simply because of economic necessity, this pathway has been a deliberate choice and strategy pursued by visionary political leaders, supported by the captains of industry, desirous of raising the nation's status onto a global stage. The opening up of the country in ways reminiscent of the entrepreneurialism of the colonial period will no doubt once again transfigure the spaces and sociality of its residents. Not surprisingly, these transformations will be felt most intensely in the network of large urban centres, old and new, that dot Malaysia.

Notes

1 All figures cited are from Department of Statistics 2011.
2 It was observed that British Malaya had an 'unusual degree of urbanisation for a country where half the working population is engaged in agriculture and with very minor industrial development' (Cooper 1951: 118). Between 1911 and 1970, urban growth in the peninsula outstripped the growth rate for the total population (Aiken and Leigh 1975: 546).
3 This definition was adjusted with the 1970 census to 10,000 persons and above, then again with the 1991 census to reflect a more realistic level of urbanisation. *Inter alia*, 'urban areas' are gazetted areas and their adjoining built-up areas have urban characteristics and a combined population of 10,000 persons or more.
4 For a recent critical evaluation of the achievements of the New Economic Policy, see the collection edited by Edmund Terence Gomez and Johan Saravanamuttu (2013).

5 Conurbations are demarcated according to travel times from employment centres of core cities. For main conurbations, this would be forty-five minutes and for other conurbations, thirty minutes.
6 See http://pemandu.gov.my/gtp (accessed 3 October 2013).
7 See http://etp.pemandu.gov.my (accessed 3 October 2013).
8 See www.tar.com.my/upcoming-projects/malaysia-truly-asia-attraction; see also www.theedgemalaysia.com/property/245165-land-matters-delay-khazanahs-cultural-park.html (accessed 4 October 2013).
9 Surveys conducted in the late 1960s and 1970s had revealed that up to one-third of Kuala Lumpur's resident population was made up of 'squatters'. While a more explicit 'anti-squatter policy' took gradual shape from the late 1970s, it was only during the economically buoyant 1990s that a 'squatter-free city' discourse became normalised, in line with aspirations for a 'World Class city'.

Bibliography

Abdul Rahman Embong (2001) *State-led Modernisation and the New Middle Class in Malaysia*, Basingstoke: Palgrave.

Aiken, Robert S. and Colin H. Leigh (1975) 'Malaysia's emerging conurbation', *Annals of the Association of American Geographers*, 65(4): 546–63.

Azizah Kassim (2011) 'Transnational migration and the contestation of urban space: emerging problems and possible solutions', in Abdul Rahman Embong and Tham Siew Yean (eds), *Malaysia at the Crossroads*, Bangi: Penerbit Universiti Kebangsaan Malaysia, pp. 86–117.

Barker, Joshua, Erik Harms and Johan Lindquist (eds) (2014) *Figures of Southeast Asian Modernity*, Honolulu: University of Hawai'i Press.

Brookfield, Harold (ed.) (1994) *Transformation with Industrialization in Peninsular Malaysia*, Kuala Lumpur: Oxford University Press.

Brookfield, Harold, Abdul Samad Hadi and Zaharah Mahmud (1991) *The City in the Village: The In-Situ Urbanization of Villages, Villagers and Their Land around Kuala Lumpur, Malaysia*, Singapore: Oxford University Press.

Bunnell, Tim (2006) *Malaysia, Modernity and the Multimedia Super Corridor*, London and New York: Routledge.

Cooper, Eunice (1951) 'Urbanisation in Malaya', *Population Studies*, 5(2): 117–31.

DeBernardi, Jean (2004) *Rites of Belonging: Memory, Modernity and Identity in a Chinese Community*, Stanford: Stanford University Press.

Department of Statistics (2011) *Population Distribution and Basic Demographic Characteristics 2010*, Government of Malaysia, http://www.statistics.gov.my/portal/download_Population/files/census2010/Taburan_Penduduk_dan_Ciri-ciri_Asas_Demografi.pdf (accessed 3 October 2013).

Evers, Hans-Dieter and Rudiger Korff (2000) *Southeast Asian Urbanism: The Meaning and Power of Social Space*, New York: St Martin's Press.

Gomez, Edmund Terence and Johan Saravanamuttu (eds) (2013) *The New Economic Policy in Malaysia: Affirmative Action, Ethnic Inequalities and Social Justice*, Petaling Jaya and Singapore: Gerakbudaya, NUS Press and ISEAS.

Government of Malaysia (1984) *Kuala Lumpur Structure Plan*, Kuala Lumpur: Kuala Lumpur City Hall.

Government of Malaysia (2001) *Eighth Malaysia Plan*, available at www.epu.gov.my/en/eighth-malaysia-plan-2001-2005 (accessed 3 October 2013).

Government of Malaysia (2004) *Kuala Lumpur Structure Plan 2020: A World Class City*, Kuala Lumpur: Kuala Lumpur City Hall.

Government of Malaysia (2006a) *National Urbanisation Plan*, available at www.kpkt.gov.my/kpkt_2013/fileupload/dasar/DPN_BI.pdf (accessed 3 October 2013).

Government of Malaysia (2006b) *Ninth Malaysia Plan*, available at www.epu.gov.my/en/ninth-malaysia-plan-2006-2010 (accessed 3 October 2013).

Government of Malaysia (2010a) *Tenth Malaysia Plan*, available at www.epu.gov.my/en/tenth-malaysia-plan-10th-mp- (accessed 3 October 2013).

Government of Malaysia (2010b) *Economic Transformation Plan*, available at http://etp.pemandu.gov.my/Download_Centre-@-Download_Centre.aspx (accessed 3 October 2013).

Government of Malaysia (2010c) *National Physical Plan*, available at www.kpkt.gov.my/kpkt_2013/fileupload/dasar/NPP.pdf (accessed 3 October 2013).

Hamzah Sendut (1966) 'Contemporary urbanisation in Malaysia', *Asian Survey*, 6(9): 484–91.
Hoffstaedter, Gerhard (2011) *Modern Muslim Identities: Negotiating Religion and Ethnicity in Malaysia*, Copenhagen: Nordic Institute of Asian Studies.
Jackson, J.C. (1968) *Planters and Speculators: Chinese and European Agricultural Enterprise in Malaya, 1786–1921*, Kuala Lumpur: University of Malaya Press.
Kahn, Joel (2006) *Other Malays: Nationalism and Cosmopolitanism in the Modern Malay World*, Singapore: National University of Singapore Press.
Kaur, Amarjit (1985) *Bridge and Barrier: Transport and Communication in Colonial Malaya*, Kuala Lumpur: Oxford University Press.
King, Ross (2008) *Kuala Lumpur and Putrajaya: Negotiating Urban Space in Malaysia*, Singapore: National University of Singapore Press.
Lee Boon Thong (1997) 'Emerging urban trends and the globalising economy in Malaysia', in Fu-Chen Lo and Yue-man Yeung (eds), *Emerging World Cities in Pacific Asia*, Tokyo: United Nations University Press, pp. 335–76.
Lee, Julian (2010) 'Oversanctification, autonomy and Islam in Malaysia', *Totalitarian Movements and Political Religions*, 11(1): 25–43.
Lee, Raymond and Susan Ackerman (1997) *Sacred Tensions: Modernity and Religious Transformation in Malaysia*, Columbia: University of South Carolina Press.
Lefebvre, Henri (1991) [1974] *The Production of Space*, trans. Donald Nicholson-Smith, Oxford: Blackwell.
Lim Heng Kow (1978) *The Evolution of the Urban System in Malaya*, Kuala Lumpur: Penerbit Universiti Malaya.
Lim Teck Ghee (1977) *Peasants and Their Agricultural Economy in Colonial Malaya, 1874–1941*, Kuala Lumpur: Oxford University Press.
Mandal, Sumit (2004) 'Transethnic solidarities, racialisation and social equality', in Edmund Terence Gomez (ed.), *The State of Malaysia: Ethnicity, Equity and Reform*, New York and London: Routledge, pp. 49–78.
Mayaram, Shail (ed.) (2009) *The Other Global City*, New York: Routledge.
Morshidi Sirat and Ghazali Suriati (1999) *Globalisation of Economic Activity and Third World Cities: A Case Study of Kuala Lumpur*, Kuala Lumpur: Utusan Publications.
Peletz, Michael (2002) *Islamic Modern: Religious Courts and Cultural Politics in Malaysia*, Princeton: Princeton University Press.
Reid, Anthony (1988) *Southeast Asia in the Age of Commerce, 1450–1680 1*, New Haven: Yale University Press.
Rimmer, Peter and George C.H. Cho (1981) 'Urbanisation of the Malays since Independence: evidence from West Malaysia, 1957 and 1970', *Journal of Southeast Asian Studies*, 2(2): 349–63.
Rimmer, Peter and Howard Dick (2009) *The City in Southeast Asia: Patterns, Processes and Policy*, Singapore: National University of Singapore Press.
Roy, Ananya and Aihwa Ong (eds) (2011) *Worlding Cities: Asian Experiments and the Art of Being Global*, Chichester: Wiley-Blackwell.
Sassen, Saskia (1994) *Cities in a World Economy*, Thousand Oaks: Pine Forge.
Schottmann, Sven Alexander (2013) 'God helps those who help themselves: Islam according to Mahathir Mohamad', *Islam and Christian–Muslim Relations*, 24(1): 57–69.
Thompson, Eric (2007) *Unsettling Absences: Urbanism in Rural Malaysia*, Singapore: National University of Singapore Press.
Wain, Barry (2009) *Malaysian Maverick, Mahathir Mohamad in Turbulent Times*, Houndmills: Palgrave.
Willford, Andrew (2006) *Cage of Freedom: Tamil Identity and the Ethnic Fetish in Malaysia*, Ann Arbor: University of Michigan Press.
Williams, Raymond (1981) *Culture*, London: Fontana.
Wong, David (1975) *Tenure and Land Dealings in the Malay States*, Singapore: Singapore University Press.
Yeoh Seng Guan (2009) 'Limiting cosmopolitanism: Streetlife Little India, Kuala Lumpur', in Shail Mayaram (ed.), *The Other Global City*, London and New York: Routledge, pp. 131–60.
Yeoh Seng Guan (ed.) (2014a) *The Other Kuala Lumpur: Living in the Shadows of a Globalising Southeast Asian City*, London and New York: Routledge.
Yeoh Seng Guan (2014b) 'Actually existing religious pluralism in Kuala Lumpur', in Chiara Formichi (ed.), *Religious Pluralism, State and Society in Asia*, London and New York: Routledge, pp. 153–71.

Part III

Social policy and social development

Overview

Meredith L. Weiss

Famously glossed as a 'plural society', Malaysia remains complex, in terms not just of ethnicity, but also class, religion, gender, sexuality, and other dimensions. Known equally, too, for its developmentalist aspirations (as discussed in the last section), which have required both ambitious educational and social service expansion and a degree of media and other openness, and for a restrictive human rights regime, Malaysia struggles with endemic tensions among competing goals and along varied axes, as inequalities and unmet benchmarks put prescriptions and policies to the test.

Shamsul A.B. and Athi S.M. kick off the discussion by seeking the historical roots of the ethnic categories so pervasive and internalised in Malaysia today. They trace this organisational rubric to colonial authorities' administrative and functional demarcation of communities and the eventual reification of these categories in everyday life. Key to that process was a colonial division of labour that effectively separated 'Malays', 'Chinese', and 'Indians', and which persisted, with much the same parameters, well beyond independence. It was only with the expansion of industrialisation and urbanisation, as well as state-organised agricultural restructuring and resettlement schemes, particularly after 1970, that patterns began to change. In particular, with increasing occupational and social mobility, Shamsul and Athi argue, intra-ethnic distinctions have come to rival inter-ethnic ones.

Alberto G. Gomes highlights a particularly stark manifestation of Malaysia's inter-ethnic disparities. However impressive Malaysia's accomplishments overall in reducing poverty and boosting opportunities across ethnic categories, indigenous minorities in particular remain deeply disadvantaged. Gomes focuses on the Orang Asli (indigenous peoples) on the Peninsula, whom he describes as endemically marginalised in the face of market forces – willingly embraced or otherwise – as well as government-sponsored development plans, forcible resettlement, and social engineering, including Islamisation. He argues, among other measures, for security of land tenure, for both economic and cultural/identity reasons, and for more appropriate and higher-quality education, better healthcare and nutrition, and political and economic power broadly.

Echoing and expanding upon Gomes's call for empowerment, John Liu examines the ups and downs of civil liberties in Malaysia, over the course of successive administrations. While the Malaysian constitution grants a full raft of civil liberties and both positive and negative rights, these are contravened or curbed by enactments that prioritise aspects of public order over individual rights. While particular enactments and events represent these dynamics especially well, the overall picture is relatively consistent: one of side-lining civil liberties in conjunction with, and in support of, larger political contests and arguments for Malaysia's exceptionalism.

We move next to a more positive story, as Molly N.N. Lee details Malaysia's well-developed, well-supported primary, secondary, and tertiary education system. Here, too, though, she finds room for improvement. From a perspective of national unity, different language streams across school types limit ethnic mixing at the primary and secondary levels, and matters of media of instruction remain controversial. From a more material perspective, Malaysia has not met its own targets either for overall higher education enrolments or for the share of graduates in science, technology, and engineering fields. Echoing Shamsul and Athi's as well as Gomes's findings, Lee notes a lack of equity not just across ethnic groups, but also, for instance, between urban and rural students, across classes, and between men and women. Moreover, Malaysia has performed below expectations in international assessment exercises, at all levels, and issues of graduate employability remain keen. She recommends updating and revising standards for educators as well as student achievement, thinking seriously about the appropriate economic model for higher education (e.g. state support versus corporatisation and privatisation), and determining the right mix of central regulation and institutional autonomy, especially, but not exclusively, in higher education.

We turn next to healthcare, another much-touted Malaysian success story, but one similarly subject to pressures and plans for reform. Chee Heng Leng and Por Heong Hong examine healthcare financing and access, including the latest system rebranding, '1Care'. Healthcare expenditures have been rising and private healthcare has expanded – neither of which development is likely optimal. Opposition to the '1Care' plan has come both from healthcare practitioners and advocates and from the public, given concerns over potential (and substantially unknown) escalating costs and bureaucracy as well as potentially worse access to services, accessibility, and patient choice. Yet the latest bout of civil society opposition is in line with responses to prior rounds of privatisation and restructuring of healthcare financing. After detailing several alternatives proposed, Chee and Por recommend a well-designed social health insurance fund as the best option.

Carolina López C. picks up the thread of civil society, but in a different context. She focuses on Malaysia's longstanding cultural and religious pluralism, recent tensions disrupting interfaith relations, and initiatives, originating both with government and with civil society, to sustain harmony. Structural features of the Malaysian state, she argues, socialise Malaysians toward a deeply internalised dichotomy between Malays/Muslims and 'others' – a dichotomy perpetuated in laws and policies. That framework lays the ground for potential inter-group conflict, as has periodically emerged in Malaysia. The sorts of efforts at collaboration López describes, she suggests, offer a way out of or around these impasses, but to be effective, must address that underlying dichotomy.

Kathy Rowland similarly engages with sparring cultural visions, but on the terrain of visual, musical, and performance art. She sketches the arts in Malaysia as a site of ongoing contest, between the state's hegemonic vision and ambitions and generations of artists' alternatives. While local arts practitioners have taken advantage of discursive openings from changes in Malaysian cultural policies as well as increasingly available private and public sponsorship, much development, especially in recent years, has been in parallel to more mainstream forms and venues. In particular, in the face of increasing efforts by the state and its allies to police identity and conceptions of the nation and 'the public', artists working across genres and languages have offered their own, varied imaginings.

In their chapter on gender in Malaysia, tan beng hui and Cecilia Ng describe a similarly thorny process of engagement with state policies and visions. In terms of covenants signed and quantitative indices, Malaysia has made progress over the past several decades toward women's empowerment and gender equality; however, closer attention to context and nuance suggests important lacunae. The authors argue for a critical, rather than merely instrumental, approach to gender, to explore the distribution of power and resources in Malaysian society, as well as how gender aligns with or intersects other social constructs and structures. Lack of systematic, gender-disaggregated data or innovative approaches to undercut essentialism in assigning/presuming tasks, and deeply entrenched structural inequalities as well as legal provisions and cultural norms limit the scope of women's advance.

Pang Khee Teik depicts an even more fraught discursive and embodied landscape as he parses the controversy over Seksualiti Merdeka, a recent Malaysian sexuality rights initiative. The banning of Seksualiti Merdeka served to raise popular awareness of sexuality and gender diversity as well as the ways in which these challenge normativity – or in the apocryphal language of opponents, threaten the very fabric of the nation and Islam. Debate over the festival brought to the fore questions of LGBTs' (lesbian, gay, bisexual, and transgender) own identification and priorities, engaged local and international norms and laws, and amplified both the exclusionary boundaries of full Malaysian citizenship and the limits of ethnonationalist or economic alternatives. Pang closes the section with an appeal for a more inclusive, but also more flexible and empowering, national imaginary.

21

Ethnicity and identity formation

Colonial knowledge, colonial structures and transition

Shamsul A.B. and Athi S.M.

The evolution of a social group into an ethnic group in a national context is largely the result of a modernist project of nation-state formation, and closely related to power relations; however, competing power relations functioning at different levels, in different periods, produce a plurality of understandings. Hence, ethnic identity is always subject to contestation and renegotiation – evidence of its versatile and adaptive nature. Even so, certain fundamental notions regarding racial and ethnic construction tend to persist, given the habituation of epistemological space.

In Malaysia, the origins of ethnic groups lie in the construction of colonial knowledge about Malaysia. This knowledge became applied, institutionalised and embedded into official use, bureaucratic tools and public policy formulations, such as through censuses, land enactments, birth certificates, identity cards, vernacular school systems, and so on. These functions continued largely uninterrupted in the post-colonial period, extending the notion of defining ethnic and racial categories according to physical and cultural markers.

Under colonial and post-colonial rule alike, defining and classifying ethnic and racial categories at the administrative level and applying these on the ground can be a difficult task. As a way out, 'popular perceptions are usually [accepted as] sufficient to sort most of the population into standard classifications' (Hirschman 1987: 557). This compromise suggests the existence of multilayered notions of ethnicity. It is thus vital to probe the origins of ethnic and racial classifications and key terms regarding race, nationality, dialect group, community and ethnicity.

On the other hand, the complexity of ethnic identity can be observed in the fact that the study of ethnicity and identity may yield different results when pitched at a different level of analysis. For instance, at the individual level of self-identification, a person is 'Hakka' or 'Cantonese', 'Tamil' or 'Telugu', or 'Javanese' or 'Bugis', but at the communal level, he will be 'Chinese', 'Indian' or 'Malay'. If religion is used as a primary marker, then self-identification will shift once again. This is not merely a problem of conflating categories with groups or confusion in distinguishing among idiosyncratic complexities arising at the individual or group levels. Rather, this complexity suggests that the focus should be on the social and political formation of ethnic identity.

We employ the term 'ethnicity' instead of other value-loaded referents in the Malaysian context. Ethnicity permeates all aspects of the complexities exhibited in Malaysian social life, both seen and unseen. Ethnicity has a dominant influence in defining and shaping the identity of Malaysians, consciously as well as unconsciously. To unpack this complexity in identity formation among Malaysians we need an analytical tool that is simple enough to be understood and applied across the board in the humanities and social sciences.

We therefore use the 'two social realities' framework of 'authority-defined' and 'everyday-defined' reality introduced by Shamsul (1996a). This framework provides, perhaps for the first time, the following conceptual and empirical tools: first, an alternative analytical device to examine the internal dynamics of ethnicity and identity formation in Malaysia; second, a demonstration of the defining role of colonial knowledge in shaping the landscape of modern knowledge production, particularly in Malaysia; and, third, an understanding of the significance of the phenomenon of social mobility and its material base in the reshaping of ethnicity and identity formation, so as to highlight not only the inter-ethnic, but also intra-ethnic dimensions that complicate post-1969 discourse.

The 'two social realities' approach

We contend that, like most social phenomena, identity formation takes place within what we would call a 'two social realities' context: the 'authority-defined' social reality as laid out by members of the dominant power structure and the 'everyday-defined' social reality experienced in the course of normal life. These two social realities exist side by side at any given time. Although intricately linked and mutually constitutive, these social realities are rarely identical. Both are mediated through the social class position of those who observe and interpret social reality and those who experience it.

Woven into the relationship between these two social realities is social power, articulated in various forms, such as a majority–minority discourse and state–society contestation. In concrete, familiar terms, social power involves social collectives such as religious or environmental or nationalist movements, political parties, NGOs, professional groups, trade unions, charity associations, literary groups, the intelligentsia, academia and the like. Its discourse takes both oral and written forms, some literary and others simply statistical, informed usually by various dimensions of ideas about 'social justice' and reflecting wider, inherent social inequality.

In the authority-defined context, we would include debate and discourse, both in the past and at present, within the government and between government and non-government collectives, amongst members of the intelligentsia and within the sphere of *realpolitik*. The discourse in an authority-defined context is not homogenous. In fact, it has always been characterised by vigorous and tense discussions on a broad range of themes and issues, both minor and major in nature, usually involving a number of social groups, each representing particular interests. For instance, discourse on ecological issues between the government and opposition political parties or NGOs may be viewed as a majority–minority discourse, but conducted in the confines of an authority-defined context. Generally, discourse in an authority-defined context is textualised, both in published and unpublished forms, some of which are woven into official policies and others, written up as academic publications. In short, the text of such a discourse is usually recorded, either in printed form (official reports, policy documents, newspaper reports, books, magazines, academic journals, photographs, etc.) or in audio-visual electronic and digital forms (tape and video cassette recordings, diskettes, CD-ROMs, films, YouTube clips, etc.).

Discourse in an everyday-defined context is usually disparate, fragmented, intensely personal and conducted mostly orally. Since it is overwhelmingly an articulation of personal experience, not meant to be systemised or positioned for a particular pre-determined macro objective, it is not textualised for future reference, except occasionally by researchers, such as anthropologists or historians who record or write down, as ethnographic notes, 'personal narratives'. These narratives are often captured, too, in what is generally categorised as 'popular forms of expression' or popular culture, such as cartoons, songs, poems, short-stories, rumours and gossip, poison-pen letters, and the like. Irrespective of what each narrative has to tell, how widely it has been accepted across society, and whether or not it represents contemporary public concerns, it is usually considered as an individual or personal contribution from the 'author' (cartoonist, singer, poet, short-story writer, etc.) (Shamsul 1982). As such, it remains a subjective 'text', often considered as unrepresentative of empirical reality or 'truth', and not dissimilar in status from legally unacceptable hearsay evidence.

Until recently, some social scientists have rejected such texts outright as a source or form of research data because they are deemed not objective; those social scientists would prefer instead 'scientific' statistics, even if concocted or manipulated. The subjective nature of texts of everyday-defined social reality has never been in doubt, but consistent rejection of these as valid sources of information and data is tantamount to the political suppression, or exclusion from mainstream consideration and concern, of 'voices from below' or subaltern voices. While reminiscent of the 'orality–literacy' contest (Sweeney 1987), this rejection – often subtle and taken for granted – is not simply that, but has been 'normalised' into our daily life. One has only to read the newspapers, which invariably represent authority-defined voices of all types and rarely everyday-defined ones, except perhaps in the 'letters to editor', editorial, or entertainment sections.

This juxtaposition reflects the inter-connectedness and dialectical nature of the relationship between authority-defined and everyday-defined social reality, which, of course, has a material basis. Often the politics and poetics of this relationship are ignored, or its material basis unexamined. This is most obvious in the intellectual realm of society, in which there has been a tendency to disconnect 'social theory', on the one hand, from public intellectual life and the moral concerns of real people, on the other hand, with the former assumed the authority. Many of us perceive the status of and relationship between authority-defined and everyday-defined discourse in much the same way, and tend to favour the former.

Colonial origins: define and rule

Colonial knowledge defined and created ethnic and other social categories, thus enabling the colonial administration to govern in a divide-and-rule-manner (Shamsul 2001). This phenomenon has recently been well captured and elucidated by Mamdani in his book *Define and Rule* (2012), drawing on African experience. Relevant here are the methods of accumulating facts that resulted in the formation and organisation of the corpus of colonial knowledge. The approach that anthropologist Bernard Cohn developed to make British rule in India more understandable is extremely useful. The British managed to classify, categorise and connect the vast social world that was India so it could be controlled by way of so-called 'investigative modalities', or devices to collect and organise 'facts' which, together with translation works, enabled the British to conquer 'epistemological space'.

An investigative modality includes the definition of a body of information that is needed and the procedures by which appropriate knowledge is gathered, ordered and classified, and then transformed into useable forms such as published reports, statistical returns, histories, gazettes, legal codes and encyclopaedias. Some of these investigative modalities, such as historiography and museology, are of a general nature, whereas the survey and census modalities are more precisely defined and closely related to administrative needs. Some of these modalities have been transformed into 'sciences' or 'disciplines', such as economics, ethnology, tropical medicine, comparative law and cartography. Their practitioners became professionals. Each modality was tailored to specific elements and needs on the administrative agenda of British rule; each became institutionalised and routinised in the day-to-day practice of colonial bureaucracy.

The 'historiographic modality', the most relevant one for our argument, had three important components. First, the production of settlement reports, on a district-by-district basis; these usually consisted of a description of local customs, histories and land-tenure systems, and a detailed account of how revenues were assessed and collected by local, indigenous regimes. Second, descriptions of indigenous civilisations; these eventually provided the space for the formation of the discourse that legitimised the British civilising mission in the colony. Third, the history of the British presence in the colony, which evoked emblematic 'heroes and villains' and led to the erection of memorials and other 'sacred spaces' in the colony (and in the motherland, as well).

The 'survey modality' encompassed a wide range of practices, from mapping areas to collecting botanical specimens, from the recording of architectural and archaeological sites of historic significance to the minute measuring of peasants' fields. When the British came to India, and later to the Malay lands, they sought to describe and classify every aspect of life in terms of zoology, geology, botany, ethnography, economic products, history and sociology by way of systematic surveys; they also created a colony-wide grid in which every site could be located for economic, social and political purposes. In short, 'surveys' came to cover every systematic and official investigation of the natural and social features of indigenous society; their vast amounts of knowledge were transformed into textual forms such as encyclopaedias and archives.

The 'enumerative modality' enabled the British to categorise indigenous society for administrative purposes, particularly by way of censuses that were to reflect basic sociological facts such as race, ethnic groups, culture and language. The various forms of enumeration that were developed objectified and classified social, cultural and linguistic differences among indigenous peoples and migrants. These differences were of great use for the colonial bureaucracy and its army, to explain and control conflicts and tensions.

Control was primarily implemented by way of the 'surveillance modality': detailed information was collected on 'peripheral' or 'minority' groups and categories of people whose activities were perceived as a threat to social order. Methods such as anthropometry and fingerprinting systems were developed for surveillance, and in order to be able to describe, classify and identify individuals rather accurately for 'security' and other general purposes.

The 'museological modality' started out from the idea that a colony was a vast museum; its countryside, filled with ruins, was a source of collectibles, curiosities and artefacts that could fill local as well as European collections, botanical gardens and zoos. This modality became an exercise in presenting the indigenous culture, history and society to both local and European publics.

The 'travel modality' complemented the museological one. If the latter provided the colonial administration with concrete representations of the natives, the former helped to create a repertoire of images and typifications, if not stereotypes, that determined what was significant to European eyes; architecture, costumes, cuisine, ritual performances and historical sites were presented in 'romantic', 'exotic' and 'picturesque' terms. These often aesthetic images and typifications found expression in paintings and prints as well as in novels and short stories, many of them created by colonial scholar-administrators, their wives and their friends.

These modalities represented, according to Cohn, a set of 'officialising procedures' which the British used to establish and extend their authority – a system of

> control by defining and classifying space, making separations between public and private spheres, by recording transactions such as sale of property, by counting and classifying populations, replacing religious institutions as the registrar of births, marriages, and deaths, and by standardizing languages and scripts.
>
> *(Cohn 1996: 1)*

The colonial state introduced policies and rules that were organised by way of these investigative modalities, in the process framing locals' minds and actions in an epistemological and practical grid.

The relevance of Cohn's approach for analysing developments in the Malay lands is obvious. The Malay Reservation Enactment 1913, to mention just one example, offers a revealing illustration: the Enactment defined, first, who is 'a Malay'; second, it determined the legal category of people who were allowed to grow rice only or rubber only; and third, it was bound to exert a direct influence on the commercial value of land. This particular enactment was instituted in the state constitution of each of the eleven *negeri* (states) on the peninsula separately, and in each, offered a slightly different definition of who was a 'Malay'. For instance, a person of Arab descent was a Malay in Kedah but not in Johor; whereas a person of Siamese descent was a Malay in Kelantan but not in Negeri Sembilan. It could be argued, then, that 'Malay' and 'Malayness' were created and confirmed by the Malay Reservation Enactment. However, there is more to this than meets the eye: the Enactment also made 'Malay' and 'Malayness' contested categories.

In different ways, the growth of public education and its rituals fostered beliefs in how things were and how they ought to be: schools were (and still are) crucial 'civilising' institutions, seeking to produce good and productive citizens. By way of schools, many 'facts' amassed through investigative modalities, and resultant officialising procedures, were channelled to the younger population; in this process governments directed the people's perception of how social reality was organised. What is more, with the creation of Chinese, Malay, Tamil and English schools, ethnic boundaries became real, and ethnic identities became solidified and essentialised by way of language and cultural practices.

The most powerful and pervasive by-product of colonial knowledge on the colonised has been the idea that the modern 'nation-state' is the natural embodiment of history, territory and society. In other words, the 'nation-state' has become dependent on colonial knowledge and its ways of determining, codifying, controlling and representing the past as well as documenting and standardising the information that has formed the basis of government. Modern Malaysians have become familiar with 'facts' that appear in reports and statistical data on commerce and trade, health, demography, crime, transportation, industry, and so on; these facts and their accumulation, conducted in the modalities designed to shape colonial knowledge, lie at the foundation of the modern, post-colonial nation-state of Malaysia. The citizens of Malaysia rarely question these facts, and thereby depict the fine and often invisible manifestations of the process of Westernisation.

What we have briefly sketched here is the 'history of an identity', since these 'facts', rooted in European social theories, philosophical ideas and classificatory schemes, form the basis of Malaysian historiography. It is within this history that modern identities in Malaysia, such as 'Malay', 'Chinese' and 'Indian', have been described and consolidated.

Structural change, ethnic identity and social mobility

The construction of ethnic identity is intricately linked to the material basis of social groups, itself originally the creation of colonial capitalism. Shifts in that material base result in social and economic differentiation through realignment of the inter-ethnic and intra-ethnic status quo and transformations in social position at the individual and collective levels. These critical changes inevitably influence ideas and meanings associated with particular social and economic positions, which in turn shape debates on ethnic identity. We will now outline the processes that shifted the social and economic bases of ethnic groups in Malaysia, and the economic and social polarisation that ensued. Our focus is on the labouring class of each ethnic group.

State-facilitated capitalist development and socio-economic policies since the early 1970s were mainly responsible for this transformation. In exact terms, rapid changes in the social and economic base of ethnic groups was rooted in structural transformation especially of the labour market as well as demographic transformation. The advent of export-led industrialisation in that period created vast employment opportunities for the unskilled and semi-skilled. Employment opportunities created labour mobility in the new sectors, drawing workers mainly from more poorly paid sectors. Sprouting industrial estates along the west coast of Peninsular Malaysia not only created employment opportunities, but also produced rapid urbanisation, with a demographic transition in terms of class and ethnic indicators.

Labour migration highlights these processes. Migration within Malaysia was prompted by differential distribution of income and other opportunities, mediated by network and social ties. For instance, the state with the highest in-migration, Selangor, had the highest acreage of industrial estates – more than half the total in Peninsular Malaysia by 1977. The combination of independent economic migrants as well as state-promoted labour migration, including to federal land schemes, resulted in considerable spatial and occupational mobility among ethnic groups. State and/or market forces function at different levels among the different ethnic groups and within different categories of employment, given state preferential policies. Ethnic identity can be enhanced when it is the state that charts the direction of mobility for many, while also playing a moderating role where market forces are dominant, especially in large industries offering employment for the unskilled and semi-skilled.

The changes caused by labour migration affect both the 'origin' and 'destination' of migration. In the 'origin' – say, the village or the plantation – remittances began to differentiate the economic and social bases of families. Flows of non-agricultural income from a commuting labour force also became a new form of household income in the 'origin'. One estimate was that, with the opening of a new highway between Kuala Lumpur and outlying towns with industrial estates, workers were willing to commute 100 km to work instead of changing residential locations (Chan 1980: 420). More importantly, development triggers ever more outmigration through the established links of earlier migrants. These subsequent migrations were precipitous because the economic and psychological cost of migration also substantially decreased. Changes also occur in the demography of 'destination' areas, with the presence of large numbers of migrants defining the urban social space (or that of 'land schemes') along class and ethnic divides.

The impact of labour migration among the poorest groups cannot be overstated. Categories such as farmers and agricultural labourers were recorded to be among Malaysia's poorest in the early 1970s; by the late 1970s, the agricultural sector was suffering a labour shortage. For example, an acute labour shortage was announced for the plantation industry as early as 1978, both in private and state-promoted land schemes (Athi 2014b). Most migrants moved to urban areas for employment, mainly in the industrial sector. The exodus has permanently changed the labour composition in plantations and eventually paved the way for increased reliance on foreign labour. Thus, social mobility through spatial and occupational mobility became a possibility.

Transition: spatial and occupation mobility of ethnic groups

Notions of ethnicity, as discussed above, are rooted in the colonial power's authority, worldview and needs. One of the factors that sustained these notions in the post-colonial period has been the social and economic reality of productive activities linked with ethnic groups. The original economic function of the various ethnic groups invented during British rule and the spatial distribution of these groups did not change much with independence. This persistence partly legitimised the construction of ethnic identity by the colonial power – a trend that has persisted to the present day.

We witness meaningful transformation in the occupational structure when spatial resettlement is accompanied by economic expansion. The initial mass resettlement of ethnic groups, however, occurred at different periods, under different conditions, and not necessarily under economic expansion. The mass movement of Chinese from rural and fringe areas to 'new villages' was engineered by the British to curb Communist insurgency. More than one million people are estimated to have been resettled from 1948 to 1960 (Sandhu 1964). This movement was followed by two waves among Indians, first following the sub-division of plantation lands from 1950 to 1968, when more than 22,000 labourers alone (excluding their families) were displaced. Next came a second wave of outmigration from the 1970s that depleted the bulk of Indian labour in the plantations. By the time the second wave subsided, Indians had ceased to be the main workforce in an industry in which they once predominated (Athi 2014b). Among Malays, mass rural–urban as well as rural–rural mobility was largely a phenomenon of state rural development programmes of the 1970s. The Federal Land Development Authority (FELDA) scheme alone saw more than 715,000 people resettled between 1956 and 1990 (Sivalingam 1993). The scale of these movements permanently changed the spatial character and occupational patterns of ethnic groups. By 2010, 71.0 percent of the Malaysian population was designated as urban, compared with 26.8 percent in 1970.

At the micro level, this phenomenon also transformed ethnic groups' social and economic organisation, and to a certain extent, their political organisation. The shift from colonial-inherited economic activities – mainly commercial agriculture and mining – in the 1970s was evident in all ethnic groups in Peninsular Malaysia to varying degrees. The shift from supporting the largest rubber and tin industry in the world to retaining only a meagre status in tin and a declining position in rubber reflects the (re)development of colonial industry and employment patterns, especially in Peninsular Malaysia. The locus of this transformation was the spatial and occupational mobility among members of the respective ethnic groups, or even entire family units, since the kinship system and communal ties played a key role – sustained by rapid economic expansion.

For instance, on the eve of independence, the majority of Malays were subsistence peasants (Shamsul 1979), confined to rural areas and involved in rice cultivation (Purcal 1971) and in growing cash crops, mainly rubber (Swift 1965; Wilson 1967), as well as coastal fishing (Firth 1946). They owned small-sized and often fragmented land to till, which limited their productivity. Many rented the plots that they cultivated – landlordism was a common phenomenon in rural Malay areas. Social and economic stratification took on similar patterns among Malays throughout the Peninsula. After World War II, however, an increasing number of Malays with Malay primary school education joined the salariat as low-ranking members of the police and the army and as schoolteachers, or found employment in the government offices (Nordin 1976).

The economic function and spatial character of the community were soon to change. All categories of employment among the Malay labouring class, such as farmers, plantation workers and fishermen, were to experience occupational mobility. Incidentally, these are also the categories of employment identified as 'poverty groups' in various Malaysia Plans. These categories' share of employment in 1970 was 52.2 percent, but dropped to 14 percent in 2008 (Jones 2012: 264), reflecting the magnitude of change in occupational structure. For instance, coastal communities traditionally dependent on the sea as fishermen for generations (Firth 1946; Ishak 1990) moved to shore to seek employment following the creation of new forms of employment in these areas (Nor Hayati 2010). Similar changes in occupational pattern can also be observed among paddy farmers and Malay smallholders. Paddy farmers recorded high rates of outmigration and some even abandoned their land (Courtenay 1988). In fact, this phenomenon also engulfed FELDA settlements, where ageing labourers, absenteeism and outmigration became common occurrences (Sutton and Buang 1995).

Similar changes can also be identified among the Chinese in new villages. Almost 86 percent of the original new village dwellers were Chinese and, for many, their livelihood abruptly halted with resettlement. Soon after the Emergency ended in 1960, some returned to their lands, but the majority remained in the new villages. With the gradual closure of tin mines, changes in employment patterns could be observed. The Chinese working class in new village settlements were heavily involved in agricultural activities, mainly cultivating vegetables, rearing livestock and cultivating cash crops (Loh 1988). The government recognised one-quarter of Chinese households, mostly in the new villages, as living below the poverty line in 1970 (Heng 1997). As economic expansion since the 1970s created new forms of employment, however, outmigration consistently reduced the number of new village residents, especially in settlements in rural areas (Khoo and Voon 1975; Voon 2011). The number of residents in Chinese new villages is now estimated to be about 1.2 million, comprising almost 21 percent of the total Chinese population (Ooi 2009). In settlements close to urban areas, the residents commute to work, mostly in the new economy, benefiting from low-cost urban dwellings.

Indians, on the other hand, were largely confined to plantations, mainly on the west coast of Peninsular Malaysia. The most labour-intensive crop, rubber, was still the primary crop at independence. In the Indian case, disruption in plantation work and life occurred with mass retrenchments and displacement from the early 1950s through the late 1960s, caused by the sub-division of plantation lands into smaller plots for immediate sale, mainly by foreign owners. It also became clear that the plantation as a 'unit of production' should not be confused with its function as a 'unit of settlement', as retrenchments made workers homeless overnight. In short, the plantation community underwent a turbulent period in the years after independence up until the late 1960s. These changes cast serious doubt on the sustainability and security of plantation work and living (Athi 2014b). In the 1970s, outmigration continued – mainly voluntarily – as employment opportunities increased for younger workers in non-plantation sectors, facilitated through migration networks. Such employment continued to be the magnet for migration in the next two decades (Athi 2014b).

New predicament: from poverty to inequality

Developments in the post–1970 era have gradually diluted the ethnic identification with economic activities – as envisioned by state policy-makers, and sustained by market capital.

In 1970, the poverty rate was about 64.8 percent among Malays, 26 percent among Chinese and 39.2 percent among Indians. Those rates had dropped drastically, to 3.3 percent, 0.6 percent and 2.5 percent, respectively, in 2009. Mainstream concern had shifted from poverty to a new problem: inequality. For instance, the gap between urban and rural increased about fifteen times, in absolute terms, and the disparity between rich and poor increased by a factor of almost thirteen, in absolute terms (UNDP 2014). Macro processes resulting from globalisation substantially changed colonial structures of employment and demographic distribution.

The social and economic outcomes of this vast development have varied among and within ethnic groups, reflecting the range of social mobility trajectories experienced by families and communities. Spatial and/or occupational mobility fundamentally defines the outcome of the vast transformation especially among poor and deprived groups. Income mobility and social mobility are evident across ethnic lines. In the same vein, vulnerability persists among certain quarters of the poor in all ethnic groups, including both migrants and non-migrants (Shamsul and Athi 2014).

Malays and Indians are over-represented among the lower-income class, though evidence suggests a small section have become affluent. The majority have experienced income mobility and social mobility, though some remain vulnerable. By no means were these new positions stable; 'stress' and 'shocks' at the familial level and economic crises at the macro level have caused intermittent interruptions, across the ethnic groups, especially in Peninsular Malaysia (Nor Hayati 2010; Athi 2014b; UNDP 2014).

Income disparities divide ethnic groups internally. This is true in most categories of employment. Those who migrated have fared relatively better than their counterparts at the bottom stratum in place of origin, while certain privileged ones have joined the new affluent class. For instance, the rise of a class of accumulating settlers in FELDA (Pletcher 1991; Ishak 1990) or wealthy boat-owning class among fishermen (Nor Hayati 2010), or a new class of contractor-entrepreneurs in plantations (Athi 2014b) demonstrates rapid social mobility in terms of place of origin. Meanwhile, some urban counterparts employed in the industrial sector, while relatively better off than their downtrodden peers in their 'origin', may join the new class of urban poor (Ong 1983). Ironically, urban poverty has increased with each economic crisis, but rural poverty has remained stable in the same periods (Ragayah 2011).

Polarised intra-ethnic patterns among similar income categories have given rise to new forms of discourse, especially at the 'everyday-defined' social reality axis. Often, this discourse is reflected in overt reference to the 'successful' ones. In fact, we have argued elsewhere that the rise of a new discourse on the identity of the 'new rich' among Malays refers to at least two types of 'new' middle classes: *Orang Kaya Baru* and *Melayu Baru* (literally, 'The New Rich' and 'New Malay') (Shamsul 1999b).

In short, the country's development since the early 1970s has had a tremendous transformative impact on the economic, social and political position of the various ethnic groups. The social mobility of the ethnic groups, vertically and horizontally, increased at an incredible pace after that time, and in about two decades, we suddenly saw the emergence of a visible 'new' middle class, urban-based and working not only in the expanded public sector, but also in the enlarged private/corporate sector (Abdul Rahman 2002).

The differentiated experience among social groups engaged in comparable economic activities has been the result of the rapid structural changes. These shifts have given rise to new forms of discourse on ethnic identity, including on intra-ethnic notions of materialism; however, crucial agency in generating new forms of discourse and politics can be observed among the novel class – the 'new' middle class – that arises from these very processes, from the lowest stratum. Their distinct politics is said to range from promoting liberal ideas to being communalistic and safeguarding their newly acquired positions (Athi 2014a). Indeed, this range reflects the entire gamut of debate and discourse on the subject of ethnicity and identity construction.

Conclusion

Identity-formation processes in Malaysia have always been tied up with ethnicity (read: race, communal group, nationality, dialect group) and vice versa. The 'epistemological conquest' by the British set the 'define-and-rule' framework of modern colonial and post-colonial Malaya, and later, Malaysia. The construction, definition and operation of the modern nation-state in Malaysia have been wholly based on colonial knowledge, which many ordinary Malaysians do not recognise or even realise. For instance, what have been considered as 'facts' in various official reports that are taken for granted as 'the truth' and accepted as something natural and given are indeed accumulated and derived from the colonial investigative modality, a methodology that creates and defines social categories. In other words, colonial knowledge has been and remains to a great extent the foundation and pillar of the modern, post-colonial Malaysia.

Events since the early 1970s, particularly the structural changes triggered by state-facilitated capitalism and new state policies, have transformed the landscape of ethnicity and identity formation built upon colonial knowledge, which emphasised inter-ethnic relations as the primary phenomenon to be observed and understood in order to make sense of what happens in Malaysia. This transformation has made it imperative also to observe and explain the phenomenon of intra-ethnic relations. The complex dynamics of, and interactions between, these dimensions represent the social roots of non-ethnic and issue-based discourse in post–1999 Malaysia. Moreover, the attendant vertical and horizontal social mobility experienced by all ethnic groups suggests that the material basis of ethnicity and identity formation in Malaysia has gone through an irreversible change, and that the identification between ethnicity and economic activity has become blurred. It has been the aim of this chapter to highlight and elucidate the complicated social, political and economic realms within which both understandings of ethnicity and identity-formation are embedded in an ever-changing Malaysia.

Bibliography

Abdul Rahman Embong (2002) *State-Led Modernization and the New Middle Class in Malaysia*, New York: Palgrave Macmillan.

Athi S.M. (2014a) 'Positioning "new" middle class studies: regional debates and the Malaysian discussions', in *Sains Sosial dan Kajian Pembangunan: Kumpulan Rencana Penghormatan Profesor Abdul Rahman Embong* [Social Science and the Study of Development: A Tribute to Professor Abdul Rahman Embong], Bangi: Penerbit UKM.

Athi S.M. (2014b) Moving-out of the Estates: Spatial and Occupational Mobility of Plantation Labour, PhD Dissertation, University of Amsterdam.

Chan, Paul (1980) 'Regional industrial policies and employment shifts in intermediate urban centres in peninsular Malaysia', paper presented at the Meeting on Intermediate Cities in Asia, East-West Population Institute, Honolulu, Hawai'i, July.

Cohn, Bernard S. (1996) *Colonialism and its Forms of Knowledge: The British in India*, Princeton: Princeton University Press.

Courtenay, P.P (1988) 'Farm size, out-migration, and abandoned padi Landin Mukim Melekek, Melaju (Peninsular Malaysia)', *Malaysian Journal of Tropical Geography*, 17: 18–28.

Firth, Raymond (1946) *Malay Fishermen: Their Peasant Economy*, London: Kegan Paul.

Heng Pek Koon (1997) 'The new economic policy and the Chinese community in Peninsular Malaysia', *The Developing Economies*, 35(3): 262–92.

Hill, R.D. and Voo Min Shin (1990) 'Occupational and spatial mobility in an overseas Chinese agricultural community: the Hakkas of Kudat, Sabah, Malaysia', *Sojourn: Journal of Social Issues in Southeast Asia*, 5(2): 194–218.

Hirschman, Charles (1987) 'The meaning and measurement of ethnicity in Malaysia: an analysis of census classifications', *The Journal of Asian Studies*, 46(3): 555–82.

Ishak Shari (1990) *Ekonomi nelayan: pengumpulan modal, perubahan teknologi, dan pembezaan ekonomi* [Fishing Economy: Capital Accumulation, Technological Change, and Economic Differentiation], Kuala Lumpur: Dewan Bahasa Dan Pustaka.

Jones, Gavin W. (2012) 'Demographic and labour force dynamics', in Hal Hill, Tham Siew Yean and Ragayah Haji Mat Zin (eds), *Graduating from the Middle: Malaysian Development Challenges*, London: Routledge, pp. 255–75.

Khoo, S.H. and Voon Phin Keong (1975) 'Rural–urban migration in peninsular Malaysia: a case study of Sungai Ruan new village, Pahang', *Ekistics*, 39(235): 405–8.

Loh Kok Wah, Francis (1988) *Beyond the Tin Mines: Coolies, Squatters and New Villagers in the Kinta Valley, Malaysia, c. 1880–1980*, New York: Oxford University Press.

Mamdani, Mahmood (2012) *Define and Rule: Natives as Political Identity*, Cambridge, MA: Harvard University Press.

Nor Hayati Sa'at (2010) Keluar dari lingkaran kemiskinan: mobiliti sosial di kalangan komuniti pesisir pantai, Kuala Terenganu [Out of Poverty: Social Mobility Among Coastal Communities, Kuala Terenganu], PhD Dissertation, University Utara Malaysia.

Nordin Selat (1976) *Kelas menengah pentadbir Melayu* [Malay Administrative Middle Class], Kuala Lumpur: Utusan Publications.

Ong, Aihwa (1983) 'Global industries and Malay peasants in Peninsular Malaysia', in June Nash and Maria Patricia Fernandez-Kelly (eds), *Women, Men, and the International Division of Labour*, Albany: State University of New York Press, pp. 426–39.

Ooi Keat Gin (2009) *Historical Dictionary of Malaysia*, Lanham, MD: Scarecrow Press.

Pletcher, James (1991) 'Regulation with growth: the political economy of palm oil in Malaysia', *World Development*, 19(6): 623–36.

Purcal, John T. (1971) *Rice Economy: A Case Study of Four Villages in West Malaysia*, Kuala Lumpur: University of Malaya Press.

Ragayah Haji Mat Zin (2011) 'Poverty eradication and income distribution', in Hal Hill, Tham Siew Yean and Ragayah Haji Mat Zin (eds), *Graduating from the Middle: Malaysian Development Challenges*, London: Routledge, pp. 255–75.

Sandhu, Kernial Singh (1964) 'The saga of the "squatter" in Malaya: a preliminary survey of the causes, characteristics and consequences of the resettlement of rural dwellers during the Emergency between 1948 and 1960', *Journal of Southeast Asian History*, 5(1): 143–77.

Shamsul A.B. (1979) 'Development of underdevelopment of the Malaysian peasantry', *Journal of Contemporary Asia*, 9(4): 434–54.

Shamsul A.B. (1982) *Daun-daun kemarau: ceretra dan kuntuman puisi Sabar Bohari seorang seniman rakyat* [Parched Leaves: Stories and a Collection of Poems by Sabar Bohari an Artist], Subang Jaya: Penerbitan Tra-Tra.

Shamsul A.B. (1994) 'Religion and ethnic politics in Malaysia: the significance of the Islamic resurgence phenomenon', in Charles F. Keyes, Laurel Kendall and Helen Hardacre (eds), *Asian Visions of Authority: Religion and the Modern States of East and Southeast Asia*, Honolulu: University of Hawai'i Press, pp. 99–116.

Shamsul A.B. (1996a) 'Debating about identity in Malaysia: a discourse analysis', *Tonan Ajia Kenkyu*, 34(3): 566–600.

Shamsul A.B. (1996b) 'The construction and transformation of a social identity: Malayness and Bumiputeraness re-examined', *Journal of African and Asian Studies*, 52: 15–33.

Shamsul A.B. (1999a) 'Consuming Islam and containing the crisis: religion, ethnicity and the economy in Malaysia', in Mason Hoadley (ed.), *Southeast Asian-Centred Economies or Economics?*, Copenhagen: Nordic Institute of Asian Studies, pp. 43–61.

Shamsul A.B. (1999b) 'From Orang Kaya Baru to Melayu Baru: cultural construction of the Malay "new rich"', in Michael Pinches (ed.), *Culture and Privilege in Capitalist Asia*, London: Routledge, pp. 86–110.

Shamsul A.B. (2001) 'A history of an identity, an identity of a history: the idea and practice of "Malayness" in Malaysia reconsidered', *Journal of Southeast Asian Studies*, 32(3): 355–66.
Shamsul A.B. and Athi S.M. (2014) 'Conceptualising social mobility in Malaysia', in UNDP, *Malaysia National Human Development Report: Redesigning an Inclusive Future*, Kuala Lumpur: United Nations Development Programme in Cooperation with Economic Planning Unit, Prime Minister's Department.
Sivalingam, G. (1993) *Malaysia's Agricultural Transformation*, Selangor Darul Ehsan: Pelanduk Publications.
Sutton, Keith and Amriah Buang (1995) 'A new role for Malaysia's FELDA', *Geography*, 80(347): 125–37.
Sweeney, Amin (1987) *A Full Hearing: Orality and Literacy in the Malay World*, Berkeley: University of California Press.
Swift, Michael Godfrey (1965) *Malay Peasant Society in Jelebu*, London: Athlone Press.
United Nations Development Programme (UNDP) (2014) *Malaysia National Human Development Report: Redesigning an Inclusive Future*, Kuala Lumpur: United Nations Development Programme in Cooperation with Economic Planning Unit, Prime Minister's Department.
Voon Phin Keong (2011) 'The Chinese new villages in Malaysia: impact of demographic changes and response strategies', *Journal of Malaysian Chinese Studies*, 12: 73–105.
Wilson, Peter J. (1967) *A Malay Village in Malaysia*, New Haven: Human Relations Area File Publications.

22

Marginalisation of the Orang Asli of Peninsular Malaysia

Alberto G. Gomes

Since the 1970s, the Malaysian government has created several economic and social initiatives and institutions as part of its New Economic Policy (NEP) to fulfil its goal of developing a more affluent, inclusive and equal society. More than half a century later, we find that while the national poverty level has been considerably reduced and the association between 'race' and occupation is less obvious, there are several marginalised communities, such as the Orang Asli of Peninsular Malaysia and indigenous minorities in Sabah and Sarawak, who remain in the 'backwaters' of modern Malaysia (Endicott and Dentan 2004). This chapter will focus on the Orang Asli of Peninsular Malaysia, who fare poorly in almost every social, political and economic indicator relative to the national average (Nicholas and Baer 2007).

Contrary to common assumptions, Orang Asli communities have become marginalised not because they live on the fringes of Malaysian society and lack access to economic and social services, but because they have been entrapped by the tentacles of state hegemony and market economy via state projects of economic development and social engineering (Gomes 2007). Their increasing entanglement with 'modern' Malaysia has spurred their displacement and dispossession, as well as the degradation of their environments and sources of livelihood – in short, their impoverishment. They mostly live in abject poverty; 35.2 percent of Orang Asli are classified as 'hardcore poor' (*rakyat termiskin*), compared with 1.4 percent nationally (Nicholas and Baer 2007: 119). Concomitantly, they lack food security, suffer disproportionately from preventable diseases, experience high maternal and child mortality, have remarkably lower life expectancy than the average Malaysian, are more vulnerable to natural hazards, and post educational attainment levels far below the national average.

Who are the Orang Asli?

The ethnic label 'Orang Asli' literally means 'original people' in Malay. Before the 1950s, the British used the term 'Sakai', a former label for the subgroup of people now called 'Senoi', to refer to the Orang Asli in general. Apparently taking note that this ethnonym, meaning 'serf', is a derogatory term and is held to be invidious by the Orang Asli, the British dropped the term from official usage. The label 'Sakai' most likely relates to the time during the eighteenth and nineteenth centuries when the Orang Asli were the targets of brutal and cruel slave-raiding perpetrated by immigrant Malays, mostly from Sumatra (Endicott 1983). 'Sakai' was replaced with the epithet 'Aborigines' in later years of the British colonial administration; however, this term was also deemed inappropriate and was changed to 'Orang Asli' in the early 1960s.

The Orang Asli population of 158,000 in 2008, comprising 0.5 percent of Malaysia's total population, is officially divided into three main groups – Negrito (Semang), Senoi, and Melayu Asli (Aboriginal Malays or Proto-Malays) – which are further subdivided into eighteen 'tribes' (*sukubangsa*) (Rusaslina 2012: 267). Two-thirds of Orang Asli speak distinctive languages belonging to the Mon-Khmer language family (named after the two main languages in the group). Linguists have labelled these languages as 'Aslian' languages, 'because they are spoken *only* by Orang Asli' (Benjamin 2001: 101). The Mon-Khmer language family, according to linguists, is a branch of the Austroasiatic stock (Benjamin 1976; Diffloth 1979). Aslian languages are further subdivided into Northern, Central and Southern on the basis of the geographical location of the speech communities. The other Orang Asli peoples speak Austronesian languages related to the Malay language.

Most Orang Asli engage in a combination of economic activities, including hunting and gathering, fishing, swidden farming, arboriculture, and small-scale trading of forest products such as rattan, bamboo and gaharu. Since the 1970s, a growing number of them have become increasingly involved in the cash economy as small-scale rubber, oil-palm and fruit cultivators and wage labourers (Dallos 2011; Dentan *et al.* 1997; Gomes 2004; Howell and Lillegraven 2013; Nagata 1997; Nicholas 2000). Their increasing involvement in cash-cropping has progressed in tandem with their growing dependence on the market and commercial stores for most of their food and other needs. While entanglement with the market was gradual and voluntary for many Orang Asli communities as their interactions with commercial centres intensified, this was not the case for a large number of Orang Asli who became entrenched in the market economy as a consequence of government-sponsored development and modernisation programmes.

Development, dependency, and disempowerment

Orang Asli encounters with development have been in the form of either government initiatives purportedly designed to uplift the social and economic position of the beneficiaries, or a range of national projects such as resource extraction, road or highway and dam construction, commercial plantations, and land development schemes for mostly rural Malays. All in all, insurmountable evidence from numerous studies confirms that development in either form has contributed to the marginalisation of the Orang Asli (Aiken and Leigh 2011; Dentan *et al.* 1997; Endicott and Dentan 2004; Gomes 2007; Nicholas 2000).

Government policies in respect to Orang Asli in Peninsular Malaysia were formulated and passed as a statute, the Aboriginal Peoples Act 1954, by the colonial administration during the height of the anti-communist Emergency (1948–60). In 1955, the Department of Aboriginal Affairs (known by its Malay acronym, JHEOA, currently JAKOA) was set up primarily as a tool of the security forces, concerned with preventing Orang Asli from falling under the influence of communist insurgents hiding in the dense forests. One of its projects was the controversial resettlement of Orang Asli living in 'communist areas' to 'safer' sites. It is worth noting that, as Nicholas (2000: 107) contends:

> The department was modelled along the lines of the United States Bureau of Indian Affairs and the Australian Department of Aborigines, not just in terms of administrative

> structure, but also in rationale: to 'protect' a class of people deemed to be 'wards of the state'. The policy of establishing Orang Asli reserves is an example of policy similarities.

While national security remained as an important policy consideration in the 1960s, the Department embarked on a range of efforts aimed at integrating the Orang Asli into 'the mainstream of society' (JHEOA 1961: 2). The government's paternalistic attitude, a legacy of the colonial administration, of 'protecting' the Orang Asli, was evident in its early policy statements. The Aboriginal Peoples Act 1954 (1974) gave the JHEOA the power to exclude any person or 'class of persons' from entering an Orang Asli area. The discourse of Orang Asli protection is often invoked when state officials are keen to control the affairs of the Orang Asli or to maintain control of access to Orang Asli peoples by, for instance, prohibiting missionaries other than Islamic ones from visiting Orang Asli villages or disallowing activists from contacting Orang Asli (Rusaslina 2011).

In a 1976 publication, Carey (1976: 300), who was the Head of the JHEOA in the 1960s, identifies the JHEOA's three main tasks as: 'the provision of medical treatment, education, and rural development'. JHEOA rural development projects include: (1) the resettlement of Orang Asli into 'pattern settlements' where they are housed in new Malay-style dwellings, provided with a piped water supply, encouraged to cultivate cash crops such as rubber, oil palm, and trees in specially designated plots of land, and provided with facilities such as a school, community hall, health clinic, and sanitary conveniences; (2) the promotion of cash crops; and (3) the provision of agricultural skills and knowledge to previously non-settled Orang Asli. Clearly, these rural development programmes intend and operate to incorporate the Orang Asli more fully into the market economy and the Malaysian state.

In the 1990s, state policies towards the Orang Asli began to take a neoliberal turn in their promotion of privatisation as a means of reducing government intervention in, and expenditure on, development programmes and in the process facilitating greater 'free market' involvement (Nicholas 2000: 96). The government also stepped up its assimilation policy towards the Orang Asli, a policy aimed at turning Orang Asli into Malay-Muslims. Such a policy was tacitly adhered to in the early days of the state's intervention in the lives of the Orang Asli, but since 1993 there appears to have been open admission of the objective to convert the Orang Asli to Islam, especially with the establishment of a special *dakwah* (Islamic missionary) unit some time in the 1980s to fulfil the goal declared in a 1983 JHEOA document of 'the Islamisation of the whole Orang Asli community' (Nicholas 2000: 98; Dentan *et al.* 1997: 144). This is, however, not just a policy to facilitate religious conversion; it is also implicitly a policy to prevent Orang Asli from converting to another religion.

What has been dubbed as the 'Srigala Incident' exemplifies this insidious aspect of the conversion policy. Dentan *et al.* (1997: 68) provide a succinct description of the Srigala Incident:

> At the urging of a Christian missionary and using funds he supplied, the thirty Christians in the forty-person Semai settlement of Teiw Srigala' (Malay *Sungai Srigala*) in Selangor began in August, 1990, to build a M$16,000 church, which was also to serve as a kindergarten. On orders from the Malay District Officer, they applied for a building permit on September 2. On September 14 the D.O. denied their application on grounds that 'certain' relevant laws forbade it. The D.O. circulated several copies of this letter, including one to the Selangor Department of Religious Affairs. The Semai unsuccessfully appealed the decision. The D.O. ordered them to destroy the building and accused

> the Christians, particularly their leader Bah Supeh, of illegally occupying government land. But Bah Supeh remained defiant. . . . On November 27, officials from the District Office, armed policemen, and Federal Reservists armed with batons, machetes, and M–16s invaded Teiw Srigala'. With the help of two bulldozers from the Public Works Department (JKR), they levelled the church.

Since the Srigala Incident, there have been at least two other reported destructions of Christian churches in Orang Asli villages: one in Kampung Orang Laut Masai in Johor in 2005 (*New Straits Times*, 18 December 2005) and the other in Kampung Jias in Kelantan in 2007 (*New Straits Times*, 15 January 2008).

Displacement and dispossession

Government-sponsored development for the Orang Asli has mostly been implemented through resettlement projects in which Orang Asli have been enticed to leave their forest or forest-fringe homelands and settle in patterned villages resembling Malay *kampung* (villages). While the primary reason given for resettling Orang Asli in the inception of this programme in the 1950s was to 'protect' Orang Asli from the communist insurgents operating in the forests, the reasons provided for Orang Asli relocation in the 1970s onwards have included moving people closer to economic growth areas, facilitating economic development, and the provision of educational and health facilities. In almost all the resettlement projects, however, it is apparent that the Orang Asli have been moved to make way for industrial resource extraction such as mining and logging; infrastructural development like dams, roads, and airports; land development schemes for more dominant others; commercial development; universities (National University of Malaysia); and even golf courses (Dentan *et al.* 1997). In light of the negative connotations associated with the word 'resettlement', these projects were later officially referred to euphemistically as 'regroupment schemes'. Irrespective of nomenclature, these schemes have been generally unsuccessful for a range of reasons, including inadequate government support, unfulfilled promises of facilities, loss of access to traditional sources of livelihood, and insufficient land and degraded environmental conditions at the regroupment site.

Resettlement has led to increasing marginalisation of the Orang Asli by displacing them from their traditional lands, resulting in their loss of control and ownership of the land that was once theirs. Moreover, land allocated to Orang Asli settlers is invariably less than, and different from, the land they occupied traditionally. As Nicholas (1990: 71) observes, the size of the resettlement areas ranges from 1.1–15 percent of the size of their former territories. For one project, the Betau Regroupment Scheme, he notes that the 95.1 hectares of land allocated to the village amounts to a mere 1.4 percent of the approximately 7,000 hectares of their communal land.

Land or traditional territory (*sakaq*) is an important source of history and identity for the Orang Asli, who typically relate stories of past events in connection to the place where these events occurred. In other words, Orang Asli history, as in most indigenous communities, is inscribed in their land; their historical consciousness is spatialised rather than temporalised, as in conventional conception. Spaces are transformed into places as they are incorporated into people's social and cultural maps. Place is also an important symbolic source and substance for Orang Asli social identity. Defining who they are depends largely on where they are from. Hence, displacing them from their *sakaq* does not only have significant economic repercussions in terms of the diminution of their source of livelihood, but also dire implications for their sense of identity and history.

To ensure a secure future for their economy, it is of critical importance for the Orang Asli to have unambiguous ownership and control of their land. As Endicott (1979: 190) indicated some time ago, for Orang Asli, 'the amount of land acquired and the kind of rights to it that are obtained will have a crucial effect on the future of those groups'. Secure tenure to their land is certainly an issue of considerable concern as, while most Orang Asli think of themselves as owners of the land they utilise, they have yet to obtain clear legal recognition of their claims. As Nicholas (2000: 38) contends:

> The dismal record of securing Orang Asli land tenure – coupled with increased intrusion into, and appropriation of, Orang Asli traditional lands by a variety of interests representing individuals, corporations and the state itself – remains the single element that is of grave concern to the Orang Asli today.

As Hooker (1976: 180) has indicated:

> The area of state land occupied by the Orang Asli is public domain and the greatest title which the Orang Asli can get, either as an individual or as a group, is tenant at will. There is no power in any Orang Asli to lease, charge, assign or mortgage such land although some dealings are possible with the consent of the Protector. . . . Land as such cannot be owned and no one group can claim rights over it as against another group. All that may be owned is the produce of the land both cultivated and (in some cases) wild.

Orang Asli do not have secure rights to the land they occupy. Even if resettlement lands were declared as Orang Asli reserves, they would be 'tenants at will', totally dependent on the state, which has the right to revoke wholly or partly its declaration of reserve status.

The displacement of the Orang Asli is predicated on a myth that they do not have clear notions of land rights or their links to territory are weak. Nicholas (2000: 103–4) provides quotations made by several ministers and high-ranking officials illustrating this misconception. For example, a chief minister of the state of Perak stated: 'Perak will issue land titles to the Orang Asli on condition that they give up their nomadic ways and live in a certain area for a continuous period of time' (Nicholas 2000: 104).

In 2010, a proposal to amend the policy pertaining to Orang Asli land was announced. It was proposed that Orang Asli be 'given' between two and six acres of land per household (Rusaslina 2012). But this proposal repeats many of the flaws of the policy it sought to replace, such as the provision of inadequate amount of land allotted to Orang Asli, often a fraction of what they claim as theirs, and it was formulated with hardly any Orang Asli consultation. Furthermore, as Rusaslina (2012: 285) points out, the proposal 'disregards the Orang Asli's unique position as indigenous peoples with special ties to the land', a status that is being increasingly recognised by the Malaysian courts, as evidenced in the case of *Sagong Tasi v. State of Selangor*, where the Court ruled that the Orang Asli of Sagong Tasi had 'native title' to the land that the state had deemed as 'unoccupied'. While this is indeed a welcome change in the way Orang Asli land rights are perceived in the Malaysian courts, the Orang Asli struggle to defend their rights to their land continues, as many communities still face the threat of losing their customary land to outsiders or having their lands degraded by logging or mining. They will remain marginalised as long as the Malaysian state regards them as 'wards of the state', waiting to be *given* land rather than having their rights to their land recognised. Their marginality is also reinforced through government-sponsored education.

Schooling the marginalised

The introduction of schooling in Orang Asli communities has been one of the key modernisation projects implemented by the Malaysian government. Before 1995, the JHEOA carried out the Malaysian government's educational programmes for the Orang Asli, designed to prepare Orang Asli children to enter the national education system after three years of schooling. The JHEOA set up about eighty schools specifically for Orang Asli communities in remote areas (Endicott and Dentan 2004: 36). These schools were generally poorly equipped and children were taught by JHEOA Malay and Orang Asli field officers rather than by professional teachers. After completing the initial three years, the children were sent to one of several primary schools set up in larger Orang Asli communities. These schools offered education through standard six. Students passing the standard six exams were then eligible to attend government secondary schools, mainly located in towns or close to large Malay *kampung*. Orang Asli secondary students mostly stayed at JHEOA hostel accommodation in several urban areas.

The JHEOA educational programme has been declared a 'dismal failure' by government officials and Orang Asli advocates alike. A 1994 survey revealed that about two-thirds of Orang Asli children (47,141 out of 70,845) between 5 and 18 years old were not going to school at all (Endicott and Dentan 2004: 37). The proportion appears to have improved over the years, with a reported 60.8 percent of Orang Asli children having received some schooling. The number of Orang Asli children attaining secondary schooling had increased from 10.2 percent in 1991 to 15.5 percent in 2000, but only 0.8 percent had made it into a tertiary institution by 2000 (Rusaslina 2012). A key problem, however, is the high dropout rate, as Endicott and Dentan (2004: 37) indicate:

> According to JHEOA statistics, the dropout rate in the 1980s was extremely high, especially in the lower grades. . . . On average 25 percent of the children who started primary schools, mostly in JHEOA schools, dropped out after only one year, and about 70 percent of all students dropped out by the end of grade five.

The high dropout rate does not appear to have improved, as recent statistics reveal. Between 2000 and 2008, the dropout figure for Orang Asli students between primary and secondary schooling averaged 36 percent, and the average share of Orang Asli students leaving school between form one and form five was a staggering 48 percent (Rusaslina 2012). Why is the dropout rate among Orang Asli schoolchildren high? Government administrators regularly blame Orang Asli attitudes. A media statement by Jimin, a former director-general of JHEOA, quoted in Endicott and Dentan (2004: 37) exemplifies this view:

> Firstly, it must be realised that there is no formal education in Orang Asli society. None of the Orang Asli tribes have their own alphabet or writing. Moreover, the introduction of a formal education process was met with general apathy. Orang Asli children go to school because there is a hot-meal programme. They will stay away from school if they are scolded by their teachers. Then there is the problem of parents taking their children away for weeks – to look for wild fruits during the season.

Several anthropologists (see Dentan *et al.* 1997; Endicott and Dentan 2004; Nagata 1995; Nicholas 2000; Rusaslina 2012) attribute the high dropout rate to problems with the education programme. One problem raised is the relevance of the curriculum to Orang Asli needs.

It has been argued that Orang Asli parents generally felt that their children stood to gain little from subjects such as Malaysian (Malay-centric) history and mathematics. Another, perhaps more significant, issue is the quality of education provided at Orang Asli schools. In particular, a thorny issue is the appointment of 'inferior teachers' in Orang Asli schools, as Endicott and Dentan (2004: 38) explain:

> Teachers in the three-year primary schools were JHEOA field staff with no training as educators (Jimin 1983: 72; Mohd Tap 1990: 269, 295 n. 24). Teachers in six-year central schools came from the Ministry of Education, but were generally those who had failed their Lower Certificate of Education exams. Many resented being assigned to JHEOA schools (Mohd Tap 1990: 269), and they often took out their resentment and frustration on their students.

Recognising the lack of success in the JHEOA education programme, the government shifted the responsibility of Orang Asli education to the Malaysian Ministry of Education in 1995. Since then, there has been some improvement in terms of the quality of infrastructure and teachers in Orang Asli schools, which in effect means that the strategy of imprinting social and cultural values and beliefs through schooling has been enhanced.

Health, nutrition, and disease

The JHEOA was given the intrinsic role of implementing a health and medical programme in the late 1950s and it has run this programme ever since, with some assistance from the Malaysian Ministry of Health. Endicott and Dentan (2004: 36) hold the view that the programme has been a 'qualified success, although the quality of care has not improved appreciably since the 1960s'. The central aspect of this programme is the 450-bed Orang Asli Hospital at Hulu Gombak on the outskirts of Kuala Lumpur. The JHEOA also provides health and medical care through clinics established at resettlement and regroupment schemes and through flying doctor services. How effective has this medical programme been in catering to Orang Asli health care needs? Chee (1995: 63) indicates:

> There are still many problems and inadequacies [in the Orang Asli Medical Service]: it is, for instance, not based on the primary health care philosophy of community participation; largely oriented toward a curative approach with a vertical programme of disease eradication; and lacks trained staff, resources, and proper supervision, organisation, and management.

One major problem that has undermined the government medical programme is the high level of non-compliance by the Orang Asli. Generally, Orang Asli are unwilling to seek medical treatment from the government medical personnel because they are often discriminated against by the mostly non-Orang Asli medical staff. Orang Asli have told me that they are often treated in a condescending manner at the government clinics. They claim to have been ridiculed, laughed at, and scolded by medical staff. Orang Asli reticence in their communication with medical practitioners has on occasions led to misdiagnosis.

Assessing the effects of the JHEOA medical programme in disease control among the Orang Asli, Endicott and Dentan (2004: 36) note:

> Certainly many diseases, like ringworm and yaws, have declined dramatically since the 1950s. The infant mortality rate appears to be down, and the total population is increasing.

> Yet malaria and tuberculosis are still serious problems, respiratory diseases are common, pollution-caused diseases have increased, and malnutrition is widespread.

Baer (1999a) reports that Orang Asli account for about 50 percent of all reported malaria infections in Peninsular Malaysia. This amounts to roughly 450–600 reported cases of malaria per year, but the rates of inflection are likely to be even higher since many cases of infection among Orang Asli are undetected by authorities (Baer 1999a). The incidence of tuberculosis among the Orang Asli is alarming; for the state of Perak, Devaraj (2000) reports a rate of 240 cases per 100,000 of tuberculosis among the Orang Asli, which is 5.5 times higher than the overall rate for the state.

As for the health consequences of resettlement, Chee (1995: 50), among others, contends that 'Resettled communities which are at higher population densities . . . can sustain parasitical infections which could not previously be sustained; and crowding provides ideal conditions for the spread of infectious diseases.' Another factor is the settlement layout, which turns out to be conducive to the proliferation of diseases like malaria. As Baer (1999b: 303) indicates, the low-built and closely spaced houses, unlike traditional living arrangements, prevent people from 'penning domesticated or wild-caught animals (alternative blood-meal sources for mosquitoes)' or making 'smudge fires' under their houses to drive mosquitoes from the area. Having more people living close to one another, as Baer (1999b) also notes, facilitates the transmission of malaria from an infected person to others.

In my multi-temporal research (1976–2006) on an Orang Asli resettlement, Sungei Rual in Kelantan, I analysed demographic changes in the resettlement, drawing from censuses I conducted in 1978, 1988, and 1998 as well as extrapolating from genealogical records, reproductive histories, and comparative analysis. During the period from 1978–98, there were 178 deaths in the Sungei Rual population. This means that an average of nine people died each year; in a population ranging from 193 to 331, this is a rather high number of deaths in a year. From a comparison of death records compiled in different survey periods, it was evident that there were more deaths occurring in Sungei Rual annually than before. I found that approximately 96 percent of the deaths were brought about by disease. From death records kept at the Sungei Rual administrative centre that I obtained in 1988, it was reported that twelve (or 40 percent) of the thirty deceased whose deaths were registered with known causes suffered from chronic diarrhoea and blood in the stool, which are symptoms associated with such diseases as acute amoebic dysentery and cholera. Another nine (30 percent) died of respiratory-related diseases, such as acute bronchitis and tuberculosis. In 1993, there was a cholera outbreak with eighteen detected cases, which killed eight people (Gomes 2007).

My analysis indicated a very high and rising child mortality rate. A comparison of the differences in the figures for surviving children and live-born over the three census periods suggests a considerable increase in the level of mortality in the Sungei Rual population. The number of children dying before their mothers had increased from 0.67 in 1978 to a staggering 1.69 in 1988 – which meant each post-reproductive woman living in 1988 had lost one child more than her counterpart living in 1978 – to 2.13 in 1998.

As Baer (1999b), among others, has indicated, there is a correlation between medical problems and nutrition. Good nutritional status undoubtedly ensures a balanced immunochemical system and therefore good health and better protection against disease. Several studies report a decline in nutritional status in Orang Asli communities that have been resettled. On the basis of nutritional surveys carried out in several such populations, Khor (1994: 123) concludes:

> Some 15 years after relocation, the nutritional status of Orang Asli children in regroupment schemes can be described as poor with a moderate to high prevalence of underweight, acute, and chronic malnutrition. Their dietary intakes are deficient in calories and several major nutrients . . .

Similarly, from anthropometric measurements taken at a Semai resettlement, Betau in southeast Pahang, Mohd Sham Kassim (1986, in Chee 1995: 61) found that out of 499 children below the age of ten examined, '54% [were] underweight, 21% severely underweight, 70% stunted, and 47% had poor mid-arm circumference (indicating poor protein and calorie reserves)'. In another study in Kuala Betis, Kelantan, Zulkifli *et al.* (1999) discovered considerable evidence of malnutrition, such as underweight, stunting, and wasting among the 451 Temiar children they examined. The researchers attributed the malnutrition to 'the diminishing food source from hunting and gathering due to logging activities in the resettled area' and 'the impoverished state of the resettled Orang Asli communities' (Zulkifli *et al.* 1999: 125–26). In a relatively recent review of seven studies of nutritional status among several different Orang Asli communities, Khor and Zalilah (2008) reveal that one-third to three-quarters of the children examined in these studies were underweight and stunted.

Conclusion

Orang Asli remain as the most marginalised community in Malaysia in terms of their access to political and economic power. Their increasing immersion into the 'mainstream' of Malaysian society has resulted in their increased marginalisation, specifically because it has intensified the asymmetry between the Orang Asli and dominant others. Orang Asli dependence on others, especially on the government, for the fulfilment of most of their needs has induced a loss of control of their means of production and survival. They still generally lack security of tenure as far as ownership of their traditional lands is concerned. They continue to be displaced from their homelands to make way for development projects for other people, such as the building of dams, the construction of the new international airport in Sepang, plantations, and even golf courses. Through projects of social engineering, such as conversion to Islam as part of 'spiritual development' and resettlement into Malay-modelled *kampung*, they have been forced into living facsimiles of Malay lives.

Malaysia's impressive economic advancement over the past several decades appears to have missed Orang Asli communities, as many of them live in abject poverty. Orang Asli levels of educational attainment and their health and nutritional status remain relatively low. They are more vulnerable to disease and concomitantly suffer high levels of child and maternal mortality rates and have low life expectancies. They continue to be viewed and represented as 'primitive', 'backward', and naïve people needing a helping hand to advance into the 'modern' world, and their cultural practices, as inimical to modernity.

Inspired by international indigenous movements, Orang Asli have recently clamoured for social justice for their communities. In March 2010, some 3,000 Orang Asli travelled to Putrajaya to deliver a memorandum with 12,000 signatures to the prime minister, asserting their rights to their traditional lands (Rusaslina 2012). While such political activism and several court decisions favouring Orang Asli land claimants are important steps towards resolving Orang Asli marginality, there is much more that needs to be done. Most significantly, Orang Asli must be treated as equal citizens, with the respect and dignity that they so deserve.

Bibliography

Aiken, Robert and Colin Leigh (2011) 'In the way of development: indigenous land-rights issues in Malaysia', *The Geographical Review*, 101(4): 471–96.

Baer, Adela (1999a) 'Rainforest malaria, mosquitoes and people', *Malayan Nature Journal*, 53: 299–305.

Baer, Adela (1999b) *Health, Disease and Survival: A Biomedical and Genetic Analysis of the Orang Asli of Malaysia*, Subang Jaya: Centre for Orang Asli Concerns.

Benjamin, Geoffrey (1976) 'Austroasiatic subgroupings and prehistory in the Malay Peninsula', in Philip N. Jenner, Laurence C. Thompson and Stanley Starosta (eds), *Austroasiatic Studies*, Honolulu: University of Hawai'i Press, pp. 37–128.

Benjamin, Geoffrey (2001) 'Orang Asli languages: from heritage to death?', in Razha Rashid and Wazir Jahan Karim (eds), *Minority Cultures of Peninsular Malaysia: Survivals of Indigenous Heritage*, Penang: Academy of Social Sciences (AKASS), pp. 101–22.

Carey, Iskandar (1976) *Orang Asli: The Aboriginal Tribes of Peninsular Malaysia*, Kuala Lumpur: Oxford University Press.

Chee Heng Leng (1995) 'Health and nutrition of the Orang Asli: the need for primary health care amidst economic transformation', in Razha Rashid (ed.), *Indigenous Minorities of Peninsular Malaysia: Selected Issues and Ethnographies*, Kuala Lumpur: Intersocietal and Scientific Sdn. Bhd. (INAS), pp. 48–71.

Dallos, Csilla (2011) *From Equality to Inequality: Social Change Among Newly Sedentary Lanoh Hunter-gatherer Traders of Peninsular Malaysia*, Toronto: University of Toronto Press.

Dentan, Robert, Kirk Endicott, Alberto Gomes and Barry Hooker (1997) *Malaysia and the Original People: A Case Study of the Impact of Development on Indigenous Peoples*, Needham Heights, MA: Allyn and Bacon.

Devaraj, Jeyakumar (2000) 'Between myth and reality: why are Orang Asli more prone to illness?', paper presented at the World Conference of Primary Care Physicians, Kuching, March 1999, *Aliran Monthly*, available at http://aliran.com/archives/monthly/2000/05f.html (accessed 14 May 2014).

Diffloth, Gerard (1979) 'Aslian languages and Southeast Asian prehistory', *Federation Museums Journal (New Series)*, 24: 2–16.

Endicott, Kirk Michael (1979) 'The impact of economic modernization on the Orang Asli (aborigines) of Northern Peninsular Malaysia', in James C. Jackson and Martin Rudner (eds), *Issues in Malayan Development*, Singapore: Heinemann, pp. 167–204.

Endicott, Kirk Michael (1983) 'The effects of slave raiding on the aborigines of the Malay Peninsula', in Anthony Reid (ed.), *Slavery, Bondage, and Dependency in Southeast Asia*, Brisbane: University of Queensland Press, pp. 216–45.

Endicott, Kirk Michael and Robert Knox Dentan (2004) 'Into the mainstream or into the backwater? Malaysian assimilation of Orang Asli', in Christopher R. Duncan (ed.), *Civilizing the Margins: Southeast Asian Government Policies for the Development of Minorities*, Ithaca: Cornell University Press, pp. 24–55.

Gomes, Alberto G. (2004) *Looking for Money: Capitalism and Modernity in an Orang Asli Village*, Subang Jaya and Melbourne: Center for Orang Asli Concerns and Trans Pacific Press.

Gomes, Alberto G. (2007) *Modernity and Malaysia: Settling the Menraq Forest Nomads*, London: Routledge.

Hirsch, Phillip (1990) 'Review essay: marginal people on marginal land', *Bulletin of Concerned Asian Scholars*, 22: 55–59.

Hooker, Barry M. (1976) *The Personal Laws of Malaysia: An Introduction*, Kuala Lumpur: Oxford University Press.

Howell, Signe Lise and Anja Lillegraven (2013) 'Cash, culture and social change: why don't Chewong become entrepreneurs?', in Eldar Bråten (ed.), *Embedded Entrepreneurship: Market, Culture, and Micro-business in Insular Southeast Asia*, Leiden: Brill Academic Publishers, pp. 275–97.

Jabatan Hal Ewhal Orang Asli (JHEOA) (1961) *Statement of Policy Regarding the Administration of the Orang Asli of Peninsular Malaysia*, Kuala Lumpur: JHEOA.

Jimin Idris (1983) *Planning and Administration of Development Programmes from Tribal Peoples (the Malaysia Setting)*, Kuala Lumpur: Centre on Integrated Rural Development for Asia and the Pacific.

Khor Geok Lin (1994) 'Resettlement and nutritional implications: the case of Orang Asli in regroupment schemes', *Pertanika (Journal of the Society for Science and Humanities)*, 2(2): 123–32.

Khor Geok Lin and Zalilah Mohd Shariff (2008) 'The ecology of health and nutrition of "Orang Asli" [Indigenous People] women and children in Peninsular Malaysia', in Kaushik Bose (ed.), *Health and Nutritional Problems of Indigenous Populations*, Delhi: KRE Publishers, pp. 67–77.

Mohd Tap Salleh (1990) An Examination of Development Planning Among the Rural Orang Asli of West Malaysia, Unpublished PhD Thesis, University of Bath.
Nagata, Shuichi (1995) 'Education and socialisation in a Semang resettlement community of Kedah, Malaysia: the case of the Kensiu, the Kintak Bogn and the Kintak Nakil', in Razha Rashid (ed.), *Indigenous Minorities of Peninsular Malaysia: Selected Issues and Ethnographies*, Kuala Lumpur: Intersocietal and Scientific Sdn. Bhd. (INAS), pp. 86–108.
Nagata, Shuichi (1997) 'Working for money among the Orang Asli in Kedah, Malaysia', *Contributions to Southeast Asian Ethnography*, 11: 13–31.
Nicholas, Colin (1990) 'In the name of the Semai? The state and Semai society in Peninsular Malaysia', in Lim Teck Ghee and Alberto G. Gomes (eds), *Tribal Peoples and Development in Southeast Asia*, Kuala Lumpur: Department of Anthropology and Sociology, University of Malaya, pp. 68–88.
Nicholas, Colin (2000) *The Orang Asli and the Contest for Resources: Indigenous Politics, Development and Identity in Peninsular Malaysia*, Copenhagen and Subang Jaya: International Work Group for Indigenous Affairs and Centre for Orang Asli Concerns.
Nicholas, Colin and Adela Baer (2007) 'Health care for the Orang Asli: consequences of paternalism and non-recognition', in Chee Heng Leng and Simon Barraclough (eds), *Health Care in Malaysia: The Dynamics of Provision, Financing and Access*, London: Routledge, pp. 119–36.
Rusaslina Idrus (2011) 'The discourse of protection and the Orang Asli of Malaysia', *Kajian Malaysia*, 29(1): 53–74.
Rusaslina Idrus (2012) 'The Orang Asli under the New Economic Policy', in Edmund Terence Gomez and Johan Saravanamuttu (eds), *The New Economic Policy of Malaysia: Affirmative Action, Ethnic Inequalities and Social Justice*, Singapore: Institute of Southeast Asian Studies, pp. 265–91.
Zulkifli A., Khairul Anuar A. and Atiya, A.S. (1999) 'The nutritional status of children in resettlement villages in Kelantan', *Southeast Asian Journal of Tropical Medicine and Public Health*, 30(1): 122–28.

23

Civil liberties in contemporary Malaysia

Progress, retrogression and the resurgence of 'Asian values'

John Liu

The Malaysian government's position on human rights has largely been based on the arguments that it is necessary to curtail some civil liberties in order to achieve economic development and national security, and that human rights should be subjected to interpretation based on local norms, values, religious traditions and national priorities (López 2001, 2007). Such a position goes against the United Nations' formulation of human rights – that they are *universal*, that is, regardless of national, regional, historical, cultural and religious backgrounds; and *indivisible and interdependent*, that is, all rights must be respected at all times (UN 1993) – which many Asian governments, including Malaysia's, have claimed to be 'Western-centric' (Bauer and Bell 1999).

A long-term assessment of the history of human rights in Malaysia has been described by historian Cheah Boon Kheng (2001: 57) as one of 'progress and retrogression; of moving one step forward, only to step two steps backwards'. This chapter attempts to chart the progress and retrogression of civil liberties in contemporary Malaysia, with the aim of answering the following questions: how much have civil liberties in Malaysia progressed or regressed in recent years? How have changes of political leadership in the country in recent years influenced that progress or retrogression? What are the major challenges to substantive improvements in civil liberties in Malaysia?

Legal framework for civil liberties

Part II of the Federal Constitution provides guarantees of 'fundamental liberties': the rights to personal liberty, to habeas corpus, to be informed of the grounds of arrest, to be legally represented by a lawyer of one's choice, and to be produced before a magistrate within twenty-four hours (Article 5); prohibits slavery (Article 6); protects from retrospective criminal laws and repeated trials (Article 7); grants rights to equal protection under the law (Article 8), freedom of movement (Article 9), freedoms of speech, assembly and association (Article 10), and religion (Article 11); and grants rights in respect of education (Article 12) and to property (Article 13). Besides these commitments, the constitution also enumerates citizenship rights (Articles 14–31), the right be elected into parliament (Articles 47–48) and the right to universal adult franchise (Article 119); and guarantees protection against racial discrimination in the public services (Article 136), among others.

Notwithstanding these guarantees, the Federal Constitution 'subordinates individual rights to the need for social stability, security and public order', and permits the imposition of various restrictions on fundamental freedoms (Shad 1999: 137). Laws that have subordinated individual rights in the name of 'social stability, security and public order' have included the Internal Security Act (ISA) and the Security Offences (Special Measures) Act (SOSMA), in contravention of the right to personal liberty (Article 5); the Printing Presses and Publications Act (PPPA), the Official Secrets Act (OSA), and the Sedition Act, which restrict the right to freedom of expression (Article 10); Section 27 of the Police Act and the Peaceful Assembly Act, which curtails the right to freedom of peaceful assembly (Article 10); and the Societies Act and the Universities and University Colleges Act (UUCA), which impose restrictions on the right to freedom of association (Article 10).

Right to personal liberty

Article 149 of the Federal Constitution empowers the parliament to pass laws to curb 'subversion' or acts that are 'prejudicial to public order'. One such law was the Internal Security Act 1960 (ISA). The ISA was used extensively against political dissidents, students and labour activists (Koh 2004), purportedly for committing acts deemed 'prejudicial to the security of Malaysia' or threatening to the 'maintenance of essential services' or 'economic life'. The ISA empowered the police to detain individuals for an initial sixty-day detention period in secret police holding centres for the purpose of investigation, with no judicial order required. Torture and other cruel, inhuman and degrading treatment were common occurrences during the initial detention period (for instance, SUARAM 2002; SUHAKAM 2003; Kua 2010). At the end of the sixty-day period, the Home Ministry could order further detention without trial for a term of two years, which could be renewed indefinitely.

In 2012, after years of public criticism, the ISA was abolished and was replaced by the Security Offences (Special Measures) Act (SOSMA). Another detention-without-trial law, the Emergency (Public Order and Prevention of Crime) Ordinance 1969, was also repealed. The SOSMA, nevertheless, permits detention of individuals for up to twenty-eight days without their being brought before the court, merely on the basis that the police have 'reason to believe' that the person may be involved in security offences. The law refers to the Penal Code, which was also amended in 2012 to include activities 'detrimental to parliamentary democracy', such as 'to support, propagate or advocate any act prejudicial to the security of Malaysia or the maintenance or restoration of public order', in its list of 'security offences'.

Right to freedom of expression

Legitimate restrictions on freedom of expression are permitted under international human rights law, specifically Article 19 of the International Covenant on Civil and Political Rights 1966 (ICCPR) on the basis of national security or public order, but such restrictions may be imposed only if the proposed measures are proportional and necessary to meet certain narrowly defined objectives. Article 20(2) of the ICCPR further prohibits hate speech, incitement to or advocacy of national, racial or religious hatred, discrimination, violence or hostility. Restrictions on freedom of expression in Malaysia, however, have often been imposed, including through laws such as the Printing Presses and Publications Act (PPPA), the Official Secrets Act (OSA), and the Sedition Act, without being subjected to tests of proportionality and necessity.

The PPPA requires all mass-circulation newspapers to obtain publishing permits, which previously had to be renewed annually. Amendments to the Act in 2012, however – part of the Najib Razak administration's purported reforms to civil liberties and media freedom – have eliminated the annual renewal requirement. The 2012 amendments also allow publishers to challenge the Home Ministry's decisions to revoke or suspend permits, a right that was previously absent. Notwithstanding these relative improvements, the Act has maintained its press censorship function with the requirement of publishing permits from the Home Ministry, which still has the power to revoke a permit at any time if a publication contains anything that is deemed 'prejudicial to public order or national security'.

The OSA, in addition, criminalises the dissemination of information classified as 'official secrets', providing a maximum penalty of seven years' imprisonment. Meanwhile, the Sedition Act criminalises 'any act, speech, words, publication or other thing' that has a 'seditious tendency', which includes exciting disaffection against any ruler or against any government; promoting hostility between races or classes of the population; and questioning 'any matter, right, status, position, privilege, sovereignty, or prerogative established or protected by the provisions of Part III of the Constitution [provisions relating to citizenship] or Article 152 [national language], 153 [special rights of the ethnic Malays and natives of Sabah and Sarawak], or 181 of the Constitution [powers relating to the ruling chiefs of Negeri Sembilan]' (Sedition Act 1948). The Act provides a maximum penalty of three years' imprisonment, a RM5,000 fine, or both.

Rights to freedoms of peaceful assembly and association

Prior to 2012, restrictions on the right to freedom of peaceful assembly was imposed by Section 27 of the Police Act 1967, which required a police permit to be obtained fourteen days before any public assembly. Then in 2012, as part of Prime Minister Najib Razak's reform agenda, this provision was replaced by the Peaceful Assembly Act, which introduced other restrictions, including prohibiting street protests, barring organisation of assemblies by persons below the age of twenty-one, and participation in peaceful assemblies by children below the age of fifteen.

The right to freedom of association is restricted by the Societies Act 1966, through which many organisations and societies have been subjected to refusal of registration, imposition of conditions on their activities, and deregistration by the government. The Universities and University Colleges Act 1971 (UUCA), on the other hand, prohibited students and faculty members from expressing support for, sympathy for or opposition to any political party or trade union (UUCA, Section 15(5)(A)); however, amendments were made in 2012 following a Court of Appeal ruling that the provision was unconstitutional. This ruling was a result of a constitutional challenge of the Act by five university students who had been subjected to disciplinary action by their university for being present at a parliamentary by-election campaign in April 2010. With the amendments, university students are now permitted to take up membership in any organisation, including political parties, although the Act still prohibits students from joining organisations that are deemed 'unsuitable to the interest and well-being of the students or university'.

Mahathir administration (1981–2003)

Mahathir Mohamad is generally viewed by human rights advocates as being responsible for having 'inflicted serious harm to human rights in Malaysia' during his twenty-two-year premiership (SUARAM, cited in Jason 2005). He was one of the most outspoken critics of universal human rights, which purportedly focus on individualism, advocating instead for adherence to 'Asian values', which emphasise 'collective' and 'community' rights (Khoo 2002; Verma 2002). Indeed, Mahathir even publicly defended authoritarian rule 'in the interest of political stability and efficiency of governance' (Khoo 2002: 58).

In assessing Malaysia's civil liberties under the Mahathir administration, two major events – namely *Operasi Lalang* (1987) and the *reformasi* years (1998–early 2000s) – stand out, although these are far from exhaustive. Nevertheless, both instances saw highly publicised and well-documented cases of human rights abuses, and mass crackdowns on political opposition and civil society leaders. The Mahathir administration also introduced a number of legislative amendments that restrict civil liberties. Perhaps some of the most far-reaching in their impact upon civil liberties were 1989 amendments to the ISA, which removed the possibility of judicial review of the Home Ministry's two-year detention orders or their renewal.

In October 1987, 106 political leaders (predominantly from the opposition) and civil society leaders were detained without trial under the ISA in an operation named *Operasi Lalang*. The arrests came against the backdrop of a major leadership crisis and split in UMNO in late 1986 and 1987, which coincided with the emergence of several critical ethnic-related issues in the country, including the switch to Malay language as a medium of instruction for optional courses in the departments of Chinese and Tamil studies at the University of Malaya in 1987, as well as the government's appointment of more than one hundred Chinese teachers who did not possess qualifications in Mandarin as senior assistants in Chinese primary schools – resulting in demonstrations and counter-demonstrations that provided a pretext for the mass arrests (Munro-Kua 1996: 130–36; Crouch 1996: 110–11; Kua 2005a: 94–95). The government justified the mass ISA detentions on grounds of combating purported threats of racial extremism, liberation theology and communism (SUARAM 1989).

In September 1998, former Deputy Prime Minister Anwar Ibrahim was detained incommunicado under the ISA following his dismissal from all positions in the government and in UMNO, and was brought to court nine days later with a black eye, apparently resulting from assault by a police officer, who was later identified to be the then inspector general of police, Rahim Noor. Anwar was subsequently tried and convicted on charges of corruption and sodomy in a judicial process that was widely criticised for contravening international fair trial standards. Several other individuals linked with Anwar were also incarcerated under the ISA and subjected to torture in detention (Abolish ISA Movement 2005: 27–30).

Anwar's sacking and subsequent detention catalysed growing calls for reforms, giving rise to the *reformasi* movement, which manifested in frequent street demonstrations in 1998–99. The government reacted by criminalising public assemblies relating to the *reformasi* movement and deployed excessive police force to disperse and arrest demonstrators. The police deployed tear gas, water cannon and batons, often causing injuries to demonstrators while dispersing or arresting them (SUARAM 2005).

It is against a backdrop of public outcry at both national and international levels against rampant human rights abuses in the detention and trial of Anwar Ibrahim and the crackdown on the *reformasi* movement that the Human Rights Commission of Malaysia (SUHAKAM) was established in 1999. The creation of SUHAKAM was, however, seen by critics as merely a window-dressing exercise of the government to deflect criticism of its human rights record. Critics have pointed out that SUHAKAM's enabling law was hastily introduced by the government and passed in parliament without any public consultation, and as a result, falls short of the Paris Principles (Tikamdas and Rachagan 1999).[1]

Notwithstanding the criticism over the establishment and mandate of SUHAKAM, civil society groups and *reformasi* activists soon began to engage with the commission, albeit critically. They referred cases of human rights abuses to SUHAKAM, with the view that it could utilise its mandates to hold investigations and public inquiries into alleged human rights violations and make recommendations to the government.

On 5 November 2000, a *reformasi* rally held on the premises of Parti Keadilan Nasional (National Justice Party) was dispersed violently by the police using water cannon and tear gas, resulting in scores of injuries. SUHAKAM, which had then only been in existence less than a year, subsequently conducted a public inquiry into allegations of human rights abuses during the rally and concluded the police had committed several human rights violations, including using excessive force, damaging private property, causing injury to persons in detention, delaying provision of medical treatment for injured detainees and failing to provide medication prescribed for injured detainees. SUHAKAM also made a list of recommendations, including for the police to review its methods of crowd dispersal, exercise restraint when dispersing assemblies, and provide demonstrators sufficient time to disperse (SUHAKAM 2001). This was considered a landmark report, which saw the newly established official commission confirming, through a public inquiry, allegations of human rights violations in an opposition-led rally; however, Mahathir dismissed SUHAKAM's report and findings as 'influenced by Western thinking' (Ramlan 2001).

In April 2001, *reformasi* activists announced a plan to present SUHAKAM with a 'People's Memorandum' on 14 April 2001 – the second anniversary of Anwar Ibrahim's conviction on corruption charges – on ten key areas of human rights concern, including freedoms of expression and peaceful assembly, the independence of the judiciary, and the repeal of restrictive laws such as the ISA, the Sedition Act, the Police Act, the PPPA and the UUCA. The government responded to this plan by arresting and detaining seven key *reformasi* activists without trial under the ISA for allegedly planning to overthrow the government through violent means (López 2001: 55; 2007: 64). Contrary to the official allegations, however, affidavits filed by the detainees at the Federal Court later revealed that police questioning hardly touched on the actual allegations, but rather on 'political strategies, information, structure and funding of political parties and NGOs, and alternative news websites' (SUARAM 2005: 29).

In sum, the Mahathir administration's legacy in relation to civil liberties in Malaysia has had far-reaching implications – in legislation, policy and practice – deeply entrenching elements of authoritarianism that have survived subsequent changes in national leadership, as will be demonstrated below.

Abdullah administration (2003–09)

When Abdullah Badawi took office from Mahathir in 2003, human rights advocates were cautiously optimistic about the possibility of changes in attitudes towards democracy and human rights in the country (SUARAM 2004). Indeed, from time to time during his premiership, Abdullah stated his intent to promote human rights and democracy.

One of the events of greatest significance vis-à-vis civil liberties during the Abdullah administration was the establishment of a Royal Commission to Enhance the Operation and Management of the Royal Malaysian Police, mandated to make recommendations for the improvement of the police force, in response to 'allegations of torture, brutality, non-accountable shootings, deaths in custody, corruption, discrimination and abuse at the hands of the police' (Kua 2005b: 2). The Royal Commission made 125 recommendations under three broad categories: reduction of crime and the enhancement of public safety; eradication of the perception of widespread corruption within the Malaysian Police Force; and compliance with human rights. Among its main recommendations in relation to the police's compliance with human rights were the establishment of an Independent Police Complaints and Misconduct Commission (IPCMC), an oversight body mandated to receive and act on complaints regarding the police; amendments to Section 27 of the Police Act with regard to police permits for public assemblies, Section 73 of the ISA, to require detainees to be produced before a magistrate within twenty-four hours of detention; the repeal of the Emergency (Public Order and Prevention of Crime) Ordinance 1969; and amendments to Section 117 of the Criminal Procedure Code to limit police detentions to a maximum of seven days for an arrest without a warrant, and not more than twenty-four hours for arrest with a warrant.

Despite Abdullah's pledge to implement all recommendations, however, many were not implemented. The IPCMC, for instance, still has not been established, largely due to strong opposition from the police force itself. This was seen when a supposedly internal report of the police – which described the IPCMC as 'unconstitutional, prejudicial to national security and public order, victimised the people, and could cause a state of anarchy which would undermine the ruling coalition's power' – was inadvertently posted on the Royal Malaysia Police website in May 2006 (Kuek 2006).

Meanwhile, the ISA continued to be used under Abdullah's premiership. In a parliamentary reply on 9 July 2007, Abdullah said that 'the ISA is significant because we use it *to maintain peace and to ensure the security of the general public*' (cited in SUARAM 2008: 8; emphasis added). Such a statement reveals the fact that Abdullah, despite pledges to improve respect for human rights, did not depart from the Mahathir administration's line of restricting civil liberties on grounds of 'public stability'.

One of the more publicised of such cases was the detention of five Hindu Rights Action Force (HINDRAF) leaders in December 2007. Earlier, on 25 November 2007, HINDRAF had organised a massive rally in the capital Kuala Lumpur, demanding equality and fair treatment for ethnic Indian Malaysians, whom it claimed had been systematically marginalised and discriminated against (see Govindasamy, this volume). The rally was violently dispersed, with more than a hundred protestors arrested. In the run-up to the rally, three HINDRAF leaders were arrested under the Sedition Act for alleged inflammatory speeches made while on tour in several cities and towns around the country. In December 2007, after numerous repeated threats and warnings, five HINDRAF leaders were detained under the ISA. The movement was subsequently officially banned by the government in October 2008. Brown (2011: 226) notes that the Abdullah administration's heavy-handed response towards HINDRAF caused ethnic Indian Malaysian votes to swing against the Barisan Nasional (BN, National Front), causing major losses for the ruling coalition in the 2008 general election.

In March 2008, the ruling BN obtained its worst electoral result to date. That August, it then suffered a huge defeat in a by-election in Permatang Pauh, Penang at the hands of opposition leader Anwar Ibrahim. Soon after, Anwar publicly announced an invitation to members of parliament from the ruling coalition to cross over and join the opposition and to form a new government, signalling a direct challenge to power that put Abdullah's leadership in question.

Against this backdrop, in September 2008, three individuals – Raja Petra Kamaruddin, a blogger and outspoken government critic; Teresa Kok, a member of parliament from the opposition Democratic Action Party (DAP); and Tan Hoon Cheng, a journalist for Chinese-language newspaper *Sin Chew Daily* – were arrested within a period of twenty-four hours under the ISA for allegedly inciting racial tensions. Critics contend that these arrests were part of BN's 'modus operandi' during times of political crisis – invoking the ISA to censor discussions deemed 'too sensitive' in a multi-ethnic society and raising the 'spectre of racial conflict' as a form of regime maintenance, as had been seen in 1987's *Operasi Lalang* (SUARAM 2009). Criticism against the Abdullah administration's misuse of the ISA was not confined to the political opposition and civil society, but also emerged from within the ranks of the government. Zaid Ibrahim, then minister in charge of law in the Prime Minister's Department, strongly criticised the government's actions and eventually resigned from his ministerial post. Subsequently, several BN component parties also called for the review of the ISA (SUARAM 2009).

While the Abdullah administration had pledged greater respect for civil liberties, resistance from within the establishment resulted in many of the pledges remaining unimplemented. On the other hand, heavy-handed responses towards dissent against the government eroded public support towards the ruling BN, eventually leading to Abdullah's resignation in 2009.

Najib administration (2009–present)

Any assessment of the situation of human rights under Najib Razak can only be a preliminary one, since the sixth prime minister of Malaysia is currently still in office, having succeeded Abdullah Badawi in April 2009.

Having taken the helm in the context of eroding support for the BN and growing demands for reforms in democracy and human rights, Najib promised greater respect for civil liberties; however, in 2009 – Najib's first year in power – close to 1,000 individuals were arrested for various forms of peaceful protest (SUARAM 2010). A massive anti-ISA rally held on 1 August 2009 saw 589 individuals arrested, the greatest number of persons arrested in a single public assembly in recent years. The BN's takeover of the Perak state government from the opposition Pakatan Rakyat (People's Alliance) coalition following the defection of three elected Pakatan state assemblypersons also sparked a wave of protests around the country in May 2009, which were met by a police crackdown and arrests of a total of 167 persons (SUARAM 2010: 94).

In September 2011, Najib announced plans to repeal the ISA and other restrictive legislation such as the Sedition Act, as well as emergency proclamations. Then in November 2011, the government hastily introduced the Peaceful Assembly Act, which replaced Section 27 of the Police Act. While the abolition of Section 27 was welcomed, the new law drew objections for a number of reasons, including the lack of public consultation in its formulation, as well as its continued restrictions on freedom of peaceful assembly, including the ban on street protests. Several UN human rights experts have cautioned that the definition of 'assembly' in the new law is too vague and imposes overly broad restrictions, and have expressed regret that neither SUHAKAM nor civil society was meaningfully consulted in its drafting (UN OHCHR 2011).

The ISA was officially repealed in April 2012 with the passage of its replacement, the Security Offences (Special Measures) Act 2012 (SOSMA). While the new law introduces improvements in some areas, critics contend that it imposes more restrictions in others. For example, the initial police detention period under the new law is shortened to a maximum of twenty-eight days, after which the attorney general must decide whether or not to charge a suspect, as compared with the previous sixty days' initial detention followed by a possible two-year detention without trial under the ISA. Critics also note that the bill, coupled with amendments to other laws, has introduced new restrictions, including broadening police apprehension and surveillance powers (Spiegel 2012). In October 2013, another law, the Prevention of Crime Act, was amended, resulting in what critics have claimed is the reintroduction of detention without trial similar to under the ISA.

Najib's first general election as prime minister in 2013 was marred by allegations of numerous electoral irregularities and violations, including political violence, illegal campaigning, conveyance of voters and harassment of election observers (PEMANTAU 2013). Almost immediately after the elections, an opposition-led protest movement against allegations of electoral irregularities emerged, organising mass rallies, vigils and public forums. While the heavy-handed government response of the past – characterised by violent police crackdowns – was notably absent in the post–2013 election rallies, the government nevertheless embarked on a series of arrests and criminal charges under the Peaceful Assembly Act and the Sedition Act against individuals organising and participating in these events.

Human Rights Commission of Malaysia (SUHAKAM)

SUHAKAM was established through the enactment of the Human Rights Commission of Malaysia Act in 1999, amidst growing criticism of the serious human rights abuses at the height of the *reformasi* era. Civil society groups welcomed the government's announcement of its plan to establish the Commission, especially in a context 'where key public institutions such as the police, the judiciary and the Attorney-General's Chambers have come under strong public criticism', and further called for the government to hold public consultations on the drafting of the Commission's founding law (Malaysian NGOs 1999). This call was never met, however, and SUHAKAM's enabling law was enacted in September 1999 without any public consultation. The first batch of Commissioners was appointed in 2000 (Tikamdas and Rachagan 1999: 6). The Commission is mandated to:

- promote awareness and provide education in relation to human rights;
- advise and assist the government in formulating legislation and administrative directives and procedures and recommend necessary measures to be taken;
- make recommendations to the government with regard to subscription to or accession of treaties and other international instruments in the field of human rights; and
- inquire into complaints regarding infringements of human rights.

Since its establishment, SUHAKAM has been criticised for its apparent lack of independence and compliance with the Paris Principles. Among other aspects, the process of appointing commissioners has been criticised, as the prime minister has full discretion over appointments. The definition of 'human rights' in its mandate – limited to the fundamental liberties enshrined in Part II of the Federal Constitution – has also been criticised as restrictive (Rachagan and Tikamdas 1999; Burdekin 2007). The effectiveness of the commission has also been questioned, as the government has largely ignored its recommendations. None of SUHAKAM's many reports has even been debated in parliament (SUARAM 2010).

The perceived lack of independence and effectiveness of SUHAKAM has led to a generally dissenting attitude by human rights groups towards the commission. In May 2002, thirty-two NGOs announced a hundred-day boycott of SUHAKAM, suspending all forms of engagement with the commission, in protest against the government's poor response to SUHAKAM's numerous recommendations (Yusof 2002). This was not the only time SUHAKAM was boycotted by civil society groups. In September 2005, thirty NGOs boycotted its Malaysian Human Rights Day conference, for which former Prime Minister Mahathir Mohamad was invited to deliver a keynote address. The NGOs questioned the credibility of SUHAKAM's conference on human rights if it 'featured a leader who perpetrated extensive human rights violations' and noted that 'the Mahathir-led government inflicted some very serious harm to human rights in Malaysia' (Jason 2002). In September 2009, forty-two civil society groups staged another boycott of SUHAKAM's annual Malaysian Human Rights Day conference, in protest of the long-standing concerns over its lack of independence and effectiveness (Ong 2009).

In 2008, the International Coordinating Committee of National Human Rights Institutions (ICC-NHRI), the governing body of national human rights institutions (NHRIs) around the world, gave SUHAKAM a one-year notice to make improvements in its compliance with the Paris Principles – including by strengthening its independence through a more transparent appointment and dismissal process – failing which the Commission's accreditation would be downgraded from 'A' status to 'B'.[2] The government responded by introducing amendments to the founding law of SUHAKAM on two occasions – in March 2009 and June 2009 – changing to a selection process which is relatively more transparent and inclusive of public participation, among other adjustments (SUARAM and ERA Consumer 2010; Renshaw *et al.* 2011).

The establishment of SUHAKAM in 1999 was widely considered a major milestone in the history of human rights in Malaysia. Yet, questions remain about its effectiveness in substantially improving human rights in the country. In September 2009, while commemorating the tenth anniversary of the law that established the commission, a conference was held to take stock of the work of SUHAKAM in the field of human rights in Malaysia. One of the speakers at the conference, human rights lawyer Ramdas Tikamdas, termed the first ten years of SUHAKAM 'the lost decade', noting that detention without trial under the ISA continued to be abused and misused, that peaceful assemblies continued to be quashed with excessive use of force, that custodial deaths and deaths caused by police shootings continued with alarming regularity, that freedom of religion continued to be denied, and that Malaysia's rankings in press freedom indices continued to drop (Tikamdas 2009).

While some significant developments have subsequently occurred, including the repeal of restrictive laws such as the ISA and Section 27 of the Police Act in 2012, the following observation made by Andrew Khoo, chairperson of the Malaysian Bar's Human Rights Committee, at the 2009 SUHAKAM conference highlighted a larger challenge to the fulfilment of SUHAKAM's mandates, and more generally to the development of human rights in Malaysia: 'The resurgence of the argument for a culturally-appropriate set of human rights and values places enormous challenges to the development of international human rights norms and standards in Malaysia' (Khoo 2009).

Conclusion: 'Asian values' and their recent resurgence

While Mahathir's successors have not been as outspoken as him in their defence of 'Asian values', successive administrations have continued to invoke the argument that 'collective' and 'community' rights should be prioritised over civil liberties. For instance, in 2009, during a review of Malaysia's human rights record at the UN Human Rights Council,[3] the Malaysian government once again invoked the 'public stability and national security' argument as the basis for curtailing some civil liberties, while noting the 'unique character' of Malaysia implied a subtle rejection of the universality of rights. The government did so, though, without explicitly spelling out its disagreement with the supposed 'Western notion' of human rights and fundamental freedoms, as it had done, for instance, during Mahathir's administration:

> In considering the promotion and protection of human rights and fundamental freedoms, including the exercise of international obligations, *Malaysia's unique character required prime importance be given to national unity, stability and security*. . . . Today, Malaysia is a robust democracy fully committed to the principles of rule of law, good governance, integrity and accountability. Efforts have been largely devoted to *achieving inter-racial harmony, and equitable socio-economic development*, while taking into account individual human rights and fundamental freedoms.
>
> *(UN 2009: 3; emphasis added)*

Indeed, a major stumbling block for sustained improvement in the relative progress attained thus far is the government's continued rhetoric of the need to curtail some civil liberties on grounds of economic development, national security and public stability, especially in the context of Malaysia's 'unique' character. This line of argument had in the past been strongly championed by Mahathir, but there has been a resurgence of cultural and regional particularistic arguments regarding human rights in the ASEAN sub-region in recent years. The establishment of the ASEAN Intergovernmental Commission on Human Rights (AICHR) in 2009 and the adoption of the ASEAN Human Rights Declaration in 2012 demonstrate this: the AICHR reaffirms the 'ASEAN Way' of non-interference and decision-making by consensus in its work, and the declaration incorporates principles of cultural and regional particularities in relation to human rights (FORUM-ASIA 2013). Yet, these developments in ASEAN also signal some form of shift through the states' acceptance of – albeit with a view to steer – human rights discourse in the region. The same can be said about the Malaysian government, for instance, in its establishment of SUHAKAM, which as López (2001) notes, is a result of external influences, especially when linked with local struggles.

This chapter has attempted to chart the significant progress and retrogressions in civil liberties in contemporary Malaysia. The establishment of SUHAKAM in 1999 and the repeal of several restrictive laws, including the ISA in 2012, have been positive developments, but they have also been accompanied by retrogressions, such as new restrictions imposed by laws introduced to replace old ones. This trend of 'moving one step forward, only to step two steps backwards' (Cheah 2001: 57), it is argued, largely stems from the Malaysian government's continued resistance towards the full acceptance of the principles of the universality and indivisibility of rights.

A major challenge is thus to shift the focus of discourse away from whether civil liberties should be granted relative to one's location and culture, to when and under what specific circumstances limitations on civil liberties can be considered legitimate, proportional and necessary. Indeed, existing international human rights jurisprudence has already laid the foundations to questions regarding the latter. On the other hand, it is equally important to acknowledge that the progress seen in recent years – and indeed in the longer view of history – is a result of pressures, partly external, but more importantly, from the struggles of the Malaysian people.

Notes

1 The Principles Relating to the Status of National Institutions for Protection and Promotion of Human Rights (Paris Principles) establish international standards for national human rights

institutions, covering aspects including the need for independence, a broad human rights mandate, adequate funding, and inclusive and transparent selection and appointment processes.

2 'A' status is accorded to NHRIs that are in full compliance with the Paris Principles. Only 'A' status NHRIs are recognised and given the right to make interventions at general sessions of the UN Human Rights Council.

3 In 2006, the Universal Periodic Review was created under the UN Human Rights Council as a mechanism of peer review of all UN member states' human rights records.

Bibliography

Abolish ISA Movement (2005) 'Torture under the ISA', in Kua Kia Soong (ed.), *Policing the Malaysian Police*, Petaling Jaya: SUARAM Kommunikasi.

Bauer, Joanne R. and Daniel A. Bell (eds) (1999) *The East Asian Challenge for Human Rights*, New York: Cambridge University Press.

Brown, Graham K. (2011) 'Understanding horizontal inequalities: the role of civil society', in Valpy FitzGerald, Judith Heyer and Rosemary Thorp (eds), *Overcoming the Persistence of Inequality and Poverty*, Basingstoke: Palgrave Macmillan.

Burdekin, Brian (2007) *National Human Rights Institutions in the Asia-Pacific Region*, Leiden and Boston: Martinus Nijhoff Publishers.

Cheah Boon Kheng (2001) 'From end of slavery to the ISA: human rights history in Malaysia', in Jomo Kwame Sundaram (ed.), *Reinventing Malaysia: Reflections on its Past and Future*, Bangi: UKM Press.

Crouch, Harold (1996) *Government and Society in Malaysia*, Ithaca: Cornell University Press.

FORUM-ASIA (2013) *Still Window-dressing: A Performance Report on the Third Year of the ASEAN Intergovernmental Commission on Human Rights (AICHR) 2011–2012*, Bangkok: Asian Forum for Human Rights and Development.

International Coordinating Committee of National Institutions for the Promotion and Protection of Human Rights (ICC-NHRI) (2009) *Report and Recommendations of the Session of the Sub-committee on Accreditation*, Geneva, 26–30 March.

Jason, Roshan (2005) 'NGOs to boycott Suhakam event over Mahathir invite', *Malaysiakini*, 5 September, available at www.malaysiakini.com/news/39965 (accessed 10 October 2013).

Khoo, Andrew (2009) 'Human rights in Malaysia: the last 10 years', paper presented at the 2009 Malaysia Human Rights Day, 9 September, Kuala Lumpur.

Khoo Boo Teik (2002) 'Nationalism, capitalism and "Asian values"', in Francis Loh Kok Wah and Khoo Boo Teik (eds), *Democracy in Malaysia: Discourses and Practices*, Richmond: Curzon.

Koh Swe Yong (2004) *Malaysia: 45 Years Under the Internal Security Act*, Petaling Jaya: SIRD.

Kua Kia Soong (2005a) *The Malaysian Civil Rights Movement*, Petaling Jaya: Strategic Information Research Development.

Kua Kia Soong (2005b) 'Introduction: reform the Malaysian police', in Kua Kia Soong (ed.), *Policing the Malaysian Police*, Petaling Jaya: SUARAM Kommunikasi.

Kua Kia Soong (2010) *445 Days Under the ISA: Operation Lalang 1987–1989*, 3rd edn, Petaling Jaya: SUARAM Kommunikasi.

Kuek Ser Kuang Keng (2006) 'Police "attack" IPCMC in internal bulletin', *Malaysiakini*, 27 May, available at www.malaysiakini.com/news/51654 (accessed 10 October 2013).

López, Carolina C. (2001) 'Ideological-structural analysis of external influences on current human rights discourses in Malaysia', *Akademika*, 59(July): 53–73.

López, Carolina C. (2007) 'Globalisation, state and g/local human rights actors: contestations between institutions and civil society', in Edmund Terence Gomez (ed.), *Politics in Malaysia: The Malay Dimension*, Abingdon: Routledge.

Ong, Andrew (2009) '42 NGOs to boycott Suhakam's 10th year bash', *Malaysiakini*, 8 September, available at www.malaysiakini.com/news/112417 (accessed 10 October 2013).

Malaysian NGOs (1999) Memorandum on the Proposed Malaysian National Commission on Human Rights, Submitted to the Minister of Foreign Affairs.

Munro-Kua, Anne (1996) *Authoritarian Populism in Malaysia*, Basingstoke: Macmillan Press.

PEMANTAU (2013) *Clean & Fair? An Election Observation Report of the 13th Malaysian General Election*, Petaling Jaya and Kuala Lumpur: BERSIH 2.0, MAFREL and KOMAS.

Rachagan, S. Sothi and Ramdas Tikamdas (1999) 'Human Rights Commission of Malaysia Act 1999: a critique', in S. Sothi Rachagan and Ramdas Tikamdas (eds), *Human Rights and the National Commission*, Kuala Lumpur: HAKAM.

Ramlan Said (2001) 'Suhakam taken to task', *New Straits Times*, 23 August.

Renshaw, Catherine, Andrew Byrnes and Andrea Durbach (2011) 'Testing the mettle of national human rights institutions: a case study of the Human Rights Commission of Malaysia', *Asian Journal of International Law*, 1(1): 165–98.

Shad S. Faruqi (1999) 'Human rights and the constitution', in S. Sothi Rachagan and Ramdas Tikamdas (eds), *Human Rights and the National Commission*, Kuala Lumpur: HAKAM.

Spiegel, Mickey (2012) 'Smoke and mirrors: Malaysia's "new" Internal Security Act', *Asia Pacific Bulletin*, 167, available at www.eastwestcenter.org/publications/smoke-and-mirrors-malaysias-new-internal-security-act (accessed 10 October 2013).

SUARAM (1989) *The White Paper on the October Affair and the Why? Papers*, Petaling Jaya: SUARAM Kommunikasi.

SUARAM (1998) *Malaysia Human Rights Report*, Petaling Jaya: SUARAM Kommunikasi.

SUARAM (2002) *Malaysia Human Rights Report 2001: Civil and Political Rights*, Petaling Jaya: SUARAM Kommunikasi.

SUARAM (2004) *Malaysia Human Rights Report 2003: Civil and Political Rights*, Petaling Jaya: SUARAM Kommunikasi.

SUARAM (2005) 'Police brutality at public assemblies', in Kua Kia Soong (ed.), *Policing the Malaysian Police*, Petaling Jaya: SUARAM Kommunikasi.

SUARAM (2008) *Malaysia Human Rights Report 2007: Civil and Political Rights*, Petaling Jaya: SUARAM Kommunikasi.

SUARAM (2009) *Malaysia Human Rights Report 2008: Civil and Political Rights*, Petaling Jaya: SUARAM Kommunikasi.

SUARAM (2010) *Malaysia Human Rights Report 2009: Civil and Political Rights*, Petaling Jaya: SUARAM Kommunikasi.

SUARAM and ERA Consumer (2010) 'Malaysia: substantial reforms still elusive', in Asian NGO Network on National Human Rights Institutions (ed.), *2010 ANNI Report on the Performance and Establishment of National Human Rights Institutions in Asia*, Bangkok: Asian Forum for Human Rights and Development.

SUHAKAM (2001) *Inquiry 2/2000: Inquiry on Its Own Motion into the November 5th Incident at the KESAS Highway*, Kuala Lumpur: SUHAKAM.

SUHAKAM (2003) *Review of the Internal Security Act 1960*, Kuala Lumpur: SUHAKAM.

Tikamdas, Ramdas (2009) 'Human rights in Malaysia: the last 10 years – the lost decade', paper presented at the 2009 Malaysia Human Rights Day, 9 September, Kuala Lumpur.

Tikamdas, Ramdas and S. Sothi Rachagan (1999) 'Introduction', in S. Sothi Rachagan and Ramdas Tikamdas (eds), *Human Rights and the National Commission*, Kuala Lumpur: HAKAM.

United Nations (UN) (1993) *Vienna Declaration and Programme of Action*, adopted by the World Conference on Human Rights in Vienna, 25 June.

United Nations (UN) (2009) *Report of the Working Group on the Universal Periodic Review – Malaysia*, UN Human Rights Council, Eleventh Session, A/HRC/11/30.

United Nations Office of the High Commissioner for Human Rights (UN OHCHR) (2011) 'Malaysia: new bill threatens right to peaceful assembly with arbitrary and disproportional restrictions', press release, 7 December, available at www.ohchr.org/en/NewsEvents/Pages/DisplayNews.aspx?NewsID=11694&LangID=E (accessed 10 October 2013).

Verma, Vidhu (2002) *Malaysia: State and Civil Society in Transition*, Boulder: Lynne Rienner Publishers.

Yusof Ghani (2002) 'NGOs launch 100-day boycott against Suhakam', *Malaysiakini*, 4 May, available at www.malaysiakini.com/news/11309 (accessed 10 October 2013).

24

Educational reforms in Malaysia

Towards equity, quality and efficiency

Molly N.N. Lee

Malaysia aims to become a high-income nation that is both inclusive and sustainable by the year 2020. Under its Economic Transformation Programme (ETP), Malaysia hopes to increase its gross national income per capita to at least US$15,000 by 2020, from its current level of about US$10,000 (PEMANDU 2010). Education is seen to play a central role in Malaysia's economic growth and national development. Thus the government has been investing heavily in education. In 2011, the government spent as much as 3.8 percent of its gross domestic product (GDP) on education, or 16 percent of total government spending, which is higher than the OECD average of 3.4 percent GDP or 8.7 percent of total public spending (MoE 2012). Starting from 2004, there were two ministries in charge of delivering educational services in the public sector, the Ministry of Education (MoE) and Ministry of Higher Education (MoHE), but these two ministries were merged in 2013 so as to ensure better coordination and increased efficiency of the education system. These ministries had produced blueprints and strategic plans for the development of the school sector and higher education sector, respectively. MoE launched its National Education Blueprint 2013–2025 (NEB) in 2013, while the MoHE launched its National Higher Education Strategic Plan (NHESP) earlier, in 2004.

In both these documents, the emphasis is on issues of equity, quality and efficiency of the Malaysian education system. The NEB states that the five system aspirations for Malaysian education are access, quality, equity, unity and efficiency (MoE 2012). The NHESP listed 'Widening access and increasing equity', 'Improving the quality of teaching and learning', 'Enhancing research and innovation', 'Strengthening of higher education institutions' and 'Reinforcing the delivery systems' as five of its seven thrusts (MoHE 2004).

The aim of this chapter is to examine these contemporary issues facing the Malaysian education system in three sections, namely, (1) access and equity, (2) quality and relevance, and (3) efficiency and effectiveness. In each of these sections, the analysis spans both the school level and higher education level.

Access and equity

School level

Unlike in many other countries, the education structure in Malaysia is from K–13 instead of K–12, with six years primary schooling, three years lower secondary, and four years upper secondary, which includes two years pre-university. Student enrolments in each of these levels are relatively higher than in most developing countries. In 2011, the primary enrolment rate was 96 percent, the lower secondary enrolment rate was 91 percent and upper secondary rate was 82 percent. Most students were enrolled in the public school system, with the private schools accounting for only 2 percent of primary enrolment and 4 percent of secondary enrolment (MoE 2012). At the end of each level, students have to sit for a national examination, namely, *Ujian Penilaian Sijil Rendah* (UPSR, Primary Assessment Test Certificate) at the end of year six, *Peniliaian Menengah Rendah* (PMR, Lower Secondary Assessment) at the end of year nine, *Sijil Pelajaran Malaysia* (SPM, Malaysian Certificate of Education) at the end of year eleven and *Sijil Pelajaran Tinggi Malaysia* (STPM, Malaysian Higher School Certificate) at the end of year thirteen. Only two of these national examinations are selective: SPM for selecting students to enter pre-university programmes and STPM for selecting students to enter universities. Malaysia provides eleven years of free basic education. Under the NEB, MoE plans to extend the six years of compulsory education to eleven years starting at the age of six. It will also ensure that pre-school education becomes universal by 2020 for five-year-olds (MoE 2012).

Education is a federal matter in Malaysia, with the exception of some religious schools which belong to the states. To cater for the different preferences of a multi-ethnic population, there are types of schools which use different media of instruction. National schools use Bahasa Malaysia as the medium of instruction, national-type primary schools use either Chinese or Tamil, Chinese independent secondary schools use Chinese, private and international schools use English, and state religious schools use Arabic and Bahasa Malaysia. The advantage of these different types of schools is that they cater to parental choice, but increasingly, the different types of schools end up with students from one particular ethnic group only, which limits opportunities for social interaction across ethnic groups. The increasing ethnic homogenisation of schools is a major concern in terms of social cohesion and national unity. To counteract this trend, the government has introduced programmes such as the Student Integration Plan for Unity and Vision Schools, in which students from national-type schools are encouraged to share physical facilities for co-curricular activities, to give students from a particular ethnic group opportunities to socialise and interact with students from other groups.

As for equity, the issue is not only that disadvantaged groups gain access to education, but also to ensure that they have a certain degree of success after gaining admission. As the *bumiputera* group, which comprises 67.4 percent of the population, is considered a disadvantaged group in Malaysia (see Hwok-Aun Lee, this volume), special schools such as Fully Residential Schools and MARA Junior Science Colleges have been established to nurture outstanding *bumiputera* students. In addition, a special national examination known as the matriculation examination is designed mainly to select *bumiputera* students for admission to universities. Performance gaps also exist between rural and urban, gender and socio-economic groups. In general, urban students perform better than their rural counterparts, female students perform better than male students, and students from high socio-economic backgrounds perform better than do less well-off students. Under the NEB, the ministry aspires to halve current rural–urban, socio-economic and gender achievement gaps by 2020. Furthermore, it will invest in physical and teaching resources for students with specific needs, including those with disabilities, indigenous students from Sabah and Sarawak, and the Orang Asli in Peninsular Malaysia (MoE 2012).

Higher education level

The higher education system in Malaysia has expanded rapidly in the past three decades, with the active participation of the private sector. The gross enrolment ratio (GER) of the 17–23-year-old age cohort in 2011 is 36 percent. This percentage is comparable to the world average of 30 percent, but low when compared with other high-income countries. For example, the GER for Finland is 95 percent, for the United States is 90 percent, and for Japan and the United Kingdom is 60 percent. The NHESP sets a target of attaining a 50 percent GER by 2020 (MoHE 2004).

Table 24.1 shows the number of each type of higher education institution (HEI) found in Malaysia. There are a total of 573 HEIs, consisting of twenty public universities, thirty-two polytechnics, eighty-four community colleges, forty-seven private universities and university colleges, and 390 private colleges. Five of the public universities are research universities[1] and five of the private universities are foreign branch campuses.[2] While public HEIs are quite evenly spread throughout the country, most of the private HEIs are located near the capital, in the Klang Valley. In 2012, there were about 1.3 million tertiary students, out of which 58 percent were enrolled in public HEIs, 35 percent were enrolled in private HEIs and 7 percent were studying abroad.

To correct the economic imbalance among the ethnic groups in Malaysia, an ethnic quota system for admission into public universities was implemented from 1979 to 2002. This affirmative action policy was replaced by a so-called 'merit system'. It is considered a so-called 'merit-based' university selection system because *bumiputera* students are selected for admission based on matriculation examination results, whereas non-*bumiputera* students are selected based on STPM examination results. Critics call the system unjust because the results of these examinations are not comparable (Lim 2013). The equity issue does not only involve different ethnic groups, however, but it also involves gender, the poor and indigenous people. Like in many other countries, there are more female students than male students in HEIs. The overall male to female ratio is 45:55, but it is even higher in public HEIs, at 40:60 in favour of females.

To widen accessibility and increase equity, the government, through its various ministries, has established HEIs and skills development centres throughout the country. Financial assistance for students is provided by various organisations[3] in the form of scholarships and student loans. Nonetheless, the biggest funding body for HEI students is the National Higher

Table 24.1 Number of higher education institutions in Malaysia

Types of institution	*Number*
Public university	20
Polytechnic	32
Community college	84
Private university and university college	47
Private college	390
Total	**573**

Education Fund Corporation (NHEFC). NHEFC student loans are heavily subsidised by the government, and any student who is enrolled in an accredited programme is entitled to apply for a loan; however, the record shows that the number who default on their repayment is quite high and there is great concern about the sustainability of this funding mechanism (MoHE 2004).

Another increasing concern is related to qualification levels and fields of study. Currently, there are more students studying for degrees than engaged in non-degree studies. The ratio of non-degree to degree is 2:3. This imbalance is more obvious in the public HEIs, where the ratio is 1:3; the imbalance in private HEIs is much less (46 percent to 54 percent). Under the NHESP, the target ratio for non-degree to degree is 2:1. As for fields of study, the most popular ones are social science, business and law and the least popular ones are agriculture and veterinary. The challenge is to increase the number of graduates in science, technology and engineering in the country.

Quality and relevance

School level

One of the most controversial issues in Malaysian education is language policy. Although there are several different media of instruction for schools at the primary level, the point of convergence is at the secondary level, where all the public schools are taught in the national language, Bahasa Malaysia. English is taught as a second language in all public schools. In 1996, the teaching of mathematics and science in English was introduced, in recognition of the importance of English in the fields of science and technology as well as in the global economy and international trade. This policy was reversed in 2009, however, and these two subjects came to be taught in Bahasa Malaysia again as of 2012, despite protests from various quarters in Malaysian society (Soong 2012). To improve the standard of English, the ministry recently announced that English will be made a compulsory pass in the SPM examination from 2016 (Stareducate Team 2013). Under the NEB, the aim is to ensure that every child is proficient in both Bahasa Malaysia and English (MoE 2012).

The national education philosophy aims at the holistic development of all children: intellectual, spiritual, emotional and physical. The school curriculum comprises subjects that are similar to the world model (Benavot *et al.* 1991). Much emphasis is also given to co-curricular activities as well as Islamic education (for Muslim students) and moral education (for non-Muslim students). Under the NEB, the aspirations are for students to acquire knowledge, thinking skills, leadership skills, bilingual proficiency, ethics and spirituality, and national identity (MoE 2012).

Malaysia's student performance in international assessment exercises has been quite discouraging, however. Malaysia has participated in the Trends in International Mathematics and Science Study (TIMSS) since 1999 and in the Programme for International Student Assessment (PISA) since 2009. It is reported that Malaysia's student performance in both these assessments is declining (MoE 2012). These poor performances in international benchmarking exercises have led the MoE to revamp both its primary and secondary curricula. The New Secondary School Standard Curriculum and the Revised Primary School Standard Curriculum will be introduced in 2017. These new curricula will include financial education and environmental education. In a similar manner, national examinations will also be reformed, with increased school-based assessment to test for higher-order thinking skills (MoE 2012).

As mentioned earlier, racial polarisation, and sometimes even racial discrimination, are found in schools, which can be detrimental to social cohesion and national unity. Therefore, the challenge is how to inculcate shared values, how to provide shared experiences, and how to develop shared aspirations among the young so that they acquire a strong Malaysian identity, irrespective of ethnicity, religion or socio-economic status. The main thrust here is for young people from different ethnic groups to interact, to understand one another and to embrace cultural diversity.

In any discussion of quality of education, one cannot ignore the quality of the teaching force. The teaching force in Malaysia comprises both graduate and non-graduate teachers. While all teachers in secondary schools are graduates, there are still many non-graduate teachers in the primary schools. Many non-graduate teachers upgrade themselves, either on their own or through government scholarships, via open distance learning. The move is toward an all-graduate teaching force; however, the teaching profession does not usually attract talented young people because teachers' pay in Malaysia is not competitive. Under the NEB, steps will be taken to transform teaching into a profession of choice by raising the entry bar for teachers from 2013 onwards, to draw from amongst the top 30 percent of graduates (MoE 2012).

Higher education level

With the rapid expansion and privatisation of higher education, the quality of higher education in Malaysia has become a great concern among the stakeholders of higher education. After an initial period of unregulated expansion, the Malaysian government took steps to regulate and consolidate the expansion of both public and private higher education. The governance and management of universities have been reformed, with an increase in institutional autonomy in return for more accountability (Lee 2012). The institutional autonomy of private universities and corporatised public universities has increased in terms of governance structure, academic matters, financial management, staff management, leadership appointment and student intake. At the same time, higher education institutions in Malaysia are increasingly being subjected to public accountability. In 2007, the Malaysian Qualifications Agency (MQA), formed from the merger of the National Accreditation Board (established in 1997 to monitor the standard and quality of higher education provided by the private sector) and the Ministry of Higher Education's Quality Assurance Division (which monitored and evaluated the quality of higher education programmes in public universities), was established. The MQA is responsible for quality assurance in higher education, in both the public and private sectors. It accredits higher education programmes, carries out institutional audits and rates higher education institutions in Malaysia.

To improve the quality of teaching and learning in higher education institutions, the NHESP states that HEIs should undertake curriculum reviews at two- or three-year intervals, taking into consideration the views of academicians, industrial experts, government officials and members of non-governmental organisations. Curricular transformation should strive toward achieving stipulated learning outcomes such as soft skills, entrepreneurship, better ethnic relations, and proficiency in English and a third language. HEIs would leverage on the use of information and communications technology (ICT), innovative teaching and multidisciplinary approaches, and industrial training to enhance students' learning experiences. HEIs would also upgrade and expand their postgraduate programmes, targeting a national doctoral-level enrolment of 55,500 students by 2020 (MoHE 2004). To achieve this target, the credibility of academic staff is to be improved. Currently, 75 percent of the academic staff in the five public research universities possess PhD qualifications, whereas only 40 percent do in the other public universities.

Malaysia aspires to be an excellent international hub of higher education. Over the years, the national higher education global network has been strengthened and the enrolment of international students in Malaysian HEIs has increased significantly, from 40,525 in 2005 to 72,456 in 2012. The government aims to increase the number of international students to 200,000 by 2020. The aim is to attract international students by the quality of higher education and its affordability. To attract more foreign students, the government has intensified overseas promotional programmes and taken pre-emptive measures to settle visa and immigration issues.

Malaysia recognises the importance of research, development and innovation (RDI) to support its national goals of becoming a high-income country and a progressive society. Gross expenditure on research and development in Malaysia has increased constantly as a proportion of GDP over the last two decades. The ratio has increased from 0.22 percent in 1996 to 1.07 percent in 2011 (MOSTI 2012); and by 2020, Malaysia aims to increase it to 2.0 percent. HEIs play a significant role in the development of RDI in Malaysia. To enhance RDI, Malaysia has established five research-intensive universities. The roles of these HEIs are to produce a critical mass of researchers, to establish research centres of excellence and to commercialise research. Under the NHESP, the targets are that by 2020 Malaysia will have at least six research universities, twenty centres of excellence, a critical mass of one hundred researchers, scientists and engineers (RSE) per 10,000 workforce, and that 10 percent of research products will have been commercialised, to boost the country's position in the innovation capacity index (MoHE 2004).

A major concern in discussing the quality and relevance of higher education in Malaysia is graduate employability. It was reported that in 2010, about 24.6 percent of graduates had not found a job in the first six months after their graduation (MoHE 2011), while another 25 percent of graduates worked in areas unrelated to their field of study. The factors often cited for the problem of graduate unemployment include lack of core knowledge and competency in the jobs applied for, lack of communication skills and language proficiency, and lack of general knowledge. The challenge for HEIs in Malaysia is to increase the employability of their graduates by providing the right technical skills, soft skills and work ethic.

Efficiency and effectiveness

School level

The Malaysian education system is highly centralised, with authority concentrated at the Ministry of Education (MoE). A brief review of the administrative structure (Lee 2006) shows that at the national level, the MoE is responsible for the formulation of education policies, overall planning, control of all matters related to finance and expenditure, planning and implementing physical development, developing school curricula, and recruitment, training, and posting of teachers. The State Education Department (SED) in each state answers directly to the MoE. The SED functions as a regional agency, regularly receiving directives from the centre. It implements all educational programmes in schools within the state. In addition, the SED manages, monitors and supervises all matters concerning curricula, schools, teachers and students as well as public funds received from the centre. Each school is headed by a principal or head teacher, whose role is to implement all education programmes stipulated by the MoE, supervise and guide teachers to ensure the quality of teaching and learning in schools, monitor and supervise students' welfare with respect to their learning experiences, and establish good and effective relations with parents and the community.

As the number of schools, students and teachers has grown, however, the volume of work at the state level has also increased and become more complex. Therefore, district education offices were established in 1982. The roles of these offices are to facilitate administration and to liaise between schools and SEDs. The functions of district education officers (DEOs) are mainly supervisory, managing information and carrying out routine tasks. DEOs supervise schools, teachers and students at the ground level. They also establish good relations with parents and communities. They collect data on schools, teachers and students and pass that information to the SEDs, which use the information to make decisions. DEOs also disseminate information concerning rules and regulations from the SED to schools. In addition, they carry out routine tasks, such as maintaining school facilities and monitoring public examinations (Lee 2006).

To improve the efficiency of the Malaysian education system, the government aspires to 'further maximise student outcomes within the current budget levels' (MoE 2012: 14). Under the NEB, measures to be undertaken to improve the efficiency of the system include the following:

- To ensure high-performing school leaders in every school by introducing competency-based selection criteria and enhancing succession planning processes for school principals from 2013 onwards.
- To empower SEDs, DEOs and schools by allowing greater school-based management and autonomy, including greater operational flexibility over budget allocation and curriculum implementation.
- To leverage ICT to scale up quality learning across the country by providing Internet access and a virtual learning environment to all schools.
- To transform MoE delivery capabilities and capacity by strengthening leadership capabilities.

The MoE will partner with parents, communities and the private sector to improve the effectiveness of the education system. It will maximise student outcomes for every Malaysian ringgit invested by linking every programme to clear student outcomes. It will annually rationalise programmes that have low impact and shift towards outcome-based budgeting. It will also increase transparency for direct public accountability (MoE 2012).

Higher education level

In the past, the Malaysian government was the main provider of higher education. But with widening access to higher education, the state encountered tight budgetary constraints in sustaining the expansion of higher education, so it privatised higher education and corporatised the public universities. The rapid expansion of private higher education can be seen in the increased number of private HEIs and the wide range of educational programmes that are being offered. The number of private colleges has more than doubled from 156 in 1992 to about 390 in 2013. The increase in the number of private universities and university colleges is even more dramatic, from zero in 1995 to forty-seven in 2013 (Table 24.1). Over the years, private HEIs have evolved different modes of ownership. Some of them are profit-oriented enterprises, while others are not-for-profit. Besides differences in mode of ownership, private HEIs also differ in their market focus. Some of them offer a wide range of programmes in various fields of study from the pre-university to postgraduate level, while others specialise in specific areas, such as health-related fields, art and design, language, hospitality, music, and so on. As in other countries, the survival of the private HEIs depends on their ability to experiment and innovate with different kinds of educational programme so that they can offer more choices to their customers. The educational programmes offered by private HEIs in Malaysia can be broadly categorised into three groups, namely, (1) internal programmes, (2) transnational education programmes, and (3) programmes leading to qualifications awarded by external examination bodies (Lee 2004).

Besides the privatisation of higher education in Malaysia, public universities are being corporatised. In 1995, the Universities and University Colleges Act 1971 was amended to lay the framework for all public universities to be corporatised. Through corporatisation, public universities are freed from the shackles of government bureaucratic regulations and are run like business corporations. Corporatised public universities are empowered to engage in market-related activities, such as entering into business ventures, raising endowments, setting up companies, and acquiring and holding investments. The Malaysian government continues to own most of the public universities' assets and to provide development funds for new programmes and expensive capital goods, but corporatised public universities are required to generate income for their operating costs.

As the higher education system has expanded, it has become more bureaucratic and regulated, so as to ensure consistency of treatment in various areas pertaining to the governance and management of HEIs. It has also become more complex, comprising a wide variety of institutions with different missions, scattered across different geographical locations, and thus difficult to manage centrally. Therefore, more decentralised management is needed to cope with challenges. The twenty public universities are divided into three categories, namely, (1) five research universities, (2) four comprehensive universities, and (3) eleven focused universities. Many public and private universities in Malaysia have adopted 'corporate managerialism' in their efforts to improve accountability, efficiency and productivity. Management techniques from the corporate sector, such as mission statements, strategic planning, total quality management, ISO (International Organization for Standardization) certification, right-sizing and benchmarking are being institutionalised in HEIs (Lee 2004).

The liberalisation of higher education in Malaysia has also resulted in a wide range of innovative public–private partnerships (Lee and Neubauer 2009). Examples include state governments partnering with private companies to establish state HEIs, public universities franchising their educational programmes to private HEIs, public universities partnering with private companies to engage in market-related activities such as setting up industrial parks and incubators, and the practice of outsourcing to private companies to provide various student services.

One of the thrust areas under the NHESP[4] is to 'reinforce the delivery system of the Ministry of Higher Education' (MoHE 2004: 142). The objectives of this thrust are: (1) to ensure that higher education legislation and policies are always relevant and current, (2) to develop an effective delivery system, and (3) to ensure the accountability and quality of HEIs. The strategies proposed to achieve these objectives include the following:

- plan and streamline the implementation of policies, programmes and projects;
- establish a more effective higher education delivery system by widespread use of ICT;
- increase compatibility between graduates' capabilities and job market needs; and
- practise international standards of monitoring to facilitate HEIs' efforts at obtaining international recognition.

The challenge will be for the ministry to provide flexible working procedures, reduce bureaucracy and review higher education policy so that HEIs can have the space to grow and innovate as well as to be responsible and responsive to societal needs.

Conclusion

Effective, relevant, high-quality education plays a critical role in laying a foundation toward improving the nation's competitive edge at the global level (MoHE 2004). Malaysia will continue to improve the general health of its education system through widening access, increasing equity, enhancing quality and relevance, and improving efficiency and effectiveness. The challenge is to implement both the NEP and NHESP with all their set targets and timelines, efficiently and effectively. Furthermore, these strategic plans need to be reviewed on a regular basis so that the Malaysian education system can meet changing economic and societal needs.

The successful implementation of these plans will require not only adequate resources, but also that special attention be given to a whole range of educational issues. Contemporary issues include concerns over social cohesion and national identity, language policy, admission policy to higher education institutions, quality of the teaching force, the shift away from rote learning to the development of higher-order thinking skills, the employability of graduates, return on investment in research and development, and the delegation of authority and responsibility to the state level and deconcentration of routine tasks from SEDs to the district level in the administration of the school system.

Notes

1 The five research universities are Universiti Malaya (UM), Universiti Kebangsaan Malaysia (UKM), Universiti Sains Malaysia (USM), Universiti Putra Malaysia (UPM) and Universiti Teknologi Malaysia (UTM).
2 The five foreign branch campuses are Monash International University, the University of Nottingham Malaysia campus, Curtin University of Technology Sarawak, Swinburn University of Technology Sarawak and Newcastle University Medicine Malaysia.
3 For example, through the Public Service Department (PSD), Majlis Amanah Rakyat (MARA), Tunku Abdul Rahman Foundation (Yayasan Tuanku Abdul Rahman), PETRONAS, Yayasan Telekom Malaysia, Yayasan Tenaga Nasional, Khazanah Nasional, as well as foundations and state governments.
4 With the merger of MoHE and MoE, the National Higher Education Strategic Plan is currently under review.

Bibliography

Benavot, Aron, Cha Yun-Kyung, David Kamens, John W. Meyer and Wong Suk Ying (1991) 'Knowledge for the masses: world models and national curricula, 1920–1986', *American Sociological Review*, 56(1): 85–100.

Lee, Molly N.N. (2004) *Restructuring Higher Education in Malaysia*, Monograph Series, 4/2004, Penang: School of Educational Studies, Universiti Sains Malaysia.

Lee, Molly N.N. (2006) 'Centralized decentralization in Malaysian education', in Christopher Bjork (ed.), *Educational Decentralization*, Dordrecht: Springer, pp. 149–58.

Lee, Molly N.N. (2012) 'Institutional autonomy in the restructuring of university governance', in John N. Hawkins, Ka Ho Mok and Deane E. Neubauer (eds), *Higher Education Regionalization in Asia Pacific: Implications for Governance, Citizenship and University Transformation*, New York: Palgrave Macmillan, pp. 161–75.

Lee, Molly N.N. and Deane E. Neubauer (2009) 'Redefining public and private in Asia Pacific higher education', in Terrance W. Bigalke and Deane E. Neubauer (eds), *Higher Education in Asia/Pacific: Quality and the Public Good*, New York: Palgrave Macmillan, pp. 33–47.

Lim Kit Siang (2013) 'WHAT MERITOCRACY? University intake is now even "more quote than quota"', *Malaysia Chronicle*, available at www.malaysia-chronicle.com/index.php?option=com_k2&view=item&id=133321:what-meritocracy?-university-intake-is-now-even-more-quote-than-quota-kit-siang&Itemid=2#axzz2hThEAG2z (accessed 12 October 2013).

Ministry of Education (MoE) (2012) *Malaysia Education Blueprint 2013–2025*, available at www.moe.gov.my/userfiles/file/PPP/Preliminary-Blueprint-Eng.pdf (accessed 11 October 2013).

Ministry of Higher Education (MoHE) (2004) *The National Higher Education Strategic Plan: Laying the Foundation Beyond 2020*, Putrajaya: Ministry of Higher Education.

Ministry of Higher Education (MoHE) (2011) *Graduate Tracer Study Executive Report 2010*, Putrajaya: Ministry of Higher Education.

Ministry of Science, Technology and Innovation (MOSTI) (2012) *National Science, Technology and Policy (2013–2020)*, Putrajaya: Ministry of Science, Technology and Innovation.

PEMANDU (2010) *Economic Transformation Programme: A Roadmap for Malaysia*, available at http://etp.pemandu.gov.my/upload/etp_handbook_chapter_1-4_economic_model.pdf (accessed 11 October 2013).

Soong Siew Hoong (2012) 'Teaching mathematics and science in English in Malaysia: chronology of recent press releases', 19 March, available at www.chinesechamber.org.my/html/themes/chinesechamber/images/content/bulletin342/Teaching%20of%20Mathematics%20and%20Science%20in%20English%20in%20Malayisa.pdf (accessed 12 October 2013).

Stareducate Team (2013) 'NEB 2013–2025: English a compulsory pass for SPM from 2016', *The Star Online*, 6 September, available at www.thestar.com.my/News/Nation/2013/09/06/National-Education-Blueprint-English.aspx (accessed 12 October 2013).

25

'1Care' and the politics of healthcare in Malaysia

Chee Heng Leng and Por Heong Hong

Two duelling slogans, '1Care for 1Malaysia' and '*Tak Nak* [Reject] 1Care', provide a succinct representation of what can arguably be considered the most contentious issue in healthcare for Malaysian society spanning the last three decades. The tagline '1Care for 1Malaysia' invokes the health plan that was prepared by the Ministry of Health (MOH) for the Tenth Malaysia Plan (2011–2015) (MOH 2010). The health plan is a comprehensive overall policy document that sets the vision and direction for the nation's healthcare sector. Central amongst the various programmes described in the document is a statement of intent for a 'restructured Malaysian health system' (ibid.: 51) that revolves around the establishment of a long-awaited social health insurance scheme.

'1Care' refers to this proposed national health financing scheme. Its announcement by the MOH at the Tenth Malaysia Health Plan Conference on 2 February 2010 met with diverse responses, with the most vocal resistance coming from the Citizens' Healthcare Coalition (CHC), which organised a series of seminars between February and June 2012 to garner support for a stand against the plan, and a '*Tak Nak* 1Care' campaign initiated through the Internet.

This is not the first time that the Malaysian public has been informed of such a proposal to reform healthcare financing. Plans for setting up a national health financing scheme have been publicly made known several times within the last three decades. The first time that a national health financing study was announced was in the Mid-Term Review of the Fourth Malaysia Plan (1981–1985). The Sixth Malaysia Plan (1990–1995) proposed governmental support for the growth of private health services, but it still approached the issue of financing cautiously, reporting that the national health financing study that was carried out under the Fifth Malaysia Plan would be further reviewed while waiting for the completion of a National Health Plan Study in 1992 (EPU 1991: 358). By the time of the Seventh Malaysia Plan (1996–2000), however, official policy unequivocally charted the direction of healthcare as toward privatisation, corporatisation and the setting up of a national health financing scheme (EPU 1996a: 544). '1Care' is therefore merely a renaming of what used to be referred to as the national health security fund, using the '1Malaysia' branding of the current administration under Prime Minister Najib Razak.

Throughout the entire policy process, numerous consultants' reports have been commissioned but never publicly released, and official announcements have been lacking in details.

Nevertheless, it became clear from early on that the financing scheme would be based on a social health insurance model. From the 1980s onward, international organisations such as the WHO and World Bank have been strongly advocating social health insurance as the financing mechanism by which countries should achieve universal coverage of their populations (World Bank 1987, 1993). Viewed in this light, the institution of a social health insurance scheme in Malaysia would have been congruent with international trends. Furthermore, when compared with countries such as Taiwan and Thailand, it is the delay in implementation rather than its enunciation that surprises. How can we understand the official rationale to restructure healthcare financing in this country and, concomitantly, the underlying forces and tensions that hold it in abeyance?

In this chapter, we use this central question to arrive at an understanding of the current status of healthcare in Malaysia. We begin by giving an overview of the transformation in healthcare provision and financing over the last half century or so, focusing mostly on the changes that have come with the privatisation policy of the mid-1980s. This is followed by a more detailed discussion of the issues and contesting arguments surrounding the proposed restructuring of national health financing. Third, we investigate the tensions and vested interests underlying the contestations in the context of the politics of healthcare. Finally, we point to regulatory shortcomings in the current shaping of Malaysian healthcare which face the danger of being overlooked while the politics over the healthcare financing issue is being played out.

Transformational changes in Malaysian healthcare

The official rationale for the 'restructured national health system' based on social health insurance is largely presented as a need to achieve an 'integrated delivery system that enables services to be obtained from both public and private sectors' (MOH 2010: 51–52). Malaysian healthcare provision was for a long time (through the 1960s and 1970s) dominated by governmental healthcare services funded through central treasury funds. Its large network of public health clinics makes primary care available through most of the country, including rural areas. While private sector general practitioners (GPs) are the mainstay of primary care in urban areas, hospitals and specialist services were for the most part provided by government.

This pattern started to change from the 1980s onward, in parallel with the institution of the government's privatisation policy, which led to the privatisation of the government's drug manufacturing, procurement and distribution centre in 1994, and of five hospital support services in 1996. Meanwhile, the economic and policy environment allowed for a rapid growth of private hospital and specialist services. In 1980, for example, the private sector's share of hospital beds was 5.8 percent (MOH 1980); by 2000 it had grown to 24.8 percent, stabilising in the following decade at around 25 percent (Nooraini *et al.* 2011: 7). Where, before, specialist services were concentrated in the government sector, the percentage of specialists in the private sector grew until it reached 43.2 percent in 2008–09 (Lim *et al.* 2011: 1). The imbalance is particularly acute in certain specialties; for example, only one-fifth of cardiologists are working in the public sector (Lim *et al.* 2011: 1).

Likewise, over the last three to four decades, the private share of healthcare financing has increased even as total health expenditure has grown. In 1983, private health expenditure was 24 percent of total health expenditure, which was estimated to be 2.8 percent of GNP (EPU 1996b: 18). By 2004, private expenditure overtook public expenditure, and in 2009, it reached 55.4 percent of total health expenditure; meanwhile, total health expenditure as a percentage of GDP grew from 2.9 percent in 1997 to 4.6 percent in 2009 before dipping down again to 3.6 percent in 2011 (Chua and Cheah 2012: 3; WHO 2013).

The increasing share of private health expenditure is due largely to the growth in out-of-pocket payments and private health insurance. In the ten years between 2002 and 2011, the share of total health expenditure from out-of-pocket payments grew from 28.7 to 41.7 percent, while that from private prepaid plans grew from 5.6 to 8.0 percent, both in tandem with the expansion in private health expenditure from 40.2 to 54.3 percent (WHO 2013). The increased frequency and spread in the use of private health insurance is clearly reflected by nationally representative survey data from the ground. Using data from national health and morbidity surveys, Zurina and Jones (2012: 164) estimate that healthcare payments that are wholly or partially made by insurance rose from 4.2 percent (of total number of observations) in 1996, to 20 percent in 2006.

The changes in healthcare provision and financing outlined above are in line with the shift in national policy in the mid-1980s from welfare-oriented to the 'caring society' (Chee and Barraclough 2007). Contrary to what images of societal solidarity the moniker 'caring society' might give rise to, it is in fact an enunciation of the retrenchment of the welfare role by the state, concomitant with an exhortation for welfare to 'revolve not around the state or the individual but around a strong and resilient family system'.[1]

Along with other changes in Malaysian society, in particular the rise in national income, increase in urban population, and ageing of the population,[2] the governmental policy environment and its corollary action and inaction led to a transformation of the healthcare system from one that was essentially cross-subsidised through national tax funding to one that is increasingly financed through private means and hence not subject to cross-subsidisation. Policy retrenchment of the governmental welfare role has been translated into a retreat from governmental healthcare provision (stated in the Seventh Malaysia Plan), leading to an increasing reliance on the private sector, where healthcare access is differentiated by the ability to pay, particularly for hospital and specialist care.

The 1Care scheme and doctors' responses

Official documents have repeatedly laid out the main problems faced by the government healthcare sector, namely, 'shortage of skilled personnel, movement of health professionals from the public sector to the private sector, inadequate expertise in some critical areas, and difficulty in placement and retention of doctors and nurses in more remote areas' (Lim *et al.* 2011: 1). The different levels of remuneration for doctors and specialists in the private and public sectors cannot be reconciled, leading to the intractable problem of doctors leaving the public sector for the private sector. The proposed restructuring of the national healthcare system is meant primarily to address this problem of the bifurcation between public and private healthcare services, and aims at an integration between the two (MOH 2010: 51–52).

The unified healthcare financing system that has been announced will essentially be a single centralised fund functioning as a social health insurance. Premiums from employer–employee contributions will be mandatory, while the government will pay the premiums for the registered poor, disabled, elderly (sixty years old and above), government pensioners and civil servants and their dependants, up to a maximum of five. In fleshing out some of these details, the deputy director-general of health, Maimunah A. Hamid (2010), reassured the public that premiums will be community-rated and progressively structured, based on income.

A healthcare system that is based on financing through health insurance with a fee-for-service payment mechanism is linked to cost escalation.[3] The MOH policy document addresses this concern by explaining that the 1Care fund will replace the current fee-for-service system with other types of payment mechanisms based on diagnostic-related groups

(DRGs) and/or capitation to control cost escalation on the supply side.[4] To control the demand side, these new payment systems will be tied to a referral system to rationalise the utilisation of specialist care. Furthermore, the new scheme will incorporate co-payments, which may be paid out-of-pocket or through an option to buy extra coverage from private health insurance (MOH 2010: 52–53).[5]

Although the national health plan (MOH 2010) provides the most detailed exposition of the financing scheme to date, there is still much that is unclear. Public concern obviously revolves around the amount of premium that would be extracted from payroll deduction. Since this detail was not spelt out when the 1Care fund was presented, public unease was expressed when a leak led to speculation, placing it at 10 percent, with a maximum cap of six GP visits a year (*Malaysian Insider* 2012). An MOH official had to clarify that the 10 percent was actually a ballpark figure of current average healthcare spending by Malaysians each year and that six was the average number of times a person would visit a healthcare facility, while emphasising that implementation of the scheme was not yet imminent and that eleven technical working groups with members drawn from professional bodies, the government and academia were still involved in drawing up a blueprint for cabinet approval (Edwards and Lim 2012).

One of the organisations in the coalition spearheading the '*Tak Nak* 1Care' campaign is the Federation of Private Medical Practitioners' Associations of Malaysia (FPMPAM).[6] Founded in 1989, it is the largest private practitioners' association with over 5,000 members, and the most widely represented, with seven state-level association members. As spelt out by the president, its position is a conservative one that calls for 'limited reform' by way of improving the management of public healthcare, but otherwise maintaining the status quo (Chow 2011). It opposes the 1Care financing scheme on the basis that it is modelled after the National Health Service (NHS) of the United Kingdom, citing the problems of accessibility (long waiting lists), lack of choice (patients have to register with doctors for care) and failure in containing costs (Chow and Ng 2011). According to the FPMPAM's arguments, the proposed insurance body, functioning as a 'middle-man', will add a layer of bureaucracy, thereby increasing costs, while the premiums will be an additional tax burden for the citizens.

Citing a 2002 consultancy report, the FPMPAM president called for the outsourcing of public hospital ambulatory outpatients to 'the existing robust GP system thereby releasing the public system to concentrate on secondary and tertiary care' (Chow 2011). The UK NHS has a similar system of contracting care out to GPs. It would seem therefore that the FPMPAM's objection is not to the 'NHS model' per se, but more narrowly focused on the capitation payment mechanism that the NHS uses to remunerate GPs. Furthermore, in terms of overall costs of healthcare, the NHS type of healthcare system results in lower costs when compared with healthcare systems that are based on social health insurance, while both the NHS and social health insurance systems result in lower costs than the largely private-market type of healthcare system prevalent in the United States. Although the emphasis of the FPMPAM's criticism is the removal of patients' choice (for those who can afford to pay) and increasing costs, its main objection is more specifically to the part of the 1Care scheme that is envisaged to place controls and limitations on the private outpatient (both GP and specialist) sector through the proposed payment mechanism.

Different groups of doctors would be affected in different ways by a social insurance scheme, hence doctors' support for or opposition to the proposed scheme could depend on their various positions, and may be for different reasons.[7] As seen above, private medical practitioners have been against it because of their vested interest in retaining the existing public–private mixed system, with doctors in the private sector paid on a fee-for-service basis. Likewise, specialists who believe that they benefit from the current lack of a referral system in the private sector (which means that patients bypass GPs to consult specialists on a fee-for-service basis) would oppose the proposed scheme.[8] On the other hand, doctors in the government services who could look forward to higher levels of remuneration in a new financing scheme would be likely to support it.

Hence, the Malaysian Medical Association (MMA), with about 13,000 members from both government and private sectors, GPs as well as specialists, has taken a different position from the FPMPAM.[9] The MMA position is set out in its paper, 'Health for All' (MMA 1999), which in principle supports the national healthcare financing scheme, and calls for active engagement in the policy process so as to exert influence and ensure good governance in the new scheme (Koh 2011).

Three discernible positions

Current opposition to the proposed fund is only the latest in a long series of civil society opposition to governmental measures to privatise public health services and reform national healthcare financing (Chee and Barraclough 2007: 208–17). The 1997 Citizens' Health Manifesto, issued by the Citizens' Health Initiative, a loose grouping initiated by the MMA, Consumers' Association of Penang (CAP) and academics in Universiti Sains Malaysia, and endorsed by a long list of NGOs, unions and individuals, had called for a moratorium on the privatisation of healthcare and for more governmental transparency and greater civil society involvement in the policy process of national healthcare financing reform.

On the eve of the 1999 general elections, a successful campaign was waged against the corporatisation of government hospitals (Chee 2008: 2153–54). The opposition coalition at that time opposed the creation of a national healthcare security fund on the basis that the fund created, estimated to be second in size only to the Employees' Provident Fund (EPF), could be abused by the ruling regime, which had been accused of using the EPF to bail out politically linked companies (Gomez and Jomo 1997: 195; Jalleh 2005). Furthermore, throughout the time period when it seemed as though the management of the national health security fund could be outsourced, politically well-connected companies – some supported by the hiring of retired officials formerly highly placed in the health ministry – vied for this management role. The statement that the 1Care health fund will be publicly managed may be read as a strategic response to a long-standing criticism that it will benefit yet another politically well-connected 'rentier-type' management corporation (MOH 2010: 51–53).

In 2004, the media reported on a range of measures introducing private practice into government hospitals, including the setting up of private wings and allowing government specialists to engage in private practice after office hours, as well as on a consultant study for the implementation of the national health security fund which would incorporate a role for private insurance (Chee and Barraclough 2007: 213). In response, eighty-one civil society members formed the Coalition Against Health Care Privatisation (CAHCP)[10] and issued the People's Proposal, which called for consultation and full disclosure by the government in its formulation of the national health financing scheme; an increase in the government health budget to 5 percent of GDP; that the proposed national health authority be created by an act of parliament; the strengthening of the public health sector; and that any essential health package provided by the national health insurance fund minimally include all treatment options currently available in government clinics and hospitals (*Aliran Monthly* 2006; CAHCP 2006; Pillay 2005).

In response to the current 1Care proposals, the CAHCP has now taken a stronger position, calling for a pull-back from privatisation. This would involve a freeze on private hospital expansion (i.e. the government should not approve any new private hospitals nor any increase in the number of beds in existing private hospitals), and the government's taking back outsourced hospital cleaning and technical services; manufacturing, supply and distribution of drugs and pharmaceutical supplies; and compulsory health screening of foreign workers. Parallel to these demands, the CAHCP also calls for the government health budget to be increased and service conditions for healthcare workers to be improved – in particular, calling for a separate service commission to be set up so that doctors' remuneration could be released from the constraints of the Public Services Department and substantially increased (Keruah 2012).

Summing up, therefore, there are now three discernible positions in response to the 1Care proposals, namely, the FPMPAM position of rejecting 1Care and maintaining the status quo; the CAHCP position of not only rejecting 1Care but going further, to roll back privatisation; and the MMA position of supporting the proposals and engaging in the process of formulating the financing scheme.[11] While the CAHCP and the FPMPAM positions appear similar because both reject the 1Care proposals, however, the difference between them is clearly reflected in the alternatives they propose and the consequences that flow from each.

The FPMPAM position basically calls for the status quo to be maintained, the consequence of which is that the current trend of privatisation and marketisation of healthcare provision and financing will continue.[12] Since forces in society do not remain static, the growth of the healthcare market can only lead to the increasing strength of private hospital providers and private health insurance. Inequities will increase in the face of the widening gap between public and private healthcare. In contrast to the FPMPAM, the CAHCP is in fact calling for a reversal of thirty years of privatisation and closing the gap between the private and public healthcare services by putting the brakes on private hospital care. It would simultaneously put more resources into government health services in order to improve service conditions and salaries of doctors and other healthcare workers.

It is important to note that while countries such as Thailand and South Korea have turned to social health insurance from a more private-dominated system of financing, Malaysia is coming to it from the other end, that is, from taxation-based funding (Lee 2012). Analysts have pointed out that compared with other countries and WHO criteria, governmental healthcare expenditure is still low in relation to GDP (Chua and Cheah 2012; Ramesh and Wu 2008). Seen in this context, the CAHCP's proposal is entirely viable, although the details will have to be further examined. Nevertheless, it requires political will, and therein lies the crux of the matter. A reversal of privatisation is possible but highly unlikely, at least in the foreseeable future, due to the numerous challenges that such a reversal would entail.

Obstacles to the reversal of healthcare privatisation would be presented by vested interests that benefit from the status quo. The privatisation trend of the last few decades has led to the creation of corporate bodies with interests in outsourced government contracts, privatised governmental entities, and the private healthcare delivery sector with its corollary industries. Vested interests are lodged not only within capitalist ownership and professional management of these private sector bodies, but also within statist capitalist forces, such as sovereign wealth funds that own private healthcare facilities (Chee 2008; Chan 2010). For example, Malaysia's investment agency Khazanah holds the majority share ownership of Parkways, one of the largest transnational corporations that own and manage hospitals throughout Asia, including Malaysia, and the state of Johor's economic development corporation owns KPJ Healthcare, another large hospital-ownership and management entity.

It is not only the investment arm of the state that has stakes in private healthcare corporations, however. Policy-makers of both federal and state level governments and at least one part of the MOH bureaucracy view the medical tourism industry as an instrument for economic development and a source of foreign exchange. The medical tourism industry serves to expand the private healthcare market and is a major source of revenue for a substantial number of private healthcare providers. Interests in the growth of medical tourism are therefore intertwined with interests in the growth of private healthcare services; hence a moratorium on the expansion of private hospitals will also decelerate the current trend of increasing foreign patient numbers.

Two viable choices

From our reading of the various responses, we have presented three positions vis-à-vis the proposed 1Care national healthcare financing scheme. From the perspective of citizen-users of public healthcare, there really are only two viable choices, namely, either to reject 1Care and roll back privatisation and private sector growth, or to accept the scheme and actively engage in the process to fight for better terms under the health plan. The FPMPAM position of maintaining the status quo does not provide a sustainable solution, because it means that the current trend of growth in private healthcare will continue. With the healthcare market's expansion from the efforts of the medical tourist industry, the gap between private and public sectors will grow increasingly larger, with detrimental effects for those who depend on public healthcare.

The CAHCP's solution of rolling back privatisation and placing a limit on private hospital growth means that the government's role in healthcare provision would have to be increased and strengthened. In theory at least, if government healthcare of acceptable quality is easily accessible, with acceptable waiting times, the private sector will remain small, and the presumably low fees in the government sector will act as floor prices, to keep charges in the private sector down. It has been argued that governmental provision of hospital and specialist care in a healthcare system acts as an effective cost containment mechanism for total healthcare expenditures (Ramesh and Wu 2008). From the perspective of overall cost, equitable access and universal coverage, this option is most desirable for the majority of citizen-users of healthcare, but is politically difficult to achieve.

A social health insurance scheme will involve higher overall costs compared with the present public system, because it will necessarily involve more administration and regulation, as well as higher remuneration to doctors in the public services. On the other hand, in the tentative proposals of the 1Care scheme, control over pricing in the private sector will be exercised not only directly through legislation, but also through the financing and payment mechanisms of the social health insurance fund, which will act as a single payer. The proposed referral system, as well as the capitation and DRG payment methods, are essential mechanisms to help prevent the inappropriate and excessive use of healthcare which has been shown to occur under social health insurance schemes (Wasem *et al.* 2004).[13] If not controlled, over-use will lead to cost escalation, and finally come full circle back to users, in the form of higher premiums.

The imposition of healthcare premiums will present an additional financial burden for households in the immediate and short term. If well planned and implemented, however, it should result in regulated pricing of healthcare services as well as medicines that would ease inflationary pressures on healthcare costs in the longer term.

Compared with the current de facto trend of an increasing dependence on private insurance to allay increasing out-of-pocket payments, a social health insurance will provide a more equitable system of healthcare financing. There is cross-subsidisation on a national basis in a social health insurance scheme (and also in a tax-funded national health service) that is absent in a healthcare system dominated by private insurance and out-of-pocket payments. The concept of cross-subsidisation, from the healthy to ill, across time and nation, is the fundamental basis of solidarity in a national healthcare system.

Regulation

When the government announced the implementation of a health financing scheme, along with its withdrawal from the provision of medical services, its stated intention was to increase its regulatory and enforcement roles (EPU 1996a: 544). This reflects a recognition that with the proposed change in healthcare financing, as well as increased privatisation, including the corporatisation of government hospitals, the exercise of regulatory oversight would be more demanding and complex.

The Private Healthcare Facilities and Services Act 1998 (Act 586) and Regulations 2006 (PHFSA) were implemented only after more than twenty years of rapid private sector growth. A recent study (Wan Abdullah and Lee 2011: 102)[14] evaluating its implementation in the private hospital sector found that 'full compliance of these regulated corporate private hospitals remained a challenge'. Under this Act, the statutory power of the director-general of health to grant a licence of operation or to close a health facility has been greatly expanded compared with under previous legislation. This study found, however, that the powers of the MOH to carry out effective regulatory intervention are limited due to lack of enforcement capacity, in terms not only of manpower, but also of adequate information to regulate medical practice in corporate private hospitals, and that the MOH enforcement team was 'overstretched and over stressed physically and mentally' (Wan Abdullah and Lee 2011: 102).

Two empirical observations from this study serve to illustrate, however, that these difficulties stem from conflicts of interest that are structurally derived. The first observation pertains to the PHFSA regulation that holds the private hospital or health facility responsible for the employment of qualified health professionals. To comply, the hospital has to appoint a medical director from among its senior consultants to be the licensee or 'person-in-charge'. The researchers in this project found that even though the position comes with material incentives, senior clinicians are reluctant to undertake this task because it is a challenge for the person-in-charge to exercise independent decision-making that may be (and usually is) in conflict with corporate policies and business decisions. In one of their study hospitals, the senior clinician who had previously been the person-in-charge resigned from the post, and was replaced by a junior doctor-employee due to cost-containment considerations. Eventually, the hospital was found to be in violation of the law for allowing an unregistered practitioner (not holding an annual practising certificate) to practise medicine at its premises. Regardless of the actual reason that led to this particular instance of legal infraction, it is obvious that the employee-doctor would have been in an even more difficult situation with regard to making hospitals give priority to medical considerations over business ones.

A second empirical observation from this study illustrates that effective regulation requires a larger context of good governance. The researchers cite a case of a prominent clinician owning a private healthcare facility that was in violation of the medical professional code of practice due to its 'hard-selling entrepreneurial initiatives' (Wan Abdullah and Lee 2011: 101). When its application for licence renewal was temporarily suspended because of non-compliance with regulations, the facility continued to operate for a year without a valid licence, until its licence was renewed by 'invisible hands', that is, through political connections. This case reflects the intertwined political and vested interests that can work to confound state attempts at regulation.

Even while the healthcare financing scheme is being debated, and PHFSA regulations are slowly being implemented, the fast-changing healthcare system is being shaped by practices that are in the process of being institutionalised. One example to illustrate how this could be problematic is the issue of over-treatment in private hospitals. Over-treatment can be motivated by a variety of reasons, such as a profit maximisation or the practice of defensive medicine to prevent litigation. Incentives to over-treat may be further built into the system if regulatory mechanisms are not in place to prevent it. An example of this would be situations in which consultant specialists in private hospitals also have ownership interests in expensive equipment (such as MRI scanners) which accrue to them a monetary return on a fee-for-service basis. Their being in a position where they can directly increase the use of this equipment gives rise to a conflict of interest with an incentive to over-treat. The conflict is between their role as doctors in ensuring that the equipment is used only when medically necessary, and the investor's interest in recuperating costs. Some, but not all, hospitals have policies and good practices to guard against these kinds of situation. We give this example to illustrate that there are areas that urgently require the attention of the regulatory authorities.[15]

Conclusion

In this article, we assess the current state of healthcare financing and the contestation surrounding it in Malaysia. The stakes are high because the system of healthcare financing in a country influences to a large extent issues of healthcare accessibility, equity and universal coverage. The taxation-based public healthcare system is a primary welfare source for the people of this country. Nevertheless, privatisation of the healthcare sector, expansion of private hospitals, and increase in use of private health insurance and out-of-pocket expenditures have all worked to strengthen the private sector, which continually drains the public sector of medical expertise.

The 1Care national health financing scheme proposes to change the taxation-based financing structure to one that is based on compulsory, social health insurance. Three positions exist in response to this proposal: (1) reject the change and maintain the current taxation-based financing in the public sector, leaving the private sector to private (insurance or out-of-pocket) financing; (2) reject the change and roll back privatisation, that is, strengthening the current taxation-based financing of the public sector and controlling the expansion of the private sector; and (3) accept the change and actively engage in the policy process.

We have argued that the first position of maintaining the status quo is not viable, because the current trend of private sector expansion will continue to lead to an erosion of public healthcare. To actualise equitable and accessible healthcare with universal coverage through a taxation-based healthcare system, the expansion of private secondary and tertiary care has to be controlled. If this cannot be achieved, the option of a social health insurance would be more equitable than de facto growth in private (insurance and out-of-pocket) financing.

The argument that a social health fund is open to abuse by corrupt forces in power is one that can be addressed only by strong safeguards attached to the fund itself and to the institutional processes of national accounting and audit. As previously discussed, even straightforward application of legal regulations can be circumvented by corrupt political intervention. Institutional safeguards are necessary whatever system of financing is in place, and have to be protected through the political process. It may well be that a taxation-based dominant public healthcare sector would be better and less subject to abuse compared with a social health insurance scheme. If no fundamental transformation occurs in the political and economic structures, however, Malaysians may no longer have the privilege of choice.

Notes

1 It is the seventh of nine challenges outlined in 'Vision 2020', introduced in 1991 by the then prime minister, Mahathir Mohamad. Originally titled 'The Way Forward', the vision document articulated Malaysia's goals to become a fully developed nation by the year 2020. See Prime Minister's Office of Malaysia (2013).

2 GNI per capita increased from US$1,820 in 1980 to US$9,800 in 2012 (World Bank 2013); urban population from 2.79 million persons or 26.7 percent in 1970 (MOH 1980) to 20.09 million persons or 71.0 percent in 2010 (Department of Statistics 2010); the elderly, defined as those above 65 years of age, rose from 602,734 persons or 3.84 percent in 1985 (Department of Statistics 1985) to 2.02 million or 6.95 percent in 2011 (Department of Statistics Malaysia 2013).

3 For a discussion on rising healthcare costs in countries with social health insurance, see Figueras *et al.* 2004: 117.

4 The argument is that healthcare providers who are paid on a fee-for-service basis will have an incentive to increase the utilisation of their own services, which they can do because they have more medical knowledge than the user/patient. Payment mechanisms based on DRGs or capitation remove this incentive.

5 Although not explicitly spelt out, the co-payment mechanism is meant to act as a disincentive for 'over-use' of healthcare, but it seems that this mechanism would be rendered ineffective as such if co-payments are also covered by private insurance. See Wasem *et al.* 2004: 241.

6 The other visible partner is Dr T. Jayabalan, who is a politician with an opposition party and member of the Penang State Assembly.

7 We do not mean to imply from this that their arguments are therefore invalid. Some of their arguments and concerns could very well be legitimate and well founded. This caveat pertains to the above discussion of the FPMPAM position as well.

8 In the current system, doctors who have a specialist certificate can function as both GP and specialist, that is, as GPs, they can refer patients to other specialists, while as specialists, they can also be referred patients by others. According to a key informant, these doctor-specialists fear that they will lose the privilege of this dual role in the referral system that will be instituted in the new financing scheme (interview by Por Heong Hong with key informant, 12 January 2012).

9 Mary Cardosa, then MMA president, had admitted that it had been a difficult process for MMA to arrive at a position due to the different types of doctor who are members (interview by Por Heong Hong, 21 February 2012).

10 Not to be confused with the CHC.

11 We are heuristically delineating and labelling these three positions here so as to sharpen the issues for discussion and analysis. We do not imply that there are no other positions vis-à-vis the proposed national healthcare financing scheme, nor do we assume that there are no other organisations or individuals propounding these or other positions, nor that there could not be other alternative framings.

12 The FPMPAM opposes the corporatisation of government hospitals, and supports monitoring and controlling the cost of private hospital care through 'appropriate market forces and regulatory machinery' but is silent on the CAHCP's position of rolling back privatisation (Chow 2011; Chow and Ng 2011).

13 The over-use of healthcare is largely attributed to supplier-induced demand. Patients, not having as much knowledge and expertise as doctors and being in a more vulnerable position when ill, depend on their doctors' recommendations to 'demand' or use healthcare; while doctors have a self-interested tendency to increase demand on their patients' behalf.

14 This is the only academic study evaluating the implementation of the PHFSA that we could find. This section uses the evidence in this study for its arguments.

15 There is currently no regulation or mechanism to prevent the proliferation of expensive medical equipment in the country or to rationalise its usage. The acquisition of expensive equipment is not controlled in the private sector. In 2010, 122,135 out of a total 170,010 MRI procedures were performed in the private sector. The usage rate in the urban centre of Kuala Lumpur is the highest: a total of 37,481 MRI procedures were performed in 2010, or 224 MRI procedures per 10,000 population. This is twenty times the usage rate of rural Terengganu, where nine MRI procedures per 10,000 population were performed in the same year (Sivasampu *et al.* 2012: 16).

Bibliography

Aliran Monthly (2006) 'Health care at a cross-roads', *Aliran Monthly*, 25 April, available at http://aliran.com/aliran-monthly/2006/2006-1/health-care-at-a-cross-roads (accessed 6 October 2013).

Chan Chee Khoon (2010) 'Re-inventing the welfarist state? The Malaysian health system in transition', *Journal of Contemporary Asia*, 40(3): 444–65.

Chee Heng Leng (2008) 'Ownership, control and contention: challenges for the future of healthcare in Malaysia', *Social Science & Medicine*, 66: 2145–56.

Chee Heng Leng and Simon Barraclough (eds) (2007) *Health Care in Malaysia: The Dynamics of Provision, Financing and Access*, London: Routledge.

Chow, Steven K.W. (2011) 'With 1Care, the choice will not be there', *Malaysiakini*, 13 December, available at http://beta.malaysiakini.com/letters/183993 (accessed 21 January 2014).

Chow, Steven K.W. and Ng Swee Choon (2011) '1Malaysia healthcare – transforming for the better or worse', Federation of Private Medical Practitioners' Associations Malaysia (FPMPAM), 3 May, available at http://fpmpam.org/content/presidents02.html (accessed 20 September 2013).

Chua Hong Teck and Julius Chee Ho Cheah (2012) 'Financing universal coverage in Malaysia: a case study', *BMC Public Health*, 12(1): S7, pp. 1–7.

Coalition Against Health Care Privatisation (CAHCP) (2006) 'Who is calling the shots in health care?', *Aliran Monthly*, 18 March, available at http://aliran.com/archives/health/index.html (accessed 6 October 2013).

Department of Statistics (1985) *Social Statistics Bulletin Malaysia, 1985*, Kuala Lumpur: Department of Statistics.

Department of Statistics Malaysia (2010) *Population Distribution and Basic Demographic Characteristic Report 2010*, available at www.statistics.gov.my/portal/index.php?option=com_content&id=1215 (accessed 7 October 2013).

Department of Statistics Malaysia (2013) *Population Quick Info: Population by States and Age, Malaysia 2011*, available at http://statistics.gov.my/portal/index.php?option=com_content&view=article&id=471&lang=en&Itemid=0 (accessed 14 May 2014).

Economic Planning Unit (EPU) (1984) *Mid-Term Review of the 4th Malaysia Plan, 1981–1985*, Kuala Lumpur: Economic Planning Unit.

Economic Planning Unit (EPU) (1986) *The Fifth Malaysia Plan, 1986–1990*, Kuala Lumpur: Economic Planning Unit.

Economic Planning Unit (EPU) (1991) *The Sixth Malaysia Plan, 1990–1995*, Kuala Lumpur: Economic Planning Unit.

Economic Planning Unit (EPU) (1996a) *Seventh Malaysia Plan, 1996–2000*, Kuala Lumpur: Economic Planning Unit.

Economic Planning Unit (EPU) (1996b) 'Health sector development', in Robert Haas, Sulaiman Mahbob and Tham Siew Yean (eds), *Health Care Planning and Development: Conference Proceedings*, Kuala Lumpur: Malaysian Institute of Economic Research, pp. 13–24.

Edwards, Audrey and Lim Wey Wen (2012) '1Care still a long way off, says Ministry', *The Star*, 10 February, available at www.thestar.com.my/News/Nation/2012/02/10/1Care-still-a-long-way-off-says-Ministry.aspx (accessed 20 September 2013).

Figueras, Josep, Richard B. Saltma, Reinhard Busse and Hans F.W. Dubois (2004) 'Patterns and performance in social health insurance systems', in Richard B. Saltman, Reinhard Busse and Josep Figueras (eds), *Social Health Insurance Systems in Western Europe*, Glasgow: Open University Press, pp. 81–140.

Gomez, Edmund Terence and Jomo Kwame Sundaram (1997) *Malaysia's Political Economy: Politics, Patronage and Profits*, Cambridge: Cambridge University Press.

Jalleh, Martin (2005) 'The truth about privatization', *Aliran Monthly*, 25(6), available at http://aliran.com/archives/monthly/2005a/6h.html (accessed 6 October 2013).

Keruah Usit (2012) 'Yes, there is an alternative to 1Care', *Malaysiakini*, 22 February, available at www.malaysiakini.com/news/189890 (accessed 6 October 2013).

Koh Kar Chai (2011) 'The 1Care for 1Malaysia (1C1M) Issues', *Berita MMA*, 41(10): 17–18.

Lee, Nathaniel (2012) 'Social health insurance in Malaysia: lessons from Thailand and South Korea', *Kajian Malaysia*, 30(1): 51–70.

Lim T.O., S. Sivasampu, Z. Ariza and M.K. Nabilah (2011) 'Overview on hospitals and specialists services in Malaysia', in Sheamini Sivasampu, Lim Teck Onn and Noor Hisham Abdullah (eds),

National Healthcare Establishments and Workforce Statistics 2008–2009, Kuala Lumpur: Ministry of Health, pp. 1–2.

Maimunah Abdul Hamid (2010) '1Care for 1Malaysia: restructuring the Malaysian Health System', paper presented at The Tenth Malaysia Health Plan Conference, Subang Holiday Villa Hotel, 2–4 February.

Malaysia Medical Association (MMA) (1999) *Health for All: Reforming Health Care in Malaysia*, Kuala Lumpur: Malaysia Medical Association.

Malaysian Insider (2012) '1Care to be made mandatory, says Health Ministry', *The Malaysian Insider*, 9 February, available at www.themalaysianinsider.com/malaysia/article/1-care-to-be-made-mandatory-says-health-ministry (accessed 20 September 2013).

Ministry of Health (MOH) (1980) *MOH Annual Report, 1980*, Kuala Lumpur: Ministry of Health.

Ministry of Health (MOH) (2010) *Country Health Plan, 2011–2015*, Putrajaya: Ministry of Health.

Nelson, Joan M. (2008) 'Malaysia's healthcare sector: shifting roles for public and private provision', in Joan M. Nelson, Jacob Meerman and Abdul Rahman Embong (eds), *Globalization and National Autonomy: The Experience of Malaysia*, Singapore: ISEAS, pp. 218–40.

Nooraini, B., S.C. Teng, I. Lailanor, S. Ahmad Razid, S. Sivasampu, A. Afidah, M. Laili Murni, S. Amiruddin, S. Fauziah J. and O. Faridah (2011) 'Hospitals services in Malaysia', in Sheamini Sivasampu, Lim Teck Onn and Noor Hisham Abdullah (eds), *National Healthcare Establishments and Workforce Statistics 2008–2009*, Kuala Lumpur: Ministry of Health, pp. 3–18.

Pillay, Subramaniam (2005) 'Government shouldn't shirk health responsibility', *Malaysiakini*, 16 December, available at www.malaysiakini.com/letters/44619 (accessed 6 October 2013).

Prime Minister's Office of Malaysia (2013) *Malaysia as a Fully Developed Country*, available at www.pmo.gov.my/?menu=page&page=1898 (accessed 4 October 2013).

Ramesh, M. and Xun Wu (2008) 'Realigning public and private health care in Southeast Asia', *The Pacific Review*, 21(2): 171–87.

Sivasampu, Sheamini, N.Y. Akma, M.M. Laili, A. Afidah, M. Fatihah, O. Faridah and N. Ruby (2012) 'Hospital services in Malaysia', in Tahrani Periana Kovindear, S. Sivasampu, P.P. Goh, A. Faizah and A.N. Hisham (eds), *National Healthcare Establishments and Workforce Statistics (Hospital) 2010*, Kuala Lumpur: Ministry of Health, pp. 3–22.

Wan Abdullah Nik Rosnah and Lee Kwee Heng (2011) 'Impact of the Private Healthcare Facilities and Services Act 1998 (Act 586) and Regulations 2006 on the medical practice in corporate private hospitals in Malaysia', *OIDA International Journal of Sustainable Development*, 2(9): 89–106.

Wasem, Jürgen, Stefan Greß and Kieke G.H. Okma (2004) 'The role of private health insurance in social health insurance countries', in Richard B. Saltman, Reinhard Busse and Josep Figueras (eds), *Social Health Insurance Systems in Western Europe*, Glasgow: Open University Press, pp. 227–47.

World Bank (1987) *Financing Health Services in Developing Countries: An Agenda for Reform*, Washington DC: World Bank.

World Bank (1993) *World Development Report 1993: Investing in Health*, London: Oxford University Press.

World Bank (2013) *World Bank Data*, available at http://data.worldbank.org/indicator/NY.GNP.PCAP.CD/countries/1W?display=default (accessed 7 October 2013).

World Health Organization (WHO) (2013) *Global Health Observatory Data Repository*, available at http://apps.who.int/gho/data/view.country.12900 (accessed 3 October 2013).

Zurina Kefeli and Glenn Jones (2012) 'Moral hazard and the impact of private health insurance on the utilisation of health care in Malaysia', *Jurnal Ekonomi Malaysia*, 46(2): 159–75.

26

Interfaith relations in Malaysia

Moving beyond Muslims versus 'others'

Carolina López C.

Due to its favourable location on trade routes stretching across Asia, Peninsular Malaysia has long been a point of contact among civilisations and belief systems. Since the height of the Srivijaya empire, from the seventh to thirteenth centuries, the region has served as an *entrepôt*, or an international trade centre, where peoples from diverse religious and cultural traditions have met.

The presence of Muslim traders, and Melaka's first sultan's embrace of Islam in the fourteenth century, quickly led to the adoption of Islam by most ethnic Malays inhabiting the peninsula (López 2001). While Chinese and Indians have travelled to the Malayan peninsula throughout its history, their numbers increased greatly under British rule, profoundly changing the demographic makeup in the region (Table 26.1). The British brought thousands of Chinese immigrants to work in commerce, tin mines and commercial agriculture, while Indians came to labour on estates and rubber plantations, with others serving in the colonial government.

Fifty-nine years later, demographic data from the 2010 census indicated that the total population of Malaysia had reached 28.3 million, of whom 67.4 percent are Malays, 24.6 percent Chinese, 7.3 percent Indians and 0.7 percent 'others' (Table 26.2). These figures show an 18 percent increase since independence in the percentage of Malays comprising the total population, with a corresponding 13.8 percent decrease among Chinese, a 3.3 percent decrease among Indians and a 0.7 percent decrease in those categorised as 'others'.

Table 26.1 Ethnic breakdown in Malaya, 1951

Population in Malaya – 1951	*Population of Malaysia 5,317,222*
Malay	49.4%
Chinese	38.4%
Indian	10.6%
Other	1.4%

Source: 1951 Annual Report on the Federation of Malaya.

Table 26.2 Ethnic breakdown in Malaysia, 2010

Population of Malaysia – 2010	*Total 28.3 million*	*Percentage increase/decrease*
Malay	67.4%	+18.0%
Chinese	24.6%	−13.8%
Indian	7.3%	−3.3%
Other	0.7%	−0.7%

Source: Census 2010.

Table 26.3 Demographic breakdown by faith tradition

Total population of Malaysia – 2010	*28,3000,000*
Muslims	61.3%
Buddhists	19.8%
Christians	9.2%
Hindu	6.3%
Chinese Traditional: Confucianism, Taoism, others	1.3%
Unknown religions	1.0%
Non-believers	0.7%
Other religions	0.4%

Source: Census 2010.

In terms of religion, Malays are required by law to be Muslim, while ethnic Indians, Chinese and others are free to choose their religion, and to convert to a different religion if they so desire. The 2010 Census reports that 61.3 percent of the population identified themselves as Muslim, 19.8 percent as Buddhist, 9.2 percent Christian and 6.3 percent Hindu; another 1.3 percent fall into the category of 'Confucianists, Taoists, or practitioners of other traditional Chinese religions', 1 percent are of unknown religions, 0.7 percent are listed as non-believers and 0.4 percent are followers of 'other religions', a category that includes small numbers of Sikhs, Baha'i and Animists, among others (Table 26.3).

The present chapter examines interfaith relations in Malaysia and the often undiscussed structural factors which underpin inter-ethnic and interfaith relations in the country. It ends with the author's musings about the great potential Malaysia has to become an example of positive interfaith relations for multicultural societies around the world.

The legal regime and its possible impacts on interfaith relations

Article 3 of the Federal Constitution establishes Islam as the religion of the federation, while allowing other religions to be practised 'in peace and harmony' in all parts of the federation. This legal proclamation grants Islam the central position within the structures of the nation, implicitly placing other faith traditions at the margins of state power.

Constitutional Article 11(1) grants all people the right to profess and practise their religion, while Clause 4 declares that any religion other than Islam should not be propagated among Muslims. Article 153 grants Malays and natives of Sabah and Sarawak, collectively known as *bumiputera*, a 'special position', with quotas giving Malays privileged access to federal public service positions, to federal scholarships and support, to trade or business licences, and to enrolment in public tertiary education.

Article 160 of the Malaysian constitution defines 'a Malay' as 'a Malaysian citizen born to a Malaysian citizen who professes the religion of Islam, habitually speaks the Malay language, conforms to Malay custom and is domiciled in Malaysia'. People fitting this description are accorded the privileges granted to Malays and other *bumiputera* under Article 153 above, instated through the New Economic Policy (NEP), then National Development Policy (NDP) (see Hwok-Aun Lee, this volume). A Malay who converts out of Islam is no longer considered a Malay; therefore, his or her privileges granted under these affirmative action policies are revoked. Conversely, a non-Malay citizen of Malaysia who converts to Islam can claim *bumiputera* privileges.

It is noteworthy that the constitutional definition of 'a Malay' is based entirely on cultural constructs – which can be adopted by others. Nakamura (2012) writes that this open and non-racialised definition allows for others to *masuk Melayu* (become Malay), effectively increasing the numbers of 'Malay' Muslim citizens vis-à-vis those labelled as non-Malay and/or non-Muslim. That said, the construct 'Malay' has come to carry increasing weight within the Malaysian polity.

Policy shift in the wake of the 1969 race riots

In the 1969 general election, parties opposing *bumiputera* privilege gained enough seats for the ruling Alliance to lose its two-thirds majority in parliament. After the election, they organised a victory celebration during which they allegedly hurled insults at the Malay community. In response, UMNO youth held a parade which turned into inter-ethnic rioting in which scores of people were killed or injured (Kua 2007).

Shortly thereafter, Prime Minister Tunku Abdul Rahman resigned his post, after which Tun Abdul Razak assumed the premiership. One of Abdul Razak's first acts was to enact the NEP (1971–90), which aimed to ensure that a 30 percent share of the economy was in the hands of ethnic Malays. Although the NDP succeeded the NEP in 1991, privileges granted to Malays through the NEP remained largely intact. The NDP granted further privileges aimed at helping Malays become successful entrepreneurs. Among these was the stipulation that all publicly listed companies must have 30 percent Malay equity. Additional privileges include discounts on purchases of automobiles and housing. In addition, government bids are to be given to Malay-owned businesses. In this last case, it is often the Malays who are primary owners in a company, while their Chinese associates are the ones with the means and the business acumen to ensure that contracts received are successfully fulfilled (see also Varkkey, this volume).

In short, particularly since the introduction of the NEP in 1970, Malaysia's legal and policy framework has reified a long-standing 'special position' for *bumiputera*. While operationalised initially largely in economic terms, that position has developed along cultural and religious lines, as well.

Racialisation and 'othering' as the backdrop to interfaith relations in Malaysia

While science shows that there is no physiological basis for the notion of 'race', in Malaysia it is a socially constructed 'reality' into which the country's citizens are socialised from the time they are born. The existing legal regime places *bumiputera* – specifically Malays – as the default 'race', creating a juxtaposition of 'us' and 'other' in which non-Malay Malaysian citizens constitute 'others'. Since Malays are constitutionally defined as Muslims, Islam becomes the default religion, with all other faith traditions juxtaposed as 'others'. Boundaries constructed between an 'us' and a collective 'other' set the foundation for tensions and potential conflict if the default group fears that 'others' desire a larger share of the collective pie or may ask for constitutional and legal equality as citizens. The socially constructed narrative of a default Malay 'race' whose religion is Islam provides a powerful tool for political and economic interests to use at will. Just as these notions are embedded in the country's legal structures, they are also deeply imprinted within both the individual and the collective Malaysian psyche. This socio-political arrangement must be pointed out if the reader is to make sense of interfaith relations in the country.

To illustrate, Nur Farhana and Khadijah state:

> it cannot be denied that there are a number of examples of tolerance from believers of other religions towards Muslims and *vice-versa*. Without tolerance, the common relationship between Muslims and non-Muslims will complicate the effort in building a harmonious life in Malaysia.
>
> *(Nur Farhana and Khadijah 2013: 87)*

The authors then surmise that problems among Malaysia's religions arise due to 'deep rooted prejudice between two sides; Muslims and Non-Muslims' (Nur Farhana and Khadijah 2013: 88; emphasis added). The analysis first categorises all of Malaysia's non-Muslims as a monolithic 'other'. It then purports to examine how this 'other' relates with the Muslim population. So instead of a multi-sided approach to dialogue among citizens of different faith traditions, the thinking is that of 'us' vis-à-vis a monolithic 'other'. These authors are academics involved in interreligious dialogue, yet it is unlikely that the operational assumptions illustrated here will lead to an understanding of the many traditions lumped into the collective 'other' designation, as multiple differences are rendered invisible by the mode of thought applied by the analysts.

Within the broader context discussed above, the following section examines some of the more salient incidents of interfaith conflict which have occurred since the May 1969 riots.

Recent incidents of interfaith conflict

For the sake of brevity, the ensuing summaries of both conflicts and efforts at collaboration constitute simple snapshots when, in reality, each incident mentioned involves complex dynamics and contestation, with moments of collaboration found within the conflicts, and vice versa.

Banning and seizure of Alkitab

The Malay-language (*Bahasa Melayu*) version of the Bible, the *Alkitab*, has been used in Malaya since before the British colonial period, having been first published in 1612 (*News.va* 2013). In addition, *Bahasa Indonesia* (Indonesian-language) translations are utilised mainly in Sabah and Sarawak, and by some Malay-speaking Christians on the peninsula. Use of the *Bahasa* Bible was first outlawed in independent Malaysia under the Internal Security Act (Prohibition of Publications, Number 4) in March 1982. Two other *Bahasa*-language versions of the New Testament were later banned in 1983, after being deemed prejudicial to the national interest; however, the bans were generally not enforced until much later, apart from occasional confiscations. While seizure of the Christian Holy Book is not new, in 2010 Customs impounded 35,000 Bibles imported from Indonesia, which they released the following year. When Prime Minister Najib Tun Razak launched his Global Movement of Moderates in 2012, Christian groups urged him to revoke the outdated bans issued under the now defunct Internal Security Act, alleging that said prohibitions run counter to the image of religious 'moderation' which Malaysia desires for the world to see (Chong 2012).

The Kampung Medan incident

From 8 to 11 March 2001, violent clashes raged in Kampung Medan, in Petaling Jaya, Selangor between Malay-Muslims and ethnic Indians, mostly of the Hindu faith. The official death toll was six, with more than forty treated in hospital for injuries. The vast majority of the dead and injured were working-class Indians. Malays said they acted in retaliation when an irate Indian man kicked at wedding party chairs and tables placed under a tent blocking the street as the Malays prepared for a wedding *kenduri* (celebratory meal). The man was reportedly angry because the *kenduri* obstructed a Hindu funeral procession. Armed with machetes, sticks, swords and iron rods, Malay youths reportedly roamed the streets, setting upon Indians. A neighbourhood woman who prefers not to be named reports that she and others were prevented by the Malay-Muslim police from coming to the aid of an Indian man, Mr Muniratnem, who was beaten to death by a gang of enraged youths (Chandran 2002). Concerning official response to the incident, Prasana Chandran (2002) writes:

> The government has been accused of denying the racial dimension of the clashes, perhaps concerned over Malaysia's international image as it might rattle investor confidence. Until today, despite numerous memoranda sent to the Prime Minister's Department and the Human Rights Commission, there has not been a show of a response.

Lina Joy

Born in 1964, Azlina Jailani, the daughter of Javanese Muslim parents, converted to Christianity at the age of twenty-six. The Federal Court approved her request to change her name to Lina Joy; however, the application she submitted to have 'Muslim' taken off her identity card was rejected on the grounds that she was not authorised to renounce Islam. The three Muslim Federal Court judges presiding over her case were Tun Ahmad Fairuz, Sheikh Abdul Halim and Datuk Alauddin Mohd. Sheriff. They ruled that Lina Joy – now a Christian – must present her case before the *Shari'a* Court. Lina feared that in doing so, she would likely be sent to an Islamic rehabilitation centre, where she would be pressured to give up her new faith and re-embrace Islam. She appealed the Court's decision, and in May 2007 the case was closed with the definitive rejection of her appeal. Given the angry responses to media reports of her conversion, Lina was forced to go into hiding.

Cow's head

In July 2009, scores of Muslims marched with a bloodied cow's head from a mosque to the Selangor chief minister's office in protest against the state government's authorisation for the construction of a Hindu temple in an area where Muslims reside. Some of the protestors stomped and spat on the head, while making angry speeches against the planned temple construction. These behaviours deeply offended the Hindus, since the cow is the most sacred animal in Hinduism. While twelve of the leaders of the protest were fined, the state government heeded their desire and chose a new site for building the temple. This incident served to highlight frustrations among non-Muslims about ongoing restrictions on non-Muslim places of worship. Some Hindu leaders considered the sentences very light, given the deep insult to their religion, adding that, had the Hindus been less mature in their response to the Muslims, these actions could have caused a riot (*Fox News* 2010).

The 2009 Allah ruling and subsequent attacks on places of worship

In 2009, the Federal Court ruled that Christians have the right to use the Arabic word *Allah* to refer to God in their church newspaper, in sacred scriptures and in worship. After the ruling, eleven attacks were reported on churches in the Klang Valley. Twice in 2010 and again in 2012, severed pig heads were placed outside mosques, causing deep offence to Muslims, who deem pigs unclean. No arrests have been made, leading many to question who the perpetrators are. Member of Parliament Chua Tian Chang declared these incidents to be politically motivated provocations which aimed to cause tensions between Muslims and non-Muslims. He called for people 'not to fall into the trap and to, instead, remain calm' (Yow 2012). This issue has persisted up to the time of writing.

Spitting out the host

In March 2010, Attorney-General Abdul Gani Patail dropped charges against two *Al-Islam Magazine* journalists who took Holy Communion in an attempted sting operation at a Catholic church they were investigating to see if Muslims were being converted to Christianity. Upon receiving Holy Communion, they spat out the host, photographed it and uploaded it to the magazine's website. This caused deep offence among the Catholic community, with the archbishop of Kuala Lumpur, Rev. Tan Sri Murphy Pakiam, saying that the men had desecrated the church with their actions, and that he feared that the lack of charges appeared to legitimise their behaviour. Abdul Gani stood his ground, however, stating that the undercover journalists had unintentionally offended Catholics out of sheer ignorance. The journalists reported that they found no evidence of illegal conversion of Muslims at the church (*BBC News* 2012).

Johor Mufti's Department and Ministry of Education seminar

With interreligious tensions on the increase, in March 2012, the Johor Mufti's Department and state Department of Education sponsored an official seminar, originally titled 'Strengthening the Faith, the Dangers of Liberalism and Pluralism and the Threat of Christianity towards Muslims. What Is the Role of Teachers?' The name was eventually changed to 'Strengthening the Faith: What Is the Role of Teachers?' Nonetheless, the content taught was not modified to suit the new title. When asked, the director of the Johor Department of Education, Mohd. Nur Abdul Ghani, stated that the programme was aimed at strengthening the faith of Muslim teachers who will, in turn, teach the same to Muslim students. Here again, the situation is framed as 'us' – the Muslim community, which is faced with a purported threat – versus a Christian 'other', and the topic is used as a means of strengthening the faith of Muslims (*Malaysia Chronicle* 2012). To the author's mind, this is a very telling example of the state of interfaith relations in Malaysia.

A commemoration requiring ritual sacrifice

During Hari Raya Qurban in October 2013, several schools were reported to have slaughtered cows on public school grounds during school hours. The deputy president of the Malaysian Indian Congress (MIC) pointed out that cow-slaughtering is a sensitive issue, given the Hindu students present in the schools. The MIC president later added that cows could be slaughtered in mosques and surau, but that this activity on public school grounds was upsetting to non-Muslim students, particularly to those of the Hindu faith. No other actions were taken (Alyaa 2013).

Court overturns Christians' right to use the name 'Allah'

Shortly after the 2009 decision allowing Christians to use the name *Allah*, the Home Ministry filed an appeal to have the decision overturned. Six Islamic religious councils were allowed to join the appeal. On 14 October 2013, the three presiding (Muslim) judges ruled that non-Muslims in Malaysia will no longer be allowed to call God by His Arabic name, *Allah* (*BBC News* 2013). The editor of the *Catholic Herald* newspaper, Father Lawrence Andrew, responded that Christians would continue to worship Allah in their *Bahasa* services. In response, Subang UMNO President Datuk Zein Isma Ismail called for Fr. Lawrence to be charged with treason and stripped of his citizenship. At the time of writing, the inspector general of police had taken Fr. Lawrence in for questioning to decide whether he would be charged with sedition. Those against Fr. Lawrence argue that continuing to use the word *Allah* constitutes disrespect to the Malay sultans, who have symbolic authority over matters of the Islamic religion, while others argue that the Islamic authorities have no jurisdiction over non-Muslims. The outcome of the investigation has yet to be revealed.

JAIS raids Bible Society of Malaysia

On 2 January 2014, Selangor Islamic Religious Department (Jabatan Agama Islam Selangor, JAIS) officers, accompanied by two policemen, raided the premises of the Bible Society of Malaysia (BSM), seizing 320 copies of the *Bahasa*-medium Bible and ten copies of the Iban Bible. BSM President Lee Min Choon and office manager Sinclair Wong were arrested and later released on bail. The Selangor state government has claimed that the raid was legal, and that no action will be taken against JAIS or the accompanying police officers. Others consider the raid illegal since JAIS should have no jurisdiction over non-Muslims. Furthermore, the officers had no search warrant, nor do they hold the right to seize items. As of this writing, it appears that no action will be taken against the raiding officers.

Interfaith collaboration: a sampling of civil society initiatives

The author believes that ordinary Malaysians of all ethnic backgrounds want to live in peace with one another. Day-by-day, relatively peaceful co-existence prevails in the country despite the actions of the few who seem to find inter-communal tensions to be desirable. While everyday acts of neighbourliness go undetected *because they are the norm*, the following section will focus on organised civil society initiatives aimed at nurturing positive interfaith relations in the country. The proliferation and continuity of interfaith organisations and activities suggest that the divisive attitudes and actions mentioned in the section above reflect the position of a minority, rather than of the majority of Malaysians.

Interfaith Spiritual Fellowship

The Interfaith Spiritual Fellowship (INSaF) is one of the country's oldest interfaith movements and is housed at the Hindu-run Pure Life Society. The idea for INSaF was first mooted by Swamiji Satyananda shortly after World War II. Having gained the approval of the Registrar of Societies, the organisation was officially launched as the Malaysian Council for Interfaith Cooperation (MCIC) on 3 November 1958, with Dato' Zainal Abidin bin Haji Abas serving as its first president. Later, under the presidency of Sardar Singh, the MCIC took the name Interfaith Spiritual Fellowship, which it retains to this day. In 1999, Dr Amir Farid bin Dato' Ishak assumed the presidency of INSaF – a position that he retains at the time of writing. INSaF welcomes members of all faith traditions to work together for the greater good of Malaysia and the world. Faith traditions represented include Hinduism, Buddhism, Islam, Sikhism and Christianity, among others. Activities promoted by INSaF include dialogue sessions aimed at helping people see the interests, values and concerns they share with others, such as raising children in today's world, identifying common threads among sacred texts, promoting understanding among diverse communities, and organising activities for the greater common good.

Malaysian Consultative Council for Buddhism, Christianity, Hinduism, Sikhism and Taoism

Created in 1983, the Malaysian Consultative Council for Buddhism, Christianity, Hinduism, Sikhism and Taoism (MCCBCHST) acts as a liaison body for Malaysia's non-Muslim faith communities as they strive for more open dialogue and collaboration among the faith traditions. At the time of its creation, the MCCBCHST invited representatives of Islam to become part of the council; however, the leaders of the day chose not to participate. Representatives of the non-Muslim faith traditions decided to form the organisation nonetheless.

Recently, the MCCBCHST has pointed out to government authorities that religious places and people who worship there have become targets of criminal attacks. They have asked for official intervention to ensure that worshippers of all faiths may come to and go from their places of worship in safety. In 2012, the MCCBCHST put forth an initiative requesting that the Ministry of Education allow all religions to teach their holy scriptures in national and government-aided schools to children from their respective traditions. They have requested permission for the authorities from each religion to prepare and grade exams which would be recognised by both the Ministry of Education and the Department of Education. At the time of writing, the official decision of the nation's authorities is unknown to the author.

Taiping Peace Initiative

The city of Taiping, Perak is known as the City of Everlasting Peace. The Taiping Peace Initiative (TPI) was launched on 20 January 2001, pronouncing a vision of living in 'internal peace, social peace and environmental peace' on a daily basis. The TPI works with government agencies, the business sector and civil society with the aim of instilling these values. Its scope is local, national and global, and its partners include the University of Science Malaysia, UNICEF and the United Nations, among others. Examples of TPI activities include the 'Interfaith Dialogue on Common Values and Common Actions' and the 'Taiping Interfaith

Dialogue Roundtable'. The Taiping Peace Initiative is a high-profile organisation, with locally famous Dato' Dr Anwar Fazal as one of its founding members; furthermore, it enjoys links with the United Nations system. Around the time of writing, in early 2014, TPI was not seen as being very active.

Malaysian Interfaith Network

Toward the end of 2002, the Malaysian Interfaith Network (MIN) was launched as an offshoot of the Taiping Peace Initiative. Its aim is to bring concerned citizens of various faiths together to work toward a more harmonious and peaceful society. Its three focal areas include promoting dialogue among the faith communities found in Malaysia; fostering understanding of common concerns, values and areas of contention among the communities; and organising actions, sharing information and advocating for harmonious interfaith relations in the country. Its emphases include family values, action against extremism, environmental protection, human rights, interfaith understanding, multi-faith education and good governance. Its members include Muslim, Christian, Hindu, Buddhist, Sikh, Taoist, Baha'i, Sai Baba and Brahma Kumaris, as well as officially secular organisations advocating for civil society issues. The MIN acts as a platform for communication and collaboration among various organisations throughout Malaysia. While the MIN represents a broad base of faith traditions, it appears not to have been very active around the time of writing.

Nur Damai

Launched in 2007, Nur Damai (ND, 'the light of peace') is an interfaith organisation that works to foster peace by building community through collaborative action. Its mission is to promote peace for the benefit of the Earth and of all living beings. The members of ND 'unite to bring the wisdom and values of different religious traditions to be shared for mutual understanding and respect across different faiths and religions'. It supports freedom of religion and belief, as well as the rights of all individuals, 'in order to witness together the wondrous spirit of life which embraces all of our diversity'. ND supports a vision of love and protection of the Earth, reverence for life and harmony with all living beings.[1]

Nur Damai organises a variety of activities around social concerns and its members pay visits to sacred sites in order to learn about diverse religious traditions. In addition, ND co-sponsors events like the biannual Music and Dance Festival (MadFest), whose performers are youth groups performing music and dance from their respective traditions. People of all ages and all walks of life are welcome to come together and enjoy the beauty offered by each of the traditions. 'Awakening to Oneness' is another ND event in which participants come together to share sacred space and to learn from the wisdom of each other's faith traditions.

Government programmes to construct unity

The discussion turns to a number of government-led initiatives designed to foster positive interfaith relations in order to explore how these official programmes and activities align with the aims and goals of civil society organisations and ordinary citizens discussed so far. The section considers what role these official programmes might play in solving – or possibly exacerbating – the tensions and conflicts mentioned above.

Department of National Unity and Integration

The Department of National Unity and Integration (JPNIN) was launched under the Prime Minister's Office in July 1968 to enhance unity among Malaysia's citizens. JPNIN runs community centres, known as *Rukun Tetangga*, in neighbourhoods throughout the country. It also has multi-ethnic pre-schools and kindergartens called *tabika*, where children interact with peers from diverse ethnic groups. JPNIN has offices in each of the thirteen states, including Sabah and Sarawak. Presently, the author's Centre for Dialogue and Transformation has proposed conducting workshops on dialogue and conflict transformation in each of the JPNIN state offices, with the aim of providing their staff with tools for working toward peaceful conflict transformation. The department's authorisation for the proposed workshops remains pending at the time of writing.

Rukun Negara

The *Rukun Negara* (RN) is the Malaysian national philosophy, which arose in response to the race riots of 13 May 1969. It was promulgated by royal decree on 31 August 1970 at the Merdeka (independence day) celebration. Its aim is to enhance harmony and unity among Malaysia's ethnic groups. The RN is normally recited at the weekly assembly in public primary and secondary schools, and it can generally be found in the exercise books used by schoolchildren. It is sometimes read at official functions as well. The text of the RN (Jabatan Perpaduan Negara 2013) is:

> Whereas our country, Malaysia nurtures the ambitions of:
>
> - achieving a more perfect unity amongst the whole of her society;
> - preserving a democratic way of life;
> - creating a just society where the prosperity of the country can be enjoyed together in a fair and equitable manner;
> - guaranteeing a liberal approach towards her rich and varied cultural traditions; and
> - building a progressive society that will make use of science and modern technology.
>
> Now therefore, we, the people of Malaysia, pledge to concentrate the whole of our energy and efforts to achieve these ambitions based on the following principles:
>
> - Belief in God
> - Loyalty to King and country
> - Supremacy of the Constitution
> - Rule of Law
> - Courtesy and morality.

Vision 2020 and Bangsa Malaysia

In 1991, Prime Minister Mahathir Mohamad introduced the concept of Vision 2020, with the goal of ensuring that Malaysia would reach developed nation status by the year 2020. As a part of Vision 2020, the *Bangsa Malaysia* concept aimed to create an inclusive identity for all Malaysians. This framework replaced the earlier National Culture Policy, which asserted Malay identity as the central cultural norm into which all Malaysians should be assimilated.

The policy aimed to encourage all citizens to identify with the country, to speak *Bahasa*, and to accept the national constitution – which many non-Malays found challenging, due to Articles 3, 11, 153 and 160, discussed above. Critics of *Bangsa Malaysia*, like Johorian Malay nationalist Abdul Ghani Othman, oppose the concept, arguing that Malays must remain 'the pivotal race' of Malaysian identity.

Islam Hadhari

Islam Hadhari (IH, civilisational Islam) is a form of government based on Islamic principles expounded in the Qur'an. Through the IH concept, Prime Minister Abdullah Ahmad Badawi (2003–09) put forth a notion of Islam that is compatible with economic growth and technological development. Specifically, IH sought to uphold morality and ethics, to protect minority and women's rights, and to ensure a just system of government. The IH concept ceased to be promoted after Badawi stepped down from the prime minister's post in June 2009. Had it been implemented, this proposed mode of governance would have been based on Islam as the 'default' religion, placing all other faith traditions on the margins as permanent 'others'.

1Malaysia

Unveiled on Malaysia Day, 16 September 2012, by Prime Minister Najib Tun Razak, the stated aims of 1Malaysia are to exhort members of the cabinet, government agencies and the civil service to prioritise ethnic harmony, national unity and efficient governance. The 1Malaysia programme aims to promote inter-ethnic tolerance and national unity, while also improving the performance of politicians and civil servants, of whom the vast majority are ethnic Malays. Polls have shown that many non-Malays view the 1Malaysia policy as a strategy for winning the non-Malay vote, while Malay groups such as Perkasa (Pertubuhan Pribumi Perkasa Malaysia, Malaysian Indigenous Empowerment Organisation) reportedly fear that the policy could undermine Malay privileges, if all citizens are accorded the same rights (Boo 2010).

Interfaith Commission

In April 2002, the Human Rights Commission of Malaysia (SUHAKAM) initiated a dialogue among groups such as the Malaysian Islamic Development Department, the Malaysian Ulama Association, and MCCBCHST. A plan was mooted to create an Interfaith Commission aimed at promoting understanding and respect among the country's citizens. The proposal was opposed by certain quarters, such as Pan-Malaysian Islamic Party (PAS) Member of Parliament Dzulkefly Ahmad, who believed that religious pluralism would relativise truth claims, thereby implying that Islam is the same as other religions. The proposal was shelved by Prime Minister Abdullah Ahmad Badawi as a result of such concerns (Malik 2005).

The National Unity Consultative Council

The National Unity Consultative Council (NUCC) was formed by Prime Minister Najib Tun Razak in November 2013 after the fractious general election held in May of that year. Its goal is to promote national reconciliation amid rising inter-ethnic and interreligious tensions.

The NUCC is expected to produce a National Blueprint Plan on Unity before the end of 2015. Its members will organise unity dialogues in seventeen localities throughout the Peninsula and East Malaysia.

While these government initiatives strive to ensure peaceful inter-ethnic relations in the country, none of them examines, nor do they address, two core issues underlying and seemingly affecting intercommunal and interfaith relations: the privileged position of Islam vis-à-vis other religions practised in the country and the institutionalised privileges granted to a particular group of citizens based on 'race' and religion, to the distinct disadvantage of Malaysians from other religio-ethnic identity groups. Until these issues are addressed, they will undoubtedly continue to affect interfaith relations in the country.

The maturity of Malaysian civil society

At the time of writing, in February 2014, the country is steeped in interfaith tensions, especially between the Muslim and the Christian communities, largely because of the Allah issue. Why 'the pot was stirred' and the suit filed against the *Catholic Herald* over the use of the Arabic word for God is anyone's guess. Could this be a tactic used to rally 'Malays' and Muslims around the government of the day, which hopes to paint itself as champion and protector of Malay ethnicity and Islamic piety?

National governments have been known to create a virtuous 'us' and an evil 'other' as a means of gaining the votes and support of their electorate. Yet in most cases that 'other' is a constructed 'enemy' found outside the national territory. With current interfaith tensions in Malaysia, virtuous 'us' and evil 'other' constructions are found *within* the country itself. Anyone exacerbating this situation for political gain would be putting each and every Malaysian citizen at risk. Recognising this danger, Malaysians from across faith communities have taken steps to defuse tensions, whatever their origin.

With reference to the 2 January 2014 JAIS raid on the Bible Society of Malaysia, opposition leaders such as PAS's Dr Mujahid Yusof Rawa assert that the true motive behind both issues is political rather than religious. He and others remark that the latest stirrings may be a ploy to divert the attention of poor Malays from the rising cost of living as the country enters the new year (Mahavera 2014).

Threats by Perkasa and other Muslim groups to demonstrate outside churches caused trepidation among Christians as they attended Sunday services on 5 January 2014; however, those attending mass at Our Lady of Lourdes in Klang were met by some two hundred non-Christians, who showed up outside the church in solidarity with the Christian community. After mass ended, Datin Paduka Marina Mahathir presented a bouquet of flowers to the officiating priest, Fr. Michael Chua. A solidarity event called 'In the Name of Allah' had been organised through a Facebook page created by one Siti Kasim, who wrote, 'a true Muslim cannot hurt a Christian in any way'. She added, 'I think it's high time rightful thinking members of society gather together and prevent these people who are using the mask of "Islam" from creating dissention and intolerance.' She ended by urging others to gather at the church 'in solidarity with our Christian brothers and sisters' (Lim 2014).

Other shows of solidarity among people of all traditions abound, for example in the writings of *The Malaysian Insider* journalist Azrul Mohd Khalib, who continually advocates for positive relations among the communities. Respected individuals like Dr Wan Zawawi Ibrahim and Marina Mahathir, too, constantly use their Facebook accounts to promote peace among the nation's communities, as do many others. Given the deafening silence of top government leaders, it is heartening to see so many ordinary Malaysians standing up for peace and respect among all.

Note

1 www.nurdamai.webs.com (accessed 15 May 2014).

Bibliography

Alyaa Azhar (2013) 'Schools not the place to slaughter cows', *FMT News*, 23 October, available at www.freemalaysiatoday.com/category/nation/2013/10/23/schools-not-the-place-to-slaughter-cows/ (accessed 6 January 2014).

BBC News (2012) 'Arrests over pig heads found at Malaysian mosque', *BBC News*, 20 February, available at www.bbc.co.uk/news/world-asia-16388370 (accessed 9 January 2014).

BBC News (2013) 'Malaysia court rules non-Muslims cannot use "Allah"', *BBC News*, 14 October, available at www.bbc.co.uk/news/world-asia-24516181 (accessed 27 December 2013).

Boo Su Lyn (2010) 'Perkasa tells Najib to explain his One Malaysia or face rejection', *The Malaysian Insider*, 18 September, available at www.themalaysianinsider.com/malaysia/article/perkasa-tells-najib-to-explain-his-1-malaysia-or-face-rejection (accessed 27 December 2013).

Chandran, Prasana (2002) 'Remembering Kampung Medan after 1 year', *Malaysiakini*, 8 March, available at https://www.malaysiakini.com/news/10633 (accessed 30 December 2013).

Chong, Debra (2012) 'Revoke ISA ban on Alkitab, Christians tell PM', *The Malaysian Insider*, 17 April, available at www.themalaysianinsider.com/malaysia/article/revoke-isa-ban-on-alkitab-christians-tell-pm (accessed 13 December 2013).

Fox News (2010) 'Malaysia court fines 12 Muslims for parading cow head in protest against temple plan', *Fox News*, 27 July, available at www.foxnews.com/world/2010/07/27/malaysia-court-fines-muslims-parading-cow-head-protest-hindu-temple-plan/ (accessed 29 December 2013).

Jabatan Perpaduan Negara dan Integrasi Nasional (2013) *Rukun Negara*, available at www.jpnin.gov.my/rukun-negara (accessed 3 January 2014).

Kua Kia Soong (2007) *May 13: Declassified Documents on the Malaysian Riots of 1969*, Petaling Jaya: SUARAM.

Lim, Ida (2014) 'Mixed-faith "solidarity gathering" to protect Klang church from Muslim protestors', *The Malay Mail*, 5 January, available at www.themalaymailonline.com/malaysia/article/mixed-faith-solidarity-gathering-to-protect-klang-church-from-muslim-protes (accessed 5 January 2014).

López C., Carolina (2001) 'The British presence in the Malay world: a meeting of civilizational traditions', *Sari Journal of the Malay World and Civilization*, 19: 3–33.

Mahavera, Sheridan (2014) 'Muslim–Christian ties deteriorate while extremists celebrate', *The Malaysian Insider*, 4 January, available at www.themalaysianinsider.com/malaysia/article/muslim-christian-ties-deteriorate-while-extremists-celebrate (accessed 7 January 2014).

Malaysia Chronicle (2012) 'Maximus: I will ask Muhyiddin why they organized Christian threat seminar', *Malaysia Chronicle*, 3 April, available at www.malaysia-chronicle.com/index.php?option=com_k2&view=item&id=31270:maximus-i-will-ask-muhyiddin-why-they-organized-christian-threat-seminar&Itemid=2#axzz2tn322s4c (accessed 3 January 2014).

Malik Imtiaz Sarwar (2005) 'We are committed to dialogue: a response to criticism of the Interfaith Commission Initiative', *Aliran Monthly*, 25(6): 26–33.

Nakamura, Rie (2012) 'Malaysia, a racialized nation: study of the concept of race in Malaysia', *International Proceedings of Economic Development and Research*, 42: 134–42.

News.va (2013) 'El Sultán de Selangor prohíbe el uso de la palabra "Allah" para los no musulmanes: los cristianos no lo aceptan' [The Sultan of Selangor bans the use of the word "Allah" for non-Muslims: the Christians don't accept this], 9 January, available at www.news.va/es/news/asiamalasia-el-sultan-de-selangor-prohibe-el-uso-d (accessed 19 May 2014).

Nur Farhana Abdul Rahman and Khadijah Mohamed Khambali (2013) 'Religious tolerance in Malaysia: problems and challenges', *International Journal of Islamic Thought*, 3(June): 81–91.

Yow Hong Chieh (2012) 'Pig's head found outside Sentul mosque', *The Malaysian Insider*, 2 February, available at www.themalaysianinsider.com/malaysia/article/pigs-head-found-outside-sentul-mosque/ (accessed 12 December 2013).

27

Culture and the arts in Malaysia

Playing to multiple galleries

Kathy Rowland[1]

Arts and culture in Malaysia are marked by tensions that are both a result of and indicative of currents arising out of the nation's political, economic and social dynamics. While the state has made consistent efforts to shape culture and the arts to reflect and reinforce its hold on power, the field is also influenced by other factors, some of which have supported the state's hegemonic project, and others which have provided counterpoints to it. What follows is an attempt to identify the many moving parts that circulate and collide in the field of cultural practice and arts production.

Background

Modern Malaysia's arts and culture are rooted in practices indigenous to the Malay archipelago and the region's absorption of external cultural and religious influences. Traditional art forms such as *wayang kulit* and *mak yong* reveal lasting vestiges of the Hindu and Buddhist empires that dominated Southeast Asia in ancient times. Their strategic location within Indian Ocean trade routes brought indigenous Malays into contact with traders from China, the Middle East and India. Islam, which was first introduced in the twelfth century, had, by the height of the Melaka Sultanate in the fifteenth century, become a dominant force in the culture of *Tanah Melayu*, the Malay land. The Portuguese, who occupied Melaka in 1511, and the Dutch, who replaced them in 1641, contributed to this diversity. A residual effect of these early colonisers can be found in the use of Western instrumentation in ostensibly traditional Malay folk performances, for example.

The British colonial era, which began formally in Penang in 1786, was to have an enduring influence upon the shape of modern Malaysia. While Malaya had welcomed various communities to its shores for centuries, it was the British who brought in Chinese and Indians in such significant numbers as to change the socio-cultural character of Malaya significantly. The British administration practised a policy that kept these groups largely separate. After World War II, however, as the colonial government became aware that calls for independence could no longer be contained, it took steps to foster a multicultural vision of Malaya.

The National Cultural Policy

When Malaysia achieved independence in 1957, the state was largely absent from the artistic and cultural arena of the newly formed nation. There were no provisions for culture and the arts in the Constitution, although religion and language were prominent features. The Culture portfolio was first managed by the Ministry of Social Welfare (1953–57), followed by the Ministry of Information and Broadcasting (1957–964). When the Ministry of Culture, Youth and Sports was established in 1964, it was placed under a junior minister (Mohamed Taib 1988: 276).

Although plurality was a key characteristic of the newly formed Malaysian nation, state attempts to construct a national identity via the formulation of a cultural policy began only in direct response to the communal riots of 1969. A National Cultural Congress was held in 1969, with the aim of formalising a cultural policy to unify the multi-ethnic nation. The National Cultural Policy (NCP) was launched in 1971, with three principles. The first was that the national culture of the country would be based on that of the indigenous inhabitants of the region; second, elements of other cultures, where suitable and reasonable, would be incorporated if compatible with Malay-Muslim culture; and third, Islam was a crucial component of the national culture. A caveat clarified that 'Suitable and reasonable referred to in the second principle must be understood in the context of the first and third principle, and not from other values' (KKBS 1973: vii).

Miller and Yúdice note that cultural policies are a 'privileged terrain of hegemony' (2002: 8) that reproduces and supports the ideological framework of the dominant group, even as it is framed in the rhetoric of unity and nationhood. Indeed, the NCP was part of a network of prescriptive polices, including the National Economic Policy (1971), the National Language Bill 1967 and the Education Act 1961, designed to entrench Malay political and cultural hegemony in response to the riots of 1969. While the stated aim of the NCP was to create a common identity to unify the multi-ethnic nation, its ideological kinship with divisive post-1969 policies hampered its efficacy in establishing the hegemony of Malay political dominance through culture and the arts. Unlike those policies, the NCP was never tabled in parliament, nor was it supported by a clearly articulated roadmap, affecting both its legitimacy and implementation, particularly amongst those who felt themselves marginalised by it.

The NCP presented the elements of what comprised national culture, but within a set of parameters that may be described as highly subjective, if not arbitrary. The two core principles of indigenous culture and Islam are themselves fluid and would be subject to multiple inscriptions and reinscriptions over time. This would in turn modify the criterion of 'suitability' weighted against minority cultures, resulting in a highly unstable concept of arts and culture. The ambiguity of the wording of the three principles would provide more room for challenges and counter-challenges to what precisely constituted national culture by both those seeking to establish Malay-Muslim hegemony and those opposed to it. The battle over the nature of national culture was deeply fraught, given the notions of group identity embedded in expressions of culture and arts practice.

Conflicts

As issues of language, education and the affirmative action policies of the NEP grew more vexed in the aftermath of the riots, culture became the site of proxy battles between the state and those who saw their political power and influence diminish in the face of the rising influence of the Malay political elite. Early controversies included the purported unsuitability of the lion dance, an integral part of the Chinese culture, as part of national culture,[2] and Chinese and Indian groups' opposition to the use of *jawi* script on road signs.

Despite serious flashpoints over the NCP, the state did not suppress minority art forms or cultural practices outright. The NCP, while proscriptive, was intent on establishing a hierarchy of value that placed Malay-Muslim expressions of symbolic identity at the forefront of national culture rather than in repressing or eradicating minority cultures. Indeed, a system of attention versus neglect might best describe the early years of the NCP, as the state's resources and focus were assigned in favour of culture that reflected its hegemonic desires.

As is often the case when states seek to marshal the past to fit contemporary needs, some measure of reinvention was present. The original wording of the NCP references the indigenous inhabitants of the region, evoking the diverse cultural influences that had historically shaped arts and cultural practices in the Malay archipelago. The idea of Malay culture became essentialised, however. As a result, under the aegis of the NCP, traditional art forms were remade into the image of Malayness as envisioned by the state. For example, *bangsawan*, a form of Malay opera characterised by its diverse cultural elements, was refashioned by using Malay-based stories to keep with the principles of the NCP (Tan 1993: 177–80). The resurgence of Islam in the 1970s altered the scope of national culture further, with contemporary Malay-language theatre particularly vulnerable to accusations of being un-Islamic (Jit 1984).

The art forms and cultural practices relegated to the margins by the NCP were disadvantaged by a policy delegitimising their stake in the national, and limiting access to public resources. Yet, an unexpected outcome of the NCP was the resurgence, in the 1970s and 1980s, of culturally distinct art forms and practices amongst minority communities, as ethic consciousness amongst those marginalised by the NCP heightened and certain forms of arts and culture received renewed community support as emblems of ethnic identity (Tan 2000).

Liberalisation and growth

In 1991, the Mahathir government launched Vision 2020, appearing to promote a more open configuration of Malaysian identity. The liberalisation of the country's economy in the 1990s as part of global deregulations and its own economic ambitions turned previous points of contestation into assets. Francis Loh (2002: 21) describes the period as marked by cultural liberalisation. The state softened its stance against the use of English in education. In its pursuit of the tourist dollar, it began to promote a more inclusive, multicultural vision of the country internationally.

The cultural terrain appeared less stressed and the arts blossomed in this period. A number of major public institutions were established, strengthening arts infrastructure in general. The National Arts Academy was created in 1994, while the National Theatre and the National Art Gallery were finally housed in purpose-built buildings in 1998 and 2000, respectively, after decades of delays.[3] These institutions formed different sites of influence and funding that expanded arts practice and provided opportunities across a wide range of artists and art forms, signalling a more accommodative application of the idea of 'suitable' in the NCP.

The prosperity that came with economic liberalisation saw the emergence of a stronger arts market and the entry of corporate and private art galleries, such as Galeri Petronas (1992), established by the national petroleum company, Petronas, and Valentine Willie Fine Art (1996), respectively. Art critic Michelle Antoinette notes that despite their own institutional imperatives, both played important roles in the growth of arts practice in Malaysia. The growing middle class expanded the audience base for live performing arts further, although few companies could sustain themselves purely on ticket sales.

The inflow of corporate sponsorship was essential, helping to foster the growth of arts practice not only through financial support, but also through the validation of the artists as worthy of support. In particular, corporate sponsorship was instrumental in creating venues for the performing arts. These include Kuala Lumpur's first privately owned theatre, The Actors Studio's Theatre Underground (1995), which was supported by Transfield, Carlsberg and Malaysian Airlines; then Actors Studio Bangsar (2001), supported by Bandaraya Development; the Kuala Lumpur Performing Arts Centre (2005), supported by YTL Malaysia; The Annex (2007), an alternative arts space attached to the Kuala Lumpur Central Market; and mapKL (2010), housed in an upmarket mall.

Changing technology and venues

Developments in technology have also left indelible marks upon the arts and cultural fields. The increased availability of new technologies such as digital cameras stimulated the emergence of a local independent film movement, which Khoo Gaik Cheng dates to the 2000 release of Amir Muhammad's *Lips to Lips*. Khoo further notes that the movement may signal a reclaiming of the pluralist, hybrid, multi-ethnic national term 'Malaysian cinema' (2006: 123). International interest in films from beyond the traditional Western metropolitan centres has also benefited these young filmmakers. Proliferating regional and international film festivals present important platforms that offer validation that might otherwise be absent domestically. Two of Amir's works, *Lelaki Komunis Terakhir* (*The Last Communist*, 2006) and its sequel, *Apa Khabar Orang Kampung* (*Village People Road Show*, 2007), for example, are banned in Malaysia but have been screened at festivals internationally.

The influence of the global DIY-alternative ethos has spawned a number of artist collectives and alternatives spaces, particularly in the visual arts. These provide an important counterpoint to the more commercial or state-driven institutions that developed in this period (Nurhanim 2012). This independent spirit is also evident in the emergence of several arts-related publications. Artseefartsse.com,[4] established in 1997, and Kakiseni.com,[5] launched in 2001, utilised new technologies such as online newsletters, electronic mailing lists and websites to build audiences and create sites of critical discourse on Malaysian arts and culture. In 2002, Kakiseni, with the financial support of Boh Plantations, launched the BOH Cameronian Arts Awards, an important source of recognition for the performing arts in Malaysia. Since 2011, the website's new owners have focused on increasing funding for the arts and providing professional development for the arts community. *KLue*, a lifestyle and arts magazine established in 2000, launched Urbanscapes in 2002, a popular weekend creative arts festival that is now the longest running arts festival in Kuala Lumpur.

Playing to multiple galleries

The *reformasi* movement of 1998 and the new configuration of political power it spawned reinvigorated and intensified contestations over national culture. Over the past fifteen years, the opposition Parti Keadilan Rakyat (People's Justice Party), a multi-ethnic, governance-oriented party headed by charismatic former deputy prime minister and *reformasi* leader Anwar Ibrahim, and Parti Islam SeMalaysia (Pan-Malaysian Islamic Party), have eroded the governing United Malay National Organisation's (UMNO) dominance amongst Malay-Muslim voters. UMNO has sought to regain its position within its main voting block by re-establishing itself as the champion of Islamic identity and Malay rights. Following its dismal performance in the 2008 general elections (which UMNO's Barisan Nasional, or National Front, coalition nonetheless won), UMNO redoubled these efforts, with a particularly profound impact across the arts and cultural arena.

The state has taken an increasingly accommodative stance towards conservative voices in society. Concerts by international acts, most recently the pop singer Ke$ha (2013), have been cancelled following public pressure. In 2010, the annual Warrior's Day ceremony was moved from Tugu Negara (the National Monument) to Dataran Merdeka (Independence Square) because the bronze soldiers of the monument flout the Muslim prohibition against graven images; the ceremony was also changed, to eliminate the customary moment of silence and laying of wreaths. In actual fact, a *fatwa* (religious edict) against the ceremony had been announced fifteen years earlier, in 1995, but had not been enforced. A member of the National Fatwa Council noted that the *fatwa* was not new but that 'they are finally listening . . . no prime minister was brave enough to follow it. I am glad Najib had the courage to change the practice' (Adib 2010). The state has increased its policing of Muslim identity, particularly amongst the youth. Raids on nightclubs, beauty pageants and the so-called 'black metal' subculture exhibit a highly performative quality, with agents drawn from the religious department, volunteer forces and enforcement agencies, followed by lurid headlines in the tabloids.

The complexities of the terrain, however, mean that despite increasing evidence of a constricted space for arts and culture, there are also instances in which the state reconfigures itself in apparently contradictory ways. In 2006, a *mak yong* performance was denied a performance permit in Kelantan. The state is governed by opposition party PAS, which deemed the ritual elements of *mak yong* un-Islamic. The Minister of Culture, Arts and Tourism condemned the ban and asserted the ministry's support. This performance of moderation and benevolence versus PAS's hard-line position could be read as an attempt to reach out to a more moderate domestic constituency and to win political mileage over PAS. It is also possible to view the ministry's public performance of permissibility in the light of its international desires. Just four months earlier, UNESCO had designated *mak yong* an Oral and Intangible Heritage of Humanity. The prestigious award placed the state under greater international scrutiny, particularly given its ambitions of assuming an international leadership role as a moderate Muslim nation.

The fates of Amir Muhammad's *Lelaki Korunas Terakhir* (2006) and Shuhaimi Baba's *Tanda Putera* (*Mark of Prince*, 2012) illustrate the delicate balance of power, public opinion, pragmatism and constituency maintenance that have played out in the field of arts and culture in recent years. *Lelaki Komunis Terakhir* is a documentary which deals, in an oblique way, with exiled communist leader Chin Peng.[6] The Film Censorship Board approved the film for screening without any cuts in April 2006. Given the subject matter, the filmmaker was further asked to screen the film for the Special Branch, which also approved its release, again without any cuts.[7]

Before the film's release, however, *Berita Harian*, a Malay-language daily owned by UMNO, launched an attack on the documentary, criticising the authorities for not banning it. In response, a special screening was arranged for members of parliament. Once again, the general consensus was that the film was suitable for general viewing. Nevertheless, *Lelaki Komunis Terakhir*'s permit was withdrawn on the grounds that 'the public had protested'. In a blog post recounting the event, Amir notes, 'The decision to ban the documentary was based on the series of articles in *Berita Harian*',[8] highlighting the power of state-aligned media to instigate punitive actions against the arts.

Seven years later, another film, *Tanda Putera*, followed a similar path to that of Amir's film, but with quite different results. Well-known director Shuhaimi Baba's film *Tanda Putera* is a historical drama set against the backdrop of the riots of 1969. Made with a grant from the National Film Development Commission, the film was approved for screening in 2012. Following the release of the movie trailer and a provocatively captioned photo of opposition stalwart Lim Kit Siang posted on the film's official Facebook page,[9] however, *Tanda Putera* was accused of being a work of government propaganda, which cast ethnic Chinese as the sole perpetrators of the riots. The impending general election at the time further heightened tensions, leading academic Lim Teck Ghee (2012) to note that 'it is only to be expected that pro-opposition supporters would see what they regard as "the May 13 film" to be part of a pre-election smear campaign against the DAP'. Public anger against the film, expressed in newspaper articles and on social media, proliferated. There was, conversely, strong support for the film from Malay-rights groups such as Perkasa (Pertubuhan Pribumi Perkasa Malaysia, Malaysian Indigenous Empowerment Organisation). In November 2012, the Ministry of Information, Communications and Culture announced the postponement of the film's release, 'for the benefit of the people . . . as it contains scenes that may cause conflicts' (Zulaikha 2012). With its eye on the upcoming general election, the state was aware that it could not further alienate the Chinese community, which was an important voting bloc for the Barisan Nasional coalition.

The election, held in May 2013, was won by Barisan Nasional despite an overwhelming loss of urban votes. Three months after the general election, *Tanda Putera* was released. Shuhaimi announced that she had made cuts to certain scenes and rescinded her earlier claim that the film was based on historical fact, now asserting that it was a work of fiction. Nevertheless, a fresh round of public debate surfaced, with some ugly threats made against Shuhaimi by netizens. The chief minister of Penang, a member of the opposition Democratic Action Party (DAP) and the son of Lim Kit Siang, attempted, unsuccessfully, to proscribe the film in his state. *Tanda Putera* premiered in August 2013, but performed dismally at the box office. In the face of the film's commercial failure, several ministers called for the use of public institutions of education and broadcasting to ensure its longevity in the public sphere (*Sinchew* 2013). This was in contrast to the state's pre-election willingness to delay the film's release in response to public dissatisfaction.

Both *Lelaki Komunis Terakhir* and *Tanda Putera* deal with historical figures and incidents that are still sites of active contestation: the communist insurgency and the riots of 1969. In both cases, the state's initial stance was permissive; however, upon pressure from what it terms 'the people' or 'the public', the state altered its position to proscribe according to the desires of a specific public.

Rather than look at these censorious publics as weakening the state's power, it is possible to read them as the result of complex manipulations enacted by the state to maintain its hold on power. Technologies of governance shape the individual's or community's sense of itself, prompting each unconsciously to construct themselves into subjects of power, acting in the interest of the state. Control and discipline become outsourced to the public. The state, therefore, is able to mask its disciplinary nature by enabling its public to act in its – the state's – interest. As evidenced by the competing public that arose in protest against *Tanda Putera*, these practices are unstable and porous, rather than stable and totalising. Further, there is every potential for the state's assigned gatekeepers to become more strident, pushing the state into a more repressive position than it might otherwise take.

With *Lelaki Komunis Terakhir*, the result was a ban that remains in effect, seven years on. *Tanda Putera*'s short-term proscription, followed by subsequent screening and active promotion, point to a state that is able to make pragmatic shifts to accommodate conflicting interests, as easily as it is able to reassert its ideological dominance to discipline these same interests.

A recent controversy offers a prism through which to refract the moral panic and public mobilisation that have arisen out of the so-called Allah issue (see Puyok, this volume). Erykah Badu, an American neo-soul singer, was scheduled to perform in Kuala Lumpur in February 2012.[10] Two days before the concert, *The Star*, Malaysia's highest-circulation English-language newspaper, published a feature on Badu's concert, with a photo of the singer, bare-shouldered, and with what appeared to be tattoos on her body and face (de Vries 2012). The image used was similar to the ones on posters and promotional material around the city, except for one crucial difference. In the newspaper, the word 'Allah', in Arabic, is clearly visible on Badu's shoulders. Badu's promotional posters around the city, through the magic of Photoshop and with Badu's permission, had taken God off Badu's shoulders for the local market. *The Star* had used the original, unedited photo, possibly downloaded from Badu's homepage, instead of the version supplied by the local concert promoter.

Condemnation came quickly and was widespread. The next day saw intense coverage in the mainstream media and on social media sites, with the now familiar enactment of outrage by several non-governmental groups and individuals. A large number of people also argued in support of Badu. The following day, the Minister of Information, Communications and Culture announced the withdrawal of the permit to hold the concert. The minister, via his Tumblr account, explained that the 'tattoos' had 'raised objections from the community which can threaten national security and have a negative impact on the government's image' (*New Straits Times* 2012). *The Star* issued three formal apologies, indefinitely suspended two editors and was threatened with the withdrawal of its publishing licence. Although a government-owned paper, *The Star* is associated with the Chinese/non-Muslim community. Its publishing the unexpurgated image of Badu served as a kind of call to action to those who have internalised the discourse of purported Christian disrespect for Islam and evangelism towards Muslims. A public arose in response – a public that came into being as protectors of Allah by the state's manufacturing of a controversy where previously there had been none. There were, in fact, two camps, two publics: those who were for and those who were against banning her concert. The state chose to 'obey' the public that best served its interest – the public that it had constructed to begin with.

Artists' response

Despite the considerable energies spent by the state – both ideological and coercive – towards maintaining dominance, its hegemonic project remains unaccomplished. Members of the arts community are amongst a diverse set of stakeholders who have provided counterpoints to the state's agenda. Even with limited resources, arts practitioners have fashioned a diverse, robust and resilient arts landscape.

Artists working in different genres and across different sites of language have openly explored alternative imaginings of nationhood through their use of intracultural strategies and themes. These include theatre practitioners who have engaged with historical narratives, such as Mark Teh, in his *1955 Baling Talks* (2011). Instant Café Theatre's *Air Con* (2008; written by Shanon Shah) and *Parah* (2011, 2012 and 2013; by Singaporean writer, Alfian Sa'at), under the direction of Jo Kukathas, examine the impact of the state's increasingly disciplinary stance upon disenfranchised youth. In the visual arts, Sarena Abdullah (2013) notes that since the 1990s Malay artists have employed the idiom of post-modernism to present nuanced reflections on fractures and conflicts assailing the emerging Malay middle class, in addition to broader explorations of social and political currents sweeping the nation.

There has also been more direct engagement with the body politic, with practitioners directing their creativity towards activism. Visual artists, musicians and performers were actively and visibly involved in Coalition for Clean and Fair Elections (Bersih) rallies in 2007, 2011 and 2012 (see Govindasamy, this volume). The strategies employed can be described as playful, innovative and subversive. At Bersih 2.0, in 2007, Wong Tay Sy, Liew Kung Yu, Gan Siong King and Yee I-Lann conceptualised *Bola Bersih* (Clean Ball). The work involved the release of a series of giant yellow and green inflatable balls amongst the thousands of demonstrators. The crowd spontaneously responded by keeping each ball bouncing overhead. While framed as a game to keep the masses of people gathered entertained, the work instigated those present in an act of collectivism, an essential aspect of the Bersih movement. The glee with which the crowd engaged with the ball, captured and posted on YouTube,[11] was a canny way to disprove the state's demonising of Bersih participants as rabble-rousers and rioters. At Bersih 3.0, held in 2012, a group of local indie musicians, calling themselves 'Ayam & the Vanilla Boys (Girls too)', formed a percussion band with the express purpose of entertaining 'Bersih 3.0 attendee around Dataran Merdeka on that particular historical event'.[12]

On occasion, the state has attempted to reassert itself and stem these creative challenges to its authority. *Malaysian Spring*,[13] for instance, was a crowd-sourced art installation and visual campaign around Kuala Lumpur leading up to the general election in May 2013. As conceptualised by well-known architect Ng Sek San, hundreds of fabric flowers and flags were 'planted' along streets and embankments around the city. Members of the public were encouraged to set up their own installations, which quickly caught on. In the highly divisive atmosphere of the election campaign, the flags were at once whimsical and subversive. The title's echo of the Arab Spring, coupled with the strong anti-establishment sentiment in the urban areas where these flags appeared, instigated police action. The deputy inspector general of police claimed to have intelligence that the flags were a code for violence and chaos during the upcoming elections (Farik and Camoens 2013), casting a menacing quality on a creative mass moment. The accusations had little traction and the case was eventually dropped.

Two other examples concern a questionable recent death in custody. In 2007, Teoh Beng Hock, an opposition aide, was found dead at premises of the Malaysian Anti-Corruption Commission, having been detained overnight for questioning. A Royal Commission of Inquiry found that Teoh had committed suicide, a verdict that did little to convince the public that Teoh was not in fact murdered. *Sudden Death: Participatory Performance in Memory of Teoh Beng Hock* (2009) was created by Mark Teh of Five Arts Centre. The work places members of the audience on the ground, each assuming the same pose in which Teoh's body was found, as a candle burns for a timed four minutes. The audience, who in attending the performance, are automatically transformed from spectators to actors, are instructed to refrain from over-emoting or speaking. The image of Teoh's body has been replicated in mainstream and social media to the point of becoming iconic, and his death had, to some extent, become a rallying point amongst opposition politicians to denounce the government. Teh's work makes deft interventions, against both the possible culpability of the state and the apparent opportunism of the opposition. On the sixth anniversary of Teoh's death, another theatre director, Ayam Fared of Rumah Anak Teater, staged *Selak:Serak*, a devised theatre work. The work highlights both Teoh's death and the deaths of scores of others in police custody. As the nation moves from the latest scandal or crisis to another, *Selak:Serak* presents an insistence to remember. Both these creative responses to a deeply tragic incident are examples of how artists are using their creativity to reach into the crevices of that dark place that is the collective Malaysian psyche. These works show the potential for artists to rise above the increasing sectarianism, and in so doing, go deeper.

Conclusion

The field of artistic practice and cultural production in Malaysia is one that is particularly unstable. While the cultural policy framework has played an enduring role, a range of stakeholders, some of whom act in accordance with the desires of the state, and others whose contours are formed in resistance to it, are increasingly influential. Further, while competing domestic dimensions impact on the way that Malaysian arts and cultural practices have configured themselves, they are not immune to external forces of globalisation and international relations. The agency displayed by arts practitioners and different publics to pursue their own agendas and visions of cultural identity reveal that the potential for counter-hegemonic practices remains present. As the state comes under increasing pressure, however, it may well reassert itself, narrowing the parameters of what is acceptable.

Notes

1 This essay was conceptualised in discussion with Sharaad Kuttan.

2 It was the Minister of Home Affairs, and not the Minister of Culture, who announced that the lion dance, a vital part of Chinese New Year celebrations, was incompatible with the NCP (*New Straits Times* 1979).

3 The NAG was established in 1958 but only moved into its own premises in 2000. The National Theatre (Istana Budaya) was first mooted in 1964.

4 The site, created by Vernon Adrian Emuang, has been inactive since 2000 but continues to provide support to artists and events on an ad hoc basis.

5 Jenny Daneels and I were the co-founders and managing editors of the website until 2010, when it was taken over by Low Ngai Yuen.

6 Chin Peng was then still barred from Malaysia for his role in the violent campaign launched by the Malayan Communist Party to overthrow the British colonialists after World War II – the ban extended even to his ashes, upon his death in 2013. The threat of communism has long since ended, however, and Chin Peng's autobiography, *My Side of History*, was a best-seller, widely available in bookstores in the country at the time.

7 For a detailed account of the controversy, refer to Amir Muhammad's blog, http://lastcommunist.blogspot.sg/2006/05/why-is-lelaki-komunis-terakhir-banned.html (accessed 25 February 2014).

8 http://lastcommunist.blogspot.sg/2006/05/why-is-lelaki-komunis-terakhir-banned.html (accessed 25 February 2014).

9 The photo implied that Lim had urinated on a flagpole at a Malay politician's home during the riots, a claim that was debunked by various sources.

10 The material in this section is drawn largely from the author's unpublished paper, 'From bums on seats to censor', presented at the Substation Conference: *Target Audiences and the Publics of Art*, Singapore, 7 April 2012.

11 www.youtube.com/watch?v=Id8Ka2lfdmg (accessed 25 February 2014).

12 http://findars.blogspot.sg/2012/05/adventures-of-ayam-vanilla-boys-girls.html?q=Bersih (accessed 25 February 2014).

13 https://www.facebook.com/malaysianspring (accessed 25 February 2014).

Bibliography

Adib Zalkapli (2010) 'Warrior's Day to be marked the Islamic way on Saturday', *The Malaysian Insider*, 29 July, available at www.themalaysianinsider.com/malaysia/article/warriors-day-to-be-marked-the-islamic-way-on-Saturday (accessed 25 February 2014).

Antoinette, Michelle (2007) '. . . and Malaysia?', *Asiart Archive*, available at www.aaa.org.hk/Diaaalogue/Details/35 (accessed 25 February 2014).

Antoinette, Michelle (2013) 'Different visions: contemporary Malaysian art and exhibition in the 1990s and beyond', in Nur Hanim Khairuddin and Beverly Yong with T.K. Sabapathy (eds), *Reactions – New Critical Strategies, Narratives in Malaysian Art Vol. 2*, Kuala Lumpur: RogueArt, pp. 166–85.

de Vries, Abigail (2012) 'Living off the wall', *The Star*, 27 February.

Farik Zolkepli and Austin Camoens (2013) 'GE13: Police identify group planning Malaysian Spring, says deputy IGP', *The Star*, 3 May, available at www.thestar.com.my/story.aspx/?file=%2f2013%2f5%2f4%2fnation%2f20130504123504&sec=nation (accessed 25 February 2014).

Jit, Krishen (1984) 'Towards an Islamic theatre for Malaysia: Noordin Hassan and *Don't Kill the Butterflies*', *Asian Theatre Journal*, 1(2): 127–47.

Kee, Jac S.M. (2011) 'The colour yellow', *The Design Observer*, 7 August, available at http://changeobserver.designobserver.com/feature/the-color-yellow/28758/ (accessed 25 February 2014).

Kementerian Kebudayaan Belia dan Sukan (KKBS) (1973) *Asas Kebudayaan Kebangsaan*, Kuala Lumpur: KKBS.

Khoo Gaik Cheng (2006) *Reclaiming Adat: Contemporary Malaysian Film and Literature*, Vancouver: University of British Columbia Press.

Lim Teck Ghee (2012) 'Tanda Putera: dishonest or truthful reconstruction?', *Free Malaysia Today*, 7 August, available at www.freemalaysiatoday.com/category/opinion/2012/08/07/tanda-putera-dishonest-or-truthful-reconstruction/ (accessed 25 February 2014).

Loh, Francis K.W. (2002) 'Developmentalism and the limits of democratic discourse', in Francis Loh Kok Wah and Khoo Boo Teik (eds), *Democracy in Malaysia: Discourses and Practices*, Richmond: Curzon Press, pp. 19–50.

Miller, Toby and George Yúdice (2002) *Cultural Policy*, London: Sage.

Mohamed Izwan (2013) 'After Tanda Putera's poor showing, Perkasa wants it to be screened for free', *The Malaysian Insider*, 5 September, available at www.themalaysianinsider.com/malaysia/article/after-tanda-puteras-poor-showing-perkasa-wants-it-to-be-screened-for-free (accessed 25 February 2014).

Mohamed Taib Osman (1988) *Bunga Rampai: Aspects of Malay Culture*, Kuala Lumpur: DBP.

New Straits Times (1979) 'Ghazali on the basis for the nation's culture', *The New Straits Times*, 20 May, reproduced in full in Kua Kia Soong (ed.) (1990), *Malaysian Cultural Policy and Democracy*, Kuala Lumpur: The Resource and Research Centre, Selangor Chinese Assembly Hall, pp. 10–12.

New Straits Times (2012) 'Erykah Badu concert cancelled', *The New Straits Times*, 28 February, available at www.nst.com.my/opinion/columnist/erykah-badu-concert-cancelled-1.53054 (accessed 25 February 2014).

Nurhanim Khairuddin (2012) 'A decade of excess: Malaysian contemporary art since late 1990s', Catalogue Essay, *A Decade of Collecting Contemporary Art*, Wei-Ling Gallery.

Sarena Abdullah (2013) 'Malay artists and the postmodern situation', in Nur Hanim Khairuddin and Beverly Yong with T.K. Sabapathy (eds), *Reactions – New Critical Strategies, Narratives in Malaysian Art Vol. 2*, Kuala Lumpur: RogueArt, pp. 154–65.

Sinchew (2013) '"Tanda Putera" should be subject of study at tertiary institutions – Razali Ibrahim', *mysinchew.com*, 2 September, available at www.mysinchew.com/node/90773 (accessed 25 February 2014).

Tan Sooi Beng (1993) *Bangsawan – A Social and Stylistic History of Popular Malay Opera*, Singapore: Oxford University Press.

Tan Sooi Beng (2000) 'The "Huayue Tuan" (Chinese Orchestra) in Malaysia: adapting to survive', *Asian Music*, 31(2): 107–28.

Zulaikha Zulkifli (2012) 'Rais: deferment of *Tanda Putera* decided by cabinet', *Malaysiakini*, 8 November, available at www.malaysiakini.com/news/213809 (accessed 25 February 2014).

28

Filling in the gaps

The pursuit of gender equality in Malaysia

tan beng hui and Cecilia Ng

Over the past two decades, the Malaysian government has made several commitments towards realising women's rights and gender equality in the country. At the global level, it has ratified – albeit with reservations[1] – three key international human rights treaties: the United Nations (UN) Convention on the Rights of the Child, Convention on the Elimination of All Forms of Discrimination against Women (CEDAW) and Convention on the Rights of Persons with Disabilities. It is a signatory to major agreements like the Cairo Programme of Action and the Beijing Platform for Action, and outcome documents from the UN International Conference on Population and Development 1994 and the Fourth World Conference on Women 1995. It was also a prime mover behind the Putrajaya Non-Aligned Movement (NAM) Declaration 2005, which focuses on women's empowerment. At the national level, Malaysia prohibits any form of gender discrimination, via an amendment to Article 8(2) of the Federal Constitution in 2001. As well, there is a National Policy on Women (updated in 2009) and a Women's Development Action Plan.

For such efforts, which include contributions from the women's movement, Malaysia's level of gender equality, as measured by the Malaysian Gender Gap Index (MGGI) – developed by the United Nations Development Programme (UNDP) and Malaysia's Ministry of Women, Family and Community Development (MWFCD) in 2004 – appears to have shown signs of improvement. This index recorded a positive shift from 0.34 (1980) to 0.24 (2004) for the areas of health, education, economic activity and empowerment.[2] This development has not been uniform, however, with the greatest equality registered for education (0.046) and health (0.099) and the least in economic activity (0.247) and women's empowerment (0.579). Furthermore, while such indices are useful, they are limited in the categories they study – for example, violence is excluded – and are largely descriptive in aggregate terms of the existing situation.

For a more comprehensive and nuanced picture of gender relations in the country, one has to take into account the socio-economic and political context, such as the neoliberal economy, masculinist and semi-authoritarian political regime, and instrumentalisation of ethnicity and religion. In this light, this chapter will discuss gender relations and the position of women in Malaysia in relation to six areas of concern. These are: development planning, poverty, employment, violence, political representation and the law.

Development planning

'Women' were singled out in Malaysia's development agenda for the first time via a standalone chapter of the Sixth Malaysia Plan (1990–1995). Noting that 'women constitute[d] a vital economic resource', the government claimed that its goal was 'to integrate women as equal partners in nation building' (EPU 1991: 427). This acknowledgement was potentially an important milestone towards gender equality, but little has come of it. Instead, hanging on to an outdated model from the 1970s – which seeks to 'fit' women into 'development' rather than changing the development paradigm to suit women's needs[3] – every development plan until now has emphasised maximising the (re)productive capacities of women. They do not consider the complexities of women's lives, particularly in the era of neoliberal globalisation, and expect that a 'one size fits all' approach will work in a multi-ethnic, multi-religious, and multi-class context.

The Ninth Malaysia Plan (2006–2010, 9MP), for instance, spoke of 'efforts [that would] be undertaken to provide an enabling environment'. But this thrust was 'to ensure *more effective participation of women in national development*' (Government of Malaysia 2006: 281; emphasis added). Compared with earlier plans, the Tenth Malaysia Plan (2011–2015) (10MP) appeared to be an improvement insofar as it professes that the empowerment of women will be a 'key agenda'. Nevertheless, it, too, qualifies that this focus is to help women 'realise their full potential and *participate more effectively in the economic and social development of the country*' (Government of Malaysia 2010: 179–80; emphasis added). Women's interests, much less women's rights, are not the concern of these documents.

For development efforts to work for women, the way forward is to recover the concept of gender as a category of analysis that focuses on the dynamics of power relationships between men and women, in relation to the distribution of resources and knowledge in society. It is also critical that there be analysis of the linkages between gender and other social constructs and structural inequalities. This is where women's and men's multiple identities need to be addressed in relation to the intersectionalities of gender with class, ethnicity, culture, ability, sexuality, geographic location, citizenship, and so on. The government has to respect, protect, promote and fulfil human rights and monitor how development outcomes are realised. Adopting a rights-based approach would help achieve this goal.

Particularly under today's market-led development model – where economic growth has failed to bring about equality and sustainable human development, and instead led to more inequalities and exploitation – a rights-based approach has to ensure that the more vulnerable groups in society do not bear the costs of neoliberal globalisation and development. In the case of women, multiple layers of discrimination have to be unearthed and addressed to achieve gender and social justice. Given the goal of good governance Malaysian authorities have enunciated, it is important that the process of development planning involve the genuine participation of civil society, and be accountable and transparent.

Poverty

Malaysia has displayed impressive gains in fighting poverty. Officially, the incidence of poverty plunged from 52.4 percent in 1970 to 3.8 percent in 2009. The 10MP sought to reduce this figure further, to 2.8 percent. As well, at 0.2 percent, hardcore poverty has almost been eliminated (DOS 2013b: 7). Nevertheless, it is important to note that these achievements are not evenly spread. For example, the poverty gap in rural areas is more than three times that in urban areas, with higher incidences in the east coast states of the peninsula and in East Malaysia.[4] The 9MP notes a rise in income inequality from 1990 to 2004.[5] Moreover, Malaysia's Gini co-efficient is one of the highest in the region, at 0.431 (DOS 2013b), due more to intragroup than intergroup disparities (Ragayah 2009).

It is well established that poverty has a 'female' face and globally the feminisation of poverty has been a critical challenge for a number of decades. Despite this, studies of female poverty in Malaysia are hampered by the lack of official sex-disaggregated data. The most recent National Policy on Women revealed that poverty among women-headed households was 11.5 percent in 2004, a drop from 12.5 percent in 2002.[6] Such information is useful, but its randomness limits any kind of meaningful analysis. Instead, there should be data pertaining to the different categories of poor women, why and how they fall below the poverty line, and how much access and control they have over economic resources.

This gap has been partly filled by the few localised studies that deal with rural women. Research into indigenous women in two villages in Pulau Carey, for instance, concluded that the shift from subsistence production to palm oil monoculture has adversely affected gender roles and power relations (Lai 2008). A 2004 survey of women oil-palm plantation workers found that they not only received a barely liveable wage but were also exposed to health hazards due to the lack of protective gear when handling toxic chemicals.[7] Another study of dam projects and the resettlement of indigenous groups showed how women, much more than men, lose access to land and rights whenever their communities are involuntarily moved (Yong 2006).

Such research is insufficient and sometimes can produce conflicting results. In two studies about low-waged single mothers, the first, carried out in urban areas of eleven states, found that the majority of the 1,486 respondents who earned less than RM500 a month said that they were satisfied with their living conditions and the well-being of their families (Dasimah *et al.* 2009). The second, which the National Human Rights Commission, SUHAKAM (2009) conducted, found that respondents from two public housing flats – who also fell below the official poverty line – complained of difficulties in affording healthcare services and sending their children to school. Some also felt that they had been discriminated against for being poor. The availability of more structured and systematically collected data would help address this limitation.

Employment

In the space of less than one generation, Malaysian women have entered the workforce in large numbers. Since the 1980s, almost half the women of working age in the population have entered the formal work sector at some point in their lives. This is due mainly to the export-oriented industrialisation model adopted by the government in the late 1970s, which attracted many multinational companies looking to relocate their labour-intensive work, particularly in the electronics sector. As a result, the participation rate of women in the labour force grew from 37.2 percent in 1970 to 47.8 percent in 1990, before plateauing for the next two decades and never exceeding the 50 percent mark. These figures have been consistently lower than those for men, which peaked at 85.3 percent in 1990 (Table 28.1), and raised cause for concern as it is assumed that the majority of women aged between 15 and 64 are not contributing – as they are expected to – to the nation's productivity.

Malaysian government data do not fully reflect the numbers or profile of those in the informal economy. For example, the inaugural *Informal Sector Work Force Survey Report 2012* (DOS 2013a) states that there are around one million such workers, the bulk of whom are male[8] and in the construction industry; however, these figures are only for those recognised

Table 28.1 Labour force participation rates by sex in Malaysia, 1970–2011

Year	*1970*	*1980*	*1990*	*2000*	*2010*	*2011*
Male	79.3	84.8	85.3	83.3	79.5	78.9
Female	37.2	42.2	47.8	46.7	46.5	47.9

Source: Labour Force Survey Reports (various years).

as participating in the labour force *and* performing non-agricultural work.[9] The fact that there were almost five million women in 2011 officially considered as not working or looking for a job[10] raises further questions about the veracity of figures pertaining to informal employment in the country, in particular that of women.

Many women who are not captured in official labour force statistics are found in productive but informal employment. It is estimated that the majority of the world's workers are now contracted in the informal economy, in jobs with minimal or no security, and few or no benefits (Heintz 2006; Razavi 2009; Kabeer 2012). Typically too, those workers with lower skills are poorly paid, but work long and irregular hours. Some studies suggest that there is a gender hierarchy at play, in which men tend to be on top of the pecking order as industrial outworkers or employers and women at the bottom, as employees or waged workers (Chen, Vanek and Carr 2004 cited in UNDP 2010: 62).

The low female labour force participation rate can partly be attributed to the reproductive and care work that women perform (e.g. child-bearing and rearing, housework, caring for sick or older members of the family), most often for free. Even though the government has introduced several measures to support women in these roles – for example, increasing maternity leave for the public sector from sixty to ninety days,[11] offering tax deductions to employers to provide childcare facilities, and legalising flexi-work – women still bear the burden of responsibility because such initiatives do not challenge gender stereotypes, much less change them. Instead of offering longer paternity leave to encourage fathers to play a greater role in raising children, for instance, this is capped at a maximum of seven days.[12]

To help working women or those who want to stay in or re-enter the labour force, it is important that there be good and affordable childcare facilities. Not many public sector bodies offer childcare facilities, while private childcare centres are costly. In 2007, the government introduced a subsidy of RM180 per child to civil servants whose monthly household income was below RM2,000, later extended in 2009 to households earning RM3,000 and below. It also granted a tax exemption of 10 percent to private employers who establish childcare centres, but few have taken up this offer. In 2013, the government announced further incentives, amounting to as much as RM15 million, for both private and public institutions to provide quality childcare services, but their impact has yet to be seen.

Besides childcare, the idea that flexi-work opportunities be targeted at women needs to be revisited. This should be an option for both male and female workers. Otherwise, women will continue to be made solely responsible for work within and outside the home, with many opting to give up formal employment either to become full-time mothers or to juggle family life and work with little or no long-term security. One government study on time usage showed that women perform 75 percent of housework and childcare (Bernama, 8 August 2005). Another, in 2011, found that 66.9 percent of women – versus 2.6 percent of men – outside the labour force cited housework as the main reason why they did not seek employment; the majority of men cited ongoing schooling (MWFCD 2011). With more women now having tertiary education, it is a cause for worry if the country's better-qualified citizens are out of the labour force in this way.

Over time the occupational distribution by gender has shifted in tandem with structural changes in the economy. Due to the growth of the services sector, women are now over-represented as clerks (18.8 percent of all women in the formal labour force) and service workers (20 percent) (Fernandez 2009). As more women gain tertiary qualification, their numbers as 'senior officers and managers', 'professionals' and most especially 'technicians and associate professionals' have also grown (Table 28.2). Even so, they remain outnumbered by men, especially in the higher occupational groups, suggesting that they still have to overcome a sticky floor/glass ceiling as top decision-makers in their respective industries.

One other measure of gender inequality at the workplace is wages. Table 28.3 shows that the overall gender wage gap was recorded as having declined from RM234 in 2008 to RM68 in 2012. Besides the fact that, on average, men still make more than women (RM1,906 versus RM1,838 per month), the figures reveal a more worrying picture. Discounting those who are in managerial positions, every other occupation shows a rise in the gender wage differential from 2008 to 2012. This is particularly disconcerting for jobs in which women dominate (i.e. clerical support workers, and service and sales workers). Even though the gap at the managerial level is less now, women's wages remain on average almost RM1,500 less than those of male managers. Clearly, their economic contribution is still considered of lower value – even for similar kinds of work.

To address the issue of wage differentials requires continuous monitoring mechanisms that can determine the nature and extent of gender wage discrimination in the workplace. On the one hand, the Malaysian government has agreed to close such gaps, as exemplified by its ratification of the ILO Convention on Equality of Wages between Men and Women in September 1997 (MWFCD 2004). On the other hand, it has not incorporated the ILO Equal Remuneration Convention 1951 (No. 100) into existing law to ensure equal pay for work of equal value.

Table 28.2 Employment distribution by occupation and sex, 2001 and 2010 (by number employed, millions)

	2001		*2010*	
Occupation	*Male*	*Female*	*Male*	*Female*
Senior officers and managers	0.545	0.153	0.612	0.205
Professionals	0.273	0.186	0.356	0.317
Technicians and associate professionals	0.715	0.415	0.954	0.619
Clerical workers	0.315	0.578	0.320	0.755
Service workers, shop and market sales workers	0.733	0.561	1.039	0.803
Skilled agriculture and fishery workers	0.890	0.378	1.018	0.325
Craft and related trade workers	0.975	0.183	1.011	0.161
Plant and machine operators and assemblers	0.993	0.488	0.975	0.333
Elementary occupation	0.618	0.382	0.826	0.498
Total	**6.056**	**3.323**	**7.112**	**4.017**

Source: Tan and Thambiah (in press).

Table 28.3 Average monthly basic wage by occupation and sex in Malaysia, 2012

Occupation	Male (RM)	Female (RM)	Wage difference	
			2008	2012
Managers	5,644	4,159	1,774	1,485
Professionals	4,358	3,384	822	974
Technicians and associate professionals	2,474	2,354	50	120
Clerical support workers	1,853	1,663	82	190
Service and sales workers	1,506	1,003	122	503
Skilled agricultural, forestry and fishery workers	1,110	713	217	397
Craft and related trades workers	1,327	752	354	575
Plant and machine operators and assemblers	1,311	896	237	415
Elementary occupations	1,015	756	132	259
Total	**1,906**	**1,838**	**234**	**68**

Sources: Tan and Thambiah (in press); DOS (2013c).

In sum, despite economic modernisation, the majority of women employees are still in unskilled or semi-skilled jobs, with limited prospects for upward mobility. While there are some women who have completed tertiary education and reached middle-management positions, all women workers continue to face challenges, such as health and safety hazards, sexual harassment, limited upward mobility, and lack of avenues to organise and have their views heard.

Violence

The UN (1993) defines violence against women (VAW) as 'any act of gender-based violence that results in, or is likely to result in, physical, sexual or psychological harm or suffering to women, including threats of such acts, coercion or arbitrary deprivation of liberty, whether occurring in public or private life'. Those from marginalised communities like the poor, refugees, migrants or sexual minorities are especially vulnerable when it comes to crimes like rape, domestic violence, incest and sexual harassment.

Table 28.4 shows reported VAW cases in Malaysia for 2000–12. These numbers, which are believed to be the tip of the iceberg,[13] show little improvement over time, and in some instances, demonstrate a worrying upward trend. For example, rape cases more than doubled during this period. Worse, in 2007, it was reported that just over half the victims were below age sixteen (*The Star*, 7 May 2009). A 2004 memorandum by women's groups confirmed this grim situation, noting that many cases occur in spaces that are assumed as 'safe' for women; the profile of victims and assailants was increasingly younger; conviction rates are low; women are being raped in custody or by those they trust; and extreme violence, including murder, was now being used during rape.

The picture is similar with domestic violence (i.e. physical, psychological, emotional or sexual abuse) except that, as Table 28.4 illustrates, this category consistently registered the highest frequency of reported cases for the same period. This is possibly because there is greater awareness of the Domestic Violence Act 1994, which women's groups had lobbied for, or greater confidence to lodge such reports. Even so, as stated before, there are likely to be

Table 28.4 Cases of violence against women and girls in Malaysia

	2000	*2002*	*2004*	*2006*	*2008*	*2010*	*2012*
Rape	1,217	1,431	1,760	2,454	3,409	3,595	2,998
Domestic violence	3,468	2,755	3,101	3,264	3,769	3,172	3,488
Incest	213	306	334	332	334	NA	302
Outrage of modesty[a]	1,234	1,522	1,661	1,349	2,131	2,054	1,803
Sexual harassment at the workplace	112	84	119	101	NA	NA	NA

Sources: Royal Malaysian Police (PDRM); Ministry of Women, Family and Community Development (MWFCD) (various years).

Notes:

[a] This phrase 'outrage of modesty' is an archaic remnant of British colonialism and often used as a euphemism for sexual harassment.

NA = Not available.

many more cases out there that do not make it into national statistics. The narrow legal definition of the term does not help. So, for instance, women survivors of violence in a de facto relationship are not recognised under the law. A recent local study which revealed that women experience domestic violence in nine out of every hundred households supports the contention that official figures are inaccurate (see Noraida 2013).

Figures for sexual harassment in the workplace – in which women are the majority of 'victims' – seem low, despite the Code of Ethics for the Prevention and Eradication of Sexual Harassment at the Workplace 1999 and new provisions curbing sexual harassment in the Employment Act 2011. These figures do not reflect results of surveys like that conducted in 2005 by Universiti Malaya, in which more than half the 657 female respondents stated that they had experienced at least one form of sexual harassment at work (*New Straits Times*, 9 November 2009).

Indeed, amendments to prevailing laws appear to fall short of ensuring women's lives are free from violence or discrimination. Hence, even though the Employment Act was reformed in 2011 to address sexual harassment at the workplace, numerous loopholes render these changes problematic. For instance, the act applies only to the private sector and in Peninsular Malaysia; there is no independent body to investigate complaints; a complainant has no recourse to appeal a decision; there is no possibility of compensation or apology to a victim; and no action is possible against perpetrators who are not permanent employees at a workplace (e.g. contract workers, vendors, visitors, etc.). The government's latest moves to amend the Penal Code demonstrate its preference to address sexual crimes punitively rather than through rehabilitative or reparative measures.[14]

The persistence of VAW in Malaysia can be explained in several ways. First, there is a perception that such violations are acceptable because, many a time, perpetrators get away with impunity because of the ineffectiveness of the legal framework or a lack of political will to deal with such matters. To correct this, the government needs to exercise greater due diligence. While laws are important, however, it is equally crucial to conduct education and awareness-raising programmes that challenge socio-cultural beliefs that perpetuate VAW. Such changes will ensure that women are able to benefit from legal mechanisms and other services extended by the government and civil society groups. Government intervention can also remedy sexist, patriarchal and stereotypical attitudes that women face when attempting to access these opportunities, as well as women's lack of financial independence, mobility and exposure in dealing with public institutions. Experiences at NGO women's shelters show that women need assurance that they and their children will not suffer immediate poverty and indignity when they choose to act against the violence they face.[15]

Political representation

After fifty years of nation-building, Malaysian women's underrepresentation in formal politics continues. Following the last general election in 2013, women constitute just over 30 percent of appointed senators in the Dewan Negara (Upper House), and a mere 10.36 percent of those elected to the Dewan Rakyat (Lower House). Ranked 113 out of 189 countries in women's representation in parliament, Malaysia is surpassed by poorer neighbours like Timor Leste, Vietnam, Cambodia and Indonesia.[16] At an average of 8 percent, women's numbers in state legislative assemblies are likewise disappointing. Since independence, the number of women cabinet ministers has never exceeded three, a situation that has only worsened under Prime Minister Najib Razak's administration.[17] Selangor is the solitary state in which women form 40 percent of the state's executive committee. Most other states have less than 10 percent, or in Terengganu, Perak and Sarawak, zero. A similar picture is seen for local councils, where women comprise fewer than 20 percent of appointed councillors, and just 4.8 percent are local council presidents (WAO 2012: 119).

The fact that women make up about a quarter to half of the members in all major political parties in Malaysia gives some perspective on what these numbers mean. Such consistently low figures reflect the patriarchal set-up of the political regime, which limits and excludes women from public decision-making. Even when elected, women face a hostile environment, with sexist remarks being the norm. A strategy of 'fast tracking', it is argued, can help remove barriers that impede women's entry into the political arena. Underpinning that approach, however, is an assumption that a critical mass needs to be accompanied by critical acts – that is, what women elected to office do with their position is equally important.

Given this imbalance, the call to increase women's political representation – particularly through use of quotas – has grown louder recently. The 9MP, for instance, spelt out a policy objective of having at least 30 percent women in decision-making positions. In 2007, the MWFCD and the UNDP commissioned a study on this issue to recommend a plan of action to meet this goal by 2015. This effort came after it was revealed that women were lagging far behind as decision-makers in both the public and private sectors. The starkness of women's poor representation becomes clearer against the fact that even though they now dominate the public sector, women occupy a mere 20 percent of decision-making positions.

The opposition Pakatan Rakyat (PR) coalition has started to make inroads to enhance women's political representation. In 2009, a component party, Parti Keadilan Rakyat (PKR, People's Justice Party) amended its constitution to ensure that at least 30 percent of decision-making posts be held by women, the first party in the country to do so. The PR-led state of Selangor has also committed itself to this goal, while Penang has two women local council presidents and a state-funded body – the Penang Women's Development Corporation (PWDC) – to promote gender equality. Penang was also the first state in the country to adopt gender-responsive budgeting (Ng 2011a, 2012).

The law

The law is a powerful tool to engineer social change. As mentioned, Malaysia ratified CEDAW in 1995, in conjunction with the Fourth World Conference on Women. Although it has removed some of the original reservations it first made, the government has persisted with objections to five provisions concerning citizenship, and marriage and the family.[18] It is a well-established principle of international law that once a state ratifies an international treaty, it is bound to implement the treaty provisions in good faith.[19] Malaysia, however, has been slow to domesticate this pivotal women's human rights law, opting instead to delay the introduction of enabling legislation that will allow CEDAW to have the force of law locally.[20]

Even so, the non-incorporation of international human rights norms into domestic legislation has not deterred women and other human rights advocates from pushing the boundaries and trying to set a legal precedent through the judicial system. The first attempt, *Beatrice Fernandez v. Sistem Penerbangan Malaysia & Anor* (2004), failed after the Court – which narrowly interpreted Article 8(2) of the Federal Constitution – ruled that discrimination on the basis of gender was permissible on certain grounds (Box 28.1). It took another seven years before a High Court judge finally declared that CEDAW had the force of law and was binding on member states. This decision was reached when Noorfadilla Ahmad Saikin sued the Education Ministry for discrimination after the ministry retracted a job offer it made because she was pregnant. Even though the government initially chose to appeal the decision, it eventually withdrew its appeal, leading to a significant victory for women's rights in the country (Box 28.2).

Box 28.1 The Beatrice Fernandez case

In 1991, Beatrice Fernandez was fired from her job as a flight attendant with Malaysian Airlines (MAS). Under the prevailing collective agreement, any flight attendant who becomes pregnant after two pregnancies is obliged to resign. In her case, she fell pregnant for a third time but refused to resign and her employment was thus terminated. She then took her case to court, but lost after the judges ruled that:

1. Malaysian Airlines (MAS) was a private enterprise and the law protected an individual only if their rights had been violated by state or public authorities;
2. Article 8(2) of the Federal Constitution, which prohibits gender-based discrimination, does not apply, because collective agreements are not considered law;
3. the term 'gender' was included in the Federal Constitution only after 1991 – the year of the offence – and thus cannot be applied retrospectively; and
4. no discrimination took place because all female flight attendants were treated the same.

Box 28.2 The Noorfadilla Ahmad Saikin case

2008: Noorfadilla applies for a temporary teaching position in a government school.

2009: She is offered a teaching job, which she accepts; however, the offer is later withdrawn after she is discovered to be pregnant. The government (Ministry of Education) claimed it could not employ pregnant women because their absence for two months after delivering would require hiring a replacement teacher, and that if a woman encountered health problems during her pregnancy, she would be absent from the job. Noorfadilla files a court application to declare the government's actions discriminatory, unlawful and unconstitutional.

2011: On 12 July, Justice Zaleha Yusof of the Shah Alam High Court rules in favour of Noorfadilla, stating that the Ministry of Education's actions constituted gender discrimination as defined in CEDAW,[a] and violated Article 8(2) of the Federal Constitution. The Ministry appeals the decision.

2013: In June, the government withdraws its appeal. The landmark decision of the Noorfadilla case stands, and as noted by the Joint Action Group for Gender Equality (JAG), 'There can be no more excuse for an employer, be it the government or private entity, to deny a woman her right to work and to the same employment opportunities as men, on the basis of gender' (Press statement, 27 June 2013).

Note:

[a] She said, 'The Court has no choice but to refer to CEDAW in clarifying the term "equality" and gender discrimination under Article 8(2) of the Federal Constitution' (Selangor Darul Ehsan, Originating Summons No. 21-248-2010 between Norfadilla binti Ahmad Saikin and Defendants, 'Grounds of judgement', 12 July 2011, p. 16, cited in WAO 2012: 66).

Without detracting from this latest achievement, in general, the process of legal reform has been arduous and other attempts at challenging discriminatory laws have been less successful. In 2012, the Court of Appeal told a group of women factory workers who had been forced to retire at age fifty that there was no bias in having different retirement ages for male and female employees, even when this clearly violated Article 8(2), the non-discrimination provision, of the Federal Constitution.[21]

In the case of Islamic legislation, amendments from the 1990s onwards have caused Muslim women's rights to be whittled away. Prior to this, Malaysia had one of the more progressive family enactments in the Muslim world in its 1984 version of the Islamic Family Law (IFL). Without the intervention of women's groups like Sisters in Islam, the latest efforts by the central government to impose uniform legislation across all states[22] would have caused the erosion of rights that Muslim women previously enjoyed. For example, in the past, Muslim men were only able to contract a polygamous marriage if they could prove that this was 'just *and* necessary', and more importantly, that the subsequent marriage would not impair the standard of living of the existing family. The 1984 IFL was repealed in 1994 and in 2005 the government proposed several changes including rewording 'just *and* necessary to 'just *or* necessary', thus making it easier for Muslim husbands to take on additional wives.[23]

As well, there are certain provisions under Islamic law that have resulted in Muslim women's being denied rights enjoyed by women of other faiths, especially in relation to marriage and the family. For instance, the minimum age of marriage for Muslim women is sixteen; for other women, eighteen. Regardless of age, the former need the permission of a *wali* (male guardian) to marry;[24] the latter do not. Once married, a Muslim wife has to submit to and obey her husband, failing which she can be charged in court. Only Muslim women are subjected to polygamous marriages, they do not have equal rights in relation to divorce or guardianship, and where inheritance is concerned, daughters get half the share of a son. It is commonly understood that Malaysia's earlier mentioned reservations to CEDAW are made to preserve this status quo.

Finally, the regulatory powers of the law have also been used to perpetuate and uphold a particular and rigid notion of what constitutes the 'ideal' Malaysian woman. It penalises those it deems as being 'immoral' or who dress or behave 'indecently'. Although all women are subjected to sexual policing, those who are younger, less affluent, look masculine and/or are Malay-Muslim bear the brunt of such controls. This situation has worsened with the politicisation of ethnicity and religion in recent times (tan 2012).

Conclusion

On the whole, Malaysia does not suffer from a dearth of policies and programmes that can improve women's lives. As the account above shows, the government has a fairly reasonable track record of introducing changes; however, most of these have remained on paper. It has also been reluctant to take on additional progress by ensuring that the barriers that women encounter are effectively addressed. This can happen only by taking into account women's multiple identities. Unless this situation is reversed, the labour force participation rate of women will continue to stagnate at around 50 percent, since affordable childcare facilities are lacking in both the public and private sector. As well, present occupational hierarchies will continue to be reproduced under conditions of capitalism and patriarchy. While there may be slight improvements in women's decision-making positions, top posts will largely benefit elite women who have the prerequisite education, professional qualifications and network connections.

Patriarchal ideology and control over women have been difficult battles for the women's movement to overcome, particularly in the arena of violence against women. Increasingly, Muslim women have been under attack, purportedly for reasons of immorality and irreligious behaviour (see Pang, this volume). Unless there are real cultural, structural and systemic changes at all levels, the potential for *all* women to live violence-free lives in the future is bleak. Democracy and socio-economic justice are prerequisites to gender equality, and thus opening up such spaces and insisting on a more equitable distribution of the country's resources are indispensable towards realising women's rights and gender equality in Malaysia.

Notes

1 Under the United Nations human rights treaty system, states are allowed to place 'reservations' to a treaty for provisions that they do not accept and by which they will not be bound. Reservations are allowed so long as they are not incompatible with the objective and purpose of said treaty. They are meant to be temporary; over time, the state needs to demonstrate that it is making progress toward removing a reservation.

2 The range of values of the MGGI is between 0, no gender inequality, and 1, maximal gender inequality (see MWFCD and UNDP 2007). The latest MWFCD data show that this gap has been maintained (MWFCD 2009).

3 This followed the Women in Development (WID) model popularised in the 1970s by economist Ester Boserup.

4 Sabah registers the worst poverty rate, at 8.1 percent (DOS 2013b).

5 The share of the bottom 40 percent of the populace fell from 14.5 percent (1990) to 13.5 percent (2004), while that of the top 20 percent grew from 50 to 51.2 percent for the same period (Ragayah 2009).

6 It should, however, be noted that the incidence of poverty among female-headed households is still higher than among male-headed households (2.1 versus 1.6 percent), and the former's mean monthly income is RM3,671 whereas the latter's is RM5,248 (DOS 2012: 40–41).

7 See Sangaralingam 2005.

8 The official 2012 figures count 616,700 men (59.07 percent) versus 427,200 women (40.92 percent).

9 The report defines 'employed persons in the informal sector' as working for establishments that: (1) are not registered with the Companies Commission of Malaysia or any other professional body; (2) produce goods and services that are meant for sale or barter; and (3 employ fewer than ten persons.

10 In 2011, out of 9,555,700 women of working age, fewer than half (4,575,300) were in the labour force (tan and Thambiah in press).

11 For those in the private sector, maternity leave remains at sixty days.

12 The state of Selangor, ruled by the Pakatan Rakyat coalition since 2008, is an exception, with fourteen days' paternity leave.

13 It is well known that only around 10 percent of VAW incidents are reported, for such reasons as shame, culture, inaccessible reporting procedures and poor awareness levels, resulting in a stark discrepancy between incidence rates and police reports of VAW. Further research is still needed to determine if there has merely been a rise in the rate of reporting.

14 'Memorandum to Nancy Shukri, Minister in the Prime Minister's Department in charge of law, and Ahmad Zahid Hamidi, Minister of Home Affairs on the Proposed Amendments to Laws relating to Domestic Violence and Sexual Crimes in the Penal Code and Criminal Procedure Code'. Submitted by the Joint Action Group for Gender Equality (JAG), 30 September 2013.

15 See the various annual reports by Women's Aid Organisation (WAO) and Women's Centre for Change (WCC), as well as Noraida and Intan Hashimah 2011.

16 'Women in national parliaments', website of the Inter-Parliamentary Union, as of 1 July 2013, available at www.ipu.org/wmn-e/classif.htm (accessed 10 August 2013).

17 At one point, he had only one woman in his cabinet. After the last general election, this figure climbed to two out of the thirty-three appointees.

18 Reservations to Articles 5(a), 7(b) and 16(2) have been dropped, but those to Articles 9(2) (women's transferring their nationality to their children), 16(1)(a) (right to enter into marriage), 16(1)(c) (equality in marriage), 16(1)(f) (guardianship) and 16(1)(g) (a wife's right to choose a family name and occupation) remain.

19 Article 27 of the Vienna Convention on the Law of Treaties 1969 stipulates that 'a party may not invoke the provisions of its internal law as justification for its failure to perform a treaty'.

20 Any international treaty entered into by Malaysia is not self-executing; a local law must be passed to give effect to an international commitment.

21 The case began in 2001 when the jobs of the eight women from Guppy Plastics Industries were suddenly terminated after their company changed its employment regulations, including forcing female employees to retire at fifty while men were allowed to work until fifty-five. Though the women won their case at the Industrial Court, the High Court later overruled this decision.

22 Islamic family law falls under the jurisdiction of each state in Malaysia.

23 Following protests by Sisters in Islam, the government withdrew these amendments for further review; however, there has been no resolution on this matter since.

24 In some states, women can also be forced into marriage through a *wali mujbir*, a male guardian who has the right to compel a woman to marry.

Bibliography

Aminah Ahmad (2007) 'Family-friendly employment policy practices in the Malaysian Government and selected private organisations', *The Journal of Global Business Management*, 3(1): 128–35.

Dasimah Omar, Puziah Ahmad and Muna Sarimin (2009) 'Urban living condition of low income single mothers in Malaysia', *European Journal of Social Sciences*, 9(2): 193–201.

Department of Statistics, Malaysia (DOS) (2013a) *Informal Sector Work Force Survey Report 2012*, Kuala Lumpur: National Government Printers.

Department of Statistics, Malaysia (DOS) (2013b) *Household Income and Basic Amenities Survey Report 2012*, Kuala Lumpur: National Government Printers.

Department of Statistics, Malaysia (DOS) (2013c) *Salaries and Wages Survey Report 2012*, Kuala Lumpur: National Government Printers.

Economic Planning Unit (EPU) (1991) *The Sixth Malaysia Plan, 1990–1995*, Kuala Lumpur: Economic Planning Unit.

Fernandez, Jacqueline (2009) 'Work, income and gender equality: labour market outcomes in Malaysia', paper presented at the National Seminar on Work, Income and Gender Equality, 20–21 April, Kuala Lumpur, Malaysia.

Franck, Anja (2012) *From Formal Employment to Street Vending*, Gothenburg: University of Gothenburg.

Government of Malaysia (2006) *Ninth Malaysia Plan 2006–2010*, Kuala Lumpur: National Government Printers.

Government of Malaysia (2010) *Tenth Malaysia Plan 2011–2015*, Kuala Lumpur: National Government Printers.

Heintz, James (2006) 'Globalization, economic policy and employment: poverty and gender implications', Employment Strategy Papers 3, Geneva: International Labour Office.

Human Rights Commission of Malaysia (SUHAKAM) (2007) *Annual Report*, Kuala Lumpur: Human Rights Commission of Malaysia.

Human Rights Commission of Malaysia (SUHAKAM) (2009) *Annual Report 2008*, Kuala Lumpur: Human Rights Commission of Malaysia.

Kabeer, Naila (2012) Women's Economic Empowerment and Inclusive Growth: Labour Markets and Enterprise Development, SIG Working Paper 2012/1, Ottawa: International Development Research Centre (IDRC) and Department for International (DFID).

Lai Wan Teng (2008) Gender and Livelihoods in Oil Palm Plantations: Case Study of the Mah Meri in Carey Island, Malaysia, Unpublished Master's Thesis, Bangkok: Asian Institute of Technology.

Mahadeva, Sheridan (2010) 'How poor are we, really?', *Malaysia Insider*, 21 July.

Ministry of Human Resources (2009) *National Employment Returns (NER) Report*, Putrajaya: Ministry of Human Resources.

Ministry of Women, Family and Community Development (MWFCD) (2004) *Report to the UN Committee for the Convention on the Elimination of All Forms of Discrimination Against Women (CEDAW) (First and Second Report)*, Kuala Lumpur: Ministry of Women, Family and Community Development.

Ministry of Women, Family and Community Development (MWFCD) (2004, 2007, 2008, 2009, 2010, 2012) *Statistics on Women, Family and Social Welfare*, Kuala Lumpur: Ministry of Women, Family and Community Development.

Ministry of Women, Family and Community Development (MWFCD) (2009) *Dasar Wanita dan Pelan Tindakan Pembangunan Wanita* [Women's Policy and Women's Development Action Plan], Kuala Lumpur: Ministry of Women, Family and Community Development.

Ministry of Women and Family Development (MWFCD) (2011) *Perangkaan Wanita, Keluarga dan Masyarakat 2012* [Statistics on Women, Family and Community 2012], Kuala Lumpur: Ministry of Women, Family and Community Development.

Ministry of Women, Family and Community Development and United Nations Development Programme (MWFCD and UNDP) (2007) *Measuring and Monitoring Gender Equality: Malaysia's Gender Gap Index*, Kuala Lumpur: Ministry of Women, Family and Community Development.

Ng, Cecilia (2011a) 'The hazy new dawn: democracy, women and politics in Malaysia', *Gender, Technology and Development*, 14(3)(November): 312–38.

Ng, Cecilia (2011b) *Gender and Rights: Analysis for Action*, Penang: Good Governance and Gender Equality Society and Women's Development Research Centre.

Ng, Cecilia (2012) 'Right time, right place and some luck: PWDC in the making', *Penang Monthly*, 4(12)(April): 18–21.

Ng, Cecilia, Zanariah Mohamad Noor and Maria Chin Abdullah (2003) *A Pioneering Step: Sexual Harassment and the Code of Practice in Malaysia*, Petaling Jaya: All Women's Action Society and Women's Development Collective.

Ng, Cecilia, Maznah Mohamad and tan beng hui (2006) *Feminism and the Women's Movement in Malaysia: An Unsung (R)evolution*, London: Routledge.

Noraida Endut (2013) 'More equality > less violence', Letters to the Editor, *New Straits Times*, 24 October, available at www.nst.com.my/opinion/letters-to-the-editor/more-equality-less-violence-1.383363 (accessed 24 October 2013).

Noraida Endut and Intan Hashimah Hashim (2011) 'The nature and impact of domestic violence: a study of survivors of wife abuse in Malaysia', in Cecilia Ng, Noraida Endut and Rashidah Shuib (eds), *Our Lived Realities: Reading Gender in Malaysia*, Penang: Universiti Sains Malaysia, pp. 43–64.

Ragayah Haji Mat Zain (2009) *Poverty Reduction, Social Integration and Development: The Formula for Peace?*, Bangi: Institut Kajian Malaysia dan Antarabangsa [Institute for Malaysian and International Studies].

Razavi, Shahra (ed.) (2009) *The Gendered Impacts of Liberalization: Towards 'Embedded Liberalism'?*, New York and London: Routledge.

Sangaralingam, Mageswari (2005) *Plantation Workers Face Poverty and Poison*, Consumers' Association of Penang, available at http://www.socialwatch.org/node/10932 (accessed 15 May 2014).

tan beng hui (2012) 'Sexual offences in Malaysia: the role and impact of Syariah criminal offences laws', in Nursyahbani Kajasungkana and Saskia E. Wieringa (eds), *The Future of Asian Feminism: Confronting Fundamentalisms, Conflicts and Neo-liberalism*, Newcastle upon Tyne: Cambridge Scholars Publishing, pp. 348–77.

tan beng hui and Shanthi Thambiah (in press) 'Women and inclusive growth in Malaysia', in *Malaysia National Human Development Report 2013: Redesigning an Inclusive Future*, Kuala Lumpur: United Nations Development Programme.

United Nations (UN) (1993) Declaration on the Elimination of Violence against Women, adopted by the UN General Assembly on 20 December 1993, UN Doc. A/RES/48/104.

United Nations Development Programme (UNDP) (2010) *Asia and the Pacific Human Development Report: Power, Voices, Rights – A Turning Point for Gender Equality in Asia and the Pacific*, Colombo: Macmillan for UNDP.

Women's Aid Organisation (WAO) (ed.) (2012) *CEDAW and Malaysia: Malaysian Non-Governmental Organisations' Alternative Report*, Petaling Jaya: WAO.

Yong Ooi Lin, Carol (2006) 'Autonomy re-constituted: social and gendered implications of dam resettlement on the Orang Asli of Peninsular Malaysia', *Gender, Technology and Development*, Special Issue: *Gender and Environmental Governance*, 10(1): 77–99.

29
Sexual citizenship in conflict[1]

Pang Khee Teik

Same-sex sexual acts became headline news in Malaysia in 1998 when the then deputy prime minister, Anwar Ibrahim, was deposed and charged with sodomy (Spaeth 1998). Anwar had been highly critical of corruption and cronyism within his own party, the United Malays National Organisation (UMNO), while openly expressing disagreement with Prime Minister Mahathir Mohamad's economic policies. Many saw the sodomy charge and imprisonment as political retribution from the prime minister (Berman 2008). The trials imprinted upon the collective psyche of the nation the criminality of the act, the stigma of the accusation and the otherness of homosexuals in Malaysia.

In 2008, troubled by the stigma but inspired by civil society movements, my colleagues and I, who ran an arts centre called The Annexe Gallery in downtown Kuala Lumpur, felt the time was ripe for a sexuality rights festival (Tan 2008). Consisting of a programme of forums, concerts, theatre, workshops, film screenings and talks, Seksualiti Merdeka was organised by a loose coalition of artists, activists, academics, volunteers and NGOs. We built our platform on discussing and celebrating the diversity of sexual orientations and gender identities, with principles such as sexual rights, bodily autonomy, and freedom from discrimination based primarily upon the Yogyakarta Principles (on the Application of International Human Rights Law in relation to Sexual Orientation and Gender Identity) (Yogyakarta Principles 2007) and the Universal Declaration of Human Rights (UDHR).

Seksualiti Merdeka quickly gained the support of international organisations based in Malaysia, such as Amnesty International and the United Nations, as well as many local NGOs, including progressive Muslim group Sisters in Islam, human rights organisation SUARAM, Women's Aid Organisation and the Malaysian Bar Council (Parthiban 2012; Lim 2011). Many of these groups rose together with growing civil society movements that emerged after Anwar's sacking. According to Parthiban (2012), these movements represent a critical cosmopolitanism uniting Malaysians across ethnic borders. The most sizeable of these is Bersih (literally, Clean), the Movement for Clean and Fair Elections (see Govindasamy, this volume). Bersih was viewed as a threat to the present government precisely because it undermined the legitimacy of the regime's mandate while seemingly advancing the cause of the opposition. Any association with this movement therefore risked the wrath of the government.

In November 2011, Seksualiti Merdeka's organisers took that risk and invited Bersih chairperson Ambiga Sreenevesan to officiate at our launch, hoping that we could tap into the growing political consciousness of Malaysians signalled by the popularity of Bersih. News of Ambiga's involvement quickly attracted the attention of pro-government NGOs such as Malay-rights group Perkasa, which called Ambiga the 'antichrist' for 'promoting deviant teachings in encouraging homosexuality' (Hafiz 2011a). The nexus from Seksualiti Merdeka to Ambiga, Ambiga to Bersih, and Bersih to the opposition coalition lined up the usual suspects in so fortuitous a way as to allow the ruling Barisan Nasional (BN, National Front) to target Anwar by shooting through Seksualiti Merdeka and the LGBTs (lesbian, gay, bisexual, transgender). The mounting campaign against LGBTs and sustained insinuation of Anwar's support for LGBTs carried on right up to the general election held eighteen months later.

Following a number of public protests against Seksualiti Merdeka, the police announced the festival was banned (*Star* 2011). The police later claimed they received up to 154 police reports against the festival (*Borneo Post* 2011). Reasons for the ban included that many groups were protesting against the programme, fears that 'the programme could create disharmony, enmity and disturb public order', that 'the law in the country did not recognise any deviationist activity that could destroy the practice of religious freedom', and that the festival 'threatens national security' (Goodman 2011).

Responding to the ban, Seksualiti Merdeka immediately released a press statement titled 'Stop Inciting Hatred Against Us! We Are Citizens of Malaysia' (Seksualiti Merdeka 2011). The statement begins:

> We are saddened that many Malaysians, including people's elected representatives, have seen fit to relentlessly persecute, stigmatise and discriminate all those who have found a safe space to dialogue and share information and knowledge on human rights during Seksualiti Merdeka's events.
>
> We are Malaysian citizens who are being denied our rights to our identity and self-determination.

After strongly asserting our citizenship, the statement goes on to appeal to a variety of rights frameworks to which we felt entitled: Malaysia's federal constitution, the National Human Rights Commission of Malaysia, the UDHR and the United Nations Charter. The statement's three demands are that the authorities 'condemn all forms of discrimination, stigmatisation and threats of violence and murder in the name of any religion or belief system'; 'uphold the human rights of the LGBTIQ community'; and 'uphold our right to conduct peaceful forums, workshops and performances'. The statement then announces the cancellation of all public events of the festival. It ends with a note of regret for the attacks on Ambiga, and finally, thanks our supporters. The expression of thanks was strategic, to remind the authorities that we were not alone, but were part of a growing movement. Portions of this statement were reproduced in many news sites and online media.

Identification as against

It was not until the ban of Seksualiti Merdeka that the term 'LGBT' became popular in the media, even though the organisers themselves more frequently employed 'LGBTIQ', adding intersex and queer. Previously, derogatory terms from the vernacular denoting 'inverted' (*songsang*), 'soft men' (*lelaki lembut*), 'hard women' (*wanita keras*), 'social ills' (*gejala-gejala sosial*) or even specifically forms of 'transgenderism' (*bapuk, ah kua*), were more common in the media. Many of these terms reveal the slippage between same-sex sexual attraction and gender non-conformity (Ismail 2001), representing the vague, fluid and unbounded ways many Malaysians view the myriad manifestations of non-normative gender and sexual expression. But this lack of clarity provides an interesting lens to understand the complex constitution of our subjectivities and subversive potential of our sexual desires.

As state actors spoke out against LGBTs as threats to the nation, and Seksualiti Merdeka responded by defending LGBTs, many in Malaysia found themselves confronted by a term that seemed to promise freedom and threaten them all at once. So, do they want to be identified by this term? And if they do, should they embrace the politics implicit in its deployment? With whom should they align themselves? The gay imaginary is not always so homogenous as sexual rights activists imagine. Malaysian gays who refuse subjection to the term 'LGBT' and its implied politics can redeploy the term to distance themselves from the project. Self-identified gays perhaps define for themselves what it means for them to be gay and to be citizens, and whether they want to utilise citizenship norms or sexual rights to get there. Queer theorist Eve Kosofksy Sedgwick said, 'to identify as must always include multiple processes of identification with. It also involves identification as against' (Sedgwick 1990: 60). So, some Malaysian LGBTs who may identify as lesbian, gay, bisexual or transgender could also find themselves resisting human rights because the politics appear counterintuitive to their own survival strategies or antithetical to their political stances.

The contestation over the potential for sexual citizenship in the public is therefore crucial for LGBTs in Malaysia in the way they imagine their place within the nation. Sexual citizenship is not a single theory, but a lens through which to collate various conflicting frameworks through which marginalised sexual subjects demand the rights of full citizenship. But what is citizenship? Formulating citizenship *not* as a status granted by the state, but as a process claimed by marginalised communities, prominent citizenship theorist Engin Isin proposes new activist figures, 'who enact political subjectivities and transform themselves and others into citizens by articulating ever-changing and expanding rights' (Isin 2009: 368). He calls this process acts of citizenship. Sexual rights activists of Seksualiti Merdeka, deemed as threats to the nation, perform such acts of citizenships through our very existence.

But what about the gays who resist us? Literature on 'tacit subjects' (Decena 2008) and closeted self-identified gays in different countries often analyses such sexual subjectivities through ethnographic lenses rather than political ones. Caught between the state that denies their belonging and activists who are forcing them out into public, these subjects are often reduced in research to a no-man's-land between the battlefronts. While these studies do not discount their agency in choosing to remain in the closet, they nonetheless contain their subjects' discourse within a scale so small that their agency seems to bear little imprint across the varying scales upon which acts of citizenship are enacted.

I offer a discourse analysis of texts by Malaysian sexual rights activists and those who resist them to demonstrate that speaking out against sexual rights politics has implications for the work of activists, and therefore constitutes acts of citizenship. This chapter looks specifically at two online texts:

1. 'Open Letter to Seksualiti Merdeka' published on gay blog Malaysian Gay Love, which hosted chats and video channels in which young Malaysians sometimes engaged in cyber sex (Malaysian Gay Love 2011). This website is now defunct.
2. 'Does Your Seksualiti Need Merdeka-ing?', an opinion piece published on online news site *The Malaysian Insider* as well as the writer's own blog. The writer uses the pseudonym of TykeOnABike (2011).

In the former, a group which claimed to represent the Malaysian Gay Love website demanded that Seksualiti Merdeka not disgrace the country and respect the position of Islam in Malaysia. They admit to being homosexuals but believe that homosexuals should practise 'homosexual activities' in private. There are three major areas in which they claim that Seksualiti Merdeka disgraces Malaysia: in the conflation of religion and the nation; in terms of Malaysia's position among other countries, and particularly, among other Islamic countries; and finally, on the issue of the public/private nature of homosexuality. In the second piece, the writer describes himself as part of an affluent and fashionable gay scene, in which his many gay friends are accepted by families, have good jobs, are able to afford material comfort and are therefore not living in fear, as claimed by Seksualiti Merdeka. He suggests that instead of highlighting differences, the political struggles of gays should be premised on similarities with straight people.

Excluded from any form of human rights

As the Malaysian government deployed anti-colonial discourse to demonise LGBTs as traitors to the nation, sexual rights activists responded by bolstering our citizenship claims with a range of norms from international frameworks, local human rights bodies and the federal constitution. Seksualiti Merdeka organisers built much of their case around being persecuted, stigmatised and discriminated. According to Angela Kuga Thas (2013: 2), this victimisation discourse comes from a 'traditional way of pushing for social change and social justice', and the amount of sympathy it evokes depends greatly on the strength of the evidence of violence.

But what if the violence is deemed as justified? Subjects required to adopt the subjectivities of victimhood in order to secure justice are always already approaching the state as *its* victims. Human rights victims are therefore resubmitting themselves within a system that is complicit with their victimisation. Oppression is then doubly reinforced from both state and non-state actors as they draw legitimisation from each other for their actions. Feeling empowered by a government that upholds Islam, therefore, those making threats to Seksualiti Merdeka may feel justified, even expected, to do so. According to them, LGBTs are already sinners, purveyors of 'animal culture' (Fernandez 2011), deserving to be punished and persecuted, even by extra-legal means. As Joseph Goh (2012: 149) points out:

> The act of tagging the festival as a promotion of the 'culture of animals' effectively renders all queer folk and their allies as little more than beasts. Consequently, queer folk are excluded from any form of human rights by virtue of their gender and sexual identities – how could any effort in support of *human* rights achieve real cogency if they are made on behalf of *animals*?

Does this mean, then, the pleas of victims fall on deaf ears locally? Or could this statement be performed for a different audience, perhaps a transnational one? Could the organisers be trying to rally the global community of human rights networks against the government of Malaysia? Could this be a script in which two parties – local sexual rights activists and transnational networks – perform a dialogue for the viewing of another audience, the Malaysian government?

Having found ourselves abjected as citizens within our countries but interpellated as 'human' within international human rights frameworks, sexual rights activists deployed the norms and attendant politics of the global stage. But Malaysian sexual rights activists were not necessarily trying to set international human rights norms in opposition to local norms.

Instead, by appearing to be in conversation with both international and local human rights networks, these norms were performed with the goal of shaming the Malaysian government for complicity in persecution. It also reminded the state of the fact that it has already subscribed to the very same international norms, as a member of the United Nations. It is in the nature of performances, however, to be susceptible to (deliberate) misreadings. It does not help that Western LGBT rights activists sometimes declaim about universal rights as if they are fighting for the rights of all LGBTs in all countries, making the uncritical assumption that their historical route for the acquisition of rights is one everyone else should travel, too. It also does not help that the highly publicised nature of their local battles, for example marriage equality in the US and UK, becomes mistaken as the agenda for LGBTs elsewhere, giving the impression that some of us are naively advocating for marriage rights while our very identities are still deemed illegal.

The Malaysian government, therefore, easily misrepresented this dialogue with transnational rights instruments as an act of collusion between sexual rights activists and Western liberal forces to undermine Islam. In this, the government, too, deployed victimisation discourse – except that the victim in their version was not the government, but the nation, its Muslim majority and Islam itself. The success of the government's discourse can be seen in how Malaysian Gay Love expresses the same defensive attitude on behalf of Islam and the nation.

Don't disgrace our country

Acutely aware of the bias that casts us as supporters of Western imperialist projects, and hoping to demonstrate that sexual rights are not alien to a local conception of justice, Seksualiti Merdeka organisers increasingly appealed to local norms. For this reason, we turned to the federal constitution first in our press statement. Constitutionalism is an emerging platform among Malaysian activists, including members of the Malaysian Bar and Bersih. Many of these activists have criticised Barisan Nasional policies, statements and practices for being unconstitutional. According to Malaysian academic Khoo Gaik Cheng (2013: 1), elements of Malaysian civil society have

> invoked the discourse of citizenship and constitutional rights to counter the dominant politics of race perpetuated by the National Front (Barisan Nasional) . . . that constitutional patriotism manifests itself as 'creative acts of citizenship' that energise democracy, and in its attempt at forming alternative but ultimately patriotic forms of solidarity, constitutional patriotism becomes a constituting process of citizen-making.

By appealing to the constitution before drawing on the UDHR, Malaysian sexual rights activists were attempting to draw the boundaries of citizenship to include ourselves and the rights we claim. By subsuming our rights within the borders of constitutionalism and citizenship, the statement recognises the nation-state as the author of our subjection and the recogniser of our rights. Even Seksualiti Merdeka's name, meaning Sexuality Independence or Independent Sexuality, calls attention to this bonding of borders of state and of bodies: the word 'Merdeka' is the same Sanskrit word used in Malaysia to mark Independence Day. By conflating sexual autonomy with the nation's autonomy, Seksualiti Merdeka signifies that the nation's independence and its people's independence are co-extensive. Read on its own, this fusion of nation and sexuality has the force of a declaration of independence: that the emancipation of sexual citizens is parallel to the nation's independence – and by extension, that the independence project is incomplete without the freedom of sexual subjects. UMNO, which has positioned itself as the party that fought for Malaysia's independence, naturally greets any challenge to its narrative as heresy.

An appeal to constitutionalism therefore forces Barisan Nasional into the defensive. Hence, de facto law Minister Nazri Aziz offered a creative interpretation to construe homosexuality as unconstitutional:

> According to Article 3 of the constitution, there is a general statement that says Islam is the religion of the federation. . . . What it means is that even though certain acts are determined as within the rights of the constitution but are against Islam, they are inconsistent as far as Islam is concerned.
>
> *(Hafiz 2011b)*

Article 3 of the constitution provides that 'Islam is the religion of the Federation', though scholars agree that according to its original framers, this 'shall not imply the State is not a secular state' (cited in Fernando 2006). Disregarding that Nazri Aziz's interpretation would render even eating pork and drinking alcohol unconstitutional in Malaysia, his remark seems to be an effect of former Prime Minister Mahathir Mohammad's declaration in 2002 that Malaysia is an 'Islamic fundamentalist state' (*CNN* 2002).

Some scholars believe that the Malaysian government's growing Islamisation is not simply to secure the unity of Muslims within the country, but also to align Malaysian Muslims within a global polity of fellow believers – the *ummah* – thereby gaining membership in a fraternity of an even larger imagined community (Barr and Govindasamy 2010). If liberal civil society voices represent a localised mobilisation of transnational discourse, so does the image of a stable Islamic polity. The advent of the Arab Spring has destabilised this global unity, however, fuelling the Malaysian government's paranoia regarding the possibility of similar revolutions in Malaysia should critical voices go unchecked. As Parthiban Muniandy points out, the activism of Seksualiti Merdeka, Bersih, and progressive Islamic women activists signals a 'democratisation of Islamic discourses, engendered by increasing fragmentation of Islamic authority' (Parthiban 2012: 584). This multi-vocality of Islamic discourses threatens and undermines the state's authorisation of a monolithic Islam and its position as guardian of that unity. Hence, Prime Minister Najib Razak, hoping to demonise all forms of plurality, insisted, 'LGBTs, pluralism, liberalism – all these "isms" are against Islam and it is compulsory for us to fight these' (Hafidz 2012).

Echoing this script, then, the Malaysian Gay Love editors' first salvo in their letter to Seksualiti Merdeka (2011) is that 'the official religion of the country is Islam as provided by the Federal Constitution'. This statement aligns the letter immediately with two axes of affiliation, the nation and the global *ummah*. The letter speaks strongly against Seksualiti Merdeka for disgracing the country and Islam, and diminishing others' opinions of the country and Islam. In fact, it mentions this concern three times:

1. '. . . if this programme is carried out, it will bring disgrace and diminish the opinions of other nationalities towards Islam and this country'.
2. 'Don't disgrace our country.'
3. 'We apologise if this letter upsets you. But our team consisting of citizens of all races agree that this programme will only disgrace Malaysia.'

It further exhorts: 'You must understand that Malaysia is a member of the Organisation of Islamic Cooperation (OIC). As a citizen of Malaysia you should put the people and the country first.' Promotion of the rights of homosexuals, it seems, has the force of separating Islam from the foundation of Malaysia, and thus alienating Malaysia from the OIC, and by extension, the global *ummah*. Furthermore, throughout the letter, the way Islam and the country are mentioned in relation to each other suggests a certain amount of slippage between the two. The letter begins with a reminder of the position of Islam within the federal constitution, implying that Islam is at the core of the nation and thereby equating the nation with Islam. When the writers further urge that as Malaysian citizens, we should 'put the people and the country first', they are not deploying a plural, cosmopolitan definition of 'people', but rather a unified *ummah* represented by the majority, a 'people' who have agreed to put the nation (and Islam) first, and who have therefore been empowered to represent the imaginary. For these sexual subjects, to be a citizen is to surrender to the national ideology. This means that both sexual rights activists and the gays who resist them similarly appealed to the logic of the nation-state and performed its scripts in hopes of being read as citizens. But it also means that both believed there is a possibility to become part of the nation if only their preferred scripts are followed.

Respect other religions

By asking the secular nation, a constitutional monarchy, to recognise the human rights of LGBTs, Seksualiti Merdeka and its supporters were deemed as touting a (per)version of Islam, as if demanding of it to adopt what is, according to most believers, clearly not permissible. Framing the promotion of LGBT recognition as a 'deviant teaching' and a 'new religion' portrays Seksualiti Merdeka as directly contravening the government's singular version of Islam (Hafiz 2011a). The logic that regards an assertion of citizenship as an attack on Islam reveals the slippage between nation and religion.

For the deputy inspector general of police, this concern was enough to justify a ban, ostensibly to protect national security. The national security in question, then, is a state of accord – not a threat of a military incursion by external forces, but of fragmentation of the nation's unity by internal forces. It demonstrates the import of the unifying discourse of religion in the construction of the national imaginary. This imaginary is productive in many ways, not the least in constituting the identity of the people, who can then brandish this identity as a political tool (Frith 2000), and, significantly, as a tool to determine who do not belong and who are enemies. Kamarulnizam Abdullah (1999: 275) explains the nexus of national security threats in Malaysia this way:

> Security in the context of Malaysia, as mentioned earlier in this article, reflects the idea of state security and not of national security in the traditional sense. The object of this security is, in large part, the government itself. . . . However, security of a government here will also refer to the security of a regime. The regime refers to the government-led party, that is, UMNO, which is a major factor in Malaysia's political stability.

By positioning itself as defender of the Malays and of Islam, UMNO effectively solders the ideological production of the social imaginary to its foundation. In this way, the defender of Islam becomes its symbol: threatening the symbol is seen as a threat against Islam. The party and its ideology are now conjoined, their fates bound together. As the government entrenches a politicised Islam in its discourse, it styles dissenters as dissenting against Islam itself. This leads to its deployment of an anti-colonial rhetoric when dealing with critics. As Shanon Shah (2013: 276) notes, 'many movements that question the Malaysian government's commitment to democracy and fundamental liberties (as enshrined in the Federal Constitution) are cast as "foreign plots" and "threats to Islam"'. He reminds us, however, that 'this rhetoric is linked to authoritarianism'. A threat to UMNO's authority becomes refashioned as a threat to the nation; but instead of risking exposure of this self-serving agenda, all UMNO needs to do is mask all threats to it as threats to Islam.

Having constructed the national imaginary as part of a monolithic global Islam, UMNO is able to wield this norm as a weapon against its opposition and dissidents. Hence, the request not to offend Muslim sensitivities, or to 'respect other religions' as in the letter from Malaysian Gay Love, is not a treaty for reciprocal respect. It is a warning: it serves to remind us who is in charge. The Muslim homosexuals of Malaysian Gay Love are then affirming their allegiance to the national ideology of the country as well as the global community of fellow believers, which they deploy in earnest, believing Islam and Malaysia are truly under threat by Western liberal human rights forces. The self-identified homosexual Muslims from Malaysian Gay Love, who state in their letter, 'Our decision is final', seem to be asserting their dominance among Malaysian homosexuals: non-Muslim homosexuals who accept their subordination to this social contract, can, like them, become citizens. Their 'requests', therefore, articulate the political hegemony they hope to continue to enjoy within the national imaginary, so long as Seksualiti Merdeka does not compromise their performance of the heteronormative nationalist script. Malaysian homosexuals who subscribe to ethno-religious nationalist ideologies, therefore, can have political investments antithetical to the projects of sexual rights activists. Any critique of the oppressive norms they are complicit in sustaining, then, must begin with an appreciation of their political affiliations, without presuming their alliance with other homosexuals. I propose that it is possible to initiate a critical engagement with them based upon their political subjectivities, beginning with 'affirm[ing] the values of dialogue, freedom of expression, and basic human dignity and rights' through interpretations of Islam (Shah 2013: 278).

'We have jobs. We have family. We have responsibilities.'

While the advancement of Islam is regularly touted as the nation's main priority, Michael Barr and Anantha Raman Govindasamy (2010: 294–95) argue that Islamisation is

> a tool in service of [the] ethnic agenda, a program of hegemony designed to reinforce Malay occupation at the heart of Malaysia's nation-building project and to condition non-Malays and non-Muslims to accept their assimilation into the Malaysian nation as subordinate, peripheral partners.

Citizens who are abased in the nationalist imaginary have to accept the political supremacy of the Malay and their own abjection. This social contract, however, would receive little support if it did not also offer non-Malays, particularly economically dominant Chinese, compensation for political subordination. In this section, I argue that some marginal sexual subjects, much like non-Malays, have learned to focus their energies on participation in the economy and the market. For them, economic citizenship offers a way of belonging to a nation that would not claim them as her own.

TykeOnABike's article 'Does Your Seksualiti Need Merdeka-ing?' provides a great illustration of the possibility for marginal subjects to enjoy rewards in exchange for their subservience to the market and the nation. He responds at length to Seksualiti Merdeka's promotional material that proclaims 'our firm belief that all Malaysians have the right to live and love without fear'. Asking, 'Are we truly a community that is oppressed and constantly living in fear?', TykeOnABike answers by pointing out gays who go to Bukit Bintang, a highly gentrified district in Kuala Lumpur full of swanky cafés, malls and five-star hotels. Their list of visible attributes, he writes, are: 'perfectly styled hair', 'unusually fashionable take on casual wear', 'gym-toned body', 'iPhone4', 'leather folio bound iPad' and 'Mini Cooper'. He adds:

> They live thriving, successful lives within a social network (and often, net worth) comparable to, if not better than many a straight man's. . . . So call me blind or perhaps a bit presumptuous, but from where I stand, this simply doesn't seem like a community living on the brink of fear.

He assumes that material accumulation is proof that Malaysian gays are not living in fear, as if social anxiety and material consumption were inversely proportional; and more pertinently, he provides a portrait of a gay scene that appears homogenously affluent. David Evans (1993) calls this the 'material construction of sexuality', where to be gay is to consume the culture of commoditised sexuality, and to be so appeased as to relinquish the struggle for equality. This conformity to a market-driven image of being gay is crucial to TykeOnABike's later point:

> The fight for acceptance and tolerance is not won by emphasising our differences. . . . It is won, I reckon, by proving to naysayers that at the end of the day, save for our choice of partners for life, homosexuals are really no different from the average straight bloke or lass strolling the streets of Kuala Lumpur. . . . We have jobs. We have family. We have responsibilities.

He flattens sexual diversity into a desire for conformity to heteronormative citizenship: family, job security and responsibilities. His descriptions of what successful gays look like, then, takes on a prescriptive tenor. In the context of the article, he marks desirable gay subjects as those who do not 'need to scream it out loud at every opportunity' but instead quietly enjoy the privileges that economic citizenship has to offer. In other words, they are allowed in public because they are not public about it. By extension, bad gays are the 'divas' who scream, who are too public.

The gays described by TykeOnABike, excluded from full citizenship by ethno-religious nationalism, have nonetheless found a home in the nation's market, not unlike the economic citizenship proffered to non-*bumiputera* in Malaysia through the social contract or 'ethnic bargain':

> The ethnic bargain encapsulated the communal settlement in which the Chinese agreed not to challenge *bumi* political dominance with the *quid pro quo* that they would acquire citizenship rights, continue with their way of life and that their economic dominance would be unaffected.
>
> *(Tan 2001: 950)*

Muslim homosexuals are called to prioritise and defend their nationalism if they want to become citizens, therefore, while both Muslim and non-Muslim gays can also protect their vulnerable position through economic participation. As TykeOnABike suggests, the economy offers a form of social insurance against other effects of disenfranchisement, so long as one's financial means are not threatened. But political gays could end up threatening this economic security by being too public. Such gays must remain quiet and accept their reduced rights within the realm allowed to them: in the market. Just like politically connected and economically empowered elites from the Chinese community, financially secure gays like TykeOnABike have an interest in sustaining the political culture that has guaranteed their survival, and furthermore, which they are complicit in sustaining. Like Malaysian Gay Love's editors, his request to serve the 'gay agenda' quietly is also a kind of warning. A dialogue with him, then, needs to highlight the economic inequalities that prevent poorer queer subjects from achieving the same social insurance affluent gays presently enjoy. At the same time, sexual rights activists could resist careless claims of representing all LGBTs, and focus on securing rights for self-representation for all, but especially for socially and economically disadvantaged groups.

A bed big enough

My attempt here to produce knowledge about subjects who have already refused sexual rights activists' earlier attempts to represent them gives rise to the potential for doubly misconstruing their subjectivities and thereby further denying their agency. In assessing my position, I accept part of Joseph Massad's critique of Arab LGBT activists, whom he accuses of being 'native informants' to the Gay International, a term he uses for Western gay rights activists trying to liberate gays and lesbians in non-Western societies. He writes that '[i]t is the discourse of the Gay International that both produces homosexuals, as well as gays and lesbians, where they do not exist, and represses same-sex desires and practices that refuse to be assimilated into its sexual epistemology' (Massad 2002: 363). Arguing that same-sex practices in the Arab world have historically been tolerated without the need to name them through Western sexual epistemologies, Massad blames activists and Gay International for causing the Arab state to crack down on sexual subjects. Meanwhile, he problematically assumes there is some ahistorical past of Arab sexuality that can be reclaimed, ignores that the state's legal instrument is itself a Western construct, and denies the rights of those who *do* identify as lesbian, gay, bisexual or transgender. He is right, however, in borrowing Foucault's notion of 'incitement to discourse'.

Incited by the discourse of the same sexual epistemologies, some Malaysian gays found themselves part of a political debate which they felt compelled to resist. As a sexual rights activist, I acknowledge our role in this incitement to discourse. But the discourse incited is not necessarily unproductive. The portrait of our subjectivities is incomplete if we disregard the multiplicity of sexual and gendered subjectivities in Malaysia, the citizenship discourses posited by politicians and enacted by citizens, our aspirations towards a future freedom based on any number of these different, even self-conflicting, political investments, and our desires to belong – which, much like our desires for intimacy, fluctuate through inchoate impulses and counter-discourses at once seductive and threatening.

Finally, I welcome Sedgwick's invitation to reparative, as opposed to paranoid, reading of discourse. She asks, 'What does a hermeneutics of suspicion and exposure have to say about social formations in which visibility itself constitutes much of the violence?' (Sedgwick 2003: 140). This question speaks to this project: the work of sexual rights activists has made Malaysian sexual dissidents visible and placed them within the state's gaze; the effort at knowledge production here risks repeating that outcome. To read reparatively is to realise that 'there can be terrible surprises, however, there can also be good ones'. It is to read with hope, because then 'the reader has room to realize that the future may be different from the present' (Sedgwick 2003: 146). I concede that my own investments in self-representation are mired in my investments for the equality of sexual minorities in Malaysia. Both have framed my readings of the subjects in this project. They are suffused with my hope for a future markedly different from the present, a future in which we attend to rather than dismiss each other's norms and resistances, a future in which subjects are not denied spaces to be the kind of citizens they want to be, sexual or otherwise. As we lay ourselves down to awkward sleep with one another tonight, may we make a bed out of this nation big enough for all to rise as citizens tomorrow.

Note

1 This chapter is adapted from my dissertation for an MA in Gender, Sexuality & Culture, at Birkbeck College, University of London, completed on 27 September 2013. The original title is 'Sexual Citizenship in Conflict: Malaysian Sexual Rights Activists and the Gays Who Resist Them'. I am grateful for the supervision of Silvia Posocco; the guidance of the professors of the modules, Kate Nichols, Matt Cook, Eddie Bruce-Jones and Amber Jacobs; the Sexuality Summer School of Manchester University; as well as the advice of Rahul Rao, Alicia Izharuddin and Lee Jiahui.

Bibliography

Barr, Michael D. and Anantha Raman Govindasamy (2010) 'The Islamisation of Malaysia: religious nationalism in the service of ethnonationalism', *Australian Journal of International Affairs*, 64(3): 293–311.

Bell, David and Jon Binnie (2000) *The Sexual Citizen: Queer Politics and Beyond*, Cambridge: Polity Press.

Bell, David and Jon Binnie (2004) 'Authenticating queer space: citizenship, urbanism and governance', *Urban Studies*, 41(9): 1807–20.

Berman, Alan (2008) 'The Anwar saga: sexuality and politics in contemporary Malaysia', in Damien W. Riggs (ed.), *Gay and Lesbian Issues and Psychology Review*, 4(3): 188–97.

Borneo Post (2011) 'Seksualiti Merdeka: 154 reports lodged', *Borneo Post Online*, 10 November, www.theborneopost.com/2011/11/10/seksualiti-merdeka-154-reports-lodged/ (accessed 25 September 2013).

CNN (2002) 'Mahathir: Malaysia is "fundamentalist state"', *CNN.com*, 18 June, available at http://edition.cnn.com/2002/WORLD/asiapcf/southeast/06/18/malaysia.mahathir/ (accessed 22 September 2013).

Decena, C.U. (2008) 'Tacit subjects', *GLQ: A Journal of Lesbian and Gay Studies*, 14(2–3): 339–59.

Duggan, Lisa (2002) 'The new homonormativity: the sexual politics of neoliberalism', in Russ Castronovo and Dana D. Nelson (eds), *Materializing Democracy: Towards a Revitalized Cultural Politics*, Durham: Duke University Press, pp.175–94.

Evans, David T. (1993) *Sexual Citizenship: The Material Construction of Sexualities*, London: Routledge.

Fernandez, Celine (2011) 'Malaysians debate ban of gay rights festival', *The Wall Street Journal*, 5 November, available at http://blogs.wsj.com/searealtime/2011/11/05/malaysians-debate-ban-of-gay-rights-festival/ (accessed 25 September 2013).

Fernando, J.M. (2006) 'The position of Islam in the constitution of Malaysia', *Journal of Southeast Asian Studies*, 37(2): 249–66.

Frith, Tabitha (2000) 'Ethno-religious identity and urban Malays in Malaysia', *Asian Ethnicity*, 1(2): 117–29.

Goh, Joseph N. (2012) 'The word was not made flesh: theological reflections on the banning of Seksualiti Merdeka 2011', *Dialog*, 51(2): 145–54.

Goodman, J. David (2011) 'Malaysian authorities block a festival celebrating gays', *The New York Times*, 3 November, available at www.nytimes.com/2011/11/04/world/asia/malaysia-gay-festival-is-banned.html?_r=0 (accessed 13 September 2013).

Hafidz Baharom (2012) 'Najib: LGBTs, liberalism, pluralism are enemies of Islam', *The Malaysian Insider*, 19 July, available at www.themalaysianinsider.com/malaysia/article/najib-lgbts-liberalism-pluralism-are-enemies-of-islam (accessed 15 May 2013).

Hafiz Yatim (2011a) 'Perkasa: act against Ambiga, the "antichrist"', *Malaysiakini*, 5 November, available at www.malaysiakini.com/news/180332 (accessed 25 September 2013).

Hafiz Yatim (2011b) 'Nazri: homosexuality IS unconstitutional', *Malaysiakini*, 21 November, available at www.malaysiakini.com/news/181958 (accessed 15 May 2013).

Halim Salleh (2000) 'Globalization and the challenges to Malay nationalism as the essence of Malaysian nationalism', in Leo Suryadinata (ed.), *Nationalism and Globalization: East and West*, Singapore: Institute of Southeast Asian Studies, pp. 132–74.

Heng Pek Koon (1997) 'The New Economic Policy and the Chinese community in Peninsular Malaysia', *The Developing Economies*, 35(3): 262–92.

Isin, Engin F. (2009) 'Citizenship in flux: the figure of the activist citizen', *Subjectivity*, 29(1): 367–88.

Ismail Baba (2001) 'Gay and lesbian couples in Malaysia', in Gerard Sullivan and Peter A. Jackson (eds), *Gay and Lesbian Asia: Culture, Identity, Community*, New York: Harrington Park Press, pp. 143–64.

Jaya Sharma (2009) 'Reflections on the constructions of heteronormativity', *Development*, 52(1): 52–55.

Kamarulnizam Abdullah (1999) 'National security and Malay unity: the issue of radical religious elements in Malaysia', *Contemporary Southeast Asia*, 21(2): 261–82.

Khoo Gaik Cheng (2013) 'The rise of constitutional patriotism in Malaysian civil society', *Asian Studies Review*, 26 June, pp. 1–20.

Lim Chee Wee (2011) 'Press release: if Malaysia wants to be respected as a democracy, it must stop persecuting sexual minorities', *Malaysian Bar*, 2 November, available at www.malaysianbar.org.my/press_statements/press_release_if_malaysia_wants_to_be_respected_as_a_democracy_it_must_stop_persecuting_sexual_minorities.html (accessed 13 September 2013).

Malaysian Gay Love (2011) 'Letter to Seksualiti Merdeka', *Malaysiangay.co.cc blog*, 1 November, retrieved from http://Malaygay4u.blogspot.com (accessed 27 January 2013; note: blog removed).

Massad, Joseph Andoni (2002) 'Re-orienting desire: the gay international and the Arab world', *Public Culture*, 14(2): 361–85.

Maznah Mohamad (2002) 'Towards a human rights regime in Southeast Asia: charting the course of state commitment', *Contemporary Southeast Asia*, 24(2): 230–51.

Parthiban Muniandy (2012) 'Malaysia's coming out: critical cosmopolitans, religious politics and democracy', *Asian Journal of Social Science*, 40: 582–607.

Sedgwick, Eve Kosofsky (1990) *Epistemology of the Closet*, Berkeley and Los Angeles: University of California Press.

Sedgwick, Eve Kosfsky (2003) 'Paranoid reading vs. reparative reading, or, you're so paranoid you probably think this essay is about you', in Eve Kosfsky Sedgwick, *Touching Feeling: Affect, Pedagogy, Performativity*, London and Durham: Duke University Press, pp. 123–52.

Seksualiti Merdeka (2011) 'Stop inciting hatred against us! We are citizens of Malaysia', press statement by the organisers of Seksualiti Merdeka, *Seksualiti Merdeka*, Blog, 5 November, available at www.seksualitimerdeka.org/2011/11/stop-inciting-hatred-against-us-we-are.html (accessed 12 September 2013).

Shah, Shanon (2013) 'The Malaysian dilemma: negotiating sexual diversity in a Muslim-majority Commonwealth state', in Corinne Lennox and Matthew Waites (eds), *Human Rights, Sexual Orientation and Gender Identity in The Commonwealth: Struggles for Decriminalisation and Change*, London: Institute of Commonwealth Studies, School of Advanced Study, University of London, pp. 261–85.

Shamsul Amri Baharuddin (1997) 'The economic dimension of Malay nationalism: the socio-historical roots of the new economic policy and its contemporary implications', *The Developing Economies*, 35(3): 240–61.

Spaeth, Anthony (1998) 'Whose trial?', *TIME World*, 16 November, http://www.time.com/time/world/article/0,85999,2053873,00.html (accessed 27 September 2013).

Star (2011) 'Seksualiti Merdeka movement festival banned', *The Star Online*, 3 November, available at www.thestar.com.my/story.aspx?file=%2F2011%2F11%2F3%2Fnation%2F20111103172539&sec=n (accessed 13 September 2013).

Tan, Eugene K.B. (2001) 'From sojourners to citizens: managing the ethnic Chinese minority in Indonesia and Malaysia', *Ethnic and Racial Studies*, 24(6): 949–78.

Tan, Sylvia (2008) 'Malaysian heartbreak hero: Pang Khee Teik', *Fridae.asia*, 15 August, available at www.fridae.asia/newsfeatures/2008/08/15/2105.malaysian-heartbreak-hero-pang-khee-teik?n=sea&nm=pang+khee+teik (accessed 13 September 2013).

Thas, Angela M. Kuga (2013) 'No right to live? Malaysia's Islam and implications for its sexual minority storytellers', paper presented at 4th Global Conference on Storytelling: Global Reflections on the Narrative, Prague, Czech Republic, 21–24 May, available at www.inter-disciplinary.net/probing-the-boundaries/wp-content/uploads/2013/04/Thas.pdf (accessed 22 September 2013).

TykeOnABike (2011) 'Does your Seksualiti need Merdeka-ing?', *The Malaysian Insider*, 10 November, available at www.themalaysianinsider.com/sideviews/article/does-your-sexuality-need-merdeka-ing-tykeonabike/ (accessed on 27 January 2013).

Yogyakarta Principles on the Application of International Human Rights Law in Relation to Sexual Orientation and Gender Identity (2007) available at www.yogyakartaprinciples.org/principles_en.htm (accessed 13 September 2013).

Part IV
International relations and security

Overview

Meredith L. Weiss

Malaysia's international profile and engagements have been perhaps less actively contested or vacillating than its domestic politics and policy. Even here, though, Malaysia has changed tack with economic transformations, strategic realignments, security flash-points, leadership transitions, and fluctuating visions of what Malaysia's place and priorities should be. While Malaysia is an active, founding member of the Association of Southeast Asian Nations (ASEAN) and a trusted defence and trading partner with Asian and 'Western' states alike, Malaysia's regional and global position has not been entirely consistent. Rather, Malaysian foreign policy reveals both complementary and conflicting goals for the country's orientation vis-à-vis the region, a global *ummah* (Muslim community), and the international scene.

To begin, Karminder Singh Dhillon enumerates the array of challenges facing Malaysia. These present sometimes-contradictory priorities or constraints, from developing an open and competitive economy while still protecting domestic affirmative action policies, to cultivating encompassing and varied alliances without compromising the state's Islamist identity and commitments, to asserting a middle-power role regionally and globally, to ensuring foreign policy serves the interests of domestic regime maintenance. While the Mahathir years were rocky ones for Malaysia's ties with the US and Europe in particular, trade, security, and diplomatic relations have flourished since. Meanwhile, Malaysia has pursued closer economic and other ties with China, Singapore, Indonesia, and the wider ASEAN region, all while it aims to achieve fully developed and middle-power status.

The next chapter, by Lai Yew Meng, reiterates that economic partnerships are only part of the foreign policy picture. Malaysia faces, too, a range of traditional and, increasingly, non-traditional security threats, mandating careful foreign and domestic policy-making. Malaysia's most pressing security challenges in the past have been internal, most notably, communist insurgency from 1948 to 1989. Regionally, while ASEAN mechanisms, norms, and institutions offer safeguards against flare-ups, these are not independently adequate – each member state also must take independent, bilateral and multilateral safeguards. Malaysia's is a generally peaceful neighbourhood, yet subject to outbursts in the volatile South China Sea as well as intermittent territorial and maritime-territorial disputes. Radical Islam, too, presents both internal and external threat dimensions, but the state has taken strong proactive and reactive measures. 'Security' in the contemporary context, though, as Lai details, encompasses everything from maritime-territorial sovereignty, to transborder crimes, to environmental challenges, mandating similarly wide-ranging responses, including a continuing need to modernise all branches of the armed forces.

Heng Pek Koon zeroes in on the bilateral relationship that perhaps best embodies Malaysia's balance between warm embrace and arm's length distancing: its alliance with the United States. The US–Malaysia relationship has been strong throughout Malaysia's independent history, primarily in economic terms, but increasingly also in terms of security and US regional strategy. That said, especially under the less-than-tactful Mahathir, and given deep disagreement with, for instance, US policy toward Palestine, ties have been battered. Prime Minister Najib in particular has not only resuscitated the relationship, building on the efforts of his predecessor, Abdullah Ahmad Badawi, but has brought it to new highs; Malaysia has benefited from the US's increasing 'pivot' toward Asia. That said, Heng argues for a more solid, comprehensive footing for this still relatively informal, if important, bilateral alliance.

Arguably equally significant is Malaysia's relationship with the much closer, increasingly formidable China. Kuik Cheng-Chwee argues that the asymmetrical relationship between Malaysia and China previously represented more of a threat – particularly in the throes of the Cold War – but now is largely (mutually) beneficial. By the 1980s, Malaysian leaders had set aside ideological anticommunism and concerns over Chinese support for the Malayan Communist Party, to focus on economics. Kuik argues that Malaysian elites recognise the political advantages to be gained from closer economic and strategic ties with their more powerful, much larger neighbour. Moreover, development of the Malaysia–China relationship has been in tandem with, and symbiotically linked with, expansion also of China–ASEAN ties, signalling and supporting deeper, reciprocally advantageous regional integration.

Ruhanas Harun suggests that although Malaysia's relations with Europe generate far less scholarly or public attention than its ties with the twin giants of the US and China, in fact, these connections have remained quietly percolating and significant. The US and China clearly dominated Malaysia's Cold War agenda, yet even then, Malaysia moved toward closer economic ties in particular, not only with Britain (though ties with Britain have been intimate from the outset), but also with the rest of Europe. Since then, Malaysia has worked to build relations with the former communist countries of Eastern Europe, as well, with ever-deeper social and cultural linkages increasingly complementing close economic and political collaboration.

Finally, Carolin Liss takes us offshore, to the continuing prevalence of piracy in Malaysian waters. Such attacks have a long history, albeit with diverse parameters, perpetrators, and targets. Contemporary maritime pirates may be either organised gangs or opportunistic sea-robbers; they attack a wide range of vessels, sometimes violently. While the nature of these crimes often mandates transnational cooperation in response, such cooperation is hampered by concerns of national sovereignty, ASEAN's norm of non-interference, conflicting interests, and contending maritime-territorial claims. Despite fluctuations in the numbers of attacks in Malaysian waters, piracy remains a key concern for government as well as commercial interests. Yet patrols, Liss suggests, however well resourced and coordinated, are not enough; the Malaysian government needs to address root causes of poverty, radical political groups, corrupt or lax regulation, and more.

30
Foreign policy priorities

Karminder Singh Dhillon

A nation's foreign policy priorities are inevitably determined by a complex interplay among domestic and exogenous factors, regional and global realities, and national needs. As a state with middle-power aspirations and ambitions of becoming a fully developed nation by the close of the decade, Malaysia's foreign policy priorities are essentially driven by the aforementioned inputs, albeit within the parameters of its unique social and cultural setting as well as the national aspirations defined by its political leadership.

Malaysia's foreign policy priorities include keeping the nation relevant in a rapidly globalising world while preserving regional solidarity, balancing domestic constraints with the imperatives of an open economy, forging international initiatives while retaining Islamic credentials, and maintaining regime interests while pursuing national goals. Malaysia's experience has been one of embracing globalisation while attempting to keep out those aspects that are defined as undesirable by the political leadership. The foreign policy challenge is, therefore, one of finding the balance between the desire for social and cultural sovereignty and the aspiration to be globalised.

Given that Malaysia is an open and developing economy, the parameters of the nation's developmental-state aspirations present a second foreign policy challenge. The challenge is to strike a balance between the free inflow of foreign funds, technology and expertise – all considered vital for the economic leap that must be taken by 2020 – and the constrictions of affirmative action-based initiatives. Since a variety of domestic economic and industrial activities are the direct result of the government's affirmative action policies and require government intervention for their continued survival, protecting them from the foreign competition that would inevitably result from opening up the nation's economy presents yet another constraint.

A third challenge has to do with the desire of the nation for middle-power status within the region, at least, if not globally. Malaysian foreign policy is thus tasked with the responsibility of forging a wide variety of international initiatives, building a reputation as a leader within the ASEAN (Association of Southeast Asian Nations) region, and building friendships with a wide spectrum of neighbours and nations. At the same time, Malaysia desires to retain its Islamic credentials – an aspiration which can limit the parameters of these other initiatives.

The final challenge has to do with the nature of the Malaysian political system. Regime maintenance occupies a crucial position, to the extent that foreign policy initiatives are deployed towards that objective. Within such a context, safeguarding regime interests while pursuing higher national goals becomes a sticky challenge for foreign policy makers and practitioners.

Recalibrating ties with Western countries

The post-Mahathir regime inherited a foreign policy that was starkly anti-Western, both in rhetoric and substance. Of seven major foreign policy initiatives that spanned the twenty-two-year Mahathir era (Dhillon 2009: ix) four – Buy British Last, Anti-Commonwealth, Look East and Third World Spokesmanship – had explicit anti-Western orientations. A fifth initiative, Regional Engagement, was implicitly anti-Western, in that Malaysia not only strove to limit Western and US influence in the region, but sought to balance it with Japanese sway. The sixth, Islamic Posturing, was anti-Western largely in rhetoric. Only one initiative, Commercial and Developmental Diplomacy, remained devoid of any anti-Western flavour, given that Western investment, technology and expertise were crucial for the impressive structural and physical development that defined the Mahathir era. Within sixteen component foreign policy initiatives of the Mahathir era, eight – those relating to Antarctic policy, apartheid, the global environment, South–South cooperation, the New World Order, Palestine, the Gulf Wars of 1991 and 2003, and Bosnia – contained anti-Western elements. The Mahathir era also took pride in developing cordial ties with regimes such as Cuba, Sudan, Iran and Myanmar – all considered as rogue states and outcasts in the eyes of their Western antagonists.

The most strident anti-Western foreign policy stance was taken during the concluding years of the Mahathir era, which coincided with the Asian financial crisis and the attendant political predicament that resulted from the sacking of Mahathir's heir apparent, Anwar Ibrahim. Mahathir blamed both crises on the West and took stances that were decidedly anti-Western, such as condemning hedge funds, shunning the IMF and withdrawing from global currency markets. Kuik (2012b: 1) surmises that foreign policy in the Mahathir era, while considering the United States to be an economic and security partner, simultaneously viewed it as a source of immense political irritation and pain. Though in aligning itself with the US in the latter's war on terror following the events of September 11, the Mahathir regime was accorded an opportunity to rehabilitate its image, it was not enough to cleanse the two-decades-long era of its anti-Western credentials. The result was that the post-Mahathir regime inherited a foreign policy that needed to recalibrate its ties with the US and the Western world.

The Abdullah Badawi administration set the tone for reconciliation by softening the confrontational and nationalistic foreign policy tenor of his predecessor. Badawi decisively ended blunt and intemperate criticism of the US's global behaviour, anti-Semitic statements, disparagement of former colonial power Britain, condemnation of global institutions as being 'tools of the West', denigration of 'Western values', vilification of 'Western ethics' and assertions that the West was attempting to 'recolonise' the developing world. In what can be seen as the initial outcome of reprioritising its foreign policy orientations, in 2008, Malaysia won authorisation to purchase over US$269 million worth of arms from the US, more than any other state in Southeast Asia (Johnson 2010: 2). Further substantive shifts in Malaysian foreign policy in this regard were, however, weakened in the aftermath of the 2008 general election, which delivered five state governments to the opposition, denied the Barisan Nasional (National Front, BN) coalition its traditional two-thirds majority, and fatally weakened

Badawi's position within his party, the United Malays National Organisation (UMNO). Any new direction in foreign policy vis-à-vis Malaysia's ties with the Western world was further complicated by the Mahathir factor. The former prime minster, a vociferous critic of Badawi, was seemingly able to muster enough clout within UMNO to create a faction whose agenda was to revert to Mahathirism. It is on account of such dynamics that in January 2009, Malaysia suspended its free trade agreement (FTA) talks with the US.

Even though Prime Minister Najib Razak took over the reins of state in April 2009 with the tacit support of Mahathir's faction, foreign policy under his administration leveraged what Badawi had grasped with regard to reconciling with the US and West (see also Heng, this volume). Bilateral trade with the US climbed; Malaysia became the latter's sixteenth-largest trading partner, with trade flows amounting to US$44 billion in Najib's first year. Within the same period, Malaysia enjoyed US$757,000 worth of military education training. In 2010, Malaysia became the second-largest recipient of US investments in the region, after Singapore (Murray *et al.* 2012: 10). Under Najib, Malaysia has, for the first time, participated in US-led Cobra Gold regional military exercises. Najib's foreign policy further committed Malaysia to renewed negotiations on the Acquisition and Cross Servicing Agreement. In meeting with US President Barack Obama in April 2010, Najib declared that Malaysia's relationship with the US was approaching a 'new beginning' – a direct acknowledgement of Obama's Cairo speech, in which the president spoke of 'new beginnings' between America and Muslims worldwide (Najib 2010a). Najib agreed to contribute towards the US-led reconstruction of Afghanistan and to collaborate on issues ranging from nuclear non-proliferation and human trafficking to Iran and North Korea (Murray *et al.* 2012: vii). That May, Malaysia revived its FTA talks with the US and signalled its intention to join the emerging Trans-Pacific Partnership Agreement (*New Straits Times*, 31 May 2012). In July 2010, Malaysia began sending medical military personnel to Afghanistan (Ruhanie 2011: 140). In the same year, Malaysia passed the US-sponsored Strategic Trade Bill, which was designed to thwart illicit arms transactions and trafficking of nuclear and other strategic material (Bernama, 20 December 2010). Malaysia also cooperated with the US to cut off transfer payments for weapons transactions with Pyongyang.

A number of meetings among and visits by leaders of both countries, including the US secretary of state and the commander of the US Pacific Command, as well as a second Najib–Obama meeting, made clear that the recalibration of Malaysia–US ties was real. During Secretary of Defense Chuck Hagel's visit to Kuala Lumpur in August 2013, discussions touched on defence collaboration in various areas, including regional and international security, military technologies and exchanging information (*Star*, 26 August 2013). In September 2013, army personnel from Malaysia and the US took part in a ten-day joint military exercise in Kedah – another first (*Star*, 18 September 2013). In what can be described as a break from tradition, Foreign Minister Anifah Aman, in choosing not to condemn the US's position on Syria, said that bilateral ties with the US would not be affected should the US go ahead with its plans to strike Syria (*Star*, 6 September 2013).

Under Najib, Kuala Lumpur has similarly moved to improve ties with Britain. Malaysian foreign policy focuses on attracting British investments in high-technology, value-added, knowledge-based and skill-intensive industries – areas of growth vital for Malaysia to move into high-income nation status. Britain has since become Malaysia's eighth-largest investor, with investments worth US$2 billion, and eighteenth-largest trading partner, with US$4.4 billion worth of trade (*Star*, 10 September 2013).

Najib has further attempted to enhance Malaysia's political and economic cooperation with other major Western nations through the European Union (see also Ruhanas, this volume). In late 2010, Malaysia and the EU commenced negotiations focusing on trade in services, green technology and trade remedies. The talks have progressed well, with the latest round concluded in July 2013 (MITI 2013). EU exports to Malaysia in 2012 amounted to about €15 billion, while Malaysian exports to the EU reached about €20 billion. In 2012, Malaysia recorded a trade surplus of nearly €6 billion with the EU. Globally, Malaysia is the EU's twenty-third-largest trading partner; the EU is also the largest source of foreign direct investment (FDI) into Malaysia. In 2012, it invested €953 million, far exceeding Japan (€702 million) and Saudi Arabia (€652 million) (*Malaysian Insider*, 3 July 2013).

Prioritising relations with China

China factors prominently in Malaysia's foreign policy for three main reasons (see also Kuik, this volume). First, China's economic growth, in particular the opening of the nation's markets and expansion of investment outflows, are too lucrative to ignore. Malaysia's increasing foreign policy focus on trade, FDI and new markets for Malaysian exports ensures capitalisation upon China's emergence. Second, China is fast becoming the region's military superpower. Malaysian calculations relating to defence and security inevitably must factor in China's military designs and intentions. Third, China is the motherland of up to a third of Malaysia's population. A psychological link persists between China and this significant and influential minority group. Malaysian foreign policy stances towards China are expected to affect Malaysian Chinese perceptions of their own government.

The Najib administration has made enhanced cordiality and maximised engagement its guiding principles in Malaysia–China relations in economic and defence matters, respectively. Greater cordiality allows for Malaysia to maximise economic and diplomatic benefits from a fast-prospering regional neighbour, while maximised engagement allows for smaller and weaker Malaysia to deploy both bilateral and multilateral diplomacy with a rising superpower in defence and security matters.

China was the first country outside of ASEAN that Prime Minister Najib visited. The two countries have since agreed on a bilateral framework of cooperation covering thirteen areas (*Star*, 4 June 2009). Najib acknowledges that Malaysia's relationship with China is based upon Malaysia's national interests (Kuik 2012a: 16). Chief amongst these interests is the forging of business deals to enable Najib's Economic Transformation Plan (ETP) to succeed (Lim 2009). Measures taken under the auspices of the ETP include licensing China's largest bank, ICBC, to operate in Malaysia, opening a Malaysian National Bank office in Beijing, and doing away with visas for Chinese investors from government and government-linked entities.

In the Badawi period, China became Malaysia's fourth-largest trading partner, with US$39 billion in bilateral trade in 2008. In the Najib era, the regional giant has risen to become Malaysia's largest trading partner. In 2011, bilateral trade was valued at US$90 billion, one-third of which value accrued to Malaysia as surplus (*Star*, 16 March 2012). By then, China had become Malaysia's biggest export market and number-one buyer of Malaysia's main agricultural product, palm oil. In 2012, Malaysia's trade volume with the second-largest economy in the world increased by another 14 percent. Chinese Premier Wen Jiabao visited Malaysia in 2011, then Najib reciprocated with a second visit to generate even greater inflows of investment from China. Both countries have since renewed a bilateral currency swap deal for US$35 billion, allowing more businesses to settle trade transactions in local currencies. The result has been a four-fold jump in trade conducted in local currencies (*New Straits Times*, 2 April 2012). China's foreign minister, Wang Yi, called on Najib in August 2013 (*Malay*

Mail, 3 August 2013). Moreover, Chinese tourists and students have become almost as crucial to Kuala Lumpur as Chinese businessmen and investors.

Foreign policy under Najib has also attempted to improve relations within the defence and security realm. A number of high-level visits and meetings involving the Malaysian chief of defence forces, the Chinese minister of public security and the defence ministers from both countries have been undertaken in this regard. Despite pledges of 'strategic and cooperative relations' in 2011 (Bernama, 28 April 2011), 'pragmatic military cooperation' in 2012, and 'high level discussions' over cross-border crime in February 2012 (Bernama, 28 April 2012), defence cooperation remains political and diplomatic at best.

There is no evidence to suggest that Malaysia has accepted a Chinese-led regional order. In fact, the principle of 'equidistance' vis-à-vis great powers remains very much alive within Malaysian foreign policy when it comes to defence of the region. Najib articulated this position as early as 2010, saying ASEAN wants to engage China 'as much as it wants to engage with the United States' (Kuik 2012a: 27). China's assertive actions in the South China Sea with regard to the Philippines, Manila's decision to move strategically closer to the US, and China's strong protest against the joint submission by Malaysia and Vietnam to the UN Commission on the Limits of the Continental Shelf in 2009 have not gone unnoticed in Kuala Lumpur. Malaysia has also not overlooked Chinese actions in retaliation against Vietnam's maritime claims.

Yet, Malaysia's foreign policy stance is a calculated dismissal of any threat from China. Such a position pivots on pragmatism. The substantial economic, trade and investment dividends which flow from a friendly relationship with China and Malaysia's own domestic developmental priorities mandate such a stance. Pragmatism dictates that openly considering a proximate economic and military giant as a threat would not only lead to loss of economic benefits, but open Malaysia to potential strategic harm. Najib spoke of the economic side of such a calculation during Wen Jiabao's visit to Malaysia in 2011. He described Malaysia–China ties as 'having paid us dividends' and that Malaysia considered China as a 'friend, not adversary; a partner, not a rival' (Najib 2011). Malaysia is not unaware that China's GDP is expected to surpass that of the United States by around 2020 and that its economic strength will command significant regional and global influence. Malaysian foreign policy priorities in the realms of defence and security with regard to China are thus two-pronged: first, to place more reliance on multilateral instruments such as the ASEAN Regional Forum (ARF) and ASEAN Defence Minister's Meeting; and second, to remain engaged with China. This means that the focus of bilateral ties will remain in the economic sphere.

Building solidarity with neighbours and the region

Malaysia's two closest neighbours, Singapore and Indonesia, factor prominently in foreign policy formulation, albeit for different reasons. Singapore enjoys a geographical and historical proximity which is made complex by intense competition in the realms of economics, defence, foreign relations, sovereignty and territoriality. Indonesia, on the other hand, shares cultural, social, linguistic and religious affinities with Malaysia which are complicated by territorial issues, competition over leadership roles in the region and large volumes of immigrant labour upon which Malaysia is heavily reliant. Thailand, the Philippines and Brunei likewise share land and sea borders with Malaysia and enjoy a range of common issues. Yet these three nations, together with Cambodia, Laos, Vietnam and Myanmar, belong to a comparatively lesser league as far as their impact on the direction of Malaysian foreign policy is concerned.

The Badawi administration inherited a Malaysia–Singapore relationship that was fraught with tensions. Issues that had created strains included the price and tenure of a continuous supply of raw water to the island state, Singapore's massive land reclamation projects, use of Johor airspace by Singapore air force jets, the relocation of Malaysian Customs, Immigration and Quarantine (CIQ) checkpoints, withdrawal of funds from the Singapore Central Provident Fund by Malaysian workers leaving the state, and construction of a new bridge to replace the causeway (Dhillon 2009: 128–40). Underlying these issues were feelings of suspicion regarding Singapore's military prowess, intense competition for FDI, trade and port usage as well designs for the region. It did not help that the two nations were each helmed for decades by combative political strongmen who believed in the utility of rhetorical grandstanding.

Najib's policy towards Singapore clearly aims at warming ties. He visited Singapore within his first hundred days in office, announcing Malaysia's desire that contentious issues be resolved. In July 2009, Lee Kuan Yew visited Malaysia. Within a year, a long-standing dispute over three parcels of land within Singapore owned by Malaysian Railways had been resolved, with both sides agreeing to a land swap and joint development of the parcels (*Star*, 23 June 2010). This agreement represented a breakthrough in resolving the equally thorny issue of the relocation of the Malaysia and Singapore CIQ checkpoints from the heart of Singapore to the Woodlands train checkpoint in the northern part of the island (*Straits Times*, 20 September 2010). Singapore is expected to be the lead investor in the newly launched Iskandar Regional Development Plan in Johor. The two nations are also considering a third bridge to improve connectivity and accessibility, possibily at Pengerang (*Star*, 10 September 2013). Even if a number of serious issues have not been fully resolved, the overall tone of bilateral ties has remained cordial, as a September 2013 visit by Singapore's president to Malaysia, and a planned reciprocal visit by the Malaysian king, affirm.

Despite a plethora of cultural, linguistic and religious similarities, Badawi inherited a Malaysia–Indonesia relationship that was likewise testy. Suharto had opposed a number of Mahathir's favourite foreign policy stances, such as South–South Cooperation and the East Asian Economic Caucus (EAEC). As the leader of the world's most populous Muslim nation and the Non-Aligned Movement (NAM), Suharto was chagrined that Mahathir sought to become the spokesman of the Third World and the Islamic world. The fact that Suharto's Indonesia was allied to the US – the direct target of Mahathir's spokesmanship – intensified the strains further.

Given that the Badawi administration had no interest in pursuing Mahathir's proclivities, much of the friction with Indonesia dissipated. Najib visited Indonesia in April 2009 to warm up bilateral relations with Susilo Bambang Yudhoyono's economically and politically reformed Indonesia. Under Najib, Malaysia has become Indonesia's second-largest investor in industries ranging from petroleum and petrochemicals to plantations and banking (*Star*, 8 June 2009). It has been argued that two factors driving Malaysia into a cosier relationship with Indonesia are regional interests and growing trade links with China (Khadijah 2011: 444). Such is the convergence of stances on both factors that erratic but widely publicised protests in Jakarta over alleged abuse of Indonesian labour migrants in Malaysia have failed to cause any serious impact. In November of 2009, Indonesian President Susilo Bambang Yudhoyono visited Kuala Lumpur to reassure Najib that the protests had no government endorsement. Malaysia chose not to retaliate, and within a year, Najib's deputy had declared that Malaysia and Indonesia shared an 'unbreakable' bond (*Malaysian Insider*, 27 September 2010).

Regionally, ASEAN continues to remain one of Malaysia's top foreign policy priorities. The focus of the Najib administration, however, is on ASEAN as a trading bloc. Malaysia thus continues to promote free trade aggressively and has implemented three FTAs, including the ASEAN FTA, ASEAN–Australia–New Zealand FTA and ASEAN–India FTA in Goods.

Aspiring to middle-power status

Malaysia's defence budget hovers in the region of RM13 billion, peaking at RM14.6 billion in 2008 and 2009 (Malaysian Defence 2012). Such military spending – equivalent to that of Finland, Indonesia, Thailand and Venezuela – puts Malaysia on the lower rung of 'middle-power' status. Much of this money has been used to modernise military hardware and increase the strength of the armed forces. Given that the resultant military capability is unable to match the vast superiority of neighbour Singapore, and to a lesser extent, that of Indonesia, the aim of such upgrading is primarily to act as a deterrent, protect Malaysia's interests in potential flashpoints such as the Spratly Islands, acquire influence in regional defence and security groupings such as the ARF and ASEAN Defence Ministers' Meeting, and act as a backdrop for Malaysia's middle-power aspirations.

Consequently, Malaysia's foreign policy priorities vis-à-vis middle-power status are focused on a leadership role in the region supported by economic and military standing. One major aspect of such leadership is playing a mediator's role in intractable conflicts within the region by deploying soft power that leverages on cultural, religious, political and kinship ties. Malaysia's middle-power status and resultant credibility contributed to the willingness of conflicting parties in Mindanao, in the southern Philippines, to accept Malaysia as an honest broker. Malaysia has lead the international monitoring team there, whose main function is to ensure adherence to the ceasefire agreements between the Philippines government and the Moro Islamic Liberation Front (MILF) (Dhillon 2007). Despite frequent lapses, Malaysia succeeded in getting the two sides to sign an agreement to end all arms hostilities in October 2012 (Faisal 2012: 30). A September 2013 lapse caused by MILF rebel leader Nur Misuari's decision to attack Zamboaga (*Star*, 10 September 2013) notwithstanding, Malaysia is poised to leverage its middle-power status, its ASEAN-based ties with the Philippines and its Islamic bonds with the MILF to take the peace process into succeeding phases – humanitarian, rehabilitation and developmental – that will provide permanent peace to what was, by all measures, an enduring and violent conflict.

Malaysia under Najib has attempted to play a similar role in southern Thailand, where the rebels are not just Muslims but Malays. More than five thousand people have died since suspected separatists started an armed campaign a decade ago to seek independence for the three southern provinces of Narathiwat, Pattani and Yala, making southern Thailand the most serious security problem in the region. Thai Prime Minister Abhisit Vejjajiva discussed the unrest in the south during a visit to Malaysia in June 2009 (Funston 2010: 235). Najib then met with Abhisit's successor, Yingluck Shinawatra, on the sidelines of the APEC Forum in Vladivostok, Russia in September 2013 to discuss Malaysia's willingness to mediate. (Bernama, 9 September 2013). It does appear that Najib has somewhat assuaged Thailand's fears that Malaysia has been complicit in the violence. Thailand has thus accepted Malaysia's educational and economic assistance in the strife-torn region. Both sides have begun joint border patrols, as well. Mediation, if there has been any, has been conducted secretly.

Malaysia's aspirations for middle-power status are not confined to the region. At the international level, Malaysian peacekeepers are serving in some of the UN's toughest missions – in Lebanon, South Sudan and the Democratic Republic of the Congo. The continued growth of the Malaysian Peacekeeping Training Centre at Port Dickson and the substantial number of peacekeepers testify to the seriousness of the nation's priorities in this regard.

Malaysian foreign policy and national priorities

Malaysia's overarching national goal is to achieve developed-nation status by the end of this decade. For this to happen, steady and uninterrupted economic growth, leading Malaysia to become a high-income nation, is crucial. Such growth will help ensure political and social stability as well as keep its diverse people cohesive.

The Najib administration's biggest challenges are linked to this goal. In the macro sense, the nation appears stuck in the middle-income trap. At the micro level, Malaysia faces serious quality of life issues, such as growing crime rates, corruption, declines in health services and quality education, rising costs of living, reduced availability of affordable housing, environmental degradation, and rising racial and religious polarisation. As it confronts these challenges, the nation is running out of time to become fully developed by 2020.

Najib's New Economic Model (NEM) and Economic Transformation Programme (ETP) aim to put the nation back on its 2020 track, while his Government Transformation Programme (GTP) focuses on reforming the primary vehicle tasked with that job. At the collective core of the NEM and ETP lie Malaysian foreign policy initiatives and priorities. These include maximising FDI in the midst of stiff regional competition; minimising capital flight in the midst of pull factors provided by countries such as Cambodia, Laos and Myanmar; improving the nation's competitiveness; and accelerating Malaysia's globalisation process. Najib's Capital Market Master Plan has its roots in the globalisation process: it seeks to make the nation's capital market sufficiently diversified and broad-based to attract foreign investors. Malaysia's efforts towards greater trade liberalisation in the Asia-Pacific region, in particular the Trans-Pacific Partnership involving Australia, Brunei, Chile, New Zealand, Peru, Singapore, the US and Vietnam, are other Malaysian foreign policy initiatives in this regard.

Najib is acutely aware that the future of the ruling coalition as well as his own survival within his party are at stake and depend on the government's ability to resolve the nation's economic growth issues and related quality of life concerns. The outcome of the 2013 general election helped establish that premise. The prime minister is further aware that foreign policy performance must be dramatically enhanced to help resolve some of these problems – thus ensuring that domestic economic concerns remain at the forefront of foreign policy priorities.

Rebranding Islamic credentials

Analysts explaining Malaysian foreign policy during the Mahathir era have debated the role of Islam, providing a variety of theories, ranging from Islam's having a substantive role in foreign policy (Nair 1997; Saravanamuttu 2010) to its being used largely in foreign policy rhetoric, even if it remained an important factor in domestic politics (Dhillon 2009; see also Liow and Afif, this volume). Yet the consensus is that for Mahathir, Islam was always a part of foreign policy. He championed Muslim causes such as Palestine and Bosnia, flayed the West over Iraq, assumed spokesman roles in Islamic groups such as the Organisation of the Islamic Conference (OIC) and wasted no time in developing ties with Islamic Sudan and the Muslim former Soviet republics of Uzbekistan, Kazakhstan and Kyrgyzstan.

The Badawi administration introduced Islam Hadhari (Civilisational Islam), softening his predecessor's zeal. Under Najib, foreign policy seems to have shed Mahathirist Islamism and steered clear of Islam Hadhari, as well. An analysis of Najib's speeches relating to foreign policy indicates that his discourse on Islam is sparse. It has been suggested that Najib is not comfortable engaging with issues pertaining to Islam, both internationally and domestically

(Khadijah 2011: 436). The philosophical brand of Najib's Islam is *wassatiyyah*, or moderation, as espoused by his Global Movement of Moderates (GMM) (Najib 2010b). GMM calls for harnessing forces of moderation to defuse extremism and violence. Malaysia's focus on ties with the Muslim world has also shifted, from multilateral forums such as the OIC to bilateral alliances centred on trade and investment. This explains why Bahrain and the United Arab Emirates command a higher priority for Malaysia than its relations with traditional Muslim states. The Ministry of Trade and Industry has been tasked with exploring FTAs with selected Muslim countries, with a view to expanding Malaysia's industries into Islamic finance and halal food, as well as to obtain FDI for the Iskandar corridor (*Business Times*, 13 December 2010).

Foreign policy and regime maintenance

Kuik (2012a: 27) has argued that foreign policy is an extension of domestic legitimation, in the sense that state elites seek to justify and enhance their governance capacity by acting in accordance with the very foundations of their political authority. Dhillon (2009: 76) similarly contends that regime stability and maintenance comprised an integral impetus for foreign policy during the twenty-two-year Mahathir era. It is argued that regime interests continue to contend with national goals within foreign policy processes.

In 2008, the Badawi-led ruling coalition lost its two-thirds parliamentary majority, five state governments and the Kuala Lumpur federal territory. Led by Najib, the BN not only lost yet more seats in 2013, it lost the majority of the popular vote, even as it managed to reclaim two states from the opposition. These setbacks, described by some as the worst performance for BN in Malaysian history (Welsh 2013), pose serious challenges to the stability of the regime, especially when the underlying causes of the electoral losses – rising demands for democratisation; growing support for the Anwar-led opposition movement amongst the urban middle class, the younger generation and the non-Malay electorate; and economic stagnation – are factored in.

Recalibration of ties with the West, including the US, has provided the regime leverage to reduce, if not neutralise, Western support for Anwar's coalition, which has come to represent a real and present danger to the continued rule of the regime. After all, Anwar's Parti Keadilan Rakyat (People's Justice Party) had made serious inroads in the 2008 elections, then came closer towards their goal of capturing Putrajaya in 2013. Going by what transpired during recent high-level visits by US leaders to Kuala Lumpur, such recalibration seems to have yielded the results desired by the regime. Hillary Clinton did not meet personally with Anwar, opting to speak by phone instead (Sheldon 2011: 7). She also did not speak with Wan Azizah Ismail, Anwar's wife and president of Anwar's party, even though Wan Azizah attended one of Clinton's functions during the visit. Defense Secretary Hegel, too, did not meet with any opposition leaders during his visit in 2013. It was clear that regime maintenance, as an outcome of the recalibration, overrode larger concerns of not wanting to alienate the country's Muslim-majority voters, who are generally critical of US and Western stands on the Palestinian issue.

Similarly, the government's announcement that former Anwar proponent, turned Najib loyalist, Zaharin Hashim will be sent as envoy to Indonesia (*Star*, 6 September 2013) can be viewed as an attempt to limit the predilection within the Indonesian ruling elite and its media for supporting Anwar as a Malaysian leader.

Prioritising relations with China and reducing acrimony with Singapore undoubtedly served the goal of regime maintenance, as well. The outcome of the 2008 elections made clear that the political legitimacy of the UMNO-led ruling coalition had shifted to new bases such as economic performance, political inclusiveness and national competitiveness. After expanding by nearly 9 percent, on average, from the early 1990s until the 1997–98 Asian financial crisis, Malaysia's GDP growth rate has slowed by half over the past several years. In oil and gas production, the biggest drivers of growth, Malaysia has become reliant on maturing fields. Until 2010, when a rebound began, foreign investment had also been slipping. Malaysia's stock exchange, the choice destination of emerging-market investors in the early to mid-1990s, now lags behind the bourses of Indonesia and the Philippines. From the standpoint of regime maintenance, the combined effect of such economic downturns has been the inability of the regime to sustain rent-seeking enterprises to support its Malay electorate, and loss of faith amongst the ethnic Chinese community in the regime's ability to expand the economic cake.

A friendlier Singapore ensured the success of mega economic development projects such the Iskandar project in Johor. This US$28 billion port, tourism and industrial complex in a region three times the size of Singapore (*Time*, 8 July 2012) has the potential to turn around more than a decade of lacklustre growth and halt the flight of large numbers of Malaysia's most educated and enterprising citizens – Singapore takes in more than one-half of all human talent that leaves Malaysia. Furthermore, the absence of Malay-ownership quotas for companies operating in the central business district of Iskandar, which will comprise industries such as financial services, education, tourism and healthcare, may help rebuild non-Malay constituents' faith in the regime.

A productive relationship with China, even if founded on purely trade and investment considerations, has allowed Malaysia to benefit from its massive growth and outward investments. More than that, however, the alliance has had an impact on the domestic Chinese population – a group whose political support and financial clout have become increasingly crucial to both the ruling BN and the opposition coalition. The outcome of the 2008 and 2013 elections has made it clear that UMNO needs more than the majority Malay vote to maintain its political supremacy and keep the existing regime afloat. Winning the support of the numerically substantial and economically significant Chinese minority is tied, to a certain extent, to the manner in which Malaysia deals with China.

Najib's attempts to recalibrate a new balance between Islamism and Westernism within Malaysian foreign policy are also supported by regime exigencies. The opposition front's appeal is invariably linked to its ability to make universal values such as good governance, democracy, transparency, political reform and citizens' rights dominant themes in political discourse. These were the ideational issues that appealed to middle-class and younger-generation voters in the 2008 and 2013 elections. Additionally, the Pan-Malaysian Islamic Party (PAS) has successfully reinvented itself, to the extent that it has secured the support of Muslims outside of its heartlands and that of non-Muslim voters, as well. The regime's response has been to allow Islamism to recede, to portray BN as being inclusive and broad, and for UMNO to step back from undercutting PAS on the Islamic front. The expected outcomes are twofold: a foreign policy that is driven less by ideational concerns and more by national needs, and broader support for the ruling BN.

Conclusion

Relieved of the shackles of Cold War rivalry and freed from the shadows of Mahathir's grandiosity, foreign policy under Najib could afford to be driven primarily by domestic considerations – predominant among which is the health of the domestic economy, which is, in turn, inherently tied to political stability and regime maintenance. Externally, such a shift has been facilitated by the globalised international environment as well as specific factors such as the rise of China and the economic dynamism of the Asia-Pacific region. Domestically, the six years of the Badawi administration served to provide foreign policy and the nation the gumption to move away from Mahathir's mould. The Badawi years also provided Najib with some important lessons – chief amongst which was that failure to transform was a recipe for failure at the personal, political and regime levels.

Najib served as prime minister for four years without a popular mandate. The general elections of 2013, while providing him with that mandate, also laid bare the challenges that lay ahead for the ruling coalition, the regime and the nation. Given this state of affairs, Malaysia's priority remains a cooperative, conciliatory foreign policy which aims to forge better ties with the West, neighbours and the region; benefit from globalisation and the rise of China; and improve trade, defuse tensions and lessen reliance on ideology.

Bibliography

Abdul Razak Baginda (ed.) (2009) *Malaysia's Defence and Security Since 1957*, Kuala Lumpur: Malaysia Strategic Research Centre.

Dhillon, Karminder Singh (2007) 'Malaysia's involvement in the peace process in Mindanao, Philippines', in Suwit Laohasiriwong and Ang Ming Chee (eds), *Peace Building in the Asia Pacific: The Role of Third Parties*, Khon Kaen: Institute for Dispute Resolution, Khon Kaen University, pp. 69–85.

Dhillon, Karminder Singh (2009) *Malaysian Foreign Policy in the Mahathir Era 1981–2003: The Dilemmas of Development*, Singapore: NUS Press.

Dhillon, Karminder Singh (2010) 'The OIC: overcoming challenges and reinventing in an age of global terrorism', *The Journal of Defence and Security*, 1(2).

Faisal A. Nawang (2012) 'MILF rebellion in Southern Philippines: is peace still elusive?', *Journal of Strategic Studies and International Relations*, 18.

Funston, John (2008) 'Thailand's southern fires: the Malaysian factor', *UNEAC Asia Papers*, 26: 55–67.

Funston, John (2010) 'Malaysia and Thailand's southern conflict: reconciling security and ethnicity', *Contemporary Southeast Asia: A Journal of International and Strategic Affairs*, 32(2): 234–57.

Hiebert, Murray, Elina Noor, Gregory Poling and Tham Siew Yean (2012) *From Strength to Empowerment: The Next Generation of U.S.–Malaysia Relations*, Washington DC: CSIS.

Jeshurun, Chandran (2008) *Malaysia: Fifty Years of Diplomacy, 1957–2007*, Singapore: Talisman Publishing.

Johnson, Joshua R. (2010) 'Cooperation and pragmatism: Malaysian foreign policy under Najib', *Asia Pacific Bulletin*, 63.

Khadijah Md Khalid (2011) 'Malaysian foreign policy under Najib', *Asian Survey*, 51(3): 429–52.

Kuik Cheng-Chwee (2012a) Malaysia's China Policy in the Post-Mahathir Era: A Neoclassical Realist Explanation, RSIS Singapore Working Paper, 24.

Kuik Cheng-Chwee (2012b) Malaysia's US Policy Under Najib: Ambivalence No More?, RSIS Singapore Working Paper, 250.

Lim Tin Seng (2009) 'Renewing 35 years of Malaysia–China relations: Najib's visit to China', EAI Background Brief 460, Singapore: East Asia Institute.

Liow Joseph Chinyong (2001) 'Personality, exigencies and contingencies: determinants of Malaysia's foreign policy in the Mahathir administration', in Ho Khai Leong and James Chin (eds), *Mahathir's Administration Performance and Crisis in Governance*, Singapore: Times Books International, pp. 120–60.

Malaysian Defence (2012) '13 September 2012', available at http://malaysiandefence.com (accessed 5 September 2013).

Ministry of Trade and Industry (MITI) (2013) available at www.miti.gov.my (accessed 6 September 2013).

Nair, Shanti (1997) *Islam in Malaysian Foreign Policy*, London: Routledge.

Najib Razak (2010a) 'An update from Washington DC, 13 April 2010', 1Malaysia Blog, available at www.1Malaysia.com.my (accessed 3 August 2013).
Najib Razak (2010b) 'Wassatiyyah and the global movement of moderates', 1Malaysia Blog, 12 October, available at www.1Malaysia.com.my (accessed 3 September 2013).
Najib Razak (2011) 'Dato Sri Najib Tun Razak, Prime Minister of Malaysia, welcoming address at the Malaysia–China economic and trade cooperation forum, 28 April 2011', 1Malaysia Blog, available at www.1Malaysia.com.my (accessed 26 August 2013).
Nawang Faisal A. (2012) 'MILF rebellion in Southern Philippines: is peace still elusive?', *The Journal of Strategic Studies and International Relations*, 18.
Ruhanas Harun (2009) 'In pursuit of national interest: change and continuity in Malaysia's foreign policy towards the Middle East', *The International Journal of West Asian Studies*, 1: 25–41.
Ruhanie bin Ahmad (2011) Dasar Luar Malaysia Terhadap Amerika Syarikat 1957–2020: Perspektif Realisme Neoklasikal [Malaysia's Foreign Policy Towards the United States of America 1957–2010: A Neo-classical Realist Perspective], MA Thesis, Universiti Kebangsaan Malaysia.
Saravanamuttu, Johan (2010) *Malaysia's Foreign Policy, The First Fifty Years: Alignment, Neutralism, Islamism*, Singapore: Institute of Southeast Asian Studies.
Sheldon, Simon (2011) 'US–Southeast Asia relations: full court press', *Comparative Connections*, 12(4).
Tan Tuck Cheong and Wong Hock Sen (2008) *Malaysia's International Trade Issues: An Impressionistic View*, Kuala Lumpur: Pelanduk.
Welsh, Bridget (2013) 'Disturbing questions surrounding GE 13 polling', *Malaysiakini*, available at www.malaysiakini.com/news/229367 (accessed 7 May 2013).

31

Malaysia's security concerns

A contemporary assessment

Lai Yew Meng

On the fateful day of 11 February 2013, an approximately 150-strong armed militant group calling themselves the Royal Security Forces of the Sultanate of Sulu and North Borneo breached the far-eastern borders of Sabah, Malaysia, and landed in Lahad Datu to assert what they claimed as their unresolved territorial rights in North Borneo. Dispatched by one of the self-styled heirs to the throne of the now-defunct Sulu Sultanate, the armed intruders camped in at the remote village of Tanduo, located in the dense oil-palm estate of Felda Sahabat, despite repeated appeals from both the Malaysian and Philippine governments for their peaceful withdrawal. Their defiant stance unavoidably led to a month-long bloody stand-off with the Malaysian security forces that saw seventy-seven casualties, including nine Malaysian servicemen and six civilians. Not only did the 'Lahad Datu Incident' shock the nation, it also served as a timely wake-up call for Malaysia to review its national security preparedness in the face of potential and real threats, from within and externally.

This chapter examines the various national security concerns, both real and perceived, that Malaysia encounters today. Although the issues at heart are predominantly oriented towards traditional security, non-traditional, 'human security' challenges are given equal emphasis to stress their growing importance in shaping Malaysia's security assessment. The chapter is divided into three parts: the first provides a brief overview of Malaysia's national security outlook and threat perceptions, from both historical and present vantage points; the second part delves into various traditional and non-traditional security challenges, while the third and concluding part deliberates on Malaysian authorities' efforts towards defending and securing the nation.

Malaysia's security outlook: an overview of the past and present

Most observers would agree that Malaysia's traditional security concerns have been essentially internally oriented and 'emanated from within' (Tang 2010: 25; Ruhanas 2009; Sidhu 2009). From the outbreak of communist insurgency in 1948 until the signing of the 1989 tripartite peace accord among Malaysia, Thailand and the Communist Party of Malaya, the primary security threat facing the nation came from none other than the decades-long communist struggle to position Malaya (and subsequently, Malaysia) within the communist sphere of influence (see Nathan 1990; Sebastian 1991). To be sure, the communist threat was a domestic manifestation of the Cold War's structural logic, which saw the advent of global confrontation between the Western camp, led by the United States, vis-à-vis the Soviet-led Eastern bloc. Regionally, Malaysia was inextricably caught up in the 'grand strategy' of communist expansionism in Southeast Asia spearheaded by the People's Republic of China, and thus served as a vital piece to facilitate the so-called 'domino theory' that became an overarching concern for both Western policy-makers and Malaysian state-elites (Sidhu 2009: 2). Obviously, the limited resources of the Malaysian security apparatus were primarily geared towards stemming the 'Red Tide' from within, while the country hinged its nascent foreign policy on the Western bloc during the era of rigid bipolarity.

Apart from the communist insurgency during the Cold War, Malaysia also faced imminent military threats from neighbouring Indonesia, which under the stewardship of the nationalistic Sukarno, launched the ill-founded *Konfrontasi* policy, in reaction to the formation of the Federation of Malaysia in 1963. Driven by *Ganyang Malaysia* (Sweep Malaysia) rhetoric, the Sukarno government waged a series of sporadic and limited-scale military campaigns that lasted until 1966, which not only saw skirmishes at the border between Bornean Malaysia (Sabah and Sarawak) and Indonesia (Kalimantan), but also the attempted infiltration by Indonesian paratroopers in Labis and Pontian, in the peninsular Malaysian state of Johor (Sidhu 2009: 2–3). Similarly, the formation of Malaysia courted controversy from the Philippines, which, like Indonesia, refused to recognise the newly minted federation because of Manila's sovereignty claim over Sabah. Although the Filipino government did not pursue the military option, it demonstrated its displeasure vividly by severing diplomatic ties with Kuala Lumpur in 1963.

Despite the restoration of full diplomatic relations following the end of the confrontation in 1966, and the dawning of regional solidarity via the establishment of the Association of Southeast Asian Nations (ASEAN) a year later, Malaysia's relationship with Indonesia has continued to be periodically blighted by both new and unresolved issues, ranging from cultural heritage to maritime-territorial disputes. Meanwhile, Manila's cordial bilateral relations with Kuala Lumpur overshadow the fact that the Philippines' claim over Sabah remains unsettled. Like the proverbial 'thorn in the flesh', the issue has dramatically returned to torment Malaysia in the guise of the recent Lahad Datu intrusion. Yet, barring Sabahans, most Malaysians may be unaware that this was not the first time Lahad Datu had faced 'foreign' infiltration. Back in September 1985, this sleepy coastal town was jolted awake by heavily armed pirates from neighbouring islands, who raided the local police station and robbed several businesses, resulting in civilian casualties (Barraclough 1986: 203).

Apart from a waning communist threat, Malaysia's other security concerns in the 1970s and 1980s came from the radicalisation of Islam, following global events, such as the Arab–Israeli conflict, the Islamic revolution in Iran and the Soviet invasion of Afghanistan, among others, which spawned radical and deviant Islamic groups that were deemed by the Malaysian government to be a threat to Muslim unity and national security (see Noraini 1989).[1] The 'Memali Incident' in November 1985, when police laid siege to a village occupied by an Islamic sect led by the charismatic 'Ibrahim Libya', resulting in eighteen deaths, and the July 2000 Al-Ma'unah fiasco, when a group of militants from a Muslim fringe group raided an army camp and made off with a substantial cache of weapons, served as cases in point regarding the socio-political dangers manifesting from such radicalised Islamic movements. These incidents also somewhat justified the Mahathir administration's robust policy in combating this festering domestic threat, and in sanctioning the allegedly ruthless actions of Malaysian security forces, including potential human rights violations.

The demise of the Cold War not only saw some old issues persevering, but also precipitated new security concerns for Malaysia. Although Southeast Asia remains relatively peaceful, Malaysian security planners have been envisaging potential threats from unresolved maritime-territorial disputes, which, aggravated by uncompromising nationalistic impulses among claimant states, could trigger regionally destabilising inter-state conflicts. Likewise, the threat of radical Islamic movements from within has been exacerbated by the advent of global terrorism, championed by non-state extremist groups such as Al-Qaeda, Jemaah Islamiyah (JI) and Kumpulan Mujahidin Malaysia (KMM) that perpetrated global/regional acts of terror, for example the 'September 11' attack, as well as the Bali 2002 and Jakarta Marriot bombing incidents, in which Malaysian connections were implicated.

Meanwhile, other non-traditional security challenges have emerged and become increasingly problematic. The prevalence of 'human security' requires Malaysia adequately to manage non-military and asymmetric threats, such as illegal immigration and human trafficking, environmental degradation, piracy and drug smuggling, which are essentially transboundary in nature and scope (see KEMENTAH 2010). Indeed, Malaysia's strategic outlook has become what Tang (2010: 25) calls 'fuzzier', as the country strives to re-examine and enhance its national security in the face of a globalised and fluid international environment that spawns both challenges and opportunities in traditional and non-traditional dimensions of security.

To be sure, ASEAN, of which Malaysia is a founding member, has almost always demonstrated a propensity to manage, if not peacefully resolve, disputes between member states since its inception. Guided by the so-called 'ASEAN Way', which promotes norms of non-intervention and constructive engagement, and aptly supported by a compendium of legal and institutionalised frameworks, ranging from the Zone of Peace, Freedom and Neutrality (ZOPFAN) and the 1976 Treaty of Amity and Cooperation in Southeast Asia (TAC), to various Track-I and Track-II mechanisms, not to mention the emerging ASEAN Security Community, it is reasonable for Malaysia to be cautiously optimistic towards 'ASEAN's commitment to resolving conflicts without the use of force' (Tang 2010: 26; see also Caballero-Anthony 2005: ch. 2). Nonetheless, the 2008 border clashes and still ongoing territorial dispute between Thailand and Cambodia over an ancient temple site suggest the limitations of ASEAN and ASEAN states' predominantly realist worldview, when it comes to managing issues of national sovereignty and territorial integrity. Obviously, the Thai–Cambodian conflagration has elucidated that existing ASEAN safeguards are not foolproof and member states like Malaysia are cognisant of the need to enhance their national security, unilaterally through defence build-up, while concurrently maintaining their participation in bilateral and multilateral security arrangements, or confidence-building measures.

Malaysia's security concerns

The global security environment of the twenty-first century is shaped as much by traditional security issues as by non-traditional threats that require national actors to adopt the concept of comprehensive security as the basis for their national strategic thinking. As such, Malaysia's national security interests encompass both dimensions, ranging from safeguarding the nation's maritime-territorial sovereignty to managing transborder crimes and environmental challenges. Both shall be examined in the following sections.

Malaysia's contemporary national security thinking has continued to be primarily shaped by conventional security concerns, despite the salience of non-traditional challenges, which the national security community commonly acknowledges to be less of an 'immediate threat'

(Ruhanas 2009: 50). In particular, two key concerns stand out, namely, safeguarding territorial sovereignty and securing maritime interests in exclusive economic zones (EEZ). These priorities tend to be correlated, in view of Malaysia's geographical designation as a littoral state with extensive maritime boundaries.

To a large extent, Tang's (2010: 28) observation that Malaysia's security challenges 'are predominantly territorial in nature' is spot on, insofar as the country is riddled with a number of extant maritime-territorial disputes, due to unresolved land and maritime boundaries that have led to contestation and overlapping claims vis-à-vis neighbour states. These include both bilateral and multilateral disputes. The former involve Limbang and the islands and surrounding waters of Ko Kra and Ko Losin, with Brunei and Thailand, respectively; the Ambalat/Celebes Sea maritime conflict and periodical altercations at the Sarawak–Kalimantan border with Indonesia; and Manila's latent historical claim over Sabah; while the latter refers chiefly to Malaysia's overlapping claims in the South China Sea vis-à-vis five other claimant states over parts of the Spratly archipelago (Tang 2010; Emmers 2010).

The disputes over the aforesaid common boundaries with Brunei and Thailand have been latent, and thus far, peacefully managed by both disputant states via bilateral negotiations. For instance, after decades of diplomacy, Malaysia and Brunei finally reached a possible settlement of the 'Limbang Question', with the signing of the Letters of Exchange in March 2009. Both neighbours agreed comprehensively to demarcate their common border based on five agreements signed by Sarawak and Brunei between 1920 and 1939, of which two directly concern the disputed territory (Nurbaiti 2009). Meanwhile, the Ko Kra and Ko Losin dispute, which stems from a contest over the continental shelf boundary between Malaysia and Thailand, remains unresolved, but has been tabled by both countries in favour of joint development under the auspices of the Malaysia–Thailand Joint Development Area established in February 1979. The arrangement was subsequently strengthened by the formation of a joint authority in 1991 to administer the area on behalf of the two governments (see Prescott and Schofield 2001).

Although shelving a maritime-territorial dispute for the purpose of improving mutual relations has appeared feasible in the case of the Malaysia–Thailand arrangement, the effectiveness of such a modus operandi is not guaranteed, since unresolved disputes have the tendency to resurface and haunt the claimant states.[2] The Philippines' dormant territorial claim over Sabah has proved to be a compelling case. Manila's repeated failure to renounce the claim formally since 1969 (Caballero-Anthony 2005: 66–68) has unwittingly led to its recent resurrection, when non-state actors in the semblance of Sulu Sultanate descendants launched the aforementioned armed intrusion, in the name of the Philippines. To be sure, the Filipino government led by President Benigno Aquino III demonstrated willingness to cooperate with its Malaysian counterpart to end the stand-off by appealing to the intruders to engage in dialogue to address their territorial grievance, while simultaneously reminding them of possible constitutional violations for instigating an act of war (see *Official Gazette* 2013). The stand-off inadvertently turned into a highly visible 'nationalist' issue, however, that saw Filipinos sympathising with their brethren's cause, while netizens took their discontentment to cyberspace, launching attacks on Malaysian websites (Australian Network News 2013). Coinciding with the period leading to their respective general elections in May 2013, rising domestic nationalist pressure made it difficult for both Malaysian and Filipino state-elites to adopt an overly conciliatory approach towards the incident. Although eventually subdued by Malaysia's security forces after a protracted operation (*Ops Daulat*), the Sulu intrusion undoubtedly tested the spirit and solidarity of ASEAN. More significantly from the Malaysian standpoint, this national security breach exposed limitations of the country's security apparatus, in terms of their level of preparedness, outlay and outreach, especially when it comes to securing the nation's outermost border and territories. The establishment of the Eastern Sabah Security Command (ESSCOM) reflects the Malaysian government's immediate and steadfast commitment to address these national security deficits.

Close to the shores of south-eastern Sabah lies another potential flashpoint that could undermine an already strained bilateral relationship between two so-called kin states, which has been aggravated by their clashing nationalisms and competition for national prestige and power (see Lai 2013b). The Malaysian–Indonesian dispute over the hydrocarbon-rich, deep-sea blocks located in the Ambalat/Celebes Sea is undeniably a key irritant for both countries. The seeds of this debacle were first sown when Malaysia laid formal claims over the Sipadan and Ligitan islands, following its unilateral declaration of the controversial *Peta Baru 1979* (*New Map of 1979*), which included an extended maritime boundary and jurisdiction overlapping with those of Indonesia (Mak 2006: 141–43; Sutarji 2009: 188). The overlapping claims led to a territorial dispute vis-à-vis Indonesia that was subsequently referred to the International Court of Justice (ICJ) for arbitration. The Sipadan–Ligitan dispute was officially resolved on 17 December 2002, when the ICJ ruled in favour of Malaysia, much to Indonesia's chagrin. The episode, however, did not end, but has instead fed into the Ambalat dispute, when Malaysia decided to reconfigure its boundaries by making the legally acquired islands the new baseline to establish its extended maritime border in the Celebes Sea, which encompasses parts of the Ambalat deep-sea blocks (Lai 2013b: 133).

To date, the Ambalat/Celebes Sea conflict has seen two volatile episodes. The first involved provocative manoeuvres and face-offs between vessels of the Royal Malaysian Navy (RMN) and Tentera Nasional Indonesia–Angkatan Laut (TNI–AL) at the disputed waters that led to a ship collision incident between RMN's KD *Rencong* and Indonesia's KRI *Tedong Naga* on 8–9 April 2005, which almost triggered the first Malaysia–Indonesia armed conflict since *Konfrontasi* (*Tempo* 2005). The second episode took place between May and June 2009, and reached its climax when an RMN vessel, KD *Baung–3509*, was accused of venturing deep into the Ambalat waters and aggressively manoeuvring (zigzagging) so as to endanger Indonesian warships in the vicinity (Lai 2013b: 157). Although conflict was avoided when the RMN vessel left the disputed area, it was learnt that the shadowing Indonesian warships had assumed combat readiness, with the captain of one of the ships revealing 'that Indonesia was moments away from firing its first shot in anger' (Amir 2009; cf. Lai 2013b: 157). The highly charged nature of the Ambalat dispute suggests the necessity for both claimant parties to demilitarise the contested waters in favour of a mutually beneficial diplomatic resolution. Conversely, such high-sea altercations also emphasise the pressing need to bolster the RMN's capabilities, to effectively defend Malaysia's extensive maritime claims.

Another of Malaysia's maritime-territorial concerns is the Spratly archipelago, which it claims in part, vis-à-vis five other claimant states, namely China, Vietnam, Philippines, Brunei and Taiwan. This group of South China Sea islands/reefs/atolls is not only the epicentre of competing maritime-territorial, geo-economic and geo-strategic interests, but also a potential hotspot for great power politics, because of its abundant natural resources (i.e. fisheries and hydrocarbon deposits) and its strategic location, straddling the world's busiest sea lines of communication. The archipelago is claimed en masse by China and Vietnam, while the Philippines officially lay claim to fifty-three features. Malaysia entered the fray in 1978 via its invocation of the principle of continental shelf extension, making it the only party to stake claims over the area without a historical basis (Catley and Keliat 1997: 35; Emmers 2010: 69). Malaysia claims sovereignty over a total of twelve geographical features in the southern part of the disputed archipelago, and moved to occupy Swallow Reef (*Pulau*

Layang-Layang) in 1983, followed by the Ardasier (*Terumbu Ubi*) and Mariveles (*Terumbu Mantanani*) Reefs three years later (Emmers 2010: 69; Sutarji 2009: 174). After a thirteen-year hiatus, Malaysia increased its Spratly profile in 1999, by erecting structures in the Investigator Shoal (*Terumbu Peninjau*) and Erica Reef (*Terumbu Siput*) (Kuik 2013: 23).

The Spratly dispute has witnessed the use of force by claimant states on several occasions to stake claims that periodically threatened the stability of the region. As the most militarily preponderant, China has been criticised over the years for adopting 'gunboat diplomacy' to pursue its 'creeping invasion' of the archipelago. In March 1988, the People's Liberation Army-Navy (PLAN) clashed with the Vietnamese navy in 'the deadliest [Spratlys] armed conflict to date' near Fiery Cross Reef, to wrestle control over six adjacent features (Shepard 1996: 5). In 1994–95, Manila ceded control of Mischief Reef following 'strong-armed' diplomacy from Beijing. Meanwhile, Chinese fortification of Mischief Reef in the late 1990s had sceptics raising the spectre of a 'China threat' (Lai 2001). Fear of China's forceful dominance had been exacerbated earlier by the promulgation of its 1992 Territorial Waters Law, which not only reaffirmed Chinese sovereignty over the Paracel and Spratly islands, but also laid China's claim to more than 80 percent of the South China Sea (Emmers 2010: 71). Although the Chinese had maintained a status quo presence in the disputed archipelago since 1999, the extended Chinese–Filipino stand-off at Scarborough Shoal in mid-2012 has again resurrected concerns regarding China's growing assertiveness in managing the South China Sea dispute. Compounding the unease among regional states, including Malaysia, has been the strengthening of Chinese military presence and power-projection capabilities in recent years, as indicated by the establishment of the Sanya naval base on Hainan island and the huge outlay of the PLAN's South China Sea Fleet, which included commissioning China's maiden aircraft carrier, *Liaoning*, and a sizeable fleet of submarines, purportedly to assert Chinese sovereignty over the troubled waters.

To be sure, Malaysia has neither been on the receiving end of China's military assertions, nor been compelled by the Chinese forcefully to defend its Spratly outposts. For instance, Beijing's response to the Malaysian occupation of the two Spratly reefs in 1999 was low-key, possibly a sign of Chinese goodwill toward Malaysia's 'deferential' China policy that has fostered their relatively 'benign and reciprocally productive' bilateral relationship (Kuik 2013: 23). Indeed, unlike its Vietnamese and Filipino counterparts, the Malaysian government, from Mahathir to the Najib administration, has never officially declared China a security threat, but rather, has chosen to view its rise as an opportunity. Nevertheless, Kuik (2013: 38) sees Malaysia, like other ASEAN states, as becoming 'increasingly concerned about rising tensions in the South China Sea', especially following unusually strong Chinese protestation against a Malaysia–Vietnam Joint Submission to the United Nations Commission on the Limits of the Continental Shelf (UNCLCS) in May 2009. Hence, while Malaysia continues its pragmatic policy of engaging China and opting for diplomatic means to manage the South China Sea imbroglio, it has also sought to hedge against the uncertainties of the regional strategic environment by 'quietly supporting a United States military presence' (Kuik 2013: 37) (i.e. the US 'pivot' to Asia) and maintaining traditional military links with the Western powers, notably the United States and members of the Five Power Defence Arrangement (FPDA), as a critical dimension of its national strategic policy (see also Kuik, this volume).

Closely intertwined with Malaysia's maritime-territorial interests is safeguarding the nation's aforementioned extensive maritime border, which, based on the *Peta Baru 1979*, encompasses approximately 450,233 square kilometres of territorial sea and EEZ, an area much larger than its total land mass of 332,800 square kilometres (Sutarji 2009: 188). Malaysia's maritime zones are both strategically and economically salient to its national security and well-being. From fisheries to hydrocarbon reserves, the nation's EEZ contributes substantially to the sustainability of its food and economic security. Meanwhile, the Straits of Malacca, South China Sea and Celebes Sea are vital sea lines of communication for Malaysia and other trading nations, as they serve as an 'artery through which a huge proportion of global trade is transported' (Sutarji 2009: 189). Securing and enhancing the safety of its EEZ is therefore a key national security priority, especially in view of the proliferation of trans-boundary maritime threats such as illegal fishing and encroachments, piracy, maritime terrorism, illegal immigration and human trafficking, which endanger the nation's well-being.

Among the most pressing maritime security challenges is the rise of piracy or high-sea armed robbery, with the Straits of Malacca gaining international notoriety during the early 2000s as amongst the major sea routes suffering from a relatively high incidence of pirate attacks. With some 62,000 ship movements transporting more than a quarter of global commerce and half the world's oil supply passing through this narrow waterway annually (Sutarji 2009: 189), it is no coincidence that the Straits have become a hotbed for modern-day sea piracy (see Liss, this volume). In 2004 alone, the International Maritime Bureau (IMB) reported some thirty-eight cases of pirate attacks, prompting marine insurers like Lloyds to classify the Straits of Malacca as a 'war zone' (Tang 2010: 31). In fact, its high-risk environment had led then US Pacific Command Chief Admiral Thomas Fargo to suggest in April 2004 that the US Marines and Special Forces would assist the littoral states of Malaysia and Indonesia in patrolling the troubled Straits (Mak 2006: 152). Concerned by the potential 'internationalisation' of Malaysia's security, and recognising the urgent need for counter-piracy measures to convince users regarding its safety, the Malaysian authorities 'went so far as to offer naval escorts at no cost for "high-risk" vessels transiting the [Malacca] Straits' (*Straits Times* 2004; cf. Mak 2006: 153). More significantly, they began working closely with Indonesia and Singapore to stem piracy in the Straits under the auspices of the Malaysia–Singapore–Indonesia Coordinated Patrol (MALSINDO CORPAT), launched on 20 July 2004 (Mak 2006: 155). With the subsequent incorporation of aerial surveillance under Thailand's Eye-in-the-Sky programme, Tang (2010: 31–32) sees Malaysia and its littoral neighbours as having efficaciously 'reversed the tide of piracy' in the Malacca Straits since 2004; indeed, the IMB's first quarterly report in 2009 identified only one of 102 piracy incidents worldwide occurring in the Straits.

Apart from in the Malacca Straits, piracy and maritime terrorism have manifested intermittently in the nation's far-eastern EEZ, most notably in the form of hostage and abduction cases. Infamous incidents include the April 2000 abduction of twenty-one victims from a diving resort in Sipadan Island by the Abu Sayyaf Group (ASG) and a similar case a year later, at Pandanan Island in east Malaysia, by its splinter group. In November 2012, two cousins were abducted from a plantation in Lahad Datu, Sabah, and held ransom by their ASG abductors in nearby Jolo Island. The incident ended uncannily nine months later, following the escape of one of the victims; the other reportedly died in captivity (Lee 2013). Like the recent Sulu armed intrusion, these debacles clearly expose the limitations in Malaysia's maritime surveillance and capabilities.

The involvement of the Al-Qaeda-linked ASG in these abductions reveals yet another national security concern in the form of Islamist extremism and global terrorism, which since the September 11 terror attacks, has recalibrated Malaysia's security perceptions to include viewing seriously the potential threat posed by radical Islamic movements, such as KMM and JI within its shores. Although Malaysia has never directly experienced the menace of terrorism, the role of Malaysian citizens in the earlier mentioned Bali and Jakarta bombings is indicative of the clear and present danger posed by these allegedly Al-Qaeda sponsored local extremist groups, whose transboundary activities/movements have to be diligently monitored and curtailed through effective joint counter-terrorism measures with neighbour states. As such, Malaysia's establishment of the Southeast Asia Regional Centre for Counter Terrorism (SEARCCT) in 2003 was a proactive step in the right direction.

The transboundary nature of terrorism is, indeed, profoundly manifested in the Malaysia–Indonesia–Philippines 'tri-border' area, which is seen as a hub of terrorist and related criminal activities in Southeast Asia (Rabasa and Chalk 2012). Despite current trends suggesting an overall improvement in the regional security situation vis-à-vis terrorism, following the fragmentation and attrition of key militant groups as a result of concerted counter-terrorism efforts (Rabasa and Chalk 2012: ix), the Malaysian authorities have remained vigilant over the tri-border area, which they still consider a hotbed for terrorist activities. Their preoccupation is understandable, since the demographic make-up and proximity of Sabah to the southern Philippines (Mindanao/Sulu) makes the tri-border 'a suitable rear area for militants, who can blend into and develop support networks undetected among large migrant populations' (Rabasa and Chalk 2012: 5). The onus is thus on Malaysia to continue strengthening its coastal-cum-naval surveillance and operational capabilities, while simultaneously pursuing trilateral/multilateral maritime security cooperation in the tri-border area, to deal effectively with terrorism and other transnational criminal activities.

Malaysian security planners are also highly concerned with other human security issues. Illegal immigration, drugs smuggling and human trafficking are considered priority areas, since Malaysia considers itself 'on the receiving end' of such transnational criminal activities (Sato 2010: 144), owing to its porous border and strategic geographical location, as well as its vibrant economy. Indeed, Malaysia is a favoured transit point for movement of illegal migrants and victims of human trafficking from Indonesia, the Southern Philippines, Bangladesh, Myanmar, Vietnam and China, among other places, and for narcotics from the Golden Triangle. According to the Immigration Department's records, Malaysia has a 1.85 million-strong foreign workforce, many of whom are undocumented, and whose presence has exacerbated social problems, such as rising crime, spread of diseases, and culture/identity clashes, that threaten public security (KEMENTAH 2010: 11–12).

Besides increasing border surveillance and security, the Malaysian authorities have also launched periodic crackdowns (for instance, an initiative dubbed *Ops Nyah*) to curb illegal immigration, including offering amnesty and deportation, while imposing stiffer penalties on perpetrators. In late 2011, the government launched the Illegal Immigrant Comprehensive Settlement Programme or '6P' to allow illegal migrants to register and be either legalised or deported back to their home country without prosecution. About 1.3 million illegal foreign workers have since registered, of whom 500,000 were legalised and 330,000 repatriated (Gangopadhyay and Lim 2013). It is noteworthy that Malaysia's handling of illegal immigrants has occasionally become an issue of contention in its relations with Indonesia and, to a lesser extent, the Philippines.

Last, but not least, environmental threats like transboundary haze and marine pollution have highlighted the dire need for Malaysia to work closely with ASEAN member states to comprehensively manage these borderless security challenges. Transboundary haze, for instance, has become a regular problem in Southeast Asia since the 1990s, as a result of unscrupulous open burning by small farmers and large plantation firms alike, to clear land for commercial purposes. It became a contentious issue in 1997, again in 2006 and recently in 2013, following severe degradation of air quality, which forced national authorities to issue public health warnings and businesses and schools to close in Malaysia and Singapore. Since the forest fires were started and hotspots recorded mainly in Sumatra and Kalimantan, the Indonesian government has been taken to task, time and again, for its apparent lack of conviction in combating the issue. Nonetheless, allegations concerning the involvement of Malaysian-owned plantation companies in large-scale land clearing in Indonesian provinces have had Jakarta playing the 'blame game', as well, resulting in what has increasingly appeared to be a diplomatic conundrum when it comes to collective management of the haze debacle. To be sure, ASEAN has, since 2003, enforced a regulatory framework based on the Transboundary Haze Agreement to manage the problem. Indonesia's conspicuous absence as a signatory, however, remains the major obstacle in realising the agreement's full potential (Tang 2010: 34). To make matters worse, Malaysia reportedly 'struck a deal' with Indonesia in September 2013 'to withhold critical information on forest fires in Sumatra, which cause the annual haze in the region' (Zachariah 2013). This bilateral arrangement cast serious doubts on the viability of the ASEAN-proposed Haze Monitoring System, due to be launched shortly thereafter (Zachariah 2013). The spectre of transboundary haze will continue to haunt Malaysians in years to come if no concerted inter-governmental effort is made to tackle the root causes of the problem.

Enhancing national security: modernisation of the Malaysian Armed Forces

These myriad traditional and non-traditional security concerns require a sustained modernisation programme for the Malaysian Armed Forces (MAF), which not only involves the procurement and maintenance of advanced military hardware and technologies, but equally emphasises improving the standards of military personnel in terms of training, equipment, morale and welfare. Indeed, prior to the 1997 Asian financial meltdown, Malaysia was amongst the biggest defence spenders in Asia. In 1996, it was ranked the world's eleventh-largest arms importer (Sidhu 2009: 23). Since the late 1990s, however, the MAF's development has assumed an irregular pace, as a result of political, economic and fiscal constraints (Dzirhan 2012). Confounding the matter has been the dire need to replace extensive ageing MAF military equipment, which has strained the capacity of its services (army, navy and air force) to accomplish their missions effectively. For instance, the defence sector enjoyed consecutive annual budget increments between 2006 and 2008, but suffered a 10.46 percent contraction in 2009, owing to the global financial crisis (Tang 2010: 35). In 2013, the Defence Ministry received a budget of RM15.2 billion – an increase from the RM13.7 billion allocated the year before. The bulk of these annual defence allocations went to operating expenditures, while the portion for development (including procurement) was meagre, at best. This irregular pattern of expenditure, nonetheless, blurs the fact that Malaysia's annual defence spending, which averaged 2 percent or less of its gross domestic product (GDP), was comparatively higher than that of most ASEAN states during the period 2008–12, Singapore, Vietnam and Brunei notwithstanding (see World Bank n.d.). Yet, the gloomy economic outlook has raised doubts about the ability of the government to finance the MAF's modernisation agenda. In 2012 alone, all three services of the MAF took significant cuts to their procurement funding; the army requested RM1.16 billion, but was given RM541 million; the navy asked for RM4.39 billion, but received only RM759 million; and the air force was allocated RM983 million, despite requesting RM2.49 billion (Dzirhan 2012).

Despite its shoestring budget, the MAF has strived to beef up its capabilities by initiating a number of strategic procurement programmes over the last decade, to meet the operational requirements of its three services. These included, among others, the army's acquisition of

257 indigenously produced AV–8 8x8 AFVs; the navy's procurement of two French-built Scorpene submarines, six Kedah-class offshore patrol vessels (OPVs) and another six second-generation patrol vessel–littoral combat ships (SGPV-LCSs) to enhance its maritime capabilities; and the air force's purchase of twelve EC–725 Eurocopters and Russian-made SU–30MKM multi-role combat aircrafts (MRCAs), as well as the planned acquisition of another eighteen MRCAs as replacement for its MIG–29N fleet, scheduled for decommissioning in 2015 (contenders include the Boeing Superhornet, Eurofighter Typhoon, Dassault Rafale and Saab Gripen) (see *Asian Military Review* 2013). It is worth noting that while Malaysia's defence spending has generally decreased over the last few years, acute awareness of the limitations of the country's security apparatus in dealing with the likes of the Lahad Datu intrusion ensures that force modernisation will remain a priority area in years to come.

Conclusion

The demise of the Cold War precipitated a fluid international security environment that has left Malaysia facing myriad security concerns, in both the traditional and non-traditional senses. To be sure, the country has thus far enjoyed relative peace and stability, both internally and externally, and the security concerns outlined in this chapter have yet to pose any clear and present danger to national security. Nonetheless, from maritime-territorial disputes to transboundary haze, these security challenges require the Malaysian authorities not only to be continuously vigilant, but also comprehensively to review and recalibrate the country's national strategic policy better to manage the nation's security. To this end, the government has continued to emphasise the time-proven, 'skilful use of diplomacy' (via bilateral and multilateral channels) as 'the first line of defence' (Sidhu 2009: 29), while simultaneously seeking to strengthen the country's military-security option to serve as a credible deterrent against sources of threat. Although the lacklustre global economy has held back the MAF's modernisation agenda, the necessity to replace near-obsolete capital equipment to enhance force operability and reduce the gap with other regional armed forces will ensure outlays for security are given due emphasis for the foreseeable future.

Notes

1 The Malaysian government's threat perceptions of radical Islam were underlined by the publication of a white paper entitled 'The Threat to Muslim Unity and National Security' in the late 1980s (Noraini 1989: 146; see also Sidhu 2009: 12).
2 For instance, Deng Xiaoping's shelving of the Japanese–Chinese Senkaku/Diaoyudao islands dispute in 1978 has not stopped the conflict from becoming a potential flashpoint in their contemporary bilateral relationship, especially since a resurgence of domestic nationalism in both countries has rendered the issue non-negotiable (see Lai 2013a: ch. 6).

Bibliography

Amir Tejo (2009) 'Navy was set to fire on warship', *Jakarta Globe*, 4 June.
Asian Military Review (2013) 'Malaysian defence modernisation', *Asian Military Review*, 1 March, available at www.asianmilitaryreview.com/malaysian-defence-modernisation/ (accessed 7 October 2013).
Australian Network News (2013) 'Sabah sultan followers take fight to cyberspace', 4 March, available at www.abc.net.au/news/2013–03–04/sabah-sultan-followers-take-fight-to-cyberspace/4552378?section=australianetworknews (accessed 3 October 2013).

Barraclough, Simon (1986) 'Malaysia in 1985: a question of management', *Southeast Asian Affairs*, 1986(1): 185–207.

Caballero-Anthony, Mely (2005) *Regional Security in Southeast Asia: Beyond the ASEAN Way*, Singapore: Institute of Southeast Asian Studies.

Catley, Robert and Makmur Keliat (1997) *Spratlys: The Dispute in the South China Sea*, Aldershot: Ashgate.

Dzirhan Mahadzir (2012) 'Malaysia funding problems continue', *Defence Review Asia*, 19 March, available at www.defencereviewasia.com/articles/152/Malaysia-Funding-problems-continue (accessed 3 October 2013).

Emmers, Ralf (2010) *Geopolitics and Maritime Territorial Disputes in East Asia*, London: Routledge.

Gangopadhyay, Abhrajit and Shie-Lynn Lim (2013) 'Malaysia's drive to oust illegal migrants worries smaller planters', *The Wall Street Journal*, 11 September, available at http://blogs.wsj.com/searealtime/2013/09/11/malaysias-drive-to-oust-illegal-migrants-worries-smaller-planters/ (accessed 7 October 2013).

Kementerian Pertahanan Malaysia (KEMENTAH) (2010) *Dasar Pertahanan Negara*, Kuala Lumpur: KEMENTAH.

Kuik Cheng-Chwee (2013) 'Making sense of Malaysia's China policy: asymmetry, proximity, and elite's domestic authority', *The Chinese Journal of International Politics*, 6(4): 429–67.

Lai Yew Meng (2001) The Resurgence of Chinese Nationalism: Implications toward the Regional Security of East Asia, Occasional Paper 4, Kota Kinabalu: Universiti Malaysia Sabah.

Lai Yew Meng (2013a) *Nationalism and Power Politics in Japan's Relations with China: A Neoclassical Realist Interpretation*, London: Routledge.

Lai Yew Meng (2013b) *The Politics of Pride, Prestige and Power in Contemporary Indonesia–Malaysia Relations*, Fundamental Research Grant Scheme (FRGS) Project Final Report, Putrajaya: Ministry of Higher Education, Malaysia.

Lee, Stephanie (2013) 'Sabah kidnap victim returns home', *The Star*, 9 August.

Mak, J.N. (2006) 'Unilateralism and regionalism: working together and alone in the Malacca Straits', in Graham Gerard Ong-Webb (ed.), *Piracy, Maritime Terrorism and Securing the Malacca Straits*, Singapore: Institute of Southeast Asian Studies, pp. 134–62.

Nathan, K.S. (1990) 'Malaysia in 1989: communists end armed struggle', *Asian Survey*, 30(2): 210–20.

Noraini Haji Abdullah (1989) 'Leadership in Malaysia: security perceptions and policies', in Mohammed Ayoob and Chai'anan Samudvanija (eds), *Leadership Perceptions and National Security: The Southeast Asian Experience*, Singapore: Institute of Southeast Asian Studies, pp. 142–59.

Nurbaiti Hamdan (2009) 'Limbang border to be set', *The Star*, 20 March, available at www.thestar.com.my/story.aspx?file=%2f2009%2f3%2f20%2fnation%2f3518846&sec=nation (accessed 4 October 2013).

Official Gazette (2013) 'Statement of His Excellency Benigno S. Aquino III, President of the Philippines on the Sabah Incident', *Official Gazette of the Republic of Philippines*, 26 February, available at www.gov.ph/2013/02/26/statement-of-president-aquino-on-the-sabah-incident-february–26–2013/ (accessed 17 May 2014)

Prescott, Victor and Clive Schofield (2001) 'Undelimited maritime boundaries of the Asian Rim in the Pacific Ocean', *Maritime Briefing*, 3(1): 1–68.

Rabasa, Angel and Peter Chalk (2012) *Non-Traditional Threats and Maritime Domain Awareness in the Tri-Border Area of Southeast Asia: The Coastal Watch System of the Philippines*, Santa Monica: RAND Corporation.

Ruhanas Harun (2009) 'The evolution and development of Malaysia's national security', in Abdul Razak Baginda (ed.), *Malaysia's Defence and Security Since 1957*, Kuala Lumpur: Malaysian Strategic Research Centre, pp. 31–58.

Sato, Yoichiro (2010) 'Perceptions of transnational security threat in Malaysia and Singapore: windows of cooperative opportunities for the United States', in David Fouse (ed.), *Issues for Engagement: Asian Perspectives on Transnational Security Challenges*, Honolulu: Asia-Pacific Centre for Security Studies (APCSS), pp. 140–53.

Sebastian, Leonard C. (1991) 'Ending an armed struggle without surrender: the demise of the Communist Party of Malaysia (1979–89) and the aftermath', *Contemporary Southeast Asia*, 13(3): 271–98.

Shepard, A. (1996) Testing the Waters: Chinese Policy in the South China Sea, Australian Defence Studies Centre Working Paper 39, Canberra: Australian Defence Studies Centre.

Sidhu, Jatswan S. (2009) 'Malaysia's defence and security since 1957: an overview', in Abdul Razak Baginda (ed.), *Malaysia's Defence and Security Since 1957*, Kuala Lumpur: Malaysian Strategic Research Centre, pp. 1–30.

Straits Times (2004) 'Malaysia offers navy escorts through Malacca Straits', *Straits Times*, 18 April.

Sutarji Kasmin, Haji (2009) 'Maritime law enforcement agencies and auxiliary security agencies in Malaysia', in Abdul Razak Baginda (ed.), *Malaysia's Defence and Security Since 1957*, Kuala Lumpur: Malaysian Strategic Research Centre, pp. 187–217.

Tang Siew Mun (2010) 'Malaysia's security outlook and challenges', in *NIDS Joint Research Series, No. 5: Asia Pacific Countries' Security Outlook and Its Implications for the Defense Sector*, Tokyo: National Institute for Defence Studies (NIDS), pp. 25–36.

Tempo (2005) 'Senggolan kapal perang Indonesia–Malaysia' [Collision of Indonesia–Malaysia warships], 17 April, p. 20.

World Bank (n.d.) 'Military expenditure (% of GDP)', *The World Bank*, available at http://data.worldbank.org/indicator/MS.MIL.XPND.GD.ZS (accessed 3 October 2013).

Zachariah, Elizabeth (2013) 'Jakarta and KL haze deal angers Asean partners', *The Malaysian Insider*, 13 September, available at www.themalaysianinsider.com/malaysia/article/jakarta-and-kl-strike-deal-to-keep-it-hush-hush-on-haze (accessed 15 September 2013).

32

Malaysia and the United States

A maturing partnership

Heng Pek Koon

Over the past six decades, since gaining independence in 1957 from Britain and establishing formal ties with the United States, Malaysia has sought to maintain and strengthen bilateral ties with the world's leading superpower. Its primary objectives have been to build a successful multiracial nation and secure a peaceful Southeast Asian neighbourhood. With the two nations sharing fundamentally common strategic interests, the bilateral relationship has proven remarkably resilient, particularly in the area of trade and security cooperation. Just as American economic and national strategic interests drive American foreign policy toward Malaysia, Malaysia's national interests have led it to look to the US as a major source of trade, foreign investment and technology to promote economic growth, and as a key regional stabiliser in the face of security challenges.

Foreign policy decision-making in Malaysia has been in the hands of the leadership of the United Malays National Organisation (UMNO), the dominant political party in the coalition governments that have held power since independence. Ever since the traumatic May 1969 race riots, national leaders have been keenly aware that inter-ethnic imbalances, if left unaddressed, may undermine social stability. Thus, the organising principle of Malaysian domestic and foreign policy has been to implement the wide-ranging inter-ethnic redistributive and income-raising agenda of the New Economic Policy (NEP). While fundamentally a free market, the Malaysian economy is also regulated by state interventionist policies to implement Malay affirmative action measures (Gomez and Saravanamuttu 2013), requiring an uneasy balance. A second key source of Malaysian foreign policy is Islam, as a factor both in shaping relations between Muslims and non-Muslims in the country and also in colouring external relations with the west (Nair 1997).

Six Malaysian prime ministers have shaped the course of Malaysia–US ties since 1957: Tunku Abdul Rahman Putra Al Haj (1957–70), Tun Abdul Razak Hussein (1970–76), Tun Hussein Onn (1976–81), Tun Dr Mahathir Mohamad (1981–2003), Tun Abdullah Ahmad Badawi (2003–09) and Datuk Najib Abdul Razak (2009–present). In the political and economic realms, the goals of Malayan foreign policy have consistently revolved around forging racial harmony among the majority Malay and minority Chinese and Indian communities, promoting economic development and enhancing the legitimacy of the UMNO-dominated Barisan Nasional (BN, National Front) coalition. As Malaysia has looked to the

US for political, economic and military resources to advance its domestic goals, scholars have characterised the bilateral relationship in distinctive ways. Pamela Sodhy, for example, emphasises that the relationship is marked by both cooperation and tension, with cordiality strongly outweighing acrimony, on balance (Sodhy 1991, 2003, 2012). Helen Nesadurai describes Malaysia's foreign policy toward the US as one of 'rejecting dominance, embracing engagement' – a hedging posture that has allowed Malaysia to pursue more independent policies while simultaneously cultivating economic and security ties with Washington (Nesadurai 2004).[1]

Malaysia–US relations, 1957–81

Under the watch of first Prime Minister Tunku Abdul Rahman, mutually held Cold War objectives of containing communism and promoting economic growth through market capitalism drove bilateral foreign policy interests. While the Tunku placed more political and security reliance on Britain, source of military assistance and troops to defeat the communist insurgency, he looked to the US for investment and technology transfer to help transform Malaysia from an underdeveloped agricultural, raw materials-producing economy into a manufacturing, industrialised one (Sodhy 1991: 217). While Malaysia was firmly but informally aligned with the US during the Cold War, in the interest of maintaining neutrality and non-alignment, it did not join the Southeast Asia Treaty Organization (SEATO), the US-led regional anti-communist defence pact formed in 1954 (Saravanamuttu 2010: 333); and while not committing Malaysian troops to Vietnam, the Tunku fully supported the Vietnam War. Washington appreciated the Tunku's successful efforts in defeating communism on the domestic front, even if Malaysia did not participate fully in the US's regional containment strategy. During his visit as the first American president to Malaysia in 1966, Lyndon Johnson praised his host for 'valiantly [subduing] a Communist insurgency and . . . building a free and prospering countryside that can relieve the poverty and the apathy upon which communism so often thrives' (cited in D'Cruz 2013).

Impacting bilateral ties during Prime Minister Tun Razak's leadership were two fundamental transformations, one in the domestic realm and the other in the regional environment. The race riots of May 1969 brought a fundamental shift in the country's political and economic landscape. Concentrating ever increasing authority and power in its own hands, UMNO initiated the NEP to address Malay economic backwardness. In Malaysia's larger neighbourhood, President Nixon's winding down of the Vietnam War and moves to normalise ties with China enabled Razak himself to pursue new diplomatic initiatives in the region. In 1974, he established diplomatic ties with China, making Malaysia the first country in Southeast Asia to do so.

From 1970 until the present, the NEP has served as the key driver of Malaysian domestic and foreign policy, with bilateral ties with the US and other countries recalibrated to achieve its Malay economic empowerment goals. American trade and investments, vital for economic growth, job creation, wealth redistribution and poverty alleviation, were actively sought. Although the policy has posted impressive growth rates, succeeded in reducing inter-ethnic income disparities and ensured political stability, it has also retarded the task of fostering national unity and multiracial harmony. Non-Malays have become increasingly alienated from the National Front government, and growing numbers of Malays themselves have become disenchanted with the widening intra-Malay income gap as well as the money politics and cronyism that have come to characterise UMNO political behaviour. The unprecedented electoral losses suffered by the governing coalition in 2008 and 2013 provided evidence of these high levels of dissatisfaction (see, for example, Maznah 2008; Gomez and Saravanamuttu 2013: 346–56).

Under Prime Minister Hussein Onn's leadership, bilateral ties moved forward smoothly, with no fundamental departures from the objectives and strategies of his two predecessors' domestic and foreign policy agendas. Under Hussein's watch, Malaysia promoted its 'neutralism' on the international stage and signed ASEAN's landmark Treaty of Amity and Cooperation (Saravanamuttu 2010: 167–81).

Malaysia–US relations, 1981–2003

During Mahathir's twenty-two-year premiership, a period that spanned the presidencies of Ronald Reagan, George H.W. Bush, William Clinton and George W. Bush, the multifaceted bilateral relationship continued to work well in the areas of economic and security cooperation. The 'atmospherics' of the overall relationship were marred, however, by Mahathir's acerbic criticisms of US policies in the Middle East and US tepid responses to the 1997–98 Asian Financial Crisis on the one hand, and by Washington's sharp rebukes of Malaysia's human rights record pertaining to the arrest and incarceration of Deputy Prime Minister Datuk Anwar Ibrahim, on the other.

Apart from the Anwar issue, two other major contretemps seriously frayed Malaysia–US ties: Mahathir's call to ASEAN to join with Japan, China and South Korea to establish the East Asian Economic Grouping (EAEG) and his assertive championing of issues high on the international Islamic agenda, particularly support for Palestinian rights. Both initiatives were seen as underlining Mahathir's attitude of counterhegemonic antipathy and rejection of the US-dominated neoliberal global order.

Responding to the imminent creation of trade blocs in both Europe and North America, where the European Union and the North American Free Trade Agreement would come into force in 1993 and 1994, respectively, Mahathir argued that East Asia needed its own regional free trade regime in order to maintain global competitiveness (Dhillon 2009: 216). The Bush administration's response to Mahathir's initiative in 1991 to establish an Asians-only economic club that expressly excluded the US was decidedly negative. Washington regarded the EAEG as a competing regional framework, one that would threaten the institutional strength of the US-endorsed Asia-Pacific Economic Cooperation (APEC) forum. Telling his Japanese counterpart to stay clear of the EAEG, Secretary of State James Baker warned that Tokyo's participation would 'draw a line in the Pacific Ocean' and lead to 'a split between the United States and Japan' (cited in Akashi 1997: 5). In the face of strong US opposition and a lukewarm reception by Indonesia, the EAEG proposal was downgraded to the East Asian Economic Caucus (EAEC), an arrangement that placed it within APEC's purview.

While the EAEC concept spoke to Mahathir's ambitions to acquire greater stature as a pivotal player in shaping the emerging regional architecture in East Asia, his championing of Islamic issues derived from both domestic priorities and his desire to play a larger role in the Muslim world. Since the early 1980s, the widening appeal to Malay voters of opposition Party Islam SeMalaysia's (PAS) Islamic agenda had driven Mahathir to put new emphasis on pro-Islam policies in both domestic and foreign policy. His strident criticisms of US policies in the Middle East found favour with Malaysia's Muslim audiences, who were already inclined to be highly critical of Washington's pro-Israel policies. While Mahathir initially supported George H.W. Bush's conduct of the Gulf War in 1990, that support soon dissipated and was replaced by sustained forceful criticism of the US for its 'anti-Muslim' policies and its 'war against Islam' under George W. Bush's global war on terror after 9/11. Mahathir's sharp anti-US rhetoric created a decidedly uncomfortable environment for American officials charged with advancing the bilateral relationship.

These serious differences came to a head in September 1998, when Mahathir sacked his deputy over policy differences on how the country should respond to the financial crisis, as well as Anwar's power play for the top position in UMNO. When Anwar began to advocate for greater accountability in the country's governance and greater civil liberties for its people, while also being receptive to Washington's and the International Monetary Fund's policies for addressing the financial crisis, he earned the high regard of the Clinton administration, as well as that of US human rights activists and business leaders.

Tensions between the countries came to a head over Mahathir's incarceration of Anwar over abuse of power and sodomy charges, widely perceived by Washington policy-makers as trumped-up indictments. A diplomatic mini-crisis erupted during Vice President Al Gore's state visit to Malaysia in November 1998. Representing Clinton at the APEC summit meeting, Gore criticised his hosts for suppressing freedom and praised the pro-Anwar *reformasi* (reformation) movement that was then in full play in Kuala Lumpur. To his Malaysian audience, Gore's reference to *reformasi* was a direct allusion to the reform movement that had successfully toppled the thirty-one-year authoritarian rule of Indonesian President Suharto that May. Finding Gore's choice of words deeply offensive and constituting 'gross interference in the internal affairs of the country and a brazen violation of the basic tenets of relations between sovereign states', then Foreign Minister Abdullah Badawi countered that 'Malaysians would hold the United States accountable for any rupture of harmony arising from this irresponsible incitement' (cited in Landler 1998).

Despite those strains, the overall bilateral relationship remained resilient, buoyed by robust economic and security cooperation. Like his predecessors, Mahathir looked to the US as a vital partner to expand trade and investment opportunities. After formulating his 'Vision 2020' policy in 1991, which proposed to make Malaysia a fully developed nation by 2020, Mahathir was even more keenly aware that Malaysia's accession to that status depended on attracting larger US trade and investments, which he actively sought (Sodhy 2012: 18–20). In contrast to the high profile of Malaysia–US economic cooperation, defence cooperation with the Pentagon was conducted outside the glare of public attention. While Malaysian leaders had long recognised that the US military presence was indispensable for regional stability, unfavourable perceptions among the majority-Muslim population toward US military support for Israel made it politically judicious for UMNO's leaders to downplay the country's military cooperation with the US. Even while continuing to chastise the US for its policies vis-à-vis Muslim countries, however, Mahathir, just prior to relinquishing power, moved to improve his public standing with the US by backing the formation of the Malaysia–America Friendship Caucus in the US Congress, and endorsing the establishment of the US-supported Southeast Asia Regional Centre for Counter-Terrorism (SEARCCT) in Kuala Lumpur.

Malaysia–US relations, 2003–09

Bilateral ties improved rapidly under Prime Minister Abdullah Badawi. During his stewardship, two key bilateral initiatives augmented ties with the US: counterterrorism cooperation and free trade agreement negotiations. A third important development was Malaysia's initiative in persuading ASEAN to launch the East Asia Summit (EAS) in 2005,[2] a development that prompted Washington to recalibrate its role in the expanded ASEAN-led regional architecture and eventually helped lay the policy foundations of the 'pivot' to Asia under Obama.

Abdullah's more open and conciliatory demeanour produced welcome changes both in the domestic political environment and in the bilateral relationship. His decision to release Anwar Ibrahim signalled the new leader's desire to provide greater political space for opposition parties and civil society movements, and to govern in a more transparent and accountable manner, steps that won Washington's approval (Sodhy 2012: 24–51). In the area of counter-terrorism cooperation, Abdullah made good on Malaysia's pledge of enhancing cooperation with American security and intelligence agencies in breaking up alleged Al Qaeda-linked cells such as the Kumpulan Mujahidin Malaysia (Malaysia Mujahidin Movement) and in detaining scores of suspected terrorists under Malaysia's Internal Security Act. Given the transnational nature of militant Islam in Southeast Asia, Malaysia–US counterterrorism cooperation has been multilateralised to cover cooperation with both US and local security agencies in Indonesia, Singapore, the Philippines and Thailand, countries that also have comprehensive bilateral counterterrorism programmes with the US.

Abdullah's conduct of counterterrorism cooperation with the US was located within a more grandiose agenda of propagating Islam Hadhari (Civilizational Islam), a concept he developed in order to exhort the *ummah* (Muslim community), both in Malaysia and at large, to revive aspects of Islam for political moderation, social inclusion, and economic competitiveness and progress; to pursue knowledge and open-mindedness in science and technology; and to emphasise moral integrity (Saravanamuttu 2010: 239–42). In the war against Islamist terror, Abdullah pitched Malaysia as a successful democratic, tolerant and economically competitive nation and Islam Hadhari as an antidote to the tide of extremism ravaging the larger Muslim world (Abdullah 2004).

Spurred by the robustness of bilateral economic ties – Malaysia had become America's tenth-largest trading partner by 2005 – and a desire to promote Malaysia's global competitiveness, Abdullah launched a bilateral FTA with the US (USTR 2006). However, the two countries failed to reach agreement within the tight sixteen-month time frame before the expiration date in July 2007 of the Trade Promotion Act, which provided 'fast track' authority to the US president to present negotiated agreements to Congress for an up-or-down vote. A key reason for the stalled talks was Abdullah's continued reliance on government procurement and other affirmative action programmes to benefit Malay business interests, a policy that puts the country squarely at odds with neoliberal and free market trade practices the US seeks in FTAs (Heng 2007).

Malaysia–US relations, 2009–present

Of all of Malaysian leaders since independence, Datuk Najib, son of the country's second prime minister, Tun Razak, has the deepest and longest-lasting connections with senior US foreign policy-makers, particularly within military, intelligence and business circles – ties forged during previous stints as Malaysia's defence minister and finance minister. Najib has made his greatest mark in the security and economic dimensions of the relationship, while also strengthening and expanding educational and socio-cultural exchanges.

Najib's emergence on the national and international scene coincided with the US decision in 2011 to 'rebalance' or 'pivot' to Asia. As US policy-makers reassessed their strategic and economic interests in the Asia-Pacific region, they decided to give greater priority to bilateral engagement with the US's Southeast Asian treaty allies and new partners as well as elevate US multilateral ties with ASEAN and EAS (Clinton 2011). The US rebalance and emphasis on strengthening bilateral ties with Malaysia have given Najib a more prominent place in US foreign policy thinking than that accorded to any prior Malaysian leader.

In the sphere of military and counterterrorism cooperation, Najib has strengthened the collaborative programmes he initiated while serving as defence minister, such as joint naval exercises, reciprocal military training, and purchases of American military equipment. In 2013, seventy-five visits and exchanges were planned with the US military to boost Malaysia's military capability and 'help it become a more professional and flexible force' in areas of mutual concern, such as maritime security, counterterrorism, non-proliferation, humanitarian disaster and relief assistance, and peacekeeping operations (Hagel 2013). In the field of counterterrorism cooperation, Najib continued to work closely with the US to monitor Islamist militant groups that were using Malaysia as a base for both operational and terrorist financial transactions (Sodhy 2012: 60–63). At the US's behest and in response to a direct invitation from the Afghan government, Malaysia deployed a small force of military medical personnel to Bagram (*Malaysian Flying Herald* 2012). Under a new Global Movement of Moderates initiative, Najib has continued Abdullah's policy of portraying Malaysia as an exemplary, moderate Muslim-majority nation, one that Washington can rely on to help foster progress and stability in the Muslim world at large (Najib 2012: 14–32).

In the field of strategic cooperation, Najib's most notable contribution has been to advance the US's non-proliferation agenda by passing the Strategic Trade Act in April 2012 and endorsing the Proliferation Security Initiative in April 2014. This measure strengthened Malaysia's ability, with US assistance, to curb the export and trans-shipment of weapons of mass destruction (WMD) materials. Malaysia had become a smuggling and trans-shipment hub for WMD-related procurement networks, leading US ambassador James Keith to urge Malaysia in February 2009 'to contribute to international mechanisms to manage the flow of sensitive technology, including nuclear and missile-related equipment' (cited in Lieggi and Sabatini 2010). When Najib attended the Nuclear Security Summit in Washington in April 2010, his groundbreaking contribution to bilateral non-proliferation cooperation was publicly recognised by President Obama; Najib was one of only two Asian leaders granted a face-to-face meeting at the summit with Obama (the other being Hu Jintao).

Concurrently with Najib's measures to strengthen the strategic relationship, both countries moved to augment economic ties further through negotiations over the Trans-Pacific Partnership (TPP) Agreement, a plurilateral FTA portrayed by Obama's National Security Adviser Thomas Donilon as 'the centerpiece of [US] economic rebalancing . . . [which] allows the people of the Asia-Pacific – including the American people – to reap the rewards of greater trade and growth' (Donilon 2013). Representing a major step toward an ultimate FTA of the Asia-Pacific region, and envisaged to come into force in 2014, the twelve-member TPP would constitute the world's largest high-quality free trade area, comprising a total population of 800 million and holding a 38.2 percent share of global GDP in 2012 (Williams 2013: 8; Fergusson *et al.* 2013).[3]

For Najib, participation in the TPP talks offered a timely opportunity to both conclude the unfinished Malaysia–US FTA talks that had started under Abdullah, and to gain more free trade partners, notably Japan and Singapore. In 2013, Malaysia ranked as the twentieth-largest goods trading partner of the US with US$40.3 billion in two-way goods trade. US foreign investment had grown steadily, totalling US$15.0 billion in 2012, an increase of 21 percent from 2011 (Punke 2013). Najib's principal goal in seeking TPP membership was to increase trade and attract high-quality foreign investments and high-end technology deemed necessary to enhance the country's industrial, agricultural, service, biotech and science and technology sectors, toward the goal of becoming an advanced nation by 2020. While Malaysia made a swift transition from a largely agricultural to a manufacturing-based economy in the 1970s and 1980s, by the early 2000s, it appeared to have become caught in the 'middle-income trap' (Hill *et al.* 2012; Lean and Smyth 2014). Najib sought to remove the structural and economic barriers to Malaysia's graduation to high-income status through an ambitious economic reform blueprint, details of which were enumerated in his New Economic Model (NEM), Economic Transformation Programme, and Government Transformation Programme (Lean and Smyth 2014; Wan Saiful 2011). During one of his many visits to the US to court American investors, Najib stressed that liberalisation of the Malaysian economy under the NEM had, by May 2011, given foreign investors unrestricted access and 100 percent equity ownership in twenty-seven service sub-sectors, with many more to come (Najib 2011).

When Malaysia first joined the TPP talks, American and Malaysian negotiators were optimistic that they could successfully come to an agreement. Najib had given strong indications that he had the political will to deal with the remaining 'sticking points' – including services, investment, financial services and government procurement – that had earlier stymied the Malaysia–US FTA talks.[4] That optimism was buoyed in part by the notable lack of public protests from consumer, labour, environmental, agricultural and Malay business groups compared with those which had dogged the bilateral FTA negotiations (Smeltzer 2009); however, public protests against the TPP emerged after the general election in March 2013, in which the BN lost the popular vote though it kept its parliamentary majority. With the long drawn-out election campaign behind them, both UMNO and the opposition turned their attention to the TPP in July, when the eighteenth round of talks was held in Malaysia. Public opposition, led by protectionist groups in UMNO and Malay business, as well as multiracial consumer, labour and environmental groups, has gained momentum (Kyodo News International 2013a), emboldened by former Prime Minister Mahathir's assertions that accession to the TPP would require Malaysia to abandon its pro-Malay policies, regardless of the damage to Malaysian society (Mahathir 2013a).

A second obstacle faced by Najib in his quest for Malaysia to join the TPP has been the demand by the opposition Pakatan Rakyat (People's Alliance), led by Anwar Ibrahim, that any final deal be discussed in parliament, and not be approved only by executive fiat, as Najib originally envisaged; he had planned to obtain only cabinet, not parliamentary, approval for the final TPP package. Thus, despite his belief that accession to the TPP would enhance Malaysia's trade competitiveness, the domestic imperative of having to shore up his leadership of UMNO – in the face of Mahathir's objections to the TPP – has led Najib to backtrack on his reformist agenda while assuring his critics that he would only approve an agreement that is 'most favourable' to the country (Kyodo News International 2013b). He has also re-emphasised his commitment to Malay special rights through his *bumiputera* Economic Empowerment Agenda, instructing government-linked companies to set pro-Malay targets for personnel, procurement and financial incentive measures (Najib 2013).

Cultural differences between the two countries notwithstanding, it must be noted that the US and Malaysia have enjoyed more than fifty years of productive interactions among students, scholars, homestay host families, businessmen and participants in people-to-people exchanges (Sodhy 2012). During its twenty years in Malaysia, from 1962 to 1983, the Peace Corps nurtured many of those early relationships, as did high school students' travelling in both directions under the American Field Service programme and professors and students, under Fulbright and East–West Center Programs. Later came university affiliations and twinning programmes, which are still active. Most recently, Najib, citing the valuable earlier contributions of the Peace Corps, led the way in encouraging the US to send Peace Corp-like English-language specialists to conduct training in Malaysia. His proposal has been modified and subsumed under the highly successful Fulbright English Teaching Assistants (ETA) programme (*Star* 2013).[5]

While relations between the two countries are generally smooth in the security, economic and educational/people-to-people areas, one notable source of irritation has been the State Department's annual *Trafficking in Persons Report*. Over the past decade, that assessment has consistently given Malaysia low marks for how it treats both legal and illegal migrant workers, estimated by the US to stand at some four million in 2013 and comprising up to 30 percent of the total workforce (US State Department 2013: 249; Robertson 2008: 1). Malaysia has also been faulted for its problematic treatment of refugees, the majority of whom have come from Myanmar to Malaysia in transit to the US and other Western countries (US Senate 2009). Having been relegated three times to the lowest-ranking Tier 3 category and placed on the Tier 2 Watch List for four consecutive years, Malaysia is in danger of facing US sanctions that, among other measures, will withhold funding for the participation of Malaysian government employees in educational and cultural exchange programmes. Another concern raised by US-based human rights groups is that while the repressive Internal Security Act has been replaced by the Security Offences (Special Measures) 2012 Act (SOSMA), that measure has not fundamentally improved human rights protection in the country. According to its critics, while SOSMA offered some improvements, it was more retrograde in other ways, thus 'demonstrating yet again that the Malaysian government was playing "bait and switch" with human rights'; together with amendments to other laws, SOSMA is deemed to have 'broadened police apprehension and surveillance powers in new and innovative ways' (Spiegel 2012: 2).

Human rights advocates in both the US and Malaysia have also become increasingly troubled by UMNO's polarising emphasis on race and religion in ways that seek to buttress Malay 'supremacy' (*ketuanan Melayu*) and restrict interfaith relations between Muslims and non-Muslims. That posture contrasts sharply with Najib's international advocacy of moderate Muslim governance. In addition, it is seen by many Malaysians as reflecting an ironic reversal of roles in which PAS – now a member of the multi-ethnic opposition Pakatan and posting unprecedented gains among non-Muslim voters since 2008 – is in many ways today less likely than UMNO to play the race and religion card (Ahmad Fauzi 2013). Most troubling have been recent pronouncements by Islamic officials outlawing the use of Arabic words by non-Muslims, including the term 'Allah' in translations of the Bible meant only for Christians in the country (Nambiar 2014). Forthcoming versions of the State Department's annual *Report on International Religious Freedom* will likely reflect negatively on those constraints to interfaith harmony in the country.

The regional context of Malaysia–US relations: ASEAN and China

Malaysia–US relations are carried out in the context not only of domestic factors, but also of national priorities related to regional institutions, notably ASEAN and EAS, as well as major regional powers, particularly China. Consequently, bilateral initiatives in such diverse areas as free trade arrangements, counterterrorism, non-proliferation, maritime security, environmental protection, humanitarian assistance and disaster relief, and preventing transnational crime pertaining to trafficking in people, arms and narcotics have been, and will continue to be, conducted within this wider foreign policy context.

A founding member of ASEAN, originator of initiatives such as the Zone of Peace, Freedom and Neutrality (ZOPFAN) principle in 1971, and promoter of EAS in 2005, Malaysia continues to give top priority to ASEAN; the association has proven its worth by providing a more secure regional political environment, advancing greater regional economic integration and forging closer cooperative ties among its member countries. As ASEAN chair in 2015, Malaysia will preside over the official launch of two landmark ASEAN undertakings, the ASEAN Economic Community and the ASEAN-led Regional Comprehensive Economic Partnership (RCEP), a preferential trade agreement that includes China, Japan, South Korea, India, Australia and New Zealand. These developments, both of which will move forward regardless of what happens with the TPP, will in themselves significantly increase Malaysia's economic competitiveness.

The US's rebalance to Asia policy gives a central role to ASEAN as the driver of regional integration. Its membership in the EAS since 2011 has enabled the US to play a direct part in shaping the region's strategic and political agenda while opening up new avenues for multifaceted cooperation with its formal treaty allies, and with new partners such as Malaysia, Indonesia and Vietnam. In order to operationalise the multilateral dimensions of the US's pivot, a new Office of Strategy and Multilateral Affairs was created in the State Department's Bureau of East Asian and Pacific Affairs in 2011. Describing Malaysia as an important partner in the US's recalibrated strategy in Asia, a senior American official called the country 'a bridge between East and Southeast Asia and an influential voice of moderation; and a success story, strategic partner and friend' in four critical areas of US foreign policy in the region: promotion of economic ties, strengthening of East Asian institutions, joint efforts in solving global problems, and advancing people-to-people exchanges (Burns 2011).

China's emergence on the world stage as a major player presents new opportunities and challenges to both Malaysia and the US. China will play a crucial factor in their respective future foreign policy calculations because it is in both countries' interests to encourage China's peaceful rise. Working separately and in cooperation with Malaysia, ASEAN and EAS, the US seeks to maintain its pre-eminent strategic position in the Asia-Pacific region. Malaysia, as a claimant state in the territorial disputes in the South China Sea, looks to the US to uphold freedom of navigation and to support ASEAN's goal of concluding a Code of Conduct in the South China Sea with China (Thayer 2012a, 2012b). In short, both countries seek to maximise the benefits of expanding economic ties with Beijing while minimising the challenges emanating from China's rapid military modernisation and increasingly assertive behaviour in the South China Sea.

President Barack Obama's visit and the US–Malaysia Comprehensive Partnership

Washington's appreciation of Najib's role in elevating the bilateral relationship to a historic high was capped by President Obama's official visit to Kuala Lumpur in April 2014. The key outcome of Obama's visit was the upgrading of the bilateral relationship to a Comprehensive Partnership that seeks to institutionalise 'dialogue mechanisms in key areas including political and diplomatic cooperation, trade and investment, education and people-to-people ties, security and defense cooperation, as well as collaboration on the environment, science and technology, and energy' (White House 2014). In the area of democracy and human rights, while Obama did not meet with beleaguered opposition leader Anwar Ibrahim (who met with National Security Advisor Susan Rice), he promoted his views on democracy and civil liberties with Malaysian civil society leaders as well as youth leaders in Malaysia and the region in a separate town hall session (Obama 2014).

As a TPP negotiating partner and the ASEAN Chair in 2015, when the ASEAN Economic Community and Regional Comprehensive Economic Partnership will take formal form,

Malaysia is well positioned to advance US economic and strategic interests in the region. Najib and Obama emphasised their mutual commitment to further enhance Malaysia–US engagement on bilateral, regional and international issues. Both leaders underlined the need for a successful conclusion of the TPP talks, and endorsed Najib's Global Movement of Moderates to mitigate religious extremism in the Muslim world and a binding Code of Conduct in the South China Sea between ASEAN and China to manage tensions in the South China Sea. The two leaders also pledged to intensify cooperation beyond long-standing bilateral economic and strategic issues to cover educational, cultural people-to-people exchanges, with the extension and expansion of the Fulbright English Teaching Assistants programme, and promotion of youth empowerment and leadership in Malaysia and across the region through the Malaysian Global Innovation and Creativity Centre (MAGIC) and the US-funded Young Southeast Asian Leaders Initiative (YSEALI) (Obama 2014).

Conclusion

Post-Cold War strategic interests between the US and Malaysia have revolved around the mutual desire to maintain political and strategic stability in the region, particularly maritime security in the South China Sea; to deepen bilateral trade ties as well as expand regional economic linkages; and to deal with the threat of Islamist terrorism since the 2001 attacks against the US. In the past ten years, the growing salience of ASEAN as the driver of regional integration has increasingly shaped the contours of Malaysia–US relations, as both countries have looked to the grouping to advance their respective political, economic and security objectives. Another significant variable that has affected the foreign policy of both countries has been China's rise, which has presented unprecedented opportunities, but also uncharted challenges, for both countries.

Such mutually held interests have shaped Washington's perception that constructive relations with Malaysia would well serve the US's political, economic and strategic goals, both bilaterally and multilaterally, through ASEAN and the EAS. Despite Malaysia's not being a formal treaty ally, and despite policy differences and displays of anti-US sentiments during the Mahathir era, the US has long regarded Malaysia as a valuable partner in promoting Washington's key foreign policy objectives in the region, such as counterterrorism, maritime security, trade and investment promotion and advancement of democracy and human rights. The US's positive predisposition toward Malaysia in facilitating Washington's foreign policy agenda in the region has, in turn, enabled Malaysia to punch above its weight and to leverage its relationship with the world's superpower.

The bilateral relationship, which at times in the past has struggled to rise above mistrust, has become, under Najib's leadership, a 'functionally mature friendship rooted primarily in trade, defence and security' (Noor 2013). During Obama's four-country April 2014 trip to the region, Malaysia was the only non-treaty ally destination (the others were Japan, South Korea and the Philippines). Although the TPP negotiations are high on the bilateral agenda of both countries, in the final analysis, should Malaysia and the US fail to reach agreement, it would not prove a major setback to the overall bilateral relationship. The door would still remain open to Malaysia's participation at a date when the government is willing to substantially modify its pro-Malay domestic policies. Within the US itself, opposition to the lack of transparency in the conduct of the negotiations has increased, particularly from labour, environmental and special-interest groups (Johnson 2013). In addition, Obama has yet to obtain fast-track authority from Congress to secure a final up-or-down vote in the US. With the establishment of the Comprehensive Partnership, regular institutionalised dialogue will serve to foster greater cooperation that covers not only economic and strategic issues, but also matters of mutual interest and concern related to human rights and democracy, salient to the national, regional and global foreign policy agendas of both countries.

Notes

1 In the same vein, Johan Saravanamuttu argues that Malaysia pursues a posture of 'counterdominance and counterhegemony' and practises 'middlepowermanship' in its foreign policy toward big powers, a strategy that enables Malaysia to 'balance, hedge, and countervail the foreign policies of major powers' (Saravanmuttu 2010: 330).

2 The EAS, when originally conceived by Malaysia, was to comprise the ASEAN+3 countries: the ten ASEAN member countries plus China, Japan and South Korea. Due to concerns by countries such as Singapore, Indonesia and Japan that China would dominate the organisation, however, it was expanded to include Australia, New Zealand and India. The US and Russia became members in 2011.

3 The other ten negotiating parties are Australia, Brunei, Canada, Chile, Japan, Mexico, New Zealand, Peru, Singapore and Vietnam.

4 Information on Malaysia's bargaining position on the TPP was obtained from interviews conducted in the summer of 2013 with Malaysian officials in the Ministry of International Trade and Industry, American officials in the Office of the US Trade Representative and US–ASEAN Business Council figures familiar with the negotiations.

5 Launched in 2005 as an initiative of the state of Terengganu, the Fulbright ETA programme has been funded by the US and Malaysian governments since 2010. With an intake of 100 American grantees in 2014, it has grown to be one of the largest of its kind in the world.

Bibliography

Abdullah Badawi (2004) 'Speech delivered at the Oxford Centre for Islamic Studies, Magdalen College, University of Oxford', 1 October, available at www.oxcis.ac.uk/lectures/badawi.doc (accessed 26 January 2014).

Afif Pasuni and Mohamed Naweb Mohamed Osman (2013) 'Umno, Islam and Malayness: going back to roots', *RSIS Commentaries 231/2013*, Singapore: S. Rajaratnam School of International Studies, Nanyang Technological University.

Ahmad Fauzi Abdul Hamid (2013) 'Political Islam and Islamist politics in Malaysia', *Trends in Southeast Asia*, 2, Singapore: Institute of Southeast Asian Studies.

Akashi, Yogi (1997) An ASEAN Perspective on APEC, Working Paper 240, The Helen Kellogg Institute for International Studies, available at http://kellogg.nd.edu/publications/workingpapers/WPS/240.pdf (accessed 4 January 2014).

Anwar Ibrahim (1996) *The Asian Renaissance*, Singapore: Times Editions.

Burns, William J. (2011) 'Remarks by Deputy Secretary Burns on US, Malaysia and Asia-Pacific', 15 December, available at www.state.gov/s/d/2011/178872.htm (accessed 6 December 2013).

Clinton, Hillary (2009) 'Remarks with Malaysian Foreign Minister Y.B. Datuk Anifah bin Haji Aman after their meeting', 14 May, available at http://m.state.gov/md123505.htm (accessed 22 November 2013).

Clinton, Hillary (2011) 'America's Pacific Century', *Foreign Policy*, 11 October, available at www.foreignpolicy.com/articles/2011/10/11/americas_pacific_century (accessed 10 August 2013).

D'Cruz, Frankie (2013) 'When L.B.J. dropped by to say "thank you"', *Malay Mail*, 2 October, available at www.themalaymailonline.com/opinion/frankie-dcruz/article/when-l.b.j.-dropped-by-to-say-thank-you (accessed 10 January 2014).

Dhillon, Karminder Singh (2009) *Malaysian Foreign Policy in the Mahathir Era 1981–2003: The Dilemmas of Development*, Singapore: NUS Press.

Donilon, Thomas (2013) 'The United States and the Asia-Pacific in 2013', Speech delivered at Asia Society, New York, 12 March, available at http://asiasociety.org/blog/asia/donilon-us-not-containing-china-or-dictating-terms-asia-rebalance (accessed 10 October 2013).

Fergusson, Ian F., William H. Cooper, Remy Jurenas and Brock R. Williams (2013) *The Trans-Pacific Partnership Negotiations and Issues for Congress*, CRS Report for Congress, Washington DC: Congressional Research Service.

Gomez, Edmund Terence and Johan Saravanamuttu (2013) *The New Economic Policy in Malaysia: Affirmative Action, Ethnic Inequalities and Social Justice*, Singapore: NUS Press.

Hagel, Chuck (2013) 'News transcript: joint press conference with US Secretary of Defense Chuck Hagel and Minister Hishamuddin in Kuala Lumpur, Malaysia', 25 August, available at www.defense.gov/transcripts/transcript.aspx?transcriptid=5293 (accessed 12 November 2013).

Heng Pek Koon (2007) 'Negotiating the Malaysia–US Free Trade Agreement: challenges to bilateral trade liberalization in East Asia', paper presented at the 2007 Six Universities Annual Conference on Regionalism and Multilateralism in the Asia-Pacific, Korea University Graduate School of International Studies, 1–2 November.

Hiebert, Murray, Elina Noor, Gregory Poling and Tham Siew Yean (2012) *From Strength to Empowerment: The Next Generation of U.S.–Malaysia Relations*, Washington DC: Center for Strategic and International Studies.

Hill, Hal, Tham Siew Yean and Ragayah Haji Mat Zin (eds) (2012) *Malaysia's Development Challenges: Graduating from the Middle*, London: Routledge.

Johnson, Dave (2013) '"Secret negotiations": the Trans-Pacific Partnership Agreement (TPP): a corporate takeover?', *Global Research News*, May 16, available at http://www.globalresearch.ca/secret-negotiations-the-trans-pacific-partnership-agreement-tpp-a-corporate-takeover/5335348 (accessed 4 January 2014).

Johnson, Joshua R. (2010) *Cooperation and Pragmatism: Malaysian Foreign Policy under Najib*, Asia Pacific Bulletin 63, Washington DC: East-West Center.

Kerry, John (2013) 'Press statement by US Secretary of State John Kerry in Kuala Lumpur', 10 October, available at www.state.gov/secretary/remarks/2013/10/215274.htm (accessed 18 November 2013).

Khadijah Md Khalid (2011) 'Malaysia's foreign policy under Najib', *Asian Survey*, 51(3): 429–52.

Kyodo News International (2013a) 'Malaysians protest against TPP', *Global Post*, 11 October, available at www.globalpost.com/dispatch/news/kyodo-news-international/131011/malaysians-protest-against-tpp (accessed 7 January 2014).

Kyodo News International (2013b) 'Malaysia says not in hurry to sign TPP Agreement', *Global Post*, 15 August, available at www.globalpost.com/dispatch/news/kyodo-news-international/130815/malaysia-says-not-hurry-sign-tpp-agreement (accessed 7 January 2014).

Landler, Mark (1998) 'Gore scolded in Malaysia for defense of dissenters', *New York Times*, 18 November, available at www.nytimes.com/1998/11/18/world/gore-scolded-in-malaysia-for-defense-of-dissenters.html (accessed 3 January 2014).

Lean Hooi Hooi and Russell Smyth (2014) Malaysia's Past Successes and Uncertain Future: Graduating from the Middle or Caught in the Middle?, RSIS Working Paper 266, Singapore: S. Rajaratnam School of International Studies, Nanyang Technological University.

Lieggi, Stephanie and Richard Sabatini (2010) 'Malaysia's export control law: a step forward but how big?', *Nuclear Threat Initiative*, 10 May, available at www.nti.org/analysis/articles/malaysias-export-control-law/ (accessed 4 January 2014).

Mahathir Mohamad (2002) *Globalisation and the New Realities*, Selangor: Pelanduk Publications.

Mahathir Mohamad (2013a) 'FTAs actually restrict free trade', *New Straits Times*, 3 August, available at www.nst.com.my/opinion/columnist/ftas-actually-restrict-free-trade–1.331794 (accessed 25 November 2013).

Mahathir Mohamad (2013b) 'TPP will be another bad pact', *New Straits Times*, 12 July, available at www.nst.com.my/opinion/columnist/tpp-will-be-another-bad-pact-1.317645 (accessed 25 November 2013).

Malaysian Flying Herald (2012) 'Malaysia sends new contingent to Afghanistan', *Malaysian Flying Herald*, 2 May, available at http://malaysiaflyingherald.wordpress.com/2012/05/04/malaysia-sends-new-contingent-to-afghanistan/ (accessed 26 November 2013).

Maznah Mohamad (2008) 'Malaysia – democracy and the end of ethnic politics?', *Australian Journal of International Affairs*, 62(4): 441–59.

Mazwin Nik Anis and Izatun Shari (2009) 'US wants Malaysia to play a role in inter-faith dialogues', *The Star*, 28 September, available at www.thestar.com.my/story.aspx/?file=%2f2009%2f9%2f28%2fnation%2f20090928184815&sec–ation (accessed 16 December 2013).

Nair, Shanti (1997) *Islam in Malaysian Foreign Policy*, London: Routledge.

Najib Razak (2011) 'New York Invest Malaysia 2011: speech by Najib Razak', 17 May, available at www.1malaysia.com.my/en/speeches/new-york-invest-malaysia–2011/ (accessed 15 October 2013).

Najib Razak (2012) *Global Movement of the Moderates*, Kuala Lumpur: Global Movement of Moderates Foundation.

Najib Razak (2013) 'Full text of Najib's speech at 2013 UMNO General Assembly', *New Straits Times*, 7 December, available at www.nst.com.my/latest/full-text-of-najib-s-speech-at–2013-umno-general-assembly–1.425244#ixzz2qpkSi2zj (accessed 13 January 2014).

Nambiar, Predeep (2014) 'Penang Mufti outlaws 40 words to non-Muslims', *New Straits Times*, 11 January, available at www.nst.com.my/nation/general/penang-mufti-outlaws–40-words-to-non-muslims–1.459685 (accessed 30 January 2014).

Nesadurai, Helen E.S. (2004) Malaysia and the United States: Rejecting Dominance, Embracing Engagement, RSIS Working Paper 72(4).

Noor, Elina (2013) 'Empowering Malaysia–US ties', *New Straits Times*, 16 July, available at www.nst.com.my/opinion/columnist/empowering-malaysia-us-ties–1.320076?localLinksEnabled=false (accessed 20 August 2013).

Obama, Barack (2014) 'Remarks by President Obama at Young Southeast Asian Leaders Initiative Town Hall', 27 April, available at www.whitehouse.gov/the-press-office/2014/04/27/remarks-president-obama-young-southeast-asian-leaders-initiative-town-ha (accessed 14 May 2014).

Parameswaran, Prasanth (2013) *Getting to Full Bloom in US–Malaysia Relations*, Asia Pacific Bulletin 239, Washington DC: East-West Center.

Punke, Michael (2014) 'Statement by US Ambassador to the WTO Michael Punke at the WTO Trade Policy Review of Malaysia', 3–4 March, available at www.ustr.gov/about-us/press-office/speeches/transcripts/2014/March/Ambassador-Punke-statement-WTO-Trade-Policy-Review-Malaysia (accessed 28 May 2014).

Robertson, Philip S., Jr (2008) *Migrant Workers in Malaysia: Issues, Concerns and Points For Action*, Washington DC: Fair Trade Labor Association.

Russel, Daniel R. (2013) 'The Asia rebalance is here to stay', 31 December, available at www.huffingtonpost.com/daniel-r-russel/us-asia-rebalance-is-here-to-stay_b_4524853.html (accessed 7 January 2014).

Saravanamuttu, Johan (2010) *Malaysia's Foreign Policy, The First Fifty Years: Alignment, Neutralism, Islamism*, Singapore: Institute of Southeast Asian Studies.

Sheldon, Simon (2011) 'US–Southeast Asia relations: full court press', *Comparative Connections*, 12(4).

Sithraputhran, Siva (2013) 'Malaysian PM Najib entrenches race-based policies', Reuters, 14 September, available at http://news.yahoo.com/malaysian-pm-najib-entrenches-race-based-policies–081713929.html (accessed 13 November 2013).

Smeltzer, Sandra (2009) 'A Malaysia–United States free trade agreement: Malaysian media and domestic resistance', *Asia Pacific Viewpoint*, 50(1): 13–23.

Sodhy, Pamela (1987) 'Malaysia and the United States in the 1980s', *Asian Survey*, 27(10): 1074–94.

Sodhy, Pamela (1991) *The US–Malaysian Nexus: Themes in Superpower–Small State Relations*, Kuala Lumpur: Institute of Strategic and International Studies.

Sodhy, Pamela (2003) 'US–Malaysia relations during the Bush administration: the political, economic, and security aspects', *Contemporary Southeast Asia*, 25(3): 363–86.

Sodhy, Pamela (2012) *Malaysia–US Relations 2000–2011*, Kuala Lumpur: ISIS Malaysia.

Spiegel, Mickey (2012) *Smoke and Mirrors: Malaysia's 'New' Internal Security Act*, Asia Pacific Bulletin 167, Washington DC: East-West Center.

Star (2013) 'Fulbright ETA programme grows bigger', *The Star*, 12 October, available at www.thestar.com.my/News/Nation/2013/10/12/Fulbright-ETA-programme-grows-bigger–100-volunteers-set-to-boost-English-language-skills-next-year.aspx/ (accessed 19 January 2013).

Thayer, Carlyle (2012a) 'ASEAN's code of conduct in the South China Sea: a litmus test for community building?', *The Asia Pacific Journal: Japan Focus*, 10(34).

Thayer, Carlyle (2012b) 'The rise of China and maritime security in Southeast Asia', IDE-JETRO Paper, Tokyo: Institute of Developing Economies, Japan External Trade Organization.

United States Department of State (2013) *Trafficking in Persons Report 2013*, Washington DC: US Government Printing Office.

United States Senate Committee on Foreign Relations (2009) *Trafficking and Extortion of Burmese Migrants in Malaysia and Southern Thailand: A Report to the Committee on Foreign Relations, United States Senate*, Washington DC: US Government Printing Office.

United States Trade Representative (USTR) (2006) *USTR 2006 National Trade Estimates on Foreign Trade Barriers*, Washington DC: Office of the United States Trade Representative.

Vaughn, Bruce and Michael Martin (2007) *Malaysia: Political, Security, Economic, and Trade Issues Considered*, CRS Report for Congress, Washington DC: Congressional Research Service.

Wan Saiful Wan Jan (2011) 'Malaysia's new economic model: is the Malaysian government serious about economic liberalisation?', Friedrich Naumann Paper 14, Potsdam: Friedrich-Naumann-Stiftung für die Freiheit.

White House (2014) 'Joint Statement by President Obama and Prime Minister Najib of Malaysia', 27 April, available at www.whitehouse.gov/the-press-office/2014/04/27/joint-statement-president-obama-and-prime-minister-najib-malaysia–0 (accessed 16 May 2014).

Williams, Brock R. (2013) *Trans-Pacific Partnership (TPP) Countries: Comparative Trade and Economic Analysis*, CRS Report for Congress, Washington DC: Congressional Research Service.

World Bank (2012) *Malaysia Economic Monitor: Brain Drain*, Washington DC: The World Bank.

Yang Razali Kassim (2013) 'New battle lines drawn in Malaysian politics', *East Asia Forum*, 27 December, available at www.eastasiaforum.org/2013/12/27/new-battle-lines-in-malaysian-politics/ (accessed 25 January 2014).

33

Malaysia–China relations[1]

Three enduring themes

Kuik Cheng-Chwee

In one of the earliest studies on Malaysia's foreign relations, scholar Peter Boyce (1968: 145) observed that relations with China were 'the key point of reference' for Malaysia's foreign policy-makers. This observation was true throughout the early decades of Malay(si)a's existence as a newly independent small state in a volatile international environment, struggling to battle the China-backed Malayan Communist Party (MCP) against the backdrop of the Cold War. Significantly, the observation has remained generally true to the present day. Although (or precisely because) the external and internal contexts have changed drastically since the end of the Cold War, China has remained a key point of reference for Malaysia's external policy planners. This time, the reference has been cast in a largely positive light, as China has gradually emerged as a key economic and diplomatic partner since the early 1990s. Successive Malaysian leaders, from Mahathir Mohamad, to Abdullah Ahmad Badawi, to present Prime Minister Najib Abdul Razak, have all chosen to engage China at both bilateral and multilateral levels. Despite overlapping territorial claims in the South China Sea between the two countries, Malaysia has accommodated and capitalised on China's growing power, seeking to maximise commercial and geopolitical gains from the rising power while endeavouring to keep its long-term options open. Abdullah and Najib both chose China as their first country outside ASEAN to visit upon assuming the premiership in 2003 and 2009, respectively. Two weeks after his visit, Najib remarked in a key foreign policy speech that the trip was made 'because our relationship with China is fundamental to our national interests, and because there are many mutual lessons to be learnt and shared between our countries' (Najib 2009).

This chapter analyses the key factors that have made China so central to Malaysia's foreign policy planners. It argues that such persistent salience – and the turnaround in bilateral ties since the 1990s – is essentially a function of three enduring imperatives that have together characterised the dynamics of Malaysia–China ties. They are: the ambivalence of asymmetrical power relations; the gravity of geographical proximity; and the primacy of the political elite's domestic authority.

The chapter is divided into three parts. The first part elucidates the three enduring themes in Malaysia–China interactions. The second and third parts discuss how the interplay among these imperatives has shaped the evolution of Malaysia–China relations in the Cold War and the post-Cold War periods, respectively. The concluding section sums up the discussion.

The endurance of asymmetry, proximity and authority

Malaysia's relations with China are, by all measures, asymmetrical. The enormous disparity between the two countries in size of territory, population and resources necessarily results in a vast disparity in their economic and military capabilities. This immutable power gap means that, in effect, China can harm and help Malaysia's interests much more than any other actor can (with the obvious exception of the United States, and, during the Cold War, the Soviet Union). Size and strength matter in international relations; for the weak, the effects of asymmetry often go both ways, because the strong is a source of both apprehension and assistance. Such is the dominant theme that has coloured Malaysia's relations with the giant to its north, as discussed below.

The consequences of power asymmetry, significantly, are often heightened by geographical proximity, with particularly profound effects for weaker states like Malaysia. This is because proximity often means a greater range and a higher intensity of contacts between the states, thus rendering the weaker side more exposed to the consequences of the giant's might. The logic of proximity need not be always malignant. There can be benevolent aspects from the presence of a proximate power. The case of Malaysia–China interactions indicates that the effects of living with a giant neighbour are far from single-directional; rather, they are mixed and multifaceted. During the Cold War, proximity constituted security threat and political subversion to Malaysia, when communist China provided support and assistance to local communist insurgents. During the post-Cold War era, the negative ramifications of proximity include various trans-boundary challenges and territorial disputes over the South China Sea. On the other hand, however, Malaysia's post-Cold War interactions with China show that proximity has shaped the bilateral ties in a generally positive manner. Geographical closeness has encouraged a growing two-way flow of goods, services, capital and people between the two countries, which is, by and large, mutually beneficial. This has created a growing need for more bilateral cooperation.

While asymmetry and proximity are given conditions with which a smaller state like Malaysia must reckon, regardless of any changes at the domestic level, their effects are rarely straightforward. The case of Malaysia's China policy indicates that the effects of power asymmetry and geographical proximity have always been filtered through, and defined by, domestic politics, that is, the ruling elite's desire to enhance their political relevance and authority at home. The pages that follow illustrate why, despite the enduring challenges of asymmetry and proximity, Malaysia–China relations have been transformed from hostility during the Cold War to a cordial partnership in the post-Cold War era. It is argued that such transformation is, to a large extent, driven by the ruling elite's determination to prioritise economic and geopolitical benefits over potential security concerns from an essentially asymmetric power relationship, for the ultimate goal of enhancing their own domestic political authority.

The Cold War period

Throughout much of the Cold War decades, the effects of power asymmetry on Malaysia were predominantly negative. Relations between Malaya (after 1963, Malaysia) and communist China were then hostile and antagonistic. This was the result not only of ideological differences, but also of Mao Zedong's policy of supporting indigenous communist insurgencies in Southeast Asia, including the Malayan Communist Party (MCP), which had sought to establish an independent republic via armed struggle since 1948. As a result, the ruling Parti Perikatan (Alliance coalition) elite in Kuala Lumpur – comprising mainly the Malay aristocracy, predominantly Malay state bureaucrats, as well as English-educated Chinese and Indians – had come to view China as a threat to Malaya's security and internal order.

The Malayan elite's strategy was one of balancing, or aligning with Western powers to confront the source of threat. Under its first prime minister, Tunku Abdul Rahman, Malaya upon independence in 1957 entered into the Anglo-Malayan Defence Agreement (AMDA) with its former colonial ruler, Britain, and pursued an anti-communist and anti-China foreign policy (Chin 1983). In 1959, Malaya strongly deplored China's suppression of the Tibetan revolt (Jeshurun 2007: 27). In 1962, when the India–China border war broke out, Malaya was again forthright in criticising China's action (Saravanamuttu 1983: 27). Domestically, the Malayan government insulated the local Chinese community 'from the political and socio-cultural pulls reverberating from the home of Chinese civilization' (Singh 2004: 5). Publications from China were banned; travel restrictions to and from the mainland were imposed; and Bank of China branches in Malaya were all ordered to close. On 16 September 1963, Malaya merged with the former British colonies of Singapore, Sarawak and North Borneo (now Sabah) to form a larger Federation of Malaysia. From 1963 to 1966, Indonesia launched *Konfrontasi*, a low-intensity military campaign, to 'crush' the infant nation. Beijing gave support to Jakarta. This deepened Perikatan leaders' fear that Mao's China and Sukarno's Indonesia had forged a pact to establish hegemony over the region, with tiny Malaysia as the target of the two larger countries' expansionism. The end of *Konfrontasi* in 1966 ended the threat from Indonesia, but it did not ease the perceived threat from China.

The period from the second half of the 1960s to the early 1970s was a threshold for the Malaysian elite's security outlook. Developments during this period for the first time created an acute sense of uncertainty in the minds of the smaller state's elite about the long-term commitments of its security patrons. In July 1967, the British government announced that it would withdraw its forces east of Suez by the mid-1970s. In 1971, the British began the withdrawal of forces from its bases in Singapore and Malaysia. AMDA was replaced by the Five Power Defence Arrangements (FPDA) – among Britain, Australia, New Zealand, Malaysia and Singapore – which obligated all partner states to 'consult' each other in the event of external aggression against Malaysia and Singapore, but with no obligation for the partners to act. At around the same time, the United States also started to reduce its ground troops in mainland Southeast Asia, as enunciated by President Nixon's Guam Doctrine in 1969.

These developments, which highlighted the risks of abandonment, were watershed moments for Malaysia's security planners. In adjusting to the new realities that 'the British lion no longer had any teeth, the Australian umbrella was leaking, and the American eagle was winging its way out of Asia' (Sopiee 1975: 136), the Malaysian elite realised that they now had to cope with their own security problems, and to face the proximate big power largely by themselves. This realisation compelled the elite to stress self-reliance and regionalism in their security planning (Alagappa 1987).

Changing structural conditions thus called for major adjustments in Malaysia's external policy. They compelled the ruling Perikatan – now under the leadership of Tun Abdul Razak – to abandon the country's long-standing pro-West stance, and to replace it with a posture of non-alignment and regional neutralisation first enunciated by Tun Dr Ismail in 1968. This policy shift was formalised in April 1970 when Ghazali Shafie, the foreign ministry's permanent secretary, called for endorsement of the neutralisation

> not only of Indo-China area but of the entire region of South East Asia, guaranteed by the three major powers, the People's Republic of China, the Soviet Union and the United States, against any form of external interference, threat or pressure.
>
> *(Ghazali 1982: 157)*

The Malaysian elite judged that, in order to get the big powers to 'recognize, undertake, and guarantee Southeast Asia as an area of neutrality', the ASEAN states should acknowledge and accommodate the 'legitimate interests' of each of those powers, while observing a policy of 'equidistance' with all the powers (Ghazali 1982: 157). The new strategic outlook necessitated Malaysia to adjust its China policy because neutralisation 'required formal relations between the neutralized and the guarantor' (Sopiee 1975: 149). That China had now shown a more moderate external posture made it easier for Malaysia to explore reconciliation.

Malaysia's move toward rapprochement was driven not only by structural concerns, but also domestic security and political exigencies. In terms of security, the elites in Kuala Lumpur calculated that, given the perceived impending departure of their Western patrons, establishing relations with Beijing was a necessary move to reduce or neutralise the threat of MCP guerrillas, who were now restricted mainly to the Malaysia–Thailand border.

The early 1970s thus saw a process of engagement and normalisation of negotiations between Malaysia and China, culminating in Razak's historic visit to Beijing and the establishment of diplomatic ties on 31 May 1974. Malaysia was the first ASEAN member to establish such ties. Analyst Abdul Razak Baginda (2009) observes that while the external changes in the late 1960s and early 1970s provided opportunities for policy rethinking, it was domestic political developments that influenced the timing of Malaysia's rapprochement with China. In the wake of Perikatan's unprecedented electoral setback in May 1969 and ensuing ethnic riots (between Malays and Chinese), the new Razak government needed to formulate new directions for the country's internal and external policies that would serve *to restore internal stability* and *justify their authority* (Saravanamuttu 1983). Internally, the government moved to prioritise Malay interests by introducing a pro-Malay affirmative action programme in the form of the New Economic Policy (NEP) in 1971. It also moved to consolidate the United Malays National Organisation's (UMNO) dominance within the ruling coalition by co-opting most opposition parties, thereby transforming Perikatan into the enlarged Barisan Nasional (BN, National Front) in 1973. These political changes dramatically reduced the role of non-Malays in Malaysia's political and economic life (Means 1991).

Externally, the Razak government moved to steer Malaysia's foreign policy towards nonalignment, which appealed particularly to Malay nationalists and leftist groups. Given that neutralisation required Malaysia to drop its earlier anti-Chinese stance and make overtures to Beijing, this new posture also had the effect of alleviating the alienation of ethnic Chinese, winning over their support for BN and improving inter-ethnic reconciliation in the post-1969 environment (Saravanamuttu 1981). Shafruddin Hashim (1986: 159) notes that the rapprochement served to promote inter-communal conciliation, chiefly by enabling Malays 'to view the PRC, communism, and the local Chinese as separate entities'. In the general elections that were held little more than two months after Razak's China visit, the BN coalition clinched an overwhelming victory. This boosted the new government's authority.

These developments, however, did not erase the dual problems of asymmetry and proximity. Despite the rapprochement, Malaysian leaders from Razak through Hussein Onn to Mahathir Mohammad continued to view Beijing with distrust throughout the 1970s and 1980s. They were upset over China's 'dual-track policy' of separating government-to-government relations from party-to-party ties, which meant the relationship between the

Chinese Communist Party and communist parties elsewhere, including the MCP, were separate from government-to-government relations (Tilman and Tilman 1977: 153). Joseph Liow (2009: 53) notes that although China attempted to placate Malaysia's concerns by stressing that its support for the MCP was necessary in order to prevent the Soviets from exerting influence on the party, and that its support was limited only to moral support, Malaysia remained unconvinced. Malaysian elites were also suspicious of Beijing's policy of treating ethnic Chinese as 'returned Overseas Chinese' (Leong 1987). Overlapping territorial claims in the South China Sea further added to the mistrust (Mak 1991).

Notwithstanding these anxieties, the effects of asymmetry and proximity were not entirely negative during the Cold War period. Indeed, Malaysia's China policy since the 1970s has been motivated by a growing pragmatism on the part of the Malaysian elite, who saw economic benefits to be gained from the proximate giant's huge market. This was so especially after Mahathir came to power in 1981. While the new premier had paid attention to strengthening Malaysia's economic ties with Japan under his Look East Policy, he also sought to develop closer economic links with potential big markets such as China.

It was during the first decade of Mahathir's tenure that economic pragmatism was made a central theme in Malaysia's China policy. This was in part due to the leader's desire to reduce Malaysia's dependency on the West, and in part to the Malaysian elite's conviction that Deng Xiaoping's 1978 reforms were likely to continue.[2] This desire was further reinforced by the mid-1980s world economic recession. Against this backdrop, Mahathir led a large delegation to China in late 1985. The trip was significant not only because it was Mahathir's first visit to China, but also because it signalled his decision to concentrate on economic matters as the way forward to manage what was then considered to be the 'most sensitive foreign relationship' for Malaysia (Clad 1985). This top-down pragmatism cleared bureaucratic hurdles and smoothed the path for the signing of a series of important documents aimed at facilitating bilateral trade and investment (Lee and Lee 2005). Nevertheless, despite growing pragmatism in the interest of forging closer economic ties, political vigilance remained throughout the 1980s (Leong 1987). It was not until the end of the Cold War that the old political barriers were replaced by new opportunities, setting the stage for a turnaround in Malaysia–China relations in the new era.

The Post-Cold War era

Post-Cold War Malaysia–China relations are a story not so much about how the small state resists power asymmetry and proximity, but more about how it endeavours to live with, accommodate and even capitalise on these structural conditions for its own interests.

Indeed, as elaborated shortly, the past two decades have witnessed a transformation in Malaysia–China relations, from mutual suspicion to cordiality and partnership. Politically, present-day bilateral ties are at their best yet. During President Xi Jinping's visit to Malaysia in October 2013, the two countries agreed to elevate bilateral ties to a 'comprehensive strategic partnership'. Economically, since 2009, China has been Malaysia's top trading partner and Malaysia is China's largest trading partner in ASEAN, with total trade volume expected to reach US$100 billion in 2013 (the third Asian nation to exceed this figure, after Japan and South Korea). At the people-to-people level, the two nations have also seen a surge in tourism and educational links. Security-wise, while concerns linger among the Malaysian armed forces about China's future intentions, the country's political elites, by and large, hold positive perceptions of China.

What explains this transformation? What explains the shift in Malaysia's policy towards its giant neighbour, from hostility and guarded rapprochement during the Cold War to a productive partnership during the new era? In retrospect, the factors are multiple, but three are the most crucial, each concerning the ruling elite's domestic political considerations.

First, the removal of long-standing political barriers paved the way to a new era. In December 1989, MCP leader Chin Peng, who had been residing in China for years, signed a peace accord with the Malaysian government in Thailand. The accord not only put an end to the decades-long MCP armed struggle, but it also eliminated a key obstacle to Malaysia–China relations (Wang 1990). Also in 1989, China formulated a new law on citizenship, which severed the ties between the PRC and the 'overseas Chinese' diaspora. This development overlapped with a transformation within Malaysian society: since the 1970s, local Chinese have become more aware of 'their status as Malaysian citizens, and the primordial links with the homeland feature little, if at all, to them' (Liow 2009: 69) By the 1990s, the ethnic Chinese issue was no longer an impediment to bilateral ties. In August and September 1990, the Malaysian government lifted all restrictions on visits to China, in effect terminating a 'managed and controlled' policy that had aimed at insulating local Chinese from China's influence (Chai 2000).

Second, the changing source of threat to the ruling elite's domestic authority led Mahathir to reassess China's role toward Malaysia. With the dissolution of the MCP and the growing pressures of economic globalisation, Mahathir had, by the early 1990s, come to view protectionism and unfair practices in international trade as a principal threat to his rule. For him, these were not purely economic problems, but issues with profound political ramifications. According to Chandran Jeshurun (2007: 164–65), Mahathir's domestic power base was threatened in 1987 because of a political crisis sparked by the prolonged recession of the mid-1980s; this 'was one of the major factors that motivated much of his new thinking on national economic strategy and how to deal with the emerging realities of a new international economic order'.

Regional developments in the 1990s – particularly the lukewarm response from Japan and fellow ASEAN members to his idea of the East Asian Economic Grouping (EAEG), in contrast to China's supportive stance – might have convinced Mahathir to view Beijing as an indispensable partner in his quest to create a regional coalition in the post-Cold War international economic arena. In part because of China's continuous growth, its privileged position as a permanent member in the United Nations Security Council, and the emerging view that China 'would eventually replace Japan as an economic leader in the region',[3] the Malaysian elite had begun to perceive China as an emerging actor that would play an increasingly vital role in regional and global affairs. The fact that Malaysia and China saw eye-to-eye on issues like the 'Asian values' debate and multipolarity had further contributed to the elite's reassessment of China's role, from a source of fear to a source of economic and geopolitical support. Power asymmetry and proximity have, therefore, become a basis of attraction and partnership to the Malaysian elite in the new era.

Third, China's corresponding actions have made the transformation possible. Mahathir's desire to reset bilateral ties overlapped with the Chinese Communist Party's determination to improve China's relations with all the ASEAN states in the wake of Western sanctions following the Tiananmen incident in June 1989. In order to counter the West's isolation policy and ensure continuous access to markets and foreign investments, China embarked on a good neighbour policy, aimed at engaging and stabilising its relations with countries on its periphery, including the ASEAN states (Ba 2003). Malaysia, for its part, made concerted efforts to engage China.

This convergence gave rise to a process of mutual engagement. In December 1990, Chinese Premier Li Peng made a four-day visit to Malaysia. It was at a banquet for his Chinese counterpart that Mahathir proposed his EAEG idea. Four months later, in April 1991, Malaysia and China held their first bilateral consultative meeting in Kuala Lumpur.

These bilateral interactions, importantly, helped initiate a multilateral process among China and the ASEAN countries. Together with its ASEAN partners, Malaysia enthusiastically made efforts to integrate China into ASEAN activities, to which Beijing responded positively. In July 1991, three months after the first consultative meeting between the two countries, Malaysian Foreign Minister Abdullah Ahmad Badawi invited his Chinese counterpart, Qian Qichen, to attend the opening session of the 24th ASEAN Ministerial Meeting in Kuala Lumpur. Qian's attendance at the meeting, during which he also held an informal talk with other ASEAN foreign ministers, marked the beginning of the ASEAN–China dialogue process. In 1996, China became ASEAN's dialogue partner. China's actions in engaging Malaysia and other ASEAN states, as well as in responding positively to ASEAN's various regional initiatives (e.g., the ASEAN Regional Forum), have contributed to the transformation of Malaysia–China relations and development of ASEAN–China cooperation.

The 1997–98 Asian financial crisis, which highlighted a deepening economic interdependence among countries in the East Asian region, further expedited the transformation. China's decision not to devalue its currency was praised by Mahathir for helping to avert another round of currency crisis. China's positive response to Malaysia's June 1997 suggestion to hold an informal ASEAN plus China, Japan, and South Korea summit in Kuala Lumpur – held in December that year, the summit marked the beginning of the ASEAN Plus Three mechanism – along with Beijing's increasingly active participation in the various ASEAN-based regional forums, reinforced the Malaysian elite's assessment of China as an important *regional* partner. Hence, when Malaysia pushed to set up an APT secretariat in Kuala Lumpur in 2002 (unsuccessful because of opposition from other ASEAN members), then to host the inaugural East Asia Summit (EAS) in Kuala Lumpur in 2005, Beijing's strong backing was regarded as a *sine qua non*.

Beijing's receptivity to these regional initiatives, of course, was not entirely a function of China–Malaysia and China–ASEAN ties, but primarily China's own considerations about its broader geopolitical, geo-economic, and ideational interests (Kuik 2008). But the level of importance that China has attached to its bilateral relations with Malaysia – that transcends leadership changes in both capitals – should not be disregarded.

Indeed, many analysts inside and outside of Malaysia observe that, throughout the post-Cold War era, China has seemed to pursue a comparatively favourable policy towards Malaysia, even over the South China Sea issue. Joseph Liow (2009: 63), for instance, notes that while Beijing sternly condemned Vietnam for making inspection tours of the Vietnamese-held Spratly Islands in 1989, it remained silent over Malaysian king Sultan Azlan Shah's visit to the Malaysian-occupied atoll of Terumbu Layang-Layang in May 1992. In 1999, when Malaysia erected structures on Terumbu Peninjau (Investigator Shoal) and Terumbu Siput (Erica Reef), China's reaction was low-key (Razak Baginda 2002: 244).

Malaysia's outlook on China throughout the post-Cold War era reflects pragmatic acceptance of the reality of living with a proximate and rising power, which entails a determination to proactively shape the bilateral relations for mutual long-term benefit. In a 2004 speech, Prime Minister Abdullah Badawi noted:

> Malaysia's China policy has been a triumph of good diplomacy and good sense. . . . I believe that we blazed a trail for others to follow. Our China policy showed that *if you*

> *can look beyond your fears and inadequacies*, and can think and act from principled positions, *rewards will follow*.
>
> (*Abdullah 2004; emphasis added*)

Malaysia's pragmatic China policy is, first and foremost, rooted in the ruling elite's desire to maximise rewards from China's huge and growing economy. Such economic pragmatism is well illustrated by its successive leaders' high-level visits to China, which have always been accompanied by large business delegations, resulting in many joint-venture projects. That this economic pragmatism has persisted, and indeed, flourished under different administrations, reflects a sustained political will on the part of the ruling elite to prioritise mutually beneficial economic ties over other issues. The fact that the two countries' economic structures are more complementary than competitive has further contributed to the momentum of such a policy.

During the Mahathir years, Malaysia–China trade climbed from US$307 million in 1982, to US$1.4 billion in 1992, to US$14 billion in 2002 (Shee 2004: 79). In the post-Mahathir era, Malaysia's trade with China grew at a rate faster than that with the United States and Japan, the country's two traditional key trading partners. Under Abdullah, bilateral trade almost doubled from US$20 billion in 2003 to US$39 billion in 2008 (Kaur 2009). Under Najib, Malaysia's economic ties with China have grown even faster and wider, in part due to the ASEAN–China Free Trade Agreement that took effect on 1 January 2010. Since 2009, China has become Malaysia's largest trading partner. In 2011, bilateral trade reached a new high of US$90 billion, with Malaysia enjoying a large surplus of US$30 billion (*Star* 2012).

Post-Mahathir Malaysia–China economic ties have been characterised by not only growing bilateral trade, but also a conscious effort by the Malaysian government to enhance bilateral investment and financial cooperation. Under Abdullah, more government-linked companies were encouraged to make a presence in China and to establish a bilateral currency swap arrangement. Under Najib, a number of initiatives have been taken to boost bilateral investment and financial flows. In November 2009, Bank Negara Malaysia and the China Banking Regulatory Commission signed an MOU to forge cooperation on banking supervision. In February 2012, the two sides renewed their bilateral currency swap deal for RM90 billion. In April 2012, Malaysia and China launched an industrial park in Qinzhou, Guangxi. At the launch, Najib proposed a sister industrial project in Malaysia, to be located in Kuantan.

The robust two-way economic links between Malaysia and China are a result of various factors: cordial political relations, geographical proximity, complementary economic structure and socio-cultural linkages. Increasingly productive commercial links have justified and consolidated a policy of economic pragmatism. These economic benefits are particularly crucial to the present government, which seeks to promote its Economic Transformation Programme (ETP) to shore up its performance legitimacy after the 2008 and 2013 General Elections.

Yet the Malaysian elite's pragmatic disposition towards China is grounded not only in economics, but also in *geopolitical* considerations. The elite's awareness that the giant neighbour is a key, permanent factor in Malaysia's external environment – along with their deep-seated concerns about uncertainties in great power commitments, which the elite painfully learned from the Cold War years – has prompted the Malaysian elite to take a long-term view on Malaysia–China relations. Answering a question on the importance of China to Malaysia, a former senior official who headed the Malaysian foreign service commented:

> Economically, China is important for Malaysia just as it is important to other countries. Strategically speaking, China is important to Malaysia because it is a permanent neighbour

> in the region, unlike, say, the United States, which can decide to retreat to its own regional domain far away from Asia. China is here to stay forever, and it will assume superpower status sooner or later. It is pragmatic to establish friendship and understanding with superpowers. Malaysia has always held the view that the correct approach towards China is not to isolate China but to engage China. This is the best way to enable Malaysia to maintain its non-aligned posture and sustain its own independence in the international arena.
>
> *(Personal interview, 16 February 2010)*

This pragmatic view has a profound bearing on Malaysia's China policy. It has, among other effects, led successive Malaysian leaders to prefer engagement and consultation – rather than antagonism and confrontation – in dealings with China in general and the Spratly Islands issue in particular.

Malaysia's pragmatism in accepting the reality of China's growing power, however, does not mean subservience towards China. Nor does it imply an acceptance of a Beijing-dominated regional order. Given Malaysia's sensitivity about sovereignty and the complexity of its ethnic structure, a subservient approach is a non-starter for Putrajaya. In fact, preventing the possibility of domination by *any* big power in Southeast Asia continues to be an unwavering goal in Malaysia's strategic outlook. This is indicated by Malaysia's insistence on keeping an 'equidistant' relationship with all major powers.

Indeed, Malaysia's China policy throughout the post-Cold War era has continued to reflect quintessentially 'hedging' behaviour. That is, while the smaller state is determined to develop closer ties with China in order to maximise near-term economic and geopolitical rewards, it is equally determined to adopt *contingency measures* to avoid putting itself at the mercy of other states. Malaysia, like other rational actors, wants to keep its strategic options open and preserve its autonomy, for as long as structural conditions allow (Kuik 2010). These contingency measures are implemented through diplomatic and military means, that is, cultivating a balance of power at regional multilateral forums as well as pursuing limited forms of alignment and armament as a fallback position (but without directly and explicitly targeting any actor). In 2005, Malaysia under Abdullah decided to renew the Acquisition and Cross-Servicing Agreement with the US (first signed in 1994 under Mahathir), which enabled the two armed forces to share logistics and supplies for the next ten years. In 2011, Malaysia under Najib decided to upgrade its participation in the US-led Cobra Gold military exercises, from observer to participant status.

Such a hedging posture is reflected in Malaysia's approach in handling the South China Sea disputes. While the smaller state has made clear that it prefers to manage the issue through diplomatic rather than military means, it has at the same time attempted to hedge this position by quietly supporting a US military presence in the region, and emphasising that territorial disputes must be resolved peacefully, through mechanisms under international law.

There are both domestic and structural reasons why Malaysian policy elites have preferred diplomacy and rejected a confrontational approach to the South China Sea issue. A confrontational approach would require Malaysia to align with a strong military power. The United States is the only candidate on the horizon. But joining the US camp is not an option that the Malaysian elite would consider, as doing so would engender other risks. Structurally, putting all eggs in the US basket would expose Malaysia to risks of entrapment into great power conflicts and abandonment by their patron. Domestically, too, allying with Washington could erode the very bases of the UMNO-led government's authority, as it would invite fierce domestic opposition, especially from the majority Malay-Muslims, who have been critical of US policy on the Israeli–Palestinian conflict.

Domestic political considerations aside, a confrontational approach is strategically unjustified, for China is merely a security concern, and not – at least not yet – an immediate threat that must be managed by military alliance. More importantly, confrontation is strategically counter-productive, as it could galvanise a potential concern into an imminent threat. It is also economically unwise, because military confrontation would only result in the loss of vast commercial benefits that can be tapped from China. This is not merely an economic issue, but a critical political concern, given the growing salience of economic performance as a key pathway of legitimation for the ruling elites.

These bases of domestic legitimation, thus, have led successive Malaysian leaders to prioritise practical economic and diplomatic gains over potential security concerns. Given that a stronger bilateral relationship with China has enhanced Malaysian elites' capacity to strengthen their economic foundations *and* political bases over the past few decades, and given that China has remained more a potential than an imminent threat, the current policy of engaging China while keeping some contingent measures is deemed strategically sufficient, politically acceptable and economically rewarding. It is such a goal-prioritisation and ends–means assessment that has underpinned Malaysia's pragmatic approach towards China over the past two decades.

Conclusion

Malaysia's relations with China, as discussed above, have been shaped by the interplay of three enduring imperatives: the ambivalence of power asymmetry; the gravity of geographical proximity; and the centrality of the ruling elite's domestic authority. The transformation of bilateral relations from hostility to cordial partnership since the end of the Cold War suggests that, contrary to the conventional view that a rising power's growing capability and geographical closeness tend to induce fear and resistance from smaller states, the effects of asymmetry and proximity are at best mixed, and at times, a source more of attraction than of apprehension. These predetermined conditions, while important, have no inherent logic of their own. Ultimately, it is the ruling elite's domestic political needs – a desire to enhance and justify their political authority at home – that best explain how and why a smaller state chooses to respond to the evolving opportunities and challenges surrounding the rise of a big power.

Notes

1 This chapter is adapted from a longer piece first published in 2013 as 'Making sense of Malaysia's China policy: asymmetry, proximity, and elite's domestic authority', *The Chinese Journal of International Politics*, 6(4): 429–67.
2 Personal interview, Dato' Abdul Majid Ahmad Khan, former Malaysian Ambassador to China, 4 November 2009, Selangor.
3 This view was expressed to Allen Whiting by a Malaysian official in Kuala Lumpur in the mid-1990s. Cited in Whiting 1997: 311.

Bibliography

Abdul Razak Baginda (2002) 'Malaysian perceptions of China: from hostility to cordiality', in Herbert Yee and Ian Storey (eds), *The China Threat: Perceptions, Myths and Reality*, London: RoutledgeCurzon, pp. 227–47.

Abdul Razak Abdullah Baginda (2009) The Normalisation of Malaysia's Relations with China, 1970–1974, PhD Dissertation, Oxford University.

Abdullah Haji Ahmad Badawi (2004) Keynote Address to the China–Malaysia Economic Conference, Bandar Sunway, Malaysia, 24 February.

Alagappa, Muthiah (1987) 'Malaysia: from the commonwealth umbrella to self-reliance', in Chin Kin Wah (ed.), *Defence Spending in Southeast Asia*, Singapore: Institute of Southeast Asian Studies, pp. 165–93.

Ba, Alice (2003) 'China and ASEAN: renavigating relations for a 21st century-Asia', *Asian Survey*, 43(4): 622–47.

Peter Boyce (1968) *Malaysia and Singapore in International Diplomacy: Documents and Commentaries*, Sydney: Sydney University Press.

Chai Ching Hau (2000) Dasar luar Malaysia terhadap China: era Dr Mahathir Mohamad [Malaysia's Foreign Policy Towards China: The Mahathir Mohamad Era], MA Thesis, National University of Malaysia.

Chin Kin Wah (1983) *The Defence of Malaysia and Singapore: The Transformation of a Security System, 1957–1971*, Cambridge: Cambridge University Press.

Clad, James (1985) 'An affair of the head', *Far Eastern Economic Review*, 4 July, pp. 12–14.

Ghazali Shafie (1982) *Malaysia: International Relations*, Kuala Lumpur: Creative Enterprises.

Jeshurun, Chandran (2007) *Malaysia: Fifty Years of Diplomacy, 1957–2007*, Kuala Lumpur: The Other Press.

Kaur, Simrit (2009) 'Najib following in dad's footsteps', *The Star*, 31 May.

Kuik Cheng-Chwee (2008) 'China's evolving multilateralism in Asia: the aussenpolitik and innenpolitik explanations', in Kent Calder and Francis Fukuyama (eds), *East Asian Multilateralism: Prospects for Regional Stability*, Baltimore: Johns Hopkins University Press, pp. 109–42.

Kuik Cheng-Chwee (2010) Smaller States' Alignment Choices: A Comparative Study of Malaysia and Singapore's Hedging Behavior in the Face of a Rising China, PhD Dissertation, Johns Hopkins University.

Lee Poh Ping and Lee Kam Hing (2005) 'Malaysia–China relations: a review', in Hou Kok Chung and Yeoh Kok-Kheng (eds), *Malaysia, Southeast Asia and the Emerging China: Political, Economic and Cultural Perspectives*, Kuala Lumpur: Institute of China Studies, University of Malaya, pp. 3–28.

Leong, Stephen (1987) 'Malaysia and the People's Republic of China in the 1980s: political vigilance and economic pragmatism', *Asian Survey*, 27(10): 1109–26.

Liow, Joseph Chinyong (2009) 'Malaysia's post-Cold War China policy: a reassessment', in Jun Tsunekawa (ed.), *The Rise of China: Responses from Southeast Asia and Japan*, Tokyo: The National Institute for Defense Studies, pp. 47–79.

Mak, J.N. (1991) 'The Chinese navy and the South China Sea: a Malaysian assessment', *Pacific Review*, 4(2): 150–61.

Means, Gordon (1991) *Malaysian Politics: The Second Generation*, Singapore: Oxford University Press.

Najib Tun Abdul Razak (2009) 'Malaysian foreign policy: future direction for 2009–2015', Keynote Address to the 7th Heads of Mission Conference, Putrajaya, 22 June.

Saravanamuttu, J. (1981) 'Malaysia–China ties, pre and post 1974: an overview', in Loh Kok Wah, Phang Chung Nyap and J. Saravanamuttu, *The Chinese Community and Malaysia–China Ties: Elite Perspectives*, Tokyo: The Institute of Developing Economies.

Saravanamuttu, J. (1983) *The Dilemma of Independence: Two Decades of Malaysia's Foreign Policy, 1957–1977*, Penang: Penerbit Universiti Sains Malaysia.

Shafruddin Hashim (1986) 'Malaysian domestic politics and foreign policy: the impact of ethnicity', in Karl D. Jackson, Sukhumbhand Paribatra and J. Soedjati Djiwandono (eds), *ASEAN in Regional and Global Context*, Berkeley: Institute of East Asian Studies, University of California, pp. 155–62.

Shee Poon Kim (2004) The Political Economy of Mahathir's China Policy: Economic Cooperation, Political and Strategic Ambivalence, IUJ Research Institute Working Paper 2004–06, Tokyo: International University of Japan Research Institute.

Singh, Hari (2004) 'Malaysia's national security: rhetoric and substance', *Contemporary Southeast Asia*, 26(1): 1–25.

Sopiee, Noordin (1975) 'Towards a "neutral" Southeast Asia', in Hedley Bull (ed.), *Asia and the Western Pacific: Towards a New International Order*, Sydney: Nelson, pp. 132–58.

Star (2012) 'China–Malaysia trade to touch US$100b', *The Star*, 16 March.

Tilman, Robert O. and Jo H. Tilman (1977) 'Malaysia and Singapore 1976: a year of challenge, a year of change', *Asian Survey*, 17(2): 143–54.

Wang Gungwu (1990) 'China: 1989 in perspective', *Southeast Asian Affairs 1990*: 71–85.

Whiting, Allen (1997) 'ASEAN eyes China: the security dimension', *Asian Survey*, 37(4): 299–322.

34

Issues and challenges in contemporary Malaysia–Europe relations

Ruhanas Harun

In the 1980s and 1990s, Malaysia expanded its diplomacy – as well as political, economic, sociocultural and defence engagement – to many parts of the globe, putting itself on the world map. It established connections with Africa, Central Asia and Latin America and reinforced relations with China, Japan, the Middle East and Europe. While relations with other countries generated much interest among the public and in scholarly circles, Europe attracted less. It is not that relations between Malaysia and Europe degenerated or became unimportant. On the contrary, statistics showed that activities involving the two entities flourished, albeit quietly. This lack of excitement about Malaysia–Europe relations both stems from and reflects both internal and external developments affecting Malaysia and Europe.

The destructive World War II and the decolonisation that followed weakened Europe's position in world affairs and its linkages to former colonies, especially in Southeast Asia. The advent of the Cold War almost eclipsed any European presence as a result of the overwhelming influence and interests of the United States in the region. Throughout the Cold War period, the main focus of international relations in Southeast Asia was on the United States and China. Among the European powers, only Britain managed to retain its influence, owing both to its close and special relations with the United States and to the manner in which Britain managed the decolonisation of its colonies in the region. Thus, despite the long history of European countries such as France, Spain, Portugal and the Netherlands in Southeast Asia, the period was one of quiet diplomacy for Europe in the region.

In Malaysia specifically, relations with Europe during the Cold War era focused mainly on developing and consolidating political and economic relations with countries considered as traditional friends. The post-Cold War era, on the other hand, saw efforts to strengthen and expand the relationship in all domains. When he came to power in 1981, Malaysia's fourth prime minister, Mahathir Mohamad, re-prioritised Malaysia's foreign policy, with positive impacts for relations with Europe. Although many saw this re-ordering of priorities as a 'downgrading of relations' with the West, it did not necessarily lead to reduction or neglect of already close political and economic ties with Europe. Rather, it entailed refocusing on areas considered to be most beneficial to Malaysia in its relations with Europe, mainly in the area of economics. At the same time, this recalibration created the potential for forging closer social and cultural ties.

Connecting with the past

Malaysia and Europe are no strangers to each other. Contacts between the two regions for centuries have encompassed political, economic, social and cultural aspects. In the past, the Portuguese, Dutch, French and British ventured into Malaysia. The first Europeans to establish a foothold in the country were the Portuguese, who conquered the Malay kingdom of Malacca in 1511 and retained control until being ousted by the Dutch in 1641. In the fifteenth century, Malacca rose to become, in the words of Portuguese apothecary-turned-ambassador Tomé Pires, 'of such importance and profit that it seems to me it has no equal in the world' (Andaya and Andaya 1982: 38). Its importance as a trading post attracted European powers, who jostled for control of Malacca.

The Dutch arrived in Malacca in 1641, making the city the chief outpost of the Dutch East India Company, from which information-gathering missions were dispatched to the various Malay kingdoms. The Anglo-Dutch Treaty of 1824 transferred Malacca to the British, marking the beginning of the division of the Malay–Indonesian archipelago into two distinct areas of influence, one under Dutch and the other under British control. The rest of Southeast Asia, too, became divided among European powers. The French took control of Indochina, the Spanish controlled the Philippines, and Portugal retained control over East Timor until 1975.

Continuing close relations with Britain

When Malaya achieved independence from Britain in 1957, the political and security environment in Southeast Asia was dominated by the Cold War and East–West conflict. Considerations of both external and internal politics and security at that time forced Malaysia under its first prime minister to opt for a pro-West and an anti-communist foreign policy. As Europe was divided into East and West, so were Malaysia's options. Besides Britain, Malaysia also established close relations with other Western European countries, such as France, Germany, the Netherlands and the Scandinavian countries. Ideologically and politically, Malaysia saw itself as a part of the 'free world', allied with the West against the communist world. Besides this close political and ideological association with Western Europe, the Malaysian economy depended to a large extent on trade with these countries.

Malaysia's option to ally itself with the West and to maintain an anti-communist foreign policy can also be explained through an important domestic factor. Since the end of World War II, Malaysia had been engaged in fighting a communist insurgency; the conflict lasted until 1989, when a peace treaty was signed between the government of Malaysia and the Communist Party of Malaya. The communist threat was an important factor shaping Malaysia's foreign policy before 1970. Its anti-communist stance, explained Malaysia's first prime minister, Tunku Abdul Rahman Putra, was 'simply to protect our independence' (Abdullah 1985: 26). Malaysia relied on Britain to help deal with these security threats. Malaysia and Britain were members of the Anglo-Malayan Defence Agreement (AMDA), expanded in 1970 to the Five Power Defence Arrangement (FPDA), including also Australia, New Zealand and Singapore. Not only long-standing historical relations, but also the security and economic imperatives of this period made Malaysia 'conspicuously pro-Britain and pro-Commonwealth' (Abdullah 1985: 28). The British stronghold in Malaysia left little chance for other European countries to penetrate the country, nor did Malaysia have a need to push, or interest in pushing, for stronger ties with other European countries, especially given the presence in the region of the United States, a close friend and ally of Britain.

In 1970, Prime Minister Tunku Abdul Rahman stepped down and was succeeded by Tun Abdul Razak Hussein. The second prime minister reoriented Malaysia's foreign policy towards non-alignment. Several reasons accounted for this change. One was Indonesian *Konfrontasi* from 1963 to 1966, contesting the joining of Malaya, Singapore, Sabah and Sarawak in the Federation of Malaysia. Indonesia's President Sukarno also went on a political offensive against Malaysia among the non-aligned countries, declaring that Malaysia was a creation of British and American imperialism. Given Indonesia's stature and influence among the Third World countries at that time, it was able to sway these countries to its side. By 1970, too, Malaysia found it necessary to reduce its political tutelage and security dependency on Britain. Britain had announced its intention to withdraw 'from the East of Suez' by the 1970s. A foreign policy of non-alignment would enable Malaysia to broaden its external relations, maintain friendly relations with as many countries as possible, and acquire the support and confidence of others. One of the most significant steps in this direction was Malaysia's recognition of the People's Republic of China in 1974 and consolidation of relations with Eastern Europe. This foreign policy shift under Tun Razak became a lasting foundation for the balanced foreign policy followed by his successors (Ruhanas 2011: 33).

Yet, other factors help explain the strong attachment that Malaysia still has in its relations with Britain. One of the most significant is the peaceful manner in which Malaysia gained independence from Britain, which precluded the phenomenon of elite resentment towards the colonial master found in many Third World countries. Both British and Malaysian elites found it expedient to accommodate each other, which helped to avoid violent conflicts. Moreover, the particular character of Malayan foreign policy arguably reflects an elite ideology already predisposed towards certain values and norms. These values and norms were embedded in a conservatively biased elite, marked by a strong predilection for Western democratic practices, as well as for pragmatism, as nurtured in multicultural discourses and practices (Saravanamuttu 2010: 71). Britain also became intimately involved in Malaysia's difficult political experiences with its neighbours, such as during the Malaysia–Singapore split. Malaysia's then prime minister, Tunku Abdul Rahman, confided to the British that he could no longer tolerate the 'cat and dog' relationship between Malaya and Singapore and thought that it would be better for Singapore to leave the Federation (Ruhanas 2011: 33).

Britain may have left the country, but its economic, social and cultural influences remain, giving it a privileged position in its bilateral relations with Malaysia (Ruhanas 2011). Although the British hold on the Malaysian economy is no longer what it used to be, Britain remains an important trading partner of Malaysia, adding value to a close relationship forged out of a long connection. Malaysia's fourth prime minister, Mahathir Mohamad, made efforts to address what he saw as an unfair bias, to the advantage of the UK, in economic links between the two countries (Jeshurun 2007: 184). Observers suggested Mahathir was 'not very well disposed toward Britain' since 'he had no fond memories of having studied there, and he was opposed to Britain as a colonial power' (Milne and Mauzy 1999: 139). Yet despite British resentment over the take-over of British plantation enterprise, Guthrie Malaysia, by Malaysia's Permodalan Nasional Berhad (National Equity Cooperation), the 'Buy British Last' policy, and a sharp exchange of words between Mahathir and the British press (Milne and Mauzy 1999: 139), economic relations between the two countries continued to grow. British companies, some with a long history in Malaysia, such as HSBC, Standard Chartered, Shell and many others, are major players in the local market. According to the Malaysian External Trade Development Corporation, in 2009, the UK was the third most important export market for Malaysia in the European Union. According to Britain's high commissioner in Malaysia, the state of trade between Malaysia and the UK is 'pretty healthy' and there are no specific trade issues that could derail the good relations between the two countries (Ruhanas 2011: 38).

Besides close economic links, Malaysia and Britain enjoy strong cultural, educational and social ties. Traditionally, Malaysians look to Britain as a source of overseas education. Over the years, thousands of Malaysians have graduated from British universities, bringing back with them not only degrees, but also memories of and fondness for Britain. This affinity is evidenced, for example, in the widespread use of the English language, which remains the de facto language of economics, social standing and political power. Recent estimates count more than 11,500 Malaysian students in the UK, making them Britain's fourth-largest group among non-EU students (Ruhanas 2011). Many British educational institutions operate in Malaysia, too, including Nottingham University and the Newcastle Medical School of Malaysia. Others are expected to announce branch campuses in the country in the next few years. Reflecting close Malaysia–Britain social relations, too, are frequent official and private visits of leaders to Britain, as well as rising numbers of British tourists to Malaysia.

The legacy of colonial ties, national security needs and familiarity with each other are some of the most important factors shaping and influencing Malaysia's strong relations with the UK. The lack of cultural barriers and continued expectation of mutual economic and political benefits will likely continue to strengthen the relationship (Ruhanas 2011). Still, as former Prime Minister Mahathir demonstrated, a policy of diversification in Malaysia's foreign relations serves to safeguard national independence and interests. It is in this direction that Mahathir moved, in building stronger relations with other European countries that can respond to Malaysia's evolving national interests.

Europe: more than Britain

Malaysia's relations with the rest of Europe are necessarily less complex than with Britain. Malaysia established relations with major Western European countries soon after gaining independence in 1957. In general, political relations with these countries have been consistently good, without many issues to mar them. Since 1970, Malaysia has made efforts to establish and consolidate relations with the countries of Eastern Europe, too, even though they were still under communist rule at that date. By the 1980s, and in line with a new foreign policy direction under Mahathir, Malaysia–Europe relations saw an expansion of scope and of political will to venture beyond traditional partners (Ruhanas 2011: 38).

Opportunities and challenges in Malaysia–France relations

France presents a key example of a European power on par with Britain in terms of global political influence and cultural prestige, yet with no historical baggage attached to Malaysia. During his tenure as prime minister, Mahathir made efforts to develop strong relations with France in economic, political and socio-cultural domains. Besides having particular potential to counterbalance the overwhelming British influence that so disturbed Mahathir, given centuries of British–French rivalry in world affairs, cultivating close relations with France also provided Malaysia with an opportunity to expand and diversify its economic partnerships and cultivate a more independent foreign policy stance.

Malaysia established diplomatic relations with France upon independence in 1957, although its first ambassador arrived in Paris only in 1959. Few issues have disrupted the Malaysia–France relationship since (Ruhanas 2011: 34). One of these issues was French nuclear testing in the Pacific in 1995: Malaysia and some twenty-one other countries sponsored a draft resolution at the UN condemning the nuclear testing. This action resulted in a cool period in their relations. In general, though, Malaysia–France relations initially lacked visibility. Apart from the fact that Malaysia tended toward the Anglo-American sphere of influence, France's presence in Southeast Asia diminished after it left Indochina in 1954. Developments in Europe during this period also forced France to focus its attention on that region, where it was a major actor. Owing to different domestic and foreign policy priorities, prior to the 1990s, Malaysia and France did not represent high-value allies for each other strategically, politically, economically or culturally. As such, there seemed no urgency to push for a stronger relationship. As the French appropriately summed it up, Franco-Malaysian relations suffered from a reciprocal lack of knowledge about each other (Ruhanas 2011: 34).

Initiatives towards closer Malaysia–France relations developed during Mahathir's tenure as prime minister. The close political and economic relations that ensued were the result partly of the good personal relations between Mahathir and the French President Jacques Chirac, and partly of a convergence of views on international issues. As a major power, France has been known to strive to safeguard its independence and sense of mission in world affairs. It has sought to balance the overwhelming influence of the United States in European and world affairs and, at the same time, to project an image as a protector to Third World countries. Malaysia under Mahathir had a similar vision of its role in international relations. Mahathir assumed the voice of the Third World, championing the rights of the weaker nations. Points of convergence in the Malaysian and French positions on international issues can be seen in their attitudes towards the crisis in Iraq and the Palestinian question and in their uneasiness – sometimes even defiance – towards American behaviour in world affairs. Mahathir's close personal relationship with Chirac is apparent in the close contact they maintained. Not only was Mahathir present at symbolically important Bastille Day celebrations in Paris in 1997, but between September 2002 and July 2003, for example, the pair met five times, although sometimes briefly (Ruhanas 2011: 35).

The two countries also developed closer relations in the area of defence. The French have shown a great deal of interest in defence cooperation, especially with the Royal Malaysian Navy and the Royal Malaysian Air Force. France has also participated regularly in the Langkawi International Maritime and Aerospace (LIMA) Exhibition since the mid-1990s. Since 2000, there has been a sharp increase in the quality of military relations between the two countries, especially in the exchange of officers and experts, cooperation in training and more frequent calls by vessels of the French navy to Malaysia. French industry has responded well, establishing cooperation with Malaysian partners in the military industry. For example, the French naval shipbuilding company DNC, which designs, tests and maintains various kinds of warship, has been active in Malaysia. Perhaps the height of these burgeoning defence relations was Malaysia's purchase of two Scorpene submarines from France (which generated much public interest because of the sensationalist controversy surrounding the purchase). Defence purchases have contributed substantially to bilateral trade between Malaysia and France. According to French Embassy sources in Kuala Lumpur,[1] in 2012, the bilateral balance of trade was in favour of France due to the large number of aircraft purchases from France by the Malaysian armed forces. Indeed, the area of defence cooperation and business has become a major highlight of Malaysia–France relations in recent years, amplified by high-level visits from France to Malaysia – for instance, French Prime Minister Jean-Marc Ayrault's July 2013 visit included discussions with the Malaysian government regarding future defence procurements – and active consultations through a Malaysia–France bilateral defence working committee.

The increase in trade and economic interactions between the two countries has not been confined to defence purchases, however. In a statement released recently, the French Ambassador in Malaysia, Martine Dorance, said that trade between Malaysia and France is expected to increase further, with more French companies expected to set up business in Malaysia, including in the Iskandar Malaysia Economic Region in the Malaysian state of Johor. There have also been encouraging developments in cooperation in the fields of education and culture. Although educational cooperation is not new in Malaysia–France relations – the French government has provided grants and scholarships to Malaysian students to study in France since the 1960s – the 1990s saw an uptick, especially in the science and technical fields. It is estimated that as of 2013, one thousand Malaysian students were studying in French institutes of higher learning, in various fields.

Awareness of these mutual interests, and of opportunities to cooperate further, remains limited, however. Moreover, relations in areas other than defence and military procurements have not flourished as hoped and expected, for several reasons. First and foremost, defence relations are limited in scope, as they involve only a select group of people and do not favour people-to-people diplomacy. Strong defence relations must thus be complemented with connections in other areas for the alliance to thrive.

Economic priorities

Emphasising economics as the 'bread and butter' of Malaysia's diplomacy, Prime Minister Mahathir took advantage of growing economic relations between Malaysia and several European countries to further strengthen their relations. Malaysia's ties with Germany exemplify this thrust. The two countries have developed active economic, trade and educational linkages, not least because of Germany's reputation as a European and global economic powerhouse. Malaysia and Germany have a long history of close economic ties. Malaysia (along with Singapore) has for many years been one of Germany's leading suppliers and the second-largest market for German goods. Trade in the year 2004, for instance, amounted to €6.9 billion, an increase of 1.5 percent from the previous year. Another visible area of economic relations is German investment in Malaysia. With more than 300 German companies with offices in Malaysia, and over seventy operating production plants, German investment has created more than 30,000 jobs.[2] For a period of five years, between 2000 and 2005, Germany ranked as the second-largest foreign investor in Malaysia.[3] The main focus of Malaysia–Germany economic relations has been in the area of electro-technical products, office and other machinery, motor vehicles and hardware. Besides direct economic exchanges, Malaysia has also benefited from German vocational and technical cooperation programmes. One such example is the contribution of GTZ (*Deutsche Gesellschaft für Technische Zusammenarbeit*), which provided assistance in reorganising vocational and technical education in Malaysia along the lines of the German system. The flagship project in this area is the German–Malaysian Institute (GMI) in Kuala Lumpur, which began as a GTZ project in 1992 (Ruhanas 2011).

Despite efforts of NGOs from both countries since the 1990s to develop stronger socio-cultural ties between Malaysia and Germany, the results have not been encouraging, in terms of creating greater public awareness about each other. German foundations such as the Konrad Adenauer Foundation and the Friedrich Ebert Foundation have been active in organising seminars and workshops on socio-cultural and political issues in Malaysia, working closely with local institutions. Their activities seem to have declined, however, despite hopes that the visit of then Chancellor Gerhard Schroeder to Malaysia in May 2003, the first ever by a

German chancellor, could inject new momentum toward fostering stronger cultural and social relations between Malaysia and Germany. Still, the countries maintain good political and beneficial economic relations.

Strengthening relations through regional cooperation

In Southeast Asia, the end of the Cold War helped speed up the process of regionalism, as seen in ASEAN's expansion from six countries to ten. Vietnam joined the Association in 1995, followed by Laos and Myanmar in 1997 and Cambodia in 1998. By the end of the 1990s, ASEAN was able to unite all the countries of Southeast Asia, as envisaged by its founding fathers in 1967. An expanded and consolidated ASEAN provided greater opportunities to enhance relations between the region and Europe, especially in economic areas. Europe was accepted as an ASEAN dialogue partner through the ASEAN–Europe Meeting (ASEM) created in 1995. Previously, Europe and ASEAN had engaged via the Special Coordination Committee of ASEAN when the first European Economic Community (EEC)–ASEAN ministerial meetings were held in Brussels in 1978. The second EEC–ASEAN ministerial meeting, held in Kuala Lumpur in March 1980, established a framework for closer economic and trade relations between the two regional groupings. It focused on the promotion of trade, investment and business, including small and medium enterprises. Both parties have since held regular meetings, with the aim of expanding ASEAN–EU dialogue.

Despite the Asian financial crisis of 1998, European business and economic interests remained in the region. The EU remained one of Malaysia's top trading partners, behind China and the United States. Within ASEAN, Malaysia is the EU's second-largest trading partner, after Singapore. Economic relations between Malaysia and the EU continued to improve with the establishment of the EU–Malaysian Chamber of Commerce in early 2003 and further negotiations. In the view of the EU, however, opportunities remain, especially in trade in services, as Malaysia has increasingly liberalised its economy and trade.

Besides facilitating economic relations, regionalism has also brought ASEAN and EU leaders into regular political interaction. During ASEM meetings, ASEAN and EU leaders take the opportunity to hold bilateral talks and discussions on the sidelines, a tradition born out of these formal gatherings. Examples include the bilateral talks between Malaysian Prime Minister Abdullah Ahmad Badawi and Chancellor Angela Merkel of Germany, held during the ASEM Summit in Hanoi, in September 2004. Abdullah and Merkel held another such meeting in Helsinki in September 2006, during the ASEM Summit. The EU has been present on the ground in Malaysia, too, with the establishment of its office in Kuala Lumpur. Although its main interest is developing and facilitating economic interactions between its members and Malaysia, the EU office has extended its activities to include connecting with the public through engagements with civil society groups, professionals and academic circles via cultural and socio-political discussions, to generate better mutual understanding.

Opportunities in Eastern Europe

Prior to the collapse of the Soviet Union and the end of the Cold War, Malaysia did not neglect communist Eastern Europe, despite the differences in their political systems and ideologies. The USSR was the first communist power to be recognised by Malaysia, with the establishment of diplomatic relations between the two countries in 1968. Despite being clearly in the 'free world' camp, Malaysia did not want to exclude either superpower from its list of friends. Politically, this was useful in balancing the might of the West and the fear of

China that dominated the security thinking of many Southeast Asian countries, including Malaysia. Diplomatic relations with Moscow also contributed to the 'rehabilitation' among socialist and non-aligned countries of the image of Malaysia, which had been dented as a result of the confrontation with Indonesia and Malaysia's overall pro-West, anti-communist foreign policy under its first prime minister. Economically too, Malaysia was looking for opportunities to diversify and expand economic relations and for markets for Malaysia's export commodities, previously monopolised by Western countries.

This move by Malaysia was considered as 'bold' for the time and raised concern among many of its friends, including the United States. But Tun Razak Hussein, the Malaysian prime minister who reoriented Malaysia's foreign policy towards non-alignment and who was responsible for developing relations with communist countries of Eastern Europe and with China, was quick to reassure them that the aim was economic and not political. To further allay fears among the major powers of external involvement in Southeast Asia, Malaysia proposed a Southeast Asian Zone of Peace, Freedom and Neutrality (ZOPFAN) in 1971. Tun Razak made a visit to Moscow to explain the concept of ZOPFAN in relation to Southeast Asian security. Mahathir later emphasised this idea again, when he visited Moscow in 1987. Over time, the political relations between Malaysia and the USSR first established during the administration of Tunku Abdul Rahman Putra, Malaysia's first prime minister, were enhanced under Tun Razak and further refined during the tenure of Mahathir.

Challenges and opportunities of enhancing ties with Eastern Europe

Although ideologically different, Malaysia and Eastern Europe attempted to bridge the gap by exploring ways to take advantage of opportunities in other areas within the limited political confines of the Cold War era. This was especially so with the Soviet Union. The two countries agreed to promote cultural ties through the exchange of radio and television programmes, artists and museum artefacts, and in the educational field. Collaboration grew at a slow pace, however, owing not least to unfamiliarity about each other, reinforced by the geographical distance that separates the two countries and peoples. Malaysia and the USSR also differed in opinions on many international issues. The Soviet intervention in Afghanistan in 1979 was opposed by many countries, including Malaysia. Malaysia was also concerned about Soviet intentions in Indochina and the Indian Ocean. It was not until the end of the Cold War that Malaysia and Russia found new opportunities to expand and consolidate their relations in many aspects, including developing greater political, economic, social and defence ties.

While there is potential to strengthen relations between Malaysia and Russia, there are also numerous challenges. Russia is still a far-away country, whose society and culture seem almost alien to many in Malaysia. Because of distance, though, the two countries are spared the neighbourly disputes or disagreements traditionally associated with neighbours in close geographical proximity, which could provide for greater opportunities for unhindered development of political, socio-cultural, educational and economic ties. The countries have developed close cooperation in defence matters, particularly in defence purchases. Russian arms sales to Malaysia began in the 1990s, when it obtained a contract to supply eighteen MiG-29 aircraft to the Malaysian Armed Forces. In 2003, Russian President Vladimir Putin visited Malaysia in conjunction with the latter's purchase of Russian jets worth US$600 million. Malaysia and Russia have also pursued increasing cooperation in the field of science and technology. In 2007, they started talks regarding collaboration on the training of Malaysian astronauts. Moreover, many Malaysian students now look to Russia to study, especially in the field of medicine.

The end of the Cold War and subsequent political, economic and social developments in Europe have provided increased opportunities for Malaysia and the countries of Eastern Europe to look for common ground and interests in expanding their relations. The new environment in Europe has also provided an opportunity for Malaysia to contribute towards the region's security and political stability, through multilateral cooperation. The conflict in the former Yugoslavia highlighted yet another dimension in Malaysia's foreign relations: its commitment to peace.

Enhancing relations through commitment to peace and stability

Malaysia has a long history of participation in the United Nations Peacekeeping Operations (UNPKO). Its first such involvement was in the Congo in 1960. After a long lull, Malaysia became active again with the coming to power in 1981 of Mahathir Mohamad, whose active international diplomacy included contributions to the UNPKO. Since the 1980s, Malaysia has been involved in peacekeeping operations under the UN in several countries, including Angola, Cambodia, Lebanon, Somalia, Timor Leste and Bosnia-Herzegovina. Its participation in the UNPKO was motivated by its commitment to international peace and to the principle of justice enshrined in Malaysia's foreign policy.

Malaysia expressed its wish to join the United Nations Protection Forces (UNPROFOR) in the former republic of Yugoslavia in February 1992 and was accepted by the UN in February 1993. Malaysia's participation in the peacekeeping operations in former Yugoslavia included the sending of three battalions under the UNPKO and two contingents under NATO, which received a mandate to protect Bosnia-Herzegovina after the Dayton Agreement of November 1995. Malaysia's participation in these missions was the first of its kind for the Malaysian armed forces in Europe (Ruhanas 2011). The Malaysian forces involved included the Royal Malay Regiment, the Special Forces and the Royal Armour. Their tasks included building roads, schools and houses, and providing medical aid. In addition, the Malaysian battalions were given the task of mediating among groups such as the Muslim Bosnian forces and the Croatian forces.

As Prime Minister Mahathir Mohamad explained in a speech at the Commonwealth Heads of States Meeting in Cyprus in October 1993, what motivated Malaysia's involvement in the peacekeeping operations in Bosnia was its concern about the lack of attention by the international community to violations of human rights in the war-torn country. Prior to this, in May 1992, Malaysia had recognised Bosnia-Herzegovina, Croatia and Slovenia as independent, and established diplomatic relations with these nations. Consequently, Bosnia-Herzegovina established an embassy in Kuala Lumpur in March 1994. As an indication of its concern about the conflict in Bosnia-Herzegovina, Malaysia also called on the Organisation of the Islamic Conference (OIC) in 1995 to step up measures to help that newly independent European country. Malaysia's participation in the peacekeeping mission in Bosnia-Herzegovina exposed Malaysians to the complexities of the political, economic and social situation in a part of Europe relatively unknown to them before. At the same time, it succeeded in creating awareness among the countries of Central Europe about Malaysia and opened prospects for further interaction between the two areas (Ruhanas 2011).

Even if by now forgotten by many, Malaysia's participation in peacekeeping operations in Bosnia-Herzegovina helped to develop people-to-people diplomacy between Malaysians and Bosnians. Besides facilitating the work of Malaysian NGOs such as ABIM (Angkatan Belia Islam Malaysia, Malaysian Islamic Youth Movement) in humanitarian assistance to Bosnians, Malaysian participation in the UNPKO helped familiarise Malaysians and Bosnians with each other in a relatively short period of time. As a result, several educational and public institutions in Malaysia came to receive Bosnian students, especially the International Islamic University of Malaysia. Since the 1990s, too, the Malaysian Armed Forces Staff College at the Ministry of Defence in Kuala Lumpur has been accepting a Bosnian officer to be trained there each year.

These efforts aside, in general, the potential to expand relations between Malaysia and Eastern Europe in most areas is yet to be tapped. But at least the political and psychological barriers that once kept Malaysia and Eastern Europe apart have been removed, making it easier now to maximise opportunities to develop relations.

Conclusion

Malaysia's relations with Europe have focused mainly on Western Europe, particularly with Britain. This bias was shaped by history, and political and post-World War II security developments. Malaysia's close relationship with Britain in many domains was conditioned and shaped by British colonial rule in the country from the nineteenth century until its independence in 1957. The regional political and security environments contributed greatly to Malaysia's maintaining this close relationship for an extended period. The end of the Cold War ushered in new priorities and opportunities for Malaysia's foreign policy, however, which resulted in more conscious efforts to expand relations with Europe beyond the United Kingdom and to balance the overwhelming Anglo-American presence in the country. Relations with several major countries of Europe, such as France and Germany, considered as 'traditional' friends of Malaysia, have been strengthened. Since the 1990s, relations with France especially have been greatly enhanced, encompassing political, economic, educational and defence matters.

In recent years, however, issues of contention have arisen that could put a dent in efforts to cultivate friendship and understanding between peoples in Europe and others, especially Muslims. A trend of concern is the 'Islamophobia' that seemed to be on the rise after the events of 11 September 2001 in the United States. Besides that trend, other issues relating to the cultural integration of minorities in Europe have created uneasiness in Malaysia, where the majority of the population is Muslim. Nevertheless, this tension has not weakened the strong political and economic relations that have been established between Malaysia and Europe, based on mutual interests. These relations are expected to increase further, given the globalisation, accessibility and greater openness so characteristic of international relations today.

Notes

1 Personal communication, Embassy of France, Kuala Lumpur.
2 www.auswaertiges-amt.de/www/en/laenderinfos/laender/print_html (accessed 28 March 2011).
3 Dato' Seri Abdullah Ahmad Badawi's address at the Malaysia–Germany Business Forum, Frankfurt, Germany, 17 May 2005.

Bibliography

Abdullah Ahmad (1985) *Tengku Abdul Rahman and Malaysia's Foreign Policy 1963–1970*, Kuala Lumpur: Berita Publishing House.

Ahmad Mokhtar Selat (2006) 'New directions in Malaysia's foreign policy: from Tunku to Abdullah Badawi', in Ruhanas Harun (ed.), *Malaysia's Foreign Relations: Issues and Challenges*, Kuala Lumpur: University of Malaya Press, pp. 13–28.

Andaya, Barbara Watson and Leonard Y. Andaya (1982) *A History of Malaysia*, London: Macmillan Press.

Jeshurun, Chandran (2007) *Malaysia: Fifty Years of Diplomacy, 1957–2007*, Kuala Lumpur: The Other Press.

Milne, R.S. and Diane K. Mauzy (1999) *Malaysian Politics under Mahathir*, London: Routledge.

Rastam Mohd Isa (2006) 'Prvi Ambassador', in Fauziah Mohamad Taib (ed.), *Number One Wisma Putra*, Kuala Lumpur: Institute of Diplomacy and Foreign Relations, pp. 97–118.

Ruhanas Harun (2011) 'Beyond the UK: looking at contemporary Malaysian–European relations', in Christoph Marcinkowski (ed.), *Malaysia and the European Union: Perspectives for the Twenty-first Century*, Zurich: LIT, pp. 27–44.

Saravanamuttu, Johan (2010) *Malaysia's Foreign Policy, The First Fifty Years: Alignment, Neutralism, Islamism*, Singapore: Institute of Southeast Asian Studies.

Syed Hamid Albar (2005) *Selected Foreign Policy Speeches*, Kuala Lumpur: Institute of Diplomacy and Foreign Relations.

35

Contemporary maritime piracy in Malaysia

Carolin Liss

Underway from Thailand to Indonesia, a Singaporean tugboat pulling a barge was attacked by six armed robbers in Malaysian waters on 9 June 2013. The pirates climbed aboard and forced the crew to pump fuel from the tug into a fishing boat. The perpetrators then tied up the crew, stole their belongings and other valuables and escaped in a white speedboat (ReCAAP 2013b: 47). As this incident demonstrates, pirates still ply Malaysian waters today, even though – or perhaps because – international attention is focused firmly on Somali piracy. This chapter overviews contemporary piracy in Malaysia. It first looks briefly at the changing nature of piracy in Malaysia and Southeast Asia, before discussing developments from the late 1990s to the mid-2000s. It explains why piracy emerged as a security concern in Malaysia in this period, and considers the nature of attacks, the perpetrators and the Malaysian, regional and international responses to the piracy threat. The remainder of the chapter focuses on the period from the mid-2000s to the present, examining changes and continuities in contemporary piracy in Malaysia and beyond.

Piracy: past and present

Piracy in Malaysia and the wider Southeast Asian region has a long history. Long before the arrival of the Europeans in the sixteenth century, opportunistic attacks by maritime people such as fishers and petty traders were common throughout the region, but particularly in the waters adjacent to the kingdoms and entrepôts of Kedah, Perak, Selangor, Malacca and Johor. Furthermore, certain maritime ethnic groups conducted more sophisticated and well-organised attacks and slave raids against coastal communities, which intensified with the arrival of the European powers in Southeast Asia and the ensuing transformation of the global and regional economy. The raiding vessels originated from places such as the Riau-Lingga archipelago and south-eastern Sumatra. They were sponsored and supported by sultans and the local elite of Johor between the mid-seventeenth and the early nineteenth centuries (Warren 2001: 8; Teitler 2002: 69). The scale and severity of piracy in Southeast Asia eventually prompted anti-piracy countermeasures by all European powers present in the region, which brought an end to organised pirate raids in Southeast Asia by 1880 (Warren 2001: 40–47; Andaya and Andaya 2001: 134–36).

Even though piracy has a long history in Southeast Asia, its nature has changed over time, as 'piracy' has been associated with a variety of economic and political activities. Colonial powers ascribed the term 'pirates' to local 'marauders' – whether individuals or ethnic groups – to characterise as criminal and barbaric those activities that thwarted European interests, but that local inhabitants generally considered legitimate political or commercial endeavours (Trocki 1988). Contemporary piracy in Southeast Asia differs in scope, character and nature from the long-distance maritime raids of the past. Today, the booty sought by the perpetrators is no longer slaves, but cash, valuables, cargo or vessels themselves. Most important, however, is that now piracy is an act of either opportunistic pirates or organised criminal gangs, conducted for private ends. Piracy is no longer a political or economic instrument to strengthen or support the structure of states.

Piracy in Malaysia: the late 1990s to the mid-2000s

While the anti-piracy efforts of the colonial powers proved successful in fighting sophisticated organised pirate attacks and slave raids, piracy never disappeared entirely from Southeast Asian waters, and opportunistic attacks on merchant vessels and small craft continued. Large numbers of attacks in Southeast Asia were reported again only from the mid-1970s onwards, however, when the Vietnamese 'boat people' suffered horrendously at the hands of pirates in the Gulf of Thailand (Boulanger 1989; Eklöf 2006: 17–34). Yet, it was not until the 1990s that piracy in Southeast Asia, including Malaysia, re-emerged as a serious security concern in the region.

The period between the 1990s and the mid-2000s is significant because, at the time, Southeast Asia was the most pirate-prone region in the world. The level of attacks and the serious nature of some incidents triggered international concern about the safety of international shipping in the region's waters and led to the establishment of organisations and initiation of cooperative measures that have shaped the fight against piracy ever since. Malaysia played a central role, particularly because international concern focused largely on the safety of ships passing through the Malacca Strait, a strategic waterway consisting mainly of Malaysian and Indonesian waters.

For the period from the late 1990s to 2007, piracy data from the International Maritime Bureau (IMB) are the most comprehensive, even though IMB representatives themselves estimate that more than 50 percent of all pirate attacks remained unreported.[1] The IMB included in its data for this period any 'act of boarding any vessel with the intent to commit theft or any other crime and with the intent or capability to use force in the furtherance of that act' (ICC 1998: 2). The IMB data show that in this period between three (2004) and seventeen (2000 and 2001) actual attacks were reported in Malaysian waters. Additionally, some attacks reported in the Malacca Strait, the Singapore Strait and the South China Sea may also have been conducted in Malaysian waters (Table 35.1).

Pirates active in Malaysian waters attacked vessels of any nationality, type and size, with the exception of very large vessels. Smaller or medium-sized cargo vessels were preferred targets. Fishing boats were also attacked, but these incidents were rarely reported to the IMB or local authorities. The perpetrators were not necessarily Malaysian and did not always operate from Malaysian territory. Indeed, piracy is often a transnational activity, with pirates from countries such as Indonesia and the Philippines able to cross into Malaysian waters to attack ships. Regardless of their origin, the perpetrators can be divided into two types: opportunistic sea-robbers and sophisticated, organised pirate gangs.

Between the 1990s and mid-2000s, the vast majority of pirate attacks in Malaysian waters were simple hit-and-run robberies, committed by what can best be described as common

Table 35.1 IMB statistics: actual and (attempted) attacks

IMB data	*1998*	*1999*	*2000*	*2001*	*2002*	*2003*	*2004*	*2005*	*2006*	*2007*	*2008*	*2009*	*2010*	*2011*	*2012*
Malaysia	10	15	17	17	12	3	6	3	10	9	10	13	15	14	12
	(0)	(3)	(4)	(2)	(2)	(2)	(3)	(0)	(0)	(0)	(0)	(3)	(3)	(2)	(0)
Malacca Strait	1	0	37	8	13	9	17	7	6	3	0	2	0	1	2
	(0)	(2)	(38)	(9)	(3)	(19)	(20)	(5)	(5)	(4)	(2)	(0)	(2)	(0)	(0)
Singapore Strait	1	9	3	6	2	1	6	3	1	2	5	6	3	10	6
	(0)	(4)	(2)	(1)	(3)	(1)	(2)	(4)	(4)	(1)	(1)	(3)	(0)	(1)	(0)
South China Sea	4	0	2	1	0	1	5	0	1	1	0	12	22	10	2
	(1)	(3)	(7)	(3)	(0)	(1)	(3)	(6)	(0)	(2)	(0)	(1)	(9)	(3)	(0)
Southeast Asia[a]	69	123	162	116	127	122	117	91	66	63	56	55	89	92	101
	(24)	(40)	(95)	(49)	(38)	(64)	(51)	(27)	(22)	(17)	(9)	(12)	(24)	(10)	(9)

Source: International Chamber of Commerce (1998–2012), *Piracy and Armed Robbery against Ships*, Annual Reports, Barking: International Chamber of Commerce International Maritime Bureau.

Note:

[a] Southeast Asia here includes: Indonesia, Malacca Strait, Malaysia, Myanmar, Philippines, Singapore Strait, Thailand, Vietnam and South China Sea.

sea-robbers. The perpetrators operated in small groups of men who most likely had known each other for some time. They attacked ships at sea, at anchor or in ports and usually did not share their booty with anyone outside the pirate gang, except for bribes paid to outsiders to ensure their silence or cooperation. The attacks were often brief affairs, lasting no longer then fifteen to thirty minutes, and required little organisation or planning. When merchant ships were targeted, the sea-robbers skilfully slipped aboard, usually under cover of darkness, and took anything of value before leaving the vessel. Violence was limited mostly to occasions when the perpetrators' escape route was blocked or when they were confronted or threatened in some other way (ICC 1998: 3, 7). Hit-and-run incidents on small vessels such as fishing boats or yachts were often violent. In such attacks, the pirates invariably confronted their victims directly and had to be prepared to use violence and intimidation.

The second group – organised pirate gangs, or syndicates – is characterised by greater organisation and sophistication. These gangs predominantly attacked medium-sized vessels, including cargo ships, bulk carriers and tankers, and were responsible for 'long-term seizures' and hijackings. For attacks far from shore, pirate gangs employ a mother-ship. The mother-ship serves as a forward base for the pirates at sea and carries technical equipment to locate targeted vessels, fuel stores, and other logistical equipment and weapons necessary for attacks (Stewart 2002: 158). An example of an attack by an organised gang was the seizure of the MT *Petchem* in the early hours of 25 September 2000 while on its way from Port Dickson, in peninsular Malaysia, to Kuching, in the western part of Sarawak. Armed with guns and *parang* (machetes), twenty-one Indonesian pirates overpowered the crew and changed the vessel's name to *ETC*. The following day, the crewmembers, incarcerated in the cabin, felt the tremor of a second vessel coming alongside the *Petchem* and heard pumps siphoning off the cargo. The pirates left the hijacked vessel via the second ship, and the crew were able to free themselves and alert the owner of the vessel and the Singaporean and Malaysian authorities.[2]

Piracy hot spots

While pirate attacks were reported from different parts of Malaysia, two areas were particularly associated with pirate activities: the waters off Sabah and the Malacca Strait. Sabah borders Kalimantan, Indonesia, and is only a short distance across the Sulu Sea from the southern Philippines. A large number of small vessels, including fishing boats and both passenger and trading ships, ply the waters between Sabah, Kalimantan and the southern Philippines. Assaults on these vessels were common. Attacks in this area were often shaped by the conflict in the southern Philippines between the government and various separatist and terrorist groups. Some of these groups were believed to be involved in piracy, and both the lawlessness created by the conflict and the availability of firearms facilitated piracy. Indeed, many of the attacks in this area were conducted by perpetrators originally from the southern Philippines. Attacks off Sabah were characterised by a comparatively high level of violence, with the perpetrators often carrying firearms. Exemplifying the ruthless nature of attacks was an incident in the late 1990s, when three fishermen were shot dead in the strait between Basilan and Zamboanga. The armed pirates approached their victims in a motorboat, opened fire, and stole the fishing boat's engine and fishing gear (Associated Press Newswire 1999). Fishing boats were arguably most affected by piracy in these waters, but boats used for inter-island trade or smuggling, and other small transport vessels were also targeted. The actual number of attacks in this area is difficult to estimate as they were seldom reported to local authorities or the IMB (see Liss 2011).

More attacks were reported from the Malacca Strait area. The Strait connects the Indian Ocean with the South China Sea and is one of the busiest waterways in the world. Concern about piracy in the Strait was triggered by a sudden rise in the number of attacks in 2000, with reported incidents jumping from two actual and attempted attacks in the area in 1999 to seventy-five the following year (Table 35.1). While the number of incidents declined again in 2001, numbers remained comparatively high until 2005. Prevalence aside, the serious nature of some of the incidents and the fear of possible collusion between pirates and terrorists caused concern. One serious incident was the hijacking of the MT *Selayang* on 20 June 2001 in the Malacca Straits. The ship was travelling from Port Dickson to Labuan when nineteen pirates climbed on board, overpowered the crew and held them captive. The hijacking was first noticed on 21 June, but despite the ship's tracking system, the *Selayang* was not intercepted by the Indonesian authorities until 27 June, when anchoring near Samarinda, north of Balikpapan, Borneo.[3]

Beyond the attacks recorded by the IMB, fishing boats and their crew were frequently targeted in the Malacca Strait, particularly in the northern part. These attacks were often not reported because the fishermen saw no advantage in reporting the incident, were concerned about revenge by pirates, or were attacked while fishing illegally and therefore could not ask for help from authorities. Many attacks on fishing boats were serious and included hijacking vessels, kidnapping crew for ransom and killing fishermen. Examples are two attacks on the same fishing boat from Kuala Perlis in 2002 and 2004. In the first incident, the vessel, with thirty-five Thai crewmembers on board, was attacked by eight Indonesian pirates. The perpetrators stole the catch, cash and diesel oil from the vessel, and tragically, shot dead a Thai child on board the fishing boat. Two years later, the same vessel was hijacked and two crewmembers were taken hostage.[4] Also common in the Malacca Strait area was the collection of up-front protection money from boat owners to ensure their boats were not attacked. As well as opportunistic and organised pirates, members of the Free Aceh Movement (GAM) and the Indonesian armed forces were believed to be responsible for attacks on both merchant and fishing boats in the Malacca Strait (see Liss 2011).

Responses to piracy

Even at the height of attacks in the Malacca Strait, piracy remained only one of several, often much more pressing, security concerns in Malaysia (and Southeast Asia). This becomes clear when the number of pirate attacks is compared with the number of crimes committed on land. In 2000, for instance, the Malaysian police recorded 167,173 attempted and committed crimes (United Nations Office on Drugs and Crime 2004). The total of twenty-one actual and attempted pirate attacks reported to the IMB in the same year in Malaysian waters and ports seems insignificant in comparison. Even if the seventy-five attacks recorded that year in the Malacca Strait are included, the statistical impression that the vast majority of crimes are committed on land remains uncontested.[5] Yet, piracy – especially in the Malacca Strait area – drew international attention and significant efforts were made to fight it.

International concern over the safety of ships in the Malacca Strait was a major driving force behind efforts to curb piracy. Internationally, commercial organisations and governments showed concern and contributed to the introduction of new anti-piracy measures. On the commercial side, the marine underwriters Lloyds played a noteworthy, albeit controversial, role in focusing attention on piracy in the Malacca Strait. In June 2005, Lloyds Joint War Committee decided to include the Strait in its Hull War, Strikes, Terrorism and Related Perils Listed Areas, which raised insurance premiums for ships transiting the Strait and was challenged by both representatives of the shipping sector and regional governments. In August 2006, Lloyds removed the Malacca Strait from the list, stating security in the waterway had improved (*Insurance Journal* 2006). Nevertheless, Lloyds' initial decision to list the Malacca Strait prompted local governments to act against piracy.

Governments around the globe also expressed concerns about the safety of ships in the Malacca Strait. Some, such as the Japanese and the United States governments, offered assistance to increase maritime security in the area. Offers included active involvement of foreign powers in providing security, such as the suggestion that foreign naval vessels should patrol the Malacca Strait, and more indirect foreign assistance in the form of training for regional maritime agencies or donations of funds or military hardware to local government agencies.[6] While indirect assistance has generally been accepted, direct 'foreign' involvement has been viewed with suspicion in the region and refused. Sensitivities about sovereignty are often cited as the main reason behind the refusal (Storey 2006: 4; Bradford 2010). Instead, Southeast Asian countries, including Malaysia, have taken it largely into their own hands to combat piracy, individually or jointly. Malaysia, for example, has increased patrols in piracy-prone waters such as the Malaysian waters of the Malacca Strait. To improve coordination and cooperation among the seven agencies responsible for maritime security in Malaysia, the Malaysian Maritime Enforcement Agency (MMEA) was established and became operational in November 2005 (MMEA 2013).[7] In Sabah, the large-scale abduction of foreign tourists and resort workers from the Malaysian island of Sipadan in 2000 by the Philippines-based Abu Sayyaf prompted the Malaysian government to significantly increase maritime security in the area. While the hostages were still being held in the Philippines, Malaysian government representatives announced that additional navy personal would be stationed in Sabah, and that it would build a new naval base in Semporna, the town closest to the island of Sipadan; the base officially opened in July 2005 (*Daily Express* 2005).

Given that piracy is often a transnational crime, local governments have made efforts to combat piracy jointly; however, close and meaningful cooperation is often hampered by concerns about sovereignty, contending national interests, and contested claims of ownership of islands or water areas (Mak 2006). While a range of bilateral and multilateral efforts were made to combat piracy in Southeast Asia, three are particularly significant in the Malaysian context: ASEAN's efforts; the Malacca Straits Patrol Network; and the Regional Cooperation Agreement on Combating Piracy and Armed Robbery against Ships in Asia (ReCAAP). ASEAN (and the ASEAN Regional Forum, ARF), has made various efforts over the years to address piracy. For example, member states' commitment to forming an 'ASEAN Community' by 2015 (Roberts 2010: 1) includes more extensive maritime cooperation in addressing transnational crime, including piracy. ASEAN's efforts to increase security have so far, however, been limited by its policy of non-interference in domestic affairs and have seldom, if ever, resulted in any direct action (Emmers 2003: 430; Emmers and Tan 2009). MALSINDO, in contrast, a trilateral agreement among Singapore, Malaysia and Indonesia to combat piracy in the Malacca Strait, included active anti-piracy measures from the outset. It started with coordinated maritime patrols in 2004; two years later, with the introduction of coordinated air patrols over the Malacca Straits, named 'Eyes in the Sky' (EiS), the initiative was renamed Malacca Straits Patrol Network. Although the initiative has shown some success and all three states clearly cooperate in the network, the depth of their collaboration remains limited. Significantly, while surveillance planes are allowed to fly up to three nautical miles into the territorial seas of the participating states, naval patrols remain coordinated rather than joint, meaning that hot pursuit into, and patrolling of, waters of neighbouring countries is not permitted (Raymond 2010).

ReCAAP, the first regional government-to-government agreement to combat piracy, was finalised in 2004 and came into force two years later. The initiative focuses on the Asian region and most signatories are Asian countries. ReCAAP was initially proposed by Japan and aimed to facilitate the sharing of information related to piracy, especially through establishing an information-sharing centre. While the centre was set up in Singapore in 2006, the agreement does not 'obligate members to any specific action other than sharing information that they deem pertinent to imminent piracy attacks' (Bradford 2005: 69). Furthermore, even though a large percentage of pirate attacks in Southeast Asia are conducted in Malaysian and Indonesian waters, neither country is party to the agreement. Nevertheless, both Malaysia and Indonesia cooperate with the organisation, and ReCAAP reports cover incidents in the two countries' waters.

Piracy in Malaysia 2007–13: change and continuity

After the introduction of anti-piracy measures such as the Malacca Straits Patrol Network and the establishment of ReCAAP, international attention on piracy in Asian waters began to fade, for two reasons. First, the number of reported incidents in the Malacca Strait declined significantly and, second, the Gulf of Aden area became the focus of international concern after the number of serious pirate attacks began to increase sharply off the east African coast.

The decline in the number of attacks reported in the Malacca Strait area from 2007 to 2012 is clearly apparent in IMB data (Table 35.1). ReCAAP data, first published in 2006, combine attacks conducted in the Malacca and Singapore Straits and confirm that the number of reported incidents in this area remained low, at least until 2011 (Table 35.2).[8] The drop in reported incidents in the Malacca Strait can be explained partly by the introduction of the Malacca Straits Patrol Network and individual efforts by the Malaysian and Indonesian governments to increase patrols and arrest perpetrators. The 2005 peace agreement in

Table 35.2 ReCAAP ISC piracy statistics: actual and (attempted) attacks

ReCAAP	*2006*	*2007*	*2008*	*2009*	*2010*	*2011*	*2012*
Malaysia	10	7	13	12	18	14	11
	(1)	(1)	(0)	(3)	(0)	(3)	(0)
Straits of Malacca and Singapore	6	3	7	6	5	24	12
	(7)	(4)	(4)	(3)	(3)	(2)	(1)
South China Sea	3	1	5	11	17	12	7
	(0)	(5)	(2)	(2)	(8)	(6)	(0)
Southeast Asia[a]	65	55	63	58	99	113	103
	(20)	(18)	(10)	(14)	(21)	(15)	(8)
Asia[b]	100	77	83	82	134	135	123
	(35)	(23)	(13)	(20)	(33)	(22)	(9)

Source: ReCAAP ISC (2006–12), *Piracy and Armed Robbery against Ships in Asia*, Annual Reports, Singapore: Information Sharing Centre.

Notes:

[a] Southeast Asia here includes: Gulf of Thailand, Indonesia, Malaysia, Myanmar, Philippines, Singapore, South China Sea, Straits of Malacca and Singapore, Thailand and Vietnam.

[b] Asia here includes: Southeast Asia plus China, Arabian Sea, Bangladesh, Bay of Bengal, India (and Sri Lanka until 2011).

Aceh also contributed to the decline in incidents, including the drop in hijackings and kidnappings of crew. Also, many ship-owners are likely to be reluctant to report minor incidents in the Malacca Strait to avoid a renewed rise in insurance premiums, as occurred in 2005 after Lloyds classified the Strait as a risk area.

A further reason for the decline is that pirates shifted their operations to less-patrolled waters, especially the waters east of the Malacca Strait. As Tables 35.1 and 35.2 demonstrate, incidents in the Singapore Strait and the South China Sea (particularly the waters between the east coast of Peninsular Malaysia and Indonesia's Anambas Islands) increased around 2009. Indonesian pirate gangs based in the Riau Archipelago and the Anambas Islands are believed to be responsible for the attacks, with some groups also involved in other illegal activities, especially smuggling. Even though these pirates are mostly Indonesians operating from Indonesian territory, Malaysian vessels and other ships travelling from and to Malaysian ports are among those attacked (Hoesslin 2012). An example is the hijacking of the Malaysian tanker *Zafirah* on 19 November 2012 in the South China Sea on its way from Johor to Sarawak. The vessel was captured by Vietnamese authorities three days later and all eleven pirates were arrested (ReCAAP 2013a: 66).

While the number of reported incidents in the Malacca Strait has declined, piracy has not been eradicated in the Strait – or in other piracy hot spots in Malaysia. ReCAAP and IMB statistics demonstrate that, since 2005, usually between ten and twenty pirate attacks have been reported annually in the country's waters. As earlier, these include hit-and-run robberies conducted by opportunistic pirates and more serious attacks such as hijackings for which organised gangs are responsible. In Malaysian waters, the Malacca Strait and the South China Sea, however, pirates have changed their modus operandi to some extent in recent years. Most importantly, hijacking of merchant ships is less common, with pirates' increasingly targeting smaller vessels, such as tugs and barges. Such vessels are particularly vulnerable; they are easier to board because they have a low freeboard, travel slowly (8–10 knots) and carry a small crew. An example is a tug and barge travelling between Sarawak and Port Klang, Kuala Lumpur, attacked by twelve masked men on 25 May 2011. As usual for such incidents, the crewmembers were stripped of their belongings and set adrift. Fortunately, the crew was rescued by Vietnamese fishermen, while the tug was discovered on 2 June by the Royal Malaysian Navy in the Spratly Islands. The barge was not found until early December 2011, when it was discovered abandoned and run aground in the Philippines (ReCAAP 2012: 82–83). In such incidents, it appears the pirates had prior knowledge of the targeted vessels. Once the ships were hijacked, they were taken to a shipyard for refurbishment before being delivered to a pre-arranged buyer (see ReCAAP ISC and the Information Fusion Centre n.d.).

Arguably less has changed in the waters off Sabah, despite substantial efforts to increase maritime and border security in the area. Today, naval bases operate in Sandakan, Lahad Datu, Semporna and Tawau, and additional units from agencies such as the General Operations Force, the Marine Operations Force and the Maritime Enforcement Agency have been deployed to the area. Despite this, pirate attacks on merchant ships and smaller vessels, including fishing boats, remain a concern in the waters off Sabah. In August 2013, for example, a group of armed men held nine fishermen hostage for several hours in the waters off Semporna. Following the incident, Sabah police stated that they had identified two foreign-based pirate gangs responsible for attacks on fishers in Malaysian waters (*Borneo Insider* 2013).

In addition to attacks on vessels, armed men travelling by boat have been responsible for a spate of raids on villages, estates and plantations in Sabah. In 2010, for example, two employees of a seaweed plantation off the coast of Semporna were abducted by armed men and released after a ransom was paid. In November 2012, heavily armed men turned up in Kampung Indra Sabah and took off with 'a few hundred ringgit worth of anchovies', while a few days earlier, two hostages had been taken from an estate near Lahad Datu (Queville 2012). The most serious incident, however, occurred in 2013. In early February, an estimated two hundred men from the Royal Security Forces of the Sulu Sultanate arrived by boat near Lahad Datu and settled in the area. They were sent by Jamalul Kiram, one of several claimants to be sultan of Sulu, and led by his brother, Abgimuddin Kiram. The group's aim was to reinforce the Philippines' claim to Sabah. The situation remained stable for several weeks while negotiations ensued between the group and the Malaysian government. When negotiations failed and the militants refused to leave, however, violence broke out in several towns along the coast, with casualties on both sides. The Malaysian government deemed the conflict so serious that it bombed the area where the militants were hiding and increased efforts to secure the maritime border between the Philippines and Sabah. While the so-called stand-off was eventually resolved, details about the incident remain hazy (Felongco 2013);[9] however, it demonstrated clearly the prevalence of unresolved political issues and tensions in the area and focused attention once again on the porous maritime borders there. While this incident was not a pirate attack (even though several newspapers referred to it as such or likened the perpetrators to pirates), it generated insecurity and uncertainty, which are conducive to the occurrence of criminal activities such as piracy.

Conclusion

Piracy in Malaysia and other Southeast Asian waters claimed international attention in the early 2000s, mainly because of a rise in reported attacks in the busy Malacca Strait. After regional states increased their efforts to combat piracy – with some assistance from countries beyond the region – and the number of attacks in the Malacca Strait began to decline, international concern about piracy shifted away from Southeast Asia to a new piracy hot spot in the Gulf of Aden area.

Malaysia has played an important role in combating piracy in Southeast Asia, not simply because it is partly responsible for maritime security in the Malacca Strait. Naval bases have been opened in piracy hot spots, especially Sabah, new equipment and boats suitable for pursuing pirates have been purchased, and cooperation between Malaysian agencies has been enhanced by the establishment of the MMEA. Malaysia has also cooperated closely with neighbouring states, as reflected in the introduction of the Malacca Straits Patrol Network. These efforts have shown some success, as demonstrated by the drop in reported attacks in the Malacca Strait and the capture of perpetrators by Malaysian authorities. One recent example is the arrest of eight Indonesian pirates by the MMEA in December 2012. The perpetrators were apprehended while attacking a ship off the coast of Pengerang, facing the Singapore Strait (Gasper 2012). These efforts by the Malaysian authorities signal that Malaysia is interested in, and committed to, combating piracy. Indeed, Malaysia is even using its experience to contribute to anti-piracy efforts in the Gulf of Aden area. Malaysia not only sent warships to patrol the pirate-prone waters off Somalia, but also arrested perpetrators and brought them to trial in Malaysia. In September 2013, for example, a Malaysian court sentenced seven Somali pirates to between eight and ten years in jail for attacking a Malaysian-operated chemical tanker and shooting at Malaysian troops (International Transport Workers' Federation 2013).

Yet despite these efforts, piracy persists. Attacks are still reported in Malaysian waters, including serious incidents such as hijackings. This can be explained in part by the limits in cooperation between Malaysia and its neighbours. For example, sensitivities about sovereignty have so far prevented states in Southeast Asia from allowing hot pursuit of pirates into other countries' waters. Similarly, multiparty maritime patrols still remain coordinated, rather than joint patrols, and Malaysia and Indonesia are still not members of ReCAAP. Even more important in explaining the persistence of piracy, however, is that Malaysia and other Southeast Asian countries mostly focus on addressing the symptoms, but not the root causes of piracy. Combating piracy is a difficult and complex task, requiring more than patrolling piracy-prone waters. Indeed, so long as the root causes of piracy – including poverty, overfishing, lax maritime regulations, corruption of law enforcement agencies and the presence of radical politically motivated groups in the region – are not addressed, piracy will not be eliminated.

Notes

1 Author's interview with Noel Choong, Regional Manager, International Maritime Bureau, Piracy Reporting Centre, 23 October 2002, Kuala Lumpur, Malaysia.
2 Documents provided by Petrojaya Marine Sdn Bhd, Singapore, 21 October 2003.
3 Documents provided by Petrojaya Marine Sdn Bhd, Singapore, 21 October 2003.
4 Author's interview with local fishers and Shamsul bin Chin, Pengurus Besar, Persatuan Nelayan Kawasan Kuala Perlis, 29 October 2004 and 10 November 2004, Kuala Perlis, Malaysia.
5 Many of the attacks recorded in the Malacca Straits, however, most likely occurred in Indonesian waters.
6 One example is Japan's decade-old programme to build up regional coastguards (Fackler 2012).
7 The official launch occurred in March the following year.
8 ReCAAP data is included here because the organisation offers at present the most comprehensive data collection on piracy in Southeast Asia. Although both ReCAAP and the IMB now make a distinction between piracy and armed robbery against ships, both crimes are included in the statistics. For piracy (on the high seas), the definition in Article 101 of the United Nations Convention on the Law of the Sea (UNCLOS) is used; armed robbery against ships is defined in accordance with the Code of Practice for the Investigation of Crimes of Piracy and Armed Robbery against Ships of the International Maritime Organization (IMO) Assembly Resolution A.1025(26).
9 Author's interviews with people from the area, Sabah, October 2013.

Bibliography

Andaya, Barbara Watson and Leonard Y. Andaya (2001) *A History of Malaysia*, Honolulu: University of Hawai'i Press.

Associated Press Newswire (1999) 'Pirates rob, shoot to death three fishermen off southern Philippine province', Associated Press Newswire, 12 April.

Borneo Insider (2013) 'Police identify two groups of pirates in East Sabah waters', *Borneo Insider*, 30 August, available at http://borneoinsider.com/2013/08/30/police-identify-two-groups-of-pirates-in-east-sabah-waters/ (accessed 19 September 2013).

Boulanger, Pascal (1989) 'The Gulf of Thailand', in Eric Ellen (ed.), *Piracy at Sea*, Paris: ICC Publishing, pp. 83–96.

Bradford, John F. (2005) 'The growing prospects for maritime security cooperation in Southeast Asia', *Naval War College Review*, 6: 63–86.

Bradford, John (2010) 'US strategic interests and cooperative activities in maritime Southeast Asia', in John Bradford, James Manicom, Sheldon W. Simon and Neil Quartaro (eds), *Maritime Security in Southeast Asia: US, Japanese, Regional, and Industry Strategies NBR Special Report*, Seattle: National Bureau of Asian Research, pp. 17–30.

Cerquone, Joseph (1984) *Vietnamese Boat People: Pirates' Vulnerable Prey*, New York: US Committee for Refugees, February, pp. 83–96.

Daily Express (2005) 'Semporna RMN Base Opens', *Daily Express*, 13 July, available at www.daily-express.com.my/print.cfm?NewsID=35748 (accessed 27 September 2005).

Eklöf, Stefan (2006) *Pirates in Paradise: A Modern History of Southeast Asia's Maritime Marauders*, Copenhagen: NIAS Press.

Emmers, Ralf (2003) 'ASEAN and the securitization of transnational crime in Southeast Asia', *Pacific Review*, 16(3): 419–38.

Emmers, Ralf and See Seng Tan (2009) The ASEAN Regional Forum and Preventive Diplomacy: A Failure in Practice, RSIS Working Paper 189, Singapore: S. Rajaratnam School of International Studies.

Fackler, Martin (2012) 'Japan is flexing its military muscle to counter a rising China', *New York Times*, 26 November, available at www.nytimes.com/2012/11/27/world/asia/japan-expands-its-regional-military-role.html?pagewanted=all&_r=0 (accessed 30 October 2013).

Felongco, Gilbert P. (2013) 'Philippines, Malaysia increase sea patrols in aftermath of sea intrusion', *Gulfnews*, 16 February, available at http://gulfnews.com/news/world/philippines/philippines-malaysia-increase-sea-patrols-in-aftermath-of-sabah-instrusion-1.1146984 (accessed 30 October 2013).

Gasper, Desiree Tresa (2012) 'Malaysia maritime enforcement nab eight pirates looting ship', *The Star*, 12 December, available at www.thestar.com.my/story.aspx?file=%2f2012%2f12%2f12%2fnation%2f12446209&sec=nation (accessed 1 November 2013).

Hoesslin, Karsten von (2012) 'Piracy and armed robbery at sea in Southeast Asia: organized and fluid', *Studies in Conflict & Terrorism*, 35: 542–52.

ICC International Maritime Bureau (ICC) (1998) *Piracy and Armed Robbery against Ships: A Special Report*, revised edn, March 1998, Barking: International Chamber of Commerce International Maritime Bureau.

Insurance Journal (2006) 'Malacca Straits removed from war risk list', *Insurance Journal*, 9 August, available at www.insurancejournal.com/news/international/2006/08/09/71308.htm (accessed 15 November 2006).

International Transport Workers' Federation (2013) 'Malaysia jails seven Somali pirates', 9 September, available at www.itfglobal.org/news-online/index.cfm/newsdetail/9470/region/4/section/0/order/1 (accessed 1 November 2013).

Liss, Carolin (2011) *Oceans of Crime: Maritime Piracy and Transnational Security in Southeast Asia and Bangladesh*, Singapore: Institute of Southeast Asian Studies.

Mak, J.N. (2006) 'Unilateralism and regionalism: working together and alone in the Malacca Straits', in Graham Gerard Ong-Webb (ed.), *Piracy, Maritime Terrorism and Securing the Malacca Straits*, Singapore: Institute of Southeast Asian Studies, pp. 134–62.

Malaysian Maritime Enforcement Agency (MMEA) (2013) 'MMEA's background', 20 March, available at www.mmea.gov.my/v25/eng/index.php/en/about-us/background (accessed 18 May 2014).

Marine Department Malaysia (2007) 'Mandatory ship reporting system in the Straits of Malacca and Singapore', available at www.marine.gov.my/service/index.html (accessed 22 June 2007).

Queville To (2012) 'Sabah needs real protection, not "show-piece" defence', *Free Malaysia Today*, 14 December, available at www.freemalaysiatoday.com/category/nation/2012/12/14/sabah-needs-real-protection-not-%E2%80%98show-piece-defence/ (accessed 19 September).

Raymond, Catherine Zara (2010) 'Piracy and armed robbery in the Malacca Strait: a problem solved?', in Bruce A. Ellerman, Andrew Forbes and David Rosenberg (eds), *Piracy and Maritime Crime: Historical and Modern Case Studies*, Newport: Naval War College Press, pp. 109–20.

ReCAAP (2012) *Piracy and Armed Robbery against Ships in Asia: Annual Report January–December 2011*, Singapore: Information Sharing Centre.

ReCAAP (2013a) *Piracy and Armed Robbery against Ships in Asia: Annual Report January–December 2012*, Singapore: Information Sharing Centre.

ReCAAP (2013b) *Piracy and Armed Robbery against Ships in Asia: Half-Yearly Report January–June 2013*, Singapore: Information Sharing Centre.

ReCAAP ISC and the Information Fusion Centre (n.d.) *Tug Boats and Barges (TaB) Guide: Against Piracy and Sea Robbery*, Singapore: Information Sharing Centre.

Roberts, Christopher (2010) ASEAN Institutionalisation: The Function of Political Values and State Capacity, RSIS Working Paper 217, Singapore: S. Rajaratnam School of International Studies.

Stewart, Douglas (2002) *Piraten. Das organisierte Verbrechen auf See* [*Pirates. Organised crime at sea*], Hamburg: Marebuchverlag.

Storey, Ian (2006) 'China's "Malacca dilemma"', 12 April, available at www.asianresearch.org/articles/2873.html (accessed 26 September 2013).

Teitler, Ger (2002) 'Piracy in Southeast Asia: a historical comparison', *Mare Centre*, available at www.marecentre.nl/mast/documents/GerTeitler.pdf (accessed 26 September 2013).

Trocki, Carl A. (1988) 'Piracy in the Malay world', in Ainslie Thomas Embree (ed.), *Encyclopaedia of Asian History: Volume 3*, New York: Charles Scribner's Sons, p. 262.

United Nations Office on Drugs and Crime Division for Policy Analysis and Public Affairs (2004) 'Seventh United Nations survey of crime trends and operations of criminal justice systems, covering the period from 1998–2000', available at www.unodc.org/pdf/crime/seventh_survey/7pc.pdf (accessed 17 May 2005).

Warren, James Francis (2001) 'A tale of two centuries: the globalisation of maritime raiding and piracy in Southeast Asia at the end of the eighteenth and twentieth centuries', paper presented at the KITLV Jubilee Workshop, Leiden, 14–16 June.

Index

For Product Safety Concerns and Information please contact our EU representative GPSR@taylorandfrancis.com
Taylor & Francis Verlag GmbH, Kaufingerstraße 24, 80331 München, Germany

www.ingramcontent.com/pod-product-compliance
Lightning Source LLC
LaVergne TN
LVHW080803011026
849160LV00015B/1518
9781138312807